25421
15.00
MW00632845

BAKER'S HANDBOOK OF PRACTICAL THEOLOGY

BAKER'S HANDBOOK OF PRACTICAL THEOLOGY

RALPH G. TURNBULL, EDITOR

BAKER BOOK HOUSE
Grand Rapids, Michigan 49506

Copyright 1967 by
Baker Book House Company

Library of Congress Catalog
Card Number: 67-18199

ISBN: 0-8010-8880-1

Formerly published in hardback as
Baker's Dictionary of Practical Theology

Printed in the United States of America

Text (where indicated) from *The New English Bible, New Testament.* © The Delegates of the Oxford University Press and The Syndics of the Cambridge University Press 1961. Reprinted by permission.

The Bible text (where indicated) is from the Revised Standard Version of the Bible, copyrighted 1946 and 1952 by the Division of Christian Education of the National Council of Churches, and used by permission.

The General Editor and the Publishers wish to acknowledge the services of H. C. Brown, Jr., L. I. Granberg, H. H. Hobbs, N. V. Hope, H. Lindsell, B. L. Ramm, G. E. Thomas, and R. A. Ward for their assistance.

Preface

This volume is neither an encyclopedia nor a history. It lies in between as a source book for pastors and students. Dictionaries of the Bible and of Theology are available, but there is no book for ready reference in the field of Practical Theology. Theology has been classified in different ways: Biblical, Systematic, Philosophical, Exegetical, Symbolical, Moral, and Practical Theology.

Earlier books on Practical Theology include *A Manual for Theological Students,* J. J. Van Oosterzee, 1878; *Library of Biblical and Theological Literature,* G. R. Crooks and J. F. Hurst, 1891; *A General Introduction to the Study of Theology, Historical, Systematic, and Practical,* P. Schaff, 1892; and *Modern Practical Theology,* F. S. Schenck, 1903. These books are out of print and rarely available secondhand. A new century and a new era have emerged since their publication, and a store of new knowledge is now available. In addition, there are scores of articles in the standard encyclopedias and dictionaries, in the histories of preaching, and in the well-known series of lectures on preaching. Not all of these are accessible to the pastors and students who need a volume of this kind.

The format of the book is not that of the regular dictionary where each word or term is treated separately. Ten divisions of the minister's work are given classification, and within each are articles of a longer exposition. In this way it is felt that a deeper work of interpretation is obtained and the writers are not limited unduly in their presentation.

The contributors come from all branches of the Christian Church and from several countries. They readily cooperated when invited to participate. The Publishers and the General Editor are grateful for their willing response and enthusiastic writing. We trust this dictionary will become a guide to stimulate further investigation and reading in other books in the various subjects discussed.

The educated layman and laywoman in our churches will find this a volume to enlighten them about the tasks of the minister, and help their understanding of the difficulties involved in his work. The various essayists have been given freedom to write as they expressed their own knowledge and convictions. We have imposed no restrictions in that respect. The end result, we trust, will prove the value of this volume as a means to enriching this field of study. In diversity is unity of purpose.

The Editor thanks all who shared with him in this enterprise. We do not claim to have edited or written a final word on every subject. Only as Baedeker or guide can this be judged as it leads others into the vast hinterland of study yet possible in Practical Theology.

RALPH G. TURNBULL

The First Presbyterian Church
of Seattle, Washington

Contributors

Adams, Arthur M.
Dean of Field Education and Professor of Practical Theology, Princeton Theological Seminary

Anderson, Marvin W., B.D., Ph.D.
Associate Professor of Historical Theology, Bethel Theological Seminary

Babbage, S. Barton, Ph.D.
Visiting Professor of Practical Apologetics and Church History, Columbia Theological Seminary

Bast, Henry, A.B., B.D.
Pastor, Bethany Reformed Church, Grand Rapids, Michigan

Berry, William G., A.M., D.D.
Pastor, St. Paul's – Avenue Road United Church, Toronto, Canada

Blaiklock, E. M., A.M., Litt.D.
Professor of Classics and University Orator, University of Auckland, New Zealand

Blanchard, John F., Jr., M.Ed.
Executive Director, National Association of Christian Schools

Booth, F. Carlton, Mus.D.
Professor of Evangelism, Fuller Theological Seminary

Bower, Robert K., B.S., B.D., Ph.D.
Professor of Christian Education and Acting Professor of Pastoral Counseling, Fuller Theological Seminary

Briggs, Edwin A., B.D., Th.D.
Associate General Secretary of Section on Stewardship and Finance, General Board of Lay Activities of the Methodist Church

Brown, H. C., Jr., B.D., Th.D.
Professor of Preaching, Southwestern Baptist Theological Seminary

Clinchy, Russell J., D.D.
Minister Emeritus, The Church-in-the-Gardens, Forest Hills, New York

Cochrane, Elvis E., Th.M.
Professor of Philosophy and the Bible, Seattle Pacific College

Cully, Kendig Brubaker, B.D., M.R.E., S.T.M., Ph.D.
Dean and Professor of Christian Education, New York Theological Seminary

Davis, H. Grady
Emeritus Professor of Functional Theology, Lutheran School of Theology at Chicago

Dressler, Hermigild, Ph.D.
Associate Professor of Greek and Latin, The Catholic University of America

Fallon, George A., S.T.B., D.D.
Executive Secretary, Field Services, General Board of Evangelism of the Methodist Church

Frank S. Fitzsimmonds, A.B., B.D., Th.M.
Tutor in Biblical Languages and Exegesis, Spurgeon's College, London, England

Frame, John D., M.D.
Consultant, Interdenominational Foreign Mission Association, and Adjunct Assistant Professor, School of Public Health and Hospital Administration, Columbia University

Gerstner, John H., Th.M., Ph.D.
Professor of Church History, Pittsburgh Theological Seminary

Gibson, George Miles, D.D.
Professor Emeritus of Preaching, McCormick Theological Seminary

Granberg, Lars I., B.S., Ph.D.
President, Northwestern College of the Reformed Church in America

Grounds, Vernon, B.D., Ph.D.
President, Conservative Baptist Theological Seminary

Hakes, J. Edward, A.B., B.D.
Professor of Christian Education, Trinity Evangelical Divinity School

Hall, Dick H., Jr., B.S., Ph.D.
Pastor Emeritus, First Baptist Church, Decatur, Georgia

Harmon, C. Robert, B.S.S., A.M.
Assistant Professor of History, Seattle University

Harmon, Nolan B., A.M., Litt.D., D.D., LL.D.
Bishop and Editor of Encyclopedia of World Methodism

Hayden, Eric W., A.M.
Pastor, Leominster Baptist Church, Leominster, England

Hershey, Robert D., B.D., S.T.D.
Pastor, Evangelical Lutheran Church of the Holy Trinity, New York City

Hiemstra, William L., Th.M., Ph.D.
Chaplain, Pine Rest Christian Hospital, Grand Rapids, Michigan

Hintz, August M., D.D.
Pastor, First Baptist Church, Seattle, Washington

Hobbs, Herschel H., Ph.D.
Pastor, First Baptist Church, Oklahoma City, Oklahoma

Hope, Norman V., B.D., Ph.D.
Professor of Church History, Princeton Theological Seminary

Jones, Ilion T., A.M., B.D.
Professor Emeritus of Practical Theology, San Francisco Theological Seminary

Koller, Charles W., Th.D.
President Emeritus, Northern Baptist Theological Seminary

LaSor, William Sanford, Ph. D., Th.D.
Professor of Old Tesatment, Fuller Theological Seminary

Laurin, Robert B., B.D., Th.M., Ph.D.
Professor of Old Testament, California Baptist Theological Seminary

Levine, Raphael, H., A.B. LL.B., B.H.L.
Rabbi, Temple De Hirsch, Seattle, Washington

Leypoldt, Martha M., M.R.E., Ed.D.
Professor of Christian Education, Eastern Baptist Theological Seminary

Lindsell, Harold, B.S., P.h.D., D.D.
Associate Editor, *Christianity Today*

Macleod, Donald, A.M., B.D., Th.D.
Professor of Homiletics, Princeton Theological Seminary

Marshall, I. Howard, B.D., Ph.D.
Lecturer in New Textament Exegesis, King's College, University of Aberdeen, Scotland

Martin, James P., B.A.Sc., B.D., Th.D.
Professor of Biblical Interpretation, Union Seminary

Martin, W. B. J.
Pastor, First Community Church, Dallas, Texas; Lecturer in Modern Poetry at Dallas College, Southern Methodist University

McGraw, James, Th.B., A.M.
Professor of Preaching and the Pastoral Ministry, Nazarene Theological Seminary

Miller, Donald G., S.T.M., Ph.D.
President, Pittsburgh Theological Seminary

Mostert, John, B.D., Th.D.
Accrediting Association of Bible Colleges

Nelson, Wesley W., A.M.
Associate Professor of Pastoral Studies, North Park Theological Seminary

Nicole, Roger, B.D., Ph.D.
Professor of Theology, Gordon Divinity School

Oates, Wayne E., A.B., B.D., Litt.D.
Professor of Psychology of Religion, Southern Baptist Theological Seminary

Ockenga, Harold J., B.D., Ph.D.
Pastor, Park Street Church, Boston, Massachusetts

Orr, J. Edwin, B. Litt., Ph.D., B.D., Th.D.
Visiting Professor of the History of the Expansion of Christianity, Fuller Theological Seminary

Paschall, H. Franklin, B.D., Th.D.
Pastor, First Baptist Church, Nashville, Tennessee

Pattison, E. Mansell, M.D.
Assistant Professor of Psychiatry, School of Medicine, University of Washington

Pearce, Gordon, J. M., Ph.D.
Dean and Senior Tutor, Regent's Park College, Oxford, England

Perry, Lloyd M., B.D., Th.D., Ph.D.
Professor of Practical Theology, Trinity Evangelical Divinity School

Peters, George W.
Professor of Missions, Dallas Theological Seminary

Pitts, John, Ph.D.
Interim Pastor, Calvary Presbyterian Church, Pompano Beach, Florida

Prior, William, A.B., B.D.
Professor of Homiletics and Pastoralia, Wycliffe College, Toronto

Ramm, Bernard L., B.D., Ph.D.
Professor of Systematic Theology, California Baptist Theological Seminary

Reid, W. Stanford, Th.M., Ph.D.
Professor of History, Wellington College, University of Guelph, Canada

Robertson, James D., M.Ed., Ph.D.
Professor of Preaching, Asbury Theological Seminary

Roddy, Clarence S., Th.D., Ph.D.
Professor of Homiletics, Fuller Theological Seminary

Roth, Robert P., B.D., Ph.D.
Dean of Graduate School, Northwestern Lutheran Seminary

Sangster, Paul E., Litt.B., Ph.D., L.R.A.M.
Vice-Principal, Worcester College of Education, Worcester, England

Schroeder, Gordon H., B.D., Th.M., D.D.
Pastor, Redford Baptist Church, Detroit, Michigan

Simpson, John A., A.M.
Lecturer in Worship and Church History, Oak Hill College, London, England

Stanfield, Vernon L., Th.D.
Professor of Preaching, New Orleans Baptist Theological Seminary

Stoa, Norris W., A.B., Th.B.
Pastor, Denny Park Lutheran Church, Seattle, Washington

Stowe, Walter H., A.B., B.D., S.T.D.
Historiographer, Protestant Episcopal Church in the U.S.A.

Strauch, Paul E., A.B., B.D.
Secretary, Stewardship Council, United Church of Christ

Swaim, J. Carter, S.T.M., Ph.D.
Pastor, Church of the Covenant, New York City

Sylling, Adrin C., A.B., M.S.W.
Administrator, Pasadena Community Counseling Center; Assistant Professor, Graduate School of Clinical Psychology, Fuller Theological Seminary

Taylor, John B., A.M.
Vice-Principal, Oak Hill College, London, England

Thomas, G. Ernest, B.R.E., S.T.B., Th.D.
Pastor, First Methodist Church, Birmingham, Michigan

Turnbull, Ralph G., A.M., B.D., Th.M., D.D.
Pastor, First Presbyterian Church, Seattle, Washington

Tweedie, Donald F., Jr., Ph.D.
Graduate School of Psychology, Fuller Theological Seminary

Tyrrell, Charles, A.B., Th.B., M.R.E., Ed.D.
Professor of Christian Education, University of Dubuque College of Liberal Arts

Vayhinger, John M., B.D., Ph.D.
Professor of Psychology of Religion and Pastoral Counseling, Iliff School of Theology

Wallace, David H., B.D., Th.M., Ph.D.
Professor of Biblical Theology, California Baptist Theological Seminary

Ward, Ronald A., B.D., Ph.D.
Rector of the Stone Church, Saint John, New Brunswick,, Canada; Formerly Professor of New Testament, Wycliffe College, Toronto

Whitesell, Faris D., B.D., A.M.
Professor Emeritus of Homiletics, Northern Baptist Theological Seminary

Wilson, Leland
Director, Department of Interpretation, Church of the Brethren

Wirt, Sherwood E., B.D., Ph.D.
Editor, *Decision* Magazine

Woodbury, Newton B., A.B., B.D.
Executive Director, Division of World Mission Support, American Baptist Convention

Table of Contents

PREACHING

HOMILETICS

EVANGELISM – MISSIONS

COUNSELING

ADMINISTRATION

STEWARDSHIP

WORSHIP

EDUCATION

SECTION 1

PREACHING

"Go ye into all the world and preach the gospel."
— Mark 16:15

	Title	Author
1.	The Biblical Background of Preaching	Donald G. Miller
2.	The Art of Preaching	Faris D. Whitesell
3.	Planned Preaching in the Christian Year	George Miles Gibson
4.	British and American Preaching Since 1900	John Pitts
5.	Emphases in Preaching	Charles W. Koller
6.	Imagination in Preaching	W. B. J. Martin
7.	Preaching Doctrine	J. Carter Swaim
8.	Preaching in the Jewish Tradition	Raphael H. Levine
9.	Puritan Preaching	Ralph G. Turnbull
10.	Roman Catholic Preaching	Hermigild Dressler
11.	The Literature of Preaching	Ilion T. Jones

The Biblical Background of Preaching

What does it mean "to preach"? Is one of the definitions given in *Webster's New International Dictionary* (2nd ed., unabridged, 1947), which has wide current acceptance, an adequate one: "to discourse publicly on a religious subject"? If so, then the ideas of a speaker on a given religious theme, set forth to an audience of listeners, would constitute a sermon. In this case, a sermon could be preached with no reference to the Bible or to God's saving action in Jesus Christ. Or, if God in Christ were mentioned, he could well be the object of man's thought about him rather than the subject of the truth presented. A sermon would be speech about God rather than God himself speaking. It would be human speculation about the divine rather than the divine disclosing himself to man.

1. PREACHING IS DECLARING GOD'S WORD AS RECORDED IN THE BIBLE

A careful examination of preaching in the Bible indicates that it centers not in human ideas about God but in what God has done for man; that it must therefore be derived from the Scriptures, which are the record of what God has done for man, rather than from human speculation; and that it is authoritative because it is God himself speaking through his servant, the preacher, so that the preached word actually becomes the Word of God. As it is stated in *The Second Helvetic Confession* of 1566, Chapter I, "when this Word of God is now preached in the Church by preachers lawfully called, we believe that the *very Word of God is preached*" (*italics added*).

That true preaching is God's Word to man rather than man's word about God is to be seen in various Biblical descriptions of the nature of preaching. False prophets spoke a word of their own which was worthless because, said God, "I did not send them, nor did I command them or speak to them" (Jer. 14:14). On the other hand, the true prophet was sometimes the bearer of a word which ran so counter to his own thought that he would rather not have been born than to speak it (Jer. 20:14ff.). Yet he was overpowered (Jer. 20:7) by the Almighty who insisted, "I have put my words in your mouth" (Jer 1:9). He was called to say to his people, "Thus says the Lord God" (Ezek. 2:4). It is plain, then, that God was the subject of prophetic speech more than its object. The prophets were not so much speaking about God as they were men through whom God himself spoke.

The writer to the Hebrews insists that the same God who spoke through the prophets spoke the same word through his Son Jesus Christ (Heb. 1:1). Although in him God's word which was before partial and metaphorical is now total and real, the nature of the word remains constant. Jesus was less one who spoke about God than he was one in whom God himself spoke. In fact, the writer of the Acts goes so far as to call God a preacher, "God . . . sent to Israel, preaching good news of peace by Jesus Christ" (Acts 10:34ff.). Christ was a word spoken by God rather than about him.

The apostles who recounted to others this word God had spoken in his Son, however, declared that their word to men was no less a direct word of God than that which was spoken through the prophets and through Jesus Christ. Paul wrote to the Corinthian believers, "So we are ambassadors for Christ, God making his appeal through us" (II Cor. 5:20). God was not the object of Paul's thought but the subject who spoke through Paul. Paul's was an ambassadorial word which conveyed the thought and carried the authority of the one who sent him as surely as though that one himself were speaking. Paul reiterates this conviction in unmistakable terms to his Thessalonian readers, "when you received the word of God which you heard from us, you accepted it not as the word of men but as what it really is, the word of God, which is at work in you believers" (I Thess. 2:13). The word which God spoke through prophets, apostles, and Jesus Christ is the expression of himself through them. This word is recorded in the Bible.

The Bible, then, becomes the preacher's charter. It is as the Bible is preached that God's Word is preached. It is not the preacher's skill in speaking, nor his own observations on life, nor his own religious thoughts, nor his own powers of persuasion which make a sermon a sermon. It is only when the preacher becomes the contemporary instrument through which the ancient word of prophet, or apostle, or Jesus speaks, that a sermon is a sermon. Preaching, said P. T. Forsyth, "is the Gospel prolonging and declaring itself. . . . It is an eternal, perennial act of God in Christ, repeating itself within each declaration of it" (*Positive Preaching and the Modern Mind,* New York: Eaton & Mains, p. 5f.). It is only when the living God, who himself spoke in the history recorded in the Bible, speaks again through the preaching of the Bible that a sermon becomes a sermon. Otherwise, it is a speech or an address on a religious topic; the speech of a man about God, not God speaking of himself to man.

The nature of Christianity as a historical religion underlies this fact. The term "historical religion" in this sense does not mean merely a religion with a history, the development of which historians can objectively study. This would be true of any extant religion. It means rather that Christianity consists supremely in a series of unique events in which the Christian believes God acted uniquely for the salvation of the world. Christianity is a witness to something *done.* It consists primarily in events, and what flows from them. It does not move first and foremost in the realm of religious ideas. It is not primarily a theology, nor a philosophy, nor a way of life. Although theology, philosophy, and ethics may and, indeed, should be developed from it, these are accompaniments rather than constituents of the faith. Christianity consists in a series of historic events which took place over a span of centuries from Adam to the Christ. All the events in the series were leading up to and consummated by the final event in Christ. If God was active in the whole series of events, and if he acted uniquely in the final event, then Christianity is made true by happening. It is not something created by human reflection or religious genius.

This means that the proclamation and promulgation of the Christian faith must ever arise out of the continued rehearsal of the events recorded in the Bible. The word "remember" is characteristic both of the Old Testament and the New (see Deut. 7:18ff., 8:2ff., 18ff., Luke 24:8; I Cor. 11:25; II Tim. 2:8f.). Remembrance, in the Biblical sense, is not merely psychological recall. It is, rather, the reconstituting of the realities involved in the past event and involving oneself in those realities by identification with what they represent. The question of the Negro spiritual, "Were you there when they crucified my Lord?" captures the Biblical quality of "remembrance." Do you know that you were involved in that past event? And do you now identify yourself both with the judgment and the grace which flow from the past event into the present moment? The command, therefore, "remember Jesus Christ" (II Tim. 2:8), or "drink it in remembrance of me" (I Cor. 11:25), involves identification with God's saving act in Christ by believing it and by taking action appropriate to it. "Remember Pearl Harbor" means more than a date. It means identity with a nation both past and future, emotional involvement in its welfare, a sense of implication in its destiny. So it is with "remembrance" of the Biblical events. Hence, to preach is to "remember" the whole series of events begun with Adam and climaxed in Jesus Christ, so that they are reconstituted as present realities in which our destiny depends. I have stated it elsewhere: "The Bible is the unique record of the unique Act which creates, sustains, and controls the life of the church, and is as final and unrepeatable as that Act because it is really a part of the Act. If, then, preaching is to reproduce the effects of that Act in human lives now, it can normally do this only by so rooting itself in the Bible that the Deed there recorded is transfigured into living reality now" (*Fire In Thy Mouth*, New York: The Abingdon Press, p. 61).

2. FORMATION OF THE CANON

The historic justification for this is the church's formation of the canon. By sifting the many written documents which circulated in the early Christian decades and by finally setting up certain ones as authoritative over the life of the developing community, the early church was indicating that the faith witnessed to in these Christian books was that by which its own life had been created and nurtured, and by which all future developing tradition in the church was to be measured.

Four aspects of the formation of the canon should be noted. First, although the Bible came out of the life of the church and the canon was finally established by the decision of the church, it was not the church which gave to these books their authority. It is one thing to impart authority, it is another to recognize it. The canon is not authoritative because the church said it was. The church said it was authoritative because it contained the gospel which they recognized as authoritative, the authority of which they gladly accepted.

Second, the canon was formed through long process. The final formation of it by church councils was but the official recognition of what the life of the worshiping community had accomplished by the use of these books. Councils of men are quite fallible. Had the canon been set up deliberately by one such council called for that purpose, the possibility of a wide margin of error would have been strong. These works, however, circulated widely throughout the worshiping community in all parts of the Roman empire, and were used in the worship and instruction of the whole church. Those which spoke authoritatively to the life of the church rose to the top like cream, while the others were discarded. The councils later merely gave official recognition to what the consciousness of the worshiping community had already done. By this process the likelihood of major error was greatly reduced.

Third, although the Bible came out of the life of the church, in a deeper sense the church did not create the canon. Historical priority is one thing; real priority is another. Although the community may have had a large hand in editing the books of the Bible as they now stand, most of them came from inspired individuals who were often at odds with the community. It was men such as Jeremiah, Isaiah, and Amos, not the community of Israel, who produced the Old Testament, as it was Paul and Mark and Luke and others who produced the New Testament. These men, of course, were a part of the life of the community but they often stood above the community, bringing God's judgment to bear on it and guiding it in ways independent of the community. These works, then, are God's gift to the church rather than the church's achievement. Furthermore, it was the gospel, the *kerygma*, lying behind both the church and the Gospels, which produced them both. It was the message which the apostles preached which brought the church into being, and it was this same message which was finally put down in the Bible. The gospel was a message before it was a book. It is, therefore, the Bible's gospel which is authoritative over the life of the church, which authority in no way derives from the church. The church did not produce the gospel: the gospel produced the church. This gospel came to the church and brought it into being. It was the "gospel God announced" to the church and confirmed "by a mighty act in that he rose from the dead" (Rom. 1:2, 4 N.E.B.). "It was declared at first by the Lord," and then "attested . . . by those who heard him" (Heb. 2:3). The Bible, therefore, is authoritative simply because it contains the record of that which God brought to the church in his Son. The church put its stamp of approval on that which it recognized as the source of its life and the medium of its nurture.

Fourth, inasmuch as the major books of the canon were quickly and almost universally recognized as authoritative, while others were recognized by only a part of the church and had a difficult time getting into the canon, this suggests that not all the books of the Bible are on the same level. Luther wanted to eliminate the Epistle of James, and Calvin did not know what to do with the Book of Revelation. This attitude did not suggest any irreverence toward the Bible, but rather the recognition of the historic process by which the Bible came into being and the fact that historic processes, partly human as well as divine, may have in them a margin of error. The reason the Reformers had difficulty with the above named books was that they did not find the gospel imbedded in them as they did in the other parts of the Bible. Since, however, the church included these, and other less valuable works, in the canon, it is perhaps better to listen for whatever Word of God the church found in them rather than to propose casting them out as did the Reformers. Nonetheless, it is plain that the authority of the canon lies in the faithfulness and depth with which the books contained in it convey the gospel to the church. For this reason, since the absolute and infallible authority of the church does not lie behind the books in the canon for the Protestant, as it does for the Roman Catholic, it has been rightly said that the problem of the canon is the "Achilles heel of Protestantism." This means that for the Protestant the authority of the Bible is the authority of the gospel. And the authority of the gospel has behind it the authority of Jesus Christ. And this authority must be accepted by faith. To the extent, then, that Protestantism is true to its basic premise, *sola fide,* it will keep its preaching centered in the Christ to whom our faith is directed. And the place where he is to be found is in the Bible. Hence, the Bible becomes the only authoritative source for authentic Christian preaching.

3. PREACHING THE WHOLE GOSPEL

Properly to preach the Bible, however, means to view the Bible as a whole and to allow it to determine the central emphases around which Christian preaching should center. The story of the Old Testament has two foci – the Exodus and the coming Messianic deliverance. The first runs like a golden thread throughout Israel's history: "As the Lord lives who brought up the people of Israel out of the land of Egypt" (Jer. 23:7). Both worship and law, both cult and ethical instruction, are in the Old Testament consistently related to God's deliverance of his people at the Exodus. The text of the Old Testament might well be Exodus 19:4f.: "You have seen *what I did* to the Egyptians, and how I bore you on eagles' wings and brought you to myself. Now therefore, *if you will obey* my voice and keep my covenant. . . ." But since Israel did not obey, the second refrain became necessary: "Behold, . . . I will make a new covenant with the house of Israel. . . , not like the covenant which I made. . . when I took them. . . out of the land of Egypt, my covenant which they broke, . . . I will put my law within them, and I will write it upon their hearts; and I will be their God, and they shall be my people" (Jer.

31:31ff.). The entire Old Testament is organized around God's redemptive act at the Exodus and his coming redemptive act in the future.

The New Testament centers in the New Covenant established by God's redemptive act in the death and resurrection of Jesus Christ. Approximately one-fourth of the entire gospel story is given over to Jesus' death and resurrection. Furthermore, as Luke indicates by having Jesus' face set toward Jerusalem long before he actually sets out for the city (9:51), the intervening teaching is all to be understood in the light of the fact that it is given by one who is on his way to Jerusalem to die. Many of the teachings of Jesus can be paralleled in the teaching of the rabbis. The unique thing about his teaching was his own Person. He *was* what he taught, and supremely so in his death and resurrection. This is so plain in the Acts and the Epistles that it hardly needs pointing out.

In the light of this, Christian preaching should center in God's redeeming action set forth in both Testaments, climaxed in Jesus' cross and resurrection. This is not to say that this is all that should be preached. It is to say, however, that this is the presupposition of all Christian preaching. Ethical instruction, light on contemporary events, guidance in worship, or whatever might be undertaken in a Christian pulpit are made Christian by their relation to Christ. And Christ is the Suffering Servant of the Old Testament, the dying and rising Lord of the New.

It is instructive to follow through with a concordance the words translated "preach" in the New Testament to examine the grammatical objects of these verbs. They are so almost unanimously related directly to the central figure of Christ that were it not for the gloriousness of this central figure the New Testament preaching would suffer from monotony. New Testament preaching consisted in the announcement that the Kingdom of God anticipated in the Old Testament has come in Jesus Christ who, in his lifetime, did many "mighty works" to manifest his Lordship over all forms of evil; who died, who was raised from the dead and made Lord of the universe, through whose Lordship salvation is offered to all men and final judgment is to be made. Beyond this, New Testament preaching called men to repentance and belief in this "good news," and to the ethical response in their total living appropriate to the Lordship of Christ. If, therefore, the New Testament is to be our guide, these same emphases should be found in current preaching. The form in which this "good news" is cast may change, and most certainly the ethical response of our time will differ in shape from that of the first century. The form of contemporary preaching may change; its essence remains unchanged.

The same result is reached by examining the verbs in the New Testament which are translated "preach." They reinforce the proclamation nature of preaching, its center in the events of Christ's life, death, resurrection, ascension, and future coming. Friedrich, in Kittel's *Theologisches Wörterbuch zum Neuen Testament* (Stuttgart, W. Kohlhammer, Verlag), indicates that the most frequently used New Testament word for preaching, *evanggellizō*, is a *terminus technicus* for "news of a victory." Originally it was used by the Greeks to announce any joyous event, but finally it came to be used more exclusively in the sense of reporting a victory on the field of battle. It was appropriately selected by the Christians to describe their preaching. It consisted mainly in the announcement of the victory of Christ over sin and death, and what that entailed for human life here and hereafter. The second most frequently used verb to describe preaching, *kerussō*, means "to be a herald." The third is *katanggellō*, which means "to announce, declare, proclaim publicly." All of these verbs suggest that New Testament preaching was centered in the events which constituted God's saving action in history, which events and the victory they achieved must be heralded from generation to generation, to the "last syllable of recorded time."

Insofar as preaching in any age is Christian, therefore, it must be centered in the same message which formed the heart of the New Testament. It was this message which brought the church into being. It is this message which has enabled it to weather the vicissitudes of its long history. It is this message by which alone the contemporary church can be nurtured and empowered to witness to the world. The message does not originate with us. It is a "given." The message of the Scriptures is the source and norm of the Christian faith, when quickened by the Holy Spirit. Preaching the Bible makes preaching Christian.

BIBLIOGRAPHY

Dodd, C. H., *The Apostolic Preaching and Its Developments.* London: Hodder & Stoughton, 1936.

Farmer, H. H., *The Servant of the Word.* New York: Charles Scribner's Sons, 1942.

Forsyth, P. T., *Positive Preaching and the Modern Mind.* New York: Eaton & Mains, 1907.

Miller, Donald G., *Fire in Thy Mouth.* New York: Abingdon, 1954.

————————, *The Way to Biblical Preaching.* New York: Abingdon, 1947.

Mounce, Robert H., *The Essential Nature of New Testament Preaching.* Grand Rapids: Wm. B. Eerdmans, 1960.

Ott, Heinrich, *Theology and Preaching.* London: Lutterworth Press, 1965.

Ritschl, Dietrich, *A Theology of Proclamation.* Richmond: John Knox Press, 1960.

Wingren, Gustaf, *The Living Word in the Preaching and Mission of the Church.* Philadelphia: Muhlenberg Press, 1960.

The Art of Preaching

If art means to look at life the same way the poets, musicians, dramatists, and painters do, then preaching is an art. If science means a relentless search for facts which are then dissected, weighed, analyzed, and classified, preaching is not a science. The artist's approach is more essential in preaching than the scientific approach, though both have their place. The artist's use of the imagination and his effort to find the good, the beautiful, the true, and the eternal compare favorably with a preacher's responsibility. Preaching searches for the eternal values in the Scriptures in order to relate them helpfully to life.

The art of preaching has developed through the Christian centuries from the simple running commentary, or homily, to the many elaborate and varied sermon forms of today. We can observe this by mentioning some of the great preachers and indicating their influence on preaching trends.

The *apostolic* and *post-apostolic* Christian preachers hesitated to use the devices of heathen rhetoric and oratory lest the Word of God be nullified. They sought to keep preaching simple and Scriptural in order that the faith of believers might stand in the power of God and not in the wisdom of men.

But in *the second Christian century* the gospel began to reach more people in the upper classes. Some of the Greek and Roman teachers of rhetoric were converted and came into the church. They could neither forget nor ignore the grammatical and public speaking principles they had used before conversion. It was but natural that they should apply the principles of rhetoric and oratory to Christian preaching.

Justin Martyr (*c.* 100-165) tried out the various systems of heathen philosophy of his day in vain until he finally found peace in Christianity. He became a strong apologist for the faith. While not an ordained presbyter, he was a preacher and traveling advocate of the Christian faith.

Tertullian (*c.* 150-220) received a good classical education and became a lawyer. Converted when about forty years of age, he became a Christian orator and writer of first rank.

Origen (*c.* 185-254) was born of Christian parents and trained in Christian learning. He turned to the ministry of the Word and became one of the greatest exegetes, scholars, and expositors of all time. A voluminous writer, he was a careful scholar who tried to make the sacred text the real basis of preaching. However, he did considerable mischief by advocating the allegorical method of interpretation.

The preaching art remained rather static until *the fourth century* when John Chrysostom (347-407) of Antioch and Augustine (354-430) of Hippo appeared. Chrysostom, called "the Golden Mouth," was a notable preacher and orator. He brought the power of learning, eloquence, and imagination to bear upon the preaching task. He preached from the Bible directly to the needs of his listeners. His messages centered on themes but still adhered to the running commentary pattern. He preached through many of the books of the Bible, using the orator's arts to command attention and drive his message home. Chrysostom made the first known attempt to write a book on preaching. It was entitled *On the Priesthood*, but it deals more with the preacher's character and pastoral work than with the art of preaching.

Augustine was one of the world's greatest scholars, theologians, and preachers. He had been a teacher of rhetoric before his conversion, but he did not carry as much of his rhetorical skill over into his preaching as might be expected. He did not care so much for the graces of style as he did for depth of matter and power of effect. He sought to convince, persuade, instruct, and win his hearers. Like Chrysostom, he preached through much of the Bible in homily fashion. He also wrote a book, entitled *On Christian Teaching,* which contains his views on preaching. He taught that right character was essential, that there must be correct interpretation of the Scripture, and that a sane and skillful employment of accepted rhetorical principles are justified as far as these are available and servicable.

After Chrysostom and Augustine, preaching fell upon bad times and never recovered until the thousand-year period of *the Dark Ages* had passed. Allegorical, fanciful, and superstitious interpretations came in like a flood and almost displaced the true preaching of the gospel of saving grace. Preachers preached more about the virgin, the saints, the holy days, and apocryphal miracles than about Christ and the Bible.

During *the twelfth and thirteenth centuries,* Scholasticism became the fashion. Albert Magnus (*c.* 1193-1280), and Thomas Aquinas (1227-1274) were leading figures. Scholasticism meant the application of the logic of Aristotle to the interpretation of Scripture and the findings of theology. It majored on speculation, analysis, and reasoning. Preachers not only had a dozen or more main points, but dozens of subpoints and subpoints of subpoints. Though minute analysis was carried too far, sermons ever after were more orderly and logical than those of Chrysostom and Augustine.

Two preachers of the Scholastic period who had a more practical view of preaching were Dominic (1170-1221), and Francis of Assisi (1182-1226). Both of these men founded preaching orders which sought to take Christianity from the monasteries to the people. These preaching friars went out to find the people in the villages and fields and preach the Word of God to them.

Another pair of preachers of note were the Franciscans, Anthony of Padua (1195-1231), and Berthold of Regensburg (1220-1272). Both of these men preached with passion and fervor, giving the Word to the multitudes, though mingled with scholastic, mystical, and evangelical elements.

Among the Dominicans, three preachers developed the mystical emphasis still further. Master Eckhart (1260-1327), Henry of Suso (1295-1360), and John Tauler of Strasburg (1290-1361) were men of sincere lives, lofty ideals, and Christian dedication. They emphasized strict discipline, prayer, union with Christ, and the mystical interpretation of the Bible. John Tauler taught that salvation come not by works but by faith in Christ.

The ignorance and superstition of the Dark Ages gradually passed and the light of *the Protestant Reformation* came by stages. The revival of learning, the discovery of new lands, the advance of science, and new stirrings in political and social life helped to bring on the Reformation. But one of the most important factors was the work of the great humanist, Desiderius Erasmus (1468-1536), in editing and publishing the Greek New Testament. He also wrote a long and labored work on the theory of preaching entitled *Gospel Preacher.* But it is a summary of current practices rather than making any real advances.

Among the great preachers of the Reformtion, the best known are Huldreich Zwingli (1464-1531), Martin Luther (1483-1546), and John Calvin (1509-1564).

Zwingli did his work in Switzerland. Erasmus' edition of the Greek New Testament appeared in 1516 and became a mighty instrument in the hands of Zwingli. In January, 1519, he began a course of expository sermons through the Gospel of Matthew, an unheard of thing in his day. Multitudes attended his preaching. Not only did he preach through Matthew but also through the Acts, Galatians, and I and II Timothy. Preaching was the main thing with him. He had broken with almost all the major errors of Roman Catholicism. He preached without notes and did not write for publication. Therefore, few of his sermons remain.

Martin Luther moved the German nation Godward by preaching. He translated the Bible into the native tongue of the German people, and preached to them in the language they understood. His preaching was mostly the running commentary style, but was vigorous, direct, relevant to life, and loyal to the whole of Scripture. He never used much in the way of formal outlines, but was strong on explanation, argument, illustration, imagination, and application. His sermons are still read by multitudes.

John Calvin did his work in Geneva, Switzerland. He has been called "the Paul of the Reformation." Thoroughly trained in law and theology, he was the intellectual superior of both Zwingli and Luther. He became one of the notable Bible expositors of all time, as well as one of the most profound and influential theologians. He adhered closely to the Scriptures, preaching in the running commentary style, but in simple, direct, and convincing language. He made less use of imagination and illustration than Luther. His style was heavy but clear and Scriptural rather than rhetorical.

The French court preachers of *the seventeenth century* developed new emphases in preaching. Well-known ones are Jacques B. Bossuet (1627-1704), Louis Bourdaloue (1632-1704), and Jean B. Massillon (1663-1742). They preached before King Louis XIV and his court. Majoring on style, elaborate description, and oratory, these men were outstanding scholars and preachers. However, obvious flattery, fawning condescension, and overdependence on the rhetorical arts tend to mar their contributions.

Jean Claude (1619-1687) was a French Protestant preacher who introduced the method of taking a subject from a text and discussing the subject on its own merits. His famous essay, "An Essay on the Composition of a Sermon," had a wide and beneficial influence. Charles Simeon (1759-1836), the famous Cambridge expositor, translated it into English and republished it in the next century.

The Puritan movement in England and America brought into prominence a great many noble preachers. These men sought to return to the purity of Scriptural standards in preaching and church life.

Among the Puritans was Jeremy Taylor (1613-1677), a vivid, flowery, rhetorical preacher who spoke with imagination and eloquence. Some said, "He was an angel come from heaven," and Coleridge ranks him with Shakespeare, Bacon, and Milton as one of the four great masters of the English language.

Two Puritans who broke with the old method of many divisions and subdivisions were John Tillotson (1630-1694) and Robert South (1633-1716). Tillotson tried rather to develop a plain and edifying style. South disdained the elaborate fancifulness and labored conceits of the preceding age, even criticizing the overwrought style of Jeremy Taylor. Though South's thought was good and his style fresh, vigorous and moving, he lacked spirituality and tenderness.

Richard Baxter (1615-1691) is one of the most famous Puritans. His preaching and pastoral ministry transformed the town of Kidderminster during his sixteen years there. His books, *The Saints' Everlasting Rest* and *The Reformed Pastor,* have blessed all succeeding generations. He preached with deep dedication and earnestness "as never sure to preach again, and as a dying man to dying men."

John Bunyan (1628-1688), the immortal dreamer and author of *Pilgrim's Progress* was an eminent preacher of the grace of God, whose images and parables appealed to the common people, but whose written sermons do not measure up to his other writings.

Matthew Henry (1662-1714), a nonconformist Welshman, was pastor of a Presbyterian congregation in Chester, England, for twenty-five years. He became famous as a devotional and expository preacher, and his commentary on the Bible has enriched and inspired preachers ever since.

Two of the most celebrated preachers of Christian history were responsible for the Evangelical Awakening in England during the *eighteenth century.* They were John Wesley (1703-1791) and George Whitefield (1714-1770), both of whom stand in the vanguard of evangelistic preachers.

John Wesley made an enviable record as an evangelist, preacher, scholar, writer, administrator, and man of God. As an itinerant evangelist traveling up and down England for nearly sixty years, he had no equal in number of sermons preached and influence exercised. He could preach both to the head and the heart. His sermons were intended to convert sinners, to bring the Christians into the experience of the pure love of God, and to instruct all hearers. He hesitated to preach outside the dedicated church buildings until the Anglican authorities closed the churches against him. Then he followed the example of George Whitefield and took to the open air where he gathered his largest audiences and did his most lasting work.

Wesley's preaching was organized, logical, Scriptural, and didactic. Though an outstanding Oxford scholar, he spoke in the language of the people, simply, directly, earnestly, doctrinally, persuasively, and extemporaneously.

George Whitefield, a fellow-member of the Oxford "Holy Club" with John and Charles Wesley, did not measure up to Wesley in scholarship, organizing ability, or literary productions, but for pulpit eloquence and popularity as a preacher he surpassed Wesley. Endowed with a marvelous preaching voice, he has been called "the Demosthenes of the pulpit." He preached with boldness, directness, eloquence, pathos, deep feeling, and perfect gestures. With vivid imagination and sonorous voice he charmed the multitudes. He loved to preach and lived to preach the new birth. Much of his evangelizing was done in America, where he died at the age of fifty-six after crossing the Atlantic thirteen times. He literally preached himself to death to win souls.

Contemporary with Wesley and Whitefield and equally zealous to win the lost was Jonathan Edwards (1703-1758), who labored on the American side of the Atlantic. A strong Calvinist and a key figure in the Great Awakening in the colonies, Jonathan Edwards was a scholar and preacher of first rank. He held evangelical convictions and unbending views of Christian morality. His famous sermon, "Sinners in the Hands of an Angry God," is typical of his sermonizing but does not represent his major preaching emphasis. A careful analysis of his written sermons shows that he preached much more on the love of God than on his wrath. His sermons were long, heavy, and contained many divisions.

Popular preaching in *the nineteenth century is* represented by Henry Ward Beecher (1813-1887) and Phillips Brooks (1834-1893) in America and Joseph Parker (1830-1902) in England.

Beecher, one of the most brilliant and influential preachers of his century, was eloquent, imaginative, popular, and always preached out of the overflow. His sermons were not well-organized or profound, but were kindling, suggestive, and moving. Perhaps his greatest contribution to preaching was in establishing the Lyman Beecher Lectures on Preaching at Yale in 1872 in honor of his father. This lectureship on preaching has had more influence on preaching in the English language than any other factor since the Reformation.

Phillips Brooks was an Episcopal minister at Trinity Church, Boston. He made an enduring impact on American preaching. A huge man physically, with a powerful personality, he preached from manuscript at a rapid pace. His messages had such beauty, vigor, and sweeping flow that he held his hearers spellbound. A great thinker, he usually dealt with one major idea, turning it around and around to point out its facets.

Joseph Parker of City Temple, London, was colorful, original, imaginative, oratorical, and popular. His affluence of thought, richness of fancy, range of resources, combined with rare genius made him one of the great preachers of his generation. In his later years he concentrated on expository preaching, publishing *Parker's People's Bible* in several volumes.

Frederick W. Robertson (1816-1853), an Anglican who made his record in six short years at Trinity Chapel, Brighton, England, is an outstanding name in preaching literature. He died at age thirty-seven relatively unknown, but in the years since his printed sermons have had a worldwide circulation, and his popularity seems to be growing. His orginality, imagination, spiritual insight, and balance give his sermons a distinctive and lasting power. He emphasized the balanced two-point sermon and preached suggestively rather than exhaustively. His method was expository even when the sermon at first seems to be textual or topical. He had a unique capacity to penetrate to the heart of a Scripture passage, and then to set forth its primary teaching with simplicity, clarity, vividness, and force.

Classical preaching, based upon the principles of the classical Greek and Roman orators, combined with the best in Christian rhetoric is represented by John A. Broadus (1827-1895). He was a profound Christian scholar who preached with simplicity and grace. His book on homiletics, *On the Preparation and Delivery of Sermons,* has passed through numerous editions and revisions, and has been the most used such textbook in America. In this same tradition stands Austin Phelps (1820-1890) of Andover, a great preacher and teacher of preaching, whose book, *The Theory of Preaching,* emphasized classical organization and rhetoric. A pastor and preacher who demonstrated the best in this tradition was John Henry Jowett (1863-1923) of England and America, whose attainments in sermonic style, evangelical loyalty, and richness of thought are well-nigh perfect.

Following the evangelistic pattern of Wesley and Whitefield have come other great preachers. Charles Haddon Spurgeon (1834-1892) through powerful Pauline evangelistic preaching made his Metropolitan Tabernacle in London a world center of evangelism for more than a generation. D. L. Moody (1837-1899), while not a great preacher, popularized evangelistic preaching. Others have followed in their train.

The Reformation emphasis on expository preaching has also continued down through the years. Alexander McLaren of Manchester (1826-1910) and G. Campbell Morgan (1863-1942) of London achieved highest standards of perfection as expository preachers.

In *the twentieth century* psychological preaching became popular. Intense studies in psychology and personality produced such rich material for preaching that many men have centered their sermons around its use. Harry Emerson Fosdick (1878-........) believes that a sermon should begin with a life-problem rather than a Scripture passage. George A. Buttrick (1878-......), Ralph W. Sockman (1889-........) of New York, and Leslie Weatherhead (1893-........) of London have carried on this trend.

The neo-orthodox or crisis theology has made quite an impact on preaching. Originating with Karl Barth (1886-........) and Emil Brunner (1889-1966) in Europe, this theology puts great emphasis on preaching the Word. The Word of God is not identified with the written Scriptures, but the Scriptures precipitate the Word in the process of true preaching. The preacher must preach to make the Bible come alive and confront the hearer with Almighty God and his present claims.

The necessity of communication in preaching is a strong one today. Unless the message comes through to the listener, preaching fails. Halford E. Luccock (1896-1961) specialized in this area.

Today sermons must be short — not over fifteen to twenty-five minutes; they must be properly adjusted to their place in the total worship service; they must seek to involve the audience in the preaching situation, and must be Biblically oriented and vitally relevant to the needs of the people.

Preaching is a dynamic experience involving the preacher, the congregation the message, and the setting. It demands the total dedication of physical, spiritual, and intellectual powers plus the presence and power of the Holy Spirit. Then the preacher can speak with authority.

The art of preaching has never been totally static nor can it be. The Word of God does not change but the preaching situation and the needs of people change. Given the constant elements of the Word of God, the man of God, the people of God, and the Spirit of God, preaching will always be exciting. Redeemed men can do nothing nobler than to preach.

BIBLIOGRAPHY

Blackwood, Andrew W., *The Preparation of Sermons.* New York: Abingdon-Cokesbury Press, 1948.

Broadus, John A., *On the Preparation and Delivery of Sermons.* Rev. ed., Jesse B. Weatherspoon. New York: Harper & Bros., 1944.

Brooks, Phillips, *Lectures on Preaching.* London: Griffith, Farrar & Co., 1877.

Davis, H. Grady, *Design for Preaching.* Philadelphia: Muhlenberg Press, 1958.

Jones, Ilion T., *Principles and Practice of Preaching.* New York: Abingdon Press, 1956.

Pattison, T. Harwood, *The Making of the Sermon.* Philadelphia: American Baptist Publication Society, 1898.

Brown, H. C., Clinard, H. Gordon, and Northcutt, Jesse J., *Steps to the Sermon.* Nashville: Broadman Press, 1963.

Planned Preaching in the Christian Year

Part of the genius of preaching is its timeliness. The sermon is a deliverance addressed to a particular people in a particular situation. In a sense it stands alone as an urgent challenge or appeal for the hour in which it is spoken. The particularity marked the preaching of the New Testament. The sermon of Jesus in the Nazareth synagogue, and those of Peter at Pentecost, Paul at Mars Hill, and Stephen at the moment of his martyrdom, were in no sense planned with a liturgical framework. They were spontaneous deliverances with high relevancy to the particular moment. The main need was the proclamation of the evangel, and to serve that need Paul decried the formality of days and seasons and the whole conception of the ordered calendar of Judaism.

By the time of Augustine the early church had developed an ordered ministry, a theology, and a liturgy, and was well along in establishing an ecclesiastical calendar which would be complete by the fifth century. Preaching was contained within this larger framework of the church as a worshiping community, and regularly celebrated the great memorial events and doctrines of the faith.

American preaching, during the frontier days, however, had much in common with the preaching of the New Testament. The need determined the form, or rather the formlessness, of frontier evangelism. Individual souls were to be won before much attention could be devoted to the cultivation of the community of the church through theological instruction within a liturgical framework. There is a rough parallel between the change from the primitive preaching of New Testament times to that of the third and fourth centuries, and the reshaping of American preaching from frontier times to the present.

In our time the rise of the theological movement with its emphasis on the church, the revival of Biblical scholarship, the liturgical movement, the ecumenical emphasis, and the promotion of the ministry of all believers, all serve to charge the preacher with concern for the long-range goals of the church's mission, and for consistent planning for the year as well as for the current week. The ordered calendar of the Christian Year is the first means at hand for a planned program of preaching which will adequately treat the major events and themes of the worshiping community, and promote the education of the faithful in the life of faith.

The Christian Year, substantially as completed in the fifth century, has been the framework of the communal life of the Roman Catholic, Lutheran, and Anglican fellowships. It has been revived in the free churches during the past quarter of a century, though with many modifications. Each denomination is free to omit such celebrations as have no meaning for their own experience, such as days for the saints and Mary, and special periods of penance; and each denomination may add to its calendar the memorials peculiar to its own life. The civil calendar, also, presents the preacher with recurring times and themes subject to Christian interpretation. Allowing for modifications and additions, the drama of the Christian Year expresses the unity of the church and ensures continuity in its experience of worship and education. It requires long-range planning of the ministry of preaching, with the whole year as the unit, rather than the passing week.

The scheme of the calendar includes the central events of revelation with their appropriate doctrines and themes, and a lectionary which pays respect to the whole Bible. The first half of the Year, from Advent Sunday to Pentecost (or Trinity) deals with God's initiative in the divine deeds. The second half of the Year, to the end of the Pentecost (or Trinity) season, calls for man's response to God's acts of grace, expressed in personal faith and in the ministry of the church to the world.

The Year begins with Advent Sunday and continues a christological emphasis through the first half. The four Sundays of Advent are in preparation for Christmas, each Sunday having an appropriate theme, i.e., Creation, The Bible, Prophecy, and the Forerunner. Christmas emphasizes the Nativity story and the doctrine of the Incarnation. Epiphany on January 6 opens a season of from three to six weeks, concentrating on the various manifestations of God and the world-mission of the church. This is followed by the pre-Lenten Sundays, Septuagesima, Sexagesima, and Quinquagesima which offer the preacher a variety of possibilities. Lent, the oldest season, prepares for Easter and extends from Ash Wednesday through the Saturday before Easter. It is a season of penitence and growth which leads to the high climax of the Holy Week observances. Easter Day, with its triumphant celebration of the resurrection, opens the six-week season of Eastertide, continuing the theme of the risen life and its meaning for personal faith and the ministry of the church. Ascension Day is infrequently observed in the free churches, though the Sunday following is appropriate for emphasis on the transcendence of Christ. The division of the year is at Pentecost in the Roman Catholic and Lutheran usages; and, with the Anglicans, on Trinity Sunday the following week. Thus, the last half-year is called Sundays after Pentecost, or Sundays after Trinity, respectively.

The last portion of the year is not so clearly marked by events and their preparatory seasons. On the whole the emphasis is on Christian life and the church's ministry. The preacher has considerable freedom through this period in the selection of sermon themes and the organization of series on evangelism, Christian ethics, and Biblical exposition.

The lectionaries of the liturgical churches are substantially the same. The readings include pericopes from the Psalms, with lessons from the Old Testament, the Epistles, and the Gospels. Thus the whole Bible is covered in cycles through the readings and expositions. Many denominations have official lectionaries based on the traditional scheme but with variations, and unofficial reading lists by individuals are often used.

Planned preaching, with the year as the unit rather than the week, is an integral part of the evangelism, worship, education, and ministry of the church universal.

BIBLIOGRAPHY

Service books of the three major liturgical churches:

The Roman Catholic Missal.

The Book of Common Prayer of the Protestant Episcopal Church.

The Common Service Book of the Lutheran Church. The Board of Publication of the United Lutheran Church in America, 1917.

Background books on the history and theory of the Church Year:

Peter Archer, *The Christian Calendar and the Gregorian Reform.* Fordham University Press, 1941.

John Dowden, *The Church Year and Kalendar.* Macmillan Company (Cambridge Press), 1910.

Stanley Vernon, *The Liturgical Year.* A. R. Mowbray & Co., London, 1907.

Frank E. Wilson, *An Outline of the Christian Year* (pamphlet). Morehouse-Goreham Co., 1941.

Edward T. Horn III, *The Christian Year,* Days and Seasons of the Church. Muhlenberg Press, 1957.

Books of sermons and worship materials based on the Church Year:

Howard A. Johnson, ed., *Preaching the Christian Year.* Scribner, 1957.

Sixty-five Lutheran Pastors, *The Gospel We Preach.* Augustana, 1959.

Samuel J. Schiechen, *Pastoral Prayers for the Christian Year.* Abingdon, 1957.

David A. MacLennan, *Resources for Sermon Preparation.* Westminster, 1955.

Andrew W. Blackwood, *Planning a Year's Pulpit Work.* Abingdon, 1952.

George M. Gibson, *Planned Preaching.* Westminster, 1954.

British and American Preaching Since 1900

Preaching is a specialized form of the art of communication. With pardonable exaggeration it has been called "the finest of fine arts" (A. T. Pierson). It is "the mediation of Divine Truth through human personality unto eternal life" (A. E. Garvie). Its characteristic form is the sermon, which is "an oral address to the popular mind, upon some religious truth as contained in the Scriptures, and elaborately treated with a view to persuasion" (Austin Phelps). And its aim, broadly speaking, is "to bind eternal truth be present fact."

A sermon is a speech (Latin *sermo*) but Christian preaching is much more than speechmaking — it is the communication to sinful men of the good news of God in Christ. As such it is centered in Christ as the Supreme revealer of God and the only redeemer of man. In its various forms it seeks to bring men into living fellowship with the eternal Christ that they may experience the fulness of the divine salvation. This means the realization of a new standing before God, and as its concomitant the reconstruction of the sin-distorted and sin-distrupted personality. "By Christ redeemed, In Christ restored" is the *motif* of all genuine Christian preaching. That is why a lecture is no more a sermon than a platform is a pulpit or an auditorium is a church (though many a compeling sermon has been delivered from a platform in an auditorium).

1. BRITISH PREACHING

In 1900 Britain was just at the end of the fabulous Victorian Era. The nineteenth century (especially the latter half) was a time of intellectual ferment, of social idealism, of political upheaval, of religious awareness, of ecclesiastical disturbance, of scientific and theological debate. New concepts of the universe and of man's place in it were much in evidence; revolutionary social and political movements (Socialism, Marxism, Anarchism) were gaining momentum; a marked reaction from the hitherto rigid orthodoxy was dominant; and there was a considerable importation from the Continent of the "higher critical" theories of the Bible.

Of course, Christian people were much disturbed by this "new way of ideas." This was especially true of orthodox believers; but even those with a more liberal theology had their difficulties. There was widespread irreligion among the lower classes, yet much of the vigor of the British people went into their religion – despite the fact that many of the leading intellectuals (T. H. Huxley, Herbert Spencer, Matthew Arnold, George Eliot, and others) were definitely anti-Christian. The Free Churches were increasing their hold on the lower and middle classes; the Church of England was in the throes of the Anglo-Catholic Revival; and even the Roman Church had made significant gains, both politically and socially.

Many preachers attempted either to combat the "new way of ideas" or to come to terms with it; and most of the sermons of that Age of Uncertainty were characterized by (one or more) Altitude, Latitude, Platitude, or Longitude. But there were gifted preachers – some strictly orthodox, others less so – who sought to assure the Christian public that the certitudes of the faith were unshaken. Chief among these were Frederick William Robertson, whose deep spiritual insight and broad human sympathies had a powerful influence on the working classes; Frederick Denison Maurice, whose ecclesiastical career was a stormy one on account of his unorthodox eschatology and advanced political ideas; Frederick William Farrar, Dean of Canterbury, who influenced greatly the religious feelings and attitudes of the middle classes; Arthur Penrhyn Stanley, who as Dean of Westminster sought to make the Abbey a house of prayer for all Christians, irrespective of their dogmatic creed; William Boyd Carpenter, Bishop of Ripon, an evangelical orator of the first order; and Henry Parry Liddon, whose powerful preaching as Canon of St. Paul's Cathedral attracted immense crowds, and who was regarded by his fellow Anglicans as the greatest preacher of his time. The above mentioned were all Anglican clergymen; they were illustrious representatives of a tradition wherein the general level of preaching was none too high.

In the Free Churches the pulpit was more highly regarded than the altar; hence the quality of the preaching ministry was somewhat superior. And there were outstanding preachers too. Robert William Dale, of Birmingham, was the intellectual leader of the Congregationalists; indeed, of the Free Churches generally. He was a first class theologian (as witness his volume on *The Atonement*), who was not afraid to preach doctrinal and ethical sermons which called for the closest attention of the hearers. Thomas Charles Edwards, a Welshman, was another great theologian who was also a great preacher. Another Welshman was Herber Evans, who for overwhelming eloquence Sir William Robertson Nicoll placed above every other preacher he had heard. Yet another Welshman was Hugh Price Hughes, a fiery yet cultured follower of John Wesley, who never wearied in his sermons to "pursue sinners."

The Scottish pulpit also had its luminaries. Henry Drummond, a Free Church of Scotland layman and close associate of D. L. Moody, was keenly interested in lessening the conflict between science and religion. His preaching made a great impact on college students. George Matheson was blind from young manhood. Yet he soon came to be recognized as a great orator, a powerful thinker, and a master of expression – "potentially the greatest man given to the Scottish churches since the days of Thomas Chalmers" (W. R. Nicoll).

The preaching ministries of Alexander Whyte and James Stalker belong to this period, though both lived until after the close of World War I. Whyte was a "high Calvinist," who was sometimes described as "the last of the Puritans." In his sermons he revealed an intense consciousness of the sinfulness of sin. He denounced the shams and vices and respectable sins of his highly respectable congregation; nevertheless Free St. George's Church, Edinburgh, was always crowded to the door. Two of his junior colleagues may be mentioned here. John Kelman succeeded J. H. Jowett at Fifth Avenue Presbyterian Church, New York. Hugh Black became a distinguished member of the faculty of Union Seminary, New York. His brother James Black succeeded Whyte, carrying on a great preaching tradition.

James Stalker was a distinct loss to the regular preaching ministry when he exchanged his Glasgow pulpit for the Aberdeen professorship. An outstanding preacher, he knew how to fuse sound scholarship and clear thinking into memorable discourses. He too was a Calvinist, but he liked to stress in his thinking that "the death of Christ is sufficient for all, adapted to all, and freely offered to all."

During the latter half of the Victorian Era three evangelical preachers of genius stood out above all others. First and foremost was Charles Haddon Spurgeon who, with one exception, was the greatest Baptist who ever "prepared the way of the Lord." He died in 1892, his end probably hastened by the unhappy Downgrade Controversy in which he was involved. The general Christian public, and not a few of the intelligentsia, considered him the greatest preacher of the century. By today's standards his formal ministerial education was meager, but he was widely read, especially in Puritan theology. He possessed great natural gifts – a magnificent "bell voice," a rare and ready command of homespun English, a racy style of speaking, a saving sense of humor, a deep insight into the spiritual needs of the common man, and utter devotion to Christ. His impact on the religious life of Britain (and of America) was tremendous. His theology was moderately Calvinistic, his sermons warmly evangelistic, and his presentation of the gospel so fresh and refreshing that within a few months of entering upon his London ministry, at nineteen years of age, the crowds flocked to hear him and continued to do so for thirty-eight years.

His most distinguished Baptist contemporary was Alexander Maclaren, for forty-five years minister of Union Chapel, Manchester. Maclaren was called the "Prince of Expositors." Indeed, he was described as "the supreme example, the perfect type, of the classic Protestant tradition of expository preaching" (Ernest H. Jeffs); and his many volumes bear ample testimony to that fact.

Joseph Parker was a Congregationalist, the first minister of the City Temple, London. He was eccentric, emotional, theatrical, often sensational. To see his leonine figure in the pulpit was a never-to-be forgotten sight, and to hear him preach was to enjoy oratory at its highest. And the note he liked to strike was not so much the need for repentance; rather he sought to create in men's hearts "a warm, human sentiment of wondering love for Jesus Christ."

Parker's successor was Reginald John Campbell, a man with much personal charm, high preaching ability, but with an unstable theology. Parker profoundly disliked the new liberalism in religion, but Campbell welcomed it with open arms. Soon he was involved in the New Theology Controversy, owing to his over insistence upon the immanence of God and his radical views of Scripture. Yet he remained the "idol" of a vast number of people, even when he surprised everyone by "going over to Anglicanism." It was then that Campbell recanted his theological aberrations. Yet even in the midst of bitter debate he could say sincerely, "Jesus Christ is central for my spiritual life. . . . I worship Him and trust my soul to Him" (*A Spiritual Pilgrimage*).

Peter Taylor Forsyth, "a Barthian before Barth," was a preacher of considerable influence before he left the pastorate for the presidency of a Congregational seminary. Yet his sermons were far from easy to understand. He used to say, "People say that I preach above their heads. My reply is 'Lift up your heads.'" He was a vigorous opponent of Campbell's New Theology which he characterized as being "like a bad photograph, under-developed and over exposed."

Three outstanding Methodists belong to this period, namely, William L. Watkinson, who attracted crowds of men to his famous noonday lectures in Manchester; John Ernest Rattenbury, a worthy successor to Hugh Price Hughes at the West London Mission; and Frederick Luke Wiseman, whose dramatic handling of Bible incidents was unforgettable.

Two outstanding preachers who belonged to pre-1914 days were John Watson ("Ian Maclaren") and Charles Silvester Horne. Watson's twenty-five year ministry in Liverpool was phenomenal. He was a brilliant writer and a compelling preacher who never treated any theme "without a strong sense of moral responsibility." Silvester Horne was a natural-born speaker, who at times could rise to matchless eloquence. He managed to combine a great ministry in Central London with being a Member of Parliament. He believed in taking his religion into politics, holding that the latter is the natural extension of the former.

August, 1914 saw the beginning of World War I. It was also the beginning of a new era for Christianity. The church had come to that momentous date on a rising tide of expanding influence, having counteracted the secularizing currents of the preceding period with considerable success. This new era — "post-Christian" according to some — came with apparent suddenness. Humanity was now on the march, and in some ways the march seemed to be away from the Christian faith.

Such a world-shaking event as the war was bound to put its mark on the preaching of the gospel. The most obvious and significant example of this was the changed attitude to the problem of war. Prior to 1914 most British (Free Church, at any rate) and American preachers regarded armed conflict between nations as a blatant denial of the teaching of Christ, and cherished the illusion that war on a grand scale was a thing of the past. Indeed, prior to America's entrance into the conflict, many of the nations's outstanding preachers continued to denounce war as anti-Christian. But in the British Commonwealth it was different. The war was proclaimed to be a just one, even a holy crusade; and by the time the United States had become a participant most American preachers were saying the same thing. Even Harry Emerson Fosdick had not then been converted to absolute pacifism. He, like most preachers, regarded *The Challenge of the Present Crisis* (the title of the book written when he was a chaplain) as a call to go out and fight the enemy.

Furthermore, the coming of the war, and its awful slaughter, severely discredited the facile social and political optimism inherited from the nineteenth century. The secular doctrine of the inevitable progress of the human race, so often stressed in liberal pulpits, lost its hold despite the hope that this was the war to end all wars and so "make the world safe for democracy." Man's "Total Depravity" was an old doctrine now become less suspect; even that of "Original Sin" seemed more respectable. Then, with the coming of World War II, piling horror upon horror, and presaging a new era in which the nuclear annihilation of all mankind became possible, this swing to the theological right was given further impetus.

During World War I and the decades following there were many distinguished preachers in Britain. The National Church could boast of Charles Gore, Bishop of Oxford, who sought to come to terms with the higher criticism of the Old Testament while remaining loyal to his High Church theology; William Ralph Inge, Dean of St. Paul's ("The Gloomy Dean"), who because of his caustic comments on religion and social matters gained a reputation out of all proportion to his oratorical ability; H. Hensley Henson, Bishop of Durham, who, like Dean Inge, was a Broad Churchman, and a staunch champion of the reasonableness of the Christian faith; William Temple, Archbishop first of York, then of Canterbury, called "the greatest churchman of this century," who was a philosopher-theologian par excellence, and who could be quite at home in the greatest intellectual company; H. R. L. ("Dick") Sheppard, an unrepentant pacifist whose broadcast preaching during the earliest days of radio was phenomenal; G. A. Studdert-Kennedy ("Woodbine Willie"), whose unconventional and passionate preaching captivated the British troops in France; and J. Stuart Holden, an evangelical preacher of rare power.

In the English Free Church pulpits there

were giants: George Campbell Morgan, who had inherited McLaren's mantle as the "Prince of Expositors," and was exercising a mighty ministry in the shadow of Buckingham Palace; John Henry Jowett, "the greatest living preacher" of his day, who returned from New York to succeed Campbell Morgan, and to continue to preach "a Gospel of delicate sympathy rather than of sturdy strength" (Horton Davies); Dinsdale T. Young, a Methodist of the old school, a "royal preacher" with great oratorical ability, and who was followed by W. E. Sangster, "an evangelical greatheart," whose intellect matched his spirituality"; Frederick B. Meyer, who as a young Baptist minister had learned from D. L. Moody "the art of winning men for Christ"; Joseph Fort Newton, a liberal American who fulfilled a brilliant, though short, ministry in the City Temple during the war, and who was succeeded by the Australian Baptist, Frederick W. Norwood, through whose vigorous preaching the City Temple was saved from extinction; Leslie D. Weatherhead, who made skilfull use of the widespread interest in the New Psychology to commend the gospel, becoming the most popular British preacher of the time; John Clifford, the intellectual and spiritual leader of the General Baptists; John D. Jones, a Welshman who came to the forefront among the English Congregationalists, whose preaching ability was matched by his great skill as an organizer; Robert F. Horton, another Congregationalist, whose very effective ministry to the intellectuals of North London was not unlike that of Harry Emerson Fosdick at the Riverside Church; and William E. Orchard, a most unorthodox preacher until he left his Presbyterian-Congregationalist heritage for the Church of Rome.

Two who were unordained are deserving of mention: Terence Reavely Glover, Public Orator of Cambridge University, a Baptist layman whose unconventional sermons influenced students; and Miss A. Maude Royden, an Anglican who became Fort Newton's colleague at the City Temple.

Scotland has long been a country of great preaching, where there were many outstanding pulpiteers during and after World War I. Chief among these were: George H. Morrison, Arthur John Gossip, John A. Hutton, Hubert L. Simpson (all of Glasgow); William M. Clow and J. R. P. Sclater (both of Edinburgh).

Morrison was, at the height of his ministry, the most popular preacher in Scotland. He was described as "the average preacher raised to the nth degree." His was positive preaching based on Biblical truth; and through his many volumes of sermons became widely known in Britain and America. Gossip was a torrential speaker, racing from point to point and idea to idea so rapidly that his hearers were left breathless. But his sermons made their mark. Hutton and Simpson were "clever" preachers, richly imaginative, and well able in their sermons to find "a foothold in Scripture for the uneasy mind of the age." Clow was a rare combination of scholar and evangelist. His sermons were richly Biblical, characterized by an unmistakable note of urgency. Sclater had phenomenal success with college students.

During the last two decades James S. Stewart of Edinburgh has been in Scotland. He is as popular in America as he is in Britain. A fine exponent of Pauline theology, his is preaching with the cross at its center.

2. AMERICAN PREACHING

America has had a fine tradition of great preaching, especially during the last 100 years. There have been a few pulpit giants, and more than a few near-giants – men of marked intellectual achievement, outstanding oratorical ability, and true spiritual eminence. Some have been strongly conservative theologically, like John Hall, George W. Truett, Mark A. Matthews, T. De Witt Talmage, Walter A. Maier, and Clarence Macartney. Others have been just as strongly liberal theologically, like George A. Gordon, Francis Greenwood Peabody, Charles Reynolds Brown, Henry Sloan Coffin, Lynn Harold Hough, and Reinhold Niebuhr. But the majority of distinguished American preachers have been somewhere in-between, being well represented by such influential pulpiteers as S. Parkes Cadman, Peter Marshall, George A. Buttrick (and his successor David H. C. Read), Joseph R. Sizoo, Paul E. Scherer, Ralph W. Sockman, Charles E. Jefferson, and Harris E. Kirk. Cadman, Marshall, Buttrick, and Read are importees from Britain.

The great evangelists of the period have all been emphatically conservative, which fact contributed mightily to their preaching appeal. Dwight L. Moody was followed by B. Fay Mills, Reuben A. Torrey, J. Wilbur Chapman, William A. Sunday, and William F. Graham. Two outstanding Roman Catholic preachers may be mentioned: Father Charles E. Coughlin and Bishop Fulton J. Sheen.

The two preaching giants of the nineteenth century were Henry Ward Beecher and Bishop Phillips Brooks. For forty years Beecher ("the American Spurgeon") reigned from his pulpit throne in Brooklyn; and by his vigorous — sometimes sensational — preaching made Plymouth Church a national institution. In an era of challenging social and intellectual change, he stood forth as a prodigious figure, voicing the hopes and thoughts of the common people.

Phillips Brooks, like Beecher, was a preacher of genius, though the latter surpassed him in sheer oratorical power. He was much influenced by the liberalism of F. W. Robertson and F. D. Maurice; and this fact wedded to passionate sincerity and deep spiritual insight profoundly impressed his hearers.

Horace Bushnell, an older contemporary of Beecher and Brooks, was the real father of American theological liberalism. He emphasized the immanence of God in nature and in man, the atoning work of Christ as a concrete expression of divine love, and the fundamental need of religious education of the children.

Walter Rauschenbusch, "the most creative spirit in the American theological world," was the father of the Social Gospel — "the most significant contribution to the great ongoing stream of Christianity."

Washington Gladden was also a pioneer in the social application of the principles of Jesus. He was a vigorous champion of the rights of labor and a brilliant defender of the faith as he understood it.

From the end of World War I to the end of World War II the most outstanding American preacher was Harry Emerson Fosdick, a most prolific sermonizer and a widely read author. He was an unabashed exponent of a pronounced liberal theology, the advocate of an "Adventurous Christianity." Fosdick has been the storm center of theological controversy through most of his ministry. His famous sermon on "Shall the Fundamentalists Win?" evoked an answer from John Roach Straton, a doughty champion of orthodoxy, entitled: "Shall the Funnymonkeyists Win?" Yet the evangelical core of Fosdick's preaching has been noted even by some of the most conservative among his critics.

British preaching on the whole has tended to be Biblical and expository. American preaching is not altogether lacking in this respect, especially where the preacher has been influenced by the Neo-orthodoxy of Karl Barth, Emil Brunner, and Reinhold Niebuhr. However, "problem preaching" and "life situation" sermons are very much in evidence in the American pulpit today. Robert James McCracken, Fosdick's able successor at the Riverside Church, has largely departed from the Scottish tradition of preaching in which he was reared, and has adopted the type of sermon so closely associated with his distinguished predecessor. There is a good deal of "suburban preaching" in the American pulpit, by which is meant preaching "which makes its home in the fringes and outskirts of Christian truth rather than in the center and citadel."

As for the Social Gospel, it is still a strong factor in the American presentation of the Christian faith, though it is now characterized by changing emphases. There are some pulpiteers "who preach the social gospel because they have no other gospel to preach" (James Denney); nevertheless, there are staunch evangelicals who know how to stress the social implications of Christ's teaching without any lessening of their "passion for souls."

There are some other changing emphases in the contemporary pulpit. Conservative evangelicals have, with some minor reinterpretations, remained loyal to the traditional orthodox theology; for example, they lay undeviating stress upon the deity of Christ, His virgin birth, His physical resurrection, and His second coming. In extremely liberal pulpits, especially where Bultmannism and Tillichism are influential, these cardinal Fundamentalist doctrines are anathema. But there are also changes among moderate evangelicals. Some form of the Moral Influence theory of the death of Christ has been substituted for the older substitutionary theory of the atonement, giving rise in some instances to a "cross-less" Christianity. The fact of Christ is stressed, but this often goes hand-in-hand with an attenuated Christology. A subtle humanism has gained access to some prominent pulpits; and this secularized gospel can be clothed in specious psychological jargon in which "peace of mind" and "adjustment to life's tensions" are regarded as life's *summum bonum* and the quintessence of personal salvation.

BIBLIOGRAPHY

Chrisman, Lewis H., *The Message of the American Pulpit.* New York: Richard R. Smith, 1930.

Davies, Horton, *Varieties of English Preaching 1900-1960.* New York: Prentice Hall, 1963.

Gammie, Alexander, *Preachers I Have Heard.* Glasgow: Pickering & Inglis, 1946.

Garvie, Alfred E., *The Christian Preacher.* New York: Chas. Scribner's Sons, 1920.

Jeffs, Ernest H., *Princes of the Modern Pulpit.* London: Sampson Low, Marston & Co., n.d.

Jones, Edgar DeWitt, *The Royalty of the Pulpit.* New York: Harper & Brothers, 1951.

Marchant, Sir James, *British Preachers.* New York: G. P. Putnam's Sons, 1928.

Nicoll, W. Robertson, *Princes of the Church.* London: Hodder & Stoughton, 1921.

Porrit, Arthur, *The Best I Remember.* New York: George H. Doran Co., n.d.

Sinclair, Hugh, *Voices of Today.* London, James Clarke & Co., 1912.

Emphases in Preaching

Preaching emphases may shift, but only within limits which are unalterably fixed:

1. *That which the minister proclaims must be truly the Word of God.* The minister stands in direct succession with the apostles and prophets who declared, "Thus saith the Lord." The minister's message is not his own; he is an "ambassador for Christ" (II Cor. 5:20). The true ambassador does not presume to originate a message of his own; he conveys the message entrusted to him by his sovereign.

The world is not greatly interested in the opinions and speculations of the preacher; but the world listens when he declares, humbly, intelligently, with spiritual concern and spiritual attractiveness, "Thus saith the Lord!" The word of man does not become the Word of God by being loudly proclaimed, and no amount of noise and lather can substitute for the note of authority. God does not promise to bless the proclamation of our own clever ideas; but he does promise ". . . my word . . . shall not return unto me void . . ." (Isa. 55:11).

2. *The message must be complete.* A half truth might be as hurtful as an untruth. To neglect either half of the Great Commission may be as dangerous as outright heresy. The responsibility of the minister is to "make disciples" and to "teach them." His calling is thus a calling with a twofold thrust – salvation and nurture, salvation and the "things that accompany salvation" (Heb. 6:9).

After salvation there is need for indoctrination (Eph. 4:14), consecration (Rom. 12:1), inspiration (Neh. 8:10), comfort (I Thess. 4:18; Isa. 40:1), strengthening (Col. 1:11), conviction (Acts 4:20), and action (James 1:22).

But the primary concern is to "make disciples." A "disciple" is a willing learner, with his heart open to the truth of the gospel, responsive to it, and ready to be led further. We are not merely to inform our hearers, or to provoke thought, but like the Gospel of John, to induce belief; not merely to improve their manners, or to make them more comfortable on the way to destruction, but to save them from destruction. Only when they have become "disciples," are they ready to be taught "all things whatsoever. . . ."

3. *The message must be rightly motivated.* The greater part of the human family is out of fellowship with God – alienated, unreconciled and suffering all the consequences. The minister is therefore essentially a minister of reconciliation, and the test of his labors is, What happens to the man in the pew? The supreme tribute is that which was accorded to John the Baptist: When his disciples "heard him speak . . . they followed Jesus" (John 1:37). Nowhere is the Scriptural conception of the minister's task more perfectly expressed than in the familiar words of the Apostle Paul: "We are ambassadors for Christ, as though God did beseech you by us; we pray you in Christ's stead, be ye reconciled to God" (II Cor. 5:20). The

preacher whose ministry is steeped in the spirit of this text can not possibly go far wrong in doctrine, spirit, procedure, or emphasis.

The apostles have set an excellent example, and there is much to learn also from those who have ministered before us on the American scene.

1. THE EMPHASIS OF THE APOSTLES

The ministry of Peter and those associated with him is presented with amazing completeness in the second chapter of the Book of Acts. Here is evangelism at its best, and the spiritual nurture that should follow. Here, with vivid recollections of his Lord, and mindful of the twofold thrust of the Great Commission, Peter presents the Christ of the Gospels – His Messianic identity, His sinless life, His atoning death, His bodily resurrection, and His eternal sovereignty. The sermon is strongly doctrinal, containing the greatest body of truth ever put together in one sermon. So frequently do these doctrinal points recur in the messages of the apostles in the New Testament that they came to be known as "The Apostolic Formula."

Here the minister sees what to preach, what kind of an "invitation" to give, and what to do after baptism. Here also is the complete program of Christian nurture – the "all things whatsoever" of Christ's Great Commission. The believers "continued steadfastly in the apostles' doctrine and fellowship, and in breaking of bread, and in prayers" (Acts 2:42), and in witnessing, worshiping, and giving. This Spirit-filled church, with its fully rounded program, has never been equaled in spiritual attractiveness and spiritual effectiveness. It was a happy church – "with gladness . . . praising God"; it was a popular church – "having favor with all the people"; and a fruitful church – "The Lord added to the church daily . . ." (Acts 2:42-47).

The ministry of Paul, like the ministry of Peter, is notable for the inclusiveness of its emphases. In Acts 20, a number of arresting phrases account for his phenomenally fruitful ministry of three years in Ephesus:

a. *"All seasons"* (v. 18). His spiritual concern was not seasonal, but perennial; not occasional, but unceasing. The fruitage of such a ministry is not seasonal, but continuous, like that of the orange tree in continuous production bearing buds, blossoms, tiny oranges, half grown and full grown oranges, and fully ripe oranges simultaneously.

b. *"All the counsel of God"* (v. 27). This means a balanced spiritual diet, emphasizing both the theological and the ethical, the doctrinal and the practical. An unbalanced diet produces unsymmetrical saints; obsessions produce cranks, controversies and schisms; omissions leave the soul unfortified against sin and error. In touching every area of human experience, Paul labored for "the perfecting of the saints" (Eph. 4:12), and the fulfillment of both "the first and great commandment" ("Thou shalt love the Lord thy God") and "the second . . . like unto it" ("Thou shalt love thy neighbour as thyself") (Matt. 22:37-39). To observe the Golden Rule is not enough; there must be "glory to God," as well as peace among men (Luke 2:14).

c. *"Publicly and from house to house"* (v. 20). Either without the other is incomplete. There is no substitute for preaching; nevertheless, there are more lost souls in "the highways and hedges" (Luke 14:23) than in our houses of worship.

d. *"Jews and . . . Greeks"* (v. 21). Paul's ministry reached across racial barriers and smoldering resentments. He has a gospel for "both sides of the tracks," for the high and the low, "the wise and the unwise." Like the Lord Jesus, who was compassionate toward the cultured Pharisee Nicodemus and the fallen woman of Samaria, Paul witnessed with equal concern to King Agrippa and the slave Onesimus.

2. THE EMPHASIS OF AMERICAN PREACHERS

Voluntariness in religion has made American Christianity the most diverse in the world. There is more religious activity and probably less bitterness of religious feeling than in any other country. With liberty of soul and freedom of speech the preacher addresses himself to the needs of his people as he conceives them to be. Changing times and circumstances bring changing emphases. Wars, depressions, disasters, political upheavals, theological controversies, and spiritual decadence call for light and guidance from the Word of God. Perhaps the minister reacts to some prevailing error or the neglect of some vital doctrine. His preaching then reflects the age in which he is living. But, as Ernest Trice Thompson points out in *Changing Emphases in American Preaching* (Westminster Press), the preaching that seeks to correct inadequacies of previous generations may itself become distorted and partial, and neglected truth may be emphasized at the expense of other truth which is no less deserving of emphasis. Illuminating and sobering indeed is the record of those pulpit giants who have made the greatest impact upon American Christianity.

Roger Williams, 1604-1683. One of the most significant contributions to American life was that of religious freedom, in which the prime mover was Roger Williams. In the days of the "established church" of Massachusetts and Connecticut, beginning with the First Church of Plymouth, church membership was necessary to citizenship, and support of its ministry was required of members and non-members alike. Dissent and bitter controversy arose, and life became increasingly difficult for dissenters. Roger Williams fled to Rhode Island, where he established, at Providence, the first Baptist church in America. For the colony of Rhode Island, there was established in 1638, a government under which absolute religious freedom was guaranteed so long as its exercise did not disturb public order. This emphasis upon religious liberty in which Roger Williams pioneered led ultimately to religious freedom for all the American colonies, and for oncoming generations.

Jonathan Edwards, 1703-1758. Under the earnest preaching of Jonathan Edwards there occurred, in his (Congregational) parish in Northampton, Massachusetts, the spiritual revival which became the prelude to the "Great Awakening" of 1740 and the years following, in which Edwards was the leading spirit. This revival, which was taken up by other and less notable men, swept over most of the colonies, with markedly beneficial effects on the whole life of the colonies, both public and private. The emphasis of Jonathan Edwards upon conversion as a condition for acceptance into church membership placed him at variance with prevailing practice, and resulted in bitter opposition. He was a profoundly spiritual man, always humble and serene, and widely recognized as one of the ablest thinkers of his generation.

Horace Bushnell, (1802-1876). The emphases of Horace Bushnell are closely related to the beginnings of American liberalism. He preached some of the most influential sermons of his generation. Basically, he was protesting against the revivalism of Jonathan Edwards, which he regarded as stifling to the intellect. He believed in the inherent goodness of the natural man, and insisted that the child should "grow up a Christian and never know himself as being otherwise." His emphasis on "Christian nurture" gave a mighty impetus to the development of modern religious education. Unfortunately, he also set a trend toward "an attenuated Christology."

Henry Ward Beecher, 1813-1887. Beecher's ministry began in a time of controversy and schism. Reacting against hyper-Calvinism and the prevailing spirit of contention, he resolved that he would never engage in religious contention, but would emphasize the love of God as revealed in Christ Jesus. One blessed experience helped to crystallize his thinking and gave direction to his entire ministry. Having just read through one of the Gospels in a single sitting, he was overwhelmed with the consciousness of the love of God for lost sinners. It was, he explained, like the love of his mother, to whom his wrongdoing brought tears, but who never pressed him so close to her bosom as when he had done wrong, and whose every concern was to lift him out of his trouble. The evangelistic impact of his ministry was tremendous. Through the tumultuous years of the Civil War, the problems of slavery, and the distresses of the Reconstruction Period, his sermons became largely ethical in content; and he embraced the theory of evolution, with its unorthodox implications. He spoke his mind freely on the great moral issues of his time, but never ceased to deal with individual needs and the sufficiency of God's love.

Dwight L. Moody, 1837-1899. Inseparably associated with the high tide of mass evangelism is the name of Dwight L. Moody. Few men have labored so zealously, so lovingly, and so successfully in bringing God to man and man to God. Moody began with Sunday School evangelism, then attained phenomenal success in mass evangelism. The "Great Revival" which had begun under Jonathan Edwards had waned with the approach of the Revolutionary War, and the spiritual life of the nation had gone into woeful decline. A tiny flicker of the revival spirit still remained in the South, and this ultimately burst into flame in the "Second Great Awakening." Through a succession of powerful evangelists, including such men as Finney, Moody, Billy Sunday, and Gypsy Smith, the church gained new heights; and church membership climbed from about seven per cent to more than fifty per cent of the population. In the course of time, with lesser men entering the field, the movement came into disrepute through sensationalism, high pressure methods, and the taint of commercialism. But time can not erase the enormous good accomplished by Moody and his type of evangelists.

Walter Rauschenbusch, 1861-1918. Rauschenbusch did not launch the "Social Gospel," but surpassed all others in advancing it, in what he termed the "Social Awakening." He began his ministry in a small Baptist church in New York City, adjacent to an area known as "Hell's Kitchen," in the midst of grinding poverty with all its attendant evils. It was said that he and all the other ministers could not save souls as fast as they were being destroyed in "Hell's Kitchen." Rauschenbusch insisted on "a combination of personal regeneration and social reform." He made much of the "Fatherhood of God and the brotherhood of man," perhaps without sufficiently emphasizing that the fatherhood of the Devil is no less a Scriptural doctrine than the Fatherhood of God (John 8:42, 44; I John 3:10). His "Christian Socialism" was noble in concept, while overly optimistic in its estimate of human nature. Rauschenbusch was a voluminous writer, and is said to have influenced the life and thought of the church more than any other single individual of his generation.

The twentieth century has produced its full share of truly great preachers. Among them was the incomparable *George W. Truett,* with his earnest appeal to love and altruism, who served the First Baptist Church of Dallas, Texas, for more than forty years and built it from a small, struggling congregation to a membership of more than nine thousand. Of like stature and spirit was *Lee R. Scarborough,* who served as President of Southwestern Baptist Theological Seminary at Fort Worth, Texas, and also as Professor of Evangelism, for more than thirty years. His professorship became widely known as "The Chair of Fire," and through his tremendous evangelistic zeal he imbued successive generations of students with the spirit of soul-winning. Perhaps the widest hearing ever given to a minister of the gospel is that which has been accorded to Evangelist *Billy Graham,* with his marvelously effective emphasis on "Decision."

3. THE EMPHASIS NEEDED TODAY

The minister of today faces problems which are formidable indeed. Religion is probably more widespread than ever before, and correspondingly more shallow. Worldliness, Sabbath desecration, cocktail Christians, and broken homes are too largely taken for granted. Every form of evil increases from year to year. The statistics on crime, vice, drunkenness, narcotics addiction, and divorce reflect the sad spiritual state of our generation. Where should the preacher begin; and what is the most effective approach?

"*Life situation*" preaching is one favored approach. In a sense, all relevant preaching is "life situation" preaching. Whether the sermon is topical, textual, or expository, it must touch the lives of the hearers where they are. In "life situation" preaching, the preacher finds his point of contact in some current incident or situation, and deals with the issues in the light of Scripture. Peter, in his Pentecostal sermon, tied into the phenomena which his hearers had just witnessed, and explained, "this is that . . ." (Acts 2:16). Paul, at Mars Hill, began his sermon by referring to the altar inscribed "To the Unknown God" (Acts 17:23). John, in addressing the seven churches of Asia, began each message with the words, "I know thy works," followed by something in the church life that called for correction or commendation.

Closely related to the "life situation" approach is the "*problem solution*" approach, which offers the same advantages and is subject to the same limitations and hazards. To be sure, "there is a problem in every pew"; but many of these problems are too delicate for topical treatment in the pulpit, and some of the most acute problems may never become known to the preacher.

Sustained *expository preaching,* made alive with well-chosen illustrations, offers the one best hope for reaching the individual who needs help. The hearer gets the message without feeling that he is being singled out, and so do others of whose need the preacher may not even be aware. The wide coverage of expository preaching does more. It illuminates and fortifies the soul for problems not yet existent, and testings which cannot be foreseen; and it covers areas of truth which are no less important than the solution of problems which happen to appear on the surface.

Biographical preaching which is only one form of expository preaching, seems never to have received the emphasis which it deserves. Excellent books are available on the subject, with comprehensive treatments and with extensive bibliographies for further help. As Faris D. Whitesell points out, in *Preaching on Bible Characters* (Baker Book House), biographical preaching is perhaps the easiest way to preach the Bible, the way that most appeals to audiences generally, and especially to young people; and the way that is most likely to be remembered. And, for freshness and variety, there are approximately four hundred Bible characters from which to choose. Andrew W. Blackwood's *Biographical Preaching for Today* (Abingdon Press), is similarly excellent, with its plea for more biographical preaching, especially on the *good people* in the Bible. The minister owes it to himself to explore carefully the possibilities of biographical preaching.

Whatever the prevailing emphasis or approach, three needs are crucial in this troubled age; three goals deserve unceasing emphasis:

a. *Establish our people more securely in the obvious means of grace.* Whether in churches that are warmly alive, or cold and apathetic, an appalling proportion of church members "lack assurance," because they are neglecting the known means of grace: (1) Prayer, daily communication with the Lord. This is the very breath of life to Christian living. (2) Scripture reading. The Christian life begins when the soul responds, "Lord, what wilt thou have me to do" (Acts 9:6)? And the way to know his will is through his Word. "If ye continue in my Word, then are ye my disciples indeed; and ye shall know the truth . . ." (John 8:31-32). (3) Church attendance. If the Christian is not in the Lord's house on the Lord's Day with the Lord's people, it is practically certain that he is not doing anything else that a Christian should be doing. He is not praying, not studying the Bible, not giving, nor witnessing to others. (4) Service. For growing and for experiencing "the joy of the Lord" (Neh. 8:10), there must be an adequate spiritual outlet as well as spiritual intake.

b. *Reach and enlist our men.* A recent survey on one of our denominations, with one and a half million members, revealed a proportion of twice as many women and girls as men and boys. Among "dropouts" the ratio is generally reversed. "They that wait upon the Lord shall renew their strength . . ." (Isa. 40:31). Too many men are not waiting "upon the Lord," and not renewing "their strength," but are breaking down before their time. This factor doubtless helps explain why men have a much shorter life expectancy than women.

c. *Organize our families for Christ.* It is probably true that "America's number one problem is the unhappy home." Unresolved conflicts result in broken hearts, broken homes, and broken lives. The minister faces no greater challenge than that of completing the family circle and establishing the family altar and the family pew. No household is ever secure until the last member is safely "in Christ." Perhaps the solving of "America's number one problem" should be the "number one concern" of the minister in this atomic age.

BIBLIOGRAPHY

Blackwood, Andrew W., *Biographical Preaching for Today.* New York: Abingdon Press, 1954.

Brown, H. C. Jr., *Southern Baptist Preaching.* Nashville: Broadman Press, 1959.

Jones, Edgar DeWitt, *American Preachers of Today.* Indianapolis: The Bobbs-Merrill Co., 1933.

Mead, Frank S., *The Pulpit in the South.* New York: Fleming H. Revell Co., 1950.

Thompson, Ernest Trice, *Changing Emphases in American Preaching.* Philadelphia: The Westminster Press, 1943.

Thomson, D. P., *The Modern Evangelistic Address.* New York: George H. Doran Co., 1925.

Whitesell, Faris D., *Preaching on Bible Characters.* Grand Rapids: Baker Book House, 1955.

Imagination in Preaching

"The mind of man is more like a picture gallery than a debating chamber," said W. MacNeille Dixon in his famous Gifford Lectures, *The Human Situation.* Therefore, if our preaching is to be effective it must penetrate below the level of man's conscious intellect and his official ideologies. It must speak to the unexamined assumptions, and the hidden images, symbols and pictures that a man entertains in the secret places of his heart, and which are often the real driving force of his personality. As Amos Wilder has said in his *Theology and Modern Literature,* "Society lives by its symbols . . . . It is more important to discern the actual operative myths of civilization than the formal clichés of its political orators. A democratic society may proclaim its democratic dogmas, but the same society may be governed by undemocratic nostalgias and passions fed by obsolete dreams. The church itself may proclaim its Christian principles, but Christians may be ruled by sub-Christian images."

The great preachers of every age have known this. They have not been like lawyers arguing a case, or salesmen pushing a product; rather have they been like poets seeking to suffuse the mind with light, to empower the emotions with the splendor of revelation, and so to capture the will for God. In the discharge of this task they have used all the resources of imagery, picture, parable and metaphor. For, as the Scottish poet Edwin Muir once put it: "Nothing is wholly real until it finds an image as well as a formula for itself. The image is the record that the conception has been steeped in the unconscious, and there accepted by the deeper potencies of the mind."

1. MARKS OF IMAGINATIVE PREACHING

Cultivating the imagination in preaching is more, much more, than collecting illustrations and anecdotes. It is rather a habit of mind, and a way of attending to the actualities of life. We are told in I Samuel 9:9 that "he that is now called a Prophet was beforetime called a Seer." That is the first step in cultivating the imagination – to *see* what is before our eyes. Many men are so accustomed to gazing at the world through borrowed spectacles that they see only conventional stereotypes; they experience reality at second hand as it has been reported by others, and so their vision is a series of clichés. What made the old prophets such disturbing people was that they actually saw for themselves; they had a gift much rarer and perhaps more valuable than second sight, namely, first sight. And what made them such powerful communicators of their vision was that they reported it in concrete imagery, in the earth-laden speech of daily life, and in metaphors and analogies that were close to the soil and to the actualities of human existence.

The seer of Patmos was divinely counseled to "write the things which thou hast seen, and the things which are, and the things which shall be hereafter" (Rev. 1:19). No man has ever *seen* a long string of abstractions. Yet how much preaching is abstract, both in content and expression. In this regard we are all apt to be captive to our age. The novelist and teacher, Lionel Trilling, has said, "A specter haunts our culture – it is that people will eventually be unable to say, 'They fell in love and married,' let alone understand the language of Romeo and Juliet, but will, as a matter of course, say, 'Their libidinal impulses being reciprocal, they activated their erotic drives and integrated them within the same frame of reference.' " This kind of "gobbledygook" is sometimes encountered in theological writing, as witness this choice specimen from a recent article in a learned journal, "It is not the people as a collectivity that is the resolvent term of the divine action; this reaches each man in the singular." But even the best theological writing is apt to be abstract and conceptual, necessarily so. But the place for theological terms is the classroom, not the pulpit. Preaching will derive more strength and sap from the language of the Bible than from the language of the theologians, for the language of the Bible is concrete, earthy, and visual.

"Write the things which thou seest!" When we study the sermons of great preachers, we quickly discover that they have the gift of pictorial imagination. For example, when that fine Methodist preacher, Percy Ainsworth, wished to speak to his people of the incarnation, he did not use that abstract term; he said, "Christ is not God's messenger, but God's message." When Peter Taylor Forsyth wished to warn his congregation of the perils of introspection, he did not use the current psychological jargon; he said, "It is better, and safer, to pray over the Bible than to brood over the self." On the same subject, an old Rabbi once put it picturesquely, "Rake the muck this way and rake the muck that way, it is still muck." Or again, when William Robertson Nicoll wished to indicate the desolating sense of loss he felt at the death of Charles Haddon Spurgeon, he told his public, "He has fallen like a tower, and there is a gap in the landscape of life."

The great orators of our time have all cultivated the same poetic concreteness and particularity. Winston Churchill did not hearten the British people during the war by making general statements; he said "We will fight on the hills, we will fight in the streets, we will fight on the beaches . . . we will never surrender." The wartime President of the American people had the same gift of vivid imagery. When one of his script writers produced a speech that read, in part, "We are trying to construct a more inclusive society," the presidential blue pencil reshaped this to read, "We are going to make a country where nobody is left out." The abstract "construct" became the concrete "make"; the general term "society" became the particular word "country," and the colorless "inclusive" became the factual "where nobody is left out."

In all these examples there are certain common factors. For one thing, the speaker uses as few words as possible. "The great secret of style," said Robert Louis Stevenson, "is to omit." Much preaching is altogether too wordy; the thought becomes smothered by the cotton-wool of verbiage. In this connection, it is wise to watch the use of adjectives. A careful stylist once said, "The adjective is always the enemy of the noun." He meant that such general adjectives as "very," "great," and so forth, usually weaken the force of the word to which it is attached. If a crisis is always a "serious crisis," what happens to the perfectly good word "crisis"? If we never refer to a danger except as a "great danger," what connotation can we give to danger itself. Can there be a little danger?

For another thing, the speakers we have cited resolutely avoid the use of the passive voice, in favor of the active: they never say that "a thing was done," but that "he did it" – which is a more vigorous expression.

But above all, they eschew abstractions! And here surely they are in line with the Bible, and with the Lord of the Bible. When Jesus spoke of sin, for example, he did not generalize; he dealt in particulars. He spoke of salt without savor, of light hidden under a bushel, of a son leaving home, of a builder neglecting the foundations, of a wedding guest too proud to enter into the spirit of the party, of a worshiper praying for show. These are timeless images which stir the imagination, alarm the conscience, and enlighten the mind.

When that sensitive Christian poet, Edwin Muir, sought to put his finger on the weakness of the pulpit of his boyhood memory, he said,

> "The Word made flesh was here
> made word again"

and he called preachers back to the practical importance of the incarnation for preaching – to clothe our words in flesh, the flesh of palpable imagery and concrete speech. He reminded them that a sermon should be more like a poem than an abstract discussion, and that the preacher is more akin to the poet than to the propagandist or the salesman. Percy Ainsworth said, "When you watch a religion at work, you find a morality; when you converse with religion in its thoughtful moods you find a theology; but when you get to the heart of religion you find a song."

The singer and the poet do not argue, they reveal. They do not exhort and upbraid, they uncover the nature of reality; they bring to light the hidden assumptions upon which men are actually living their lives, very often in flat contradiction to their official creeds.

They aim to evoke the response of recognition. In the words of the playwright Arthur Miller: "What the dramatist works for is, to hear the audience say, not, 'What happens next?' or 'Why?' but 'O God, of course!' "

Luther wrote to his friend Eoban Hess, "I am persuaded that without knowledge of literature pure theology cannot at all endure. There has never been a great revelation of the Word of God unless He first prepared the way for it by the rise and prosperity of language and letters. By the study of literature as by no other means people are wonderfully fitted to grasp sacred truth and to handle it skilfully and happily." And surely one of the great gifts of literature is that we may learn to use words in such a fashion that that may march into the castle of Mansoul "as terrible as an army with banners," and take that castle for the Lord of All Good Life.

2. THE USE OF ILLUSTRATIONS AND POETRY

I have said that we do not become imaginative preachers by ransacking literature for "illustrations," and certainly not by compiling an anthology of pious poems and moralizing anecdotes. This does not mean that we are never to use illustrations. But if we do we should observe certain rules. We should, of course, be careful to verify our references and quote with accuracy. But even more important, we should quote sparingly. Nothing lulls a congregation to sleep more effectively than the reading of a long and involved extract from somebody else's work. Nothing is more boring than listening to a man attempting to outline the plot of a novel or a film or a play. If one wishes to quote the Shakespearean line, "Love is not love which alters when it alteration finds," it is not necessary to quote the whole of the sonnet in which the line occurs, or to discourse on the "problem" of the Sonnets. In the case of such a well-known line it is not even necessary to say "As Shakespeare said," and it is certainly not necessary to patronize the author by paying him superflous compliments, such as "the famous poet, William Shakespeare" or "that great genius, the Bard of Avon." If one wishes to make use of the parable of the Grand Inquisitor in Dostoyevsky's novel, *The Brothers Karamazov,* with its searing indictment of a religious organization that, in the name of Christ, brushes Christ aside in order to appeal to the masses, it is not necessary to quote the whole of that long and elaborately detailed parable, and certainly not to talk at large about the whole novel. It is sufficient to concentrate on the key passages. The view of the Grand Inquisitor was that "there are three powers, three powers alone, able to hold captive forever the consciences of these impotent rebels for their own happiness; these forces are Miracle, Mystery, and Authority." So, out of genuine but ill-considered love for weak humanity, he goes on to say, "We have corrected thy work. We have founded it upon Miracle, Mystery and Authority, and men rejoice that they are brought again like sheep, and that the terrible gift [of freedom] that had brought them so much suffering was at last lifted from their hearts."

In quoting poetry from the pulpit, it is wise to bear in mind a distinction that Vincent Buckley once made between "devotional verse," which seeks to give easily remembered utterance to familiar religious sentiments without probing them, and poetry which is the utterance of the whole man, desperately engaged in realizing his covenant relation with God. Many devotional poems are poems of slack devotion, without any marshaling of the whole affective personality behind them. Religious poems, on the other hand, involve the entire man — believer and doubter at the same time, caught between the "mighty opposites" of heaven and earth, crying "Lord, I believe, help Thou my unbelief." Many hymns are "devotional verse" at their best, but they lack the intensity of the poetry of a man like John Donne, with his:

> Wilt Thou forgive that sin that I
> have done,
> Which was my sin, though it were
> done before;
> When Thou hast done, Thou hast
> not done,
> For I have more.

The conclusion of that anguished poem reaches a crescendo rarely attained by the purveyors of easy sentimental verse that often passes for the real thing. Besides, it is not merely a "religious" poem, it is a Christian poem. That is, it probes, dissects, questions, affirms within the context of Christian revelation. It does not generalize in a devotional mood; it takes seriously the redemption offered to mankind in the incarnation, crucifixion and resurrection of the Son of God. Its intensity is due to its tension — the tension experienced between the reality and the promise, between the actual condition of man and the solution offered to him in Jesus Christ.

Fortunately in our day there are a host of poets who are writing from within the Christian drama; not peddling easy consolation or expressing vague nature mysticism or pious sentiments. What age has been so rich in literary men who are also committed Christians? Seldom has a single generation been able to call a roll so illustrious as T. S. Eliot, W. H. Auden, Edwin Muir, Christopher Fry, Allen Tate, Robert Lowell, John Betjeman, Elizabeth Jennings, and Phyllis MacGinley. These are all persons who are commanded by the Christian revelation, who seek to bring the "light of the knowledge of the glory of God" to bear upon the murk and obscurity of our times. But they do not so with facile ease. T. S. Eliot stabs us awake to the aridity and sterility of the "Waste Land" before he leads us out into the ample serenity of "The Four Quartets." He has shown us with devastating clarity the land where the wind shall say:

> Here were decent godless people:
> Their only monument the asphalt road
> And a thousand lost golf balls.

But in that "desert of the heart" he has pointed man to the vital meaning of the Christian faith for his life, in words that are understood by sophisticated modern people.

Similarly, the poet W. H. Auden, writing out of vast erudition and intimate acquaintance with the pilgrimage of twentieth century man, has brought alive in contemporary terms the existential significance of the incarnation in his *Christmas Oratorio.* Much of that long poem is not suitable for direct quotation from the pulpit (if only because like much modern poetry it is too close-packed with thought and imagery to be directly available at one hearing), but the insights afforded by the poem are invaluable for a preacher who wishes to relate the timeless gospel to his own age. Even so, there are memorable single passages which light up whole areas of experience:

> We would rather be ruined than changed,
> We would rather die in our dread
> Than climb the cross of the moment
> And let our illusions die.

When a poet like Edwin Muir returns in his maturity to the Christian faith, which, as he says, he now recognizes he had never left — or rather had never left him — he brings to its contemporary statement a freshness that many of us lack. There can be few men who have entered so deeply into the inner meaning of the doctrine of the second coming of Christ than Muir with his poem "The Transfiguration," or seized with such contemporary relevance the meaning of the Word made flesh as in his poem "The Incarnate One," or entered so personally into the Genesis story of creation as in the poem "One Foot in Eden."

Horace Bushnell once preached a sermon he called "The Gospel: A Gift to the Imagination." It is that, but it also requires imagination if it is to be presented effectively. It is here that the poets and dramatists and many novelists of our age can be our mentors and allies. They are not the source of the gospel, but they often probe more deeply the questions and problems to which the gospel is the answer and solution; and when they themselves are grasped by the gospel they can teach us how to set it to music, so that our hearers will learn to say, "Thy statutes have become my songs in the house of my pilgrimage."

BIBLIOGRAPHY

Fowler, H. W., *Modern English Usage.* Oxford, 1965.

Gowers, Sir Ernest, *Plain Words: A Guide to the Use of English.* Knopf, 1954.

Hopper, Stanley R., *Spiritual Problems in Contemporary Literature.* Harper, 1957.

Mueller, William, *The Prophetic Voice in Modern Fiction.* Association Press, 1959.

Palgrave, F. T., *The Golden Treasury.* Macmillan.

Scott, Nathan, ed., *The Tragic Vision and the Christian Faith.* Association Press.

Wilder, Amos, *Theology and Modern Literature.* Harvard Press, 1958.

The works of T. S. Eliot, W. H. Auden, Edwin Muir, and Christopher Fry.

Preaching Doctrine

The English word doctrine is derived, as is the word doctor, from the Latin *docere,* meaning "to teach." Doctrine, presumably, is what is taught by a doctor, or learned man. Doctrine is the ordered arrangement of those truths by which the church lives. Doctrine differs from dogma in that the latter demands acceptance on the grounds of its being authoritatively delivered. The former invites the kind of consideration which will lead to acceptance of the truths laid down.

Both the philosopher and the politician use the word doctrine. Since the year 1823 the Monroe doctrine has been a cornerstone of American foreign policy. The teacher of philosophy acquaints his students with the doctrines of Aristotle, Epictetus, Pythagoras. The preacher's concern is with doctrines by which all these must be judged. One of the grimmest things described by the prophet Isaiah is that men and women accepted popular catchwords as embracing all the meaning of life; the people, he says, "honor me with their lips, while their hearts are far from me, and their fear of me is a commandment of men learned by rote" (29:13 R.S.V.). Noting how the Pharisees assigned the highest place to human tradition, Jesus found Isaiah's words still applicable, "in vain do they worship me, teaching as doctrines the precepts of men" (Matt. 15:9, R.S.V.). Some popular notions are worse than merely human. People are sometime found "giving heed to deceitful spirits and doctrines of demons" (I Tim. 4:1). The angel-worship and ascetic practices which flourished in Colossae Paul emphatically rejects. These are "human precepts and doctrines" (Col. 2:22), and those whom Christ has delivered from darkness ought not any longer to live as if they "still belonged to the world" (Col. 2:20).

a. *Jesus Proclaimed Doctrine.* Jesus was from the outset, a proclaimer of doctrine; he "came into Galilee, preaching the gospel of God, and saying, 'The time is fulfilled, and the kingdom of God is at hand'" (Mark 1:14f.). II Peter 1:21 assures us that "men moved by the Holy Spirit spoke from God." Perhaps there is no better place to begin in expounding the doctrine of Scripture. Luke 24:44 indicates that Christ has come to fulfill everything written about him "in the law of Moses and the prophets and the psalms." This indicates the three canons of the Hebrew Bible, with psalms representing the Writings. In the Psalms Jesus found the pattern for his Beatitudes, and a Psalm phrased his feelings on the cross. In Matthew 5:17 Jesus announces that he has come to fulfil "the law and the prophets." The former has often been emphasized at the expense of the latter. The author of the letter to Hebrews stresses the way in which Christ fulfilled the law. Perhaps we do not often enough draw attention to the way in which he fulfilled the prophets. We rightly note the animal types of sacrifice, but too often neglect the way in which Micah's concern for the poor and Amos' demand for justice and Hosea's concern with the family also found their fulfilment in him. Isaiah's picture of the suffering servant and Jeremiah's doctrine of the New Covenant also foreshadowed Jesus' Messianic office.

b. *The Doctrine of the Ministry.* It is important for the preacher, as well as for his hearers, that the doctrine of the ministry should be dealt with from time to time. The call of Elisha, the call of Isaiah, the call of Jeremiah all serve to introduce the doctrine of divine vocation. Habakkuk standing on his watchtower, Jeremiah and the wake tree, Revelation's man with the measuring rod all suggest facets of the minister's work. Ephesians 4:11 describes four (not five) kinds of ministry. Apostles, prophets, and evangelists were itinerants, while the pastor-teacher was settled in a particular place. The doctrine of the ministry leads on to an inclusive doctrine of Christian vocation, in which all men are summoned not only "to be ready for any honest work" (Titus 3:1), but to "press on toward the goal for the prize of the upward call of God in Christ Jesus" (Phil. 3:14).

c. *Treatment of Doctrines.* In treating of great doctrines, it is desirable to deal at different times with the various places in which they are taught. Paul assures us in one of the best known passages of the New Testament that "faith, hope, love abide." It is impressive to note this same trinity in another context, such as I Thessalonians 1:3, where Paul, praising his friends in Thessalonica, remembers their "work of faith and labor of love and steadfastness of hope." The Trinitarian formula, which did not become dogma until the fourth century, is implicit in the great commission (Matt. 28:19), and in the apostolic benediction (II Cor. 13:14). It is impressive also to note how it is embedded in such a passage as I Peter 1:1, where the letter is addressed to the exiles of the Diaspora "chosen and destined by God the Father and sanctified by the Spirit for obedience to Jesus Christ."

One's sermons on doctrine may predominantly start in the New Testament, but that is no reason to neglect the Old. There is indeed something to be said for a New Testament approach to the Old Testament. Genesis tells of Abraham's departure from Ur of the Chaldees and of the vicissitudes which led to his becoming the father of many nations. It is the New Testament, however, which enables the Christian to see Abraham in true perspective. Hebrews 11:8 tells how "he went out not knowing where he was to go." James 2:23 records that his faith "was reckoned to him as righteousness; and he was called the friend of God." Galatians 3:7 makes it clear that now "it is men of faith who are the sons of Abraham."

Genesis records the disaster which overtook our race in the days of Noah. Luke 17:27 sums up what was wrong with the antediluvians: "They ate, they drank, they married they were given in marriage" – nothing wrong with any of these things, except that the men of that day lived as if they were the be-all and the end-all of existence. Luke 11:30 indicates that the true "sign of Jonah" was his preaching to the men of Nineveh, thus proclaiming God's love for foreigners. Genesis 11 is the record of the sinful origin of the multiplicity of languages on our planet, while John 19:20 and Acts 2:8 suggest how, in Christ, this shadow cast by the tower of Babel is being lifted.

d. *The Entire Round of Doctrine.* While it is good for man to specialize in one doctrine and learn everything possible about some theme as grace, repentance, or forgiveness, it is desirable not to preach too often upon one's favorite theme but to force oneself to deal with the entire round of Christian doctrine. Although Paul affirms his intention of proclaiming nothing except the doctrine of the cross (I Cor. 1:9), he did not preach every Lord's Day on the atonement. After three years in Ephesus he could say, "I did not shrink from declaring to you anything that was profitable" (Acts 20:20). Liturgical churches have lectionaries which compel preachers to deal with truth in its variety. Preachers who do not follow lectionaries should have some other device to keep them from riding homiletical hobbies.

e. *The Situation of the Hearers.* The preaching of doctrine must take into account the situation of the hearers. To the Corinthians, newly called out of heathendom, Paul writes, "I fed you with milk, not solid food; for you were not yet ready for it" (I Cor. 3:2). The doctrine of the Trinity is hardly the place to begin with the kindergarten department. On the other hand, one must not underestimate the capacity of the young to receive thoughtful teaching. I Peter 2:2 advises persecuted Christians, "Like newborn babes, long for the pure spiritual milk, that by it you may grow up to salvation." The one thing the newborn babe can do is long for milk. He cries when it is not available to him, and when it comes near he frantically reaches for it, and when it is within reach he suckles furiously. The rabbis spoke of the law as milk and honey and wine. The appetite of the young for "the pure spiritual milk" suggests their ability to appropriate bone building substance, and the preacher must not dull this appetite nor try to satisfy it with pap.

The letter to Ephesians, however, urges us all to grow up "to mature manhood, to the measure of the stature of the fulness of Christ, so that we may no longer be children" (4:13f.). It is this development of adult Christian judgment which enables one to resist being "tossed to and fro and carried about with every wind of doctrine" (4:14). The letter to Hebrews insists that we should "leave the elementary doctrines of Christ and go on to maturity" (6:1). If the doctrine of the Trinity is not appropriate for the infant class, married couples have a special way of understanding it, since, as Augustine observed, every family is in some measure trinitarian, with a lover and one who is loved, and love. The child may appreciate the father's love and thoughtfulness in providing the necessities of life, but only a parent can know what it means to the father to keep a lonely vigil for the prodigal who has not yet realized where enduring love is to be found.

f. *Starting Points of Doctrine.* Events transpiring in the world often give occasion for proclaiming one aspect or another of Christian doctrine. Jesus set the example. Luke 14:28-33 records two parables, that of the Impetuous Builder and that of the Thoughtless King. Jesus lived in an age of ostentatious building and reckless warfare, and was perhaps here alluding to instances of such folly that were currently in the popular mind, such as the operations of Judas the Gaulonite, credited by Josephus with having founded the "fourth sect" of the Jews, composed of violent revolutionaries and assassins.

Objects at hand can often be used as the starting point for the proclamation of doctrine. The Palestinian countryside in the spring is a riot of color, with the growth of a simple but variegated flower, the anemone. It was no doubt at this season of the year that Jesus said, "Consider the lilies of the field" (Matt. 6:28), and went on from there to outline the doctrine of God's providential care for His creation. In one of His sermons Jesus said, "If you had faith as a grain of mustard seed, you could say to this sycamine tree, 'Be rooted up, and be planted in the sea,' and it would obey you" (Luke 17:6). The demonstrative pronoun "this" suggests that it was not sycamine trees in general that Jesus had in mind but a particular tree, at that moment visible to all his hearers. In Luke 12:37 Jesus says, "Where the body is, there the eagles will be gathered." The word translated "eagles" is a generic term that could be rendered vultures, which, unlike eagles, do fly in flocks and feed on carrion. But this may well be an allusion to the eagle standards of the Roman empire, ever-present emblems of the army of occupation.

Paul often began his sermons with objects clearly in the sight or mind of all. The Athenian altar to the unknown god is the starting point of a sermon about the God in whom the whole of humanity has its being and before whom each individual will one day stand in judgment (Acts 17:22-31). The Corinthian games, in honor of Poseidon, were probably under way when the Apostle wrote to the Corinthians, "Every athlete exercises self-control in all things" (I Cor. 9:25): When Paul speaks of our receiving "adoption as sons" (Gal. 4:5; Rom. 8:23), he has in mind a provision of Roman law in which the position of the adopted son was more secure than that of the natural son. The natural son could be disinherited, but not the one who had been chosen and adopted.

Paul, too, took advantage of the calendar to set forth truth that would be remembered because spoken at a particular time and place. Although the Feast of Unleavened Bread properly came after the Passover, the two in New Testament times had come to be looked upon as a kind of double feast. It may be that at this time Paul wrote to the Corinthians about leaven and dough and the sacrificial lamb (I Cor. 5:7). Among the Jewish festivals associated with the sabbath was the first day of the seventh month, described in Numbers 29:1 as "a day for you to blow the trumpet" (cf. Lev. 23: 24). With such a convocation as background Ephesians 5:14 springs to life: "Awake, O sleeper, and arise from the dead, and Christ shall give you light."

The author of the Apocalypse arouses an interest in Christian doctrine by beginning with circumstances familiar to his readers. Laodicea was famous for the manufacture of a black, glossy cloth with which the proper Christian attire is set in contrast: "I counsel you to buy . . . white garments" (Rev. 3:18). Blind and unable to discern its true condition, the church at Laodicea is bidden also to purchase "salve to anoint your eyes." Phrygian powder was a well-known ophthalmic ointment of the time, even as the Greek word here used is perpetuated in our "collyrium." Revelation 8:8 describes how "something like a great mountain, burning with fire, was thrown into the sea." Conceivably, this could be an allusion to the eruption of Vesuvius, which occurred in A.D. 79, or to some other volcanic disturbance in the Aegean islands.

The ethical aspect of doctrine comes out clearly in the letter to Titus, where even those in humble positions are bidden "to show entire and true fidelity, so that in everything they may adorn the doctrine of God our Savior" (2:10). The term translated "adorn" is one from which we derive both "cosmos" and "cosmetics." The committed life exemplifies a doctrine that is not chaotic but orderly, not repulsive but attractive.

The King James Version, in Acts 2:42, describes how the members of the early church "continued steadfastly in the apostles' doctrine and fellowship, and in breaking of bread, and in prayers." The Revised Standard here reads, "And they devoted themselves to the apostles' teaching and fellowship, to the breaking of bread and the prayers." Here is indication that the proclamation of doctrine is done not simply in formal public discourse but is bound up with the entire life of the congregation. Believers gave earnest attention to the teaching received from the apostles. They did this not in isolation but in the context of the apostles' fellowship, the beloved community established by Christ and his apostles.

This was accompanied by a sharing of this world's goods (Acts 2:44f.; 4:32), motivated not by any economic theory but by awareness that possessions are not to be cherished and guarded as one's own but shared with less fortunate brethren "as any had need." It was evidently this combination of teaching and example, doctrine and life, that made the early church so powerful and winsome in evangelism. Theirs was a fellowship irresistible. "And the Lord added to their number day by day those who were being saved" (Acts 2:47).

g. *Translation and Doctrine.* Variety in translation often serves to display the several facets of a doctrine. Luther learned from the Greek New Testament that God was continually summoning men to repent and not merely to do penance. The RSV rendering of John 3:17 is, "For God sent the Son into the world, not to condemn the world, but that the world might be saved through him." The earlier KJV translation reads, "For God sent not his Son into the world to condemn the world." The emphasis varies, depending on where the word "not" is placed. KJV at Ephesians 1:4f. reads, "that we should be holy and without blame before him in love: Having predestinated us unto the adoption of children." RSV has it, "that we should be holy and blameless before him. He destined us in love." Predestination apart from love can be a grim and cheerless thing. Predestination in love puts the doctrine in quite a different light.

Variety of translation in single words can throw light on important doctrines. For *paracletos* it is so difficult to find a single satisfactory word that there is something to be said for transliterating it as Paraclete. Wyclif's rendering, "Comforter," was intended not as Consoler but in the original Latin sense of Strengthener. Both KJV and RSV at I John 2:1 render the term "Advocate," a Latin word which is the precise etymological equivalent of *paracletos.* It means "called to one's side." This is what the ancient Paraclete was, a friend called in to plead one's case. "Advocate" today has a little too much the suggestion of a professional who does this for pay. "Helper," "Counselor," "Friend at Court" are other terms that have been used.

Paul says the law was given as a *paidagogos.* RSV renders this "our custodian until Christ came" (Gal. 3:24). "Pedagogue" transliterates the term which KJV renders by "schoolmaster." The Greek office was different from that of our teacher. It described the tutor-slave entrusted with the supervision of a child until he came of age. Clement of Alexandria was sure that philosophy was for the Greeks what the law had been for the Hebrews, a means of disciplining them and so making them ready for the coming of Christ.

The doctrine of prayer might well begin with prayer's crowning word. The Heidelberg Catechism thus defines Amen, "it shall truly and surely be; for my prayer is more certainly heard of God than I feel in my heart that I desire these things of him." In the Old Testament Amen was the people's assent to declarations made at solemn assemblies, and the response to prayers offered in the synagogue. From I Corinthians 14:16 we learn of its continued use in the Christian church. The Fourth Evangelist represents Jesus as introducing a novel use of the term, twice repeated at the beginning of a solemn assertion (John 3:3, 5, 11; 5:19, 24, 25, etc.).

Perhaps it would gain in impressiveness if we left it untranslated in such instances:

"Amen, Amen, I say to you, every one who commits sin is a slave to sin." (John 8:34). RSV renders the phrase "truly, truly," precisely the rendering given to it by Wyclif in the first English translation of the New Testament. Wyclif's great concern was to make doctrine "understanded of the people." His is the first of many English versions that are useful to the preacher of doctrine. Finally, Wyclif exemplified the doctrine he taught. Chaucer's "pauvre Persoun" is thought to have been inspired by Wyclif:

> Christes lore, and his apostles twelve,
> He taughte, but first he folwèd it him-selve.

BIBLIOGRAPHY

Oman, John, *Concerning the Ministry.* London: SCM Press, 1936.

Flew, Robert Newton, *Jesus and His Church; a study of the ecclesia in the New Testament.* New York: Abingdon Press, 1938.

Parker, Pierson, *Inherit the Promise; six keys to New Testament Thought.* Greenwich, Conn.: Seabury Press, 1957.

Richardson, Alan, *An Introduction to the Theology of the New Testament.* London: SCM Press, 1958.

Knox, Ronald Arbuthnot, *The Trials of a Translator.* New York: Sheed and Ward, 1949.

Swaim, J. Carter, *New Insights into Scripture.* Philadelphia: Westminster Press, 1962.

Goodspeed, Edgar T., *Problems of New Testament Translation.* Chicago: University of Chicago Press, 1945.

Mackintosh, Hugh Ross, *The Christian Experience of Forgiveness.* New York and London: Harper and Bros., 1927.

Moffatt, James, *Grace in the New Testament.* London: Hodder and Stoughton, 1931.

Chamberlain, William Douglas, *The Meaning of Repentance.* Philadelphia: Westminster Press, 1943.

Preaching in the Jewish Tradition

Preaching in terms of interpreting the Bible was unknown in Judaism until after the Babylonian Exile.

The Hebrew prophets were preachers — but they were primarily exhorters, interpreters of the will of God; not preachers of the Bible (for the Bible as we know it was not yet the authoritative word of God), but as men impelled by their vision of God as a God of justice, holiness, love, and the one and only God in a polytheistic world. The Hebrew prophets preached when the Spirit moved them, often during festive occasions, because that is when the people would come to the population centers, either to offer their sacrifices in Jerusalem or to visit the great market places on market days, but there were no fixed times for their appearance and no fixed places.

Preaching, in the sense that we understand the word (interpreting the will of God through explanation and interpretation of Biblical texts) came into Judaism with Ezra and Nehemiah about the fifth century B. C. The Torah (now accepted as the Word of God) was read to the public on the Sabbath and other important occasions — read and interpreted so that the people might know what God expected of them, (Neh. 8:1-9; 9:3).

The interpretation was a translation of the Hebrew text into Aramaic, which had become the vernacular of the people, accompanied with some explanation. Thus, preaching began in Judah about 400 B.C. Josephus speaks of the custom of translating and interpreting Scripture as a very ancient custom, and Philo refers to it as an important element of public worship. Certainly by the first pre-Christian century, preaching in the synagogue was an integral part of the Sabbath worship service.

1. THE DARSHAN

The two heads of the Sanhedrin — Shemiah and Abtalion — of the first century B.C. were known as "darshanim," i.e., interpreters of the Bible.

After the destruction of the Temple in A.D. 70, expounding the Torah and using it not merely to teach the meaning of the text but to edify and to inspire, to encourage the people with hope in difficult times, became a regular part of the worship. In the early Talmudic times, the expounder used to explain the Torah through an interpreter — a meturgamon, or an amora. The interpreter was not regarded with esteem by scholars. On the contrary, the Midrash says, "It is better to hear 'darshanim' than the 'metergamanim,'" who sometimes embellished the explanation, thus distorting the meaning of the preacher.

In Talmudic times the sermon had a definite form. It consisted usually of three parts (1) the introduction (*pesichta*); (2) the exposition of the text (*drush*); and (3) the conclusion.

The technique of a Talmudic sermon adhered to the following pattern: The preacher began by quoting a verse from the Bible other than the Pentateuch, explaining it and gradually leading to his Bible text. This connection of the introductory verse with the text was known as "*haruz*" (stringing together), a term taken from the custom of stringing pearls together by piercing them. Thus when preaching from the text, "And Abraham was old" (Gen. 24:1), the preacher began by quoting the verse "The hoary head is a crown of glory; it shall be found in the way of righteousness" (Prov. 16:31), and continued by illustrating with the following incident:

"Rabbi Meir went to Minla where he noticed that all the inhabitants were black-haired. He said to them, 'Tell me, are you all descended from the House of Eli? as it is written "and all the increase of thy house shall die young men." They answered him 'Rabbi, pray for us,' whereupon he said, 'Go and practice righteousness, and you will become worthy of old age.'

" 'Whence did he derive this reason for his statement? From the words "a hoary head is a crown of glory," and where is old age found? – in the way of righteousness. From whom dost thou learn this? From Abraham of whom it is written: "He will command his children to observe the ways of the Lord, to do righteousness and justice"; therefore he was found worthy to reach old age, as it is written, "And Abraham was old, well stricken in age"'" (Genesis Rabbo – 49:1).

The preacher, having come to his text in this way, then began to explain it and to embellish it with various illustrations – parables, stories, fables, etc. The final portion of the homily consisted of a brief repetition of the ideas drawn from the text, and the preacher closed with a prayer of praise, usually the Kaddish. In addition to the darshan, in later Talmudic times, the maggid, a preacher in the more modern sense, developed.

2. THE MAGGID

The maggid was often an itinerant preacher skilled in telling stories, using parables to illustrate an ethical or spiritual message. He was much more popular than the darshan, being more entertaining and less difficult to understand for the layman. It is said that people used to leave the lecture room of Rabbi Hiyya (a great darshan) and flocked to Rabbi Abahu, a maggid. To appease the sensitive Rabbi Hiyya, Rabbi Abahu said. "We are like two merchants, one selling diamonds, the other selling trinkets. Which will the people buy more readily?" (Sotah 40 a).

Some of the great rabbis, like Meir (second century A.D.) combined both – the erudition of the scholarly darshan and the story-telling talents of the maggid. He was called the Jewish Aesop, because he was skilled in using stories of animals and parables to teach his moral lessons. But the darshanim often regarded the maggidim as distorting and twisting Biblical verses (the Word of God) to suit their momentary fancy and their roving imaginations. One rabbinic scholar, a darshan, estimated the work of the maggidim as no more value than books on magic.

In the Geonic period (from the eighth century on into the middle ages), the darshan would preach only before the great holy days and festivals, and his discourse was usually a halachic legal interpretation of the holy day and its observance.

The maggid's function was to preach to the people usually on a Sabbath afternoon when the people gathered for the Micha and Maariv services. His sermon was usually based on the Sidra (portion of the Torah), for the week. His mission was to inspire the people to righteous living, either by pointing up the virtues of Paradise which was the reward of the righteous, or by instilling in them the fear of hell, the punishment of the wicked. During the centuries of persecution the maggid would tend to give encouragement to the people by dwelling on the messianic hopes.

A very famous maggid was Isaac Abravanel, who arose after the expulsion of the Jews from Spain in 1492. His homiletic commentary on the Bible became a source book for later maggidim. His method was to explain a Biblical chapter by asking a number of rhetorical questions, which he would then answer in a lucid argumentation, embellished with illustrative material. One of the most famous of the maggidim was Jacob Kranz of Dubno, Poland, who died in 1804. He was known as the Dubner Maggid – the preacher from Dubno. His fame rested not only on erudition, but on his unique power to use the story and parable to illustrate his message. A great nineteenth century preacher was Moses Isaac ben Noah Darshal (the Kelmer Maggid), 1828-1900. His coming to a community was looked forward to as a great event, like the revivalist preachers of our own time.

Maggidim followed no special pattern. Each expressed his preaching in terms of his temperament and abilities. Thus there were the "Terror Maggidim," who preached on the terrors of hell for those who failed to live the commandments of God; the "Messianic (or hopeful) Maggidim"; the "Philosphical Maggidim"; and the "Penitential Maggidim," who preached especially during the penitential season urging people to prepare for the day of judgment. Many of the maggidim were itinerant preachers who wandered from town to town, arriving for the Sabbath afternoon to deliver their sermons. Occasionally a famous maggid would be hired by a community as their permanent preacher. Such a resident maggid was called the city preacher, whose function was to go from synagogue to synagogue in a large city.

3. PREACHING IN THE GEONIC AND POST-GEONIC PERIODS

The great period of homiletic activity was in the Geonic period (the sixth to the tenth centuries) among Sephardic Jews. It was during this period that the great midrashic collections developed. The derasha of the Geonic period was not so much an elucidation of a text as a string of midrashic passages.

The exposition of texts came in the post-geonic period by Spanish darshanim in the thirteenth and fourteenth centuries in Spain and Portugal; and in Holland, Turkey, Italy, and England from the fifteenth to the eighteenth centuries. Their sermons had a definite form. They usually had double texts – a verse from the Bible, and a midrashic verse from the Talmud. An introduction followed that led to the derasha proper. This consisted of a number of Scriptural verses and midrashic quotations which the preacher expounded, each quotation serving as an explanation of preceding, and the last being used to interpret the text itself. The sermon ended with a prayer for redemption.

Among the Ashkenazi (Jews of Germany and Eastern Europe), the sermon was largely neglected as part of the regular Sabbath worship. The accumulation of special prayers made the service so long that there was no time for a lengthy discourse. So preaching was restricted to a few times during the year when the rabbi would give a legal discourse on the observance of the holy day. Thus a legal sermon would be given on the Sabbath before the Passover, on the Sabbath of repentance between Rosh Hashanah (New Year), and Yom Kippur (Day of Atonement), and sometimes on the eve of Atonement in which the preacher dealt with the problems of sin, repentance, and atonement. The Musar (ethical sermon) was delivered by a maggid on a Sabbath afternoon, if he happened to be in the community, or by the permanent preacher.

Preaching in the modern manner began in Germany in the early part of the nineteenth century with the advent of Reform Judaism, when a sermon in the vernacular became an integral part of the worship service. The sermon was essentially an interpretation of a Biblical text, with emphasis on its moral, ethical and spiritual implications. This has now become the general practice, even in Conservative and in most Orthodox synagogues, certainly in Western Europe, in America and in other English speaking countries. The modern Jewish sermon is still based on a Biblical text, although many rabbis will speak on anything that is of contemporary concern to their congregations and to the community. It may be topical or textual. The format of the sermon follows the generally accepted format of most modern preaching.

BIBLIOGRAPHY

Morris, Joseph, *J.Q.R.*, "About Preaching." Vol. III, pp. 125-145

——————, *Jewish Encyclopedia,* "Homiletics: Darshan-Maggid.

Puritan Preaching

No one living and ministering in the English speaking world can afford to dismiss the influence of Puritan preaching. It is part of the inheritance of all who would proclaim the everlasting gospel in our generation. The themes and emphases, the style and skills, are woven into the fabric of our tradition. If this age does not have a Puritan preacher in the historical sense, overtones of Puritan preaching are still to be heard and a rich evangelical faith is still being expressed. These would remind us that we are the heirs of a glorious legacy of preaching.

1. BACKGROUND

The word "Puritan" came into use in England during the period of 1559-1567. There were those in the life of the churches who sought to purify what was to them defection and debasement of doctrine and morals. The Reformation had become an accepted fact with all its variety of expression on the continent of Europe. The Lutheran strain influenced many and the Calvinistic view was eagerly welcomed by others both on the Continent and in Great Britain. From Calvin's Geneva came views of the Bible and the Christian life which permeated English and Scottish churches. These intermingled with already existing interpretations common to the post-Reformation period. William Tyndale and others in England influenced Episcopal, Presbyterian, and Independent groups. John Knox in Scotland had laid the foundation of church life which would withstand the test of centuries.

In the midst of the political-social struggle for the rights of men over against all tyranny and despotism, the religious ideas of faith and worship found expression. Here began the "gathered church" and the "federal or covenant theology." Ever seeking a pure church the preachers of that day tried to spell out their convictions in sermons. At the heart of all preaching lay this element. "The covenant or federal theology was only an intellectual formation into which older English piety, practice and preaching was fitted" (cf. Trinterud). Thomas Cartwright of England was exiled to Holland and is known as "the father of Puritanism." Holland received many refugees and was a link between the old world and the new by the coming of the Pilgrim Fathers to America. The one thing held in common was the need for theological learning in the Reformed tradition and "the liberty of prophesying" in the apostolic manner. Thus to expository preaching was given exegetical and prophetic discipline with evangelical application to the contemporary life.

2. PURITAN PREACHERS

a. *English Preachers.* Those who stand out in this period are selective of a greater number. Their sermons and books represent a variety of expression. Woven into their message are the rich overtones of Augustinian theology, the influence of Calvin, the covenant theme, the allegorical interpretation of Scripture, and the favorite motif of the Pilgrim. The following are mentioned as samples of this emphasis: John Foxe (1517-1587), Thomas Cartwright (1535-1603), Richard Hooker (1553-1600), John Smyth (1554-1612), Lancelot Andrewes (1555-1626), William Perkins (1558-1602), Richard Sibbes (1577-1635), Thomas Goodwin (1600-1679), Richard Baxter (1615-1691), John Owen (1616-1683), and John Bunyan (1628-1688).

b. *Scottish Preachers.* In association with England the Scottish churchmen held much in common but later came to separate. John Calvin held a special place in the esteem of Scottish preachers who copied his style and method. The exposition of Scripture, characteristic of Calvin at Geneva, held priority for many years. Theology and exegesis were always in company. Puritan preaching in Scotland held sway and so molded the life and thought of its people that even today the tradition persists in spite of major defections from its historic base. Those who stand out include the following: John Knox (1505-1572), Andrew Melville (1545-1584), Samuel Rutherford (1600-1661), William Guthrie (1620-1665), Alexander Peden (1626-1686), Richard Cameron (1648-1680), James Renwick (1662-1688), and Thomas Boston (1677-1732).

c. *New England Preachers.* The Pilgrim Fathers in coming to the shores of the new world brought with them the Puritan heritage of preaching. Enriched as they were from their stay in Holland and their contact with the Low Countries of Europe they brought with them an emphasis which has never died away. Outstanding among the preachers of the new world are the following: Thomas Shepard (1605-1649), Roger Williams (1603-1683), Francis Makemie (1654-1708), Cotton Mather (1663-1728), William Tennant (1673-1746), Theodorus J. Freylinghuysen (1691-1747), Jonathan Edwards (1704-1758), and John Witherspoon (1722-1794).

d. *In the Puritan Tradition.* Puritan preaching has its historical background and its influence largely in the seventeenth century. Thereafter it continued to recede in Great Britain but continued much longer in America. Looking back from this era we can trace its revival from time to time.

In the British Isles there was Charles Haddon Spurgeon (1834-1892), whose lifetime was characterized by a ministry unparalleled in modern days. Converted at sixteen years of age, he became a preacher at twenty-two, and continued unabated until his death. For two generations he ministered at the Metropolitan Tabernacle, London. He was a Baptist by persuasion, but in spirit and style of preaching he was a Puritan. His vast library (one of the largest of private libraries then) of thousands of volumes was exceedingly rich in Puritan literature. He reveled in their writings and fed his soul at their fountain. His voice had singular charm and beauty. His preaching was direct and personal. Taken down in shorthand, his sermons were printed and circulated by the million. His unquestioned belief in the inspiration and integrity of the Scriptures gave him a power and influence in his day beyond that of any other preacher.

Alexander Whyte (1836-1921) of Scotland rose from obscurity to be the best known preacher of his country. High honors were bestowed upon him, such as the Moderatorship of the Church and Principal of New College, but he remained throughout a humble spirit, a pastor, and a preacher. He was known at his death as "the last of the Puritans." This recalls his vivid imagination, his stress on the conscience, his preaching of sin and judgment, and the grace of God ready to remake character. He preached experimentally, unveiling sin. Imaginative reason fired his utterance. The Bible and Bunyan were always at hand, and his heart was steeped in the writings of Thomas Goodwin as well as the other major Puritans.

Clarence E. Macartney (1879-1957) of Pittsburgh, is the one of recent years who recalled something of the Puritan preaching. He toiled strenuously in sermon preparation and when he preached without notes he poured forth from a well-filled and well-stored mind. His grasp of history and of human nature, his Bible knowledge, and his passionate evangelistic thrust showed that he was a Puritan of his age in America. By some sixty books he has left his legacy for all to read. Although he did not expound in detail the Scriptures as the early Puritans, his proclamation of "the grand particularities of the faith" revealed the shepherd heart and the evangelistic spirit. The simplicity, sincerity, and gravity of his utterances reminded a generation that the Puritan spirit was still among us.

3. STYLE

The genius of Puritan preaching, whether that of the seventeenth century or later, lay in its simple, unadorned, plain style. As Jonathan Edwards put it in his book of *Resolutions*: "Never to speak in narrations anything but the pure and simple verity." In his *Manductio ad Ministerium,* Cotton Mather taught that, "after all, every man will have his own style." This text was used by Puritans as well as that of William Perkins, *The Art of Prophesying* (1592). The latter taught: "Human wisdom must be concealed, whether it be in the matter of the sermon, or in the setting forth of the words: because the preaching of the word is the testimony of God, and the profession of the knowledge of Christ, and not of human skill: and, again, because the hearers ought not to ascribe their faith to the gifts of men, but to the power of God's word. . . .If any man think that by this means barbarism should be brought into pulpits; he must understand that the minister may, yea and must privately use at his liberty the arts, philosophy, and variety of reading, whilest he is framing his sermon: but he ought in public to conceal all these from the people, and not to make the least ostentation . . . it is also a point of Art to conceal Art."

Other works of that period included *The*

Marrow of Sacred Divinity (1638), by William Ames, a standard text used at Harvard and Yale until the middle of the eighteenth century. In it the plain style is defended. Others who wrote for their fellow Puritans included Richard Bernard of Cambridge, England. *The Faithful Shepheard* (1607) by him is a popular treatise on the whole duty of the preacher, describing the proper conduct of life, the learning required, as well as the method and style to be observed in the sermon, and an eloquent insistence upon the glorious function of the pulpit. Thomas Hooker, in *The Soules Preparation* (1632), warned against the evil of consequences of a too ornate sermon style: "I have sometimes admired at this: why a company of Gentlemen, yeomen, and poore women, that are scarcely able to know their A.B.C. yet have a Minister to speake Latine, Greeke, and Hebrew, and to use the Fathers, when it is certain they know nothing at all. The reason is, because all this stings not, they may sit and sleepe in their sinnes, and goe to hell hoodwinckt, never awakened."

Richard Sibbes, one of the greatest of Puritan preachers in England, wrote about style. In writing the Preface to John Smith's *Introduction to The Creed,* he stressed: "This good man's aim was to convey himself by all manner of ways into the heart, which made him willingly heard of all sorts; for witty things only, as they are spoken to the brain, so they rest in the brain, and sink no deeper; but the heart (which vain and obnoxious men love not to be touched), that is the mark a faithful preacher aims to hit. But because the way to come to the heart is often to pass through the fancy, therefore this godly man studies by lively representations to help men's faith by the fancy. It was our Saviour Christ's manner of teaching to express heavenly things in an earthly manner and it was the study of the wise man, Solomon, becoming a preacher, to find out pleasant words, or words of delight, Eccles. 12:10." William Chappell, *The Preacher and The Art and Method of Preaching* (1656) found that his book was used for several decades before the settlement in New England by the leaders of thought. He stressed "the only legitimate order of the sermon" and gave impetus to the plain style.

The Puritan style then was modest, unadorned, and such as appealed to the lowliest in knowledge as well as reaching the well-educated. The sermon was an attempt to extract from a Biblical text an axiom of theology and to dispute of this in creedal order. In procedure the text was taken apart by the method of analysis into its constituent elements, and then set out again in a proposition. After the logical analysis of Scripture the practical appeal was made by the pastor-preacher. If the speech lacked adornment in pleasing phrases, nevertheless it was convincing, straightforward speech, and easy to be understood. Some preachers tried to be "witty" and used word-play and quips, whereas the "metaphysical" or intellectual emphasis was also intermixed. The Puritan might be fully aware of his skill in so speaking, but he was counseled to avoid these conceits of Elizabethen imagery.

The background of the Puritan preacher lay in the classics and the languages of Latin, Greek, and Hebrew. He was the best educated man of his day, acquainted with the best general literature then published. Outstanding in the field of literature was the King James Version of the Bible. The "simple and pure verity" of style was encouraged by the use of this monument of the English tongue. Its cadences and beauty of word and sentence, its surge and thunder of thought gripped the mind and molded the spirit. Puritans were steeped in the Bible. No one can estimate its profound influence upon the speech and ideals of a generation. The English tongue in its rugged Anglo-Saxon was then at its flowering and height of expression, making of the King James Version a monument of unsurpassed excellence. Nothing is comparable to it. From its reading and study came a lively selection of word and thought. Thus the Puritan style owed the most to this well of pure and undefiled English. Cogent, terse, and spiritual was the style which is known as the plain style.

4. EMPHASES

The "whole counsel of God" was expounded by the faithful pastor, but a recurring theme of three principal doctrines pervaded most of the sermons.

a. *The Sovereignty of God.* Basic to all theological views lay this one truth. Reformer and Puritan held to a world view in which God was supreme. History was the outworking of divine providence and God was the architect of the ages. The Calvinism of Geneva and the Puritanism of England had this in common. The ever changing forms of government under which men had to live forced the church to think in terms of divine sovereignty. As Andrew Melville (1545-1622) of Scotland expressed it in the struggle for religious freedom, "there are two kings and two kingdoms in Scotland." Melville was the architect of Scottish Presbyterianism and what he said summed up the truth for all Puritan preaching. Man was absolutely dependent upon God. Man's freedom of will was accepted but God had the right to dispense his salvation to whomsoever he would.

b. *The Sinfulness of Man.* The Puritan was aware of his sense of need. He stressed that man in himself lacked the ability to lift himself up. The heinousness of sin was ever before him. Man was forever involved in guilt and depravity. Such depravity implied that the whole person was tainted by sin and the whole of life was limited in what it could become – apart from the grace of God. The natural man could not understand the things of God. He needed spiritual enlightenment and renewal. This called for a supernatural work of God. The aim to convert sinful man found its thrust in the conviction of man's moral inability and the prevalent belief in the doctrine of hell.

c. *The Grace of God.* The end of preaching for the Puritan lay in the awakening of the soul to the knowledge of God's grace and love in redemption. The sermon was no casual oratorical effort. It was a serious business to prepare and preach a sermon. Eternal destiny was wrapped up in its message and in its reception or rejection. Thus the sermon must stress the personal note and appeal to the individual.

Here was the wooing note in the Puritan whose preaching sought to bring in many to the kingdom of God. Hell-fire preaching was also present (perhaps to the extent of 10 per cent of the sermons), but God's love could save and renew. The way of salvation was ever present and the appeal of the gospel was effective. In the mind of the Puritan was the conviction that the sermon was God's agency of conversion. It is true that the faithful came to hear the voice of God that they might conform their lives to an ethical pattern of right and good. But the preacher had in mind those "without the camp," and to them he came with earnest concern for their souls. They too were to be won for the kingdom of God.

5. STRUCTURE

Puritan preaching was not an artificial product, hurriedly put together. Solid, serious thought and writing prepared the way for the sermon to be preached. The writing habits of the Puritan are well-known. W. F. Mitchell, *English Pulpit Oratory from Andrewes to Tillotson,* has opened up this phase in research. There was a well-defined standard in vogue. First, the text is stated, then the doctrine is stated in a proposition. For example, Jonathan Edwards of New England, following his Puritan mentors, in the sermon "Sinners in the Hands of an Angry God" begins with an Introduction which had four points. Then he outlined the Proposition which contained ten divisions in logical order. This was the body of the sermon. Finally came the Application which included an Improvement, Illustrations, and Inferences. It is interesting to note that in this sermon there are four pages of Exposition and five pages of Application.

Structure then had an unfailing regularity of outline and development. Divisions are named; points under each one are numbered; objections are stated and answered. The sermon was a closely reasoned outline of theological thinking. Usually there was a searching application with practical insights regarding life and conduct. If the sermon did not begin with any "life situation" common today, it certainly found its climax in the situation to be met in that day. The sermon was usually written and then read, but many Puritan preachers were not tied to their manuscript, preferring to have freedom of utterance in the pulpit and often in the open air.

The stress upon one idea was characteristic. One truth and not several were dealt with in the main stream of Puritan homiletics and preaching. The main theme was repeated throughout the body of the sermon for emphasis. There was unity of thought and orderliness of movement, with each division adding to the development of thought. Truth was interpreted on the basis of careful exegesis. The text and its doctrine determined the theme. Undiluted exposition and clear divisions marked the work of the preacher. There was little "surprise" element in the sermons. Because of the Puritan style, the witty or clever sermon was not to be found alongside the plain style. Structure followed the well-chosen method already laid down by the homiletical and hermeneutical teachers. While the strong structure made for easier recollection on the part of the listener, the sermons tended to be unvaried, repetitious, and lengthy. However, in that period the pulpit had no competitors and the sermon was the highlight of the week. An expectant and ready congregation came to hear "acceptable words."

6. IDEALS

The ideals of the ministry held by the Puritan were high. He did not come to his calling lightly. To be called of God as "a messenger of the Lord of Hosts" was no light thing. No Puritan minister wished to be thought of as an hireling, for God had given him a unique place among men as the mouthpiece of God. As he labored within the context of his parish he was accorded respect and given a hearing. By reason of his education he usually stood above the rest of the community. And his status as a pastor or minister of the Word of God gave him a special place in the minds of his auditors. Generally an evangelical conversion experience was the background out of which a man received the call to this holy task. Whether in the Episcopal or Presbyterian order this was so. Similar convictions existed in the Independent groups with their "prophesyings."

The ideal for the Puritan preacher is set forth by Jonathan Edwards in his *Works*, I: "Take care . . . that he be a man of thoroughly sound principles, in the scheme of doctrine which he maintains. Labor to obtain a man, who has an established character, as a person of serious religion and piety. If you should happen to settle a minister, who knows nothing truly of Christ, and the way of salvation by Him, nothing experimentally of the nature of vital religion; alas, how will you be exposed as sheep without a shepherd. You will need one that shall stand as a champion in the cause of truth and godliness." The picture of the Puritan has also been idealized in the inscription on John Bunyan's statue at Bedford, England, which reads:

> A very grave person:
> Eyes lifted up to heaven.
> The best of books in his hand.
> The law of truth was written upon his lips.
> The world was behind his back.
> He stood as if he pleaded with men.
> A crown of gold did hang over his head.

Puritan preaching is to be assessed in the light of the times when in State and in church there was tension and purifying of ideals and convictions. The shepherd heart was the basis of the preacher's concern. As Jonathan Edwards described it when the Puritan movement had well-nigh spent itself in New England, "I have given myself to the work of the ministry, labouring in it night and day, rising and applying myself to this great business to which Christ appointed me. I have found the work of the ministry among you to be a great work indeed" (*Works*, I). Puritan preaching also expressed the conviction that the man of God was not only the pastor of a local congregation, but also that he was espousing the cause of the church of Christ in general. The evangelical and reformed spirit was also linked to a universal view of the church. Their sermons and writing are finding a place today as we rediscover their enduring value and abiding standards.

BIBLIOGRAPHY

Brown, J., *Puritan Preaching in England,* 1900.

Bunyan, J., *Works.*

E. F., *The Marrow of Modern Divinity,* 1645.

Grierson, H., *Cross Currents in English Literature of the Seventeenth Century.*

Haller, W., *The Rise of Puritanism,* 1938.

Miller, P., *The New England Mind – The Seventeenth Century,* 1939.

Milton, J., *Poetry and Works.*

Perkins, W., *The Art of Prophecying,* 1631.

Turnbull, R. G., *Jonathan Edwards the Preacher,* 1954.

Works by Sibbes, Charnock, Gill, Goodwin, Preston, Mather, Edwards.

Roman Catholic Preaching

One would naturally expect a Christian sermon to be modeled after the sermons of the Master. A verbatim report, however, of a full length sermon preached by Christ has not come down to us. While it is a matter of record that the first Christians gathered for the breaking of the bread and for prayer (Acts 2:42), there is no surviving evidence of a sermon delivered on such occasions. True, seven discourses delivered by Peter are mentioned (Acts 1, 2, 3, 5, 10, 11, 15) and six by Paul (Acts 13, 14, 17, 20, 22, 26). These accounts may faithfully reproduce the preaching of these apostles, or may be an account of it as reported by a Christian writer near the end of the first century A.D. In either case, this record yields little direct evidence for the history of the sermon preached within the Christian community itself. It is difficult to judge accurately how widespread the charismatic speaking mentioned by Paul (I Cor. 12: 1-11, 27-31; 14; Eph. 4:7-16) actually was, and the phenomenon disappeared as the Christian communities developed. In general, surviving evidence points to the apostles and those whom they placed in charge of the Christian communities as the normal preachers during the apostolic age.

1. THE SUBAPOSTOLIC AGE AND THE THIRD CENTURY

The earliest extant evidence showing the sermon as a part of the Eucharistic worship service dates from the time of Justin Martyr. In his *Apology I* 67, written between A.D. 150-155, he says that the Christians gathered on Sundays and that the memoirs of the apostles and the writings of the prophets were read. When the reader had finished "the bishop gives the admonition and invites us to imitate these noble men" (T. Jalland, *Studia Patristica,* vol. 5, pp. 83 85). Justin's account continues with a description of the rest of the service. The preacher, it should be noted, is the bishop. Slightly later Tertullian refers to preaching under similar circumstances (*Apology* 39.3; *On the Soul* 9.20) without, however, identifying the preacher. None of these references give much information on the actual content of the sermon.

The so-called *Second Epistle of Clement* merits attention as the oldest extant Christian sermon. Written in Greek by an unknown author between A.D. 150 and 170, this unliterary sermon of general content emphasizes belief in the divinity of Christ, exhorts the hearers to bear witness to Christ by their exemplary lives, stresses the need for good works, and ends with a doxology.

Eusebius has preserved the earliest evidence that, in some regions at least, preaching was not restricted to bishops. Early in the third century Origen went to Palestine "and although he had not yet received the presbyterate, the bishops there requested him to discourse and expound the divine Scriptures publicly in the church" (*Ecclesiastical History* 6.19). Demetrius, bishop of Alexandria, protested strenuously against the procedure but the bishop of Jerusalem and the bishop of Caesarea cited the example of their brother bishops in Asia Minor at Laranda, Iconium, and Synnada and were inclined to think that "this thing happens in other places also without our knowing it." Origen's sermons generally followed this pattern: exordium, practical application of a selected Scriptural text explained according to the allegorical method of interpretation, exhortation, and finally a doxology. The discourses of this gifted speaker were taken down in shorthand by scribes according to the testimony of Eusebius (op. cit. 6.36). The meager extant evidence for preaching in Latin during this period centers around the church of northern Africa. Cyprian, bishop of Carthage, who died as a martyr in A.D. 257 was the outstanding preacher. Lactantius found it difficult to decide whether Cyprian was "more ornate in eloquence, or more successful in explanation, or more powerful in persuasion" (*The Divine Institutes* 5.1)

With the end of the persecutions and the peace which came to the church with the accession of Constantine a new era for preaching began. The outstanding preachers educated in the best schools of the day, e.g., Athens, Antioch, Alexandria, trained by such eminent rhetoricians as Himerius and Libanius, brought to the office of preaching in addition to their professional rhetorical training an astounding familiarity with the sacred Scripture. As the church attracted converts from the more educated circles of society an audience was at hand which could relish the artistic accomplishments of the speakers.

2. GREEK PREACHING

Fourth century Greek preaching is dominated by Basil the Great, John Chrysostom, and Gregory of Nazianzus. Basil's significant contribution to preaching is found in the exegetical homily which he enhanced with the embellishments of Greek rhetoric. The homilies on the six days of creation are his masterpieces and in their Latin translation exerted an equally powerful influence in the Latin church for many centuries. The largest legacy of discourses in Greek has been left by Chrysostom who was a master not only in the exegetical homily but also in the occasional discourse and the panegyric. The pleasing rhetorical harmonies and cadences of his sermons frequently elicited spontaneous applause from his audience. Gregory of Nazianzus won renown for the panegyric – Christianized as a sermon form by Gregory the Wonderworker in his eulogy of Origen in 238 – and his magnificent funeral orations. His discourses, like those of Basil, translated into Latin were long studied as models by following generations of preachers.

Of all the forms of preaching the panegyric was the most cultivated long after the golden age of Greek preaching had passed. It was used to commemorate the feast days of martyrs and other saints, especially those of the virgin Mary. In the long line of panegyrists the emperors themselves found a place of honor. Leo VI and Constantine Porphyrogennetus are noteworthy examples.

The decline of Greek preaching, however, seems to be clearly indicated in the legislation of the Trullan Synod (692). In its nineteenth canon the Synod instructed bishops to preach to the faithful especially on Sundays, and to adhere to the Fathers, "the luminaries and teachers," in expounding the Scriptures rather than to compose their own sermons. This synodal enactment explains, at least in part, the proliferation of collections of homilies during the following centuries.

3. LATIN PREACHING

Evidence for preaching in Latin in Gaul, Spain, and Italy becomes more specific by the fourth century as the names of Hilary, bishop of Poitiers, and Zeno, bishop of Verona, clearly indicate. The first real Latin rival of the great Greek preachers is Ambrose, bishop of Milan. His proficiency in the exegetical homily, but especially his notable contributions to the Christianizing of the Latin funeral oration, gained for him a place of honor in the history of Latin preaching.

Augustine, bishop of Hippo, dominates fifth century Latin preaching. Upon his ordination to the priesthood in 391 this office was entrusted to him although this was not a common practice at the time in the Latin church. For more than thirty years both as priest and as bishop Augustine preached frequently, at times twice a day. While the training of the former teacher of rhetoric is usually very evident in his discourses Augustine could become almost colloquial when he was addressing audiences which lacked formal training. The fourth book of his treatise *On Christian Instruction,* which gives practical guidelines for preaching, is more important for the history of the sermon, however, than the legacy of his discourses.

While Jerome, Maximus of Turin, and Pope Leo I deserve mention at least in passing, the year 529 is far more significant for the progress of preaching in the Latin church. In this year the second Council of Vaison, at which the zealous preacher Caesarius, bishop of Arles, presided, authorized priests to preach "for the edification of all the churches and the benefit of all the people not only in the cities, but also in the rural areas." If illness prevented the priest from preaching the deacons were to read the homilies of the fathers (Hefele-Leclercq, *Histoire des Conciles,* vol. 2 p. 112). Juridically this conciliar legislation ended the bishops' monopoly on the right to preach in the west. While the homilies of Pope Gregory I were widely used as models for preachers, his *Pastoral Rule* with its practical hints for preaching had an even greater influence. It was even translated into Greek during the pope's lifetime. The meager surviving evidence on preaching during the seventh century makes it impossible to determine the extent to which the legislation of Vaison in 529 was implemented, or what results it produced.

In the eight century the collection of patristic homilies made by Paul the Deacon, though primarily intended for use by monks in the choral performance of the monastic office, also was of service for the clergy in their office of preaching. By the year 789, however, a deplorable state of preaching existed at least in the Frankish kingdom. There were complaints that the clergy did not even know the Lord's Prayer and that they were not preaching the Scriptures. To remedy this defect the General Admonition (*Monumenta Germaniae Historica, Capitularia,* 1, pp. 52-56) issued an outline of essential sermon material to be followed by the clergy. An equally gloomy picture of preaching is presented by Theodulf of Orleans in 797 when he complained that some priests could scarcely do more than remind the people to turn away from evil and do good (J. P. Migne, *Latin Patrology* 105, 200A). The ninth century homiliaries compiled by Alcuin, Rabanus Maurus, and Haymo of Auxerre were invaluable aids for preachers. The history of preaching, however, was more vitally affected in 813 by the third Council of Tours and the second Council of Reims. Both councils directed bishops to provide themselves with homilies containing the necessary teachings for the instruction of the people and to translate these sermons into the early Romance language or German "so that all could more easily understand what is being said." Some thirty years later the fourth Council of Mainz (847) repeated this legislation concerning the use of the vernacular in preaching.

After this legislation the Crusades, the flowering of scholasticism, and the founding of the mendicant orders were the most significant factors that influenced subsequent preaching in the Latin church. From the tenth to the early thirteenth century important preachers were active, e.g., Peter Damian, Bernard of Clairvaux, Anselm of Canterbury, Ivo of Chartres, Robert of Arbrissel, Alan of Lille. That the sermon texts of medieval preachers have come down to us in Latin is not conclusive evidence that the sermons were delivered in that language. Jacques de Vitry clearly states that while sermons for clerics were in Latin, the vernacular was used for the laity, and Adam of Perseigne complained that the quality of many sermons suffered in the process of translation. Toward the end of the twelfth century the scholastic method of teaching left its mark on preaching. The logic and dialectic of the schools were applied to the sermon topic. The preacher announced his theme much as one of the schoolmen would state his thesis, and then went on to definition, division, subdivision, and distinction citing numerous passages from Scripture and the fathers and concluded by adding arguments from reason to prove his point. Such sermons were preached to faculty and students chiefly in the university cities such as Paris, Oxford, and Cambridge.

Distinct from this scholastic preaching was the popular preaching which by the end of the twelfth century was generally of poor quality. One factor contributing to this low ebb was undoubtedly the low literacy of many of the parish clergy about which the Fourth Lateran Council complained in 1215. Unauthorized preachers and laymen moved in to remedy the unfortunate situation. Among these initially well-intentioned persons were the Humiliati and the Waldenses. Their lack of formal training for preaching eventually involved them in doctrinal errors. Pope Alexander III forbade them to preach and Pope Lucius III finally excommunicated them for refusing to obey. The founding of the Dominicans and Franciscans was a far more effective and correct remedy in this plight. While some of these mendicant friars gained distinction in the more academic type of preaching, e.g., Hugh of Saint-Cher, Thomas Aquinas, Peter of Tarantasia, John of Rupella, Bonaventura, Guibert of Tournai, and Matthew of Aquasparta, far greater numbers devoted themselves to apostolic preaching among the people. Their sermons were in the vernacular on concrete themes, with practical applications to daily life. Homely examples and expressions as well as examples from sacred Scripture and the lives of the saints were used to convey the message. The Council of Vienne (1311-1312) considered this type of preaching so timely that it empowered the Dominicans and Franciscans with apostolic authority to preach freely and ordered prelates and parish priests to cooperate with the friars. The council went even further and granted the Dominicans and Franciscans permission for street preaching and bade prelates and parish priests not to look askance at this procedure (*Conciliorum oecumenicorum decreta,* pp. 342-344). Famous preachers among the mendicants at this time were Berthold of Regensburg, Bartholomew of Vicenza, Guido of Evreux, James of Lausanne. The mystical sermon, the beginnings of which can be seen already in Bernard of Clairvaux, received an impetus from Bonaventura, and was especially developed as a sermon genre by Meister Eckhart, Johannes Tauler, Henry Suso, and Jean Gerson.

As the various types of sermons were developing a wealth of sermon literature was also being produced. Technical treatises (*artes praedicandi*) giving instructions for the preparation and directives for the delivery of the sermon were composed. Some of these *artes* were veritable sermon encyclopedias, as the work of Humbert of Romans. The most widely used medieval sermon aids were the *Examples* (*Exempla*) of Jacques de Vitry, *The Golden Legend* (*Legenda aurea*) of James of Voragine, the *Book of Examples* (*Liber exemplorum*) and *Mirror of the Laity* (*Speculum laicorum*) compiled by two unknown Franciscans. Of almost equal popularity was the *Preachers' Summa* (*Summa praedicantium*) written by the Dominican John of Bromyard.

Though not regarded primarily as an outstanding preacher, Nicholas of Lyra significantly influenced the progress of preaching through his *Postilla litteralis.* This treatise clearly distinguished between the mystical, allegorical, and literal interpretation of Scriptural tests used for sermons. He thus provided the preacher with a new exegetical approach which was a radical departure from the patristic tradition. This work had the distinction of being the first explanation of Scriptural texts to be printed.

The fifteenth century witnessed an even greater increase in the publication of collections of sermon materials. The most popular work in this category was that of Johannes of Werden with the forthright title *Sleep Free from Care* (*Dormi secure*) which may be a significant commentary on preachers and sermons of that period. The most ambitious "sermon encyclopedia" was produced by Meffreth (*c.* 1447) under the title *Queen's Garden* (*Hortulus reginae*). This work supplied at least three sermons of considerable length for each Sunday and certain feast days with suitable quotations not only from sacred Scripture but from Greek and Latin authors as well.

This century likewise gives evidence of the increasing popularity of the special sermon for Lent, and the so-called mission sermon. The latter type of sermon attained a special eminence in the preaching of Vincent Ferrer, Bernardine of Sienna, John Capistran, and James of the Marches. The most widely known preacher of this era was undoubtedly Girolamo Savonarola.

That the quality of preaching at the beginning of the sixteenth century, at least in some regions, left much to be desired can readily be gathered from statements made in the eleventh session of the Fifth Lateran Council on December 19, 1516. In a document entitled *Concerning the Manner of Preaching* the Council complained that the gospel was not being preached, but that fictitious miracles, false prophecies, idle tales, the arrival of anti-Christ, and even the imminence of the last judgment found their way into the sermon (*Conciliorum oecumenicorum decreta* pp. 610-614).

4. PREACHING DURING AND AFTER THE REFORMATION

The Reformation placed a new emphasis on preaching and gave the sermon a decidedly more focal point in the revised divine worship. The duly authorized minister based his sermon on the literal meaning of the Scriptures. The sermon was regarded as the living voice of the gospel, and God spoke through the words of the preacher (*Die Religion in Geschichte und Gegenwart,* vol. 5, p. 522). This renewed emphasis on preaching can also be seen in the legislation of the Council of Trent which in its fifth session clearly placed the obligation of a sermon on all Sundays and feast days on the local bishops and pastors. Added emphasis on this obligation was again brought forward in the twenty-fourth session of the council in the *Decree on Reformation,* canon 4, which also strongly recommended special sermons for the seasons of Advent and Lent (*Conciliorum oecumenicorum decreta,* p. 739). In addition to determining the responsibility for preaching the Council of Trent also took steps to secure training for preachers in the seminaries it ordered to be established. The last half of the seventeenth and the beginning of the eighteenth century witnessed an era of particularly brilliant preaching in Jacques Bossuet, Louis Bourdaloue, Francois Fénelon, and Jean Baptiste Massilon. Comparable fame was won by Henri Lacordaire, Gustave Ravignan, and Joseph Felix in their memorable conferences in the venerable cathedral of Notre Dame in Paris. The well-known English cardinals, Wiseman, Manning, and Newman hold places of distinction in the annals of preaching.

In the United States during the years of immigration, preaching generally followed the practices which were traditional in the home lands of the immigrants. The parish mission in the European tradition was a regularly recurring event. Priests of a religious order or congregation, though some dioceses had their own diocesan mission band, were invited to preach twice daily for a week or even longer as the site of the parish would suggest. The topics of the sermons dealt with fundamental truths of salvation, the reception of the sacraments, and almost invariably included special sermons on death, judgment, heaven, and hell. In some instances the missionaries would conduct a type of debate from two specially prepared pulpits. By the time of World War II the parish mission was quite generally on the decline. With the founding of the *American Ecclesiastical Review* (1889) and the *Homiletic and Pastoral Review* (1900), considerable interest began to focus on preaching a sermon with more appeal to an audience now more acclimatized to the American scene. One of the most representative authors of articles on preaching was Msgr. H. T. Henry who wrote quite regularly for the periodicals mentioned. The influence of Cardinal Gibbons' *The Ambassador of Christ* on American preaching was also considerable.

A more recent trend, having its beginnings in Europe, is the so-called kerygmatic approach designed to give greater theological dimension to the sermon. As this approach becomes more widespread it may well prove to be the factor which differentiates preaching of today from earlier forms of the sermons. In terms of this approach the preacher is not simply to set before his hearers a series of truths and precepts, no matter how essential, but to present them as a unified whole forming part of the history of salvation accomplished through Christ. The beginnings of this approach are said to go back to the work of J. A. Jungmann, *Die Frohbotschaft und unsere Glaubensverkundigung* (*The Good News and our Proclamation of the Faith*), published in 1936. There are many today who think that this type of sermon is the one envisaged by the *Constitution on the Sacred Liturgy* promulgated December 4, 1963. In the directive concerning the sermon the statement is made that preaching is a "proclamation of the wondrous deeds of God in the history of salvation (*Acta Apostolicae Sedis* (56) 1964, p. 109). Whatever the congency of the reasoning may be the Second Vatican Council in three of its most recent documents gives unmistakable evidence of the importance it attaches to preaching. in the *Dogmatic Constitution on the Church* (*Acta Apostolicae Sedis* (57) 1965, p. 28), the council reiterates the statement of the Council of Trent which assigns to preaching a place of pre-eminence among the principal duties of bishops. In the decree: *On the Pastoral Office of Bishops in the Church,* issued October 28, 1965, the council became more specific. It declared that bishops are to explain Christian doctrine in a way adapted to the needs of the times. It went on to say, "In expounding this teaching let them give proof of the Church's maternal solicitude for all men, whether they be of the faith or not, and show particular concern for the poor and those in straitened circumstances to whom the Lord has sent them to preach good news." Whether these words imply the use of the kerygmatic approach mentioned above is not clear from the context. The same must also be said about the words of the council in which it took cognizance of the priest's role in preaching. "Priests too, as collaborators with the bishops have the preaching of the gospel as their principal duty. . . . The preaching of the priest, frequently very difficult in the conditions of the modern world, must explain the word of God not merely in a general and abstract way, but by applying the eternal truth of the Gospel to the concrete circumstances of life in order to move the hearts of his hearers" (Decree: *On the Ministry and Life of the Priests,* December 7, 1965).

BIBLIOGRAPHY

Brilioth, Y. T., *Landmarks in the History of Preaching*. London, 1950.

Caplan, H., *Medieval Artes Praedicandi: A Handlist*. Ithaca N. Y. 1934.

————, *Medieval Artes Praedicandi: A Supplementary Handlist*. Ithaca, N. Y., 1936.

Caplan, H., King, H. H., "Pulpit Eloquence: A List of Doctrinal and Historical Studies in English," *Speech Monographs* 22 (Special Issue 1955). Columbia, Missouri.

————, "Pulpit Eloquence: A List of Doctrinal and Historical Studies in German" **Speech Monographs 22 (Special Issue, 1956).** Columbia, Missouri.

Dargan, E. C., *A History of Preaching*, 2 vols. Grand Rapids, 1954.

Huesman, W., *The Good News Yesterday and Today*. New York, 1962. This is an abridged translation of J. Jungmann's work with essays in appraisal of his contribution.

Jungmann, J., *Die Frohbotschaft und Unsere Glaubensverkündigung*. Regensburg, 1936.

Owst, G. R., *Literature and Pulpit in Medieval England*, 2nd ed. New York, 1961.

————, *Preaching in Medieval England*, Cambridge, England, 1926.

Schian, C., *Realencyklopädie für protestantische Theologie und Kirche*, 3rd ed., vols. 15 and 24. Leipzig, 1896-1913.

Zwart, A., *The History of Franciscan Preaching and of Franciscan Preachers 1209-1927* (Franciscan Studies 7). New York, 1928.

The Literature of Preaching

1. OVERALL SURVEY

A good general introduction to this is the article, "Preaching," in *The New Schaff-Herzog Encyclopedia of Religious Knowledge* (Funk and Wagnalls, 1911), Vol. IX (reprint, Baker Book House, 1953). A long section of the article is devoted specifically to the History of Preaching. It concludes with a bibliography of the subject to the year 1909.

2. HISTORIES OF PREACHING

a. *General*

The value and importance of the history of preaching for the preacher cannot be overemphasized. This history is concerned with the lives and personalities of past preachers, the social situations in which they lived and labored, the character of their times, the particular nature of the services they rendered, and their methods of sermonizing. Such studies are indispensable for the person who seeks to understand the place preaching has occupied in the history of Christianity and the changes it has undergone and in turn brought about through the ages.

The scholars tell us that the definitive history of preaching has yet to be written. Nevertheless there are a number of reliable histories on the subject that are sufficient for the needs of the average minister.

1. *In Print*

Webber, F. R., *A History of Preaching in Britain and America*. 3 vol. Milwaukee: Northwestern Publishing House, 1952, 1955, 1957.

Brilioth, Yngve, *A Brief History of Preaching*, (Paper). Muhlenberg, 1965.

2. *Out of Print*

Broadus, John A., *Lectures on the History of Preaching*. New York: A. C. Armstrong and Son, 1891.

Pattison, T. H., *The History of Christian Preaching*. Philadelphia: American Baptist Publication Society, 1903.

Petry, Ray C., *No Uncertain Sound*. Westminster, 1948.

—————, *Preaching in the Great Tradition*. Westminster, 1950. Four lectures on the same general subject as his earlier book and a useful companion to it.

Dargan, E. C., *A History of Preaching*. Vols. I and II combined. Grand Rapids: Baker Book House, 1954.

b. *Histories of Preaching in Different Periods and Countries.*

1. *In Print*

Smyth, Charles, *The Art of Preaching: A Practical Summary of Preaching in the Church of England*, 747-1939, Allenson, 1953.

Owst, G. R., *Literature and Pulpit in Medieval England*. Oxford: Basil Blackwell, 1961.

Mitchell, W. F., *English Pulpit Oratory from Andrews to Tilletson: A Study of Its Literary Aspects*. New York: Russell and Russell, 1962.

Davies, Horton, *Varieties of English Preaching, 1900-1960*. London: SCM Press, 1963.

Blench, J. W., *Preaching in England*, 1460-1600. Oxford: Basil Blackwell, 1964.

2. *Out of Print*

Blaikie, W. G.: *The Preachers of Scotland from the 6th to the 19th Century*. Edinburgh: T. and T. Clark, 1888.

Ker, John, *Lectures on the History of Preaching* (Medieval and Modern Germany down to 1875). London: Hodder and Stoughton, 1888.
Brown, John, *Puritan Preaching in England* (Yale Lectures). Scribner, 1900.
Brastow, Lewis O., *Representative Modern Preachers.* Macmillan, 1904.
Hoyt, A. S., *The Pulpit and American Life.* Macmillan, 1921.
Owst, G. R., *Preachers in Medieval England* (1350-1450). London; Cambridge University Press, 1926.
Byington, E. H., *Pulpit Mirrors.* Geo. H. Doran, 1927.
Howard, Henry C., *Princes of the Christian Pulpit and Pastorate.* Nashville: Cokesbury Press (Two series), 1927, 1928.
Richardson, Caroline Frances, *English Preachers and Preaching,* 1640-1670. Macmillan, 1928. A fascinating account of the human side of preachers of the times: their training, habits, foibles, social standing, how they were characterized by their contemporaries, their money problems, their avocations, recreations and hobbies.
Kessling, E. D., *The Early Sermons of Luther and Their Relation to the Pre-Reformation sermon.* Zondervan, 1935.
Herr, A. F., *The Elizabethan Sermon: A Study and a Bibliography.* Philadelphia: The University of Pennsylvania Press, 1940.
Kerr, Hugh T., *Preaching in The Early Church.* Revell, 1942.
Thompson, Ernest Trice, *Changing Emphases in American Preaching.* Westminster, 1943. A Study of 5 Protestant preachers whom he considers typical of the changes in Protestant preaching in the 19th century.
Levy, Bababette May, *Preaching in the First Half Century of New England History.* Hartford, Connecticut Society of Church History, 1945.
Foster, J. *After the Apostles: Missionary Preaching of the First Three Centuries.* London: SCM Press, 1951.

3. PRINTED SERMONS

A steady stream of books of sermons, singly and in sets, has been coming off the presses of British and American publishers for the last hundred years or so. Although a few preachers boast that they never read the sermons of other preachers, there are valid reasons why, for his own benefit and for the benefit of the congregation, every preacher can wisely form the habit of studying printed sermons as a part of his self-discipline and of his continuing education for the practice of his calling.

a. Sets of Books of Sermons of Individual Preachers

Sets of books of sermons by noted preachers of other days may be found in all theological libraries. Most of these books are out of print. But from time to time publishers still put out single volumes of sermons of some of these preachers of past generations, thus making it possible for preachers of our day to get acquainted with them. For example, sermons of John Donne, that are now attracting the attention of scholars and publishers, can be secured in single volumes:

Gill, Theodore A. ed., *The Sermons of John Donne.* Meridian Books Inc. (paper), 1957.
Fuller, Edmund, ed., *The Showing Forth of Christ* (a group of Donne's Sermons). Harper, 1965. Also a group of the Sermons of Frederick W. Robertson have been recently published.
Gilbert E. Doan Jr., ed., *The Preaching of Frederick W. Robertson.* Muhlenberg, 1964.

b. *Collections of Sermons in Sets or Single Volumes of so-called Great Preachers*

Theological libraries are also usually well-stocked with these collections. They include not only regular sermons but a wide range of sermons preached for special groups, such as laymen, university congregations, young people and children; sermons for special occasions such as revivals, communion services, special days of the Christian year; and sermons of special kinds such as biographical sermons, sermons on art, and sermons on different types of literature.

1. *In Print*

Butler, G. Paul, *Best Sermons* (annual volume of 1945 or any year thereafter). Macmillan.
Blackwood, Andrew W., *The Protestant Pulpit.* Abingdon, 1947.
Blackwood, Andrew W., *Evangelical Sermons of Our Day.* Abingdon, 1963.
Brown, H. C. Jr., ed., *Southern Baptist Preaching.* Broadman, 1959.
McGraw, J., *Great Evangelical Preachers of Yesterday.* Abingdon, 1961.
Kemp, Charles, ed., *The American Pulpit.* Bethany, 1963.
Sadler, William Alan Jr., ed., *Master Sermons Through the Ages.* Harper, 1963.
Whitesell, Faris D., ed., *Great Expository Sermons.* Revell, 1964.

2. *Out of Print*

Fish, H. C., *History and Repository of Pulpit Eloquence.* Dodd, Mead, 1877. One of the best single volumes of sermons up to that time.

Kleiser, Grenville, ed., *The World's Great Sermons.* 10 vols. Funk and Wagnalls, 1908.

Scott, Rob't and Stiles, W. C., eds., *Modern Sermons by World Scholars.* 10 vols. Funk and Wagnalls, 1909.

Currier, Albert H., ed., *Nine Great Sermons.* Pilgrim Press, 1912.

Morrison, Charles Clayton, ed., *The American Pulpit: Twenty-five Foremost Preachers.* Macmillan, 1925.

Stelze, Charles, ed., *If I Had Only One Sermon To Preach.* Harper, 1927.

McKeehan, Hobart D., ed., *Anglo-American Preaching.* Harper, 1928.

Marchant, Sir James, *If I Had Only One Sermon To Preach.* English Series. Harper, 1928.

Keller, Edward L., ed., *Great Sermons by Young Preachers.* Richard R. Smith, Inc., 1931.

Jones, Edgar DeWitt, *American Preachers of Today.* Bobbs-Merrill, 1933.

Atkins, G. G., *Master Sermons of the 19th Century.* Chicago: Willett, Clark and Co. 1940.

Frost, S. E. Jr., ed., *The World's Great Sermons.* Halcyon House, 1943. 100 sermons from the time of Jesus to date of publication.

American Pulpit Series. 15 vols. Abingdon, 1945.

Gifford, Frank G., *The Anglican Pulpit Today.* Morehouse-Gorham, 1953.

Motter, Alton M., ed., *Sunday Evening Sermons.* Harper, 1950. Preached before the Chicago Sunday Evening Club.

Baird, Paul J., *From Out of the West.* Stockton: The Lantern Press, 1962.

c. Single Volumes of Sermons by Individual Preachers

In his *History of Preaching,* F. R. Webber says that in the English speaking countries alone one might easily name over 1,000 men, who, for one reason or another, may be called famous preachers. It is no wonder, then, that the shelves of theological libraries are loaded with single volumes of sermons by individual preachers. A reader who desires a book of sermons by any particular preacher will undoubtedly be able to find it in the nearest theological library.

d. Periodicals Specializing in Publishing Sermons

1. Older Periodicals

Homiletical Review, published by Funk and Wagnalls, New York. It began publication in 1883.

The Christian World Pulpit, published in London.

The Expository Times, a monthly magazine that has been published since 1889 by T. and T. Clark, Edinburgh. It contains some sermons but specializes in expositions of the Scriptures.

2. Present-Day Periodicals

The Pulpit, a monthly magazine for ministers. It is published by the Christian Century Foundation, Chicago, since about 1936.

The Pulpit Digest, a monthly magazine for ministers. It is published in Manhasset, Long Island, New York, since 1929.

Familiarity with both of these magazines enables a preacher to keep abreast of the trends in sermonizing among his contemporaries.

e. Tape and Disc Recordings

Here is a distinctively modern opportunity for studying sermons: through the living voices of preachers themselves. *The Churchman's Recorded Library of Taped Sermons and Addresses,* maintained by Sermons and Pictures Inc., Atlanta, Georgia, an organization that cooperates with the Protestant Radio and Television Center. This library was established as a non-profit organization by Mr. Harlow M. Russell of Boothbay Harbor, Maine and St. Petersburg, Florida. It lends and sells tapes covering a wide variety of subjects by a variety of religious leaders. This organization appears to be the central source of supply for recordings for all other institutions in the country. *The Charles G. Reigner Recording Library* of Union Theological Seminary, Richmond, Virginia, has a large catalog of recordings. Union Theological Seminary in New York; San Francisco Theological Seminary, San Anselmo, California, and doubtless other seminaries are also prepared to provide tapes, and in some instances discs, for ministers.

4. LECTURESHIPS ON PREACHING

Among the lectureships in theological institutions in our day three stand out above the others. Two of these are devoted primarily to preaching, and the other one has occasional important lectures on preaching.

a. The Lyman Beecher Lectureship on Preaching

This lectureship, popularly known as the Yale Lectures, is the best known lectureship in the English speaking world. It was established in the Divinity School, Yale University in 1871, by a gift from Henry W. Sage, in memory of Lyman Beecher of the Class of 1797, Yale College, who died in 1863. Although it was established specifically for lectures on preaching by preachers, the terms were soon modified so that lectures could be given on any "topic appropriate to the Christian Ministry," and by laymen as well as by ministers. Dr. Henry Ward Beecher of Brooklyn, the son of the man in whose honor the lectureship was established, and the pastor of the donor, delivered the first three lectures in 1872, 1873, and 1874.

The lectures have been given annually in ninety of the ninety-four years since they began. Of the ninety series given, only eight have not been published. The large majority of the lectures have dealt with preaching. Together they constitute the most valuable homiletical material in any language or in any comparable period of Christian history. The homiletical knowledge of any Christian minister is deficient if he has not read a sizable number of these volumes.

The lectures that did not deal with preaching were published and became outstanding books, such as:

Trumbull, Henry Clay, *The Sunday School.* Philadelphia: John P. Wattles, 1888.

Fairbairn, A. M., *The Place of Christ in Modern Theology.* Scribner, 1893.

Watson, John (Ian Maclaren), *The Cure of Souls.* Dodd Mead, 1896.

Smith, George Adam, *Modern Criticism and the Old Testament.* New York: A. C. Armstrong and Son, 1901.

Jefferson, Charles E., *The Building of the Church.* Macmillan, 1910.

Fosdick, Harry Emerson, *The Modern Use of the Bible.* Macmillan, 1924.

Sclater, J. R. P., *The Public Worship of God.* Doubleday Doran, 1927.

The list of lecturers who talked about preaching includes practically every notable preacher in Protestantism in both America and Britain in the last century. Some years ago two overall studies of the series were published. They are:

B. B. Baxter, *The Heart of the Yale Lectures.* Macmillan, 1947. It summarizes the principles of preaching found in the lectures.

Jones, Edgar Dewitt, *The Royalty of the Pulpit.* Harper, 1951. It is primarily concerned with the persons who gave the lectures. Both of these books contain a complete list of the lectures up to the time of their publication. Since Jones' book was published fourteen lectures have been added to the list. Eighty-two of the ninety-four lectures have been published. For the purposes of this article it is sufficient to list the volumes still in print and a selected group of others that are widely regarded as of permanent worth.

1. *In Print*

Only three of these lectures, previous to the late 1950's, are still in print. They are:

Brooks, Phillips, *Lectures on Preaching* (1879). Now available under the title, *Eight Lectures on Preaching.* Seabury, 1959.

Forsyth, P. T., *Positive Preaching and the Modern Mind* (1907). Allenson reprint, 1953.

Stewart, James S., *A Faith to Proclaim.* Scribner, 1953.

The following lectures, given since 1957 are still in print:

Sittler, Joseph, *The Ecology of Faith.* Muhlenberg, 1961.

Bartlett, Gene, *The Audacity of Preaching.* Harper, 1962.

Miller, Samuel, *Faith and Secularity: The Dilemma of Modern Preaching.* Published as *The Dilemma of Modern Belief.* Harper, 1963.

Barr, Browne, *A Provincial and Parochial Report.* Published as *Parish Back Talk,* Abingdon, 1964.

2. *Out of Print*

A selected group of outstanding lectures, in addition to the books of Brooks, Forsyth and Stewart, already mentioned, are:

Dale, R. W., *Nine Lectures on Preaching.* New York: A. S. Barnes and Co., 1878.

Simpson, Matthew, *Lectures on Preaching.* New York: Nelson and Phillips, 1879.

Van Dyke, Henry, *The Gospel for an Age of Doubt.* Macmillan, 1896.

Faunce, W. H. P., *The Educational Ideal in the Ministry.* Macmillan 1908.

Jowett, J. H., *The Preacher: His Life and Work.* Geo. H. Doran, 1912.

Horne, Charles Sylvester, *The Romance of Preaching.* Revell, 1914.

Pepper, George Warton, *A Voice from the Crowd.* Yale University Press, 1915.

Brown, Charles Reynolds, *The Art of Preaching.* Macmillan, 1922.

Buttrick, George A., *Jesus Came Preaching.* Scribner, 1931.

Tittle, Ernest Fremont, *Jesus after Nineteen Centuries.* Abingdon, 1933.

Park, John Edgar, *The Miracle of Preaching.* Macmillan, 1936.

Sperry, Willard L., *We Prophesy in Part.* Harper, 1938.

Sockman, Ralph W., *The Highway of God.* Macmillan, 1942.

Oxnam, G. Bromley, *Preaching in a Revolutionary Age.* Abingdon, 1944.

Scherer, Paul, *For We Have This Treasure.* Harper, 1944.

Phillips, Harold C., *Bearing Witness To The Truth,* Abingdon, 1949.

Luccock, Halford E., *Communicating The Gospel.* Harper, 1954.

Kennedy, Gerald, *God's Good News.* Harper, 1955.

b. The Warrack Lectures

These lectures were established in 1920 as "The Preachers' Lectureship" by a gift of Frank Warrack that was placed in the hands of the General Trustees of the Church of Scotland to be used for lectures "by preachers who have proved their power to attract and hold the people." The terms of the lectureship specified that the lectures should be delivered in each of the colleges of the Church: Aberdeen, Edinburgh, St. Andrews and Glasgow. A number of these lectures were quickly recognized throughout the English speaking world as of superior merit.

1. *In Print*

Farmer, H. H., *The Servant of the Word.* Scribner, 1942.

Stewart, James S., *Heralds of God.* Scribner, 1945.

Keir, Thomas H., *The Word in Worship,* Oxford University Press, 1962.

Cleland, James T., *Preaching To Be Understood.* Abingdon, 1965.

2. *Out of Print*

Black, James, *The Mystery of Preaching.* Revell, 1924.

Smith, David, *The Art of Preaching.* London: Geo. H. Doran, 1924.

Coffin, Henry Sloane, *What To Preach.* Geo. H. Doran, 1926.

Scott, W. Boyd, *Preaching Week by Week.* New York: Richard R. Smith, 1928.

Burnet, Adam W., *Pleading with Men.* Revell, 1935.

Macgregor, H. C., *The Making of a Preacher.* Westminster, 1946.

Jeffrey, George J., *This Grace Wherein We Stand.* London: Hodder and Stoughton, 1949.

Read, David H. C., *The Communication of the Gospel.* London: SCM Press, Ltd., 1952.

Craig, A. C., *Preaching in a Scientific Age.* Scribner, 1954.

MacLennan, David A., *Entrusted with the Gospel.* Westminster, 1956.

c. The Sprunt Lectures

This lectureship was inaugurated during the 1912-1913 academic year at Union Theological Seminary, Richmond, Virginia. It was endowed by Dr. James Sprunt, an elder in the First Presbyterian Church, Wilmington, North Carolina. It was not set up specifically for lectures on preaching but for presenting to the students any important subject engaging the attention of the Christian world at any given time. Of the fifty-four lectures given to date, only six have dealt primarily with preaching. All of these were either not published or are now out of print. But all were of high quality. They were:

Burrell, David James, *The Sermon, Its Construction and Delivery.* Revell, 1913.

Morgan, G. Campbell, *The Ministry of the Word.* Revell, 1914.

Vance, James I., *Being a Preacher: A Study of the Claims of the Christian Ministry.* Revell, 1923.

Black, James, *The Mystery of Preaching.* Revell, 1924.

Alexander, Maitland, *The Minister in Action,* 1926.

McCracken, Robert J., *The Place of Theology in Preaching,* 1951.

5. MISCELLANEOUS BOOKS ON PREACHING

The number of these books published in the last few decades is enormous. They constitute a collection of the type of material that every preacher needs to be familiar with in order to keep informed about what his contemporaries think about the importance of preaching, about methods of preaching and about problems of the preacher.

1. *In Print*

Blackwood, Andrew W., *The Fine Art of Preaching.* Abingdon, 1937.

Oman, John, *Concerning the Ministry.* Harper, 1937. Reprint: John Knox, 1963.

Handy, Francis J., *Jesus the Preacher.* Abingdon, 1949.

Kennedy, Gerald, *With Singleness of Heart.* Harper, 1951.

Chappell, Clovis G., *Anointed to Preach.* Abingdon, 1951.

Cleland, James T., *The True and Lively Word.* Scribner, 1954.
Caldwell, Frank H., *Preaching Angles.* Abingdon, 1954.
Gresham, Perry Epler, *Disciplines of the High Calling.* Bethany, 1954.
MacLennan, David A., *Pastoral Preaching.* Westminster, 1955.
Spurgeon, Charles, *Lectures to His Students.* Reprint: Zondervan, 1955.
Knox, John, *The Integrity of Preaching.* Abingdon, 1957.
Ritschl, Dietrich, *A Theology of Proclamation.* John Knox, 1960.
Pike, James A., *A New Look at Preaching.* Scribner, 1961.
Pearson, Roy, *The Ministry of Preaching.* Harper, 1959.
Come, Arnold B., *An Introduction to Barth's Dogmatics for Preachers.* Westminster, 1963.
Abbey, Merrill R., *Preaching to the Contemporary Mind.* Abingdon, 1963.
Ott, Heinrich, *Theology and Preaching.* Westminster, 1965.
Stevenson, Dwight E., *The False Prophet.* Abingdon, 1965.

2. *Out of Print*

Slattery, Charles L., *Present Day Preaching.* Longsman, Green and Co., 1909.
Hoyt, A. S., *The Preacher.* Macmillan, 1909.
————, *Vital Elements of Preaching.* Macmillan, 1914.
Gardner, Charles S., *Psychology and Preaching.* Macmillan, 1918.
Cadman, S. Parkes, *Ambassadors of God.* Macmillan, 1920.
Garvie, Alfred E., *The Christian Preacher.* Scribner, 1921.
Dargan, E. C., *The Art of Preaching.* New York: Geo. H. Doran, 1922.
Smyth, Patterson, *The Preacher and His Sermon.* New York: Geo. H. Doran, 1922.
Gossip, Arthur John, *In Christ's Stead.* New York: Geo. H. Doran, 1925.
McComb, Samuel L., *Preaching in Theory and Practice.* Oxford University Press, 1926.
Oxnam, G. Bromley, *Effective Preaching.* Abingdon, 1929.
Newton, Joseph Fort, *The New Preaching.* Abingdon, 1930.
Prichard, H. A., *The Minister, the Method and the Message.* Scribner, 1932.
Atkins, G. G., *Preaching and the Mind of Today.* New York: Round Table Press, 1934.
Robbins, Howard Chandler, *Preaching the Gospel.* Harper, 1939.
Piper, Otto, *Reality in Preaching.* Muhlenberg, 1942.
Schloerb, Rolland W., *The Preaching Ministry.* Harper, 1946.
Rogers, C. F., *The Parson Preaching.* London: S.P.C.K., 1949.
Sizoo, J. R., *Preaching Unashamed.* Abingdon, 1949.
MacLennan, David A., *A Preacher's Primer.* New York: Oxford University Press, 1950.
Ferris, Theodore P., *Go Tell the People.* Scribner, 1951.
Coffin, Henry Sloane, *Communion through Preaching.* Scribner, 1952.
Sangster, W. E., *The Approach to Preaching.* Westminster, 1952.
Schroeder, Frederick W., *Preaching the Word with Authority.* Westminster, 1954.
Morris, Frederick M., *Preach the Word.* Morehouse-Gorham, 1954.
Wedel, Theodore, *The Pulpit Discovers Theology.* Seabury, 1956.
McCracken, Robert J., *The Making of the Sermon.* Harper, 1956.
Pearson, Roy, *The Preacher, His Purpose and Practice.* Westminster, 1963.

SECTION 2

HOMILETICS

"Study to show thyself approved unto God, rightly dividing the word of truth."
—II Timothy 2:15

The History of Homiletics

Christian preaching is a calling, a calling to speak for God. However, as preachers proclaim God's message, they do so in the forms of their own generation and their own times. Often in the history of the church skilled rhetoricians, practiced orators, and experienced speakers have been converts to the faith and then have felt constrained to speak for God. It is only natural that the message which they preached would be couched in the forms which they already knew. These forms have followed patterns of development. Some of the developments were pre-Christian.

The science of homiletics had certain historical antecedents, i.e., Hebrew preaching and ancient rhetoric. While the Jewish religion had only occasional preachers, men among their fellow men did speak for God. These early preachers were "laymen," who felt impelled to deliver a message from their God. The Hebrew prophets were the grandest representatives of Hebrew preaching. As a divine message welled up within, they were forced to declare it. The scribes continued Hebrew preaching; however, they were not initiators; rather they were conservators. They interpreted the history, the law, and the prophets. From these Hebrew preachers came the term homily, meaning a talk based on Scripture.

At the same time rhetorical theory was developing in the ancient world. It is commonly believed that rhetorical principles were first recorded by Corax and his pupil, Tisias, in Sicily about 465 B.C. These rules were formulated to help private citizens prepare talks to give before the courts in an effort to regain property which had been confiscated. From this simple beginning, rhetorical theory developed rapidly.

Greek rhetoric culminated in the writing of Aristotle (384-322 B.C.). His *Rhetoric* was the first major work in the field.

Aristotle developed ideas which had been stated by Plato and others.

When Rome became the cultural center of the ancient world, the great Latin rhetoricians, Cicero (106-43 B.C.) and Quintilian (A.D. 35-95), made significant contributions. Cicero wrote several books, his most helpful being *De Oratore*. Quintilian's major work was *Institutes on Oratory*. Both of these men drew heavily on Aristotle's *Rhetoric*.

The primary divisions of ancient rhetoric were invention, arrangement, style, delivery, and memory. The principles of public speaking taught today are amazingly similar to those formulated by these first rhetoricians.

Thus these two antecedents of the art of preaching developed at the same time; yet they were independent of each other. In Christian preaching, the two streams of "speech art" were to merge. The contribution of Hebrew preaching was primarily content, i.e., Scripture. The basis for the Hebrew message was the Word of God. Ancient rhetoric made its contribution primarily to form, i.e., the rules of rhetoric.

1. THE EARLY CHURCH

The first Christians naturally followed the preaching method used by the scribes and elders in the synagogues. They presented the gospel in a simple, artless, homily form. Since the congregations were primarily Jewish and the groups were small, formal rhetoric would have been inappropriate. Yet, Paul's sermons give evidence that he had rhetorical training.

However, the Christian gospel was soon being presented to the Gentiles, who were familiar with rhetorical principles. Gradually the form of the message began to change. Before long trained rhetoricians were among the converts, and some of these men responded to a divine call to preach. The evangel was now presented in forms already familiar to these preachers. The rules of rhetoric began to refashion the presentation of the Christian message.

Clement of Alexandria (160-220) and Tertullian (150-220) both had training in rhetoric, and the works of both men reveal this instruction. However, it is with Origen (185-254) that rhetorical principles are clearly applied and taught. Before Origen's time the homily had been an informal comment on the Scripture. Origen's example and teaching led to a trend in the direction of a more formal discourse. However, Origen's contribution was actually more in the field of hermeneutics than homiletics. Along with his emphasis that the preacher should be a devout man, Origen stressed that the message should be drawn from the Scripture. Origen taught that Scripture had these meanings: (1) somatic or historical; (2) psychic or theological; (3) pneumatic or spiritual. Origen is the real father of allegorical interpretation; he popularized "spiritualizing" a text.

It is in the fourth and early fifth centuries that homiletical theory underwent major development and that the first important manual on the art of preaching was written. Several factors contributed to this: (1) Christianity was a recognized religion, and it became popular to attend services; (2) rhetorical instruction received primary emphasis in the schools; (3) the men who became the outstanding preachers were all rhetorically trained.

Basil (330-379) had the best training in leading universities. His sermons reveal unusual skill in the art of preaching. While he did not write a treatise in the theory of preaching, he made frequent references to homiletic principles which show a knowledge of and interest in them.

John of Antioch (347-407) had been instructed by Libanius, the most famous teacher of rhetoric of the day. John was trained for the legal profession, and his early speeches gave promise of great oratorical ability. When he became a Christian and began to preach, this training was utilized. While not primarily on preaching, his work *On the Priesthood* has relevant sections on the preacher's life and his preaching.

Ambrose (340-397), the bishop of Milan and a former governor, was such an accomplished speaker that Augustine, a teacher of rhetoric, went to hear him. However, Augustine was not only impressed with the oratorical ability of Ambrose but also his spiritual message.

Augustine (354-430) was to write the first major work on the art of preaching. Before his conversion, he was a teacher of rhetoric. After years of Bible study and experience in preaching, he wrote *On Christian Teaching*. It contained four books and most of the first three were written in 396 or 397. A part of Book III and all of Book IV were written in 427. The first three books deal with the principles of interpretation, but Book IV is a book of homiletics. Augustine relates the principles of rhetorical theory to the task of preaching.

During the Renaissance, Book III of *On Christian Teaching* was published under the title, the *Art of Preaching*. It was widely used during the Middle Ages. Augustine drew heavily on the works of Cicero and Aristotle. He gave special stress to the need for clarity, force, and variety.

2. THE MEDIEVAL PERIOD

After Augustine's work, little of value is added to the theory of preaching until the time of the Reformation. A few authors and their works stand out as lights in a time of darkness. In reality the theory of preaching was far superior to the actual preaching which was done in the parish churches or in the monasteries.

One early medieval writer of note was Isidore of Seville (d. 636). He was the archbishop of his city, a man of notable learning, and an exceptional preacher. In his *Etymologies*, a twenty volume compilation of learning, he discusses preaching. However, the principles are rhetorical rather than distinctively homiletical and add almost nothing to the art of preaching.

A more important contribution was made by Rabanus Maurus (776-856), the archbishop of Mainz. His treatise, *On the Institution of the Clergy*, written early in his ministry, contains his teaching on homiletical theory. He follows Augustine almost slavishly and does not make an original contribution.

Another writer was Alan of Lille (d. 1203). His homiletical work was entitled *Summary of the Art of Preaching*. He stressed the place of the Scripture and insisted that a preacher should have a special knowledge of both the Old and New Testaments. Alan felt that preaching should be done only by those authorized by the church. The *Summary* introduces a more scholastic method and was probably the most important work on the theory of preaching since Augustine's *On Christian Teaching*.

Some revival of preaching came in the twelfth and thirteenth centuries, due primarily to the preaching orders, the Dominicans and the Franciscans. Not only Francis and Dominic, but men like Anthony of Padua, Berthold of Regensburg, and Bonaventura preached the Scripture with a telling effect. Bonaventura wrote an *Art of Preaching*. It too, follows Augustine's work closely. He warned against minute division and subtle analysis but was not able to heed his own warning.

The other treatise of note in this period is that of Humbert of Romans, *On the Education of Preachers*. This work was translated and reissued by Newman Press in 1951. While it had some suggestions for preaching, it was concerned essentially with training the preacher for specific pastoral duties.

All in all, preaching was at a low ebb during the medieval period. Scripture was used less and less as a basis for preaching. Following the scholastic method of minute analysis, the form of the sermons was characterized by numerous divisions and subdivisions. The minutely organized sermon was often cold and lifeless. The Renaissance and the Reformation were to bring new method and new life to the theory of preaching.

3. THE RENAISSANCE AND REFORMATION

The renewed study of the Greek and Latin classics by the Humanists led to a study of homiletical theory. Scholastic method was evaluated and criticized by earlier writings.

While several writers made significant contributions, the most important author was the famous scholar Desiderius Erasmus (1457-1536). His book, *The Gospel Preacher*, was published in 1535 and was an important addition to the art of preaching. The work is a long, poorly arranged book, but it covers almost every aspect of preaching and discourse construction. It remains a source book on homiletics.

An Englishman, John Colet (1466-1519), had studied on the continent and became acquainted with Erasmus and other humanists. When he returned to his native land he began consecutive exposition of the Scripture. This was one of the real recoveries of the Renaissance. Scripture again became the basis for Christian preaching.

The Reformers were to take this emphasis on proclaiming the Word of God and implement it more fully. For the Reformation was not only a recovery of preaching, it was also a recovery of preaching from the Scripture. The sermon was once again central, and the text was a central thread upon which the sermon was woven. The simple homily was once again a popular method of preaching.

None of the leading reformers – Luther, Zwingli, Calvin, Knox, or Latimer – wrote a definite work on the theory of preaching. However, every reformer gave priority to preaching and gave instruction on preaching in their works.

In his *Table Talk* Luther (1483-1546) made many references to preaching and has a section entitled "On Preachers and Preaching." Luther declared that a preacher should have these virtues: "First, to teach systematically; secondly, he should have a ready wit; thirdly, he should be eloquent; fourthly, he should have a good voice; fifthly, a good memory; sixthly, he should know when to make an end; seventhly, he should be sure of his doctrine; eighthly, he should venture and engage body and blood, wealth and honour, in the word; ninthly, he should suffer himself to be mocked and jeered by everyone." Luther insisted that the "Preacher should be logician as well as rhetorician," that he must be able "to teach and to admonish." Luther gave this advice on sermon delivery, "To speak deliberately and slowly best becomes a preacher; for thereby he may the more effectually and impressively deliver his sermon."

John Calvin (1509-1564) restored a basic emphasis of the art of preaching by returning to consecutive exposition of the Scripture as a plan for preaching. Calvin used the homily as a method and preached through various books of the Bible. Calvin declared that it was the preacher's task not to give truths about God but to share God's revelation given once and for all in Jesus Christ. In *The Oracles of God,* T. H. L. Parker has brought together and summarized Calvin's theory of preaching. Calvin desired that the preacher should be a scholar, a student of the Word of God. The preacher must study the Bible; then as the Holy Spirit instructs him, he in turn could teach others.

Calvin made a worthwhile addition to the theory of preaching by suggesting that the congregation had a vital place in preaching. They assist the preacher by listening in a proper spirit. They must be obedient to the Word of God which they hear.

Hugh Latimer (d. 1555), the English Reformer, was a popular preacher and ridiculed the "unpreaching prelates." He inspired other ministers to proclaim God's message.

Philip Melanchthon (1497-1560) wrote two little treatises on the art of preaching, i.e., *Elementorum Rhetorices Libri Duo* and *Ratio Brevissima Concionandi.* These works contain nothing original but follow the principles of classical rhetoric, with an application to Christian preaching.

A more original contribution was made by Andrew Hyperius (1511-1564). His work, *On the Making of Sacred Discourses,* was a treatise of first importance for the art of preaching. His work consisted of two books, containing sixteen chapters each. It has been called a scientific treatise on the art of preaching, and Dargan feels that it should have received more attention than it did. The book gives special attention to the moving of the feelings by the preacher. The preacher was not to create mere excitement, rather he was to awaken the spiritual life and produce spiritual fruit.

A treatise which came somewhat between the Reformation and the seventeenth century was William Perkin's *The Art of Prophesying.* This work was first written in Latin but was then translated into English. Its emphasis on interpretation and exposition greatly influenced English preachers, especially the Puritans and Separatists who came to America.

4. SEVENTEENTH AND EIGHTEENTH CENTURIES

Some of the positive gains from the Reformation for the theory of preaching were lost in the seventeenth and eighteenth centuries. The scholastic method was revived, and the minute, analytical structure again became prominent. The end result was a method of preaching that had little relation to the needs of the people. Nonetheless, certain books stand out as milestones in the history of homiletics.

One outstanding work was an *Essay on the Composition of a Sermon* by Jean Claude (1619-1667). It was published in 1688 after Claude's death, and it was accepted immediately. When it was translated into

English by Robert Robinson, it had wide usage in England and in America. The materials in the book were first presented as lectures to candidates for the ministry. They are unusually sensible, practical, and helpful.

Perhaps a more important work was *Lectures on Preaching* by Philip Doddridge (1702-1751). These *Lectures* were students' notes, which were edited and published. Therefore, the work is more of an outline or a syllabus. In Chapter V Doddridge gave "Rules for Composing Sermons." Said he, "When we are composing a sermon, we are to consider: first, what subject is to be chosen; second, in what strain is it to be handled; third, the style of the composition; fourth, what thoughts we are to introduce; fifth, in what order we are to throw them. I shall therefore give rules for each of these" (p. 34). The suggestions which follow are most direct and practical.

Doddridge also gave some pertinent advice on the delivery of the sermon. He urged his students to be composed and sedate. He taught them not to "scream," but at the same time, he wanted to express true feeling. Declared he, "Feel all you say. If a tear fall, do not restrain it" (p. 69). He taught his students to be natural and unaffected and not to use notes. "To be able to preach without notes raises a man's character. Accustom yourselves to look much upon your auditory" (p. 70).

Mention should be made of a treatise on preaching by Cotton Mather. Mather (1663-1728) was the first preacher of note to be trained in this country and his work was the first book on the theory of preaching produced in this country. *Directions for a Candidate for the Ministry* had only a brief section on preaching. While it offers useful suggestions on preaching, its distinction is that it marks the beginning of homiletical instruction in this country.

An unusual contribution to the spirit of eighteenth century American preaching was made by the Log College group. William Tennent, Sr. (1673-1745) taught his sons and other young men. These men were instructed in personal piety, evangelical zeal, and extemporaneous delivery. Similar "colleges" developed in other areas. A majority of the preachers delivered sermons which were long, philosophical, and dull. They were dissertations which were read to congregations. In contrast, the Log College men preached evangelical sermons which were direct, animated, and which called for decision. This began a trend in American preaching which has characterized evangelical preachers.

5. MODERN HOMILETICS

The nineteenth century was a century of development and expansion in every area. This was true in the intellectual realm, and the literary productions in all fields were numerous. A vast new literature was developed in homiletical theory. While the nineteenth century writers did not add much which was new, the literature was broader in scope and more complete in detail. As the century progressed, homiletical theory became more informal, more varied, and more interesting.

A work of first magnitude was Alexander Vinet's *Homiletics.* This book was published after Vinet's death in 1847 and had immediate acceptance in France and Germany. The book was translated and edited in 1854 by Thomas H. Skinner, Professor of Sacred Rhetoric and Pastoral Theology in Union Seminary, New York. It became a standard textbook in its field in this country for many years. *Homiletics* was an adequate and appropriate treatment of the subject. It subsequently influenced other writings, including the famous work of John A. Broadus.

The outstanding book on the art of preaching in the United States during the nineteenth century was written by John A. Broadus. *A Treatise on the Preparation and Delivery of Sermons* was first published in 1870. The book has gone through many publications, two revisions, and has been widely used in seminaries and colleges. Moreover, it is still being used. Perhaps the reason for its continuing success is the completeness of the discussion of the theory of preaching. Dr. Broadus discussed almost every aspect of the theory of preaching. The revisors, Dr. E. C. Dargan and Dr. J. B. Weatherspoon, rearranged and updated the material. Many current books have used different parts of Broadus as a basis for discussion of certain facts of preaching.

Other important works on preaching began to appear. While they do not rank with the Broadus' book, they were adequate treatments. Some important titles and authors are: *The Theory of Preaching* (1890) by Austin Phelps, *The Making of the Sermon* (1898) by T. Harwood Pattison, and *The Preacher* (1909) and *Vital Elements of Preaching* (1914) by A. S. Hoyt.

The Lyman Beecher Lectureship on Preaching (called Yale Lectures) established at Yale University in 1871 has contributed many important titles to the theory of preaching. The first series given by Henry Ward Beecher was a notable series. Perhaps the most notable and most quoted series was delivered by Phillips Brooks in 1877. A series overlooked for many years was the series by P. T. Forsyth, *Positive Preaching and the Modern Mind* (1907). In more recent years it has provided the concepts which many writers have developed.

During the last fifty years few monumental changes have come in the theory of preaching, but certain movement are discernible. For a time there was a tendency to depreciate structure and few books were written on formal sermon organization. The books on preaching tended to be more inspirational in content. Many books followed a format of (1) the preacher, (2) his purpose, (3) his message, and (4) his method. This was even more true in Great Britain than in the United States. The topical sermon became the most widely used method. Often sermons were little more than religious talks.

Certain aspects of preaching have been treated in more detail. One of these is illustration. Some helpful books have appeared in this area, i.e., Dawson Bryan, *The Art of Illustrating Sermons* (1938); W. E. Sangster, *The Craft of Sermon Illustration* (1946); and Ian Macpherson, *The Art of Illustrating Sermons* (1964).

Halford Luccock in *In a Minister's Workshop* stressed "life situation" preaching as a sermon pattern. This has gained wide acceptance as one method. In *The Craft of Sermon Construction*, W. E. Sangster has suggested a psychological method. Many efforts have been made to relate the knowledge of depth psychology and social psychology to sermonic methods and forms. An example of such writing is *Preaching and Pastoral Care* (1964) by Arthur L. Teikmanis.

Increasing attention has also been given to the relationship between preaching and theology. C. H. Dodd's *The Apostolic Preaching and Its Development* (1936) gave impetus to this. *The Pulpit Rediscovers Theology* by Theodore O. Wedel; *Preaching and Biblical Theology* by Edmund P. Clowney; *A Theological Preacher's Notebook* by D. W. Cleverly Ford are more recent examples of this trend. The current emphasis on Biblical studies and Biblical theology is, therefore, to be seen in present day theory of preaching.

Moreover, the last twenty-five years have seen more attention being given to the importance of structure. A. W. Blackwood, famous homiletician of Princeton Theological Seminary, stressed the centrality of structure in *The Preparation of Sermons* (1948). Ilion T. Jones, *Principles and Practice of Preaching* (1956); Grady Davis, *Design for Preaching* (1958); Brown, Clinard, and Northcutt, *Steps to the Sermon* (1963) all give thorough attention to a renewed emphasis on a more complete sermon organization.

Perhaps the most significant current emphasis is the renewed and often reiterated stress on the use of the Bible in preaching. This represents a recovery of the early church and Reformation pattern. A. W. Blackwood made a contribution here in *Preaching from the Bible* (1941) and *Expository Preaching for Today* (1953). Helpful recent books in this area are *Fire in Thy Mouth* and *The Way to Biblical Preaching* by Donald G. Miller; *The Living Word* by Gustaf Wingren; *The Authority for Biblical Preaching* by Charles W. F. Smith; *Preaching and Congregation* by J. J. Von Allmen; *The Essential Nature of New Testament Preaching* by Robert H. Mounce; and *Expository Preaching without Notes* by Charles W. Koller.

These books call for a Biblical basis for sermons and the expository method as a primary way of preaching. Thus the expository and textual methods are beginning to replace the topical method. All this is wholesome. For the essence of homiletics is Scripture, and ideally, preaching is giving the Bible a voice.

BIBLIOGRAPHY

Augustine, *De Doctrina Christiana.*

Broadus, John A., *On the Preparation and Delivery of Sermons.*

Cicero, *De Oratore.*

Cooper, Lane, ed., *The Rhetoric of Aristotle.*

Dargan, E. C., *The Art of Preaching in the Light of its History.*

———————, *History of Preaching,* 2 vols.

Jones, Edgar DeWitt, *The Royalty of the Pulpit.*

Kepler, Thomas, ed., *The Table Talk of Martin Luther.*

Mitchell, W. F., *English Pulpit Oratory from Andrews to Tillotson.*

Owst, G. R., *Preaching in Medieval England.*

Parker, T. H. L., *The Oracles of God.*

Petry, Ray C., *No Uncertain Sound.*

Quintilian, *Institutes of Oratory.*

Smyth, Charles, *The Art of Preaching.*

Vinet, A., *Homiletics.* Tr. by T. H. Skinner.

Pulpit Speech and Rhetoric

Preaching is speaking. Good preaching means good speaking. The great preachers of history made effective use of their voices and rhetorical devices. George Whitefield, for example, made extremely effective use of rhetoric. He swayed audiences by the sheer force of his eloquence. It is abundantly clear from Whitefield's published works that it was not so much the matter of his sermons as the manner of delivering them that so impressed his congregations. As one eyewitness recorded, "his face was language, his intonation music, and his action passion." Though preaching is not entertainment, preachers who are outstanding speakers have always been able to draw and hold large crowds. The techniques of voice production, then, cannot be neglected by the preacher.

The first essential of good speech is relaxation. While nervousness can be a positive help in that it keys up a preacher to give his best, fright can paralyze the organs of speech. Tautness of the body, particularly in the chest and throat, impairs good speech. Breathing, which most take for granted, is often incorrect. Different types of breathing are used for different purposes, and normally adjustment is automatic. Under nervous strain, however, it often is not. Those whose voices tend to become squeaky, breathy, or inaudible need the help a speech therapist can offer.

The note of the voice is made in the vocal cords, and these, if not misused, will look after themselves. The commonest misuse is to try to force power from the larynx. The result is a harsh tone. Good full tone comes with ease; with effort tone becomes harsh or thin. Tone should be forward, from the front of the mouth, the lips, teeth and tongue. It should be fluid with an underlying music, but without a sing-song effect. It should accompany the sense, phrase by phrase. And it should be flexible, enabling the preacher to vary his voice.

Speech sounds are first divided into vowels and consonants, then subdivided according to their function. A vowel is a speech sound made by the free, unobstructed passage of air; a consonant a speech-sound interrupted by one or more of the articulative organs. As far as intelligibility is concerned the consonants are more important, and practice in articulation is an important study for the preacher. Local accents are more readily heard in the vowel sounds which can vary considerably from district to district. The tendency is for most inexperienced preachers to be slovenly with their consonants, forgetting that much more care is needed from a pulpit than it is in private conversation. The commonest defects in speech-sounds are in the S, R and L sounds, in the glottal stop, and in a harsh attack on initial vowels.

There are three important things to vary in good speech – pitch, pace and volume.

Most people prefer to have a deeper pitched rather than a high pitched voice. It should be noted, however, that we cannot alter the pitch of our voice (though some men, thinking it will make them sound more manly, attempt to do so and thereby ruin the quality of their tone), and the pitch does not matter nearly as much as the quality of the tone. The middle notes of the various voices are as follows: for women – soprano: B above middle C; mezzo-soprano: a third below this; contralto: a third lower again; for men – tenor: the A below middle C; baritone: a third below this; bass: a third lower again. Once pitch is established it is of the first importance to vary it, or a voice can become monotonous. At the same time, the other extreme would become pitch hysteria. Some speech experts have gone to elaborate lengths to make systems of pitch variation, annotating passages accordingly. Such rules are of little practical value, however, as a self-conscious observance of such rules would make the changes worthless. It should be sufficient to be aware of the need for variety in pitch, and to practice reading passages with this in mind.

Inflection is the rise or fall of the voice within single words. An uninflected voice is dull; an overinflected voice very irritating. A common fault among preachers is a sheer inflection — a dropping of the voice at the end of a sentence so sharply that the last sound is lost.

In pace there should be an avoidance of extremes. Nervousness tends to make the inexperienced preacher speak too rapidly, but a slow ponderous voice is a worse evil. An average of about a hundred words a minute is a good pace, but it is the variety that matters. Speed should vary considerably according to sense.

Pause may be considered as a subsection of pace. Physically we must pause for breath, and most preachers manage to let these pauses coincide with pauses for sense, as frequently at commas and full stops. Few preachers, however, use dramatic pauses, by which an important word or phrase can be emphasized more subtly than by any other method. Whitefield, his biographers say, was the perfect master of this device.

Speech should be loud enough for the whole congregation to hear the voice without difficulty, but no louder. They should not need to listen. A voice can be trained to "focus" itself on the person most remote from it, and so be certain that all can hear. It is astonishing how a preacher with quite a "small" voice can fill a great church by speaking forward on the lips and teeth and tongue, articulating carefully. Just as pitch and pace must vary, so must volume. Extremes should be employed rarely; the volume should be matched to the needs of the congregation.

In normal conversation the important words of a sentence are slightly stressed. This should be so also in the pulpit but nervous tension can prevent it. Wrong words, the trivial ones, are sometimes stressed; occasionally the right ones are overstressed, giving to the sermon a patronizing air, as if very small children formed the congregation.

All of the matters mentioned above are matters of technique, and they can be acquired with a minimum of trouble and a maximum of practice from an expert in that field. There are concerns in pulpit rhetoric, however, far beyond technique.

Manner is fundamental. The curious mixture of humility (in the preacher's recognition of his own shortcomings) and pride (as the ambassador of God) are as much part of pulpit rhetoric, in its widest sense as the use of the voice. So also is gesture. It is interesting to note that while actors spend many hours practicing these studies, preachers, whose chief work is to preach, rarely do so. More curiously still, some preachers seem so inhibited by the sacred nature of their work that they dare not let their emotions be seen in their preaching. Some of these men would even defend their point of view by contemptuously referring to actors, whom they refuse to imitate. The truth is, however, that they become actors when they refuse to let their feelings be heard in their voices. The man who allows his emotions to color his intelligence is an honest man; the man who shows no feeling in his preaching should not be preaching. One can only assume that he does not really believe what he is saying.

The perfection of Christ as a preacher was that he showed preaching and life to be one. This has been so also of his greatest followers. Jesus not only instructed people with facts, but communicated his own way of life. The preacher, more so than any other man, is called on to practice what he preaches. Beyond a technical brilliance which Whitefield, for instance, clearly had, was his saintly character. More of man's nature is revealed in his voice than in any other way. It therefore follows that a preacher's soul can and should be revealed through his voice. Essentially, the concern of the preacher is not his sermon but his soul. As Bishop Quayle put it, "Preaching is the art of making a sermon and delivering it. Why no, that is not preaching. Preaching is the art of making the preacher and delivering that. Preaching is the outrush of soul in speech. Therefore the elemental business in preaching is not with the preaching but with the preacher. It is no trouble to preach, but a vast trouble to construct a preacher. What then, in the light of this, is the task of a preacher? Mainly this, the amassing of a great soul so as to have something worthwhile to give — the sermon is the preacher up to date."

BIBLIOGRAPHY

Kirkpatrick, R. W., *The Creative Delivery of Sermons.* New York: Collier-Macmillan, 1944.

Lantz, E., *Speaking in the Church.* New York: Collier-Macmillan, 1954.

Mitchell, W. F., *English Pulpit Oratory from Andrews to Tillotson.* London, 1932.

Sangster, P. E., *Speech in the Pulpit.* London: Epworth, 1958.

Smyth, C., *Art of Preaching: A Practical Survey of Preaching in the Church of England.* London: S.P.C.K., 1940.

Tyerman, L., *Life of the Rev. George Whitefield.* London, 1882.

The Classification of Sermons

Sermons are generally classified under three major categories: (1) according to subject matter such as, Doctrinal, Moral, Political, Evangelistic, Experimental, etc.; (2) according to the relation of the structure to the text, often called "Homiletical Structure," such as Topical, Textual, and Expository; and (3) according to the structural development of the subject in relation to the type of outline or plan, such as Problem-solution, Roman Candle, Classification, Hegelian, etc. This article will have reference to the second and third categories, the first being treated elsewhere.

1. TYPES OF SERMONS ACCORDING TO STRUCTURE OR TEXT

The three main divisions used are the topical or subject sermons, textual sermons, and expository sermons. Some texts use additional forms, such as topical-textual, inferential sermons, etc. Many forms are possible, but for all practical purposes the three major divisions are satisfactory. It must be recognized that these standard forms are flexible, dovetailing into each other. They are not rigid nor frozen, which a casual perusal of any volume of sermons by the masters will reveal. After all, the structural forms are but secondary tools to serve the vital communication of the truth embodied in the sermon.

a. *The Topical or Subject Sermon*

It must be kept in mind as we treat sermon structure that the vital area of distinction is the relation of the body of the sermon to the text, and particularly the relation of the divisions of the sermon to the divisions of the text. The topical sermon derives its name from the fact that in such a sermon the topic or subject is the dominating factor in the sermon's development. The entire treatment of the sermon depends upon the topic. All the sermon receives from the text is its topic. These, of course, must be definitely related. The topic must be true to the text. But the development of the thought divisions of the sermon are not dependent upon the thought divisions of the text, but upon the logical development of the topic as determined by the preacher. They may coincide. It is then often termed a topical-textual sermon. The title may mislead, by minimizing the fact that the sermon is controlled and dominated by the topic.

This kind of sermon is by far the most popular form used by preachers. A casual survey of almost any volume of sermons will substantiate this. Since the Reformation, when the classical forms of oratory, developed by Aristotle, Cicero and Quintilian, were wedded to preaching, relegating the "running commentary" of the ancient church to the limbo of forgetfulness, the freedom of expression and organization derived from the rhetorical and literary forms of oratory have made this form a peculiar favorite for preachers of the Word. The topical form, unrestricted by the Scriptural portion being used, makes it easier to obtain unity, the indispensable element to any good sermon. It also gives freedom in the development of logical and emotional climaxes. Freedom of expression is the word. It has often been objected that such kind of preaching tends to minimize and obscure the Word, and as a result congregations become Biblical illiterates. Such a danger is present, but it is not inherent in the form of the sermon, but rather in the disposition of the preacher. Again, it has been said that such preaching becomes stultifying because it puts too much pressure upon the average man to provide variety, and not even the most fertile thinker is adequate for the task. There is abundant evidence for lack of variety in the pulpit, but again it can not be attributed to the form of the sermon. Every verse in the

Word is a dormant seed awaiting a living mind and heart. Forms do not control the man. The topical sermon, therefore, permits wideness of treatment, aids unity of thought, provides direction of aim, and grants great latitude of literary creativity. Good examples of such sermons can be seen in the words of Thomas Chalmers, Philip Brooks, Horace Bushnell, Charles Spurgeon, James Stewart, Billy Graham, Clarence Macartney and a host of others. A. W. Blackwood's *The Protestant Pulpit*, provides superb examples.

b. *The Textual Sermon*

This type, like all sermons, must be controlled by the general principles of logic and grammar. It must have a text, a subject, and divisions. A textual sermon is one in which both the topic and the divisions of development are derived from, and follow the order of the text. While the topical sermon was dominated by the topic,th e text controls and dominates both topic and the developmental divisions in this type. For example, Romans 1:16 reads, "For I am not ashamed of the gospel of Christ; for it is the power of God unto salvation to every one that believeth." Topically treated, it might have the general theme of "The Power of the Gospel," which is derived from the text. The development of the sermon into divisions would then be at the will of the preacher, or under the control of his concept of the topic. A textual form, however, would follow the thought of the text as: (1) The Gospel is the power of God; (2) It is the power of God unto salvation; and (3) It is the power of God unto salvation to those who believe. Of course, there is liberty of expression, but the basic ideas of the text control the divisions. The divisions need not be exhaustive but they must be so related to the subject and to each other as to form a unified whole. There has been some question as to how large a portion of Scripture is involved in such sermons. The very meaning "textual" seems to imply a rather short unit. The consensus of opinion appears to be that not more than four verses would qualify. A larger portion borders on the expository type.

The textual sermon has practically all the advantages of the topical form with the added advantage of staying with the thought of the Scripture. This definitely aids in the production of variety in thought and freshness of treatment. The young preacher will find this type a good introduction to expository preaching. It will teach him to come to grips with the Word itself. It is also a help to the hearer for he can follow the sermon in his Bible, and much of the sermon will not only be remembered at the time of the preaching, but in later years the Bible when read will bring back the message.

c. *The Expository Sermon*

To many, this is the sermon "par excellence." The declaration is often made that all sermons should be expository, that is, an explanation and application of Scripture. There is some confusion in this area because of the failure often times to clearly define terms. Every sermon is expository if by that is meant any explanation of a portion of Scripture, whether a single word, a sentence, a paragraph, a chapter or an entire book. In a broad sense this is true, but in the technical homiletical sense the term has a much more restricted meaning. That meaning stems from the rhetorical and grammatical peculiarities of the inherent construction of the sermon in relation to the text and its divisions, coupled with oratorical techniques and arrangements. The expository sermon is not a religious essay, or an exegetical paper, or a commentary, or even a "running commentary," but a sermon with all the attributes and characteristics of such. Perhaps the simplest definition would be: an expository sermon is one that involves the treatment of a Bible unit more than four verses long. A possible comparison is that the textual sermon is an expository treatment of a short passage while the expository sermon is a textual treament of a long passage. However that is by no means complete or entirely satisfactory. A better statement of comparison would be that the topical sermon derives its topic from the text and is dominated in its development by the topic; the textual sermon derives its topic and its divisions directly from the text and is therefore dominated by the text; whereas the expository sermon receives text, divisions and the vast weight of the supporting material from the unit under consideration.

Expository sermons are without doubt the most difficult of all to prepare. All the facets of homiletical skill are required. The fact that one is almost entirely bound to the portion used creates difficulties that increase with the size of the unit. While all the difficulties of the other forms are present, expository sermons present the preacher with two very formidable challenges. They are the ability to find and produce unity, and the ability to select and use only those materials that sharply focus upon that unity. Many expository sermons fail because they lack a unifying dominating idea, being rather a trite collection of little sermonettes. Others fail because the factor of selectivity is neglected. When everything in the passage is used, the sermon becomes a plethora of irrelevant and confusing details.

Nevertheless, by constant study and hard work, one may engage in what is in many ways the ideal treatment of the Scriptures. A study of the sermons of Alexander Maclaren and G. Campbell Morgan will prove rewarding. The advantages of such sermons are that they: (1) fit the general idea of preaching; (2) develop a greater knowledge of the Book upon the part of both the preacher and the people; (3) provide a vast variety of ideas; (4) provide opportunity for discussing ideas generally ignored or avoided; and (5) reduce the temptation to misinterpret the Scriptures, or to rely too heavily upon personal ideas. The disadvantages are those of all forms. Shoddy work wrecks all.

2. TYPES OF SERMONS ACCORDING TO OUTLINE OR PLAN

Speech designs or patterns centering in the outline of development are most common. Someone has suggested that for every mind there is another outline. That is an exaggeration, but the number is legion. Nevertheless the common mind of man has unconsciously brought forward certain rather permanent and logical forms. A few of the more common are: past, present and future; local, state, national, and international; cause and effect; problem and solution; theoretical and practical; physical, mental, and spiritual; thinking, feeling and willing; and political, economic, and social. In homiletics there is also a variety of forms which can be used profitably.

a. *The Use of Points*

The "point" in a sermon is not an arbitrary device designed by the homiletician to inflict the congregation. Rather, it represents a definite movement of thought in a very live, dynamic process of communication. There is no hard and fast rule which determines and limits the number of points a sermon should have. It should have as many as the thought warrants, whether this be the commonly thought of three points, or more or less. No one has presented cogent reasons as to why the mind seems to like the trinity, but apparently men do.

b. *The Two Point or Twin Sermon*

This type, made famous by F. W. Robertson, presents ideas in contrast, such as positive versus negative. A doctrinal sermon might be explanation and application; a character sermon, data and lessons; a narrative sermon, descriptive narrative and lessons. This type lends itself well to purposes of clarification.

c. *The Interrogative Sermon*

Each point is a question. Use is made of Kipling's "famous six." Who? Which? Where? When? Why? and How? These fundamental questions are so apparent that discussion is not needed. This type of sermon has been referred to as the "Lazy Preacher's Sermon."

d. *The Ladder or Telescope Sermon*

This form proceeds from point to point like a ladder or grows out of one into another like the telescope. It is the type for logical argument, persuasion, debate and the appeal to reason. It is used for the pressing of the claims of Christ and of Christian service and obligation. For an example, see the treatment of Romans 1:16 in the section on the Textual Sermon.

e. *The Jewel Sermon*

The development here consists in turning one idea around like a gem and viewing all aspects or facets of it. Great unity of theme, with great diversity of application is inherent in this form. A sermon on "Understanding the Incarnation" by Lynn Hough is suggestive:

1. Look backward to the Creation of Man.
2. Look upward to the Nature of God.
3. Look inward to the Soul of Man.

f. *The Classification Sermon*

This is one of the oldest, and most common, and most honored forms of sermon outlines. It consists of dividing people and things into classes or types. It is an effective form for, almost from the cradle to the grave, people indulge in such. The parables of Jesus abound in such classification. Examples are: the prodigal and his elder brother; the publican and the Pharisee; the wise and foolish virgins; fountions of sand and rock; soils: hard, rocky, infested with thorns, and good.

g. *The Hegelian Type*

Though having little or nothing to do with the philosophy of the German thinker, his thought method has given its name to this pattern. The sermon falls into three parts, thesis, antithesis and synthesis. We might have: 1. This is the way things ought to be (ideal). 2. This is the way they are (realism). 3. This is how they may be with God's help (solution). This type requires the power of cogent thinking.

h. *The Thematic Type*

This has also been called the "symphonic" sermon. Like a poem, or a song, a striking phrase or line which epitomizes the idea of the sermon, is used throughout the message. It is on the order of a Wagnerian motif. It rings throughout and haunts one ever after. James S. Stewart, in a message on the "Wonders of the Christian Faith" uses the phrase "Wonder upon wonders and every wonder true" with telling effectiveness and compelling eloquence. Often the text itself is so used. This is perfection itself, holding both text and subject together. A famous sermon on the text "Judas – not Iscariot" rings, thrills, and trembles with that phrase in every point and ends in a climax of splendor and power with those significant words, "Judas – Not Iscariot." This is a glorious type.

i. *The Rebuttal Sermon*

This type should be used sparingly, but it should be used. It is used to refute a statement which the preacher believes to be palpably false, and therefore definitely dangerous. A vivid statement is quoted and then the question is asked, "Is this true?" The answer is a resounding "Nay," the sermon then proceeding to prove that it is most certainly not true. Jesus used this technique in Luke 13:2 ff. when he discussed the death of the Galileans at the hand of Pilate. "Suppose ye that these Galileans were sinners above all the Galileans because they suffered so much? I tell ye Nay!" This was a vigorous rebuttal to the accepted theory. We might take the modern phrase, so often on the lips of the modern unbeliever, "We are now in the post-Christian Age, Christianity has failed being proven irrelevant to life." Then the preacher gives a strong "Nay!" and goes on to present his evidence. Or the current cry, "Modern life demands a new morality. It has outmoded the Christian morality." Then the resounding "Nay!" followed by the folly of so doing. Such preaching demands deep moral concern and dedication, coupled with the ability to engage in apologetic.

j. *Life-situation or Problem-solution Sermon*

This is a very popular form today. It has both many advantages and disadvantages. This item needs much more attention than we can give here. See *In The Minister's Workshop* (Abingdon Press) by H. E. Luccock for an extended discussion. The sermon grows out of a life situation known to the pastor. It presents an existential problem which calls for a solution from the Word of God. For example, despondence may find its answer in the experience of Elijah; doubt in the experience of Thomas; grief in the experience of Mary in the garden. However, it must always be kept in mind that the solution is not found in the characters involved but in their *God or Christ*. A sample outline might follow this order: 1. Problem or situation. 2. Principle – base of solution. 3. Program – way of doing it. Or we could treat it thus: 1. Where are we? 2. How did we get this way? 3. Where do we go from here? 4. How do we go? These presented are in principle only, various forms are possible.

The big disadvantage is the very real tendency never to get out of the problems and the situations. People today are strong on analyzing the troubles of mankind, but rarely are able to prescribe a cure. The preacher is no exception. Again and again the problem is eloquently described and the solution is given weak and inadequate treatment. This form presents the very subtle temptation really to neglect the exposition of the Word. Nevertheless in the hands of a Biblically oriented preacher it is a powerful method in making the gospel relevant.

BIBLIOGRAPHY

Blackwood, Andrew W., *The Preparation of Sermons.* New York: Abingdon Press, 1948.

Broadus, John, *On the Preparation and Delivery of Sermons.* New York, Harper & Bros., 1944.

Davis, Henry Grady, *Design for Preaching.* Philadelphia: Meulenberg Press, 1958.

Gibbs, Alfred E., *The Preacher and His Preaching.* Fort Dodge: Iowa, Walterick Printing Co., 1939.

Jones, Ilion T., *The Principles and Practice of Preaching.* New York: Abingdon Press, 1956.

Luccock, Halford E., *In the Minister's Workshop.* New York: Abingdon Press, 1944.

Paterson-Smyth, J., *The Preacher and His Sermon.* London: Geo. H. Doran Company, 1922.

Sangster, W. E., *The Craft of Sermon Construction,* London: Epworth Press, 1949.

Sermon Illustration and Use of Resources

1. NEED. Henry H. Farmer says that abstractness is in some ways the greatest curse of all our preaching, not so much because people fail to understand us or are bored, but because God reaches men not through abstractions but through persons and through concrete situations of day-to-day personal life. The truths of the Christian faith come to us in the form of symbols, e.g., the Cross, Baptism, and the Lord's Supper. No man can adequately communicate Christian truth without the aid of concrete imagery. John Hutton once said, "Truth cannot be taught by formulas and propositions and arguments; but only by an illustration and a tale, as our Lord acknowledged who educated the human race on God by telling half a dozen stories." The need of preaching pictorially is a psychological necessity in our picture-minded generation. "How is it possible," asks a recent writer, "to pierce the mentality of an age that is film-fed, radio-glutted, and jazz-intoxicated unless we master the art of vivid presentation and succeed in turning the ear into the eye?"

To preach in pictures is to follow the example of the Master-Preacher. "Without a parable spake he not unto them." Ian Macpherson states that approximately seventy-five percent of the whole of Christ's recorded teaching is pictorial in form.

2. USES. Illustrations are used for various reasons: (1) To clarify. The spiritual is interpreted by the natural, the unknown by the known. Often an illustration is the bridge between truth and the mind. (2) To persuade. Apt examples or stories can compel assent to an unpalatable fact. An argument may be resisted because it taxes the hearers' attention, but one can hardly escape the impact of a picture set squarely before the eyes. (3) To impress. For instance, God's love as presented in the story of the father's readiness to welcome the returning prodigal plumbs man in a depth commonly unreached by truth in the abstract. (4) To ornament. In his *Lectures on Preaching* Brooks says, "We confine too much the office of illustration if we give it only the duty of making truth clear to the understanding, and do not also allow it the privilege of making truth glorious to the imagination." Many a sermon is enhanced by introducing into an appropriate illustration remarkable for the elegance of its language. Care must be exercised, of course, to see that the illustration really adorns the truth preached and does not itself become the center of interest. (5) To afford relief. In matters of scholarly exposition, logical and theological reasoning, and sustained argumentation, the attention span of the average congregation is strictly limited. A commendable way of reducing mental tension, without deflecting the mind of the hearer from the theme under consideration, is to place apt, telling illustrations at strategic places in the discourse. (6) To aid repetition. A sermon seeks to emphasize a single truth. It may represent that truth in its several aspects and relationships but all to the end that a significant fact may be driven home. Only by judicious reiteration can this goal be achieved. Freshness of illustration is a chief means to this end. (7) As an aid to argument. This is particularly true when illustration takes the form of analogy. If certain social conditions were the prelude to the fall of the Roman Empire,

similar conditions in any society will be followed by its destruction. Although illustration is not actual proof, it often has the force of proof.

3. TYPES. An illustration may be in the form of a word, a phrase, a sentence, or a paragraph or more. Length is no criterion. Actually, the preacher whose language is luminous with meaning is less likely to feel the need of what are commonly called illustrations. Some men employ a word or two to say what others express in a paragraph – "He has a *jaundiced* view of life"; "Her mind is *hermetically sealed* to the Christian faith"; "He is a *voluble, retail* talker." He will be well rewarded who cultivates speech which is itself an illustration of thought.

Pictorial words and phrases often come in the form of *simile* or *metaphor*. The simile says that one thing is *like* another; the metaphor that one thing *is* another. Regarding similes, Christ taught us that the kingdom of heaven is "like" to leaven hid in a meal; "like" to a grain of mustard seed, etc. Speaking metaphorically Jesus said, "Ye are the light of the world," and John the Baptist is "a reed shaken by the wind." D. C. Bryan finds fifty-six metaphors in the Sermon on the Mount.

An illustration often takes the form of an *example*. Examples are of two kinds: an individual used to represent a class; or a particular instance of the working of a law or principle (e.g., apples falling from a tree may illustrate the law of gravity). Frequently examples consist of a brief series of striking sentences setting forth various aspects of a single truth. Spurgeon, emphasizing the stewardship of life, says, "Let the *potter* tremble lest he be like a vessel marred upon the wheel. Let the *printer* take heed that his life be set in heavenly type and not in the black setting of sin. *Painter*, beware! for paint will not suffice; we must have unvarnished realities."

The *parable*, an "earthly story with a heavenly meaning," is by no means the easiest method of illustrating. When truth by means of an apparently innocent tale is demonstrated objectively in the life of someone else, its lesson is likely to reach the unsuspecting hearer unobtrusively. The well-constructed parable needs not to explain or moralize, for these functions are implicit within the story. Christ's parables are drawn from nature and from the social, political, and domestic life of the time. They are remarkable for their force, structural perfection, and economy of words.

Illustration by *analogy* proceeds on the theory that things which are alike in some respects will be alike in others. Thus the ancients observed that since the living butterfly emerged from the apparently dead chrysalis, the living soul of man would emerge from his dead body. Drummond's *Natural Law in the Spiritual World*, on the basis of a certain parallelism between natural and spiritual things, presents an extremely plausible argument of this kind.

An *allegory* is a piece of sustained personification. In its greater length, and in the element of personification, it differs from the parable and the fable. In Bunyan's *Pilgrim's Progress*, the best-known example of an allegory, virtues and vices are personified into a metaphorical scene. This type of illustration has in years past been much abused. Many of the Fathers of the early church were apt to spiritualize "widely and wildly" the language of Scripture.

The *anecdote* is a brief story told not so much for its historic or biographic interest as for its narrative value. It is frequently the telling of an incident or event of curious interest. Anecdotes can be homiletically valuable when they are in good taste and not employed excessively.

Because he who talks about people interests people and because biography yields rich insights into human nature, the *biographical episode* is one of the most widely used types of sermon illustration. There is no aspect of life that does not have its counterpart somewhere in biography. Here the preacher uses life to interpret life. Here he finds concrete exemplification of every Biblical truth pertaining to man.

Then there is the *historical illustration*, a word picture of scenes and events of the past. Here prudence calls for caution in linking past happenings with God's providence. Still, he who believes that "through the ages one increasing purpose runs," will not be altogether blind to providential happenings in the lives of men and nations.

4. SOURCES. When used with discrimination, *books of illustrations* can be

helpful. But too often materials taken from them are ill-fitted to the discussion in hand. There is, moreover, always the danger of these already chiseled examples stifling individual initiative. Such omnibus collections are likely to be used more effectively by seasoned preachers who are able to separate the wheat from the chaff and who are skilled in adapting materials to their own sermon contexts.

The *Bible* itself is, of course, the greatest source of sermon illustrations. Biblical narratives and Biblical characters should hold a freshness of appeal to an age notoriously deficient in Biblical knowledge. Within the pages of Scripture is every conceivable type of illustration on every possible preaching topic. Although times and customs have changed, God and man and his needs remain the same. Every man continues to see himself in the pages of Holy Writ.

Literature is another inexhaustible source of homiletical values. Writes Andrew Blackwood, "Where better than in the noblest works of prose and poetry can the spokesman for God find what he needs to fill out the pattern of many a sermon?" Of course, the real value of literature for the preacher, whether it be poetry, drama, the essay, biography, or fiction, lies in what it does for the man rather than in what it will do for his sermons. Literature should be read not primarily to be put into sermons but to create the kind of mind and heart out of which sermonic values will flow. The pulpit masters of yesterday and today are sparing in their use of quotations. Ideas and illustrations from their readings are more likely to appear indirectly in their sermons.

Through literature we extend our acquaintance with human nature by sharing vicariously in the experiences of others. The poet, the novelist, and the essayist can draw us into the inner sanctuary of human nature and open before us the hidden ambitions and aspirations of men, the secret prejudices and hatreds that lodge within. More than anything else, it is his ability to create characters that gives Shakespeare his place in letters. Great literature, moreover, is the handmaid of religion because its writers are champions of the moral law. Every one of Shakespeare's tragedies drives home the truth, "Whatsoever a man soweth, that shall he also reap." All classic literature is confessional in that it deals with the soul of man as the home of great issues.

Reputable *fiction* yields vivid insight into the human drama. Nemesis is always on duty in the novels of George Eliot. Witness in Herman Melville's *Moby Dick* one man's gigantic struggle against fate. Where will one find a drama of deeper anguish and remorse than in Hawthorne's *The Scarlet Letter.*" To learn about man's struggle with blindness read Kipling's *The Light That Failed.* Watch the spiritual disintegration of a soul in Thomas Mann's *Death in Venice.* See in Edith Wharton's *Sanctuary* how one mother tried to save her son from the consequences of a moral taint inherited from his father. Nowhere are the widespread frustrating experiences of personal life more vividly described than in novels, dramas, poems, and biographies; yet this storehouse of case studies has been greatly neglected by preachers.

Poetry, which had its beginning as the handmaiden of religion, is a widely used source of pulpit illustrations. It not only contains the sublimest thoughts of the human mind but it explores and unfolds the depths and complexity of human nature, a fact to which the great dramas amply testify. In using poetry in the pulpit the minister should lean heavily on the masters. While it is true that much modern verse is pagan and obscure, there is much also that evidences a sincere search for religious values.

Since nothing illustrates life like life, *biography* provides a wealth of sermon resources. Much of the preacher's lighter reading may well be in this area. Sir William Robertson Nicoll listed these as the five greatest biographies: Boswell's *Johnson,* Lockhart's *Scott,* Gaskell's *Charlotte Bronte,* Trevelyan's *Macauley,* and Morley's *Gladstone.* To which may be added Sandburg's *Lincoln* and Franklin's *Autobiography.* Ministers should read standard lives of preachers, particularly those whom they admire, such men as Thomas Chalmers, John Wesley, F. W. Robertson, Phillips Brooks, Henry Ward Beecher, and Alexander McLaren. Nor should they neglect spiritual autobiographies like Augustine's *Confessions, The Autobiography of Mark Rutherford, and* Schweitzer's *Out of My Life and Thought.* Devotional literature in general, it may be added, is much neglected by the modern minister.

Fables, brief fictitious moral tales in which animals speak and act like human beings, may at times furnish apt illustrations. Among the better-known collections are those of Aesop, Hans Christian Andersen, and Lewis Carroll. Even in an age when the mental climate is more receptive to scientific fact and historical accuracy, the fabulists, when wisely used, command respect.

Granted that modern standards of journalism often leave much to be desired, it is nevertheless true that *newspapers and periodicals* are chronicling history as it is being written. They reflect the kind of world to which we are called to minister. He who never reads a newspaper finds himself out of touch with life. Christ had a keen eye for what was happening all around him. It is said that John Wesley consulted his paper to see what God was doing in the world.

The *nature scene* is an unlimited source of sermonic illustration. Goethe once said that nature is the only book upon whose every page a significant message is written. Here intimations of God and the spiritual world are all about us. Paul writes, "The invisible things . . . from the creation of the world are clearly seen, being understood by the things that are made, even his eternal power and Godhead" (Rom. 1:20). To the Christian the visible is a sacrament of the invisible. All nature was tributary to Christ. The wind blowing illustrated the mystery of being born of the Spirit, the forecasts of the weather suggested the blindness of the people to the ominous signs of the times, the barren fig tree proclaimed that character determines destiny. He bids us consider the lilies of the field and the birds of the air with their messages of trust, and the fields white unto harvest with their invitation to service. For variety of approach in using nature, study the sermons of Spurgeon, James S. Stewart, and Alistair Maclean. Read also Canon Mozley's "Sermon on Nature" in his *University Sermons.*

Many of the great *works of art* are rich in moral and spiritual values. Excellent reproductions of the great paintings are now generally inexpensively available. From a careful, personal study of some of them, with the assistance of available helps, one may come upon illustrations that will crystallize and enhance many an abstract doctrinal truth. Consider paintings like Michelangelo's "The Last Judgement," Raphael's "The Transfiguration," Murillo's "The Assumption," and Millet's "The Gleaners." Clarence Macartney sometimes draws on sculpture to heighten his meaning: "In an art museum I once saw a piece of statuary by Carpenter. . . Out of a block of marble two figures are emerging. One is bestial, fierce, cruel, sensual; the other, desperately striving to get free, is refined, noble, spiritual, intellectual. It is a study for which any one of us might sit as a model."

In a day of extensive diffusion of popular *scientific knowledge* a congregation should occasionally find an abstract sermon point come to life through some allusion to biology, chemistry, space science, or other science peculiar to the preacher's interest. Here one may proceed with confidence when he knows whereof he speaks and when the illustration is clear and uninvolved in technical terminology. At times, he will feel the need of supporting his statements with the name of a reputable scientist. One age warms to illustrations based on factual accuracy.

"A man's study," said Beecher, "should be everywhere – in the house, in the street, in the fields, and in the busy haunts of men." From *observation of life* about him the preacher will find many a rich sermon picture. Like his Master, he will gather illustrations in fields familiar to his hearers, and learn from him the art of casting the commonplace in a new light. Our Lord's preaching is steeped in the setting and action of everyday life and experience: the domestic scene, pastoral life, agricultural operations, trades, civil and national life, social relations, religious life, physical nature, and the human body. Beecher visited ships and sailors, observed the ways of the business world, acquainted himself with the way of life on the farm, and with the forms of rural life, and was ever drawing lessons from life in the home. The sermons of George W. Truett and Clovis Chappell may serve as modern examples of facility in drawing lessons from life at first hand. Insights gained in pastoral visitation can sometimes be adapted to pulpit use, but care must be taken lest a problem be too precisely dealt with. Dr. Fosdick, adept in using preaching values gained from his counseling with individuals, was careful not to publicize detailed facts of particular cases.

The modern preacher should make wider use of the *hypothetical illustration.* To demonstrate a truth it is quite proper to invent an example or even a story, provided these are true to life and at the same time clearly understood to be imaginary. Phillips Brooks was expert at inventing comparisons. His sermon, "The Fire and the Calf" contains at least thirteen hypothetical cases. The average preacher has a much greater potential for imagination than he himself suspects.

Some Rules Concerning the Illustration. (1) The illustration should hold to one central truth. (2) It should never be told merely for its own sake. No illustration is an end in itself. (3) It should usually be brief. (4) It should be in keeping with the dignity of the pulpit. (5) Seek variety in illustrative materials. (6) Avoid threadbare illustrations. (7) Avoid the overuse of illustration. (8) Beware of inaccuracy in statement. (9) The illustration that needs to be explained needs to be omitted. (10) As a rule, the thought being explained should be clear to the hearer before the illustration is introduced.

BIBLIOGRAPHY

Bryan, D. C., *The Art of Illustrating Sermons.* New York: Cokesbury, 1937.

Jeffs, H., *The Art of Sermon Illustration.* London: James Clarke & Co., n.d.

Macpherson, Ian, *The Art of Illustrating Sermons.* Nashville: Abingdon, 1964.

Resker, R. R., *Our Lord's Illustrations.* Edinburgh: T. & T. Clark, 1950.

Robertson, J. D., *Handbook of Preaching Resources from English Literature.* New York: Macmillan Co., 1962.

Sangster, W. E., *The Craft of Sermon Illustration.* Philadelphia: Westminster Press, 1950.

The Sermon in Worship

The place of the sermon in worship is determined by the goal of the liturgical act and the means chosen to achieve it. Richard Davidson defined worship as "what we say and what we do when we stand before God, realizing in high degree who he is and what we are" (*The Presbyterian Register,* XVII, 10, p. 292). The phrase "what we say" indicates that a rite is involved; "what we do" implies ceremony; and the combination of these forms the ritual. These, however, are the means, but the goal of worship is a high encounter between who God is and what we are. Its aim is to know God better and ourselves more deeply, and by means of this knowledge to praise and serve his name. In this total transaction, according to the Reformed tradition especially, the sermon has a useful, and indeed indispensable, place.

Now the sermon, at the beginning of the Christian era, already had its undisputed place in the worship of the Jewish synagogue. As an established institution or custom of his own people, Jesus accepted it and the only record in the gospels of his participating in an act of worship in the synagogue featured a sermon (Luke 4:16-21). What is more, the presentation of this exposition as an act of personal testimony and as a means of instruction became not only a bridge between Christianity and its Jewish ancestry, but has formed a distinctive feature of traditional Christian worship unique among world religions.

With such an authentic beginning one might conclude, and justifiably so, that the sermon would have had a fairly consistent career in the worship of the Christian era. But the chapters of church history present a story of worship practices in which the position of the sermon has waxed and waned. In the early formative years of the Christian witness the apostles were preachers primarily. Christianity was a "preached" religion. A remark by H. H. Farmer in *The Servant of the Word* tells much about this era: "Whoso says Christianity, says preaching" (p. 18). Preaching was the acceptable activity on the growing edge of the church; the message and the means of making it known were inseparable. As C. W. F. Smith has described it, "the method arises from the nature of the message and its source" (*Biblical Authority in Modern Preaching,* p. 35). This was definitely true of the missionary outreach of the apostolic church, but concurrently as churches became localized and stable institutions in new communities the confluence of the service of the synagogue and the simple rite of the upper room not only gave the sermon a definite context but provided a basic shape for the act of Christian worship which even the Reformation did not alter or discount. Changes of focus and the shift of emphases have contributed to the erratic career of the sermon in worship, but the authenticity of its basic role in Christian worship has never been discredited or lost.

The presupposition behind all Christian worship is a revelation. This revelation consists of God, by his very nature, wanting to make himself known to his creatures. Moreover, this revelation, which was earlier a matter of human faith, became historically real in him who was born as a child and lived, died, and rose again "for us men and our salvation." This is the great eternal fact without which there would be no Christian worship at all. In view of the impact of this reality upon our moral condition, however, man is constrained to respond. And the constant presentation of this theological and evangelical fact and the human response to it is the *raison d'etre* of our worship. Something is declared and someone listens. God speaks and man answers. But no one man is a solitary unit; he becomes his fuller self only as he is in fellowship with God and with other selves. Hence the *koinonia* of the church emerged, as Sunday by Sunday Christians joined together in a spiritual act of hearing again in reading and preaching the old, old story of what God has done for them and of their response in thanksgiving and dedication of their lives to his service.

Through the centuries of the Christian era there has not been, however, a constant method of how this message is heard or responded to by man. It is around the matter of "how" that the major traditions of Christian faith and practice have crystallized or solidified. Prior to the Reformation and as a result of emphases exceedingly difficult to identify, the character of Christian worship was largely sacramental. Both Roman Catholic and Eastern Orthodox celebrations of worship were oriented towards offering; something is offered to God through Christ who was himself the only perfect sacrifice. Here the emphasis leans more towards the ascending aspect, the man to God-ward phase of the cultic act.

With the theological reorientation of the Reformation, the character of man's relationship and of the method of his approach to God was reinterpreted. Protestant worship became less sacramental and more of an encounter between God and man through his Word. Hence the new worship was Word centered, and in consequence the emphasis upon the reading and exposition of Scripture was more pronounced. The sermon came into its own with this new emphasis upon the descending aspect, the God to man-ward phase of the cultic act. In this attempt to restore a greater balance in the act of worship, the Reformers felt they were merely restoring what had been lost. This was more true of John Calvin than Martin Luther, yet the best intentions of both men were misdirected by Zwingli and others, including the Puritans later, which disrupted the sound theological shape of Protestant worship through succeeding centuries even to our day.

Through their efforts to free Christian worship of the excesses of the medievalism — the superstitions, pagan practices, and sacramentalism — the reformers gave us a form of worship that was marked by much of the forms and customs of the early church. But an imbalance was created when the sermon emerged as the all-important factor, to the disregard of other aspects, including the human response. Protestant worship became a listening activity only and the preacher the center of the congregation's focus. The personality and prowess of the minister was exaggerated beyond everything else and the conception of the church as a community of God's people responding to the preached Word was lost. The sermon and the preacher were identified as the sole factors of the service of worship and little concern was given to the idea of the congregation making its corporate response. The complementary character of Word and sacrament was not fully grasped or understood. Hence in the Puritan tradition the sermon claimed the major part of an already lengthy act of worship. It was regarded mistakenly as the climax of the service of worship and as the only means whereby the hearers were edified. Perhaps the greatest error, however, was the tendency to consider the sermon as replacing the sacrament. Nothing could be further from the thinking of the reformers. Theirs was the conviction that both Word and sacraments were the most appropriate means of communion with God.

The sermon, therefore, has had an indisputable and indispensable place in worship and its position is being reidentified in this era of liturgical renewal from both practical and theological perspectives.

1. PRACTICAL

a. There is a sense in which preaching calls the church into being. Through preaching the early apostles planted the church. When they entered a new town or city they told the people what God had done for men in Jesus Christ. In consequence a unit of fellowship was formed as part of the body of Christ. It was instructed and nurtured by the Word read and explained, and through "the breaking of bread and prayers." Preaching was on the growing edge of the primitive church.

Similarly with new church developments in the mid-twentieth century in Great Britain, Canada, and the United States, new towns and suburban areas emerge and expand rapidly and each becomes the responsibility of the Christian church. The initial thrust into such a community is a "preaching" service. Preaching becomes the spearhead or "bringer together." The sermon takes on a pivotal character in such an adventure and the sacraments follow in order to give identity and integrity to the church, and nurture for its spiritual maintenance and growth.

b. There is a sense in which preaching or the sermon represents the most creative act of the minister. The whole pastoral ministry of the preacher comes to focus on Sunday morning in the sermon. With the background of a week of pastoral counseling and service in which he has become sensitive to his people's failures, needs, and sins and social ills of the community, the minister bears witness in his sermon to how the gospel works. He brings to reality that singular facet of Reformed worship described by William Nicholls as a miracle in which "God makes the word of man the Word of God" (*The Unity We Seek*, No. VI, p. 5). Or as William D. Maxwell expressed it in *Ways of Worship*: "True preaching therefore can come only by constant prayer, beseeching the Lord himself to witness to his promise and by the power of his Spirit to make the weak words of men the living Word of God" (p. 127).

c. There is a sense in which the sermon supplies the theme for the act of worship. This observation is both very obvious and practical. The theme of the act of worship in most Protestant traditions is arrived at by means of a lectionary or a careful recognition of the seasons of the Christian year. But if the preacher is creative at all, the service will not be an annual stereotyped reproduction in detail of what has always gone before. The framework is determined by theology and tradition but the materials that form the substance — hymns, prayers, lections, anthems — are unified in theme around the sermon. Its central idea becomes the integrative factor in the choice of subjects just as the Holy Spirit unifies the various acts and personal actions into a symphonic whole of praise and glory to God.

2. THEOLOGICAL

a. The sermon gives content to the service of worship. Since worship comes to a climax in the expression of the people's response in faith, it must be an informed faith. Calvin recognized early that the people's faith must be forever refreshed and strengthened by the growth of knowledge, else it would be in danger of deteriorating into emotionalism and superstition. "We ought not to attempt anything in religion rashly or at random," he said, "because, unless there be knowledge, it is not God that we worship, but a phantom or idol." A true sermon must present a rehearsal of the mighty acts of God which culminated in him who was the highest redemptive event of all, and hearing it the congregation experiences a personal encounter with Christ. The sermon evokes faith, but it also adds knowledge to faith. The sermon is intended to produce an informed faith. Worship marked by an effective sermon will call from the people a response not merely of heart and soul, but also with all their mind.

b. The sermon is the occasion par excellence for living witness in worship. The sermon can never be simply another self-contained item in the act of worship. It is preceded by the written Word that is read in the presence of the congregation, and then it becomes itself a witness to that Word through the personality of the preacher. Preaching, rightly conceived, is a living Word. It is, as J. G. Davies put it, "an actualization of the Word which is read." Or, as John Marsh defines it, in preaching "the Word comes into contemporaneous effectiveness." Or, as *The Directory for Worship* states, ". . . the preached Word, like the written Word, points to the incarnate Word, and shows forth the presence of Jesus Christ with power to save." The sermon then is the preacher's own act of witness in which he testifies to God's acts of love and grace and through which God's "Thus saith the Lord" confronts humanity. The sermon is the preacher's most creative and prophetic act. It involves and claims all his powers as scholar, pastor, and disciple in order that his witness may evoke a true venture of faith on the part of the congregation. Moreover, the more fully he is himself grasped by the Word, the more likely will his preaching be seen and felt as a demonstration of the power of the Holy Spirit.

c. **The sermon must be determinative in** the act of worship. In a properly regulated service of worship, the sermon provides a bridge between two actions: the reading of the Holy Scripture and the celebration at the Lord's Table. As Richard Davidson said, "The sermon is the proclamation of the message in the preacher's own words. It begins at the Scripture read; it ends at the Upper Room. If the sermon does not take the people there it has failed." The sermon then is not an end in itself, nor is it done simply for its own sake. It is part of a corporate activity. A congregation of listening people is involved, and spiritually they are on the move. Every sermon has a dialogical character. Its elements — declaration, probing, encounter, confrontation — are accompanied step by step by the willing assent of the people. This dialogical action reaches its climax when the living witness and claim of the sermon bring the congregation to the offering of themselves to Christ as the family of God around his table. Luther translates Romans 10:17, "So belief comes of preaching, and preaching by the Word of God." Through such preaching Sunday after Sunday God provides for men the possibility of living by his grace.

d. The sermon must be seen in worship as an instrument of grace. This occurs in two ways: in an immediate, vertical sense as encounter; and in a horizontal developmental sequence as fulfillment.

True worship begins with God; he takes the initiative. Within the context of such worship, preaching channels to the people "the vertical inbreak of the Word of God" (T. H. Keir, *The Word in Worship*, p. 41). For the soul that listens and receives, it is a gift of grace. Or as Paul Tillich said, "The church is primarily a group of people who express a new reality by which they have been grasped" (*Union Seminary Review*, VII, 5, p. 10). This happens whenever the faith-filled preacher by whom the Word is preached confronts a community of people met with one accord in one place. In this unique fellowship, through the instrument of the sermon, God's Word becomes a dynamic and redemptive factor reminding men that through Christ one dies unto the old self and is recreated into the new.

Preaching is marked by a *hic et nunc* complexion, but it has also an eschatological character that points to "one far-off divine event to which the whole creation moves." Along with baptism and the Lord's supper, the sermon is a means of grace by which men are nourished spiritually unto life eternal. Through baptism a man comes into the fellowship of the family of God; through preaching his faith is articulated and given structure and substance; at the Lord's table at each stated season his whole life is fed and renewed. The sermon is therefore the forerunner of the Lord's supper. Without it, this sacrament would easily become a mere work of magic. On the other hand, as J. J. von Allmen put it, "without preaching the sacrament has nothing to prove." A sermon that would end with itself would be merely the discussion of an idea or the presentation of Christ as an acceptable model for moral character. But preaching that creates faith bears fruit finally in a union with Christ.

The place of the sermon in worship is summed up cogently by Julius Schweizer when he wrote, "The proclamation of the Word of God, through which the Lord speaks to his people, gathers them and keeps them close to him, cannot be replaced in the service by anything else. There is no true divine service, nor is there any true celebration of the Sacrament without the proclamation of the Word. The reformers are agreed in this, that the exposition of the Word is a constitutive part of divine service: a worshipping congregation first comes into being through being addressed by the Word" (*Ways of Worship*, p. 128).

BIBLIOGRAPHY

Cullman, Oscar, *Early Christian Worship.* Chicago: H. Regnery, 1953.

Edwall, P., Hayman, E., Maxwell, W. D., *Ways of Worship.* New York: Harper and Brothers, 1951.

Forsyth, P. T., *Positive Preaching and the Modern Mind.* Grand Rapids: Wm. B. Eerdmans, 1965.

Keir, Thomas H., *The Word in Worship.* New York: Oxford University Press, 1962.

Macleod, Donald, *Presbyterian Worship.* Richmond: John Knox Press, 1965.

Von Allmen, J. J., *Preaching and Congregation.* Richmond: John Knox Press, 1962.

Wingren, Gustaf, *The Living Word.* Philadelphia: Fortress Press, 1965.

Sermon Structure and Design

If a sermon were always the same kind of thing, one might talk with more confidence about sermon structure and design. As it is, since a sermon may be so many different things, or so many different things may be called sermons, the question of design and structure is never a single question with a clear answer. Design, structure, form in general, are not independent values or qualities that can be imposed on the material in order to make a proper sermon.

Consequently this article, if it is to have any real value, cannot deal with the sermon as a set form of speech. The history of preaching, in the synagogue and throughout the Christian church, has seen numerous and widely variant forms of the sermon. A sermon can be a very simple and artless thing. It can also be a very elaborate literary or artistic achievement. Significantly, both the Greek word *homily* and its Latin translation, *sermon,* mean nothing more definite than the act of speaking to the people in a public assembly. Both words are also used to designate informal and private speech or conversation.

So this is the unpretentious way it all started in the first century. In our own restless day, when preaching along with everything else must be reappraised, when the newsworthy fashion is iconoclasm and the mass mind equates honesty with disbelief, it is necessary once more to strip preaching down to its basic elements. A sermon is primarily an act of speaking and only secondarily a linguistic composition. It is something done rather than something said. A sermon is always a situational speech; it speaks for a definite time and place. Believers are gathered together for worship and mutual help. A member of the community stands up and talks to all and for all the others about the important concerns of the whole community. The result is a sermon, and its importance lies in the purpose of such speaking and the urgency of what is said. The form is the inevitable by-product of the act of speaking in this kind of situation.

1. THE SERMON SITUATION

So understood, preaching is a community process, a vital function of community life and a natural function. A member speaks to his fellows within the assembled community, and the result is preaching of the kind we recognize as pastoral preaching, instruction, admonition, encouragement, and so on. Even when the speaking is done outside the assembly, it has its origin within the community. A member speaks from within the shared experience of the community to people outside of it, and the result is a form of preaching we call evangelistic. Such a sermon almost inevitably takes the form of announcement, proclamation, invitation, and so on. The community gives the sermon its form. Without a community there would be no preaching. Homiletical theory has not always recognized this fact. Today we have to begin with it.

The really important concerns of the whole community determine the proper subject matter of the sermon. This statement may not sound religious or theological enough for some. But if the community is the Christian community, the church of Jesus Christ, its real concerns are not trivial or ephemeral. They have to do with nothing less than the faith by which Christian people live, the hope which they share among themselves, and the love that lives and acts in them toward one another and all the people of the world. The right word spoken about such matters will be genuine preaching, whatever its form or lack of form. It will be historical and orthodox preaching. It will also be Biblical preaching.

The sermon does not require a special kind

of language. Language recognizable as pulpit language should be avoided in the pulpit. A sermon can succeed only by a successful use of language, for language is the indispensable medium of communication. Language is the material in which thought takes form, as a sculptor's vision takes form in wood or metal. A Christian may use language for a Christian purpose, but, as there is no such thing as "Christian" wood or stone or metal, so there is no such thing as "Christian" or "sacred" or "holy" language. Even in the Bible, especially in the Bible, language is human, true to the reality of human life. The requirement for preaching, as for any genuine communication, is that language be really human, native to the human heart and spirit.

Thus the only valid thing that can be said about sermonic form as such, about the techniques of constructing a sermon, turns out to be negative. There simply is no one right structure or design for a certain kind of speech called a sermon. Does it then follow that form is not important, that the preacher need not be concerned about the form of his sermon? Quite the contrary. The reason why there can be no one right form is that no two sermons are alike, and each one must find its own right form at every step. Form and content are not separable entities.

Authentic preaching, preaching that catches up and expresses a people's faith and hope and love, is like a people's music. It may be a simple and artless tune, it may be gay or sad, it may speak of life or of death or of the love that is stronger than life and death. But above all it is a native music, a shared music, a music learned "by heart."

The preparation of a genuine sermon, no matter how fresh its theme, is somewhat like playing such music "by ear." That is to say, when working on the sermon the preacher cannot be conscious of rules in the book or in the memory. He can only listen to the theme, and he can be guided only by his disciplined intuition. In *Design for Preaching* I called it "skill in doing, controlled by an inner sense of rightness, a sense that is nearer to feeling than to calculation, nearer to intuition than to deliberation." I would not change that, but now I would give still more credit to the theme itself for showing what is right to do.

2. SERMON DESIGN

Design begins as purpose, intended use. The designing of a sermon begins as a question: what is this particular sermon designed to do? It is important to ask the question, though at the point of beginning the intention may not yet be clear. Later in the homiletical process, but not too much later, the purpose should become clear and definite in the preacher's mind. Design should take shape as a plan that will govern the whole work.

The design of a finished sermon includes much more than this. It means the final form and character of the production, the amount and quality of material used, plus the way that material is organized, controlled, adapted to the purpose and plan, plus the success or lack of success in accomplishing the purpose, plus the degree of value of what was intended in the first place. All these, as measured in the experience of the people who listen to the sermon, come under the head of design.

The principles of design apply to the sermon as to all other works of the human mind. The commonest faults of the third-rate sermon, its pointlessness, its lost motion and wasted effort are more often due to lack of design than to poverty of content. Design begins as purpose, but the preparation of the routine Sunday address too often does not begin with a purpose definite enough to do any good. It does not begin by asking what this particular sermon should do or expecting it to do anything in particular. It does not turn out to be successfully designed to do something definite that needs to be done in the Christian community. In other words, the importance of design has not been felt, design has not been seriously attempted, and the sermon is consequently less pertinent than it needs to be.

Design in this sense of intention is a basic factor in all communication as well as in the manufacture of products for the market. That is at once its value and its risk, a risk from which the preacher is no more exempt than the advertiser. Design makes possible the mass production of an unlimited number and variety of useful articles, enough to supply everybody. It also exposes everybody to the risk of buying articles that are designed for sale rather than for use. The risk in preaching is very great to both preacher and people.

Design, intention, purpose, whether it be conscious or unconscious, is always at work. The preacher is human. He will not avoid the risk of design by giving no thought to his own designs. The sermon will intend to do something or other, if nothing more than to entertain his people, keep their interest, win their approval of a performance they expect of him and pay him for. The sermon may intend to impose the preacher's personal views, prejudices, "convictions" on his listeners, to manipulate people, exploit them. The sermon may be designed merely to propagate a party line, or promote the policies and attitudes of an institution. The prevalence of such abuses of the sermon as these and others that could be mentioned should alert us to the crucial importance of basic design, not only in the preparation and criticism of particular sermons, but also in the theoretical understanding of what preaching is.

No doubt most readers of this volume work within the presuppositions of a Christian theology of preaching, of the church, of the Word of God and its Biblical attestation. Theological and Biblical scholars of our generation have brought back an exceedingly high estimate of preaching, but they have not simplified the task of sermon preparation. They say that theology exists for the sake of preaching, yet preaching is not theologizing, and the discussion of theological concepts is not preaching. They say that the word to be preached is the Biblical word, yet it is the word of a Bible that must be historically and critically reinterpreted. A lofty theology of preaching can give courage, but it cannot guarantee good preaching. After all the talk about what preaching ought to do and can do, the actual work of sermon designing has still to be begun.

Whatever the sermon is designed to do it must do by means of language. The preacher has all the resources of language at his disposal, and he is free to do whatever he can do with it. But language can be managed and controlled for a purpose only when its nature is understood and its laws obeyed. The unique importance of language as a human function, how it operates, its limitations and possibilities, in fact the whole question of language has become central in studies of mankind today, and in none more decidedly than in Biblical interpretation.

Every Biblical text or passage consists of language used for a purpose, and the form of the language reflects the purpose. Every passage will almost certainly fall into one of the four traditional types of discourse: exposition, argument, description or narrative. In each of these familiar types there is a different use of language, corresponding to the specific purpose for which language is used in each. An understanding of language and its operation is thus as necessary for the right interpretation of the Biblical text as for expressing the shared faith of the community.

At some moment in the community's ongoing experience of itself, within the design and movement of some sermon or other, there will be a place and need for any and every form of living speech. The best new uses of language will be spontaneous, the result not of calculation but of an urgent need to speak the truth. All the resources of language should be used with the boldness, the imagination, and the freedom of the Christian man.

However, language does take definite forms according to the intention of the speaker. There are functional forms which keep turning up even in the most informal preaching. Proclamation, teaching, therapy (exhortation, persuasion, etc.) are the most important of such forms. Each has its place and its right use, which means that each is wrong when used in the wrong place. A competent workman should know how to distinguish between them, and be able to use each of these forms effectively in the right place and for the right reason. But there are no foolproof rules.

3. SERMON STRUCTURE

Function precedes form and leads to form, not only in the basic intention and design, but also in the *structure* of the sermon as a single continuous utterance. The necessity for the sermon to be a clear, orderly, integrated structure of meaning is not the necessity that the rules of linguistic art shall be observed; it is the necessity that people shall be able to hear the sermon and take it in. Everything that needs to be said about sermon structure can and should be said from the point of view of people in the hearing situation.

The preacher stands up to speak, and the people fix their eyes on him in expectation. He must begin, continue for some minutes, and then stop. What takes place during this interval is an action, the preacher's act of speaking and the people's experience of hearing and reacting. Theology says the sermon is an event, a potentially redemptive event. The clock says the sermon is an event in time, lasting certain precious minutes. This elemental fact of the situation makes certain demands which must be met by sermon structure, if the hearing experience is to be significant.

a. The sermon structure must show continuity. There must be continuity in time and continuity of thought that matches the continuity in time. There must be a beginning and a continuance and a completion. There must be a beginning because one cannot say everything at once and therefore must start with only one thing among many that he has to say. It is not possible to say the right second thing unless one has said the right thing in the first place. If the thing said first and second are the wrong things, it will hardly be possible to say the right thing in the third place.

b. There must be movement, a sense of one thing following another in a sequence so natural as to seem inevitable. This is in fact an additional aspect of continuity. Another name for it is a sense of progress. It is not possible to remain longer than necessary on one point without tiring the listener. It is disagreeable and inconsiderate to jump from one point to another without warning, or back and forth between several points for no apparent reason. If the sermon is to hold people's interest to the end, its thought must move forward in an orderly succession of steps that are clearly indicated and easy to follow.

c. There must be a goal toward which the whole sermon moves, a climax, a final issue and resolution, a point of culmination. The sermon cannot simply end, it must finish. The last thing said could not be said or heard so well till everything else has been said. Once everything else has been said, the last thing then simply has to be said. And when the last thing has been said and heard, there is a sense of finality about it, as if it were foreordained from the very first sentence of the sermon. This is accomplished by structural design, and it is conveyed by the feel of it.

d. To produce a strong or lasting impression on its hearers, a sermon must have unity of thought and unity of structure. People cannot take in a succession of unrelated or loosely related thoughts. From twenty minutes of talk, from thousands of words in hundreds of sentences, a single thought structure must take shape in the listener's mind. If this is to happen, the structure must be natural and not artificial, organic and not mechanical. Above all, it must be clear and simple.

e. The one indispensable requirement for structural unity is unity of subject matter. One can say several things about a single subject, and if they are pertinent they will hold together. But one cannot talk about two or more things without destroying unity, unless the things fall into place under a larger subject. The functional difference between subject matter and predication is decisive. Not every good sermon can be contained in one sentence, that is, one predicate. Not every integrated sermon says only one thing, but every integrated sermon talks about only one thing.

These all add up to the requirement that the sermon shall be an organic structure of meaning of some kind. But organic forms are not all of one kind. In *Design for Preaching* I described five such forms that are persistent in the history of literature: a subject discussed (much overused today), a thesis supported, a message (one sentence) illumined, a question propounded (not necessarily answered), a story told. A teacher friend adds "a problem solved," and I will agree if we say "faced" instead of "solved," for I am suspicious of a preacher's solutions. Any of these forms can serve as structural design, and any of them, especially the story, is capable of unlimited variation. Any can go on being a vital form of speech, no matter how often it is used, so long as it embodies the stuff of life. A simple, clear thought structure can be compared to nature's scheme of stem, leaf, petal, stamen, pistil, which the life process repeats endlessly without shame and with no sense of boredom with its stereotypes.

Thus it is possible to say quite dogmatically that some things have to be done for success in the speaking-hearing situation, and to name some things that have to be done. To say *how* they can be done is a different matter, a lifetime matter. That is what a lifetime calling is for.

BIBLIOGRAPHY

Bornkamm, G., *Jesus of Nazareth.* Harper, 1960.

Davis, H. Grady, *Design for Preaching.* Fortress Press, 1958.

Ebeling, Gerhard, *Word and Faith.* Fortress Press, 1963.

Knox, John, *The Integrity of Preaching.* Abingdon, 1957.

Ott, Heinrich, *Theology and Preaching.* Westminster, 1965.

Robinson, James M. & Cobb, John B., *The New Hermeneutic.* Harper, 1964.

Wilder, Amos N., *The Language of the Gospel.* Harper, 1964.

Wingren, Gustav, *The Living Word.* Fortress, 1960.

Sermonic Style in Contemporary Terms

1. IMPORTANCE OF STYLE

The first and most urgent problem of the public speaker is to make himself understood. In achieving this aim of communication through public address no part of rhetoric is more difficult to master than style, with the one possible exception of invention. Jefferson stated, "Next to the baptism of the Holy Spirit the most indispensable gift for every American preacher is a mastery of the English tongue. No time should be begrudged that is spent in perfecting the preacher's style." Style, or language, is important to the extent that it helps to prepare and subsequently to open the minds of the hearers to the ideas developed in the speech.

It is unwise to emphasize content to the exclusion of style, or vice versa. Substance and style must go together. Paying too much attention to style can lead to disastrous results. Since the best style attracts the least attention to itself, only the most critical observer is likely to appreciate its excellence. The prevalent tendency is to attach greater significance to the matter presented than to the manner of presentation. Such highly regarded homileticians as Beecher and Greer stated in their Yale lectures on preaching that style was not absolutely necessary to accomplish the task of persuading men.

The Sophists, who were the early speech teachers on the island of Sicily from 500 B.C. to approximately A.D. 100, stressed style as an end in itself. Their doctrine of plausibility made the winning of a case in the courts of more consequence than style as a factor in the speech itself. The stylists Longinus, Dionysius, and Demetrius, on the other hand, were not sophistic in their view of style. They regarded it as a part of the whole process of rhetoric and not as an end in itself.

The word style comes from the Latin *stylus,* which referred to the pointed iron pen with which the Romans wrote on their tablets. Style is one's manner of expressing thought whether in writing or in speaking. It is the expression in language of the thought, qualities, and spirit of the man. It is his characteristic way of expressing his thoughts. It involves the use of the right words in the right places. Style is the manner, as distinguished from the matter.

2. TYPES OF STYLE

The three-way classification of the types of style got its start as early as 85 B.C. with the publication of *Rhetorica Ad Herennium,* the earliest Roman work which we know that is in anywhere near its complete form. The three types were the grand, the middle, and the plain. These were referred to by Cicero as being the three complexions of eloquence. When Quintilian adopted these three types, he defined the plain as being that adapted to the duty of stating facts, the grand as that given to the moving of feelings, and the middle as that of pleasing or conciliating. Style at the time of the classical rhetoricians was referred to as *elocutio* and was one of the five parts of rhetoric; the others being invention, arrangement, memory, and delivery. Style, therefore, referred to the process of phrasing in language the ideas invented and arranged.

There were three classical works on style written about A.D. 100. Dionysius wrote a twenty-six chapter work entitled *On Literary Composition.* This was concerned with the style of public address. The work of Longinus had forty-four chapters and was more concerned with style as it pertained to poetry. The work by Demetrius entitled *On Style* dealt with four main types of style. These four types were the elevated, which made use of metaphors and comparisons; the elegant, which was noted for its charm and vivacity; the plain, noted for its clearness and simplicity; and the forcible style. Style to Demetrius included both diction and composition.

Fénelon in the second of his dialogues concerning eloquence condemned what he called the florid, swelling style. He felt that the style of the true orator has nothing in it that is swelling or ostentatious. It was his feeling that in most cases an easy simplicity and exactness are sufficient, though some things do require vehemence and sublimity.

3. INFLUENCES ON STYLE

a. *Culture.* There are certain influences which will tend to shape a preacher's style. One of these influences is culture. This will inevitably condition the character of his speech. Another influence upon style is that of the subject matter. The technical content of the material will, for instance, have definite bearing upon the speaker's style of presentation. Personal character is revealed by the speaker's style of expression. A man speaks as he does because of what he is. "Out of the abundance of the heart the mouth speaketh" (Matt. 12:34).

b. *Function.* Appropriateness is the most functional aspect of the whole problem of style. The mode of expression should be consistent with the nature of the message. The speaker must accommodate himself to the purpose in view. One of the four basic purposes for speaking will be chosen by the speaker and this major purpose will serve as a controlling factor in his style of message and in its preparation. The four purposes from which one major one will be chosen are to inform, to persuade, to impress, and to entertain. The last of the four listed will have little pertinence to the sermonizer since he will have a greater goal than merely to entertain. When the speaker seeks to inform, a didactic style will be adopted in which he will analyze, synthesize, and logically organize his material. When his purpose is to persuade, he will add emotional appeals to the logical unfolding of his subject. His employment of the purpose to impress will be evidenced by extended use or repetition of words and ideas through the main channels available to him.

c. *Audience.* There are four types of audiences with respect to the attitude which they have toward the speaker and toward his material. The apathetic audience challenges the speaker to include attention-getting material. The speaker's style must be varied, forceful, and uniquely interesting. A style is more interesting when it is direct. The introduction of the message must begin where the listeners live. The sermonizer should avoid the temptation to start his sermon by citing material which is two thousand or more years old. If he fails to catch the interest of his audience in the introduction, he may never get it throughout the time of his message. The believing audience demands that the speaker dramatize his idea by making use of statistics, telling details and vivid figures of speech. The hostile audience demands that the message be formulated in such a way that the hostility can be eased before the main import of the message is set forth. The doubting audience demands that the speaker include an abundance of factual material. The speaker must make clear in his presentation the distinction between facts and inferences.

4. RULES FOR STYLE

a. *Sentences.* The preacher will find that short sentences are always easier to understand than long ones, and that short words are as important as short sentences. Deliberate variety in sentence structure will serve to break any possible tendency to monotony. The varied sentence structure will create mood without any noticeable attempt to force itself into the attention field of the listener. The tempo of the style will be affected by sentence types as well as by sentence length. Mastery of style is more a matter of absorption and ability to adjust to the needs of the audience than it is a matter of learning rules. The main thing to be desired in a sentence is strength. The subject should be kept close to the predicate. The mastery of the use of the periodic sentence is said to afford conclusive proof of a man's education and culture. The mixture of short and long sentences will add to force, clarity, and swiftness in the presentation of the material.

b. *Words.* There are certain general rules for style pertaining to words. Words should be short and simple. The use of Latin, Greek, French, and Hebrew words is pedantic except in the company of people who are able to understand them readily. It is well to be sparing in the use of adjectives. The speaker should avoid pleonasm, or the use of more words than necessary to express the idea. The preacher will be wise to avoid slang words, vulgar words, colloquial words, hackneyed words, foreign words, barbarisms, solecisms, and exaggerated expressions. There are other types of words which should be used only sparingly. The list would include technical or scientific words, heavy theological words, philosophical words, abstract, and ambiguous words. The speaker should concentrate on using simple words, plain words, picturesque words, concrete words, short words, vivid words, exact words, and words of action.

Robert J. McCracken has wisely said, "It is a misfortune when a preacher has no feeling for the magic of words and no flair for word-weaving. We should care for words, should select them judiciously and lovingly." This zest for words can be enhanced through a study of the etymology and meaning of words. The wise use of the dictionary and thesaurus is essential. The small handbooks available for vocabulary building are valuable tools. A study of good poetry will sharpen one's taste for words which are expressive both through their meaning and their sound.

The preacher should learn to express himself in as few words as possible. The preacher should strive to use not only short, strong words but also words which sound well within their sentence surroundings. It is wise to give preference to words related to the five senses, rather than to abstract words. It is wise to remember that strong nouns and verbs carry the weight of the thought. Adjectives and adverbs do not convey thought but merely color it. These should therefore be used sparingly. Francis Bacon (1560-1626) stated that the speaker should strive for words of "similitude," and make extensive use of the words of Scripture.

c. *Paragraphs.* Good style demands that each paragraph begin with a key sentence which is clear and crisp. The remaining portion of the paragraph has as its purpose the explanation and enforcement of the idea which is contained in the opening sentence. Each paragraph contains one main idea with its development.

5. QUALITIES OF STYLE

It has been said that if there were a perfect orator, men would come away from his discourse without having any conscious recollection regarding the quality of his style. More space in American homiletical texts and tradebooks is given to the discussion of qualities of style than to the nature and improvement of style. Several writers have attempted to establish a compact list of qualities of style. George Campbell in his *Philosophy of Rhetoric* stated that the qualities of style which are strictly rhetorical are perspicuity, vivacity, elegance, animation and music. Richard Whately stressed three qualities of style, namely, perspicuity, energy, and elegance or beauty. The quality of energy is that which Campbell referred to as vivacity. Ebenezer Porter emphasized grammatical purity, perspicuity, strength, beauty, and sublimity. The classical tradition generally accepted four qualities of style, namely, correctness, clearness, ornateness, and propriety. Gregory stated that the essential qualities of good style are perspicuity, purity, and a moderate portion of ornament.

a. *Clearness.* Perspicuity, or clearness, would appear to be the first excellence of style. Nine of the Yale lecturers on preaching mentioned clearness as the first requisite of a good style. This depends first of all on the choice of words, and secondly upon their arrangement. The wise use of connectives and special attention to the relationship of qualifying phrases to each other also helps. The speaker should try to put himself in the place of the listener and then use words which will be familiar to his listeners. His metaphors should be drawn from objects which are familiar to his hearers. His relative pronouns must be close to their antecedents. It is wise to avoid the extremes of either conciseness or prolixity by making a careful use of repetition and illustration.

Perspicuity, which Blair defines as the conveying of ideas clearly, is hampered by the obscure and the unintelligible. These would include such matters as the use of technical terms, long sentences, poor arrangement of material, and the use of the same word with different meanings. Ferris states that the preacher who cannot speak in terms that at least a high school student can understand should not speak at all.

The lectures on style written by Hugh Blair emphasized three requirements for perspicuity. The first of these was purity of words and construction. The second was that of propriety. This involved the selection of words according to the best usage. The third requirement was that of precision. The words used should express the idea and no more.

Perspicuity, or clarity, begins in the mind of the preacher. It involves his identity with the people as well as the structure of language. A logically arranged basic structure for the message will tend to promote clarity. It is wise to reduce the message to one concise, simple, timeless truth, known homiletically as the proposition. A clear objective for the message will make for clarity of presentation. This can be stated in the objective sentence of the sermon, which is the first sentence of the conclusion. Although it may not be stated until that point in the delivery, it should be formulated by the sermonizer early in his process of preparation.

Conversational style will aid clarity. In this style the speaker converses with his audience as a gentleman converses with his friends. Conversational style makes use of personal pronouns, personal names, words of definite masculine and feminine gender, and words of definite personal description. It also uses what are known as personal sentences, such as questions, commands, exclamations, direct and indirect quotations, and sentences addressed directly to the audience. Contractions are also used in preference to the longer forms of a written style.

There are several hindrances to clarity. These include the lack of clear apprehension of the ideas to be expressed, the use of obscure words, and obscure constructions. When the speaker fails to put himself in the place of the listener, he has difficulty in sensing that which will appear clear to his audience. If he proceeds to employ technical jargon, the process of clear communication will be hampered. Clearness also suffers from a faulty choice of words and poor arrangement.

b. *Energy.* Energy of style is promoted by conciseness. Energy, or vivacity, depends upon word choice, the number of words used, and the arrangement of words. In choosing words, figures of speech should be used rather than abstract and general terms. Metaphors are preferred to plain comparisons. In arranging words, it is wise to make use of periodic sentences. The use of short sentences, interrogative sentences, balanced sentences, and parallel structure will also help to impart energy to style. Force of style does more than win attention; it demonstrates the conviction of the speaker. It helps to elicit conviction and decision from the hearer. Force is gained through personality, the wise use of pronouns, and the employment of virile language. The wise arrangement of material pointing toward a climax will enhance energy of style.

c. *Beauty.* In gaining beauty, or elegance of style, one must avoid smothering his work with ornamentation. The development of that terseness of expression known as the epigram, and the occasional use of antithesis will lend elegance. Of the six Yale lecturers who referred to elegance of style, only Broadus spoke of it as being a desired characteristic.

d. *Expressiveness.* It has been said that the sole office of speech is mental communication, or making known to others the speaker's mental state. The all-inclusive quality of style is expressiveness. It is extremely important, therefore, that the speaker have the right mental attitude. This point is made by Sarett and Foster in their list of the seven basic principles of speech. It is imperative that the speaker be in a good mental state toward himself, his material, his audience, and his God. Such an attitude of mind will go a long way toward insuring naturalness of presentation.

e. *Imagination.* Consideration should be given to the cultivation of an imaginative style. Imagination is awakened and invigorated by communion with nature and contact with art and literature. The study of poetry develops penetrating vision, lofty aspiration, quick sympathies, concreteness of thought, and choice diction.

f. *Economy.* Oftentimes the length of a sermon is more dependent on style than we normally recognize. A sermon is made to seem long as the speaker dwells unduly upon the obvious. Economy of style demands that the ideas be presented in such a way that they may be apprehended with the least mental effort. The chief quality of personal communication is that it says a great amount and suggests even more in a very few words.

6. ORAL STYLE

A preacher is a public speaker and not a public reader. As such his style should be the spoken rather than the written style. Skinner stated, "The style fitting for a public discourse is so different from that which becomes matter intended for the press that, if it be given to the public through that means, such important changes may be necessary as to require recomposition." The speaker has the advantage over the writer in two ways. He is permitted greater latitude and more repetition. He may interpret his meaning not only by words but by intonations, gesticulations, and changes of facial expression. His main disadvantage is that he must make his meaning apparent at once. He must try not only to communicate to the audience but also to interpret as well. Many works on style, such as Newman's, stress only written style, to the exclusion of oral style. Edward Channing, who held the Boylston chair of oratory at Harvard, made his contribution in the area of style for writing, not for speaking. Since antiquity, however, the rhetoricians and critics have recognized two distinct styles, namely, oral and written.

a. *Relation to Written.* There are several differences between oral style and written style. In written style the sentences are longer and more complex in form; whereas in oral style more use is made of the compound sentence. Repetition is more characteristic of oral than of written style, the reason for this being that when a matter has been recorded the reader may go back to it and check. In oral address it can only be checked if the speaker repeats it. Repetition must be varied by changing the language slightly. This may be accomplished by using stories, by making comparisons, and by applying figures of speech. More illustrations are used in oral than in written style. Direct address is more characteristic of the oral style. This would include the use of personal pronouns, exclamations, and commands. Terminology is more concrete and specific in oral style, and it makes use of a greater number of rhetorical questions. The use of epigrams, which are condensations of wisdom into short, striking sentences, improves oral style. Climactic order is one of the constituents of oral style. Climax is emphasized by increased rates of speed in speaking and heightened enthusiasm on the part of the speaker.

The use of image-producing words is an important feature of oral discourse. Word symbols are effective in direct proportion to the strength of the experiences with which they are associated. Some words are better than others to create images. It is wise to give special attention to details. Visual imagery is strengthened by mentioning size, shape, color, movement, and relative position. Auditory imagery is clarified by noting the pitch, volume, rhythm, quality, and duration. Gustatory imagery is most easily created by comparison with objects you remember tasting, rather than by the mere use of adjectives. In enhancing the olfactory imagery, it is well to mention not only the odor itself, but also the object producing the odor. Tactual imagery is based upon the various types of sensation received through the skin when it is touched. One should describe the shape, texture, pressure and heat. Kinesthetic imagery involves reference to muscle strain and movement. Organic imagery deals with one's present condition such as hunger, dizziness, etc.

b. *Used for the Radio.* The manuscript for the radio program is a unique form of literature. This is largely due to the fact that radio is a one-dimensional medium. Its message is received, interpreted and understood only through the medium of the ear. The radio script is written for an audience of one person, never a crowd or a congregation. The radio speaker must speak in terms which the listener can understand. He should cultivate broad sympathies and interests in order that he may be able to sense the listener's problems, interests, limitations, and tastes.

Many of the precepts pertaining to good radio style are also positive suggestions for good sermonic style. Radio style demands that the script have one core idea which is interesting to the one presenting it and which stirs conviction in his own being. It must also be an idea which is interesting to the listener. This core idea and the supporting ideas should be stated positively and not negatively. The speaker should use plenty of illustrations to throw light upon these ideas. Human interest stories or personal experiences are especially effective. He should seek for a variety of words and expressions to convey the same thought. He will concentrate upon specific, concrete terms, avoiding generalities and abstractions.

Brevity is the handmaiden of clarity. One may read widely but should quote sparingly. It is not necessary to quote an entire poem in order to place two lines which emphasize the point before the listener. A script written from a well-considered outline will not only have a strong structure but will also aid the speaker in keeping within practical time limits. Length does not insure value. The Declaration of Independence covers only one page and the parable of the Good Samaritan consists of just 165 words.

7. IMPROVEMENT OF STYLE

a. *Reading*. The acquirement of a good style is largely an unconscious process. Some general helps, however, can be given. There are great advantages in the use of a Scriptural style. It is profitable to read the English Bible audibly as a means of improving one's style. Phelps suggests that for improving one's style the speaker would do well to read Carlyle for strength, Shakespeare for words, Emerson for intellectual tone, Washington Irving for smoothness, Milton for dignity and simplicity, Fosdick for figurative imagery, and Stevenson for the perfection of English style. The reading of Chaucer might help one to gain a mastery of the English language. The accurate use of language is outstanding in the works of Bishop Hall, Lord Jeffrey, Archbishop Whately and Robert South. Dabney encourages the reading of sermons by Samuel Davies, John Mason and Robert South since these were masters of sermonizing. One can freshen and enrich his style by reading secular writers such as Stevenson, Tennyson, Defoe and Swift. Graves recommends the reading of sermons by Beecher, Brooks, Spurgeon and Maclaren. General suggestions for reading with a view toward improvement of style might include the reading of history for perspective, philosophy for depth, science for objectivity, and current literature to maintain close contact with life.

b. *Writing*. Some suggest that writing is a good means of developing a good style. This is especially true if one puts in written form that which he would say. This will give him an oral style in written form. Transcribing and reproducing one's message on a tape recorder is especially profitable. The sermonizer should develop the habit of constant revision of his message. This process should go on until the moment of delivery.

c. *People*. The preacher will be able to improve his style as he learns more about the people to whom he is to speak. He should be interested in the size of the audience, its cultural climate, economic status, and educational level.

d. *Listening*. It is helpful to listen to good speakers for the purpose of improving one's style. Such speakers may be heard on television or radio. The program might be tape recorded if desired, thus making it available for study for some time to come.

e. *Laws of Language*. Care should be taken to obey the general laws of language. Extensive use should be made of a dictionary, a dictionary of synonyms, and a thesaurus in order to determine the best word for the expression of a particular concept. A study both of semantics and general semantics will aid communication and clear thinking.

The speaker should keep in mind the fact that his purpose is to communicate ideas and not to display artifices. Style, or language, is important only to the extent that it helps to prepare the minds of the listeners for the understanding and reception of his ideas. The expression which he gives to his thoughts together with the rhetorical devices which he may use to strengthen his effectiveness may be called his style.

Individuality is an outstanding characteristic of the successful speaker. Rules become relative rather than definite because of the many influencing factors in any speaking situation. There is no absolute ideal of speaking style. Every preacher's rhetorical method must of necessity be his own. It must be natural. This natural style can be cultivated. The good qualities can be improved and the poor ones overcome. Good speaking style will leave the impression that it is produced with ease and a limited amount of effort. Actually, however, it is the product of constant work and polishing. The stimulus for improving sermonic style is the improvement of the majority by imparting a message rather than the gratifying the refined taste of a few to the end that God may be glorified.

BIBLIOGRAPHY

Baird, A. Craig and Knower, Franklin H., *General Speech: An Introduction.* New York: McGraw-Hill Book Co., 1949.

Baxter, Batsell Barrett, *The Heart of the Yale Lectures.* New York: The Macmillan Co., 1947.

Blair, Hugh, *Lectures on Rhetoric.* New York: Funk & Wagnalls Co., 1911.

Borchers, Gladys L. and Wise, Claude M., *Modern Speech.* New York: Harcourt, Brace & Co., 1947.

Brastow, Lewis Orsmond, *The Work of the Preacher: A Study of Homiletic Principles and Methods.* Boston, New York: Pilgrim Press, 1914.

Broadus, John Albert, *A Treatise on the Preparation and Delivery of Sermons.* New York: A. C. Armstrong & Son, 1889.

Burrell, David James, *The Sermon: Its Construction and Delivery.* New York: Fleming H. Revell Co., 1913.

Caemmerer, Richard R., *Preaching for the Church.* St. Louis: Concordia Publishing House, 1959.

Campbell, George, *Campbell's Lectures.* Philadelphia: Hopkins and Earle, 1810.

Cooper, Lane, *The Rhetoric of Aristotle.* New York: D. Appleton-Century Co., Inc., 1932.

Davis, Henry Grady, *Design for Preaching.* Philadelphia: Muhlenberg Press, 1958.

Ferris, Theodore Parker, *Go Tell the People.* New York: Charles Scribner's Sons, 1951.

Fisk, Franklin Woodbury, *A Manual of Preaching: Lectures on Homiletics.* New York: A. C. Armstrong and Son, 1895.

Garrison, Webb Black, *The Preacher and His Audience.* Westwood, N. J.: Fleming H. Revell Co., 1954.

Gilman, Wilbur E.; Aly, Bower and Reid, Loren D., *The Fundamentals of Speaking.* New York: The Macmillan Co., 1951.

Graves, Henry C., *Lectures on Homiletics.* Philadelphia: American Baptist Pub. Society, 1906.

Hoppin, James Mason, *The Office and Work of the Christian Ministry.* New York: Sheldon and Co., 1869.

Jefferson, Charles Edward, *Quiet Hints to Growing Preachers in My Study.* New York: Thomas Y. Crowell & Co., 1901.

Johnson, Herrick, *The Ideal Ministry.* New York: Fleming H. Revell Co., 1908.

Kern, John Adam, *The Ministry to the Congregation: Lectures on Homiletics.* New York: Jennings and Graham, 1897.

Loveless, Wendell P., *Manual of Gospel Broadcasting.* Chicago: Moody Press, 1946.

McBurney, James H. and Wrage, Ernest J., *The Art of Good Speech.* New York: Prentice-Hall, Inc., 1953.

McCracken, Robert J., *The Making of the Sermon.* New York: Harper & Brothers, 1956.

Monroe, Alan A., *Principles and Types of Speech* (rev.). Chicago: Scott, Foresman & Co., 1939.

Oliver, Robert; Dickey, Dallas C. and Zelko, Harold P., *Communicative Speech.* New York: The Dryden Press, 1949.

Parker, Everett C.; Inman, Elinor and Snyder, Ross, *Religious Radio.* New York: Harper & Brothers, 1948.

Patton, Carl S., *The Preparation and Delivery of Sermons.* New York: Willett, Clark & Co., 1938.

Perry, Lloyd Merle, *Trends and Emphases in the Philosophy, Materials, and Methodology of American Protestant Homiletical Education as Established by a Study of Selected Trade and Textbooks Published Between 1834 and 1954.* Evanston: 1961.

Phelps, Austin, *The Theory of Preaching.* New York: Charles Scribner's Sons, 1894.

Porter, Ebenezer, *Lectures on Homiletics and Preaching and on Public Prayer.* Andover and New York: Flagg, Gould and Newman, 1834.

Sarett, Lew and Foster, William Trufant, *Basic Principles of Speech* (rev.). Chicago: Houghton Mifflin Co., 1946.

Schubert, Leland, *A Guide for Oral Communication.* New York: Prentice-Hall Co., 1948.

Sherrer, Paul Ehrman, *For We Have This Treasure.* New York: Harper and Brothers, 1944.

Skinner, Thomas Harvey, *Aids to Revealing and Hearing.* New York: J. S. Taylor, 1839.

Thonssen, Lester, *Selected Readings in Rhetoric and Public Speaking.* New York: The H. W. Wilson Co., 1942.

Thonssen, Lester and Baird, A. Craig, *Speech Criticism.* Ronald Press, 1948.

Whately, Richard, *Elements of Rhetoric.* London: John W. Parker, West Strand, 1850.

Whitesell, Faris Daniel, *The Art of Biblical Preaching.* Grand Rapids, Michigan: Zondervan Publishing House, 1950.

Sermon Preparation in Contemporary Terms

Sermon preparation in current language involves eight steps. By following in sequence these fundamental procedures a minister can prepare authentic and effective sermons.

1. SERMON PREPARATION BEGINS WITH A PREPARED PREACHER

The world may doubt, the skeptic may scoff, but the Bible abounds in references to men under orders from God. These men, in the main, were spokesmen for God. Today, sermon preparation still must begin with men who are under orders from God and who regularly experience a living, vital relationship with God. Apart from men in dynamic contact with the Lord there can be no authentic preaching.

a. *The Biblical Witness*

On the barren, parched plains of Midian, Moses' attention was arrested by the presence of a burning bush. Following a brief verbal skirmish with Jehovah, who spoke from the bush, the reluctant shepherd heard God say "Come now therefore, and I will send thee unto Pharaoh, that thou mayest bring forth my people the children of Israel out of Egypt. . . . And he said, Certainly I will be with thee; and this shall be the token unto thee, that I have sent thee: when thou has brought forth the people out of Egypt, ye shall serve God upon this mountain" (Exod. 3:10, 12).

Following his participation in a dramatic vision, Isaiah heard the voice of God and answered "And I heard the voice of the Lord, saying, Whom shall I send, and who will go for us? Then I said, Here am I; send me" (Isa. 6:8). Early in the Gospel of John there appears the dramatic announcement, "There came a man, sent from God, whose name was John" (John 1:6). Later, Mark tells in strikingly simple terms the story of the appointment of the apostles "And he appointed twelve, that they might be with him, and that he might send them forth to preach, and to have authority to cast out demons:" (Mark 3:14).

Paul in eloquent language described his conversion and call for King Agrippa. Paul related the circumstances of his journey toward Damascus, the almost incredible bright light, and then said "And when we were all fallen to the earth, I heard a voice saying unto me in the Hebrew language, Saul, Saul, why persecutest thou me? It is hard for thee to kick against the goad. And I said, who art thou, Lord? And the Lord said, I am Jesus whom thou persecutest. But arise, and stand upon thy feet: for to this end have I appeared unto thee, to appoint thee a minister and a witness both of the things wherein thou hast seen me, and of the things wherein I will appear unto thee; delivering thee from the people, and from the Gentiles, unto whom I send thee, to open their eyes, that they may turn from darkness to light and from the power of Satan unto God, that they may receive remission of sins and an inheritance among them that are sanctified by faith in me. Wherefore, O King Agrippa, I was not disobedient unto the heavenly vision" (Acts 26:14-20).

Jehovah in personal self-disclosure revealed himself to prophets and apostles and commissioned them to give faithful witness to what they had seen, heard, and experienced. The witnesses first gave oral testimony to revelation and later committed or had committed to writing that witness. Embedded in the written account are the incidents cited above concerning the setting apart of prophets and apostles.

b. *The Historical Witness*

The phenomena of men serving under God's orders existed not just during the days of active Biblical revelation, but it has existed throughout the history of the church. As strange and unusual as were Biblical calls to chosen men so have been God's ways of selecting ministers throughout the centuries.

Time would fail to tell of Ambrose, and the voice of a child calling, "Ambrose for Bishop"; of Augustine turning from sin and debauchery under the guidance of Monica and Ambrose; of Luther, Calvin, Zwingli, and

Knox striding forth at the call of God to lead the Reformation; of the Wesleys and Whitefield; and of Spurgeon, Maclaren, Jowett, Truett, Maier, Chappell, and Graham. An indisputable fact of Christian history is that God calls out men for each hour and each need.

c. *The Personal Witness*

Mystery thrusts itself upon each confrontation between God and man. Neither the one called by Jehovah nor those who observe his response can fully penetrate the divine will, though all can know that God has spoken. When God does call a man to minister for him, the minister's life and conduct give witness concerning a new center of devotion.

Thousands of men have experienced the same divine compulsion as did the prophets, apostles, and religious giants and geniuses of the ages. They have heard God speak as did Isaiah, "Whom shall I send, and who will go for us?" and they have answered as did he, "Here am I, send me." Most likely the fact that one reads these words will be evidence that he has an inner certainty concerning his commission to serve God as "one under divine orders."

2. SERMON PREPARATION DEMANDS A VALID IDEA TO PREACH

a. *The Point of Beginning*

God revealed himself in sacrificial self-disclosure to man, chose selected men to give witness to this revelational self-disclosure, and inspired them to record their witness. Thus we "got our Bible," and thus we have delegated authoritative content for preaching.

The logical starting point, therefore, for a sermon is the Bible, since the Bible is the only authentic source of divine revelation. The recognition of this fact developed early in Christian history as the Bible established itself as the source and supply for sermonic materials. By the use of the word text, a term borrowed from the production of textiles during the second and third centuries A.D., ministers declared that the Bible was the fabric of the sermon. Texts comes from textus, fabric, which came from *textere,* to weave. The initial meaning of text was that Scripture served as the component foundational element in sermons and that the preacher supplied explanation, argument, illustration, and application. In spite of contemporary carelessness concerning this concept of text, its basic meaning still obtains.

The Bible, however, is not the only starting place for sermons. Because ministers differ in personality traits, in professional training, and private judgments, some men find the original sermon idea in non-Scriptural sources. There are four broad non-Scriptural areas from which sermon ideas may emerge: (1) from the needs of the congregation; (2) from a flash of inspiration; (3) from the preacher's personal experience; and (4) from a planned program of preaching. These are usually non-Biblical in nature, although not absolutely so. At times any or all of the four may be united with a Scripture text.

If the minister is to understand congregational needs, he must grasp the essential meaning of homiletic purpose or homiletic objective. The word "objective" means goal, purpose, or desire on which one sets his heart. In scope three divisions of the word "objective" stand out. First, the total objective, or the ultimate or comprehensive goal, identifies the total desire a minister has for his ministry and for his people. The purpose of Jesus was that men might have life and this purpose of Jesus best serves as a minister's total purpose. Secondly, the major objectives, which represent six broad areas for helping people obtain life eternal and life abundant. These are: (1) the evangelistic, which seeks the salvation of unregenerate men; (2) the doctrinal, which seeks the instruction of Christians; (3) the ethical, which seeks Christian conduct from God's children in all relationships of life; (4) the consecrative, which seeks the Christian stewardship of all a man is and has; (5) the supportive, which seeks strength, grace, and comfort for troubled Christians; and (6) the devotional, which seeks for Christians to love, adore, and worship God. The first major objective is reached when people enter the Kingdom of God, and the last five when they grow in all areas of Christian nature. Thirdly, the specific objective, which represents the specific desire the minister has for one sermon on one occasion for one congregation. Thus, there are three dimensions to sermon purpose: total, major, specific. They represent progress from general to particular, and afford an adequate methodology for understanding and ministering to the basic spiritual needs of the people.

A second alternate starting place for a sermon is a "flash of inspiration." These almost indefinable flashes may take multiple forms and may occur any time or place. The minister with careful homiletic habits recognizes such flashes, identifies them as to nature, and makes a note of them immediately. Sermon ideas to a preacher are like gold nuggets or diamonds to a miner. One does not carelessly leave gold nuggets or diamonds lying around unclaimed.

A third alternate point of departure for a sermon is the preacher's personal experiences. The minister may locate and utilize effective sermon ideas by examining his personal needs, by carefully observing people as he has contact with them, by taking notes on sermons and speeches by others, by reading with alertness, and by noting his personal experiences on vacation, at play, and while engaged in non-ministerial duties.

The fourth alternate point of departure for a sermon idea is a planned program of preaching. The increasingly heavy responsibilities of the modern ministry force more and more ministers to plan their preaching program around some systematic chronological, Biblical, or topical structure. The minister may plan a program of preaching to cover one, three, six, twelve or more months. He may plan a preaching course to cover great Bible books or interesting topics systematically.

Into the plan should go texts, references to special days and programs, anotation of major objectives, illustrations of all types, and structural ideas in varying degrees of completeness. All these may be filed by individual folders, placed on note paper and attached to a sermon clip board, recorded in a preaching plan book, or tossed into "a sermon seed barrel." It makes little difference as to the nature of the mechanics of the preaching plan as long as it succeeds in producing usable messages. The preaching plan will succeed if the preacher plans carefully, deposits sermon seeds systematically, cultivates constantly, and draws out regularly.

b. *The Task of Correlation*

The sermon idea and Scripture must be matched. If the sermon idea starts with a Scripture passage, correlation between sermon idea and Scripture is immediate and complete. If, however, the sermon idea starts in one of the four alternate places of beginning, the minister must secure a Scripture passage which is correlate with his alternate starting idea. There must be no exception to this principle. To violate this high Biblical standard is to risk the preparation and delivery of shallow humanistic sermons in contrast to sermons filled with revelation content.

In selecting and using Scripture for the sermon, the minister must make several decisions concerning that Scripture. He must decide which one or more sermonic uses to make of Scripture, such as text, context, illustration, and support. The first three constitute the best sermonic structural uses for Biblical passages. He must decide what size or length text to utilize in his sermon. The minister may use Scripture in the following lengths for his sermonic text and/or context: (1) the entire Bible; (2) the Old Testament; (3) the New Testament; (4) the great blocks of Scripture as Law, History, Prophets, or Gospels; (5) the great books of the Bible as Mark, Amos, or Jonah; (6) the major sections of a book as Matthew 5-7; (7) choice chapters as Luke 15 and John 3; (8) pleasing paragraphs as Luke 24:1-12 and Luke 10:25-37; (9) striking sentences as Psalm 32:1 and Psalm 34:1; (10) vivid verses as Amos 5:24 and Hosea 11:1; and (11) Biblical atoms as Luke 24:6, "He is . . . risen." He must decide on the composition of his text in three additional choices: a text from one location (the one passage sermon); a text from numerous locations (the multiple passage or multiple Scripture sermon); and a text from a Biblical concept or theme (the thematic Biblical sermon). Normally, the minister can study, organize, and preach the one passage sermon with more skill than the other two. Moreover, more hermeneutical and theological perils await the preacher in the multiple Scripture and thematic Biblical sermon than in the one passage sermon. However, with careful study and precise homiletical procedures the multiple Scripture and thematic Biblical methods may be used with profit.

And, by reason of the richness of Scripture, he must decide how to use the text following interpretation. This points forward to the next step in sermon preparation, but needs to be clarified here with the other decisions of this type. Three broad choices await the minister after he studies his text and determines the central idea or central meaning of his passage. The preacher may use it in one of three ways: he may use all of the central idea or meaning of his text; he may use only a portion of the central idea due to its richness in details and suggestions; or he may use a minor or secondary idea of the text. All three are valid and Biblical. The first suggestion normally is best, however.

3. SERMON PREPARATION STANDS ON PROPERLY INTERPRETED SCRIPTURE

a. *Principles of Interpretation*

Two fundamental principles of interpretation confront the minister when he turns to the task of discovering the meaning of the text. These two basic principles emerge from the divine and human nature of Scripture. In order to understand all or any of the Bible one must make full note of God as the giver of revelation and man as the recipient and recorder of revelation. To ignore either in the task of interpretation presents a one-sided view of the Bible.

b. *Factors of Interpretation*

A careful investigation of a text demands that at least nine facets of the Scripture be investigated. The minister seeks to discover as much data as possible concerning the following items relating to his text: (1) the historical setting and background; (2) the grammatical structure; (3) the lexical meaning of all key words; (4) the syntactical items for consideration; (5) Scriptural or cross-references to check; (6) homiletical or practical suggestions; (7) the mood or emotional coloration of the text; (8) the sympathetic or spiritual factor, and (9) the theological meaning of the text.

c. *Sequence of Interpretation*

By following a practical order of interpretation, such as the following, the minister can determine the meaning of his text. (1) The minister should read his text many times in a favorite version of the Bible, as well as in several other versions. (2) If possible the preacher should read his text in the original language. However if he cannot read Hebrew, Aramaic, or Greek, he should not despair of knowing the true meaning of his text. He can use the best Bible translations available plus scholarly technical works written in English about the Bible and in this way determine the true meaning of his text. (3) He should prepare his own tentative interpretation after reading multiple translations by writing down a summary statement concerning each verse in the text, and a one sentence summary statement concerning the meaning of the central idea of the entire text. (4) He should turn to the best technical books available and begin the search for all needed data. At this stage of interpretation, the minister will begin his search for the answers to the nine facets or factors of interpretation listed above. (5) He should read popular works, and available devotional and sermonic literature on the text. (6) On the basis of careful personal and technical study, he should state in precise terms the central idea of his text. This central idea is the historical thesis and will guide all remaining sermon preparation. (7) The minister should next translate the historical thesis into a contemporary thesis or proposition for his sermon. This contemporary affirmation is a present tense summary sentence setting forth the meaning of the text for a modern audience. This contemporary thesis should move in a straight line from the historical thesis. When this is done, direct or pure Biblical preaching becomes an exciting possibility. (8) Finally, the preacher should state the purpose which this text will best accomplish. Purpose or objective, as indicated previously, consists of the total, major, and specific aspects. At this stage, the minister will discover which major purpose his text covers, and should then write out a one sentence statement of desire for this particular sermon. This one sentence statement of desire is the specific objective.

4. SERMON PREPARATION ENRICHES ITSELF WITH CREATIVE RESEARCH

a. *Developing a Systematic Study Habit*

One tragedy of the modern ministry is that ministers in large numbers have all but stopped studying. Samuel W. Blizzard, in his now well-known studies of more than seven hundred modern ministers, discovered that these men averaged only thirty-eight and one-half minutes a day in study. No man, no matter how brilliant or how well-trained, can prepare and preach effective and appealing messages on a poverty diet of less than forty minutes of study per day. If the the minister would prepare and preach with power, he must return to his study, lock the door, and wrestle with great books which will nourish his mind and enrich his sermons.

b. *Utilizing the Fruits of Study*

From all possible sources the preacher can draw rich illustrative material for his sermons. Basic study for sermons, it is true, centers in Scripture, but one must never neglect the reading of theological, ethical, historical, psychological, and practical literature. Moreover, the careful student will read the daily newspaper, current news magazines, current fiction, and literature, and whatever appeals to him. All of these provide rich data for enriching the sermon under construction.

c. *Filing Results of Creative Study*

One will not complete his task of studying and using creative materials until he prepares some satisfactory method of filing those materials. If it is true, as is often claimed, that most students of all ages lose about ninety per cent of the data which passes through their minds, it becomes important to devise or to secure some method of retaining the best of creative research. The minister may simply develop his own personal file system. This may be done easily by setting up folders with topical headings, or by setting up folders divided according to the various books of the Bible, or by setting up folders divided and subdivided by the major objectives of preaching. Ready made filing systems are also available: (1) *Baker's Textual and Topical Filing System* by Neal Punt (Grand Rapids: Baker Book House, 1960); (2) *The Efficiency Filing System* by L. R. Elliott (Nashville: Broadman Press, 1959); (3) The Eureka Filing System (available from Carl Potter, Fort Worth, Texas); (4) the Memory-o-matic filing system (available through the Mount Vernon Foundation, Mt. Rainier, Maryland); and (5) the Rossin-Dewey system (Minneapolis: Donald F. Rossin Co., Inc., 1961).

5. SERMON PREPARATION INVOLVES PURPOSEFUL MATURITY

a. *Nature of Sermon Maturity*

Sermon maturity is the process of utilizing both quantity and quality chronological, mental, and spiritual factors in the preparation of sermons. Sermon maturity involves taking time for the message to grow and develop. It uses a number of mental and spiritual devices in the process of this creative use of time.

b. *Justification for Sermon Maturity*

The human mind recoils in the face of hasty judgments, immature thoughts, and premature conclusions. The justification for sermon maturity is that the minister may enter the pulpit with more assurance in personal convictions, more accuracy in Biblical interpretation, more fully developed and accurate theological concepts, and more pertinent application for the people. In effect, the justification for mature sermons is that the minister will be better prepared, the message will be more relevant, and the people will be better strengthened with strong spiritual food.

c. *Procedures for Sermon Maturity*

Five procedures for securing sermon maturity are available: (1) The minister may make a creative use of time during sermon preparation. A creative use of time requires adequate time between the sermon origin and the completion of the message; taking care to think intently about the message; taking care to examine the message over and over; and taking time to make notes about the sermon as they flood into the mind during the days or weeks of preparation. (2) The minister may make a creative use of his subconscious mental resources. Students of the human mind are generally agreed that it has an active and inactive state or a conscious and subconscious state. Into the subconscious state have passed all the meaningful experiences of life. By cultivating the power of concentration and recall one may pull out of the subconscious treasures for use in preaching. (3) The preacher may mature his message through divine leadership as he meditates, reads the

Bible, prays, and waits on the Lord. (4) The minister may mature his message by engaging in stimulating dialogue with a friend. In dialogue one may test and experiment with ideas and discover which ones are mature and which ones are hastily formed. (5) The preacher may mature his message by careful study. By reading strong provocative books one may create a dialogue with Fosdick, Barth, Thielicke and other theologians and preachers. Maturity achieved by one or more of the five procedures will assist in enriching the message.

6. SERMON PREPARATION ORGANIZES THE MESSAGE THROUGH CREATIVE RHETORICAL PROCEDURES

a. *By Using Correct Principles of Outlining*

A sermon body marked out by clear and definite lines or divisions is to be preferred to one which "rambles" all over the Biblical, theological, and homiletical planet. In outlining the sermon body, fourteen basic principles should be used as needed: (1) For the major points of the message, use Roman numerals. (2) For the primary subpoints, use Arabic numbers and indent. However, as an alternate method some preachers prefer A, B, C, and D for these subpoints. (3) Unless the minister is forced by his sermonic material to do so, he should use only two degrees of steps for sermon structure (as major divisions and subpoints: I. 1, 2, 3, 4 and II. 1, 2, 3, 4). As many Roman and Arabic points as needed may be used but one should seldom divide his Arabic points. (4) If, however, sub-subpoints become necessary, divide the Arabic points into parenthetical divisions [(1) and (2)] and indent. (5) As a rule sermon divisions (both major and subpoints) should be stated in sentence or phrase form rather than a key word form. (6) Since nothing can be divided into less than two parts, each point which is divided must have two or more parts. (7) Care should be taken to insure that a subtopic actually divides the point of which it is a division. (8) Illustrations should not be considered as divisions in an outline. (9) Scripture references used as illustrations or support for points should not be given numbers in the outline. (10) The functional elements of preaching – explanation, argument, illustration, and application – should not be assigned numbers in the outline. (11) The structural parts of the sermon – the introduction, sermon body, conclusion, and invitation – are not assigned numbers in the outline. (12) No point of any rank – major point, subpoint, sub-subpoint – should contain more than one idea. (13) If verb tense is used in the title or in any division, each point below the title and point should be consistent with the tense used. (14) If a point or title names a person, place, or object, then each point which follows should treat the same person, place, or object.

b. *By Using Correct Principles of Development*

Since an outline cannot be a complete message if left undeveloped, the outline must be "clothed with content." The method of adding content to an outline is commonly called "functional development." Functional development consists of four elements: explanation, argument, illustration, and application.

Explanation means to make plain, to make clear, to interpret data, and to tell the true meaning of something. Contrary to common assumptions, explanation presents a wide variety of ways for making something clear and plain. Explanation uses one or more of the following eleven methods: (1) the presentation of text and its background; (2) the presentation of context and its relationship to the text; (3) the presentation of the background of the context; (4) the setting out of cross-references which aid the text; (5) the presentation of the results or "fruits" of technical exegesis; (6) the narration or recitation of the material in the Scripture passage; (7) the description of one or more items relating to the text (as a rule description is considered a subdivision of narration); (8) the setting out of the natural parts or divisions of the text; (9) the concise use of definition of key words of text, central idea of the text, affirmation, purpose, or title as needed; (10) the judicious use of illustration; and (11) the comparison and contrast of the item under consideration.

Argument means reason and discussion in a homiletical context. Argument may be used to mean controversy and dispute but is not considered here with such meaning.

Argument is used in this discussion to mean to reason and to discuss.

There are three major forms of argument available to the preacher. First, there is argument by testimony. At all times, in using argument by testimony, care must be taken concerning the person quoted and the nature of his testimony. The person must be a reliable individual who should possess data needed. The data cited should be identified as to whether it is fact, opinion, hypothesis, or illustration. An audience will accept any of the four if they are clearly distinguished. Secondly, argument by reasoning makes use of argument *a priori* which reasons forward from cause to effect or result; argument *a posteriori* which reasons from results or effects back to cause; argument *a fortiori* which reasons from weaker examples to stronger ones; argument by the use of dilemma which presents two choices and explains that either one chosen is evil and wrong; argument *ex concesso* which reasons from what has been conceded; argument *reductio ad absurdum* which argues by reducing the issue to an absurd proposition; and argument *ad hominem* which argues by appealing to the personal feelings of the hearers. Thirdly, argument by refutation makes primary use of *reductio ad absurdum* and *ad hominem*. Good taste and courtesy should be used in argument by refutation. All processes for drawing conclusions, induction, deduction, and analogy, may be used to bring conclusions to the various forms of argument. All of these lead to proper conclusions when managed accurately.

Illustration means to add luster or light to something for purposes of clarity. Types of illustrations vary widely and are quite numerous: (1) expressive and attractive words; (2) figurative language (figures of speech); (3) anecdotes and stories; (4) narration and history; (5) poetry; (6) dialogue; (7) object lessons; (8) testimony; (9) personal experiences; (10) and statistics. Moreover, sources for illustration are inexhaustible: (1) Scripture; (2) literature; (3) pastoral work and experience; (4) history; (5) science; (6) sports and games; (7) the congregation; (8) the arts; (9) the field of politics and government; and (10) visual aids of all types.

Application means to relate the sermon content so that the audience sees that it is appropriate, fitting, and suitable for them. Application shows the audience how they can use the truth of the sermon. Application may be best used when the individual is kept in focus. Application should show why the individual should listen and respond to the message, and indicate how the individual may receive the truth of the sermon and live by it. Further, application may be best made when the minister calls for immediate commitment. It is appropriate to ask for personal involvement.

These four functional elements — explanation, argument, illustration, application — may be used in five flexible ways. First, they may be used in a blended fashion as two, three, or four of them are used in single paragraphs for the development of the message. The blended use of the functional elements requires a high degree of grammatical and rhetorical skill. Secondly, they may be used singly to build one or more paragraphs to fill out and develop major points. Thirdly, they may be used singly to build one or more paragraphs as needed for the development of Arabic or subpoints. Fourthly, they may be used to build as many paragraphs as needed to develop the title. In this form, known also as the jewel sermon, there will be no sermon points but there will be various paragraphs of explanation, argument, illustration, and application. Fifthly, they may be used in combination with the outlining procedure. The following sketch shows how able preachers often use the functional elements in combination with subpoints:

Introduction:

Text, title, thesis, and purpose used in any order in the introduction.

Sermon Body:

I. First major point: a division of the title.
   1. a division of I.
   2. a division of I.

II. Second major point: a division of the title.
   Paragraph(s) of explanation as needed
   Paragraph(s) of argument as needed
   Paragraph(s) of illustration as needed

Paragraph(s) of application as needed

Conclusion:

The emphasis in the conclusion falls on the specific objective or purpose for the sermon.

This fifth form for using the functional elements requires a brief explanation. Rhetorical consistency, a valid principle, seems to be violated by the last illustration above. However, some texts seem to be best treated as described here. In such cases, the nature of Scripture takes precedence over having exact balance in the use of major and minor points. The exception is valid.

c. *By Using Correct Procedures of Construction*

At this point in sermon preparation, four basic sermon items have already been secured and prepared for use: (1) the text and context; (2) the central idea of the text through proper Biblical study; (3) the thesis through the reformation of the historical thesis into a contemporary affirmation; and (4) a statement of the major objective and specific objective. In addition to these four foundational items, five other items remain to be prepared: the title, sermon body, conclusion, introduction, and invitation. These are listed in the order of preparation.

The title or the name of the sermon is used with the same meaning as the word "topic." The word "subject" is reserved for a general sermon idea, as "love," which is broader than the specific title or topic. The sermon title should possess qualities which show it to be appealing, contemporary, fresh, and divisible. In order for a title to be divisible, the title will need a key word or phrase which points out the line of direction for the sermon. This key word or phrase may be placed in a title by a question form of the title, an imperative form of the title, or an assertive form of the title. Also, the key word or phrase may be placed in a sermon title through the use of an emphatic word and a modifying word. Examples of these five types of titles follow with the key word or phrase italicized:

1. *Why* Do Men Worship God?
2. *Build* Your Life on Christian Principles
3. *Jesus Is* God's Only Son
4. The *Supremacy* of Christ
5. The *Second* Mile.

Sermon body means the primary section or basic portion of the sermon which fills out, develops, and completes the original idea and text. The sermon body may be completed by two broad methods: the informal form of the homily, or the formal method of rhetorical outline and development. The homily is a simple and informal sermon form. In the earliest days of preaching, the minister usually talked simply and informally about God. No introduction, sermon body, or conclusion were in evidence. Rather, the prophet, apostle, and early preacher simply talked or preached by explaining, illustrating, arguing, and applying. Later, after Christianity moved out of the Bible lands and met the pagan world, sermon form picked up the procedure of occasionally having an introduction, sermon body, and conclusion. Even though form increased slightly, the sermon body still remained simple, free, and informal. Usually the homily body was a free running commentary on the text. Variations of these two homily forms have existed from the early Christian centuries until this day. When used with rich Biblical materials, creative illustrations, and relevant applications both are useful and valid. The rhetorical sermon uses the best elements of form in each generation. The rhetorical sermon utilizes an introduction, body, and conclusion, and is usually outlined and developed carefully.

The conclusion of a sermon is the normal target area for the message. By every possible means the specific objective should be stressed as the minister urges the hearers to make personal decisions for the Lord. Five types of sermon conclusions may be identified in sermonic literature: (1) The application type stresses personal application. In sermons which have used a large amount of historical data, application tends to be slighted. The conclusion affords a final opportunity to relate the truth of the message to the congregation. In those messages which have utilized application throughout, the preacher will still use the conclusion as the final opportunity for applying the truth to the people. (2) The illustration type conclusion uses illustration to focus light on the specific purpose of the sermon. (3) The poetic type conclusion, in reality a form of the illustration type, uses religious poetry, hymns, and classics of poetry in order to focus attention on the basic purpose of the message. (4) The summary type conclusion restates or re-emphasizes the text, central idea of the text, thesis, specific objective, title, or body points. When used routinely, the summary type becomes wooden and dull. When used with thoughtfulness, however, this type may be used appealingly. (5) The direct appeal or exhortation type uses direct appeals for the hearers to respond to and act on the basis of the truth of the message.

The introduction for the sermon is best prepared following the original idea and text, central idea of the text, thesis, purpose, title, body, and conclusion. The reason for this order is simple. The introduction introduces or presents the entire sermon and the seven items listed above constitute the whole sermon with the exception of the introduction and the invitation.

In an introduction, one may usually find a presentation of the text, the central idea of the text, and a statement of the thesis. Some ministers also present the specific objective. The introduction has two key points: the opening sentences, and the bridge or transition sentence or sentences to the sermon body. Great care should be taken with the opening and transition sentences. The text, central idea of the text, thesis, and specific objective – one or more – may be used for the opening of the introduction or for the transition to the sermon body. They may also be used at any point in the introduction.

The basic forms of the introduction are ten in number: (1) the textual type which uses the text, context, and relationship and background of either or both as desired; (2) the thesis and purpose type; (3) the title or topical type; (4) the life situation approach; (5) the object lesson type; (6) the illustration beginning; (7) the striking quotation approach; (8) the special occasion beginning; (9) the question type; and (10) the preview type. The first three should normally be used in each introduction and the other seven may be used as desired.

The invitation for the sermon is the public invitation by the preacher for the people to make individual responses to God's promptings. The invitation should be carefully prepared and simply and prayerfully presented. No pressure of any kind from minister or people should be used. The Lord should supply all the pressure and power needed.

d. *By Using Correct Methods of Sermon Classification*

See article on "The Classification of Sermons."

In identifying a sermon as to form, the preacher may classify it as homily or rhetorical depending upon body development.

7. SERMON PREPARATION SECURES EFFECTIVE STYLE

See article on "Sermonic Style In Contemporary Terms."

8. SERMON PREPARATION CULMINATES IN DELIVERY

See article on "Pulpit Speech and Rhetoric."

BIBLIOGRAPHY

Blackwood, Andrew W., *The Preparation of Sermons.* New York: Abingdon-Cokesbury Press, 1948.

Broadus, John A., *On The Preparation and Delivery of Sermons.* Revised edition by Jesse B. Weatherspoon. New York: Harper & Bros., 1944.

Brown, H. C., Jr., *A Quest for Authentic Biblical Sermons.* New York: Harper and Row, Publishers, 1966.

Brown, H. C., Jr., H. Gordon Clinard and Jesse J. Northcutt, *Steps to the Sermon.* Nashville: Broadman Press, 1963.

Brown, H. C., Jr., *Southern Baptist Preaching.* Nashville: Broadman Press, 1959.

Bryan, Dawson C., *The Art of Illustrating Sermons.* Nashville: Abingdon-Cokesbury Press, 1938.

Davis, H. Grady, *Design for Preaching.* Philadelphia: Muhlenberg Press, 1958.

Dodd, C. H., *The Apostolic Preaching and Its Development.* New York: Willett, Clark & Co., 1937.

Faw, Chalmer E., *A Guide to Biblical Preaching.* Nashville: Broadman Press, 1962.

Garrison, Webb B., *The Preacher and His Audience.* Westwood, N. J.: Fleming H. Revell Co., 1954.

Jones, Ilion T., *Principles and Practicel of Preaching.* New York: Abingdon Press, 1956.

Luccock, Halford E., *In the Minister's Workshop.* New York: Abingdon-Cokesbury Press, 1944.

Miller, Donald G., *Fire in Thy Mouth.* New York: Abingdon Press, 1954.

Mounce, Robert H., *The Essential Nature of New Testament Preaching.* Grand Rapids: Wm. B. Eerdmans Publishing Co., 1960.

Whitesell, Faris D., *Power in Expository Preaching.* Westwood, N. J.: Fleming H. Revell Co., 1963.

The Study of Sermons

This article falls into the general area of preparation for preaching and will answer the question whether the reading and study of other men's sermons has any homiletical value.

The first question to be faced, is whether it ought to be done at all. Some preachers feel no need of it, and say that they rarely or never read other sermons. However, there is real value for the preacher in the reading and study of sermons. Anyone who wants to improve his own preaching can profit by reading widely in sermonic literature. There is even greater value in a careful analytical study of sermons.

1. WRONG REASONS

There are wrong reasons for reading and studying other men's sermons, and also wrong ways of doing it. The most obvious is preaching other men's sermons. This becomes literary plagiarism when such sermons are published, and there have been instances when this has caused considerable embarrassment to the publisher and to the author. Apart from the ethical question involved, it must be stated that the practice is unwise because no man will ever become a good preacher if he consistently uses another man's outline. Preaching is the proclamation of the Word of God. The given content of preaching is the revealed Word of God, but the freshness and penetration of the message lies in the preacher's skill in bringing that Word to bear on a contemporary situation and on the lives of the people. Preaching is a skill in communication. The message is given but it is the preacher's personal responsibility to make the message meaningful and relevant. For this reason every ordained minister of the Word of God should prepare his own sermons.

Another wrong reason for reading and studying sermons is only to look for illustrations and quotations. This is often done. In fact, the popularity for preachers of the publication of many contemporary sermons lies in the number of usable illustrations and quotations they contain. This caution does not mean that we ought never to use illustrations or quotations found in published sermons, but there is a wide difference between reading a sermon for the impact it makes on the mind, and flipping through a book of sermons to collect quotations from literature or illustrations. It is also poor homiletical procedure to select a text, read four or five sermons on that text, and take a little from each to make up an outline. This method of preparation gives the congregation a diet of lukewarm homiletical hash.

The best way to avoid these homiletical pitfalls is in the observance of two simple rules. First, never borrow extensively from another sermon without acknowledging it. And, secondly, never read a sermon on the text on which you are preaching. The only exception to the rule of not reading sermons on the text on which you are working is the expository preachers, particularly the Reformers and the Puritans, whose sermons often read like commentaries on the Biblical passage.

Each preacher must strive for originality and creativity. While Phillips Brooks' famous definition of preaching as "truth through personality" is inadequate, it contains an element of truth. God's Word is communicated through men who speak it. Originality in sermon preparation comes from hard work with the text, the lexicons, the critical and exegetical commentaries, the theological word books, and the various English translations available now in such rich abundance.

There are numerous advantages in making one's own outline instead of taking it in full or in part from other sermons. One is that as time goes on it makes preaching easier. For young preachers it will be harder at first and the result will not always be satisfactory. But constant practice will measurably increase proficiency, and as the years go on preaching will become easier instead of more difficult. The man who starts out preaching other men's sermons, or borrowing extensively from them, soon finds himself on a homiletical treadmill from which he cannot get off.

2. VALID REASONS

There are, however, valid reasons for the study of sermons, and profitable ways of doing it. A preliminary remark is in order here. The preacher should read not only contemporary sermons, but sermons from all the great ages of preaching. We all suffer today from what C. S. Lewis calls chronological snobbery, and there are preachers who feel that no sermons preached before the twentieth century could have any possible value for the man who must preach in this scientific age. Every sermon, of course, must be judged by the age in which it is preached; every sermon will to some extent show the marks of the age. But if we believe in revelation the validity of preaching is established and the necessity of studying how others have communicated this everlasting gospel in other ages becomes apparent.

The first reason for reading and studying sermons from all periods of time is the preacher's own devotional life, for his own upbuilding in the faith. No man can constantly put out without taking in. The busy pastor seldom has time to hear another man preach. He will, of course, read the Bible faithfully and prayerfully. He will also read the great devotional classics, but there is also much spiritual value in reading the sermons of the great preachers of the ages. We may be reminded how rich the heritage of sermonic devotional literature is if we go back only to the Reformation where we have Luther, Calvin, Bullinger and Knox; or the Puritan age where we have Baxter, Bunyan, Sibbes, Boston, Goodwin, and Owen. And then we have Wesley, Whitefield, and Edwards from the Evangelical Revival; F. W. Robertson, Chalmers, Spurgeon, Maclaren, Liddon, and Newman from the nineteenth century; Jowett, Macartney, Campbell Morgan, F. B. Meyer in the early part of this century; and Martin Lloyd-Jones in our own day. This list is not meant to be exhaustive, for anyone who has read widely in the field of preaching will think of many more.

A second reason for the reading and study of other men's sermons may be called an evangelistic reason. Preaching is essentially the communication of the gospel, so ministers can be greatly benefited by the study of the preaching of other men who were called to do this in another age, and who succeeded in doing it. Alexander Whyte in his classic *Thirteen Appreciations* shows what he owes to other preachers, and he himself is an example of how to study sermons. Whyte once made a list of all the texts Wesley preached on, both as they were given in his published sermons and recorded in his *Journal,* in order that he might discover the secret and power of the great evangelist of the eighteenth century.

Helmut Thielicke's *Encounter with Spurgeon* is a warm tribute from one of the most brilliant preachers of our day to what he learned from the gifted preacher of the nineteenth century. Thielicke says, "It would be well for a time like ours to learn from this man. For our preaching is, to be sure, largely correct, exegetically 'legitimate,' workmanlike and tidy; but it is also remarkably dead and lacking in infectious power." After this great German preacher has recognized the value of theoretical homiletics he continues, "For, since preaching encompasses a tremendously broad complex of procedures – ranging from prayer for the miracle of the Spirit through study of the text itself and the structuring of a sermon outline to the workmanlike mastery of effective speech – real standards can be found only in living examples. . . . One must therefore read sermons like Spurgeon's in order to learn what a sermon can be and what it can give." This highly educated university professor and Lutheran theologian continues for forty-four pages to tell us what the self-educated nineteenth century Baptist preacher had done for him.

If the purpose of reading sermons is to improve our own communication of the gospel, then we must read them with questions like these in mind: Does this sermon preach the historical gospel of Jesus Christ? If the preacher is attempting to communicate this message, how does he do it? Does he reason? Does he use analogies? Does he merely repeat the words of the text, or related texts? In other words, read and study the sermon to discover how in another age a man was attempting to communicate the historic gospel to the people of his day. A good exercise here is to compare Wesley and Butler. Both were from the eighteenth century. Wesley was the evangelist; Butler was the apologist for the faith. Read Butler's famous *Analogy*, or sections of it, then read Wesley's sermon on *The Marks of the New Birth*. And see what conclusions you can draw from this study in the comparative value of apologetics and evangelistic preaching in the communication of the gospel. Another exercise in such study of the communication of the gospel is Phillips Brooks' sermon, *The Light of the World*. Analyse this sermon from one point of view – was Brooks preaching the historical gospel of Jesus Christ in that sermon, or was he preaching the nineteenth century doctrine of progress. Studies like these, made in the critical reading of sermons, ought to sharpen our ability to communicate the gospel today.

A third reason for the study of sermons is for the homiletical pattern or structure of the sermon. Must a sermon always have three points? Must the division be stated, and if so how? How important is structure, and how do you achieve it? These are areas in the art of preaching where we can learn much from other preachers. Harry Emerson Fosdick was a skilled homiletician, and it will repay any person to study his sermons for their excellent structure. This kind of study of the sermon will eventually bring the preacher to F. W. Robertson of the nineteenth century who was a two point preacher, and to Thomas Chalmers, the gifted Scotch preacher of the nineteenth century, who was a one point preacher. His sermon, "The Expulsive Power of a New Affection," is a classic example of a one point sermon.

This study of the sermon for homiletical pattern will also take us back to the period of the Reformation, before the time when our traditional three point alliterative outline was used at all. The basic pattern of preaching from the second century through the Reformation was the homily, though eventually it deteriorated into a tedious commentary on the text. This pattern in the hands of Chrysostom, Augustine, Calvin, and Luther was a powerful way of presenting the message of the Bible. It had at least one advantage. It covered Scripture. For a classic example of a homily, see Calvin's eighteenth sermon on Job as outlined by T. H. L. Parker in *The Oracles of God*.

3. SERMON ANALYSIS

Sermons should also be studied analytically. Andrew Blackwood in his preface to *The Protestant Pulpit* recommends sermon analysis as one of the best ways of studying homiletics. Martin Lloyd-Jones, in the preface to his two volumes of sermons on the Sermon on the Mount, says, "I am constantly being asked to give lectures on expository preaching. I rarely accede to such requests believing that the best way of doing this is to give examples of such preaching in actual practice." The following outline in question form can be used as a guide for scientific sermon analysis.

a. The title

What does the title do? Does it merely identify the sermon? Does it state the theme of the sermon? Does it arouse interest in the subject? Is it sensational or dignified? Is it an accurate representation of the content of the sermon, or is it misleading?

b. The text

Is it a familiar passage of Scripture or an obscure verse? Is it the basis for an important Biblical truth? Is it a complete statement of a truth or a fragment? Does it consist of one verse or a more extended passage?

c. The treatment of the text

Is the treatment of the text sound exegetically? Is there any exegesis of the passage in which it occurs? Is it used as a point of departure, or a motto? Is it allegorized? Is it broken into fragments with each part handled separately? Do the divisions of the sermon express the whole truth contained in it?

d. The classification of the sermon

How is it to be classified according to form – topical, textual, expository, or biographical? How is it to be classified according to content – doctrinal, historical, ethical, or experimental?

e. The homiletical pattern of the sermon

What kind of an introduction is used – contextual, life situation, problem approach? What is the theme? Is it stated in one sentence? What are the main divisions and subdivisions? Are they all announced in advance, as they occur, or not at all? Is the conclusion hortatory, resumptive, or applicatory?

f. The application

How are the truths of the sermon applied to the hearer? What practical suggestions are offered as the means of performing the duty urged? What appeals are made to secure the desired response? Are there sections of application in the body of the sermon, or is the application only at the end of the sermon?

g. The style and content

Does the preacher quote much? What kind of material is quoted – prose, poetry, or hymns? Is the sermon in the language of the people? Are there difficult and technical terms?

h. The message

Does the sermon contain the essential message of the gospel? Is it Biblical in doctrine? Is it in keeping with the historic Christian faith?

The results of such an analysis can then be compared with one's own sermons and with textbooks on homiletics as a means toward becoming a more effective preacher.

BIBLIOGRAPHY

Dargan, E. C., *A History of Preaching.* Grand Rapids: Baker Book House, 1954.

Jones, Ilion T., *Principles and Practice of Preaching.* New York: Abingdon Press, 1946.

Macpherson, Ian, *The Burden of the Lord.* London: Epworth Press, 1955.

Parker, T. H. L., *The Oracles of God.* London: Lutterworth Press, 1947.

Spurgeon, C. H., *Lectures to My Students.* Grand Rapids: Zondervan Publishing House (new edition), 1954.

The Literature of Homiletics

This article and its companion article, "The Literature of Preaching," are designed primarily to provide tools for the pastor and the theological student. Lists of the best books in English are given in both articles and divided into two groups: those still in print, and those out of print.

These lists are intended to be helpful in locating books in libraries and in selecting books for the pastor's and seminary library.

Homiletics is properly defined as the art of preaching. Like all other arts the art of preaching is acquired partly by study, partly by observation, and partly by experience. The English statesman Benjamin Disraeli once said, "The more extensive a man's knowledge of what has been done, the greater will be his power of knowing what to do." This is as true in the field of preaching as in any other important field. Before one undertakes to practice the art of preaching, therefore, he should make a study of the principles and methods used by successful preachers in all the ages since the early Christian centuries. Fortunately the literature essential for such a study is available. Preachers and preachers-to-be can neglect this literature only at the risk of their effectiveness.

1. OVERALL SURVEY

A helpful introduction to the literature of Homiletics may be found in the *New Schaff – Herzog Encyclopedia of Religious Knowledge,* Vol. V, Funk and Wagnalls, 1911 (reprinted, Baker Book House, 1950). It also has an extensive bibliography through 1908.

2. TEXTBOOKS ON HOMILETICS

After reading widely in the history and literature of the ancient Greeks, someone remarked, "The Greeks stole all of our modern ideas." One main value of making a study of the literature of homiletics of past generations is the discovery that not much new can be said on the subject, that the principles of effectual preaching are not only antique but fairly constant. Basically they have remained the same throughout the centuries regardless of the variety of social conditions that prevailed in any particular period or place.

a. *In the Ancient Period*

Although preaching was commonly practiced in the Christian church from the very beginning, writings comparable to our modern textbooks on homiletics did not begin to appear until about the third century. Even then, these were not always separate or single treatises, but were frequently interspersed throughout the general writings of the various leaders of the times.

The writers on homiletics in the ancient period who are most often referred to by the historians are: (1) Origin. He was one of the first writers to deal with principles and problems of the preacher's art, though not formally. His chief emphasis was on the wisdom of Christians making use in their preaching of the non-Christian principles of rhetoric. For centuries thereafter he also exerted a wide influence on the interpretation of the Scriptures. (2) Gregory of Nazianzus. His *Flight to Pontus* has sections on the preacher's art. He was one of the earliest writers to warn preachers against the temptation to adopt the tricks of the professional orator. (3) John Chrysostom, whose *On the Priesthood,* dealt briefly with the form and content of sermons and outlined the preacher's task. (4) Saint Augustine. One writer says of his treatise, *On Christian Doctrine,* "This might well be required reading for every student in hermeneutics and homiletics." (5) Guibert de Nogent whose *A Treatise on the Method of Preparing a Sermon* is mentioned with praise. (6) Alain de Lille, whose *Summary of the Preaching Art* is spoken of as "the most important work on homiletical theory since Augustine."

The only one of the above works now available in English in a single volume is (L) Augustine, *On Christian Doctrine.* Bobbs-Merrill (n.d.) But (L) Augustine, *Enchridion* is available from two publishers: Allenson, 1950, and Regnery, 1961.

b. *In the Medieval Period*

The period from 600 to 1200 has been referred to as "the long night of preaching." During these centuries the treatises on the theory and practice of preaching are few and of little value for modern students. But a genuine renewal of preaching and of interest in it as an art began in the twelfth century. This renewal arose among the preaching orders, the Franciscans and the Dominicans. Their writings on homiletics were in the form of Manuals for use in training the members of the orders for their extensive preaching missions. The amount of this particular type of literature is considerable. Scholars declare that in many ways they are equal in value to modern textbooks on homiletics. One historian asserts that "modern homiletical procedures seem to have little, if anything, superior to these manuals" (Petry, Ray C., *No Uncertain Sound.* Westminster, 1948).

c. *In the Pre-Reformation Period*

One of the most interesting developments in the Pre-Reformation period was the widespead use of sermon illustrations. The three Christian preachers, whose works are most often mentioned in this connection, are: (1) Jacques de Vitry, who is described as "the master of sermon illustration" by Petry. (2) Humbert de Romans, whose work *On the Education of Preachers* is described by Petry; and (3) Nicole Brozon, an English Franciscan, who became noted in his own land for his fascinating use of illustrations. An interesting account of the work of these preachers is given in the introduction to Petry's book.

Some of the other preachers of this general period, who are regarded as significant for a study of homiletics, are (1) Thomas Aquinas, whose (*Pseudo*) *Tractate* gives a fair indication of the aspects of homiletics discussed in medieval sermonic writings. In the appendix to this document Aquinas explains in detail his famous "Preaching Tree," in which he likens the sermon to a tree with a trunk, main branches, smaller branches, etc. (2) Erasmus. The writings of Erasmus in which he expresses his ideas on preaching are *Enchiridion,* "Great Mercy of God," "Inquisitio de Fide," and "Colloquies." Of these *Enchiridion* is the only one available in a single volume in English (University of Indiana Press, Bloomington, Indiana. 1963). (3) John Wycliffe, who deals with preaching in a manner in his "On the Truth of Holy Scriptures," "Christian Mirror" and "The Priestly Mirror." (4) Savonarola, whose contribution is found mainly in his sermons; and (5) Hyperius (Andreas Gerhard of Ypes) often mentioned by the historians but with no emphasis on a particular treatise.

With the exception of Erasmus' *Enchiridion* none of the homiletical writings of these medieval leaders is available in English in single volumes.

d. *In the Early Reformation Period*

All of the early leaders of the Reformation — Luther, Calvin, Zwingli, Melancthon, and others — had many significant things to say about homiletics. But no work of these leaders on the subject is now available in single volumes for the average reader.

Although it is necessary to keep saying that few of the treatises on homiletics by the Christian leaders of the first twelve or fifteen centuries are available in English for ordinary readers, it must be emphasized that these documents *are* available to the scholars. These writings were originally in an ancient language that for long periods of time could be handled only by a limited number of scholars. In recent years, however, English translations of these and other ancient classics have appeared in print. These have been published in sets of books that can be found only in public or institutional libraries because they are too expensive for the budgets of the average pastor or theological student. Hence, anyone interested in reading translations of these ancient documents must have access to one of these sets.

The four outstanding sets of the classics now in English are: (1) *The Nicene and Post-Nicene Fathers,* originally published by the Christian Literature Publishing Co., New York, from 1886-1900, in two series of fourteen volumes each. More recently, the Wm. B. Erdmans Company of Grand Rapids published two sets of these writings: *A Select Library of Nicene and Post-Nicene Fathers of the Christian Church,* 1954; and *The Ante-Nicene Fathers,* 1956. (2) *The Library of Christian Classics,* Westminster, 1952. (3) *Great Books of the Western World,* Chicago: Encyclopedia Brittanica, 1952; and (4) *The Fathers of the Church,* New York: The Fathers of the Church, Inc. (Roman Catholic), different volumes having different dates of publication.

Fortunately a study of these ancient writings, adequate for the needs of the average preacher, is made in Ray C. Petry's *No Uncertain Sound* mentioned earlier. In fact, the writer is indebted to Petry for the information given in this article about a number of these writings. His book is primarily an anthology of sermons of Christian preachers from the third to the sixteenth centuries. But in a long introduction he summarizes these writings and explains their historical significance. This is an invaluable book for the average reader and also for the scholars, because much of the material is newly translated into English and made available for the first time. For anyone who wishes to make a further study of the writings, Petry gives an extensive bibliography in the appendix. Regretably, this important book is no longer in print.

It should also be said that important information about these ancient writers and their writings is given in all first class histories of the church and in the histories of preaching. For a list of the histories of preaching see the article, "Literature of Preaching" in this Dictionary.

e. *In the Post-Reformation and Modern Period*

Yngve Brilioth, the noted Swedish scholar, says that the homiletical literature since the time of the Reformation is "prodigious in dimension." But only within the last 150 years, more or less, have textbooks on homilitics, comparable to those we are so familiar with in our day, appeared in any large numbers. They have been published with an increasing rate in the last century by publishing houses representing the theological viewpoints of all Protestant bodies and by some Roman Catholic publishers.

These books are so numerous that it is neither desirable nor necessary for any one person to make a study of all of them in order to discover for himself the principles and practices of preaching now generally accepted as valid. There is a continuous repetition of material in these books from generation to generation. Very little *new* light of any great significance is thrown upon the subject by any one author. Though, to be fair to all writers, it must be said that each new book is worth studying and offers something helpful for the perceptive reader.

1. *Textbooks Proper*

The turnover in books in recent years has been so rapid that old books go out of print almost as rapidly as new ones come off the presses. This is true of textbooks on homiletics as well as of all other books. The span of life of these books is rarely longer than ten years. But even so, some of them can suitably be called "classics" in their field, can rightly be commended as worthwhile to each new generation of preachers, and as worthy of a place in their libraries, provided those out of print can be found in secondhand bookstores. A selected list of these books, in the order of their publication, follows.

a. *In Print*

Evans, William, *How to Prepare Sermons,* Chicago: Moody Press, 1913.
Reu, J. Michael, *Homiletics,* Chicago: Wartburg, 1924. (Reprinted by Baker Book House, 1967.)
Weatherspoon, J. B., *On the Preparation and Delivery of Sermons,* Harper, 1944. A revised and somewhat abbreviated edition of Broadus' famous book by the same title.
Blackwood, Andrew W., *The Preparation of Sermons.* Abingdon, 1948.
Luccock, Halford E., *In the Minister's Workshop.* Abingdon, 1944.
Pattison, T. H., *The Making of a Sermon* (Revised). Judson, 1946.
Liske, Thomas V., *Effective Preaching* (Roman Catholic). Macmillan, 1951.
Bowie, Walter Russell, *Preaching.* Abingdon, 1954.
Jones, Ilion T., *Principles and Practice of Preaching.* Abingdon, 1956.
Davis, Henry Grady, *Design for Preaching.* Muhlenberg, 1958. Widely commended especially for its instruction about the proper statement of the subject and the careful unfolding of the germ idea of the sermon.

b. *Out of Print*

Vinet, Alexander, *Homiletics.* New York: Ivison and Phinney, 1866. Still found in most theological libraries, and still worthy of careful study because he set the pattern for later Protestant understanding of preaching.
Phelps, Austin, *The Theory of Preaching.* Scribner's, 1894.
Hoppin, James, *Homiletics.* Funk and Wagnalls, 1883.
Fisk, W. F., *Manual of Preaching.* New York: A. C. Armstrong and Son, 1884.
Kern, John A., *The Ministry to the Congregation.* Nashville: Publishing House of the M.E. Church, South, 1897.
Broadus, John A., *Preparation and Delivery of Sermons.* New York: A. C. Armstrong and Son, 1901. Used since its first publication in practically all seminaries as a standard textbook. For this reason it has often been spoken of as "The Blackstone of Homiletics." Now available in revised form. See J. B. Weatherspoon's book in the "In Print" list above.
Hoyt, A. S., *The Work of Preaching.* Macmillan, 1905.
Johnson, Herrick, *The Ideal Ministry.* Revell, 1908.
Breed, David R., *Preparing to Preach.* Geo. H. Doran, 1911.
Burrell, David James, *The Sermon: Its Construction and Delivery.* Revell, 1913.
Bull, Paul B., *Preaching and Sermon Construction.* Macmillan, 1922.
Davis, Ozora S., *Principles of Preaching.* University of Chicago Press, 1924.
Newton, J. Fort, ed., *If I Had only One Sermon to Prepare.* Harper, 1952. A group of ministers explain their methods.
Patton, Carl S., *Preparation and Delivery of Sermons.* Chicago: Willett, Clark and Co., 1938.
Montgomery, R. Ames, *Preparing Preachers to Preach.* Zondervan, 1939.
Rhoades, Ezra, *Case Work in Preaching.* Revell, 1942.
Stevenson, Dwight E., *A Road-Map for Sermons* (Pamphlet). Lexington: The College of the Bible, 1950. Outstanding.
Sangster, W. E., *The Craft of Sermon Construction.* Westminster, 1951.
Jordan, G. Ray, *You Can Preach.* Revell, 1951.
MacLeod, Donald, ed., *Here Is My Method.* (Another group of ministers explain their methods) Revell, 1952.

2. *Textbooks on Special Aspects of Homiletics*

Learning the art of preaching involves disciplines in a number of specific subsidiary arts such as preparation of the sermon, the style (rhetoric, the old word) of the sermon, the delivery of the sermon, the use of illustrations and how to make effective use of the Bible in preaching. Each of these areas receives some attention in every complete textbook on homiletics, but each has been the subject of extensive treatment in separate volumes, so much so, that there is a veritable library of books in these subordinate subjects. Ilion T. Jones, *Principles and Practice of Preaching,* Abingdon, 1956, contains a fairly complete bibliography on these special aspects of homiletics.)

a. *Style*

(1) *In Print*

Quiller-Couch, Arthur, *On the Art of Writing.* Putnam, 1916. (Paper reprint, 1961).
Shipley, Joseph T., *Dictionary of Word Origin* (2nd Ed.). New York: Philosophical Library, 1945.
Flesch, Rudolph, *The Art of Plain Talk.* Harper, 1947.
Webster's *Dictionary of Synonyms.* G. and C. Merriam, 1951.
Miller, Geo. A., *Language and Communication.*

McGraw-Hill, 1951.

Howland, Carl L., et al, *Communication and Persuasion.* Yale University Press, 1953.

Gowers, Sir Ernest, *Plain Words, Their A.B.C.* Alfred A. Knopf, 1954.

Chase, Stuart, *The Power of Words.* Harcourt, Brace and Co., 1954.

Kraemer, Henrik, *The Communication of the Christian Faith.* Westminster, 1956.

Oliver, Rob't T., *The Psychology of Persuasive Speech.* Longman's Green and Co., 1957.

Brown, Roger, *Words and Things.* Glencoe, Illinois: The Free Press, 1958.

deWire, Harry A., *The Christian as Communicator.* Westminster, 1960. Contains a bibliography on every aspect of the subject.

Howe, Reuel, *The Miracle of Dialogue.* Seabury, 1963.

(2) *Out of Print*

Phelps, Austin, *English Style in Public Discourse.* Scribner, 1883.

Jones, E. W., *Preaching and the Dramatic Arts.* Macmillan, 1948.

Crocker, Lionel, *Interpretative Speech.* Prentice-Hall, 1952.

Garrison, Webb B., *The Preacher and His Audience.* Revell, 1954.

Dillistone, F. W., *Christianity and Communication.* Scribner, 1956.

Boyd, Malcolm, *Crisis in Communication.* Doubleday and Co., Inc., 1957.

b. *Illustrating Sermons*

All of the following, though out of print, are worthwhile:

Spurgeon, Charles H., *The Art of Illustrating Sermons.* New York: Wilbur B. Ketcham, 1894.

Bryan, Dawson C., *The Art of Illustrating Sermons.* Abingdon, 1938.

Sangster, W. E., *The Craft of Sermon Illustration.* Westminster, 1950.

c. *The Delivery of Sermons*

(1) *In Print*

Macartney, Clarence E., *Preaching without Notes.* Abingdon, 1946.

Phelps, Arthur A., *Public Speaking for Ministers.* Baker Book House, 1958.

Prochnow, Herbert V., *The Successful Speaker's Handbook.* Prentice-Hall, 1951.

Grace, Wm. J., and J. C., *The Art Communicating Ideas.* New York: Devin-Adair, 1952.

Stevenson, Dwight E., and Diehl, *Reaching People from the Pulpit: A Guide to Effective Pulpit Delivery.* Harper, 1958.

(2) *Out of Print*

Bautain, M., *The Art of Extempore Speaking.* New York: Devitt-Wilson, Inc., 1921.

Crocker, Lionel, *Henry Ward Beecher's Speaking Art.* Revell, 1937.

Kirkpatrick, R. W., *The Creative Delivery of Sermons.* Macmillan, 1944.

Hollingsworth, H. L., *The Psychology of the Audience.* American Book Co., 1948.

Lantz, John Edward, *Speaking in the Church.* Macmillan, 1954.

d. *How To Make Effective Use of the Bible*

Many and varied books have been written over the years in this general field. Some have dealt with the problems of interpreting the Scriptures as a whole, some with the proper use of single texts, some with the use of longer passages (expository preaching), some with the use of parables, miracles, Biblical characters, and Psalms, and still others with using whole books at a time as the basis of sermons.

(1) *In Print*

Morgan, G. Campbell, *Living Messages of the Books* (4 vols.). Revell, 1911-12.

Luccock, Halford E., *Preaching Values in New Translations of the N. T.*, Abingdon, 1928.

Blackwood, A. W., *Preaching from the Bible.* Abingdon, 1941.

Blackwood, A. W., *Preaching from Samuel.* Abingdon, 1946.

Blackwood, A. W., *Preaching from the Prophetic Books.* Abingdon, 1951.

Blackwood, A. W., *Expository Preaching for Today.* Abingdon, 1953.

Blackwood, A. W., *Biographical Preaching for Today.* Abingdon, 1954.

Dodd, C. H., *The Apostolic Preaching,* Harper, 1950.

Miller, Donald G., *Fire in Thy Mouth,* Abingdon, 1954.

Miller, Donald G., *The Way to Biblical Preaching.* Abingdon, 1957.

Stevenson, Dwight E., *Preaching on Books of the the New Testament.* Harper, 1956.

Stevenson, Dwight E., *Preaching on Books of the Old Testament.* Harper, 1958.

Luccock, Halford E., *Preaching Values in the Epistles of Paul* (2 vols.). Harper, 1959, 1961.

Tombs, Lawrence E., *The Old Testament in Christian Preaching,* Westminster, 1961. Exceptionally valuable.

Smart, James D., *The Old Testament in Dialogue With Modern Man.* Westminster, 1964.

(2) *Out of Print*

Farrar, F. W., *The Messages of the Books.* Macmillan, 1927. A Classic. The original treatise on preaching on single books of the Bible.

Jeffs, H., *The Art of Exposition.* Pilgrim Press, 1910.

Luccock, Halford E., *Preaching Values in New Translations of the O. T.*, Abingdon, 1933.

Patton, Carl S., *The Use of the Bible in Preaching.* Willett, Clark and Co., 1936.

Luccock, Halford E., *The Acts of the Apostles in Present Day Preaching.* Willett, Clark and Co., 1938.

Roach, Corwin C., *Preaching Values in the Bible.* Louisville: The Cloister Press, 1946.

Whitesell, Faris D., *The Art of Biblical Preaching.* Zondervan, 1950.

Weatherspoon, J. B., *Sent Forth to Preach: Studies in Apostolic Preaching.* Harper, 1954.

Whitesell, Faris D., *Preaching on Biblical Characters.* Baker Book House, 1955.

3. *Lectures on Preaching and Books of Sermons*

A complete bibliography of the literature of Homiletics would necessarily include lectures on preaching and books of sermons by outstanding preachers, because, for the most part, both of these types of books are written, not by theoreticians but by technicians, or practicioners. Dr. Theodore O. Wedel once said, "Every preacher after a few years in the pulpit, could write his own textbook on sermon writing." If the truth were known, most books about preaching, textbooks and otherwise, are put into print by preachers who desire to pass on to others the "theory" of preaching they have proved by testing formal principles of preaching in the laboratory of actual experience.

The reader will find lists of books in both of the above categories at the end of the article, "The Literature of Preaching," in this Dictionary.

SECTION 3

HERMENEUTICS

"Who is as the wise man? Who knows the interpretation of a thing?"
—Ecclesiastes 8:1

Biblical Interpretation

1. INTRODUCTION

The Protestant ministry is based upon the Word of God as expressed in the inspired canonical literature and as perpetuated in preaching. Whereas in Roman Catholicism the Christian servant is a priest whose primary function is sacramental, in Protestantism the Christian servant is a minister whose central function is the ministry of the Word of God. Although the Christian ministry is manifold and ought not to be seen exclusively as preaching, without doubt it reaches its fullest expression in the preaching of the Word of God.

If this is the nature of the Protestant ministry it follows that one of the most important considerations of the Christian ministry must be the right use of the Word of God. Paul tells Timothy that he is to handle rightly the word of truth (II Tim. 2:15. Greek: *orthotomēo,* to cut a straight line, to guide the word of truth along a straight line). A cardinal sin of false ministers is that they abuse (*kapēleuō,* to be huckster, to adulterate) the Word of God (II Cor. 2:17).

The main concern in the right use of the Word of God is its proper interpretation. Whether preaching is textual or topical or expository it rests ultimately upon the minister's interpretation of the Word of God. That theological discipline which takes as its goal the proper interpretation of Scripture is hermeneutics. A solid hermeneutics is the root of all good exegesis and exegesis is the foundation of all truly Biblical preaching. Therefore a sound hermeneutics is an absolute *desideratum* for the minister of the Word of God.

Although traditionally hermeneutics has been treated as a special theological discipline, recent studies have endeavored to enlarge the scope of hermeneutics. These studies wish to see hermeneutics in a wider perspective as a function of the human understanding (German: *Verstehen,* the grasping of meaning in depth in contrast to *Erkärung* which is merely technical explanation). Understanding is the capacity which people have to give and receive meaning. When a person speaks or writes he gives meaning; when he listens or reads he receives meaning. Hermeneutics is then deeply imbedded in the larger structure of communication. Stemming from Schleiermacher, Dilthey, and Heidegger there has arisen a new movement in hermeneutics which is so comprehensive that it is a philosophy and a theology (Fuchs, Ebeling, Gadamer). Within this larger comprehension of hermeneutics is the more technical kind of hermeneutics known as sacred or Biblical hermeneutics. In this article our concern is with the latter.

When a person is familiar with the materials he reads or hears the process of understanding occurs without effort. Interpretation is present but it functions so spontaneously that it is not evident. When a person is confronted with strange materials his process of understanding becomes self-conscious. An effort is made to find rules that will guide the interpreter through such materials. These rules are necessary because interpretation is as much art as it is science, and therefore there must be protection against arbitrary interpretation made in the name of art. Arbitrary interpretation may be a wrenching of the truth of the text or it may be the overapplication of a legitimate procedure (as in typological interpretation). The conscious setting up of rules is hermeneutics (from the god Hermes, messenger of the gods, hence *hermēneuein,* to interpret; *hermēneia,* interpretation, commentary; and *hē hermēneutikē technē,* the skill or art of interpretation).

General hermeneutics is that set of rules employed in all materials which stand in need of interpretation. It is used, with proper adaption to the subject matter, in art, history, literature, archeology and translation. Something stands in need of interpretation when something hinders its spontaneous understanding. To put it another way a gap exists between the interpreter and the materials to be interpreted and rules must be set up to bridge this gap. In that the interpreter is separated from his materials in time there is a historical gap; in that his culture is different from that of his text there is a cultural gap; in that the text is usually in a different language there is the linguistic gap; in that the document originates in another country there is the geological gap and the biological gap (the flora and fauna). In that usually a totally different attitude towards life and the universe exists in the text it can be said that there is a philosophical gap (German: *Weltanschauung,* the metaphysical manner in which the universe is put together; *Weltbild,* the physical [scientific or pseudo-scientific] manner in which the universe is put together).

Biblical hermeneutics is the study of those principles which pertain to the interpretation of Holy Scripture. In that all of the usual gaps exist between the interpreter and the text of Scripture rules for interpretation are mandatory. In that the Holy Scripture has some problems peculiar to itself (e.g., the relationship of the Old to the New Testament), other principles are necessary for the complete system of Biblical hermeneutics.

Biblical hermeneutics is capable of further division. Some works on hermeneutics present the hermeneutics of the Old Testament, then of the New Testament. Others speak of general hermeneutics as the ascertaining of those principles which apply to the entire Bible, and special hermeneutics as those principles which apply to special literary segments of the Bible (e.g., prophecy, parables).

Hermeneutics is both an art and a science. It is a science in that it can reduce interpretation within limits to a set of rules; it is an art in that not infrequently elements in the text escape easy treatment by rules. Some writers have argued that the giving and taking of meaning in understanding (*Verstehen*) is more art than science. But at least it is not all art and what is not art can be treated by rule.

It has been customary to specify hermeneutics as the theory of interpretation and exegesis as the application of the theory to the text. Hermeneutics studies the theory of interpretation and refers to exegesis only to illustrate its points. Exegesis deals concretely with the text and refers to hermeneutics only to argue a point. But recent studies in hermeneutics indicate that hermeneutical principles are distilled from the activity of exegesis itself. Therefore any division between exegesis and hermeneutics is somewhat artificial. Scholars did not develop a theory of hermeneutics from abstract considerations, but the practical issues of exegesis (as well as controversy in interpretation) drove them to the formulation of hermeneutical theory.

Hermeneutics, exegesis, and preaching form one continuum. The minister who stands in the tradition of the Reformation that the minister is the minister of the Word of God (*ministerium verbi divine*) believes that the center of gravity in his ministry is the Word of God. This means that the greatest responsibility of a ministry is the ministry of the Word of God to the congregation. Preaching must be centered in the interpretation and application of Holy Scripture. The message from the pulpit will be Biblical, exegetical, and expository. Holy Scripture is the source and norm of preaching; exegesis is the scientific ascertaining of the meaning of the text; and exposition is its relevant proclamation to the congregation. The concept which binds these three together is the concept of the Word of God. The Scripture is the Word of God written; exegesis is the Word of God understood; and preaching is the Word of God made relevant to time and place. This high view of preaching as an important form of the Word of God is in keeping with the high view of preaching maintained at the time of the Reformation by both Luther and Calvin.

Exegesis and exposition bear a special relationship to each other. Exposition grows out of exegesis. In exegesis the preacher concentrates on the meaning of the text *historically* understood. He is not immediately concerned with the relevance for the present generation. In so bracketing off present concern he is free from all those forces that would distort his search for the meaning of the text whether these forces be social, ecclesiastical, or political. Illustrative of this point were the researches of Luther into the original meaning of the Psalms, Galatians, Romans and Hebrews. In exposition the minister is concerned with the application and relevance of the text for the contemporary generation — again illustrated by Luther who made the text relevant to his day and so started the Reformation. Exegesis without application is academic; exposition that is not grounded in exegesis is either superficial or misleading or even both.

There must be no separation of exegesis and application. The twentieth century has witnessed too many instances in which exegesis was carried on without fulfilling itself in application. Christians could have had any number of cell Bible studies and never passed judgment on the Hitler regime. Christians all over the world may enjoy their in-group Bible study and ignore the grave political, social, and racial injustices and evils that surround them. Application is not a second and dispensable activity after exegesis, but in the normal situation exegesis leads inevitably to application.

If the Word of God is the center of the ministry then the minister must treat his text exegetically before he treats it homiletically. If he is to be a responsible exegete he must have a responsible working theory of Biblical hermeneutics. Otherwise his exegesis will be willy-nilly and uneven. This will reflect itself in the quality of one's preaching. Therefore if the minister is to be a faithful steward of the Word of God he must have a mature working theory of Biblical hermeneutics as the basis of his homiletics.

2. GENERAL BIBLICAL HERMENEUTICS

In that Holy Scripture is to a large measure similar to other literature the science of general hermeneutics is applicable to Biblical hermeneutics. The point of beginning in Biblical hermeneutics is to explore how the principles of general hermeneutics apply to it.

Prior to the minister's actual working with the text itself he has already made certain fundamental decisions. He has, for example, a certain conviction about the theological nature of Holy Scripture. To him the Scripture is the Word of God written which has been the universal faith of the church regardless of particular theories of inspiration, and regardless of debates whether the Bible *is* or *contains* the Word of God. Holy Scripture had its origin in the divine speaking and acting; it was transmitted to the prophets and apostles who were special agents of divine revelation; and it was cast into writing by the process of divine inspiration. This is not a dry, rational faith in a static body of literature. The evangelical preacher believes in the animating power of the Word of God, and in the quickening power of the Holy Spirit. He knows that in every generation the Word of God is to be brought to a new hearing by more vigorous exegesis and fruitful application. From the same Word of God came Augustine's great critique of pagan culture; Thomas' great attempt at synthesis of reason and revelation in the Middle Ages; and Luther's great reformulation of the Christian gospel.

This Word of God the evangelical minister accepts in the canon of Holy Scripture. The canon is the list of books which the church has deemed part of the organism of revelation and therefore the divine authority within the church. The Protestant minister works with the canon that came out of the Reformation (but not in blind unawareness of the critical problems of canon formation). The concept of the Word of God determines the concept of a canon; the historical formulation of the canon was a human decision in which it is believed that the Holy Spirit was operative.

The evangelical minister works with an accepted critical edition of the Hebrew Old Testament and the Greek New Testament. As a general rule he trusts the scholarship that has striven to give the church the purest text possible. If a preacher is not competent in the original languages he must use English translations that are based upon a critical text of the original languages as the American Standard Version and the Revised Standard Version. If the minister prefers for personal reasons to preach from the King James Version he must at least acquaint himself with the variant readings attested in the other English versions of the Holy Scripture.

Textual criticism is to be followed by a study of Biblical introduction as it relates to the text to be interpreted. The routine matters of Biblical introduction are concerned with authorship, dates, where the book was written, who were its recipients, and the conditions that prompted the writing of the book. In that each book of the Bible has its own set of critical problems the interpreter will inform himself of these. Only as the book is set in its wider historical and literary perspectives can justice be done to it in its interpretation.

At this point it is now possible to discuss those principles of general hermeneutics which carry over into Biblical hermeneutics.

a. *Literary Genre.* In the interpretation of a literary text the first matter to be concretely settled is its *literary genre.* It is the literary genre of the text which determines the frame of reference in which the words are used, and therefore the frame of reference is logically prior to the words. Some Scripture is poetry, some proverbs, some history, some sermonic, some parables, etc. The determination of the literary genre of the text determines the interpreter's mood and stance.

b. *Word Study.* Once the literary genre of a passage has been settled the piecemeal work of exegesis begins. It usually begins with a study of words because the word is the ultimate unit of meaning. There are various ways words can be studied. Words can be studied *etymologically.* The knowledge of the components of a word and its formation may be instrumental in unlocking its meaning. Words can be studied *comparatively.* Words usually occur many places in Scripture and tracing a word through a concordance is basic home work for good exegesis. There are Hebrew and Greek concordances and critical concordances as Strong and Young that aid the person who does not know the original languages. Bible dictionaries and theological word books are also sources of information about major Biblical words. There is some merit in studying synonyms for it reveals what words the writers of Scripture considered blood relatives. Words may be studied *historically* (*usus loquendi*). We have the classic example of this kind of research in Kittel's famous *Theological Dictionary of the New Testament* (in process of translation from the German). A word is studied in its classical Greek usage; then in the Hebrew Bible; then in the Septuagint; then in the inter-Biblical period with special regard to the Aramaic; then comprehensively in the Greek New Testament; and in some instances in the early Patristic literature. The historical study of words always includes research in cognate languages and in the great translations of the Old and New Testaments of antiquity.

It would be unrealistic to expect a parish minister to do extensive research in Biblical words. But there are things he can do to compensate for this. He can develop a sensitivity to words as such in the English language and make extensive use of an unabridged dictionary. He can use the latest lexicons which classify most of the uses of the Hebrew and Greek words. Bauer spent a life time to give us an accurate classification of the words of the Greek New Testament (in Arndt and Gingrich's translation, *A Greek English Lexicon of the New Testament*).

c. *Grammatical Exegesis.* The study of words is helpful but limited. It is grammatical exegesis which presses on to the interpretation of the sentence in all its parts, and the paragraph composed of sentences. Its corollary is the priority of the literal (or normal) sense of Scripture (in opposition to the medieval scheme of the fourfold meaning of the sense of Scripture). It is neither possible nor necessary to discuss the grammar of the Biblical languages at this point.

Grammatical exegesis is sometimes called literal exegesis. By the literal meaning of words and phrases is meant their normal, natural, customary sense *in situ* in their language. Allegorical exegesis has been the bedevilment of exegesis. It was the Christocentric character of allegorical exegesis in the Patristic period which saved it from being pure trash. The Reformers saw correctly that only in literal exegesis could the church be purged from centuries of accretions in the interpretation of Scripture. Literal exegesis is the check upon all irresponsible exegesis whether it be found in the history of the church or in some contemporary cult.

Grammatical exegesis pays very strict attention to the context of a passage. It has been well said that the context of every text is the canon. There is also the context of the Old or New Testament, the context of the book, the context of the chapter, and the context of the paragraph. Paul uses the word law (*nomos*) so flexibly that its particular meaning can be settled only by appeal to the context.

The next stage in grammatical exegesis is to turn to the cultural elements in the text such as references to persons, events, social practices, matters of geography (cities, towns, rivers, mountains, etc.), and flora and fauna. This is not only a matter of learning the particular items mentioned in the text but it involves the attempt to create the political and sociological world of the past. Why were the Galatians easy victims for the Judaizers? Why did the church at Corinth become the church of ecstatic gifts? What kind of community received the epistle to the Hebrews? When were certain Psalms apt to be used in liturgy? These are the sort of comprehensive questions the interpreter must ask to bring the text to its fullest hearing.

Again it must be conceded that it is impossible for the parish minister to search out all of these matters. The best recourse for the minister is to turn to a good commentary, for a good commentary will be concerned with all the things we have mentioned here. It will give him an introduction to the book. It will discuss important textual variations. It will have excellent studies of the more important words and items of grammar. It will supply the user with good historical and cultural materials. As a rule of thumb it may be said that good hermeneutics is the use of good commentaries, and bad hermeneutics is their neglect.

The commentator on Scripture has a wide range of commentaries to draw upon. Each serves a distinct purpose from the very technical commentary with its wealth of lexical and grammatical materials to the more homiletical and devotional with their general assessments of the theological, spiritual, and practical implications of the text. Again as a most general rule it can be said that newer commentaries are better than old ones, and critical and grammatical ones will be more rewarding over the years than popular and devotional ones.

3. HERMENEUTICAL PRINCIPLES SPECIAL TO SCRIPTURE

In many ways Holy Scripture is one piece with other literature. It is written in common languages; it uses many typical forms of literary composition; it refers to thousands of matters of common experience; and much of its history is buried amidst other histories. In all these matters in which the Bible overlaps other literature it is to be interpreted as other literature. But the Holy Scripture has certain unique features which require special principles if full justice is to be done to the interpretation of Scripture.

a. *The Spiritual Factor.* It was Calvin who noted that the Word of God is spiritual and therefore could only be spiritually perceived. It was for this reason that he broke with a rationalistic apologetic that presumed that it could prove Christianity to be true by an appeal to human reason as such. There are two sides to the spirituality of the Word of God. God moves upon man by the Holy Spirit who illuminates the mind and witnesses to the veracity of the divine verities. But the man upon whom the Spirit moves must be a partaker of the Spirit in regeneration. The Scriptures are most likely to be understood when a regenerate man trusts the Holy Spirit to illuminate his mind as he interprets Scripture. Relying on the Spirit is no substitute for learning. It must be conceded that an ignorant Christian is no match for a learned unbeliever. Reliance upon the Spirit must always be in conjunction with the best possible procedures in exegesis.

Those who wish a strictly controlled scientific exegesis, or who believe that in view of the "historicity" of the text the text is understandable exhaustively by general hermeneutics, look upon spiritual considerations as illicit intrusion of the subjective into an area where it does not belong. They do not see how recourse to the Holy Spirit has operational value. If objective criteria are not forthcoming, the role of the Spirit in exegesis is rejected as subjectivism or pietism. But the issue is not so easily settled. The subjective disposition of a scholar weighs heavily upon him in his exegesis. Communists have no sympathy with existentialism, and interpret it as the dying gasp of a decadent capitalism. Marx's complete preoccupation with economics caused him to recast the philosophy of Hegel into a fantastic perversion of Hegel. Logical positivists of the old school showed only disdain for metaphysics, poetry, and religion. The scholar does not exist who is completely free from presuppositions, and completely delivered from any emotionally or culturally rooted disposition that would materially influence his interpretations.

If subjective disposition plays such a decisive role in all interpretation (in spite of the best intentions to be "scientific" or "objective"), then the subjective disposition in Biblical exegesis is of immense importance. That the Holy Spirit might significantly effect the subjective disposition of the exegete and thereby his exegesis, cannot be ruled out of court even though it is not possible to give criteria for the Spirit's action. The intangibility of the work of the Spirit might be far more real than all the scientific procedures applied to the text. Because it is believed that the great fathers of the church were Spirit-gifted men some theologians trust more to patristic exegesis than they do to modern scientific exegesis. Others think that Luther and Calvin were such men of the Spirit that they are better guides to the real substance of the New Testament then men of our day with all their aids to exegesis.

b. *The Unity of Scripture.* The unity of Scripture and the harmony of Scripture is Jesus Christ and the redemption and revelation which centers in him. Hermeneutics has always been caught between Origen and Marcion. In Marcion we have an unChristian reduction of the Old Testament, and in Origen a Christian inflation of the Old Testament. The balance between the Old and New Testaments was one of the most difficult hermeneutical issues of the Reformation. The battle continues today in that Bultmann stands for a Marcion interpretation of the Old Testament, while Barth retains a Christological exegesis of the Old Testament.

Although the church may not be able to neatly solve the particular problems of Old Testament exegesis it nevertheless believes that the Old Testament is essentially a Christian book. The one theme of both Testaments is Jesus Christ and his redemption. It is admitted that the presence of Christ in the Old Testament is not fully clear, and therefore the Christological exegesis of the Old Testament will never be free from difficulty. In spite of the fantasies of allegorical exegesis its heart was in the right place in insisting on the Christian content of the Old Testament.

In that the New Testament is the realization of the Old a special hermeneutical principle is necessary. For the Christian church the center of gravity of the Scriptures is the New Testament. In the New Testament is recorded the incarnation, the life of the incarnate Son, the saving events of the cross and the resurrection, and the interpretation of the person and work of Christ in the epistles. The granting of the priority of the New Testament over the Old Testament is not meant to be an enervating relativization of the Old Testament. The Old Testament stands in a right of its own and many of its great passages are without parallel in the New Testament (e.g., Psalm 23). That which the principle intends to grant is the priority of the New Testament in the theological understanding of salvation and the Christian life.

c. *Progressive Revelation.* The concept of progressive revelation is based upon the conviction that revelation and redemption move along a historical line and that this historical line has a certain character to it. The most obvious division of the line is its division into the Old Testament period and the New Testament period. Even in the New Testament period there is division between the events prior to Pentecost and those after Pentecost. There is a progression in Scripture and unless this principle of progression is recognized there can be no clear exegesis of Scripture.

Progressive revelation means that God takes man where he finds him and with whatever notions he has of God and ethical principles and seeks to lead him higher and higher. If revelation is to make contact with empirical man it must meet him where he is. The primeval concepts of man about God and morality is a witness of God reaching down to empirical man where he is. Progressive revelation also means that as the time line unravels, the purposes of God become clearer and fuller. It involves the enlargement of the idea of God, the purification of ethical ideals, the spiritualizing of worship, and progress in divine redemption. It is because of progressive revelation that the church has found its fulness of revelation, its supreme doctrine of God, its climax of revelation, and its final ethical imperatives in the New Testament and not the Old.

Programmatically this means two things to the interpreter. If there is any tension between the older revelation and the newer, the older must give way to the newer. Although there are some remarkable ethical materials in the Old Testament, Christian theology must consciously build its final ethical formulations from the New Testament. Furthermore, it means that there is no uniformity of importance in the Scriptures. It is true that in so-called scholastic orthodoxy, Scriptures were cited as proofs without regard to their location in Scripture (hence a passing reference in the Psalms was given as much weight as a verse in Romans). But this kind of exegesis is no longer defensible and has all but disappeared in contemporary theology. The locus of a text in the corpus of revelation determines the mode of its exegesis and the theological weight that can be assessed to it.

d. *The Self-interpretation of Scripture.* At the time of the Reformation the Roman Catholic Church insisted that it was gifted with the grace of interpretation and therefore it knew instinctively the intention of Scripture. The Reformers rejected this claim and set in its place the rule that Scripture is its own interpreter (*Scriptura sacra sui ipsius interpres*). That which raised this issue was the problem created by the darker or more difficult passages of Scripture. Luther taught the objective clarity of Scripture to be Jesus Christ, and the subjective clarity to be the Holy Spirit. But this did not mean all the Bible was clear. The Catholics appealed to their gift of interpretation to direct its way through the darker part of Scripture. The Reformers appealed to "Scripture interprets Scripture." Obviously the word "Scripture" is used in two senses in this catch phrase. What it means is that the *whole* of Scripture interprets the *part* of Scripture and thus no part of Scripture can be so interpreted as to deform the teaching of the whole of Scripture. Thus incidental references in Scripture cannot be made pillars of truth. One of the most familiar traits of a sect is that it carries on this very sort of exegesis.

"Scripture interprets Scripture" has also been called the hermeneutical circle. The *whole* of Scripture can be learned only by interpreting it *part* by *part*. No man's attention span is so great that he can ingest the whole Scripture at once. Yet no part can stand in isolation from the whole. So the interpreter must go the circle from part to whole and from whole to part.

Another version of the hermeneutical circle is to be found in the Bultmann circle. The Scripture is understood only as the exegete asks leading questions of the text; but in working with the text the exegete is himself questioned by the text. But this questioning by the text gives him a deeper existential insight so now he knows how to better question the text. Hence he moves in the circle of questioning and in turn being questioned and in turn questioning the text.

e. *The Supernatural in Scripture.* The evangelical expositor accepts the report of the supernatural in the text. Since the time of the founding of modern science and modern philosophy, educated secular man has been opposed to Christian supernaturalism. To him the only factors in the universe are the immanent laws of nature. Since the time of the German enlightenment many theologians have taken the same stance with reference to theology and the Scriptures. The result of this attitude upon the interpretation of Scripture is that all reports of the supernatural in Scripture are written off as some kind of misunderstanding. Such anti-supernatural scholars point out that in precritical cultures the supernatural is everywhere. Therefore it ought not to surprise us if we find the supernatural reported in the Scriptures for they were written in precritical times. Exegesis accordingly treats the report of the supernatural in Scriptures as it would in any document of Greek or Roman antiquity which reported a supernatural event.

The evangelical Christian believes that there is a radical difference between the report of the supernatural in Scripture and in other literature. There is a sober rationale for the supernatural in Scripture based upon the Biblical structure of revelation and redemption which is completely lacking in precritical cultures. The Christian considers the present order to be out of joint and unnatural due to sin. Part of God's revelatory and redemptive work in a humanity and cosmos darkened by sin is the employment of the supernatural. Therefore when the evangelical expositor is confronted with the supernatural in the text he does not rule it out *ex hypothesi,* but accepts it as an important element of the Biblical revelation.

f. *Theological Exegesis.* The evangelical expositor is interested in the fullest reaches of Biblical interpretation and this leads to the necessary theological exegesis of the text. This is not a *double* treatment of the text as if first the text is given a grammatical interpretation and then a "spiritual" (*pneumatische*) interpretation. Theological exegesis can be nothing else but the extension of the line of grammatical exegesis. It is true that there has been in the history of the church this doubling of exegesis. It was true in Patristic times when the allegorical interpretation of the text was superimposed on the grammatical meaning of the text. It is true in contemporary times in Paul Tillich who forces an existential calculus on the text which is foreign to its grammatical sense.

Theological exegesis extends grammatical exegesis in that theological exegesis is interested in the largest implications of the text. Propositions imply other propositions. In formal systems (logic, mathematics, geometry), the process of drawing propositions from other propositions is strictly controlled. In material systems (science, history, psychology, etc.), the implications of a proposition are not always obvious and the verification of a proposition may be very difficult. The Bible as a literary and historical document does not belong to the formal system but to the material. Therefore deducing propositions from Scripture faces all of the problems typical of deducing propositions in a material system.

Although no hard line may be drawn between grammatical exegesis and theological exegesis it may be programmatically said that theological exegesis takes up where grammatical exegesis leaves off and seeks to find the fuller implications of the text. For this reason it is forced tó used concepts (logical constructs) that would not be used in grammatical exegesis (e.g., original sin, total depravity, communion of natures, etc.), and this accounts for the rather startling difference of vocabulary beween grammatical exegesis and systematic theology. The great theologian differs from the ordinary theologian in the former's ability to draw out these larger implications of the text. It was in men like Augustine, Luther, Calvin, and Barth that the genius of theological exegesis came into its own.

In that theological exegesis deals with this creative extension of the meaning of the text it is not as strictly controllable as grammatical exegesis. Theological exegesis is more art than technique, and insight is more important to it than the linguistic details of grammatical exegesis. The proof of the pudding is in the eating and the ultimate justification of theological exegesis must be its ability to make the text meaningful in its greatest depth.

The second character of theological exegesis is that the canon of Scripture is the context of every passage of Scripture. This is the theological version of "Scripture interprets Scripture." The exegete brings all the other materials that are similar to the text to bear upon the text. Again this procedure is as much art and insight as it is exegesis. Therefore it is not easy to control.

In recent times Barth has endeavored to pioneer theological exegesis in a fresh way. To him the entire Bible is the context for each passage and therefore he has no hesitancy in bringing items from the history of Israel and the New Testament into his interpretation of Genesis 1. Or in some event of the Old Testament or in some person of the Old Testament he sees a gold mine of theological materials because he brings other parts of Scripture to this text and inflates it so to speak. Although Barth has been accused of allegorical exegesis and of spiritualizing the text he nevertheless at least gives us one version of theological exegesis. His particular exegesis may be seriously questioned, but his notion of exegesis as demanding that the entire text of the Bible be brought to bear on particular texts is sound.

BIBLIOGRAPHY

Ebeling, Gerhard, "Hermeneutik," *Religion in Geschichte und Gegenwart,* (third edition), III, 242-262.

Frör, Kurt, *Biblische Hermenutik.* Munich: Chr. Kaiser, 1961.

Mickelsen, A. Berkeley, *Interpreting the Bible.* Grand Rapids: Wm. B. Eerdmans, 1963.

Ramm, Bernard, *Protestant Biblical Interpretation* (revised edition). Boston: W. A. Wilde, 1956.

Smart, James, *The Interpretation of Scripture.* Philadelphia: Westminster Press, 1961.

Terry, Milton, *Biblical Hermeneutics.* New edition; New York: Eaton and Mains, 1883.

Weber, Otto, *Grundlagen der Dogmatik.* First edition; Neukirchen: Verlag der Buchhandlung des Erziehungsvereins, 1955. Vol. I, pp. 341-384.

Interpretation of Parables

A parable is an extended metaphor or simile which compares a religious truth with a common experience or circumstance in life. As a didactic device its roots are to be traced to the Old Testament where it is found mainly in Proverbs. The Greek word *parabolic* is found nearly fifty times in the Gospels in connection with the teaching ministry of Jesus. Therefore, the parable was obviously a favorite and central teaching instrument of Jesus. In this respect he stood with the rabbis who also made extensive use of the parable. However, two features distinguish Jesus' parabolic teaching from that of the rabbis: (1) Jesus' parables were marked by freshness, simplicity and creativity, whereas those of the rabbis tended towards the ponderous and pedantic; and (2) Jesus' parables related to the coming kingdom, while the parables of the rabbis focused upon the Torah and its manifold implications.

1. RELATIONSHIP TO ALLEGORY

Because parable and allegory share many common attributes, from earliest times confusion has existed within these two literary genres with the unhappy result that parabolic interpretation has been allegorized, and the distinctive thrust of the parabolic form has been attenuated and often eclipsed. Briefly stated, a parable exists to establish one point, so that individual details serve this one purpose and have no great significance in themselves. On the other hand, an allegory may establish several points by virtue of the meaningfulness of the several details which comprise the allegory. Perhaps the outstanding example of allegory in the New Testament is found in Paul's discussion of Hagar and Sarah in Galatians 4:21-31. However, it should be noted that this custom is rare and furthermore, Paul specifically identified his handling of the theme as an allegory (vs. 24). The allegorization of the parables of Jesus commenced perhaps even within New Testament times, but its greatest development took place under Origen who, following the hermeneutical scheme of Philo, adopted allegorization as the most fruitful method of Biblical interpretation.

His baneful influence affected not only the church fathers for centuries, but continues up to the present, especially in the interpretation of the parables of Jesus.

The dominating hold of allegory upon parabolic interpretation was broken by the German theologian A. Jülicher (*Die Gleichnisreden Jesu,* 1888). He rightly perceived the difference between allegory and parable, affirming that the latter teaches one central point, all elements of a parable being secondary and subordinate to that one point. His thesis that the parables are distinct from allegory, and are to be interpreted differently, is a major contribution to this area of investigation and is of lasting value. The later labors of C. H. Dodd (*The Parables of the Kingdom,* 1936) and J. Jeremias (*The Parables of Jesus,* 1954), while they modify some of the puristic overclassifications of Juulicher, rest upon and proceed from his work. Since Juulicher's time it has come to be recognized that he differentiated too sharply between allegory, metaphor, simile, and parable. As literary and oral didactic genres which evolved out of dynamic human situations, these forms inevitably blend at some points. It should be remembered that the Old Testament prophets, the rabbis, and Jesus were not concerned with scholastic niceties of classification and were not therefore obliged to follow rules of distinction. On the other hand, the expounder today has no right to ignore the proper characteristics of a parable and proceed to allegorize upon it. With good reason the allegorical scheme has been called the "wax nose" method of interpretation because of the uncontrollable nature of allegory which gives free reign to every vagrant imagination about the sense of the text. Allegorizing of parables has for centuries been a source of mischief to correct historical interpretation of the parables of Jesus.

2. TYPES OF PARABLES

Jesus exercised considerable freedom within the general parabolic style so that it is difficult to type his sayings with systematic precision. In general, three types may be discerned: (1) short, pithy similes which vividly characterize someone or something, e.g., salt of the earth, light of the world, blind leaders of the blind, lamp on a stand; (2) a saying which explains a normal event in life, e.g., the servant is not greater than his master, you cannot serve God and mammon, the kingdom of heaven is like a net; (3) the lengthier narrative parable which has no formula of comparison and which is a fully worked out story in itself, e.g., the good samaritan (Luke 10:30-37), the prodigal son (Luke 15:11-32), the wedding feast (Matt. 22:1-14), the sower (Mark 4:3-8), the great supper (Luke 14:16-24), the rich man and Lazarus (Luke 16:19-31), the pharisee and the publican (Luke 18:9-14). It should be borne in mind that not only do the parables defy strict classification, but also at times, especially in John, it is difficult to decide whether a given saying is a parable or an allegory, as in the example of the vine and the branches (John 15:1f.). As a rule, a parable exhibits a formal, stylized introduction, expecially in the cases of the sayings about a normal event of everyday life, and the narrative parable. In the one, the introductory formula is "The kingdom of heaven is like . . .," and in the second, "A certain man. . . ." Such formulae are useful for identification of a parable and the consequent method of interpretation applied to it. One of the chief examples of difficulty of classification is the parable of the sower (Mark 4:3-8). It is generally agreed that the central point is that the proclamation of the gospel elicits a wide variety of responses from the hearers. The controversy exists, however, over verses 10-23 which are alleged in the text to be Jesus' own interpretation of the parable. Many critics assert that this is an example of Mark's editorializing tendency to explain Jesus' words. Some scholars go so far as to state that Mark failed to understand the nature of a parable, and hopelessly allegorized the original parable of Jesus. Over against this view it may be urged that Jesus was not bound by modern literary distinctions, and could in fact have allegorized his own parable, much as appears to have been done in the story about the vine and the branches. This possibility, however, is not free of difficulty for the reason of its rarity within the synoptic gospels.

3. VARIED USE OF PARABLES

An analysis of the way Jesus' parables are reported and couched in the Gospels, especially the synoptics, reveals that each evangelist handled an original saying of Jesus with some latitude and variety, depending upon the general purpose of the context. That they did not observe rigid rules of reportorial precision, either in respect to the words of Jesus or to the context in which they were originally uttered, will prove disagreeable to some because it leads to a diminution of confidence in the historical reliability of the gospels themselves. However this may be, it is undeniable that such shaping and alteration of Jesus' words did in fact take place. A clear example of this editorializing interest is seen in a comparative study of the parables of the great supper (Luke 14:16-24) and the wedding feast (Matt. 22:1-14). Originally this was one parable spoken by Jesus which Matthew adapted to a court setting which mirrors by implication some of the Jewish-Christian controversy at the time of the writing of this gospel, whereas Luke's interest is almost purely eschatological, anticipatory of the messianic banquet. Various details are altered so that the servants in Matthew's narrative are the prophets but in Luke's account the servant is Jesus. The central point in both accounts is the same: many are invited to the table of God, but not all will come. It might be argued that both gospels preserve two independent sayings. This is formally possible. But it is clear that adaptation and variation of reporting did take place among the several evangelists. The baptism, temptation, sermon on the mount, transfiguration, crucifixion, and resurrection narratives all vary in individual details. Of critical importance is not whether the evangelists preserved accuracy in specific detail, but substantial fact. Two further examples will illustrate this tendency by the evangelists Matthew 5:25-26 and Luke 12:58-59 contain the parable of the man who must appear before a judge. Luke's interest is again eschatological, anticipating the day of judgment before God. On the other hand, Matthew's interest is directed to the requirements of human legal procedures; it is prudential morality which is uppermost in Matthew's mind as he adapted Jesus' original saying to this new purpose. Indeed, Matthew's mode of handling this parable is suggestive of the inclination in early times to make a parable assume a hortatory purpose. Matthew 13 is well-known for its collection of parables on the kingdom. There is no claim in Matthew's Gospel, nor is there any sound reason to infer, that these parables were recorded verbatim, or in the order that Jesus uttered them. Moreover, there is no reason to assume that Jesus spoke all these parables in one sermon; the movement of thought in Matthew's Gospel strongly suggests that the collection as it stands in the text bears strong evidence of Matthew's own redactional work and that it reflects his own interest to a remarkable degree. This point is supported by the fact that there is no parallel collection of kingdom parables in any of the other gospels.

This powerful evidence of adaptation in Jesus' original parabolic teaching is highly instructive for preaching on the parables today. It is perfectly clear that the gospel writers held Jesus' words to be inspired and therefore authoritative and objects of deepest reverence, but this did not mean that his words could not be reshaped to new circumstances and demands. This raises a highly significant point: to be meaningful a parable must always be interpreted in the light of new historical contexts in which the Word of God is expounded. This is not to give license to unbridled and incautious vulgarizing of Jesus' words. Rather, it means that the preacher today, as in every generation, must examine the parable as it stands in the text, ascertain as closely as possible the original setting of the parable and then make a thoughtful, penetrating application of that parable to the spiritual context of his hearers. Otherwise, preaching on the parables is simply debased either to fascinating vignettes of life in ancient Palestine, or to moralisms, neither of which is authentic proclamation of the Word of God. To make an impact upon the modern hearer, the parables of Jesus must respond to a contemporary demand and situation.

4. ESCHATOLOGICAL NATURE OF THE PARABLES

If the burden of the parables of Jesus can be summed up in one word, it would be "eschatology." It used to be the fashion to read his words as teaching the progressive improvement of the human condition by human means. Nothing could be further from the truth of Jesus' intention, for by the parables he taught the imminent inbreaking of

God's sovereign and redeeming purpose in the world. Nor did Jesus relate his parables with any intellectualistic goals, as though he were speaking some kind of abstract, timeless verity in an enigmatic manner. His interest was not in mental games and riddles, but with the kingdom of God which was dawning with a new day of redemption in his own person and ministry.

Three features of this eschatological kingdom assert themselves repeatedly in the parabolic ministry of Jesus. First, the coming of the kingdom is near. Mark 1:14 f. records Jesus' opening words in his public ministry as a call to repentance because of the nearness of the kingdom, and this theme reasserts itself in many of his parables. Of course, the presence of Jesus was itself the guarantee of the nearness of the kingdom, for he was the agent by whom the kingdom was made present and effective in the world. Therefore, the parables, like the miracles, are a sign of Jesus' deity and unique relationship to the Father. The hidden and coming glory of the kingdom of God are contained in, and progressively revealed by, Jesus Christ, the eternal Word. Secondly, the imminence of the kingdom implies a separation within the human family, some to sorrow and judgment, and some to joy and final redemption. The note of joy and delight at the revelation of God's saving intention is uppermost in Jesus' mind, for its arrival signals relief for the oppressed and restoration for the downtrodden, an emphasis found particularly in Luke. Thirdly, the eschatological character of the kingdom means that it commences with small, insignificant and inauspicious beginnings, but its end is all-encompassing, powerful and transcendent. This could be said to parallel the life of Christ and the life of the church. The promise contained in this eschatological kingdom is the final victory of God's kingdom over every opponent, tyranny, and hostility directed against God's will and sway over the created order. God's will shall be done on earth as it is in heaven.

5. THE PURPOSE OF THE PARABLES

Cognate with the nature of parable is its function. Again, Jesus was not primarily concerned with intellectual stimulation as such, but with the moral response of his audience upon hearing the parable. It was not perception of some deep, esoteric truth by his hearers, but a decisive response of repentance, faith, hope, and love that motivated Jesus' use of parables. Therefore, his parables may be likened to arrows which were aimed at man's heart, the core of his being, the place of his will and affections. Just as the entire weight and momentum of an arrow make their impact felt at one decisive point, so Jesus' parables rested their full weight upon a relentless, searching claim upon man's heart. Apocalyptic speculations, facile moralisms, and intellectualistic diversions constituted no part of Jesus' purpose in parabolic teaching. Instead, he sought to confront his hearers with the incluctable, implacable and gracious claim of God upon the soul of man.

As in the case of miracles, so also parables elicited a variety of responses, for both miracle and parable were greeted with reactions ranging all the way from scorn and derision to contrition and faith. Mark 4:11 and simliar passages appear to teach that God positively hardened the hearts of some hearers and warmed the hearts of others so they could respond with faith. A better understanding of such passages takes Jesus' words as stating a gnomic fact: faith comes to him whose spirit is ready and open, and it is withheld from the proud and scornful. This is no attempt to analyze the final mystery of the tides and impulses of human decision. It may only be observed that parables in fact accomplish two ends: revelation and concealment, understanding and nonunderstanding.

6. SUGGESTIONS FOR A PRACTICAL METHOD OF PREACHING ON THE PARABLES

a. Examine the parable closely to reconstruct the real situation in which and to which Jesus spoke his parable. What questions were put to him? What were his answers? Who asked the questions? Why did the questioners put the query to Jesus? The answer to such questions will show that Jesus avoided vague, banal generalities, and aimed his parable at specific human needs and challenges.

b. Analyze the parable for the unusual element in the story. Local color will lead the hearer to the spiritual intention of Jesus.

c. The point of the parable is often found in the last sentence of the story. Many times the homely, pungent thrust of a parable is missed in a search for some elusive and "deeper" meaning. The expositor should be willing to see the obvious.

d. A parable has one point. As an arrow has one point and one area of impact, so has a parable. A failure to focus all the force of the parable upon its one point will result in dissipation of its power. Be sure to isolate and expound the unique gift of each parable.

e. Interpretation and application of the ancient parable is a never-ending task, but great are its rewards. The expounder of the parable must not only know the parable, its circumstances and its theological weight, but he must also be sensitized to his own time, his generation, his world, and his congregation which has its ever-changing fears, demands, burdens, and aspirations.

BIBLIOGRAPHY

Dodd, C. H., *The Parables of the Kingdom,* 1936.

Frör, K., *Biblische Hermeneutik.*

Jeremias, J., *The Parables of the Kingdom,* 1954.

Jülicher, A., *Die Gleichnisreden Jesu,* 1888.

Old Testament Quotations in the New Testament

The first factor that is to be considered is the sheer mass of New Testament quotations of or allusions to the Old Testament. Roughly one-tenth of the New Testament is really Old Testament material. This proportion holds also in the recorded words of Jesus. One may gather a general impression in this area by perusing an edition of the New Testament like the Nestle *Greek Testament,* where Old Testament quotations and reminiscences are printed in boldface type. Such a perusal would make it apparent that the heaviest concentration of Old Testament materials is to be found in Revelation, Romans, and Hebrews.

A conservative count discloses some 295 separate explicit references to the Old Testament. These occupy some 352 verses of the New Testament. 278 different verses of the Old Testament are cited (some more than once, hence the difference in numbering), 94 from the "Torah" or Pentateuch, 99 from the "Prophets," and 85 from the "Writings." Out of the 22 books of the Hebrew canon (equivalent to the 39 books of the Protestant Bibles), only 8 are not expressly referred to: Judges, Ruth, Song of Solomon, Ecclesiastes, Esther, Ezra, Nehemiah, Chronicles. In view of the limited length of most of these books and the nature of their contents, this absence of quotations is in no wise surprising and could hardly be argued to indicate a failure to accept the totality of the Hebrew canon.

On the other hand, it is noteworthy that there is not a single case of definite quotations of any of the books known as Apocrypha and claimed as canonical by the Roman Catholic Church. Inasmuch as a mass of material amounting to almost twenty per cent of the canonical Old Testament is involved it would appear that this absence of reference may scarcely be deemed insignificant.

1. NEW TESTAMENT ATTITUDE TOWARD OLD TESTAMENT SCRIPTURE

Both in the manner in which they are introduced and in the way in which they are used the quotations represent a very impressive witness to the high regard in which the New Testament writings held the Old Testament Scripture.

Formulae of introduction are frequently used to indicate that a quotation is intended. These are quite variegated, ranging from the simple words "and," "it says," "it is written," etc., to much more complex forms in which the human author is named, sometimes with additional data relating to place and circumstance (for instance, Matt. 12:26; Acts 4:25; 13:33; Rom. 11:2, 4).

Frequently, by the use of words like "say," "swear," "speak," "cry," etc., the formulae bear witness to the fact that the Word of God addresses us as an oral utterance. Very often also the fact that a written text is in view is marked by the use of words like "Scripture," "it is written," "have ye not read?" etc. In some cases both types of expression are combined as in the formula "the Scripture says" (John 7:38, 42; Rom. 4:3; 9:17; 10:11; 11:2; Gal. 3:8; 4:30; I Tim. 5:18; James 4:5).

Such personification, by which the Scripture is represented as speaking, is carried even further when acts which are in fact

God's actions are ascribed to Scripture. Thus in Romans 9:17 we read that, "the scripture saith unto Pharaoh," and the statement quoted is manifestly a statement of God, in which the pronoun "I" refers to God. Similarly, in Galatians 3:8 it is stated that "the scripture, foreseeing that God would justify the heathen through faith, preached before the gospel unto Abraham," and this introduces God's promise to Abraham. As Warfield pointedly noted, "It was not, however, the Scripture (which did not exist at the time) that, foreseeing God's purposes of grace in the future, spoke these precious words to Abraham, but God Himself in His own person: it was not yet existent Scripture that made this announcement to Pharaoh, but God Himself through the mouth of His Prophet Moses. These acts could be attributed to 'Scripture' only as the result of such a habitual identification, in the mind of the writer, of the text of Scripture with God as speaking, that it became natural to use the term 'Scripture says,' when what was really intended was 'God, as recorded in Scripture, said.'" (*The Inspiration and Authority of the Bible,* S. G. Craig, editor, p. 299f.).

The divine origin of Scripture is prominently featured in the formulae of quotation. In at least fifty-six cases God is explicitly referred to as the author. Among these we may note certain citations in which the text quoted and ascribed to God is not presented in the Old Testament as a direct utterance of God, but rather belongs to the course of the narrative or even is a human statement addressed to God (Matt. 19:5; Acts 4:25; 13:35; Heb. 1:5-8, 13; 3:7; 4:4). Here again we quote Warfield, "It is not God, however, in whose mouth these sayings are placed in the text of the Old Testament: they are the words of others, recorded in the text of Scripture as spoken to or of God. They could be attributed to God only through such habitual identification, in the minds of the writers, of the text of Scripture with the utterances of God that it had become natural to use the term 'God says' when what was really intended was 'Scripture, the Word of God, says'" (*op. cit.,* p. 300).

In some cases the name of the human author of Scripture is given: Moses, David, Isaiah, Jeremiah, Daniel, Joel, Hosea. Many of the passages in which this is the case are, however, references not to personal statements made by these men but rather to divine pronouncements which they were commissioned to transmit and in which the pronoun "I" refers to God. We may take special note of passages where the divine and the human authorship appear together (Matt. 1:22; Mark 12:36; Acts 1:16; 4:25; 28:25; Rom. 9:25). This type of formula bears witness to the fact that in the mind of the New Testament writers the divine superintendence did not obliterate the individual characteristics and personalities of the human authors. Rather they were used in keeping with the divine purpose in terms of their own circumstances, language, and preparation for their holy task and these features are apparent on the record, but they are never construed by the New Testament writers as impinging upon the irrefragable authority and divine authorship of the Scriptures they were commissioned to write.

An added witness to this authority may be found in the way in which the writers of the New Testament, and indeed our Lord himself, appealed to the Scripture with the formula "It is written." This does more than emphasize the fact that a written text is in view, for it implies also an appeal to a final authority from which no exception can be taken. In this same order of thought we notice that occasionally the term "law" is used where reference is made to passages which are not found in the first five books of the Old Testament (John 10:34; 15:25; Rom. 3:19; I Cor. 14:21). These are presented in such a way not as a result of confusion as to the location of these texts in the Old Testament, but because the whole Old Testament was viewed as having legal authority. An interesting parallel may well be found in certain Psalms, such as Psalm 119, where the terminology "law," "statutes," "commandents," etc., may well have a broader reference than the legal portions of the Old Testament. Similarly the term "prophets" may refer to a broader scope of Scripture than that part of the canon designated by that name. An example may be found in Matthew 13:35. This again is due to the fact that for the New Testament writers the whole Old Testament has a prophetic character; it is an address from God and to men mediated by his spokesmen.

Another interesting feature of the formulae

of quotations is the frequent use of the present for the introductory words "He says" rather than "He said." This is reinforced by the use of the pronouns "we" and "you" in relation to ancient sayings, "That which was spoken unto you by God" (Matt. 22: 31); "The Holy Spirit also beareth witness to us" (Heb. 10:15; cf. Matt. 15:7; Mark 7:6; 12:19; Acts 4:11; 13:47; Heb. 12:5). In this wise the eternal contemporaneity of Scripture is emphasized, a truth of which explicit expression is found in Romans 15:4, "For whatsoever things were written aforetime were written for our learning" (Note also Rom. 4:23, 24; I Cor. 9:10; 10:11).

Finally it is worthwhile to pause to give attention to the circumstances in which quotations were presented by both our Lord and the apostles. They appeal to Scripture when in debate; they appeal to it when requested to answer questions, whether serious or captious; they appeal to it in connection with their teaching even to those who would not be inclined to press them for other authorities than their own word; they appeal to it to indicate the purpose of some of their own actions or their insight into God's purpose in relation to contemporary developments; and they appeal to it in their prayers. In the case of Jesus, he appealed to it repeatedly in the temptation, where he was facing an adversary who could not be imposed upon in terms of a questionable authority.

Through the whole course of their career we find a consistent note of reverence for and acceptance of the Scripture of the Old Testament as the Word of God. It is not surprising, therefore, that the historic position of the church through the ages has followed very closely their lead in this matter.

2. NEW TESTAMENT INTERPRETATION OF OLD TESTAMENT SCRIPTURE

It would probably be hazardous to assert that the way in which the New Testament interpreted particular passages of the Old Testament was meant to be the norm of all Biblical exegesis. Yet, the example given by the New Testament is a very important clue to a true interpretation of Sacred Scripture.

It is manifest that our Lord and his apostles were viewing the Old Testament Scripture as a text which did not have a merely contemporary and therefore ephemeral significance, but rather as the expression of God's truth, vested with permanent relevancy and capable of direct reference to their own times. They did not, therefore, narrowly confine their interpretation and use of the Old Testament in terms of the immediate historic context in which any particular passage was uttered or written. On the contrary, they saw throughout one pervasive unity of purpose in terms of God's plan which provides for a recurrent relevancy of particular texts. Moreover, in not infrequent cases they deemed that the complete meaning or effectuation of certain Old Testament texts may come to the fore only in the redemptive revelation connected with the incarnation and mediatorial ministry of Jesus Christ. To indicate this relation they used various terms whose exact import deserves to be weighed.

a. *Fulfill* (Matt. 1:22; 5:17, and over thirty times in the New Testament. Cf. also the interesting word *Pleroma* or "fulness," John 1:16; Rom. 13:10). The contrast is not so much "empty" versus "full" as "partially full" versus "more completely full" or even "totally full." This language, therefore, emphasizes that that which was partially disclosed in the Old Testament Scripture and context has now become more fully evident; or again that that which was simply announced in Old Testament times has now become realized in the actuality of history.

b. *Type* (Rom. 5:14; I Cor. 10:6), and *antitype* (Heb. 9:24; I Peter 3:21). Here the emphasis is upon one pattern of truth with various historical manifestations, usually increasingly articulate in their portrayal of the prototype, or ultimate design in the mind of God.

c. *Shadow* (Col. 2:17; Heb. 8:5; 10:1). It is commonly contrasted to substance, although in Hebrews 10:1 the contrasting term is "image." Here the emphasis on the pre-eminence of the New Testament realization is unmistakable.

d. In the same order of thought one might mention some use of the terms *true* or *truth*, especially in the Johannine writings (John 1:17; 6:32; 15:1; etc. Cf. Heb. 8:4), where the implied contrast appears to be with "incomplete" or "partial disclosure" rather than with "falsehood."

It is within this general framework of reference that the New Testament interpretation of the Old Testament finds its place. In spite of a few difficult passages, it has been widely acknowledged that the New Testament offers a strikingly illuminating interpretation of the Old. C. H. Dodd states, "It must be conceded that we have before us a considerable intellectual feat. The various scriptures are acutely interpreted along lines already discernible within the Old Testament canon itself or in pre-Christian Judaism – in many cases, I believe, lines which start from their first, historical, intention – and these lines are carried forward to fresh results. Very diverse scriptures are brought together so that they interpret one another in hitherto unsuspected ways" (*According to the Scriptures*, p. 109).

Even passages which have frequently been viewed as difficult, and sometimes advanced as examples of farfetched and artificial exegesis, may well receive an appropriate explanation in terms of this total understanding of the divine purpose and of the pneumatic unity of the Scriptures. For instance, Matthew 2: 15 applies to Christ the statement of Hosea 11:1, "Out of Egypt have I called my son," which in the original context has surely a primary reference to the Exodus in the time of Moses. Matthew, however, far from making an artificial and illegitimate transference of the text to Christ, simply views Moses' exodus as one element in the great redemptive pattern which runs through history, an element which bears a striking resemblance, even geographically, to certain features of the career of Jesus Christ the Messiah, through whom redemption was to be accomplished and the spiritual exodus of God's people effected. It is worthwhile to read Patrick Fairbairn's eloquent pages on this subject (*Typology of Scripture*, 6th. ed., Vol. I., p. 450 ff. Also in Zondervan reprint).

While an acknowledgement of the pneumatic unity of Scripture and of the overarching redemptive purpose of God (*Heilsgeschichte*) will greatly assist in gaining a proper understanding of passages that were sometimes alleged to be strained, it is not claimed here that this principle will automatically resolve all the difficulties that may be encountered in this area. It may be wise to keep in mind the following considerations.

a. It is not necessary to assume in every case that the Old Testament writers or their immediate audience had a clear grasp of the full scope of meaning of their pronouncement, nor specifically of its fulfillment in New Testament times. The Holy Spirit of God who inspired them may well have led them to say things which had a certain relationship to their contemporary situation, to be sure, but whose ultimate God-breathed meaning far surpassed what was immediately understood or intended. This was surely the case for Caiaphas (John 11:49-52), and it may well have occurred to a greater or lesser degree in connection with certain Old Testament Scriptures.

b. Evangelicals naturally hold that any New Testament interpretation of an Old Testament text is legitimate. They do not feel bound to assert that it is necessarily exclusive or exhaustive of the full Old Testament meaning. Certain Old Testament passages may have conveyed to the original hearers a more restricted sense than the perspective that is presented in the New Testament. The original understanding was a legitimate interpretation which is now supplemented, not cancelled, by the larger vistas of the New Testament, and which in turn does not preclude the propriety of these larger vistas, now authoritatively revealed in the New Testament.

c. It may be wise to remember that the New Testament authors were so immersed in the language and the thought patterns of the Old Testament that expressions which are drawn from it seem to come naturally to their lips or to their pen. Some people versed in a certain favorite author, like Shakespeare, frequently do express themselves in forms of language derived from his writings, without thereby meaning to suggest a complete situational correspondance. Similarly, the fact that Old Testament phrases are used does not necessarily imply that the New Testament author asserted a direct relationship between the original passage and the New Testament context. Sometimes such a relationship is explicitly asserted, but when it is not, we are not in a position to say that it is implied in the presence of verbal resemblances.

d. The New Testament authors at times amalgamate various Old Testament passages in such a way that these supplement each other and are brought into illuminating focus in terms of the New Testament situation. A good example of this procedure may be found in II Corinthians 6:16-18, in which we find a composite of references to Ezekiel 37:27; Leviticus 26:11, 12; Isaiah 52:11, 12; Ezekiel 20:34; and II Samuel 7:14.

e. The New Testament writers apparently did not hesitate in a number of cases to modify the wording of the Old Testament, or even to introduce comments of their own in order to indicate in what way they construed or applied the Old Testament text. Ephesians 6:2, 3 provides an example of this practice. Occasionally it is not easy to determine what was intended as commentary and what was meant as quotation. The whole question of the verbal accuracy of the New Testament quotations is too complex to be discussed here. For a very brief treatment of it we may perhaps be permitted to refer the reader to what we have written elsewhere in an article, "New Testament Use of the Old Testament" in *Revelation and the Bible* (Carl F. H. Henry, ed.; Grand Rapids, 1958, pp. 135-151).

BIBLIOGRAPHY

Dittmar, Wilhelm, *Vetus Testamentum in Novo.* Goettingen, 1903.

Dodd, C. H., *According to the Scriptures.* London, 1952.

Ellis, E. E., *Paul's Use of the Old Testament.* Grand Rapids, 1957.

Fairbairn, Patrick, *Hermeneutical Manual,* pp. 354-460. Edinburgh, 1858.

Lindars, Barnabas, *New Testament Apologeic: The Doctrinal Significance of Old Testament Quotations.* Philadelphia, 1961.

Mickelsen, A. B., *Interpreting the Bible.* Grand Rapids, 1963.

Sweet, L. M., "Quotations," *ISBE.*

Turpie, D. M., *The Old Testament in the New.* London, 1868.

The Use of Archaeology in Interpretation

Viewed historically the Bible is a valuable collection of ancient documents, covering, if it may be assumed that written records dating back to Abraham found incorporation in the Pentateuch, something like 2000 years of history and literary activity. It is the first task of the interpreter to determine what the writer of any given work of literature, or record of history, originally intended to communicate. For that reason all information which elucidates his language, throws light on his social context, explains allusions, or otherwise provides contemporary comment on his meaning, the understanding and outlook of his public, and his own plan and purpose, is an aid to exegesis. The sources of such information are largely archaeological in the case of the Old Testament. The New Testament, which classical historians have too commonly disregarded as an important document of first century history and the Roman peace, is contemporary with the written records of sophisticated literary societies, and is less dependent for its interpretation on the diligence of archaeological research. It is, nonetheless, richly illuminated by it, in common with the secular history of a fairly well-documented age. Surviving non-Biblical literary documents from the civilizations of the Fertile Crescent, epigraphical records of five empires, works of art, and a thousand lesser and more elusive memorials of human activity, artifacts. papyri, potsherds, and the indelible marks of man's work and worship, are all relevant material for the interpretation of the Bible.

Archaeology, in its varied forms of activity, has provided most of this material. Thanks to its skilled and scientific application it is possible today to understand the Bible in its setting of time and place as never before. To grasp with clarity the writer's first meaning and original purpose is manifestly the first step towards the elucidation of that which is permanent and universally significant in his theme. Such understanding is logically the interpreter's first task and requires an awareness of key Biblical archaeological discoveries. This article is not a survey of Biblical archaeology in its breadth and achievement. A number of competent works deal adequately with the subject as a whole. It is the present object to suggest the preacher's and teacher's approach to archaeology as an aid to exegesis. Illustration under four heads will be the most effective demonstration.

1. ARCHAEOLOGICAL MATERIAL WHICH ELUCIDATES BACKGROUND AND CONTEXT

The events of the Bible did not take place in a vacuum. They were part of ancient history. The theme of the Bible is that stream of human faith, action, and endeavor which found consummation in the New Testament. The actors, nevertheless, moved on a stage which is becoming wider, deeper, and clearer in the light of archaeological discovery. In the past, the view was held that the stories of the patriarchs were folk-tales of the sort which gather round the origins of a people and were of no historical worth. Abraham was of no more significance than Aeneas, unearthed by Greeks of Magna Graecia from a motley stock of Trojan legend, as a canny compliment to emerging Rome. It is no longer possible to hold that view. Ur of the Chaldees was first shown by Leonard Woolley to be a mature and literary society, but Ur was only one place, and her history only one chapter, of the crowded story of the Euphrates valley. Movement and migration had taken place from time immemorial round what Henry Breasted called the Fertile Crescent, and Abraham's wanderings were part of a process repeated more than once in the story of the river civilizations of the Near and Middle East. By the same path came Canaanite and Phoenician in unrecorded folk migrations.

The unique feature of Abraham's story is the wealth of detail which accompanies it in the fine literary accounts in Genesis. It is almost possible to pick the point where the laborious brevity of the clay tablet was succeeded by the more roomy and ample style which the papyrus made possible and to assess the early documents which Abraham no doubt bequeathed to his family and Moses' later editing. In accordance with ancient custom his own family must have kept a record. Truth and authenticity are embedded in detail, and it is there that the investigator must look in measuring the historical value of a story. The laws, literature, and business documents of the Euphrates valley have provided a wealth of comment on the stories of the patriarchs but comment may be confined to the striking documents from Nuzi. The Hurrians of the Nuzi texts were well-acquainted with the Habiru of the Amarna letters and the Ras Shamra tablets, and demonstrate a community of custom with the Hebrew patriarchs which goes far to support the contention that Habiru and Hebrew were the same. Sarah's search for an heir by means of her maid Hagar, her legal casting out of Hagar on Isaac's birth, Abraham's adoption of Eliezer as his heir, Esau's contemptuous sale of his birthright, Laban's and Jacob's partnership, Rachel's attempt to confirm succession by the theft of the teraphim, and Isaac's irrevocable bestowal of the blessing all find detailed parallel in the Nuzi tablets. The stories of the patriarchs are obviously authentic history, and to be interpreted as such. Genesis is vindicated as a reliable record, and interpretation can proceed with the added certainty that those who move through its pages were real people and not the figures of legend or saga.

Qumran provides a parallel illustration for the New Testament. The abiding worth of the now famous Dead Sea Scrolls for the New Testament scholar is probably the light which they throw on the "third force" in Palestine, "the Remnant" of the true and faithful, distinct from the organized groupings of Sadducee and Pharisee, in revolt against urban religion, and hitherto visible only in the New Testament. Of such were the more obscure figures of the Gospels, the fishermen of Galilee, the "common people" who "heard him gladly," the followers of John, the parents of John, Mary herself, the Bethany household, and the widow with the mite. The scrolls from the caves have demonstrated the reality of this social and religious substratum. Like masses of nonliterary papyri from Egypt, the Qumran documents show the realities of common life, and the earthy truth of the New Testament. They underline the fact that the Gospels are a document of first century history, giving what no other literary record gives in such volume, a glimpse of the proletariat and life as it was lived by common folk in Rome's most uneasy and turbulent province.

The lesson for the interpreter again emerges. Any theory of literary origins which treats the four Gospels as other than a plain record put together by eyewitnesses, must be forthwith suspect in the light of the social evidence from papyrological sources. Interpretation can begin with one advantage if it can stand on such evidence in the face of the sharp attacks of the critics.

Another lesson takes shape from the examination of the archaeological material, and that is the unique ethical and monotheistic emphasis of the Bible. Sumeria,

Babylon, and Assyria have provided in their surviving literature accounts of creation, man's innocence and fall, and the judgment of a deluge. Babylon, the Hittites, and other smaller communities, provide examples of codes of law. The interpreter and apologist has only to set this parallel, earlier, and contemporary material side by side with the Biblical documents to demonstrate that the Hebrew stood apart, reserved, free from the crudities of the pagan mythologies, related to a theme and an unfolding purpose, lofty in ethics, and austerely monotheistic. If the Bible does not invent, it appropriates, adapts, and transforms. Phrases from the Lord's prayer are to be found in rabbinical liturgies. The theological language of Paul is sometimes that of the mystery cults, Christmas was Mithras' birthday, etc. Of what significance are these facts? Simply that the divine method, here as with the personality of man, is not obliteration but sublimation, and the transformation of that which is committed.

2. ARCHAEOLOGICAL MATERIAL OF APOLOGETIC VALUE

This aspect of interpretation has been touched upon above. The era of modern archaeology burst on the world with high drama, both in the classical and Biblical spheres. Schliemann discovered Troy and Mycenae, and demonstrated the absurdity of the corrupted interpretation of the Greek epics, Aegean history, and the mythology of the Mediterranean cultures. The lesson was repeated as civilization after civilization was unearthed — the Assyrians, the Babylonians, the Hittites, the Cretans. Layard preceded Schliemann with the recovery of Nineveh; Woolley succeeded him in the excavation of Ur. A dozen great names will always be listed as the pioneers of an astonishing era of discovery which thrust back the frontiers of history for scores of centuries, and so frequently demonstrated the truth and reliability of tradition that Biblical scholars of the conservative school and Christian apologists took to quoting the work of the archaeologists with something like triumph. There is no doubt that some of this enthusiasm was justified. Confirmation of otherwise unsupported detail in the Biblical records by the documents from the Euphrates valley and Assyria, or by the epigraphical evidence of Asia Minor and of Greece, has been a constant encouragement to those who rightly see a firm foundation for Christian doctrine in the reliability and authority of the Bible. The life story and research of Sir William Ramsay, the classical and Biblical scholar in Asia Minor is striking illustration of the process by which more than one honest mind returned to a confidence in the Scriptural records from the synthetic skepticism of nineteenth century scholarship Particular illustration is found in the complete vindication of Luke as an historian, the justification of his language, and the confirmation of his casual detail. The Nazareth Decree, with its strange light on the Pharisaic account of the empty tomb is a more recent illustration (see the present writer's *Out of the Earth,* chap. 4).

Thanks to archaeology, the interpreter can turn to Scripture with a much greater confidence in the historical worth of the documents and can dismiss with firmness the neo-liberal approach which, under varied forms of "demythologizing," is paradoxically creating a new mythology. So often has the hasty assumption, and the far fetched theory, crumbled at the touch of the archaeological discovery that informed conservatism can await with some tranquillity the passing of the ephemeral fashions of the liberal school. The collapse of the assumptions of the Tubingen School on the question of the Fourth Gospel is now history, and the recovery of Tatian's Diatesseron on which a galleon of theory was wrecked, can hardly be classified as an archaeological achievement. The papyrus fragment in the Manchester University library which takes the dating of John back to A.D. 125 can, however, be regarded as an archaeological prize, and the whole story illustrates the contention set forth above. The apologetic value of archaeology to the orthodox and conservative interpreter must be ranked highly.

3. ARCHAEOLOGICAL MATERIAL OF ARTISTIC SIGNIFICANCE

Art is both a rendering and a representation of life. The realism of mural art in Egypt and Assyria is a strong light upon society and human action in many spheres. Greek vase paintings have illustrated and explained more than one obscure corner in the interpretation of the classics; and if the exegesis of the Bible has less instances of such aid to quote, the help of such representational art has nevertheless deepened understanding. Professor Yigael Yadin's sumptuously illustrated book on warfare in Biblical times demonstrates the importance of surviving samples of weaponry and surviving artwork representations of battles, sieges, and all manner of military activity for the interpretation of ancient history.

Nor is war the only sphere where archaeology similarly elucidates a Biblical context or reinforces a critical argument. Early use of the vine and branches in Christian decorative art adds weight to the argument for an early date for the fourth Gospel. And consider the throne-like altar to Zeus from Pergamum, set up today in the East Berlin Museum. It throws considerable light on the symbolism of the apocalyptic letter to Pergamum, whose church dwelt "where Satan's seat is" (Rev. 2:13). The altar somehow summed up the pervasive paganism of the place with its worship of the imperial cult, and its devotion to the serpent-ridden Asklepios. Ramsay's book on the *Letters to the Seven Churches of Asia*, a landmark in the interpretation of the elusive imagery of the Apocalypse, draws heavily on art and architecture, no less than on the artistry of coinage, for the writer's convincing elucidations.

Illustration is widespread. An ear of corn, carved on a fallen plinth in the precinct of Demeter at Eleusis, near Athens, is a reference to the symbolic significance of the uplifted ear of corn in the mystery cult once celebrated here, and considerable light on the image of the corn of wheat which Christ expounded to a group of Greeks. Since Paul must have passed through Eleusis on his way to Corinth, it is significant too that the illustration of the dying grain recurs in his epistle to Corinth. And Paul's amazing Areopagus address is illuminated by reference to the artistic wonders on the rocky platform of the Acropolis above where he spoke, but whose relevance in the quest for truth were quickly dismissed.

4. ARCHAEOLOGICAL MATERIAL OF LITERARY SIGNIFICANCE

Much of the material which might have been assembled here has found a place under other headings above. The significance of the cuneiform records of Assyria and the Euphrates valley for the interpretation of the early chapters of Genesis has already been discussed. Of equal relevance is Egyptian literature, also the gift of archaeology. A. S Yahauda showed from this source, many years ago, how unerringly accurate in detail, background, and atmosphere were the closing chapters of Genesis and the early chapters of Exodus. Akhnaton's *Hymn to the Sun*, and similar surviving poetry, demonstrates the poetic psalm in a non-Biblical context, and reveals that the Hebrew psalter was in the full stream of ancient lyrism.

The nonliterary papyri, recovered in vast numbers from the sites of ancient towns south of the rain-line in Egypt, have shed floods of light on the New Testament. The human situation envisaged in the parables of Christ can be illustrated again and again from this correspondence in a manner which emphasizes the realism and contemporary relevance of Christ's teaching and the authenticity of the documents which record it. The form of the ancient letter with its opening formalities, its body of information and request, and its personal greetings at the end is similar comment on the epistles of the New Testament. It was Adolf Deissmann, a young German scholar, who first drew attention to the worth and significance of the papyri in this regard, at the end of the nineteenth century. His *Licht vom Osten* was another landmark in New Testament studies.

5. ARCHAEOLOGICAL MATERIAL OF LINGUISTIC SIGNIFICANCE

It was part of Deissmann's thesis that the Greek of the nonliterary papyri, the common spoken Greek of everyday intercourse, was also the Greek of the New Testament. The language of the papyri has thrown light on many difficult contexts in the New Testament. Examples are too numerous to quote, but the discovery that *meris* meant "a region" set Luke's description of Philippi in its correct geographical light. If *hypostasis* means "title-deeds" as well as "substance," a vivid interpretation of Hebrews 11:1 is made possible. Since *apecho* can be shown to provide a formula for a receipt, quaint light is thrown on the use of the word by Matthew, the tax collector, in the context which dismisses the Pharisaic exhibitionists as already "paid in full." If *epiousion* can refer to the day which is beginning, and has shed its classical meaning of "tomorrow," a difficult phrase in the Lord's Prayer is cleared up. It is the meaning of the word in common parlance which is so often relevant to the correct understanding of a text, and archaeology has provided the raw linguistic material for this.

The Dead Sea Scrolls share this exegetical importance with the Egyptian papyri. The ancient texts which the scrolls provide have cleared up the numerical contradiction between Exodus 1:5 and Acts 7:14 by supporting with a contemporary text the reading followed in Acts and in the Greek Septuagint. They have proved that Hebrews 1:6 is, in fact, a quotation from Deuteronomy 32:43. The magnificent scroll of Isaiah has cleared up difficulties in 3:24; 20:1, 8; and 49:12. The teaching of the Qumran sect illustrates twice the Sermon on the Mount. The Lord directly rebukes their doctrine in Matthew 5:43, and approves it in Matthew 18:15-17. The same texts show that "the poor in spirit" means "the tender-hearted."

In conclusion let it again be stressed that all competent interpretation must begin with the basic and contemporary meaning of a document. If that is not plain, the secondary and more general meaning is likely to prove elusive. The present object has been to show that archaeology, by its recovery and description of the context and background – social, political, topical, literary, linguistic, historical, and geographical, can frequently elucidate and illuminate dark corners in a manner which the interpreter cannot well neglect. His study of the archaeological evidence is therefore of prime concern.

BIBLIOGRAPHY

Banks, F. A., *Coins of Bible Days.* Macmillan.

Boulton, W. H., *Archaeology Explains.* Epworth Press.

Blaiklock, E. M., *Out of the Earth.* Paternoster.

Bruce, F. F., *Second Thoughts on the Dead Sea Scrolls.* Paternoster.

Coburn, C. M., *The New Archaeological Discoveries.* Funk and Wagnalls.

Eisenberg, A., and Elkins, D. P., *Worlds Lost and Found.* Abelard Sherman.

Harrison, R. K., *A History of Old Testament Times.* Zondervan.

Kitchen, J. H., *Holy Fields.* Eerdmans.

Pfeiffer, C. F., *The Biblical World.* Baker Book House.

Ramsay, W. M., *Letters to the Seven Churches.* Hodder and Stoughton. Reprint 1963 by Baker Book House.

Thompson, J. A., *The Bible and Archaeology.* Eerdmans.

Unger, M. F., *Archaeology and the Old Testament.* Zondervan.

Wiseman, D. J., *Illustrations from Biblical Archaeology.* Tyndale Press.

The Dead Sea Scrolls and Interpretation

The chance discovery in 1947 of some ancient scrolls, cached in a cave near the northwestern shore of the Dead Sea, began an amazing, and ever-growing, series of archaeological expeditions and scholarly researches. Thousands of pieces of Biblical, apocryphal, and sectarian manuscripts have come to light, which have affected the interpretation of the Bible. For our purposes here, only the texts from Qumran (the area of the original finds, seven miles south of Jericho) are relevant.

1. THE RELATIONSHIP TO THE BIBLICAL TEXT

The starting point of interpretation is the establishment of the "original" text, for it is well known that the text of the Bible has not been transmitted to us free from all scribal defect. This does not mean that matters of basic doctrine are in question, but rather that the text of the Bible has various obscure and unintelligible passages. But into the midst of this difficulty the texts from Qumran have come as a tremendous help, primarily for the Old Testament, for no New Testament materials were found at this site.

a. New materials. The method by which scholars seek to resolve the difficulties of the text in order to begin interpretation is called "textual criticism." The task is carried on by three primary means: (a) comparing different manuscripts, noting their agreements and differences, and arriving at an eclectic, and what is believed original, text; (b) comparing Hebrew manuscripts with ancient versions, because these translations are often based on earlier Hebrew manuscripts than have been preserved; and (c) conjectural emendation, that is, scholarly conjecture as to the original text, based on knowledge of the ways errors may occur in transcribing manuscripts. Obviously the best means is the comparison of manuscripts. However, prior to the discovery of the Scrolls this was not possible in the Old Testament on any large scale. Because of the Jewish practice of discarding and eventually burying old manuscripts, and because of persecutions and other reasons, no manuscripts (except for a few fragments) of the Old Testament earlier than the ninth and tenth centuries A.D. have survived.

Another problem has been the fact that all these medieval manuscripts agree very closely with one another, except in minor orthographic matters. The reason for this is that all medieval Hebrew manuscripts in the dominant tradition have descended from a common ancestor or single scroll. Around A.D. 100, as a result primarily of the council of Jamnia and the labors of rabbi Aqiba, a standardized, authoritative text was established out of the various textual traditions in the pre-Christian period. All variant lines of tradition were destroyed, or at least were brought into agreement with the *textus receptus.* The result was that from then on all manuscripts were made on the basis of this one authoritative text. And this is what has come to be known as the Masoretic text.

The discovery of the Qumran scrolls breached this barrier of A.D. 100. Now, for the first time, we can get a firsthand look at the state of the Old Testament text in Christian times. The Qumran texts date just prior to the stabilization of the consonantal text in A.D. 100, that is, about the second to the first century B.C.

b. New value judgments. In the process of comparing different manuscripts of the Bible with ancient versions in order to determine the correct reading for interpretation, it is necessary to have some understanding of the trustworthiness of these versions. The study of the Scrolls has brought a new appreciation of the value of certain versional evidence. Research has shown that in the days of the Qumran scribes there were at least three different textual traditions in common circulation. In other words, the texts found at Qumran fall into three separate "families" or traditions regarding the state of the text. Many of them are very similar to the Masoretic text, and so indicate that they are the tradition which was eventually accepted and standardized in A.D. 100. Others, however, agree closely with the readings in the Septuagint (the Greek version translated between 250 and 100 B.C.), and thus show that they are in a line with the Hebrew text upon which it was based. Yet some scrolls agree with neither, and on various occasions show affinities with the Samaritan Pentateuch (the Hebrew text copied by the Samaritans after the schism in the middle of the fourth century B.C.).

What all this indicates is that in the centuries before Christ there was not just one authoritative text. Various traditions were accepted and used. This means that from now on textual criticism must not be content with using the evidence of the Septuagint or Samaritan Pentateuch as a last resort. It must, rather, give greater weight to variant textual traditions reflected in these sources.

c. New clarifications. The manuscripts from Qumran and the new appreciation of the versions have yielded information that clarifies many individual texts, particularly in the Old Testament. A few examples will illustrate this.

The Old Testament committee of the Revised Standard Version had access to the complete scroll of Isaiah (IQIs[a]) found in the first cave. It eventually decided to adopt thirteen readings in the scroll that differed from the Masoretic text. Each has been marked in the margin with the note "one ancient Ms." For example, the Masoretic text of Isaiah 21:8 reads, as translated in the KJV, "And he cried, A lion." But this does not fit the context, for the immediately preceding verses speak of the watchman seeing horsemen, asses, and camels, not a lion. The ASV, sensing this difficulty, translates, "And he cried as a lion," but this is not what the text says. The Qumran scroll of Isaiah has at this point, "then he who saw cried," as the RSV reads. The difference between the words "a lion" and "he who saw" involves basically the interchange of two consonants in Hebrew, probably a scribal error caused by confusing sounds as a text was being dictated for copying. The Qumran scroll clearly makes better sense.

In the Masoretic text of I Samuel 23:11-12 David asks two questions, and the Lord answers only the second one. David then in verse twelve repeats his first question, and finally gets an answer. The Septuagint, however, omits both the second question and the Lord's answer to the first one. The Qumran scroll (4QSam[b]) has apparently preserved the original text, for it separates the two questions and gives an answer to each, "But now, will Saul go down, as your servant has heard? O Lord God of Israel, tell your servant. And the Lord said, He will go down. Then David asked, Will the men of Keilah hand me and my men over to Saul? They will deliver you, replied the Lord."

In Hebrews 1:6 there is quoted, supposedly from the Old Testament, the phrase, "let all the angels of God worship him." But this cannot be found in the Masoretic text. However, a fragment of Deuteronomy 32(4Q Deut 32) found at Qumran contains this extra phrase. It reads, "bow down (worship) to him, all ye gods." The Septuagint (which the author of Hebrews was quoting) also contains this line, and the evidence from Qumran suggests this was original.

One should remember in all this that because a reading appears in the Qumran Scrolls does not mean it is automatically to be preferred. Habakkuk 2:15 is a case in point. In the Masoretic text we read the phrase "gaze on their nakedness," but the Qumran commentary on Habakkuk reads "gaze on their feasts." The two words "nakedness" and "feasts" are very similar in Hebrew, the only difference being one letter. But there seems to be no reason to change the Masoretic text, since the Qumran reading appears to be a deliberate change motivated by interpretational purposes. The commentary that follows this passage stresses that a certain evil event took place on the Day of Atonement, that is, on a "feast" day!

2. THE RELATIONSHIP TO BIBLICAL TERMINOLOGY AND THOUGHT

Many times the problem of interpretation rests not with a corrupt text, but rather with an obscure terminology. Biblical languages have not been spoken for 2000 years, and thus word and phrase meanings have often become lost. Or it may be that a word occurs only once or twice in the Bible, and so does not provide sufficient contexts in which to clarify its meaning. The Scrolls provide many more contexts against which to interpret the signiificance of Biblical terminology. Only a few examples will be given here.

a. *The Old Testament.* In Micah 6:8 occur the familiar words, "to do justice, and to love kindness, and to walk humbly with your God" (RSV). All of the major English versions translate this phrase in a similar fashion. But it is possible to translate the Hebrew text somewhat differently: "to practice justice and love of kindness, and to walk humbly with your God." In this case "love of kindness" would be the object of "practice." The problem, of course, centers on the word "love," which in Hebrew can be read either as an infinitive "to love" or as a noun "love." Which is correct? Here the Scrolls come as a help. W. Brownless in *The Meaning of the Qumran Scrolls for the Bible* (p. 108), has pointed out that in the Manual of Discipline 2:24-25 there is an allusion to Micah 6:8 in the sentence, "for they shall all live in unity of truth, and humility of goodness, and love of kindness, and purpose of righteousness." This series of constructs, because of the particular words used, suggests that this means "true unity and good humility and kindly love and righteous purpose." That this is correct is given confirmation by another passage in the Manual, namely, 8:1-2: "in the council of the community there shall be twelve laymen and three priests, who are perfect in all that has been revealed of the whole law, who shall practice truth and righteousness and kindly love [love of kindness], who shall walk humbly a man with his neighbor." The point of all this is that the Scrolls show clearly that the word "love" in Micah 6:8 is not an infinitive, but rather a noun with a qualifying attribute "kindly," or better (as the word "kindly" in Hebrew combines the ideas of love and loyalty) "devoted." Thus Micah 6:8 should be translated,

"He has showed you, O man, what is good;
and what does the Lord require of you
but to practice justice and devoted love,
and to walk humbly with your God."

The whole passage would then reflect the twofold path of godly living stressed in Deuteronomy 6:5 and Leviticus 19:18 (cf. Mark. 12:28-31).

The Qumran sect, however, does not always give us such clarification. It had its own method of Biblical interpretation, which shows the dangers of a predetermined point of view on the meaning of the text. The sect interpreted the Old Testament against the background of its own belief that it was living in the last days, and thus discovered, so it believed, that the prophets had prophesied almost exclusively of those days. Therefore, by allegory and variant reading and words out of context, the sect found guidance in the prophets for the last, difficult times in which they lived. A commentary on Micah from cave 1 is a good example. In Micah 1:5 we find the words, "all this is for the transgression of Jacob, and for the sins of the house of Israel. What is the transgression of Jacob? Is it not Samaria? And what is the sin of the house of Jacob? Is it not Jerusalem?" (RSV). The RSV has followed the Septuagint in reading the phrase "the sin of the house of Judah," but the Masoretic text reads "the high places of Judah"; the Micah commentary agrees with the Masoretic text, except in reading the singular "high place." But, in any case, as the context shows, the reference is to the idolatrous worship found in the capital cities of Samaria and Jerusalem. However, at Qumran, "the transgression of Jacob" was interpreted as referring to "the prophet of lies, who leads the simple astray." And "the high place of Judah" is seen as a reference to the "Teacher of Righteousness," the one who led and interpreted the law to the sect. The "prophet of lies," as other contexts indicate, was probably the leader of a rival group, perhaps of the Pharisees. Here, then, allegory has taken the place of contextual exegesis.

b. *The New Testament.* In Luke 2:14, as is usually translated, the angels sang in praise to God: "Glory to God in the highest and on earth peace, good will towards men." This is now seen to have been incorrectly translated, as the RSV reflects. The Greek word *eudokia,* usually "good will," is the equivalent of the Hebrew *ratson,* a term which occurs on various occasions in the Scrolls. But at Qumran it usually carried a special connotation, namely, "God's grace" or "God's good will." Thus in the Hymns of Thanksgiving, in a passage very reminiscent of Luke 2:14, it says that God desires men to know "the abundance of his mercies towards all the sons of his grace [*ratson*]" (4:33). Or in 11:9 the author sings that "thy mercy is towards the sons of thy goodwill." And, conversely, the writer of 10:5-6 admits that the person without this *ratson* is nothing: "I am dust and ashes. What can I devise, if thou art unwilling, and what can I contrive, apart from thy grace [*ratson*]" All this suggests that during the days of the New Testament the term *ratson,* in the kind of context found in Luke 2:14, carried the idea of "divine good pleasure." Thus the passage should be translated, "Glory to God in the highest, and on earth peace to men of God's grace." The promise is that those who know God's good pleasure, and live in it, shall have peace.

3. THE RELATIONSHIP TO CHRISTIANITY

More controversial than individual passages has been the discussion over the significance of the Scrolls for the uniqueness of Christianity. Some have taken up the old position of E. Renan that Christianity is only another form of Essenism which happened to succeed, and have sought to buttress this argument by showing that for its ideas and practices the New Testament was dependent on the Qumran community of Essenes. However, although there are many striking similarities, there are also basic differences which clearly separate the two communities.

The Gospel of John is largely constructed on the theme of the conflict between light and darkness. So John 1:4-5 reads, "In him was life, and the life was the light of men. The light shines in the darkness, and the darkness has not overcome it" (RSV). This same theme is basic to the Scrolls. We learn from the Manual of Discipline that the world is ruled by two powers, one good and one evil, both of them having been created by God (1QS 3:25). The good power is termed the "spirit of truth" or the "prince of lights" (1QS 3:18-24), while the evil force is called the "spirit of perversity" or the "angel of darkness" (1QS 3:19-21). According to Qumran thought all members of the sect were "children of light" (1QS 1:9), a designation also given to Christians in John 12:36, while all outside the group were "children of darkness" (1QS 1:10). The Gospel of John also knows of those who walk in darkness (12:35).

But we should not confuse this "dualism" of Qumran and John. They are both simply using common terminology which was well-known to their contemporaries. What is important is the meaning of the terms. At Qumran a person became a "son of light" by joining the community and obeying its strict interpretation of the Law. In John one becomes a "son of light" by faith in Christ, who himself is the light of the world (cf. John 12:36, 46). Perhaps John is addressing himself to those who had become enamored with Essene thought, and thus radically alters its content. In any case, the Scrolls show that the background of the terminology is thoroughly Jewish, and not Hellenistic (as claimed by Dodd), or Gnostic (as suggested by Bultmann).

Many have thought that in practice, as well as in terminology, there was a link between Qumran and the church. For example, the baptismal practices of Qumran are sometimes thought to be the source of Christian baptism. But at Qumran baptismal practice included daily ablutions for ritual purity, initiatory ablutions for probationary members, and annual ablutions for covenant renewal. The only similarity to some Christian usage is the mode of immersion, and the fact that it was accompanied by repentance, a slim base upon which to build a theory of dependence. The same is true of the sect's "sacred meal." In the Messianic Rule (1QSa) directions are given for a meal consisting of bread and wine, over which prayers are said by the presiding priest. Although some would see here the background to the Christian Eucharist, nowhere is anything said about a sacramental character to the meal, nor of it being a memorial.

Much has also been made of possible relationships between Qumran and John the Baptist and Jesus. As to John the Baptist, there are many possible links with the Qumran sect. He began his ministry near the site of Qumran (Luke 1:80); he was from a priestly background (Luke 1:8-9) that would have found acceptance in the priestly-run sect of Qumran, whose members called themselves the "sons of Zadok" (1QS 8:4-10); he stressed the importance of baptism being accompanied by repentance, as did Qumran (Luke 3:7-9; 1QS 3:6-11); and he found the basis of his ministry in Isaiah 40:3, the foundation text at Qumran (John 1:23; 1QS 8:13-15). It is possible, in light of this, that John may have belonged to the community for a time; at least he probably knew something about their thought and way of life. But John's basic ministry was entirely independent of Qumran, and, indeed, quite opposed to it. John's ministry was essentially prophetic; the sect's was esoteric. John issued a public call to repentance; the sect withdrew to the desert. John's message was free of the legal emphasis found at Qumran. John invited all to repent, while the Qumran community hated its enemies. John baptized once all who repented; Qumran repeated the rite.

The relationship between Jesus and the Qumran leader – the Teacher of Righteousness – is another matter. There is no reason to suspect any link at all. John at least was an ascetic, but Jesus was not (cf. Matt. 11:19). Before his public ministry Jesus did not live in the wilderness; it was only during his forty days of temptation that he was there, and this would not provide much opportunity for learning the wisdom of Qumran, particularly since Mark says he was with "the wild beasts" (Mark 1:13). Although there are clear parallels between the teachings of Qumran and of Jesus (cf. Matt. 18:15-17 and IQS 5:24-6:1), there are also striking differences, particularly in relation to the authority of the Law (cf. the constant "but I say unto you" in the Sermon on the Mount). And there is little about the lives of Jesus and the Teacher of Righteousness that is similar. The latter was not crucified, had no saving efficacy attached to his death, and was not expected to rise from the dead.

The conclusion to all this is that, first, the similarities do not suggest any immediate relationship between the Scrolls and the New Testament. Rather, they indicate simply that Jesus and the disciples used the vocabulary of their contemporaries. Jesus did not appear in an historical vacuum. He did not come speaking of things about which men had never thought, nor using a heavenly language. And, secondly, the differences indicate a tremendous gap between Qumran thought and Christian belief. The central figure in this difference is Jesus Christ; there was no one like him at Qumran. The Scrolls do not destroy the uniqueness of Christianity, nor confirm any doctrine.

BIBLIOGRAPHY

Brownlee, W., *The Meaning of the Qumran Scrolls for the Bible.* New York: Oxford, 1964.

Burrows, M., *The Dead Sea Scrolls.* New York: Viking, 1955.

————————, *More Light on the Dead Sea Scrolls.* New York: Viking, 1958.

Cross, F., *The Ancient Library of Qumran and Modern Biblical Studies.* Garden City: Doubleday, 1958.

Ringgren, H., *The Faith of Qumran.* Philadelphia: Fortress, 1963.

Vermes, G., *The Dead Sea Scrolls in English.* Baltimore: Penguin, 1962.

Reformation Interpretation (1457-1560)

For a thousand years Pope Gregory I (A.D. 590-604) dominated Latin Biblical interpretation. His commentary on Job set forth a rich homiletical harvest for the medieval world. By the year A.D. 800 Augustine, Jerome, Ambrose, and Gregory controlled early medieval Biblical exegesis. The loss of Greek and the logic of scholasticism ossified Biblical study until the marriage between homiletics and fourteenth century scholarship buried the text beyond recognition. But the men of the Reformation restored to the church sound Biblical interpretation.

1. A HUMANIST HERMENEUTIC

In March of 1457 Laurentius Valla attacked Aquinas as an interpreter, preferring Paul as a theologian. When in his notes on the New Testament Valla turned to the Greek text, a positive reform of theology began. Careful attention to that text would remove "the clamor of strangers in the presence of God's Word, for His Word is our life." Erasmus discovered Valla's notes in the Parc monastery, publishing them in 1505. Bade wrote in his preface to that edition, "Valla has deserved the greatest favour and gratitude of every studious man." Erasmus earned the gratitude of all the reformers for his 1516 edition of the Greek New Testament with its fresh Latin version, followed by critical notes. It was John Colet of England who set Erasmus to producing critical editions of the New Testament and the early church fathers.

The Strassburg reformer Martin Bucer warned his town council against multiple interpretations in a single passage of Scripture. His 1527 letter cites John Colet who in 1499 argued with Erasmus that Scripture can have but one sense, and that the simplest. Erasmus listened to Colet, describing his impact in such forcible terms that Colet "could hardly attend to anything else but the destruction of that idol of ignorance, the cobweb-divinity of the schools, and to exalt the scriptures and Jesus Christ." In his 1501 *Enchiridion* Erasmus sets forth a program of popular piety based on those Scriptures. Many vilified Erasmus. John Maier of Eck censured Erasmus from Ingolstadt on February 2, 1518. Eck carped at the new Biblical theology, "If one stagger in unbelief at the authority of sacred scripture [in Latin?] what parts will escape without suspicion of error?" Erasmus would not keep the Scripture bound in theological distinctions or in an archaic Vulgate Latin text. Long before in his *Enchiridion* Erasmus answered his critics, "To be learned falls to the lot of but few, but there is no one who cannot be a Christian, no one who cannot be pious; I may add this boldly: no one who cannot be a theologian."

The fourfold system of medieval exegesis in its literal, allegorical, anagogical, and tropological senses gave multiple insights to the Biblical scholar. In the hands of a sensitive student the text determined in its literal sense the theological expression of the church. The humanists replaced that Vulgate text with Greek editions of the New Testament and critical editions of Jerome and the Greek fathers. In replacing the Vulgate with fresh sources, the Protestant and Catholic Biblical reformers also discovered a new hermeneutic. Without that humanist return to the sources and the rejection of multiple senses in single Scriptural passages, one misses the Reformation's triumph and tragedy.

2. CHRISTOLOGICAL EXEGESIS

A reading of Luther's preface to the New Testament (1546) reflects his exegetical insights. "See to it, therefore, that you do not make a Moses out of Christ, or a book of laws and doctrines out of the gospel. . . . If I had to do without one or the other – either the work or the preaching of Christ – I would rather do without the works than without his preaching. For the works do not help me, but his words give life, as he himself says (John 6:63)."

This Christological center is the new element in Reformation interpretation. To become effective it must be preached! In its first years, word and spirit determine the exegetical contributions of the reformers. One misunderstands Luther if, like the radical Thomas Münzer, the tension is placed between letter and spirit. Luther could exercise great freedom in his use of Scripture since for him the tension was between law and gospel. The dialectic between word and spirit and gospel and law leads one directly into the great controversies between Luther and the radicals. Hans Denck summarizes the first dichotomy by attacking simple reliance on the letter of Scripture. "If a man is not in God's house, the letter is no use to him. If he is, he needs no writing to tell him God is good." Luther, as at Marburg in 1529, could hang an entire volume of divinity on a single verse of Scripture.

Ebeling describes Luther's new hermeneutics prior to 1516-1518 as unique. Luther started with the Psalms where Gordon Rupp following Vogelsang suggests his new orientation began during 1514. There the fourfold sense is rendered obsolete as the proclamation of faith in Christ appears. It was not the literalism of medieval exegesis so much as its mystical sense that silenced that proclamation. Even Aquinas who restricted exegesis to the literal sense in theological proof permitted the moral sense to dominate his hermeneutics. Lombard explained "from faith to faith" in Romans 1:17 as the movement from the "unformed faith" of James 2 to the "faith formed by charity" which is the Catholic faith "universally believed by all." Aquinas defines it, "from the faith of the Old Testament to the faith of the New Testament." Then follows a fourfold doctrinal qualification so that Aquinas loses the nature of faith in a maze of definitions. Luther's Christology is refreshing. Ebeling suggests Luther's hermeneutics was unconcerned with such verbal plays. "The fundamental problem for him is not a verbal description of God but the exposure of man's existence before God . . . the proclamation of God's judgment over man." Thus Luther exclaims in his Hebrews commentary of 1517-18: "O what a wonderful thing it is to be a Christian and to have this hidden life, not as a hermit in a cell nor in the impenetrable abysses of the human heart, but hidden in the invisible God who reveals Himself nowhere else than in the poor tokens of the Word and the hearing alone." Luther found Christ as law and gospel in both Old and New Testaments. Melanchthon taught Luther the value of Greek.

When the young Melanchthon delivered his oration on the liberal arts at Tübingen in 1517, grammar was his priority. In August, 1518 Melanchthon's inaugural address at Wittenberg so impressed Luther that he bought an edition of Homer and attended Melanchthon's class "to become a Greek." In that address he summoned his audience to drink deeply at the sources, where in the Hebrew and Greek Scriptures they would find Christ free from the discordant glosses of the Latin theologians. Luther agreed, but Eck was picqued when Melanchthon passed notes to Luther at the 1519 Leipzig debate. Luther responded, "I return to Melanchthon, whom no Eck can make me hate." Melanchthon showed Luther the Greek meaning of Hebrews 11:1-2. Luther published Melanchthon's *Lectures on Corinthians* without his permission, calling him a theologian next to Paul.

The authority of Scripture impressed Melanchthon. His *On the Church and Authority of the Word of God* expresses what Melanchthon wrote to the pastors of Saxony in April of 1550 that "The Church does not create new doctrine, but adorns the grammar of the divine words." The church cannot be bound to human succession, but only to the Word of God. Melanchthon restored the patristic exegesis of Chrysostom and Basil to the church, yet freely criticized doctrine which would not bind itself to the hermeneutical principles of faith alone and Christ alone. Where Melanchthon and Luther adorn the grammar of Scripture with faith in Christ, Zwingli insisted on the certainty and clarity of those divine words.

3. THE CLARITY OF SCRIPTURE

In his first interview with Mary, Queen of Scots, John Knox set forth the clarity of Scripture: "The word of God is plain in itself; and if there appear any obscurity in one place, the Holy Ghost, who is never contrary to Himself, explains the same more clearly in other places: so that there can remain no doubt, but to such as obstinately remain ignorant." Zwingli, too, tested everything by the light of the gospel and the fire of Paul. He remarks that philosophy and theology prevented him from devotion to the Scriptures: "But eventually came to the point where led by the Word and Spirit of God I saw the need to set aside all things and to learn the doctrine of God direct from his own Word. Then I began to ask God for light and the Scriptures became far clearer to me — even though I read nothing else — than if I had studied many commentators and expositors." Zwingli mounted the pulpit of the Great Church in Zurich, January 1, 1519 to announce a program of preaching consecutively through Matthew and ultimately the New Testament. Though Luther could not accept the militant Swiss reformer and the tragic division over the sacrament separated these leaders at Marburg in 1529, Zwingli's appeal was to divine authority.

In the Baden Disputation of 1526 Zwingli answered how one ought to listen to that Word. It must be direct and master the understanding lest one's own meaning make vain the Word of God. "If it is obscure in any place, it is to be expounded by God's Word from another place." Whether at the great disputation of January 29, 1523 or when Zwingli was at the point of death, both the preaching and hearing of the Word guided the Reformation in Zurich. There was a Zwingli Luther never knew, who wrote on October 31, 1531 before his death on the battlefield, "This is the best weapon, the only one that will be victorious, the Word of God. . . . Listen to the Word of God! That alone will set you right again." To all of this John Calvin added common sense. For the reformers Christ was the subject and sovereign of Scripture. If for Jerome to be ignorant of Scripture was to be ignorant of Christ, for them to be ignorant of Christ was to be ignorant of Scripture.

The Bible was desired in the early Reformation, says Professor Van Den Brink, as a help to find a better way to God. The Word of God "seated in the minds of the faithful" led to possession and perception of its clarity. Patrick Hamilton it seems was accused in 1528 of just that opinion that the people of Scotland were well able to understand the New Testament. In *Patrick's Places,* Hamilton expressed that better way to God:

The Law sayeth
Pay Thy debt
Thou art a sinner desperate
And Thou shalt die.
The Gospel sayeth,
Christ hath paid it.
Thy sins are forgiven thee
Be of good comfort, thou shalt be saved.

For all the reformers the clarity of Scripture led to that certainty. Its clarity and certainty provoked a crisis for Catholic exegesis.

4. CATHOLIC CRISIS

It had become fashionable to study the Bible and attend public lectures on the Scripture. All over Europe by 1540 Catholic as well as Protestant commentaries multiplied as people searched for an answer to the questions raised by the Reformation. Jedin comments that such an interest was not forced, but met a need. John Colet's Oxford lectures on St. Paul depart from medieval exegesis. When in 1496 Colet took Paul literally, Catholic exegesis entered a new age. Colet described that fascination for St. Paul in a letter. Years later he praised Erasmus' *Greek-Latin New Testament.* Parallel to Protestant Biblical study there is also a Catholic fascination for the new hermeneutic and theology. A crisis not only of vocabulary but of authority resulted.

Erasmus is well known for his influence on the followers of Valdès in Spain and the sects in Italy. Several of the reforming cardinals also wrote commentaries on St. Paul. In many of them not well known to theologians, expressions identical to those of Melanchthon occur as exegetical solutions arise from philological decisions. To select two such commentaries in the decades between Luther and Trent will clarify the crisis.

During the summer of 1535 Cardinal Sadoleto saw his *Romans Commentary* condemned in Rome. Writing under the influence of Reginald Pole in 1532, Sadoleto appealed to the Greek exegetes, especially Chrysostom and Basil. His failure is not the point; his attempt in the period of doctrinal uncertainty before Trent's 1546 decree on justification is significant. "Faith alone" occurs in several places such as his comment on Romans 1:17.

Gasparo Contarini (1483-1542) studied at Padua from 1501-1511, where he learned Greek and Patristic theology from Musurus. During Easter of 1511 the young Venetian nobleman experienced justification by faith. His letters to the Camaldolese monk, Giustiniani, describe struggles similar to those Luther endured in the monastery. By 1523 Contarini wrote that St. Paul and David are his guides; "Blessed is he to whom the Lord imputes not sin, *sine operibus.*" As a member of Pope Paul III's Reform Commission, Contarini knew the state of the Roman church. In 1541 at Ratisbon he agreed with Eck, Bucer and Melanchthon that justification by faith was held in common by Protestant and Catholic participants. Cardinal Pole rejoiced. When Rome rejected that remarkable agreement, Contarini retired to Lucca broken in spirit. There he met the Italian, Peter Martyr Vermigli. Contarini wrote comments on the Pauline Epistles in 1542 which can not be ignored.

At Romans 1:17 Contarini writes, "From faith refers to God who promises and has given us faith. To faith truly refers to us who by assent and trust in the divine promises have received faith from God." In his Galatian notes he writes that justification is by faith in Christ. These notes written before the rigidity of Trent are the finest expression of Catholic exegesis, superior to the work of Sixtus of Siena. More careful attention to Catholic commentaries may cause a fresh reading of the Reformation, free from the study of polemic and prejudice.

Peter Martyr Vermigli shared Contarini's understanding of the nature of faith. That one died a Catholic, and the other a Protestant is incidental to an understanding of that faith. When Vermigli fled Italy, his Biblical scholarship was welcomed on the continent and in England. For Vermigli the clarity of Scripture is essential. His views summarize the crisis provoked by the new Reformation hermeneutic. In his *Common Places* Vermigli argues, "But yet this perspicuity is not to be sought at the light of man's sense and reason; but at the light of faith, whereby we ought to be most certainlie persuaded of whatsoever is contained in the holie Scriptures." The dream of Protestant and Catholic Biblical theologians for unity turned to a nightmare in the reactionary theology of Trent. And ever since, both parties have argued whether Scripture authorizes bishops or bishops authorize Scripture. *The Scots Confession of 1560* formulates one answer to that crisis of authority: "As we believe and confess the Scriptures of God sufficient to instruct and make the man of God perfect, so do we affirm and avow the authority of the same to be of God, and neither to depend on men nor angels. We affirm therefore that such as allege the Scripture to have no [other] authority, but that which is received from the Kirk, to be blasphemous against God and injurious to the true Kirk, which always heareth and obeyeth the voice of her own Spouse and Pastor, but taketh not upon her to be mistress over the same."

BIBLIOGRAPHY

Bainton, Roland, "The Bible In The Reformation," *The Cambridge History of The Bible, The West From the Reformation To The Present Day.* Cambridge University Press, 1963, 1-37.

Davies, Rupert E., *The Problem of Authority in the Continental Reformers.* London: The Epworth Press, 1946.

Duhamel, P. Albert, "The Oxford Lectures of John Colet," *Journal of the History of Ideas,"* XIV (1953), 493-510.

Ebeling, Gerhard, "The New Hermeneutics and The Early Luther," *Theology Today,* XXI (1964-65), 34-46.

Grimm, Harold J., "Lorenzo Valla's Christianity," *Church History,* XVIII (1949), 75-88.

Harbison, E. Harris, *The Christian Scholar in the Age of The Reformation.* New York: Charles Scribner's Sons, 1956.

Kooiman, Willem Jan, *Luther and the Bible.* Philadelphia: Muhlenberg Press, 1961.

Lehman, Paul L., "The Reformers' Use of the Bible," *Theology Today,* III (1946), 328-344.

Mann Phillips, Margaret, *Erasmus and the Northern Renaissance.* London: English Universities Press, 1949.

Manschreck, Clyde, *Melanchthon On Christian Doctrine.* New York: Oxford University Press, 1965, vii-xlii.

McNeill, John T., "The Significance of the Word of God for Calvin," *Church History* 28 (1959), 131-146.

Montgomery, John Warwick, "Sixtus of Siena and Roman Catholic Biblical Scholarship in the Reformation Period," *Archiv für Reformationsgeschichte* 54 (1963), 214-233.

Prenter, Regin, "The Living Word," *More About Luther*. Decorah, Iowa: Luther College Press, 1958, 65-80.

Rupp, E. Gordon, "The Bible in the Age of the Reformation," D. E. Nineham, *The Church's Use of the Bible Past and Present*. London: S.P.C.K., 1963, 73-87.

Rupp, E. Gordon, "Word and Spirit in the First Years of the Reformation," *Archiv für Reformationsgeschichte* 49 (1958), 13-25.

Van Den Brink, J. N. Bakhuizen, "Bible and Biblical Theology in the Early Reformation," *Scottish Journal of Theology* 14 (1961), 337-352; 15 (1962), 50-65.

Wallace, Ronald S., *Calvin's doctrine of the Word and Sacrament*. Edinburgh: Oliver and Boyd, 1953.

Zwingli, Huldrych, "Of the Clarity and Certainty of the Word of God," *Library of Christian Classics*, Vol. XXIV. Philadelphia: The Westminster Press, MCMLIII, 49-95.

Interpretation of Prophecy

The interpretation of Biblical prophecy is a specific kind of Biblical interpretation. Valid principles of Biblical hermeneutics should therefore apply. However, this is not always admitted, and, as Ramm points out, "the real issue in prophetic interpretation among evangelicals is this: *can prophetic literature be interpreted by the general method of grammatical exegesis, or is some special principle necessary?* (*Protestant Biblical Interpretation*, 2d ed., p. 225). In this article we shall defend the position that prophecy is to be interpreted according to the same principles that apply in all Biblical study.

1. PROPHECY AND THE PROPHETS

To attempt to discuss prophecy without a thorough understanding of the prophetic movement in Israel is to open the door to every sort of subjectivity. The various kinds of interpretation applied to prophecy range from orthodoxy to the "lunatic fringe," and include denominational and sectarian groups, cultic and schismatic movements, and heretical and fanatical extremists. Merely to look at the list of groups or movements that base their right to existence upon Biblical prophecy would convince any reasonable Biblical scholar that an objective basis for the study of prophecy is of primary importance. The study of the Biblical prophetic movement provides such an objective basis.

Discussions of the terms "prophet" and "seer" can be found in Bible dictionaries and Biblical theologies. Here we can only point out that the prophets were historic persons who spoke to their contemporaries out of historical situations. The basic meaning of prophet is "to speak forth," and foretelling is but one aspect of forthtelling. A large part of the prophetic writings in the Bible deals not with prediction of things to come but with God's judgment on the behavior of his people. It is a mistake, however, to deny or ignore the predictive element of prophecy, for in declaring the judgment of God the prophet sets forth what God is threatening to do and what the outcome of God's judgment will be. Some idea of the meaning of prophet may be gained from the fact that in the Hebrew canon, the books of Joshua, Judges, Samuel, and Kings are called "the Former Prophets," and these books are almost devoid of predictive prophecy.

2. MESSIANIC PROPHECY

The interpretation of messianic prophecy should follow the same rules that apply for all prophecy. If this is done, we soon discover that some of the prophecies we have considered "messianic" either are not such or are messianic only in the fuller meaning. The word Messiah (literally "anointed"), as applied to the messianic king of David's line, does not occur at all in the Old Testament, with the possible exception of Daniel 9:25-26. There are, however, many prophecies of the Davidic king to come and of the age he is to establish. The number of such prophecies and the details contained in them increase as we move toward the time of the advent of Christ. The word Christ ("anointed") comes from the Greek translation of the Hebrew word for Messiah. We would do well to remind ourselves that most of those who lived in the time of the coming of Christ so misinterpreted prophecy that they failed to recognize the Messiah.

3. APOCALYPTIC PROPHECY

A special type of messianic prophecy is apocalyptic (such as Daniel and Revelation), in which the message is set forth almost entirely in symbolic language. Even here, the only sure guide is to begin with the literal interpretation, using "literal" in the sense to be defined. For the interpretation of the symbols "literally," we need to know the historical significance of those symbols at the time and the place of the writing. There is almost certainly no universal symbolism, as Davidson points out, but there is a regularity in the symbolism used by any given author, and sometimes this carries over from one work to another (as, e.g., in the case of the use of Daniel in Revelation). A warning should be expressed concerning the symbolism of numbers, colors, and materials, but at the same time it must be admitted that there is a high degree of regularity in the symbolic use of certain numbers (such as 7, 12, 40), and perhaps a lesser degree in the symbolic use of colors (such as white, red, and black).

4. REJECTED METHODS OF INTERPRETATION

Although confusion in terminology complicates the problem, modern scholars are basically in agreement that the allegorical method, according to which the true meaning is not in the words but in the allegorizing of the words; the mystical method, which looks for the meaning in such things as the numerical values of letters; and the dogmatic method, which reduces the Bible to a collection of proof-texts, along with modern developments of these methods, are all unsatisfactory. For a full discussion, see F. W. Farrar, *History of Interpretation,* and for a summary, B. Ramm, *op. cit.*, Chap. II.

An illustration of the allegorical method is Origen's treatment of Genesis 24:16, "[Rebecca was] a virgin, neither had any man known her"; which means, says Origen, that Christ is the husband of the soul when it is converted, and that Satan becomes the husband of the soul when it falls away (see Farrar, *op. cit.*, p. 199). The mystical method can be demonstrated by the rabbinical exegesis of the words "until Shiloh come" (Gen. 49:10). Since the numerical value of the letters in the words Shiloh shall come is 358, which is also the numerical value of the word Messiah, Shiloh means the Messiah. Examples of the proof-text method can be found almost everywhere, but many of them are accepted because the text is used to support a true theological tenet. When we turn to sectarian movements, such as Jehovah's Witnesses or Christian Science, we soon become aware of the weakness of the method. But one example of questionable proof-text methodology is to be found in the orthodox evangelical's use of the "jot or tittle" passage (Matt. 5:18) to "prove" the doctrine of verbal inspiration. Jesus was talking about the teachings of the Scripture, not about jots and tittles nor about words; some of these teachings were already fulfilled and were passing away as Jesus spoke (e.g., Moses' teaching on divorce, Matt. 5:32; 19:3-8), and many more would be swept away by the Epistle to the Hebrews. Yet it remains true that the law and the prophets were not destroyed; they were fulfilled. The verbal inspiration of the Scriptures was not questioned by his hearers, nor was it defended by Jesus: it was accepted by them.

5. THE LITERAL INTERPRETATION

The basic meaning of any Biblical prophecy is that which the author intended his hearers or readers to understand. Since we begin with the faith that God communicated with prophets, we must therefore recognize that we are speaking not only (a) of what the prophet intended his hearers to understand, but also (b) of what God intended the prophet to understand in each instance. However, let us hold this latter part of the discussion until we have clarified the former.

As many authors have noted the very word "literal" introduces a few problems. For example, when a writer or speaker makes use of common figures of speech, a "literal" interpretation accepts the figures of speech as figures. In every kind of communication (except the Bible, according to some interpreters), the common figures of speech are readily recognized and interpreted as such. This principle must be applied also in Biblical study. "The moon (shall be turned) into blood" (Joel 2:31), interpreted literally, means that the moon's color shall become blood-red, and not that the moon actually becomes blood. When God tells Jeremiah, "I am calling all the tribes of the kingdoms of the north" (Jer. 1:15 RSV), he is using hyperbole; it is not necessary to interpret "all" to mean every tribe without exception. Nor does the Lord intend the words in Jeremiah 1:18 to mean that Jeremiah is actually to become "a fortified city, an iron pillar, and bronze walls" (RSV). "Literal" interpretation means the understanding which any person of normal intelligence would get, without any special spiritual gifts and without any "code" or "key."

The literal interpretation of a prophecy is the only basis of objectivity. Without it, any interpreter, with his own system, can make any prophecy mean anything – and history has certainly shown that men and women will do just that. Every sect and schismatic group calling itself Biblical is able to find Biblical support for its doctrines. It is the hermeneutics used, the method of Biblical interpretation which they apply, that makes such confusing and contradictory claims possible. Only when we start with the literal interpretation can we establish objective guidelines for the testing of other interpretations.

So important is this principle that A. B. Davidson says,

"This I consider the first principle in prophetic interpretation – to read the prophet literally – to assume that the literal meaning is *his* meaning – that he is moving among realities, not symbols, among concrete things like peoples, not among abstractions like *our* Church, world, etc. If we make this assumption, then we know what we have before us" (*Old Testament Prophecy*, pp. 167-168).

He insists that "there is no pervasive symbolism in the prophetic language" (p. 160); in other words, we are not to give such terms as "mountain," "horn," "star," "sea," etc., regular symbolic meanings and then read these meanings back into prophecies wherever the terms occur. There is symbolism, of course, for the prophets, who received many of their revelations in the form of visions, were obliged to express many truths in symbolic form. We shall return to this later. But, says Davidson, this symbolism can be understood by us without a "system" just as it was understandable to the prophet's hearers. "The first thing in interpreting prophecy is to hold that the prophet had a meaning, that he uses language like any other writer, and that what he literally says he literally means. Thus, and thus alone, can we reach his meaning" (p. 168).

6. SYMBOLS AND TYPES

To speak of "symbolic" meaning does not necessarily imply a departure from the literal meaning. We can speak "literally" of certain facts, of persons and places and things, of actions, of concrete realities. But when we begin to speak of ideas and concepts, we find that we must often resort to the use of figures of speech in order to convey meaning. And the less the concept is related to the experience of the reader, the more important the use of symbol becomes.

Every formula or equation in mathematics, chemistry, physics, symbolic logic, and many other subjects, is written in symbols and is interpreted literally. The face of the clock, the keyboard of the typewriter, and the page of a musical score are covered with symbols. Certain symbols are capable of two or more meanings. The symbol "3" – which generally conveys the abstract idea of threeness – may indicate the route a bus can be expected to take, or the name of a football player. In combination, such as 3/4/66, it may suggest the month of March or (to a European) the third day of April, whereas 3/4 – might be read as three pounds four shillings, and 3'4" could be read as three feet four inches. To a Frenchman or a German, it would be pronounced entirely different. And the amazing fact is that most of us never stop and ask, "How is it possible to know which interpretation is the right one?" The human mind is able to set the symbol against its context and interpret it, in most cases, instantly.

When we speak about God, who is spirit and not flesh, who inhabits eternity, who is completely "other" except for whatever portion of his image may be found in us, symbolic language is almost the only means we have to describe him. When we call Him "Father" we are taking a reality from our world-system, and using it to convey certain truth about God. When we say that God "hears" us, we likewise are using symbol, for hearing is a phenomenon which requires first the production of sound waves in the atmosphere, then some physical means of receiving these sound waves and converting them to sensory stimuli in our human nervous system, and finally the connecting of these stimuli with the corresponding "bits" that have been stored in our brain as "memory," so that the present stimuli and past experiences are properly paired and the hearer receives the message which the speaker was attempting to communicate. Obviously, when we say that God "hears" we are not implying that he has the physical organs necessary for hearing, or that he is dependent on our atmosphere for the transmission of the sound waves. As a matter of fact, we believe that we can pray silently and he can still "hear" us.

In the Bible certain revelations of truth are presented through symbols which at a future time are to be replaced by reality. Such a symbol is properly called a type. An excellent illustration of a type is the tabernacle, which was a symbol of the presence of the Lord (Yahweh). The tabernacle was called *mishkan*, "dwelling place," and *ohel*, "tent," words which clearly indicate the symbolism. The significance is further defined by the presence of the pillar of cloud over the tabernacle and by the statement that "everyone who sought the Lord would go out to the tent of meeting" (Exod. 33:7 RSV). We are not to understand, of course, that the Lord actually was confined in the tabernacle or that his presence was only to be found between the cherubim of the mercy seat, for he inhabits eternity, as Solomon correctly recognized (II Chron. 6:18). But in a special way the Lord was present in the midst of his people Israel, and the tabernacle was a symbol of that fact. Later, the tabernacle was replaced by the temple, and the temple became the symbol of the Lord's presence. But the presence of the Lord became a reality in the incarnation, and the symbol became unnecessary, hence it is proper to speak of the tabernacle as a *type* of the incarnate Son of God. As a matter of fact, the New Testament suggests this very idea in the words, "And the Word became flesh and dwelt (tabernacled) among us" (John 1:14).

It is possible to develop this idea even further, and to say that the tabernacle (or temple) is also a type of the presence of the Spirit of God in the body of the believer, for our body is called the "temple of the Holy Spirit" (I Cor. 6:19) and "the temple of the living God" (II Cor. 6:16). The full and final fulfillment, of course, is found in the Holy City, the New Jerusalem, of which John said, "I saw no temple in the city, for its temple is the Lord God the Almighty and the Lamb" (Rev. 21:22 RSV). In this respect, the presence of God in the Holy City can be looked upon as the antitype of the tabernacle and the temple.

A number of writers hold that any person, place, thing, or action in Scripture can be a type. In my opinion, this is an extension of the meaning of type which is both unwarranted and dangerous. Joseph, for example, is sometimes called "a type of Christ." But Joseph is Joseph, a real or historical person, whose existence shall continue into the age to come. He is not a symbol that shall one day be replaced by a reality; he is a reality. It would be more proper to say that certain facets of his life are symbolic, such as the rejection by his brothers, his exaltation to a place of authority, his forgiveness of his brothers, etc. Perhaps these symbols could be called "types" of Christ's similar experiences, but even this usage is open to abuse. According to some teachers, if a whole is typical, then the parts are also typical. On this basis, the details of the tabernacle and its furnishings are considered as types, and a significance is sought in each detail, with an antitype in Christ. Strictly speaking, this is an application of the allegorical method, rather than the typical.

The extremes to which some interpreters have gone in finding types in Scripture have led many scholars in recent decades to reject the entire notion. More recently, however, the subject has been recognized as valid, and discussions of typology can be found in several works. For example, G. von Rad says,

> ". . . we do introduce a new element of interpretation which does not derive from the Old Testament in that we presuppose the existence of a particular kind of connexion between the saving events of the Old Testament and the transcendent saving events of the New. . . . The name given to such exegesis is relatively unimportant. If it is called typological, the term is a suitable one. . . . And yet the essence of our view differs from earlier typology . . .; we, however, can no longer say that the David or Joshua of history, or the Tabernacle, or the Passover lamb, are types of Christ [*Old Testament Theology*, Vol. II, p. 371.]

> It is in this sense — i.e., in the light of a final fulfilment and of the ceaseless movement towards such a fulfilment — that we can speak of a prophetic power resident in the Old Testament prototypes." (*Ibid.,* p. 373.)

The present discussion does not follow von Rad except in the basic principle. But that principle is important. The basis for typology must be found in the organismic redemptive and the progressive revelatory activity of God. This principle underlies the argument presented by the Epistle to the Hebrews. Since the fall of Adam, there has been only one way of salvation, namely, by the gracious redeeming activity of God. But there has been a divine educational process or revelation unfolding through the ages until the final redemptive act in his Son. Otherwise, why was Christ not crucified by Cain? We are forced to assume that the education of the race, particularly of God's representative people, was a necessary part of God's plan. But if the entire redemptive process was organismic, i.e., if each step was intended to present the basic truth that redemption was provided by God and received by faith, then we may rightly conclude that the use of symbols and types necessarily had to precede the actual event. Accordingly, von Rad correctly states that, "No special hermeneutic method is necessary to see the whole diversified movement of the Old Testament saving events, made up of God's promises and their temporary fulfilments, as pointing to their future fulfilment in Jesus Christ. This can be said quite categorically. The coming of Jesus Christ as a historical reality leaves the exegete no choice at all; he must interpret the Old Testament as pointing to Christ, whom he must understand in its light" (*ibid.,* p. 374).

7. THE FULLER OR DEEPER MEANING

Roman Catholic scholars in recent Biblical studies often speak of the *sensus plenior,* or "fuller meaning," a term attributed to Andrea Fernández in an article written in 1925. Raymond E. Brown in his dissertation on the subject offers the following definition: "The *sensus plenior* is that additional, deeper meaning, intended by God but not clearly intended by the human author, which is seen to exist in the words of a Biblical text (or group of texts, or even a whole book) when they are studied in the light of further revelation or development in the understanding of revelation" (*The Sensus Plenior of Sacred Scripture,* p. 92).

Protestant scholars have sometimes indicated a similar idea, but discussions of the subject are confused because of the terminology used. The terms spiritual, mystical, allegorical, and typological, as Ramm has shown (*Protestant Biblical Interpretation,* 2d ed., p. 223), are variously used and often overlap. We suggest that the adoption of the term *sensus plenior* or its English translation will help to clarify the problem. In his study, Brown differentiates between the "literal" sense and the "fuller" sense on the basis of the human author's clear intention. If the divine author intended more in the revelation than the human author intended to convey to his hearers or readers, this is the fuller meaning (or *sensus plenior*) of the passage. Some will object, insisting that the human author was never derogated to a position where he became a mere scribe who wrote without understanding. I would agree in principle with such an objection, for inspiration, as I understand it, is the action of the Spirit upon the author by which the author becomes the recipient of God's revelation. This action does not reduce or destroy the personal knowledge or ability of the human author, nor does it superimpose a knowledge or ability which he does not normally have; but rather it heightens, or deepens, or makes more sensitive his natural ability so that he sees what God wants him to see, hears what God wants him to hear, and communicates this under the influence of the same Spirit.

But is it not possible for God to present to the author a revelation which by its very nature contains a deeper significance? Perhaps the author, under inspiration, could see the deeper meaning, perhaps not — this is incidental to any given revelation. In either event, the author does not intentionally convey the *sensus plenior* to his hearers. But at a later date, in the light of further revelation, the fuller meaning becomes clear to readers under the influence of the Spirit who inspired the original author. At a lower level, it is true that great poets, philosophers, and other creative thinkers often express a fuller meaning — perhaps even without knowing it — which their "disciples" develop into schools or systems of thought. If a human author can send forth a message which has a *sensus plenior,* why is it unthinkable that a divinely inspired author could do the same?

Brown further distinguishes the *sensus plenior* from the "typical" sense by relating the fuller sense to the words and the typical sense to the things or actions set forth by the words. He admits that there are borderline cases where the *sensus plenior* and the typical sense can scarcely be distinguished.

8. APPLICATIONS OF THESE PRINCIPLES

At this point it may be helpful to use a few Scriptural passages to clarify the discussion. In Genesis 3:15 there is the *Protevangelium* (or first form of the gospel), sometimes taken to be a prophecy of the Messiah and even of the virgin birth: "I will put enmity between you and the woman, and between your seed and her seed; he shall bruise your head, and you shall bruise his heel" (RSV). The literal sense of the passage is clear. God is speaking to the serpent who has led Eve into the sin of disobeying God's revelation. God is saying that there will be hostility between human beings (the seed of the woman) and serpents (the seed of the serpent), in the course of which human beings will be hurt (bruising of the heel) and serpents will be killed (bruising of the head). But certainly this is hardly worthy of the setting of the story. There must be a deeper meaning. The *sensus plenior* might be expressed as follows: The spiritual crisis (temptation and fall) was brought about by a being (the serpent) hostile to God and his revealed will. This hostility will continue to be expressed throughout the ages, and human beings will be hurt by it. But at last there will be victory, because a certain man (whom we identify with Jesus Christ from later revelation) will finally destroy the tempter (whom we identify with Satan from later revelation). Is there also a typical meaning? Can we say that Eve is a type of Mary? Possibly in her name (Gen. 3:20) and in her statement when Cain was born (Gen. 4:1) she is a type of Mary — but I am inclined to reject such typology. Can we say that the "seed" of the woman is a type of Christ? I think not, for the seed of the woman is the human race, and in the fuller sense it is Christ. But a type, we have seen, is a symbol that is later replaced by a reality, and certainly the human race was not replaced by Christ.

In Ezekiel 34, God pronounces judgment upon false shepherds, and declares that he will search for his sheep, concluding with the words, "I will set up over them one shepherd, my servant David, and he shall feed them: he shall feed them and be their shepherd" (34:23 RSV). Is David a type of Christ? In this case, the language is perfectly clear, and there is little reason to seek a *sensus plenior.* But from the Christian viewpoint, it is Jesus and not David who is both shepherd and prince (cf. 34:34). Yet we know that David is not a symbol, later to be replaced by Jesus; David is a person with immortality. It would be more correct, in my opinion, to speak of the Davidic office or the throne of David as the type.

Even more accurately we can speak of the son of David as the type. This is particularly noteworthy in the promise made to David, when he desired to build a house for the Lord, and the Lord said, "When your days are fulfilled and you lie down with your fathers, I will raise up your son after you, who shall come forth from your body, and I will establish his kingdom. He shall build a house for my name, and I will establish the throne of his kingdom for ever" (II Sam. 7:12-13 RSV). It is clear from verses 14-15 that God is speaking of the actual son of David, whom we know to be Solomon, for God speaks of the iniquity that he will commit. Moreover, we know that Solomon did build the temple. On the other hand, we also know that Solomon's kingdom ended in civil war and the secession of the northern tribes. Furthermore, it is always the throne of David, and not the throne of Solomon, that is mentioned in prophecy (cf. Isa. 9:7; Luke 1:32). And again, it is recorded that David referred to this son as "Lord" (Ps. 110.1, cf. Matt. 22:43-45). Since the throne of David becomes the throne of the Messiah, we may speak of David's throne as a type, and since Solomon is replaced ultimately by the Messiah on that throne, it is possible to speak either of the fuller meaning of the expression "David's son," or to say that Solomon, in this office, is a type of Christ.

How shall we understand the prophecies in Isaiah chapters 7-11? Literally, Isaiah 7 deals with King Ahaz of Judah and the Syro-Ephraimite coalition of Rezin of Syria and Pekah of Israel (7:1), including a sign which the Lord was giving to indicate that Ahaz had nothing to fear from them (7: 7-9). The sign was to be in the birth of a child called "Immanuel" (7:14), and the sudden solution of the Syro-Ephraimite problem in the face of a greater problem, namely the king of Assyria (7:17). The fuller meaning is to be found in the fact that Israel's basic problem was not the unbelief of Ahaz, but that of the people, and the ultimate solution was not in the temporary removal of national foes but in the permanent removal of all unbelief. Hence the Christian church, following Matthew 1:23, has seen the birth of Jesus Christ to be the fulfillment of the prophecy. The virgin birth of Jesus, we should note, in no way depends on Isaiah 7:14, but on the unequivocal statements in Matthew (1:18, 25) and Luke (1:34, 35).

Isaiah 9 is of a different nature. Here Isaiah is clearly talking about a coming ruler (9:6), whose reign fits the description of the messianic reign given elsewhere (Jer. 23:5; cf. II Sam. 7:12-16). Whether Isaiah was privileged to understand the details of his prophecy we cannot tell. Quite likely this is a case of "prophetic foreshortening"or "prophetic perspective," terms often used to describe the phenomenon in which the prophet sees the near-at-hand and the distant in the same plane. Following the prophecy concerning Rezin and Pekah and concerning the king of Assyria (8:6-7), Isaiah sees light breaking through the darkness (8:22; 9:1). To judge by the words that follow (10:5-11, 20-27, especially v. 25), it would seem that Isaiah expected this light to dawn "in a very little while." We know, from New Testament revelation, that Isaiah was seeing the return from exile, the first advent of Christ, and the millennial kingdom at one time, without any indication of intervals between them.

Isaiah 11 offers an illustration of symbolic language, as well as prophetic foreshortening. The "shoot from the stump of Jesse" and its parallel "branch out of his roots" is obviously symbolic language referring to the remnant of Israel (see 6:13). The prophecy could, therefore, pertain to the remnant after the exile, and "him" in 11:2 could mean the remnant of the nation. However, verses 3 and 4 pick up some of the language of the messianic king (cf. Ps. 2:8-9; 72:12-14), and verses 6-9 present the idyllic age of the Messiah. We must therefore look for the fuller meaning, which, we know from New Testament revelation, includes both advents of Christ.

The "Royal Psalms" offer another area of study which is instructive. Since several passages from these Psalms have been quoted in the Epistle to the Hebrews, it is very difficult for the Christian to come to the original passages without a Christian interpretation already built in. But certainly, the men and women who heard and used these Psalms had no such knowledge of Christ; if they had had such a clear understanding, they would never have rejected Jesus and his claims. The "Royal Psalms" – ignoring in this article the entire problem of the New Year's festival, the enthronement ritual, and related matters – were clearly addressed to or sung in honor of the reigning king of Israel (see Ps. 45:1). But we must remember that the king who occupied the throne of David was heir to the promise made to David. He was David's "son" and his throne was David's throne. As such, it was an eternal throne, and divine titles could be ascribed to it and, in a sense, to its occupant. For example, the occupant could be called God's "son" (Ps. 2:7). It is possible that the king as God's vicegerent could be addressed as "God" – for it is an open question whether Psalm 45:6 should be translated "thy throne, O God, is for ever and ever" or "thy throne is God for ever and ever" (in the Greek of Hebrews 1:8 the same possibility occurs). Even Psalm 110 was doubtless addressed to the king, and was an assurance of the Lord's fidelity to his promise. But, as we have seen, the Davidic throne is a type of the Messianic throne, and we know from New Testament revelation that the Messiah is not merely a human king of David's line but is the incarnate Son of God. The *sensus plenior*, therefore, of Psalm 110 concerns the greater Son of David, who is in fact David's Lord.

Within the limits of this article it is impossible to take up every prophecy, or even a representative of each kind of prophecy. The mention of Bethlehem in Micah 5:2 can be taken in the literal sense merely as an indication that the line of David had not been rejected, for Micah was obviously thinking of his own day (see 5:5). But the fuller meaning refers to the messianic king, hence the Christian sees the fulfillment in the birth of Jesus.

The "servant of the Lord" in Isaiah 42-53 is somewhat more complex. Israel was the servant of the Lord (Isa. 41:8; 44:1), but Israel was an unfaithful servant and suffered because of disobedience. The remnant of Israel was the Lord's servant of whom it could be said that the righteous suffer for the sins of the unrighteous. Some of the expressions in Isaiah 53 could properly be applied to the remnant. The more obedient the servant of the Lord, the more he will be despised and rejected of men. Accordingly, the fuller meaning of the servant passages has to do with the perfect Servant, and the Christian rightly identifies this Servant with the one who came in the form of a servant and who was obedient even unto death (cf. Phil. 2:7-8).

For an illustration of apocalyptic prophecy we may turn to Daniel 7. Since this is a dream or vision in highly symbolic form (7:1), the literal interpretation requires an attempt to understand the author's meaning intended by the symbols. This is often difficult or even impossible in apocalyptic literature, but in Daniel 7 we have the author's interpretation. The "beasts" are kingdoms (7:12, 23) or their rulers (7:17), and the "horns" are kings (7:7, 24). They are obviously hostile to God's rule and persecute his people, and this hostility comes to a climax in the time of the fourth kingdom, especially under the terrible king who comes to the throne after ten who preceded him (7:21, 25). However, he does not have the final word, for "one that was ancient of days" (7:9) is in control, and the rule, an everlasting dominion (7:14), is given to "one like a son of man" (7:13), while the kingdoms of the world are delivered for ever to the "saints of the Most High" (7:27). Clearly, the author is foretelling the triumph of God's king over the kings of the world. To attempt to identify the individual kingdoms and kings is difficult, for it requires not only a thorough knowledge of the history of the period but also a knowledge of the symbolism and common expressions of the day. We can, however, carry over the symbolic interpretation to other parts of Daniel's prophecy, so that we can understand the heart of his message. When it comes to setting dates or charting the future, it is just at those points where we usually become dogmatic that we should become most humble. It is an infallible rule of prophetic interpretation that the prophecy becomes fully clear only after it has been fulfilled.

Using these principles of interpretation, we are objective and reasonable. There is nothing cultic or fantastic in the interpretations. The literal meaning is always definitive, and both the fuller meaning and the typical interpretation are developed from the literal. Scripture is compared with Scripture, but never in such way as to distort the historical or grammatical sense of the passages used in the comparison. The "theological" interpretation is not imposed on Scripture as in proof-text methodology, but rather the Bible becomes the source of theology. If this method demands more of our time and effort than other methods, this is as it should be, for in this as in all matters we usually get what we pay for. Above all, both the inspiration of the Spirit in the original revelation and inscripturation, and the illumination of the Spirit in the interpretation are duly honored. It is God's Word, and we must let God tell us what it means.

BIBLIOGRAPHY

Beecher, W. J., *The Prophets and the Promise*, 1905, reprint 1963.

Berkhof, L., *Principles of Biblical Interpretation*, 2nd ed., 1952.

Brown, R. E., *The Sensus Plenior of Sacred Scripture*, 1955.

Davidson, A. B., *Old Testament Prophecy*, 1904.

Farrar, F. W., *History of Interpretation*, 1886. reprint 1961.

Kevan, E. F., "The Principles of Interpretation," *Revelation and the Bible* (C. F. H. Henry, ed.), 1958.

Oehler, G. F., *Theology of the Old Testament*, Part II, Prophetism, 1883.

Ramm, Bernard, *Protestant Biblical Interpretation*, rev. ed., 1956.

Synave, P. and Benoit, P., *Prophecy and Inspiration*, Eng. tr., 1961.

von Hofmann, J. C. K., *Interpreting the Bible*, Eng. tr., 1959.

von Rad, G., *Old Testament Theology*, Vol. II, Eng. tr., 1965.

Typological Interpretation of the Old Testament

The history of the Christian church has shown clearly that the advent of Christ and the New Testament has raised problems in the minds of many regarding the relevance of the Old Testament. At one extreme was Marcion (A.D. 85) who sought to expunge any reference to a fierce God from the Bible, and so rejected the Old Testament *in toto,* as well as much of the New Testament. At the other extreme were the church fathers (with their followers today) who sought to retain the Old Testament by fanciful allegorical and typological interpretation. In allegory, history is of little importance, and thus the literal meaning of a text is overlooked. The persons and things and events in a document supposedly stand for spiritual processes and actions and essences, for timeless truths already predetermined from other sources. In typology, however, history and literal meaning are taken seriously. Here a person or thing or event, which had a real existence and significance of its own, symbolizes or represents or prefigures someone or something greater at a later time. But, in either case, the reason for the approach is the question regarding the relevance of the old covenant. In recent days there has come a revival of interest in typology among Biblical scholars in a renewed attempt to answer this. It is not a return to the extreme typological approach of the Fathers, who saw a correspondence between Old and New Testament in minute details, but rather a stress on a general correspondence between the events and figures and institutions of both Testaments.

1. THE OLD TESTAMENT EVIDENCE

In the life and worship of Israel there was a constant re-interpretation and re-presentation of the original revelatory acts of God, because God's will and actions were seen as basically the same in any age. Thus Israel did not distinguish very clearly between the past and the present. At the great annual festivals of pilgrimage, during which time all adult male Israelites had to appear at the sanctuaries, the important events of Israel's history were "re-presented." The feast of passover and unleavened bread was celebrated year by year in the month the Lord delivered Israel from Egypt (Deut. 16:1). Its purpose was to "remember" the events of the Exodus experience, and unleavened bread was eaten to recreate the original time of haste. This meant that annually Israel was reliving the situation of being prepared for setting-out, for deliverance from bondage. The same was true with the feast of tabernacles or booths (Lev. 23:43). The means of "re-presentation" was primarily by a retelling of the story of what God did for his people (Exod. 12:24ff.), although cultic drama may also have entered in (cf. Ps. 24). We also see this in the book of Deuteronomy, where the *parenetic* discourses are characterized by the frequently occurring expression "today," the purpose of which was to make the contemporary listener hear the law as if it were for the first time and as if it were directed solely at him, as if he were at Mt. Sinai (cf. Deut. 5:3; 6:21; 26:16-19). The important point to realize is that these "re-presentations" were made, not merely to glory in the past (as if it were an ancient Fourth of July celebration), but that the present Israel might continually be taught the nature of the God she served and the response that was necessary, for God was active in the same way in the present. The wilderness wandering, for example, was retold to show the result of rebelliousness among the fathers, but also to warn the present people of a similar fate if they also rebelled.

But, furthermore, Israel also looked to the future, and saw a correspondence between it and the past. G. von Rad has pointed out in *Essays on Old Testament Hermeneutics* (pp. 17-39), that the Old Testament form of "analogy" or "typology" is quite different from that found in non-Israelite thought. Outside of Israel one finds a mythological conception of an all-embracing correspondence between heavenly and earthly things. All countries, rivers, cities, temples, etc. on earth were conceived to be only copies of the prototypes which existed in heaven. But in Israelite thought, on the contrary, there was an historical analogy between eschatological events and beginning events. Thus Amos and Isaiah speak of the eschatological return of the Paradise experience (Amos 9:13; Isa. 11:6-8). Amos also looks for the return of David (Amos 9:11), and Hosea and Isaiah mention the return of the wilderness days (Hos. 2:14-20; Isa. 52; 11-12). These prophets were not simply predicting that a particular historical event would recur. They saw a pattern in God's actions, or the repetition of a similar kind of event. It would not be merely another David; a greater than David would come. It would not be an exact return of a wilderness experience, but a greater deliverance from bondage.

This means, on the one hand, that the Old Testament writers saw a continuity to history. The judgments and acts of redemption in the Old Testament were a prefiguration of the Christ event in the New. As von Rad writes, "the same God who revealed himself in Christ has also left his footprints in the history of the Old Testament covenant people . . . we have to do with one divine discourse, here to the fathers through the prophets, there to us through Christ (Heb. 1:1)" (*op cit.*, p. 36). But it also means on the other hand, that from the standpoint of the New Testament we see meanings in the Old that the original authors missed, because the coming of Christ illumines the action of God in Israel. However, one must be careful to make a distinction between typology (or, correspondence, analogy) and allegory. One cannot look for correspondence in details or find hidden spiritual meanings, but rather must seek historical analogies alone.

W. Zimmerli in *Essays on Old Testament Hermeneutics* (pp. 89-122), has clarified this typological interpretation by his scheme of "promise and fulfillment." He distinguishes carefully between "prediction" and "promise." Prediction is the illumination of future events, but promise is the understanding that God has determined to accomplish his purposes, and is already working towards the completion of this goal. It is not just a word about something that is to come; it speaks of a future already in progress of fulfillment. Zimmerli stresses that the Old Testament depicts God's actions in history as a series of promises (not predictions) and fulfillments, with each fulfillment giving rise to the expectation of a greater fulfillment in the future. This is because the promises of God were never exhausted by one fulfillment. So the promise of rest in the promised land (Deut 12:9; 25:19) was apparently fulfilled in the conquest under Joshua (Josh. 21:45), but this was not meant to imply a final fulfillment, as Joshua 23:15-16 indicates when it looks to the possibility of the destruction of that rest, and as Hebrews 4:1ff. clarifies when it shows that Canaan was not the final intended rest. And this same movement can be seen throughout the Old Testament. In the latter prophets the final fulfillment of promise becomes eschatological, showing that the fulfillments in Israel were only the beginning phase of God's plan. The prophets found a typological significance in the historical events which enabled them to speak relevantly about God's next acts in history. So when Christ came and "actualized" the promises, he ensured the validity of the Old Testament by showing that it is part of the same divine program. Thus the Old Testament is valuable for the church, because here we can see our own situation before God, since we are still on the road to the final enrichment of that fulfillment, and so can live in trust that God fulfills his promises.

2. THE NEW TESTAMENT EVIDENCE

The coming of Christ is represented in the New Testament as something both totally new, and yet as having roots and foregleams in the Old Testament. This is centered in the *kerygma* or "proclamation of the gospel." In its fundamental form the *kerygma* consists of the proclamation of certain historical events in a context which interprets the significance of those events. The events are basically (1) the life, death, and resurrection of Jesus, and (2) the development of the church. The significance given to these events is seen most of the time in light of the Old Testament. Thus in the piece of the *kerygma* preserved in I Corinthians 15: 3-5, it is said that Christ died, and rose the third day, "according to the Scriptures." And in the further "proclamations of the gospel" found in the book of Acts, the Christ event is seen as the fulfillment of prophecies (Acts 2:16, 23). And so, in this belief, the New Testament writers constantly quote the Old Testament in reference to Christ and the church. For example, in John 15:25 the author discovers a reference to the persecution of Christ in Psalm 69:4: "they hated me without a cause." In John 2:17 he finds a description of Christ's cleansing of the temple in Psalm 69:9: "zeal for thy house will consume me." In John 19:28 he finds a prophecy of Christ's dying thirst in Psalm 69:21: "I thirst." Yet the whole psalm can hardly refer to Christ in a predictive sense, since there are also statements about sinfulness (69:5), and vindictiveness (69:22-29). Given this New Testament precedent, later Christian writers carried it on in detail to the extreme (cf. R. Grant, *A Short History of the Interpretation of the Bible*).

The modern reader is often hard pressed to justify this New Testament use of the Old, for it all appears to be so contrived. Yet we cannot dismiss the New Testament references simply as an ancient method of interpretation, for the very proclamation of the gospel is tied up with this, as I Corinthians 15 shows. What the New Testament writers meant was that the coming of Christ was the fulfillment or realization of promises and ideals and hopes and experiences found in the Old. Christ is the end of the story of God's work in the world for the redemption of mankind. The first part of the story is found in the Old Testament. There we find the same God at work, with the same purpose, that has been revealed in Jesus Christ, the second part of the story. So the experiences that came to Israel and its people are similar to those which have taken place in the days of Christ and the church; indeed, much of the Old Testament typifies or corresponds to that which occurred in the New.

This is simply because what God was doing with Israel was part of the same program destined and planned to lead to Christ. So in the quotations from Psalm 69 – they hated me without cause, zeal for thy house has consumed, thirst – John was not denying an original reference to the psalmist's own experiences, but rather he was looking over history and saying that Christ summed up all that the psalmist said about the suffering and persecution of the innocent. Christ was the supreme example of someone who suffered unjustified hate, and by his suffering brought in essence the end to suffering. The kind of thing the psalmist suffered is the kind of thing Jesus suffered – unjustified hate in the fulfilling of God's will – because both were part of the plan of God, but at different stages. In other words, the gospel is the final interpretation of God's revelation. All of Jesus' actions – his baptism by the Spirit, his identification of himself with the Servant, his claiming of the title "Son of Man," his participation in a new passover at the Last Supper – show that he understood his work as the fulfillment of the relationship between God and man promised and hoped for in the Old Testament.

C. H. Dodd, in his *According to the Scriptures*, has brought greater understanding of this. He points out that the New Testament writers used certain broad portions of the Old Testament more than others (Isaiah, Jeremiah, Psalms, and a few of the minor prophets) as a special group or body of Scriptures which was recognized as authoritative for explaining the gospel. In other words, Peter said at Pentecost that the events in Christ's life happened "according to the definite plan and foreknowledge of God" (Acts 2:23). But how could this be? In order to show this the New Testament writers continued to quote certain basic passages in the Old as especially indicative of this, because the God who was working in the Old was the same God who was working in Christ. Thus Psalm 69 was not only quoted in the three places mentioned in John, but also 69:9 is cited by Romans 15:3; 69:21 by Matthew 27:34; and 69:25 by Acts 1:20. All this suggests that Psalm 69 belonged to a group of passages which was specially drawn on by the New Testament writers for their exposition of the gospel. Now, however, the New Testament does not use isolated prooftexts out of context, that is, passages or expressions which just coincidentally bore a similarity to incidents in the gospel account, but rather it uses selected verses which point to the teaching of the whole context. The reader was thus invited to study this context, and to reflect upon the "plot" there unfolded. The New Testament writers were interested in the theme of the whole context, and used particular verses to highlight this.

One theme in particular was stressed – the suffering and triumphant servant of the Lord. Thus the New Testament writers drew on a wide range of passages, all of which in context have this same basic plot – Isaiah 52-53; Psalms 8; 22; 31; 34; 69; 80; 118; Daniel 7; Joel 2-3; Zechariah 9-14; Isaiah 6:1–9:6. The plot is that the "hero" suffers shame, ignominy, torment, disaster, and then by the sheer grace of God is delivered, raised up, glorified. The "hero" may be an individual or Israel as a whole, the deliverance may only be promised or hoped for, the reason for suffering may be due to the judgment of God upon sinful people, or to the persecution of an innocent victim, but in all cases the point is the same – humiliation and suffering turned into triumph by the grace of God.

So what the New Testament writers were saying in quoting the Old was that these experiences of suffering and these hopes of triumph have now come to fulfillment in Christ. The "day of the Lord" has arrived, and now all the tragic experiences of the past are made clear. God has had one purpose through it all, namely, that through obedient suffering and gracious triumph the world will be redeemed. The Old Testament experiences of the people of Israel were types or correspondences to the experiences of Christ and the church. What the Old Testament servant experienced (but always with the note of promise for triumph), the New Testament servant experienced (but now in fulfillment). Thus Peter in Acts 2 sees Joel's prophecy of the day of the Lord being fulfilled in his day. So typology is concerned with historical correspondence, not with detailed spiritual truths. The Old Testament hope of a land, a rest, and long life with physical pleasures becomes the hope for eternal salvation in the New. Titus' allusion to the laver (Titus 3:5), Paul's use of the veil (II Cor. 3:7ff.) and of the sin offering (Rom. 8:3), and Hebrews' reference to the altar of burnt offering (Heb. 13:10) are not exact analogies, but rather general historical correspondences with worship elements in old Israel. Therefore it is incorrect procedure to look for parallels in shape or color.

The case for a typological interpretation of the Old Testament seems to be well-established, but there are dangers for contemporary exegesis. *First,* there is the danger inherent in the use of the word "typology," because of the misuse within church history. Contemporary application of typology is quite different than the detailed use of the Fathers and others. And in order to avoid confusion many today would prefer the term "correspondence." Secondly, there is the danger that an Old Testament event or figure or institution may be regarded as important only because it provides us with a type looking forward to the New. If this takes place then we miss the meaning and importance that it had in its own context. Revelational significance is not limited solely to its typological content. Thirdly, the application of typology may limit our use of the Old Testament only to those portions where we can determine clear correspondences to the New. But the Old Testament, in large sections, is not typological in this sense. This is true, not only of whole books, such as Ecclesiastes or Job, but also of sections of books where types have been discovered (Exodus, Isaiah), but which also contain many non-typological materials. If these dangers can be kept constantly in view, however, a typological understanding can be of great service in interpretation, for it stresses the unity of Scripture in the ongoing, constant concerns of God which link Old Testament Israel and the New Testament church. The Old Testament then becomes clearly a source book for Christian preaching.

BIBLIOGRAPHY

Dodd, C. H., *According to the Scriptures: The Sub-Structure of New Testament Theology.* New York: Scribner's, 1953.

Grant, R. M., *A Short History of the Interpretation of the Bible,* rev. ed. New York: Macmillan Paperbacks, 1963.

Lampe, G. W. H. and Woollcombe, K. J., *Essays on Typology.* London: SCM, 1957.

Smart, J., *The Interpretation of Scripture.* Philadelphia: Westminster, 1961.

Westermann, C., ed., *Essays on Old Testament Hermeneutics.* Richmond: Knox, 1963.

The New Hermeneutic

The new hermeneutic is new in the sense that it departs from traditional hermeneutics. Whereas the traditional hermeneutics was concerned with the detailed principles of interpretation, the new hermeneutic looks upon this as merely a special problem within the much wider activity of interpretation. It is hermeneutic and not hermeneutics because the singular is more carefully derived from the Greek than the plural. Perhaps there is some influence from the German in which the founders of the new hermeneutic write. The Germans use *Hermeneutik* which is a singular.

The literature of the new hermeneutic has

been coming into English very slowly but the process has been expedited by the publication in 1964 of *The New Hermeneutic* by James Robinson and John Cobb as volume two in the series, *New Frontiers in Theology*.

The new hermeneutic is a development in continental theology after World War II, emerging from the hermeneutics of Rudolph Bultmann. It is therefore necessary to take a preliminary look at the thought of Bultmann. Bultmann joined with Barth in the 1920's in protest against the methodology of the prevailing religious liberalism. He heralded Barth's *Epistle to the Romans* (1919) as a new breakthrough in Biblical interpretation. Subsequently Bultmann came to the conclusion that Barth was very naive in his appreciation and understanding of critical methods in Biblical interpretation and so he broke with him. Bultmann had been thoroughly trained in critical methodology and his scholarship his entire life long has been characterized by a very critical (if not excessively critical) treatment of the Biblical text.

Bultmann is dedicated to the conviction that science (broadly conceived) and only science can settle matters of fact. This led him to incorporate into his hermeneutics a thoroughgoing anti-supernaturalism. Nothing in the Bible is acceptable that goes contrary to the scientific understanding of things. This obviously excludes miracles but also such supernatural doctrines as the incarnation and the resurrection, and such implicitly supernatural matters as holy history (*Heilsgeschichte*), prophecy, and eschatology. Prophecy involves a view of the divine action which is not acceptable to modern, scientific man. Accordingly Bultmann looks at the Old Testament as a purely human document and as *negatively* preparing the way for Christianity by showing the failure of Israel. It is thus pure law – a position he can readily come by in that as a Lutheran he operates with the law-gospel schema. There is no connected history as such in Scripture or holy history or theology of history; only events of salvation (*Heilstat, Heilsgeschehen, Heilsereignis*).

Furthermore, prescientific and precritical man casts his religious experiences into the form of an external, worldly, historical event. This is, by definition, a myth according to Bultmann. Therefore our hermeneutics demands that the interpreter locate such myths, discard the form that the myth takes because it is prescientific, and yet retain the religious intention of the myth. In this he differs from the liberalism of the nineteenth century which discarded myth and all.

Close attention must be given to the religious intention of the myth. This leads Bultmann to existentialism. According to Franz Theunis (*Offenbarung und Glaube bei Rudolph Bultmann*, 1960), Bultmann had worked out the main lines of his existentialism before he met Heidegger at Marburg but his encounter with Heidegger profoundly influenced his existentialism. There is also direct indebtedness to Kierkegaard in Bultmann. The inner side of religious experience is existential in character (and so in another way he departs from the religious liberalism of the nineteenth century), and therefore the myth is to be peeled off for the purpose of discovering the existential deposit within.

His existentialism in turn leads him to the notion that the Word of God must be address which summons a man to decision either for or against the address. Hence the message of the New Testament as address is kerygma. This in turn must lead to powerful kerygmatic preaching from the sacred desk.

If Bultmann had concentrated on any one of these issues he would have been noted as a typically capable and thorough German scholar. But his creative and dynamic synthesis of all these elements enabled him and and his students to capture the lead in theological scholarship in Germany and Switzerland after the war and so eclipse the neo-Reformed theology of Karl Barth.

The new hermeneutic accepts all of these hermeneutical principles of Bultmann intact. It believes that Bultmann represents the real continuity of the Reformation. That which Luther began with justification by faith they believe Bultmann brings to its fullest development. It is revealing how the new hermeneutic finds so much in Luther and to date has so completely bypassed Calvin. Furthermore, the new hermeneutic believes that Bultmann's hermeneutics represents a historical breakthrough back of which the theologians can never retreat.

But the new hermeneutic is critical of Bultmann on one score. Bultmann did not thoroughly exploit his breakthrough and realize its fuller implications. The precise task of the new hermeneutic is to do this very thing. It has a persuasive defender in Ernst Fuchs of Marburg and a scholar of vast erudition and meticulous scholarship in Gerhard Ebeling of Zurich. Institutes of Hermeneutics have been founded at both Marburg and Zurich. Very little of the writing of Fuchs is in English but there are now two volumes of Ebeling and certainly more to come (*The Nature of Faith,* 1961; *Word and Faith,* 1963).

The new hermeneutic takes as its task the formulation of a theory of interpretation or hermeneutics that is philosophically and theologically more comprehensive than anything heretofor. The older notion of Biblical or Sacred Hermeneutics as well as technical philological hermeneutics among the classicist were far too narrow in their understanding of the issues. Historically speaking, already such men as Schleiermacher and Dilthey had suggested that interpretation was a far more comprehensive task than philologically exegeting texts. This deeper grasp of interpretation was denoted by the German word *Verstehen* which means understanding in contrast to the more superficial and technical explanation (Erklärung) of things. It was the philosopher Martin Heidegger who really grasped this new and far more comprehensive notion of the function of hermeneutics. In his youth Heidegger studied for the priesthood and was introduced to sacred hermeneutics. This stuck within his mind and when he wrote his philosophy in later years he revived it, and, recasting it, gave it a major place in his philosophy.

Taking its clue from Heidegger the new hermeneutic asserts that language itself is interpretation. Language is also profoundly existential in character. Whenever a person speaks he is already engaging in hermeneutics for he is interpreting his world. The word itself is thus hermeneutical and existential. Here a radical shift takes place. Hermeneutics is no longer fundamentally the stating of principles whereby ancient texts are to be understood, but it is a profound investigation of the hermeneutical function of speech as such. Thus traditional hermeneutics functions only in certain special cases and in this respect must be still retained.

Part of the motivation in recasting hermeneutics was to escape the psychologism and historicism of the older critical religious liberalism. In psychologism things are explained exhaustively in psychological terms and in historicism in historical terms of causation and in both instances man never gets out of his skin and is therefore condemned to a vitiating relativism. The new hermeneutic wishes to escape this with its ontological understanding of word.

In reading the literature of the new hermeneutic one is impressed by the flexible use of "word," and grasping its different nuances is one of the more difficult problems in understanding the new hermeneutic. Sometimes "word" seems to mean the existential truth which seeks expression in speech; sometimes it seems to mean the speaking itself; other times it seems to mean the existential depth of the Biblical text; and again at other times it seems to mean the Word of God which breaks out of a sermon. It seems in order for the new hermeneutic to give a breakdown of the different kinds of sentences it uses as the logical positivists once did. Risking such a classification we can note the following kinds of sentences in the new hermeneutic. Some are *programmatic* in that they attempt to state the structure of hermeneutics and understanding as such. Some are *existential* for they seek not to communicate mere information but they intend participation and profound communication. Some are *factual* and *scientific* in that their function is merely to inform whether it be on a popular level ("there is some butter") or on a more theoretical level ("light is composed of rapidly moving photons"). Some are *formal* and only state relationships as in logic, mathematics, or grammar.

In this context of "word" as essentially existential communication the new hermeneutic formulates its concept of the Word of God. The Word of God is really more a movement than a notion. The Word of God is the existential communication of God within the text of Scripture; it is to be dug out by the exegesis and exposition of the text; it is to be formulated in a kerygmatic sermon; and it is received as the Word of God by the hearer when in decision he accepts it by faith. Existential considerations permeate each step of the procedure. For this reason the new hermeneutic is very critical of the so-called neutral, objective, scientific approach to exegesis as represented by Oscar Cullmann. No such exegesis is possible. The expositor must come to his text with existential understanding of religious matters (*Vorverständnis*), but he may not come with a prejudice (*Vorurteil*) as to what the text must say (as in allegorical exegesis).

The new hermeneutic agrees with Bultmann that faith can improperly elaborate its content. The writers of the New Testament had true faith and are our only authoritative witnesses of the Christ event. But as children of their times they were not exempt from error but into their reporting of the Christ event they introduced materials which men of today cannot accept. Although Bultmann stressed myth as that which more than anything else vitiated the reports of the New Testament that is not in accordance with the best of our knowledge, is not binding upon Christians. These foreign materials (foreign to the real existential communication of the Word of God in the texts) are subject to a special form of criticism known as "content criticism" (*Sachkritik*), which is characteristic of the new hermeneutic.

Although Barth does not accept the historic doctrine of inspiration in the Reformed tradition he does believe that once the content (*Sache*) of Scripture is determined it is binding upon Christian conscience. Quite out of step with so much contemporary theology he vigorously defends the existence of angels because he believes the revelation in Scripture commits the Christian to this (*Church Dogmatics*, III/3, p. 369 ff.). Bultmann believes that even if something is the obvious content of the New Testament (e.g., that Jesus rose bodily the third day from the dead) the interpreter is not bound to it. He may believe that this content (*Sache*) is contrary to the scientific understanding of the operation of the universe or the composition of the universe and so reject it as not binding upon Christian conscience. This content criticism came into sharpest focus in the demythologizing controversy, but content criticism in the new hermeneutic is wider than the task of demythologizing (*Entmythologisierung*), and is applicable to all the elements in the New Testament.

The new hermeneutic in extending the work of Bultmann defends a strong kerygmatic interpretation of the New Testament and of Christian preaching. The preacher is to come to the text and pose certain questions to the text. These are not thought of willy-nilly but are prescribed by existential considerations. The text in turn questions the interpreter. Thus in addition to the scientific investigation of the text there must be existential encounter with the text. Only after this is the preacher prepared to preach. Christian preaching must be textual preaching (that is, related to the text of Scripture). Christian preaching is relevant for it is not only shaped by the text, but also by the historical and cultural situation of the congregation. Christian preaching is kerygmatic for it proclaims God's love and forgiveness in Christ, and addresses the listener calling him to the decision of faith.

The new hermeneutic has not been limited to Biblical scholars and theologians but also includes philosophers and other scholars. It is the contention of the new hermeneutic that their understanding of hermeneutics or interpretation is actually the foundation for reconstruction in philosophy, for a new program in epistomology, for a fresh justification of and foundation for the liberal arts, and for a totally new formulation of the nature of Christian theology.

Some of the representative criticisms of the new hermeneutic are: (1) it is still in the liberal tradition in its critical methodology and in looking in the Scripture for the so-called "core" of its meaning; (2) in so restricting its understanding of the supernatural it destroys prophecy and with that any real significance of the Old Testament for the Christian church, and hence is a retreat to the heretical Marcionism of the early church; (3) in so stressing the purely existential and kerygmatic elements in interpretation it eliminates most of the traditional topics of systematic theology and thereby reduces the scope of Christian theology to a very small area; (4) in its notion of faith being pure existential decision it rejects all external props to faith, but only at the price of the ineluctable objective elements in the Christian faith (i.e., it is haunted by the ghost of subjectivism); (5) it has a defective anthropology in that it interprets man in an excessively existential manner and thereby loses the fullness of human nature; and (6) its concept of the Word of God is so opaque or empty (because it is existential communication and not the passing on of mere "information") that it loses real significance.

BIBLIOGRAPHY

Eberling, Gerhard, "Hermeneutik," *Religion in Geschichte und Gegenwart* (third edition), III, 242-262.

————————, *The Nature of Faith.* Philadelphia: Fortress Press, 1961.

————————, *Word and Faith.* Philadelphia: Fortress Press, 1963.

Fuchs, Ernst, *Hermeneutik.* Second edition; Bad Cannstatt: R. Muellerschoen, 1958.

Robinson, James M., and John B. Cobb, *The New Hermeneutic. New Frontiers in Theology,* Vol. II. New York: Harper and Row, 1964.

Tools of the Interpreter

The saying, "others have labored and you have entered into their labors" is particularly fitting to describe the resources available today to the interpreter of the Bible, resources which represent in many cases lifetimes of work on the part of dedicated scholars. We should not, therefore, apply too strictly the image of tools borrowed from mechanics when we speak of the tools of interpretation. For in the tools for interpreting the Bible, we meet in personal encounter the men who wrote them, and through our entering into their labors we are enabled better to engage the authors of Scripture also in such encounter, and beyond this to encounter the Lord himself who is the true and appropriate subject matter of the Bible.

We assume for the most part in this article that the interpreter is able to handle the original languages; but in case he is not so able, helps and aids are offered here which will assist him no matter what English version he may use as his study Bible. The starting point for all interpretation is, of course, a good critical text of the original languages. The standard for Hebrew is R. Kittel, *Bibla Hebraica* (Stuttgart, 1937), and for New Testament Greek is K. Aland — E. Nestle, *Novum Testamentum Graece* (25th ed., Stuttgart, 1963). A good text of the Greek Old Testament (Septuagint) is the one by A. Rahlfs, *Septuaginta* (3rd ed., Stuttgart, 1949). Pastors who depend almost exclusively on English translations should use a fairly literal and modern translation as a study edition and should compare it also with several other modern translations. Frequently, of course, an interpreter may be guided in the text he employs by a commentary written for a specific text. Commentaries frequently offer their own translations.

The primary tools for interpretation are the lexicon, the grammar, and the concordance. These tools should always be at hand, and should be used before the commentary is consulted. Grammatical exegesis precedes theological exegesis. It will be the custom in this article to cite first the most important and useful works in print, and then to refer to other worthwhile volumes. Two works are standard in the field of *Hebrew lexicography*: F. Brown, S. R. Driver, C. A. Briggs, *A Hebrew and English Lexicon of the Old Testament,* edited by G. R. Driver (1906, Oxford, 1952), and *Lexicon in Veteris Testamenti Libris,* by L. Kohler and W. Baumgartner (Grand Rapids, 1951-53). Among lexicons in New Testament Greek, one stands out above all others and has become the standard: *A Greek-English Lexicon of the New Testament and other Early Christian Literature,* translated by W. F. Arndt and F. W. Gingrich (Chicago, 1957) from Walter Bauer's Greek-German dictionary. A more compact lexicon which serves partly also as a concordance, and which lists the Hebrew equivalents for most Greek words is the work by G. Abbott-Smith, *A Manual Greek Lexicon of the New Testament* (3rd ed., Edinburgh, 1937, reprinted 1948). For serious and specialized study in the language of the New Testament, J. H. Moulton and G. Milligan's *Vocabulary of the Greek New Testament* (London, New York, 1914-1930, reprinted 1952) illustrates the New Testament vocabulary from the nonliterary papyri. The two long-popular works on synonyms should also be mentioned here: R. B. Girdlestone, *Synonyms of the Old Testament* (Grand Rapids, 1948), and R. C. Trench, *Synonyms of the New Testament* (Grand Rapids, 1948, reprinted, 1950).

GRAMMARS are normally employed as reference tools by the interpreter, which means that he enters into the riches of the grammar by way of its indexes of Scripture passages and/or Greek or Hebrew words in order to obtain help in unravelling the grammar of his text. However, the interpreter may also find it helpful to study a theme of grammar which has been brought to his attention in preparing a text, or he may study any given aspect of grammar independently of any given text. Both ways of using a grammar should be regularly followed. Some grammars serve one use better than another; and, therefore, the interpreter needs to be acquainted with several kinds of grammars. For Hebrew, the best reference grammar is Gesenius' *Hebrew Grammar* (2nd ed., Oxford, 1910), while S. R. Driver, *A Treatise on the Use of the Tenses in Hebrew* (Oxford, 1881) is excellent on its subject. The finest and most comprehensive Greek grammar available is F. Blass and A. Debrunner, *A Greek Grammar of the New Testament and Other Early Christian Literature* (Chicago, 1961), translated and edited by R. W. Funk. Another recent and fine work on syntax is Nigel Turner's volume, *Syntax*, Vol. III of J. H. Moulton, *A Grammar of New Testament Greek* (Edinburgh, 1963). The Turner book is more directly applicable to interpretation than the first two volumes of the Moulton grammar. A more concise and summary presentation of Greek grammar is provided by H. E. Dana and J. R. Mantey, *A Manual Grammar of the Greek New Testament* (New York, 1948). This treatment follows the method of the American scholar A. T. Robertson, *A Grammar of the Greek New Testament in the Light of Historical Research* (New York, 1914, reprinted by Broadman Press, Nashville, 1947), which, among other things, employs an eight-case system rather than the usual five-case system. Other grammatical helps worth having on hand are Kenneth S. Wuest, *The Practical Use of the Greek Testament* (Chicago, 1946); C. F. D. Moule, *An Idiom-Book of New Testament Greek* (Cambridge, 1953); and J. Harold Greenlee, *A Concise Exegetical Grammar of New Testament Greek* (Grand Rapids, 1963).

Turning to CONCORDANCES, most pastors will find Schmoller's *Handkonkordanz zum griechischen Neuen Testament* (13*th ed.* Stuttgart, 1963) designed as a companion volume for Nestle's Greek New Testament, adequate for their needs. One need only know Greek, not German, to use this helpful tool. A more complete Greek concordance, based on the Westcott, Hort and Tischendorf texts, is *A Concordance to the Greek Testament* (2nd ed., New York, 1900) by J. H. Moulton and A. S. Geden. Other Greek concordances available are: *The Englishman's Greek Concordance* (9th ed., London, 1903), compiled by G. V. Wigram, and J. B. Smith, and *Greek-English Concordance* (Scottdale, Pa., 1955). Studies in the Septuagint are greatly facilitated by the excellent and indispensable work by E. Hatch and H. A. Redpath, *A Concordance to the Septuagint and the Other Greek Versions of the Old Testament* (2 vols. and supplement, Oxford, 1897-1906). For Hebrew there is B. Davidson, *Concordance of the Hebrew and Chaldee Scriptures* (rev. ed., London, 1876), which is of more manageable size than the mammoth work of S. Mandelkern, *Veteris Testamenti Concordantiae Hebraicae atque Chaldaicae* (2nd ed., Berlin, 1925). Concordances to English editions of the Bible must now be classified according to the version for which they were compiled. For the King James Version there remain the long standard works by R. Young, *Analytical Concordance to the Bible* (New York, 1879-1894, rev. 1910); J. Strong, *The Exhaustive Concordance of the Bible* (London, 1903), which is indeed exhaustive; and A. Cruden's *Complete Concordance to the Old and New Testaments,* edited by A. Adams, C. H. Irwin and S. A. Waters (Philadelphia, *c.* 1949). Other works for different English versions are: J. W. Gant, *Concordance of the Bible in the Moffatt Translation* (London 1950); M. C. Hazard, *A Complete Concordance to the American Standard Version of the Holy Bible* (New York, 1922); *Nelson's Complete Concordance of the Re*vised Standard Version of the Bible, compiled by J. W. Ellison (New York, 1957); and *The Oxford Concise Concordance to the Revised Standard Version of the Holy Bible* (New York, 1962), by Bruce M. and Isobel M. Metzger.

Another indispensable tool is the BIBLE DICTIONARY. Every interpreter should possess a good multivolume Bible dictionary or encyclopedia. They are reference works for historical, geographical, literary, and theological information. An encyclopedia article is often the best introduction to the study of a subject or theme, because its concise form gives an overview of essential points and problems, and in addition usually provides additional bibliographical information. Obviously, all major encyclopedias could be mentioned here, but reference is intentionally limited to works that deserve the title of Bible dictionary; general dictionaries or encyclopedias on religion are omitted. The major dictionaries available are: J. Hastings, *Dictionary of the Bible* (5 vols., Edinburgh, 1898-1904; 12th impression, 1936); *The Interpreter's Dictionary of the Bible*, edited by George Buttrick (4 vols., Nashville, 1962); and the *International Standard Bible Encyclophedia*, edited by James Orr, and revised by M. G. Kyle (5 vols., Grand Rapids, 1930). Of these, the *Interpreter's Dictionary* is the most modern, but it has not entirely superseded the other dictionaries. The *International Standard* is more conservative theologically. Because they are still available, the two more specialized dictionaries edited by J. Hastings should be mentioned: *Dictionary of the Apostolic Church* (2 vols., Edinburgh, 1915-1918), and the *Dictionary of Christ and the Gospels* (2 vols., Edinburgh, 1906-1908). Many times the interpreter will need the information provided by a Bible dictionary but in briefer form than in the above works. In such cases, a one volume Bible dictionary is a most helpful book to have ready on hand. There are excellent ones available; and they cover a variety of theological positions, although, of course, much of the material in a dictionary does not involve theological interpretations. Among the more recent volumes the following may be recommended: *Dictionary of the Bible* (the one volume Hastings' *Dictionary*, revised and edited by F. C. Grant and H. H. Rowley; New York, 1963); *The New Bible Dictionary*, edited by J. D. Douglas, *et al* (Grand Rapids, 1962); *The Westminster Dictionary of the Bible*, edited by H. S. Gehman (Philadelphia, 1944).

Another tool which belongs with the Bible dictionary and supplements is the BIBLE ATLAS, which is essential for historical and archaeological study and, of course, serves as a useful visual aid in teaching the Bible. Among the better-known and more complete atlases in print are: *The Westminster Historical Atlas to the Bible*, by G. E. Wright and F. V. Filson (Philadelphia, 1945, revised 1956); *Atlas of the Bible*, by L. H. Grollenberg, translated and edited by Joyce M. H. Reid and H. H. Rowley (New York, 1956); *Baker's Bible Atlas,* by Charles F. Pfeiffer, (Grand Rapids, 1961); and the *Oxford Bible Atlas*, edited by H. G. May (London, 1962). A smaller, inexpensive yet excellent atlas is the Hammond atlas, *Atlas of the Bible Lands* (Maplewood, N. J., 1956).

The newest tool for the interpreter of the Bible is the THEOLOGICAL DICTIONARY, or as it is most popularly called, the wordbook. Most simply stated, this kind of book is a theological lexicon; it presents the theological meanings of important Biblical words in terms of their history. Products of the resurgence in Biblical theology, these wordbooks offer a rich and almost inexhaustible treasure of theological knowledge which will enrich the thought and life of the interpreter and help him to make the Word of God luminous. A good wordbook is an indispensable tool; it belongs along with all the other helps such as lexicons and grammars. It is not a substitute for the ordinary lexicon and grammar, but a necessary complement to them. Interpretation always commences with the text of Scripture, not with a tool, good as that tool may be. The most complete and by far the best theological dictionary produced by Biblical scholarship, G. Kittel's *Theologisches Worterbuch zum Neuen Testament,* edited after Kittel's death by G. Friedrich, is now available in an unabridged English translation by G. W. Bromiley entitled *Theological Dictionary of the New Testament* (Grand Rapids, 1964-65). Three volumes are in print; five more are scheduled. This is an expensive set but worth every bit of its cost. This dictionary is based on the Greek text and employs materials from the Old Testament, Judaism, and Hellenism as well as from the New Testament. The dictionary originally was an outgrowth of the work of H. Cremer in his *Biblico-Theological Dictionary of New Testament Greek*. Cremer's book is mentioned here because it is still available from T. & T. Clark, Edinburgh. Kittel's dictionary has spawned a large progeny. The best works only are listed in this article. Two of the most popular and good shorter wordbooks are *A Theological Workbook of the Bible*, edited by Alan Richardson (New York, 1950, also in paperback), and *A Companion to the Bible* (London edition entitled *Vocabulary of the Bible,* 1958) edited by J. J. von Allmen and translated by H. H. Rowley (New York, 1958). *Bible Key Words* (partial translations of some major articles from Kittel, New York, 1949-1964), and *A New Testament Wordbook* (London, 1955) and *More New Testament Words* (London, 1958) by Wm. Barclay are popular, shorter works; *Bible Key Words* is more theological; Barclay's work is more illustrative. Marvin Vincent's long known *Word Studies in the New Testament* (4 vols., New York, 1897-1900), while somewhat useful, does not measure up to the modern theological dictionary and is not a wordbook in the newer sense of the term.

The first help which comes to the mind of most interpreters when faced with a problem in Biblical study is the COMMENTARY. No one need speak for them; but it is difficult to speak discriminatingly about them because of the vast number of commentaries both new and old which are at the disposal of the interpreter. The other tools mentioned in this article should be used first; the commentary, of course, may be used partially as a lexicon or a grammar or a dictionary or a wordbook. But a commentary is itself a finished product of interpretation. Commentaries come in a bewildering variety of packages: separate monographs on one Biblical book, one volume commentaries on the entire Bible, or on one of the Testaments, and series of commentaries designed to cover the Biblical books one at a time and to employ a more or less uniform method of interpretation. Thus we can speak of critical commentaries, expositional or theological commentaries, and devotional commentaries, depending on which aspect of interpretation predominates over the others. Some famous commentaries, such as Barth's *Epistle to the Romans* (English translation, Oxford, 1933), are more like monuments in the history of interpretation than useful tools for present needs. Nevertheless, the influence of Barth's *Romans* is obvious in many commentaries which have succeeded it. Commentaries are recommended or selected by an interpreter because of the reputation of the author or of a series; most frequently, however, commentaries are bought on personal recommendation. Only some guidelines can be given here. A basic set for the library of an interpreter is *The Expositor's Greek Testament,* edited by Wm. Robertson Nicoll (London, 1910, reprinted Grand Rapids, 1952). One cannot help but mention the multivolume *Interpreter's Bible* (New York, 1951-1957), which is based on a double (KJ and RSV) English text, and which divides the work of exegesis and exposition among the different contributors. This is a dubious method and breaks the unity of scientific exegesis and proclamation which must characterize a proper procedure and purpose in interpretation. The interpreter should not overlook older commentaries. Patristic interpretation is worth consulting for many reasons. The commentaries of Calvin remain models of the art; most of them are still quite usable, and in the case of the New Testament commentaries are available now in new English translation. Luther on Galatians and Romans are musts; but so also is E. D. Burton on Galatians and Sanday and Headlam on Romans in the *International Critical Commentary series* (*I. C. C.*) The Pauline commentaries of Bishop J. B. Lightfoot are excellent; so also is anything by B. F. Westcott, A. Plummer and F. Godet. In the Moffatt commentaries, C. H. Dodd's volumes on Romans and the Johannine letters are very good. In the more recent *New International Commentary on the New Testament,* the volumes by F. F. Bruce (Acts, Colossians, Hebrews), N. Geldenhuys (Luke), F. Grosheide (I Corinthians), and P. E. Hughes (II Corinthians) are noteworthy. William Hendriksen's *New Testament Commentary* (Grand Rapids, 1953) merits notice. A similar series is commencing for the Old Testament, following a conservative approach. In the new *Cambridge Greek Testament Commentary,* C. E. B. Cranfield on Mark is fine; also C. F. D. Moule on Colossians and Philemon. Other series worthy of attention are the Tyndale series and the *Layman's Bible Commentary.* The interpreter should not overlook the Limited Editions Library of commentaries by Baker Book House. Individual commentaries of note among others would include H. B. Swete on Mark and Revelation; Franz J. Leenhardt on Romans (one of the best); C. K. Barrett on John; Jean Héring on I Corinthians; and E. G. Selwyn on I Peter. In the area of Old Testament commentaries, G. von Rad on Genesis is superb, and A. Weiser on Psalms is excellent.

Several recent editions of one volume Bible commentaries deserve mention. The following three commentaries are in a rough order from middle of the road to quite conservative. *Commentary on the Bible* by A. S. Peake (1919) has been rewritten as *Peake's Bible Commentary,* edited by M. Black and H. H. Rowley (New York, 1962). An evangelical work is *The New Bible Commentary,* edited by Francis Davidson (Grand Rapids, 1953), and a more conservative one is *The Wycliffe Bible Commentary,* edited by C. F. Pfeiffer and E. F. Harrison (Chicago, 1962).

Finally, brief mention may be given to expositions of the Bible which are more sermonic in content than strictly exegetical. Such works cannot really be classified as tools, but must be considered as helps and secondary ones at that. Their value, if they are used, would be for illustrative purposes, general style and aid in sermonic form; they cannot be the starting point for serious interpretation of the Bible. To be sure, one cannot despise such a work as the *Exposition of the Old and New Testaments* by Matthew Henry (New York, 1708-1710), but Biblical scholarship has moved since then; the tools are sharper; the problems more numerous; yet the possibilities and purposes remain the same, and many of the older devotional helps can remind us, if we need it, why we are interpreting at all.

SECTION 4

EVANGELISM — MISSIONS

"Where there is no vision the people perish." —Proverbs 29:18

The Biblical Basis of Missions and Evangelism

Missions and evangelism are, at heart, synonymous terms. Whoever evangelizes is a missionary whether he performs his work at home or abroad. A missionary overseas is an evangelist and if he is not an evangelist he is not a missionary. Having said this, it leaves unanswered the question "From whence do Christians get their marching orders to do missionary or evangelistic work?" To this question we must address ourselves.

Evangelism does not rest on its own foundation. Its undergirding derives from another foundation and that for a simple reason. Behind evangelism lies the gospel of Jesus Christ. The purpose of evangelism is to preach the gospel and to bring men to a decision where they are to place their faith in Jesus Christ for justification and regeneration. Thus evangelism can never be separated from the gospel. The gospel in turn can never be separated from its source. And the source of the gospel is the Bible, the Word of God written. In other words we are saying that missions, evangelism, the gospel, the knowledge of Jesus Christ, and salvation can be known only through the Scriptures. While it is true that the Scripture can be used indirectly through the medium of men who convey to other men what the Scriptures teach, it is still true that all men must ultimately turn to the Word of God written as the final source for their religious knowledge. Therefore evangelism must have a Biblical basis and if it does not it is not likely to be Biblical evangelism. What, then, is the Biblical basis for evangelism?

The Bible itself is a missionary book. The zeal for evangelism lies in the heart of God himself. Jesus Christ is the Father's missionary to a lost world. All of Scripture is the description of God who reaches down to touch man in his sin and reclaim him. Christ by his death atones for sin; he is the Lamb of God slain from before the foundation of the world.

The Old Testament is a missionary book. The choice of Israel in the Pentateuch was merely to provide a channel through which the Redeemer was to come, a people to whom the revelation of God was to be given and by whom it was to be preserved. In the Old Testament God plainly says that his concern is for all mankind (cf. the 96th Psalm). Isaiah says, "the God of the whole earth shall he be called." The Book of Jonah bespeaks the love of God for the Gentiles. The patriarch Joseph was a missionary in Egypt. Moses, likewise, was a missionary to the court of Pharaoh. Esther, the Hebrew maiden, was a missionary to Ahasuerus and his court. Daniel witnessed to the Lord his God in Babylon. Rahab and Ruth are converted Gentiles whom God graciously included in the line of promise through whom the Messiah was to come.

The New Testament is also a missionary book. From Matthew through the Revelation of St. John there is a single panoramic spread of the red thread of redemption. The Gospels portray the life of Jesus Christ – his death, burial and resurrection. The Acts of the Apostles shows the early church in outreach to the nations around it. The Epistles were written to newly established fellowships of believers. Paul traveled the Mediterranean basin to spread the good news that Jesus saves.

At the birth of Jesus the angelic hosts spoke of the good news for all men. Jesus himself taught us to pray "thy kingdom come, thy will be done on earth as it is in heaven." The first command of the risen Lord was a missionary command. When the Holy Spirit came upon the pentecostal assembly they were energized to go forth with the gospel to the people round about.

At Pentecost the church of Jesus Christ was established. This church of which the Scriptures speak has two aspects: first it is an invisible fellowship of all saints of all ages; it has in its compass the dead, the living, and those as yet unborn. The invisible church comprises all regenerate people who are known to God alone and who comprise his body. But this invisible church has visible manifestations. It can be seen empirically on this earth and at every stage in the history of the church. In a true sense one ought never to say that missions is the business of the church. Missions *is* the church. By this we mean that for the church to be the church it must act like the church. It must bring forth fruit consonant with its nature. It cannot be the church without witnessing to all men about the gospel. Just as the body that does not breathe is dead, so the church that does not witness is not the church.

The church really exists in, and to serve, the world. It is a channel through which spiritual blessings are to be conveyed. It is a church with a warfare, a church on the march, a church militant, not yet a church triumphant. God has no other agency whose duty it is to fulfill the terms of the Great Commission. If the church does not fulfill its destiny the gospel will not be preached. And God has made no other plans. Even the angels cannot preach the gospel. This is reserved for the church of Jesus Christ alone.

It is true that even if there were no command to evangelize the world in the Scriptures it would still be incumbent upon all believers to do this. The nature of the Christian faith demands it. One beggar who has received free bread without cost to himself is obligated to bring the same bread to other beggars so that they may eat and live. But this is to beg the question. It is to pose a hypothetical question and this need not, indeed should not, be done. The church has not been left in the dark about the plan of God or the mind of God for evangelism. It does not need to ask "What ought we to do in the absence of an express command to evangelize?" There is an express command. God has spoken clearly and definitively. This should be sufficient.

Matthew 28:18-20 has frequently been called the "marching orders of the church." The church is commanded to "disciple all nations," to baptise all who believe, to instruct in the holy faith those who have come, and to do so with the assurance of the undying presence of the risen Lord of the church. This command to evangelize is repeated in Mark, Luke, John and the Acts of the Apostles.

In this generation the command to evangelize has been subverted by an emphasis which has retained the word "evangelism" but which has emptied it of its traditional meaning. In too many instances to evangelize today means to change the social structures of society: to feed the hungry, to clean up the slums, to educate the illiterate, to eliminate segregation, to replace capitalism with socialism, and to bring the city of man into being. No one can overlook the need for Christian compassion nor should the gospel be limited only to proclamation. Service and proclamation are intrinsic to the gospel. But proclamation is ever to have priority over service and service which is elevated above proclamation is a deadly heresy. The absence of proclamation from much of today's evangelism means that the command of Jesus Christ has been vitiated. The great need of the hour is the recovery of proclamation in evangelism without which, whatever else it may be, it is not Biblical evangelism.

Evangelism cannot be separated from eschatology. Unfortunately eschatology today has been perverted and too frequently it has been taken to mean this present world, the Second Advent of Jesus Christ being left out. Evangelism is inextricably tied to the return of the Lord Jesus. When the gospel has gone to all the world for a witness then the end will come. Until Jesus comes the gospel has not been proclaimed to all the world.

There is a true sense in which the Church can hasten the coming of the Lord Jesus Christ. It does this by proclaiming the gospel to every creature and when this task has been accomplished Jesus will surely come. A church that is looking for the Second Advent is a church that will obey the command of its Lord. A church that really looks beyond the city of man to the eternal city of God will be busy to bring this to pass. There is a kingdom which is not of this world. This kingdom will come above and beyond history as we know it. It is, of course, already in history in the sense that those who belong to God in Jesus Christ live in this world. But it is also true that His kingdom is not of this world.

In the resurrection Jesus was not seen, according to the Scriptures, by any except those who belonged to Him. He was in the world in the resurrection but He was not visible to that world. He was visible to those who knew Him by faith. The world never has seen, and never will see, that which is discernible only to those who have faith and know Him. The world does not believe in and consequently does not look for the coming of the Lord. The Church is sometimes tempted by the world to forget what is known to it by faith and to adopt the views of an unbelieving world. Only when the Church once again realizes its divine origin, its divine destiny, and its divine obligation will His kingdom come, His will be done on earth as it is in heaven.

The only basis for evangelism, indeed the Biblical basis for evangelism, is the revelation of God in the Scriptures, the "Go ye into all the world and preach the gospel to every creature."

BIBLIOGRAPHY

Blauw, Johannes, *The Missionary Nature of the Church: A Survey of the Biblical Theology of Mission.* New York: McGraw Hill; London: Lutterworth, 1962. German tr.: *Gottes Werk in dieser Welt.* München: Kaiser, 1961.

Sets forth the results of the most important theological research of the last 30 years concerning the basis and purpose, and place and meaning of missions, from a Biblical perspective.

Carver, William O., *The Bible a Missionary Message.* New York: Fleming H. Revell, 1921.

Glover, Robert Hall, *The Bible Basis of Missions.* Los Angeles: Bible House of Los Angeles, 1946.

A very influential book in conservative circles.

Horton, Robert F., *The Bible, a Missionary Book,* Edinburgh: Oliphant, Anderson & Ferrier, 1904.

Lawrence, J. B., *Missions in the Bible.* Atlanta: Home Mission Board, Southern Baptist Convention, 1931.

Martin, Hugh, *The Kingdom Without Frontiers,* rev. ed. New York: Friendship Press, 1946.

A study in the Biblical basis of missions.

Rowley, Harold Henry, *The Missionary Message of the Old Testament.* London: Carey Press, [1945].

The Great Awakening

The term "Awakening" and even "Great Awakening" has a general and a more specific usage. Its broad reference is to the appearance of quickening of the Christian, Roman as well as Protestant, churches in both Europe and America. The more specific use of the term applies to the United States, particularly to New England, and most particularly to that awakening under Jonathan Edwards from 1740 on. The present reference is mostly to these spiritual manifestations in this country and in Great Britain.

1. DEFINITION OF "AWAKENING"

This term is rather diversely understood, then and now both by participants and by historians. Some think of awakening as a revival or the spiritual quickening of previously converted persons, others as the religious experiences accompanying the beginning of the Christian life. Still others, more correctly, see it rather as the exciting of the religious sensibilities of the unconverted both within and without the church. Probably the widespread notion that awakening was synonymous with revival is a mistake which may seriously mislead a student attempting to understand this type of religious event. Revivals are recognizable phenomena within the church of all ages and they invariably accompany or should accompany awakenings, and awakenings do or should accompany them. But they are distinguishable and separable. R. Seeberg (*RE*, 3rd ed., V, p. 486) tells us that the popular use of our word in Germany associated it with the religious experiences that were thought to mark the entrance upon the Christian life. But in the circles of Pietism in which the *Erweckungen* (awakenings) were most likely to break out they were associated with the *Erschutterunge* (strong emotions, convulsions) that were produced in many by the preaching of the Word. The same could be said of the Puritan usage generally. Edwards so understood and explained the Great Awakening. But he and his associates were careful to point out that not all who professed faith and had religious experiences were truly converted. Many were like the blossom which first appears on the tree but is not always followed by fruit. In the course of the Awakening Edwards learned much about the difficulty of recognizing genuine piety: "I am less charitable and less uncharitable than once I was. I find more things in wicked men that may counterfeit and make a fair show of piety, and more ways that the remaining corruption of the godly may make them appear like carnal men than once I knew of."

It is noticeable in this understanding of awakening that conversion may or may not occur. The proper fruit of this flower is conversion; but, it is the flower and not the fruit which symbolizes the awakening. Revival is something else: ". . . simply an increase of the best desires, efforts and exertions of persons who are already pious and benevolent, such an increase as, by the blessing of Heaven, awaken in the ungodly an anxiety for their salvation. . . . When these evidences of increased engagedness in the cause of Christ are unequivocally manifested anywhere, it is too late for an impartial observer to doubt that a genuine revival of religion has there commenced."

2. HISTORY OF THE GREAT AWAKENING

Today we think of the continent of Europe as preceding England and the United States in the production of religious ideas and movements which are imported here at a much later date. This has not always been so. In fact, in the seventeenth and eighteenth centuries at least three major movements began in the Anglo-Saxon world and from that source penetrated Europe, especially Germany. These are: the Enlightenment, whose beginning was English Deism; Pietism, which modern scholarship recognizes as springing especially from Cambridge Puritanism; and the Awakening movement, whose Anglo-Saxon origins we shall briefly sketch.

The Great Awakening in England is associated especially with the names of John Wesley and George Whitefield. But this outflowering had earlier roots. We could trace the origins of the Awakening to the "prophesyings" of the sixteenth century, but of more immediate significance for this topic are the religious societies of the seventeenth century. It was Anton Horneck, himself a German pastor in London, who first established the "religious societies" in England. These were concerned especially with the education of the poor and the provision of edifying literature which often became the means of quickening. The father of John Wesley, Samuel, who was also an Anglican pastor, was active in this movement. This was young Wesley's first contact with the new movement and the sphere of his earliest preaching. William Law, with his deep sense of true and inward religion, affected Wesley even more profoundly.

In Wesley and Whitefield the English Awakening reached its zenith. It was Whitefield who first took to the open air and mass evangelism. "The Great Awakener's" fiery zeal possessed his greater friend, Wesley, and soon all England was ablaze. In spite of the strain occasioned by the Free Grace controversy in 1740 the two evangelists were able to continue their association in worldwide evangelism. In 1770 Whitefield ended his labors in America where he became the most famous British evangelist of all time. Wesley's notable career closed forever in 1791. He had travelled 250,000 miles, preached 40,000 sermons, left about 140,000 Methodist members, as well as some 1500 traveling preachers, and had become the instrument of the awakening of unnumbered souls.

John Wesley made such a mark on the English Awakening that all subsequent movements, even outside of Methodism, bear his stamp to some degree. Conscious conversion experiences, mass meetings, social reforms, and worldwide evangelization which followed everywhere in the train of Methodist preaching are seen also in the Evangelical or Low Church wing of the Anglican Church. It is usually thought that this formation within the established church was the inevitable result of Wesley's movement taking a separate denominational existence (the Methodist Church) after his death. Without question, the English Free Churches were greatly abetted by the Wesleyan movement.

Wesley was not so successful in exporting his quickening gospel to Scotland. The awakening which broke out north of the border was introduced by two native sons, James Alexander Haldane and his brother, Robert. It had characteristic Scottish features and tended to remain within the Established Church. It was Thomas Chalmers under whom the Scottish Awakening came to its fullest expression, being closely connected with a revived diaconate and a strongly organized social activity among the industrialized workers. Whether it was in spite of or because of the Awakening, the Great Disruption of 1843 brought the great Free Church into being out of the bowels of the Establishment.

Scotland, rather than England, became the Awakening's chief port of embarkation for the Continent. The Haldane brothers spread the flame to Switzerland. Gathering seminary students around him for sound and practical studies in the Book of Romans, Robert became a center for the renewal of the gospel in the city of Calvin which by the nineteenth century was a stranger to the Reformer's teachings. Alexander Vinet was the great Swiss leader of the Revival. It was through Chalmers' influence that Germany through Fliedner and Tholuck (the developer of "Pektoral Theologie" or the theology of the heart) was awakened. Other persons were also active, and religious life in the homeland of the Reformation, which had also drifted far from the mooring of Luther, was deeply affected. The wide divergency in Germany is seen in the fact that the father of liberalism, Friederich Schleiermacher, and the pope of Lutheran orthodoxy, E. W. Hengstenberg, are both considered leaders in the Awakening movements.

The rest of Europe was also shaken. France including the Roman Catholic Church, felt this movement. Two prime ministers, Van Prinsterer and Abraham Kuyper, were leaders in the Holland Awakening. In Scandanavia the great names are N. F. S. Gruntvig, E. H. N. Hauge, and S. F. Hedberg.

It was in New England that the Great Awakening took most characteristic form. Although the "Great Awakening" often refers to the occurrences in New England especially under Jonathan Edwards between 1740-1743, speaking more comprehensively it spans the years 1726-1756 beginning with the preaching of the Dutch Reformed pastor, Freylinghuysen, of the Raritan Valley, New Jersey. Along with his revivalism the activity of the Presbyterian Tennents of the same area and the visit of George Whitefield to Georgia in 1738 were associated. Even in New England the movement began as early as 1734 under Edwards. With Samuel Davies it reached its peak in Virginia in 1748-1749. Its Baptist (Strubal Stearns and Daniel Marshall) and Methodist (Devereux Jarrett) phases followed closely.

While the Great Awakening proper may be said to have begun under the preaching of Jonathan Edwards it had been anticipated. Edwards' predecessor, Solomon Stoddard, had claimed numerous "harvests" (1679, 1683, 1696, 1712, 1718), and many other Puritan preachers likewise. And following Edwards, periodic revivals occurred (1800, 1826-1834, 1857-1858), helping to make this country the home, par excellence, of awakenings and revivals.

Both the history and the theology of the Awakening on both sides of the Atlantic are seen best in the relationships of the two leaders, Wesley and Edwards. Edwards' *Narrative of Surprising Conversions* (1734) and later works were published in England by Wesley (after deleting any objectionable Calvinistic statements), and greatly aided in implementing the British Awakening. Meanwhile Americans found encouragement in reports of the wonderful works of God in Germany, Scotland, and England. An unpublished sermon of Edwards on II Corinthians 8:10 (December 1739) bears poignant witness to this. Its doctrine was, "It may be very profitable for persons to hear of a work of God's grace being carried on in other places." After describing the Anglican decline under Charles I and Charles II, he speaks of God presently raising up certain young men, derisively called "new Methodists," to awaken the church. He mentions Wesley, Whitefield and Harris.

3. THE THEOLOGY OF THE AWAKENING

In spite of the close historical affinity of Edwards and Wesley and their common evangelical fervor, there were theological differences which played a significant role in the Awakening. There are three differences in the salvation theory of the two men which appear to have had far-reaching repercussions on their preaching. First, Wesley affirmed and Edwards denied that God had an obligation to offer salvation to sinful man. This difference not only altered their conception of grace itself in a fundamental manner, but it accounts largely for their characteristic Arminianism and Calvinism. That is to say, it was because Wesley believed that God had an obligation to give all fallen men a chance, in the fullest sense of the word, to believe and be saved that he necessarily and vigorously repudiated the doctrine of election. On the other hand, Edwards' doctrine of election, which he preached with the fervor that Wesley denied it, was perfectly consistent with his view of sin and grace.

The second great difference was on the matter of fallen man's ability to believe and be saved. Wesley maintained this as a necessary corollary is his conviction that God was under obligation to give men an opportunity to be saved, in the ultimate sense of the word "opportunity." If God were thus obliged, he would do what he was obliged to do, namely, give fallen men the full ability to believe and be saved. Wesley preached that God did give this to fallen sinners as their birthright. Sinners have "a natural propensity to sin. Nevertheless, this propensity is not necessary, if by necessary you mean irresistible. We can resist and conquer it too, by the grace which is ever at hand." Edwards, on the other hand, denied categorically that men had any such ability and he preached their inability. As we have seen, he made this very inability the basis of their seeking for ability.

The third difference bears most immediately on the preaching of Wesley and Edwards. Since one man thought that sinners had moral ability and the other did not, the appeal to these sinners was, of course, vastly different. Wesley always preached for decision. He appealed to men to believe and be saved, confidently assured that they were able to respond favorably to his invitation. Edwards, however, urged men to do far differently. He would not usually call upon them to believe and be saved (though he did do this; cf. the sermon on Rev. 3:20 which exhorts to belief without any mention of seeking), because that was not in the realm of their ability, but called them to seek to be enabled to believe and be saved because that was in the realm of their ability. (The above analysis was taken from the author's *Steps to Salvation*, 1960, with the kind permission of Westminster Press, Philadelphia, Pa.)

4. EFFECTS OF THE AWAKENING

The effects of the Great Awakening were numerous and profound. Beginning with deep repercussions on theology itself, they ranged through a broadened and more vital fellowship and tolerance. Literature poured forth and schools were built while the modern worldwide mission effort was virtually created by the Awakening. Withal the social changes that accompanied and followed the spiritual excitement were most significant for mankind in general whether participating in or merely affected by the religious upheaval.

a. *The Enlightenment Answered.* The Enlightenment, or eighteenth century form of what is commonly called "modernism" today, seemed to herald the end of Reformation Christianity. It had claimed reason was incapable of truly knowing God or the soul, whether through nature or special revelation. Proofs of religion, of the existence of God, and of the inspiration of the Bible, seemed demolished. Evangelicalism appeared reduced to superstition, a mere figment of man's stubborn imagination but not viable for the modern or enlightened man. Orthodox Christianity had persisted, of course, but its days appeared to be numbered. The modern man of the eighteenth century could no longer believe that there was either truth or power in the faith of the fathers.

This contention of the Enlightenment was refuted in kind by the evangelical scholars but the man in the pew read the refutation in the events of revival. The situation was not unlike the episode dramatized in the well-known "Owl Critic." Just as that critic who found numerous faults with the stuffing of the perched owl was devastatingly answered when the "stuffed owl" stepped down from the perch, so those who said that both God and the church were dead were silenced by the outbreak of new life within. As E. Beyreuther has written: "That the Church did not sink into the abyss of the Enlightenment and that the gospel was preserved . . . was owing above all to the Awakening" (*Religion in Geschicte and Gegenwart*, 3d Auflage, 1957, II, pp. 6, 7).

b. *Vital Orthodoxy Vindicated.* The Awakening showed the world that though the Enlightenment may have preserved the form of sound words it was without the power thereof. At the same time that the power of the gospel was bringing men alive from the dead they were asking for "that old-time religion." To be sure, in some sense Schleiermacher, the father of modern liberalism, was himself in the movement; but, it seemed to be in spite of his liberalism and because of his pietism. He subjectivized the content of Reformed Christianity almost beyond recognition, but by his emphasis on "feelings" enabled men to experience the gospel without necessarily understanding or accepting his own formulation of it. In any case, Schleiermacher and all like him were exceptions to the rule that the evangelical gospel alone brought evangelical awakening. Almost all of the outstanding preachers of the movement in Germany as well as in Britain and the United States were eminently orthodox and considered doctrine no less important than life. If there was more accent on life than doctrine this was owing to the slighting of Christian experience in the church's earlier extreme zeal for creedal correctness; not on any presumed unimportance of truth. Some of the doctrinal differences have been discussed above; here it is sufficient to note the general orthodox consensus, centering especially (as did the Reformation itself) on justification by faith alone.

c. *Christian Tolerance and Fellowship Broadened.* While doctrinal orthodoxy was essential to the Awakening its vitalization tended toward broadening. Wesley and Whitefield, for example, could have a serious controversy which divided them and their supporters yet remain good Christian friends. Moreover, while new denominations could spring up a warm fellowship pervaded all churches. Heart religion could bind together Baptist and Congregationalist, Anglican, and Methodist, even though they could not unite in the same organization. Whereas shortly after the Reformation orthodox Lutherans often considered Calvinists worse than Romanists and the Reformed looked askance at the "blemish" in the orthodoxy of Lutheranism, the Awakening was no respecter of denominations in the old sense. It was 1846 before the Evangelical Alliance could be formed but this earlier softening of the denominational ground made it possible. Nor was it a coincidence that one of the later leaders of the Awakening, Thomas Chalmers, was the moving spirit in its formation.

Corresponding to the tendency to rise above denominational confinements in the church was the moving beyond sectional divisions in the nation, especially in this nation. The quickening cut across social stratifications. The emphasis was on the hearts of men and the hearts of common men were greatly drawn toward God and one another. The Enlightenment centered on individualism and thus was centrifugal; the Awakening centered on fellowship and thus was centripetal and cohesive in principle.

There were some church splits occasioned by the Awakening but its general tendency was to heal and to unite. Many left Congregational churches in New England, for example, to unite with or to form Baptist congregations; but, this was produced by different views of children in the church and different degrees of patience toward the church. Again, the New Side-Old Side separation in the Presbyterian Church was first triggered by the revivalist sermon of Gilbert Tennent, "The Danger of an Unconverted Ministry"; but, the healing was also triggered by the same minister now sobered by the better knowledge of Christian conversion learned in the Awakening. Jonathan Edwards preached a famous sermon to the New York Synod (New Side), Newark, N. J. in 1752. This extremely searching message doubtlessly gave reconciliation a great push forward.

d. *Education Promoted.* The Enlightenment seemed to be the product of learning and certainly favored it but it was the Awakening which actually built the schools and gave men the incentive to learn. In America, Princeton, Brown, Dartmouth, and Rutgers were direct products of this sweeping movement of the Spirit. All of the colleges were affected. Even the University of Pennsylvania was an indirect product for it received its early impetus from Benjamin Franklin and he received his from Whitefield. As James H. Nichols has written, "The Awakening bore fruit in educational and evangelistic enterprises. Among the numerous academies and colleges which owe their origin to the Awakening, the best-known survivors are the Universities of Pennsylvania and Princeton . . ." (*History of Christianity*, 1650-1950, p. 75).

e. *Virtual Creation of the Modern Missionary Movement.* Some Scotsmen praying for awakening in their country wrote to Edwards in an effort to persuade likeminded Americans to join with them. This led to the writing of "An Humble Attempt to Promote Explicit Agreement and Visible Union of God's People, in Extraordinary Prayer, for the Revival of Religion and the Advancement of Christ's Kingdom on Earth" (1748). Many of those who prayed, like Edwards himself, believed they were living in the days of the "latter rain," but were expecting even greater and final blessings. They were disappointed but many have believed that the modern missionary enterprise, which began about a half century later, was God's greatest answer to those prayers. William Carey went out to India in 1793. At the beginning of the next century the Haystack Meeting took place as a part of the Awakening that was to give birth to the American mission movement. In Germany missionary societies were formed in Dresden, Langenberg, Neuendettelslau, and elsewhere. As the *Belehrung* (teaching) of the Reformation shifted its emphasis to *Belebung* (living), the *Belehrung* itself was soon to be carried to more people than in all the preceding centuries combined. Statistics show that the modern missionary movement was a ninety per cent Anglo-Saxon product. History also shows that the Awakening was pre-eminently an Anglo-Saxon experience.

f. *Profound Social Effects Produced.* Although the effects of the Awakening reached the whole world they began at home. This is the period of the beginning and intensification of the "Inner Mission" as well as foreign missions. If it is a mark of true religion to visit the fatherless and widows in their affliction, and to keep one's self unspotted from the world, then we are dealing with a revival of true religion. The anti-Antinomian character of the Awakening is seen in its strong insistence on the necessity of good works as the indispensable evidence of true faith. The quickened could not truly love God without at the same time and in the same act loving their fellow man. This was the source of vast social repercussions. The German evangelicals have a word for it. They speak of *Liebestatigkeiten*, which literally means "the actions that flow from love." When the love of God was shed abroad in the heart good deeds to men were born.

The *Gesta Christi* form a brilliant chapter in the Awakening. One of the most dynamic and graphic descriptions of the Wesleyan effects in Britain is J. W. Bready's *England: Before and After Wesley, the Evangelical Revival and Social Reform* (1938). Timothy Smith's *Revivalism and Social Reform* does something similar for the nineteenth century American Awakening, at least for its Arminian phase. It was a liberal, James Russell Lowell, who perceived the effects of the Awakening of evangelical religion if he did not clearly discern its source when he wrote, "Show me a place on the face of the earth ten miles square where a man may provide for his children in decency and comfort, where womanhood is protected, where age is venerated and where human life is held in due regard and I will show you a place where the gospel of Christ has gone before and laid the foundation."

That democracy itself was greatly fostered seems self-evident. A movement which begins with stress on personal responsibility, progresses to personal encounter with God, and reaches its climax in a call for personal decision and faith is the stuff of which democracy is made.

BIBLIOGRAPHY

Armstrong, M. W., "The Great Awakening in Nova Scotia, 1776-1809," *Studies in Church History*. vii. Chicago, 1948.

Beardsley, F. C., *History of American Revivals*. New York, 1904.

Elliott-Binns, L., *The Early Evangelicals*. London, 1953.

Finney, C. G., *Lectures on Revivals of Religion*. Oberlin, 1868.

Ferm, Robert O., *The Psychology of Christian Conversion*. Westwood, N.J.: F. H. Revell Co., 1959.

Fish, H. C., *Handbook of Revivals*. Boston, 1874.

Gaustad, E. S., *The Great Awakening in New England*. New York: Harper, 1957.

Gewehr, W. M., *The Great Awakening in Virginia 1740-90*. Durham, N.C., 1930.

Haldane, Alexander, *Memoirs of the Lives of Robert and J. A. Haldane*, 5th ed., 1855.

Kantzenbach, F. W., *Die Erweckungsbewegungen. Studien zur Geschicte ihrer Entstehung und ersten Ausbreitung in Deutschland*. Neuendettelsau, 1957.

Maxon, C.H., *The Great Awakening in the Middle Colonies*. Chicago: University of Chicago Press, 1920.

Orr, J. Edwin, *The Second Evangelical Awakening in America*. London, 1952.

Porter, *Revivals of Religion, showing their Theory, Means, Obstacles*. New York and Cincinnati, 1877.

Tracy, J., *The Great Awakening*. Boston, 1842.

Wendland, W., *Erweckungsbewegungen in Deutschland*, 1926.

Williams, Geoffry, *Flames Worth Fanning*. Newport, Monmouthshire: Riverside Works, 1944.

Woodward, J., *An Account of the Rise and Progress of Religious Societies*. London, 1698.

Evangelistic Movements

The upheavals of the late eighteenth century, especially the American and French Revolutions, were followed by a decline in Christian witness so serious that, in the judgment of Kenneth Scott Latourette, "it seemed as though Christianity were a waning influence, about to be ushered out of the affairs of men." Even in the dynamic society of the United States, the plight of the churches was desperate. Moral breakdown in individual and community life was prevalent. In despair, Christian leaders began to pray for divine intervention. The answer came in a series of six great waves of evangelical renewal and advance which made the nineteenth century up till 1914 the "Great Century" of evangelism.

1. THE FIRST WAVE

The writer long ago rejected the designation "the Frontier Revivals" commonly given to these awakenings. Even in the United States, the "1800 Awakenings" originated not on the frontiers of the westering nation but in the colleges and towns of the longest-settled communities. They were paralleled in Europe by similar revivals among the Swiss, the Norse, the Scots and others scarcely inhabiting "frontiers." *Le Reveil*, which moved the Reformed Churches of Switzerland, France, and the Netherlands, began among students in Geneva in 1816. Even in recording the revivals among the illiterate frontiersmen of Kentucky or Tennessee — as William Warren Sweet stated — there was "entirely too much stress placed upon the emotional excesses of camp meetings and all too little upon the routine work of the frontier churches and preachers." Finally, it is fallacious to consider "revivals" as "frontier phenomena" when the most widespread and effective of all such movements, the Awakening of 1858-1859 around the world, started in cities such as New York, Philadelphia, Belfast, Glasgow, London, and Birmingham. The conclusion that because the American frontier has closed, evangelical awakenings are now impossible is contradicted by facts and logic. The Revivals of 1905 began in urban Wales, Norway, and other countries.

When John Wesley died, Evangelical Christendom was confined to Great Britain, Scandinavia, parts of Germany, Holland and Switzerland, minorities in France and Hungary, and territory east of the Alleghenies in North America; while Latin America was closed by the intransigent governments of Spain and Portugal, Africa was unexplored, Islam was hostile to the gospel, the East

India Company made missionaries unwelcome in India, and none resided in China, Japan or Korea. South Seas islanders were savages.

The evangelical denominations were without Sunday Schools, Bible Societies, Home Missions, Foreign Missions – apart from Moravians – and agencies taken for granted in modern times.

The "turn-of-the-century" awakenings sent off pioneer missionaries to the South Seas, to Latin America, Black Africa, India, and China. There arose denominational missionary societies such as the Baptist Missionary Society, the American Board, and other national missions in Europe. At the same time, the British and Foreign Bible Society was founded, followed by the American Bible Society, and other national Bible Societies.

The awakenings raised up able evangelists on the American frontier, sent the Haldanes up and down to revive Scotland, produced Hans Nielsen Hauge to transform Norway, and provoked revival and evangelism in England, Germany, Holland and other European countries. Sunday Schools and a host of evangelistic agencies arose for service.

The social impact of these awakenings was tremendous. Wilberforce mobilized evangelical and political opinion in Great Britain to secure an abolition of the slave trade and the emancipation of the slaves throughout the British Empire, an achievement not won for another thirty years in the United States. John Howard pioneered prison reform, which was carried on by Elizabeth Fry in London. Theodore Fliedner adopted the same ideas in Germany, building homes and hospitals, training deaconesses and nurses, his most famous pupil being Florence Nightingale, who in turn influenced Henri Dunant in founding the Red Cross, Dunant being as ardent an evangelical as Fliedner.

Great Britain was the first of the world's countries to be industrialized, and its workers were caught in a treadmill of competitive labor which kept them straining for sixteen hours a day. Evangelical leaders, including Shaftesbury and members of the "Clapham Sect," brought an end to much of the sorry exploitation, and promoted all sorts of social improvements. No less an authority than Prime Minister Lloyd George credited to the Evangelical Revival "the movement which improved the condition of the working classes, in wages, hours of labor and otherwise." This was paralleled in the United States by what have been called "the Sentimental Years," when organized good works and betterment flourished.

These awakenings had a profound effect upon secular education, leading to the foundation of numerous schools, high schools and colleges in the expanding United States under denominational direction,and also producing free public schools, a pattern reproduced in Britain and Europe.

2. THE SECOND WAVE

The years between 1792 and 1842 produced continuous revivals in the United States, with an interruption due to the War of 1812. In its second phase, the outstanding figure Charles Grandison Finney dominated the middle third of the century as Dwight L. Moody dominated the final third. At the same time, James Caughey reaped thousands of converts in Great Britain and the United States, William Booth being impressed by his ministry.

The leaders of the Awakening in Scotland were Robert and James Haldane, who were succeeded by William C. Burns in the next generation. At this time, Charles Simeon was building up the evangelical clergy of the Church of England into its dominant force and a wave of revival produced the Primitive Methodist evangelists under whom Spurgeon was converted. Converts of *Le Reveil* begun by Robert Haldane in Geneva extended the work all over France and the Netherlands, and a parallel movement began in Germany led by great evangelists such as the Krummachers. Revival continued in Norway and a great movement began in Sweden under George Scott and Carl O. Rosenius. In the Ukraine, a revival among German settlers of Pietist and Mennonite affiliation developed into the Stundist movement among the Russians.

This second wave of revival reinforced the foreign missionary invasion of all the continents, and continued its social impact upon the sending countries. Captain Allen Gardiner pioneered in the wilds of South America and died tragically. David Livingstone explored African territories. Missionaries reconnoitered the citadels of Islam. William Carey was followed by societies ready to evangelize India. Robert Morrison opened a way for missionaries to settle in the treaty ports of China. Evangelism in Oceania was followed by extensive awakenings in Hawaii and other Polynesian kingdoms. There were setbacks also.

Missionary pioneers opened up Madagascar to the gospel and completed a translation of the Old and New Testaments before a violent persecution compelled the missionaries to abandon a couple of hundred converts to the fury of their enemies in 1836. A quarter of a century elapsed before the contact was re-established.

Evangelical Christianity faced other setbacks throughout the world in the second third of the nineteenth century. Tractarianism arose in the Church of England, an Anglo-Catholic revival, to challenge the leadership of Evangelical Church clergy. High Church parties rose among Lutherans in Germany to challenge a new rationalism. There was similar dissension in the Reformed Churches. The Church of Scotland was rent by the Disruption, which, thanks to the early Nineteenth Century Revival, strengthened evangelism and the evangelical cause in Scotland.

Among Baptists in the area of their greatest numerical strength in the United States, another exclusive movement (Landmarkism) arose and isolated Baptists from other evangelicals. The extravagances of eschatological interpretation caused dissension and decline in the United States as the churches began gaining by immigration. There were economic and political setbacks also. A gross materialism grew among Americans as political unrest gripped Europe at the mid-century.

3. THE THIRD WAVE

In the autumn of 1857, there were signs of an awakening – success in revival and evangelism in Canada, and an extraordinary movement of men to prayer in New York City which spread from city to city throughout the United States and over the world. Churches, halls, and theaters were filled at noon for prayer, and the overflow filled churches of all denominations at night in a truly remarkable turning of a whole nation toward God. More than a million of the converts were added to the churches in a short space of time.

The same movement also affected the United Kingdom, beginning in 1859 in Ulster, the most northerly province in Ireland. Approximately ten per cent of the population professed conversion in Wales and Scotland as well, and a great awakening continued in England for years. Repercussions were felt in many other European countries.

The phenomena of revival were reported in parts of India, Africa, and the West Indies. The missionaries returning to Madagascar found that two hundred converts had increased to 20,000.

Out of the 1859 Awakening in Britain arose a phalanx of famous evangelists, aristocrats, and working men. Spurgeon built his Tabernacle on the crest of the movement. The intervention of the war between the States (in which there was extraordinary revival and evangelism in every theater of war) delayed the emergence of great American evangelists of the 1858 Awakening.

The 1858-59 Awakenings extended the working forces of evangelical Christendom. Not only were a million converted in both the United States and the United Kingdom, but existing evangelistic and philanthropic organizations were revived and new vehicles of endeavor created. The Bible Societies flourished as never before. Home Missions were founded, and the Salvation Army arose to extend the evangelistic-social ministry of the revival in countries around the world. The impact upon the youthful Y.M.C.A. organization was tremendous.

The mid-Century Awakenings revived all the existing missionary societies and enabled them to enter other fields. The practical evangelical ecumenism of the revival was embodied in the China Inland Mission founded by Hudson Taylor in the aftermath of the British Awakening, the first of the "faith" interdenominational missions. As in the first half of the century, practically every missionary invasion was launched by men revived or converted in the awakenings in the various sending countries.

For example, the first permanent missions in Brazil followed the 1858-59 Awakenings. In Indonesia and India, mass movements to Christianity followed. China was penetrated by the converts of the revival from many countries. The missionary occupation of Africa was rapid, and the liberated Negro in the Anglo-American territories was thoroughly evangelized.

4. THE FOURTH WAVE

In the 1870's, Dwight L. Moody rose to fame as a mass evangelist. Beginning quietly in York in 1873, he progressed through Sunderland, Newcastle, Edinburgh, Dundee, Glasgow, Belfast, Dublin, Manchester, Sheffield, Birmingham, and Liverpool, using methods of the 1858 Revival in prayer and preaching, finally campaigning in London where about 2,500,000 people heard him in twenty weeks. In 1875 Moody returned to his native country a national figure, campaigning equally successfully in Brooklyn, Philadelphia, New York, Chicago, Boston, and other cities. From then onwards, he ministered in cities on both sides of the Atlantic. A flock of successful evangelists was associated with him. Perhaps his greatest campaign was conducted at the World's Exposition in Chicago in 1893. Moody died in action in 1899.

In the Moody period, another awakening began in Sweden, extending the work of the National Evangelical Foundation (EFS) and an offshoot, the Evangelical Mission Covenant (SMF). Revivals continued in Norway and Denmark and Finland.

As a result of the impact of Anglo-American Awakenings – including Moody – a Thirty Years' Revival began in Germany, from 1880 until 1910. Outstanding leaders were Dr. Theodor Christlieb (who founded the German Committee for Evangelism and the *Gemeinschaftsbewegung*), Elijah Schrenk and Samuel Keller.

In the same period there was both revival in the Ukrainian peasantry and evangelism among Russian upper classes, the latter begun by British gentlemen, Radstock and Baedeker. Prokhanov, converted in 1886, founded the All-Russia Evangelical Union which in the next century united in denominational organization with the Baptists.

In the 1858 Awakening in the United States, revivals among students resulted in formation of the college Y.M.C.A.'s, and in the following year, prayer meetings at Oxford and Cambridge gave rise to local Christian Unions which later united to form the Inter-Varsity Fellowship. In the local student fellowship at Princeton in 1875 were several outstanding young men – Robert Mateer, who became leader of the Inter-Seminary Missionary Alliance, T. W. Wilson, who became president of Princeton University and later (as Woodrow Wilson) the President of the United States; and Luther Wishard, who became the organizer and evangelist of the Inter-Collegiate Y.M.C.A. Wishard pleaded with Moody to begin a ministry among students, but Moody was reluctant on account of his own academic deficiencies.

In 1882 Moody was persuaded to campaign in Cambridge University, where at first he stirred up scornful opposition. Out of the awakening, the Cambridge Seven (C. T. Studd and other first-rank varsity men) stirred the student world and proceeded to China as missionaries.

Thus encouraged, Moody acceded to Wishard's promptings to arrange a conference for students at Mount Hermon, in his home state. A youthful delegate, Robert Wilder, presented the claims of the mission fields, and a hundred of the 250 present responded. Within the academic year, there were two thousand volunteers from American colleges and universities and the Student Volunteer Movement was born. Under the direction of men like John R. Mott, the Volunteers multiplied on every continent and sought to "evangelize the world in this generation." Advance was sustained.

Out of the 1859 Awakening arose the Keswick Movement for the Deepening of the Spiritual Life (1875). In the eastern hemisphere, it became a unifying force in Evangelicalism, whereas parallel movements in America, the Holiness Movement, resulted in splintering.

Christian Endeavor, a movement for training young people in church-related activity, began in a local revival in Maine in 1881, under Francis E. Clark. Within fifteen years there were two million members in forty thousand local societies. It was ecumenical and evangelical. A number of denominational copies were offered.

The 1880's witnessed advances in the evangelization of China, as well as a remarkable seven-years' revival in Japan, but the years of rapid growth were followed by a decline caused by the onslaught of rationalist theology among pastors.

The awakenings in sending countries caused an extension of missionary enterprise on every continent. Albert B. Simpson, convert of the 1858 Revival in Canada, founded the Christian and Missionary Alliance in 1886, interdenominational but later itself a denomination.

In the social impact of Mid-Century Revivals, greater effects were seen in the industrialized United Kingdom. Lord Shaftesbury continued his extraordinary parliamentary program for the betterment of humanity. Great orphanages were begun. A Society was formed for the Prevention of Cruelty to Children (1889), while Josephine Butler rallied evangelical opinion to abolish the licensing of prostitution in Great Britain (1886). The evangelical interest motivated much of the agitation for the betterment of conditions for the laboring people, many leaders in the Labor Party being avowed evangelical Christians. In the United States, there also was a growing concern with purely social issues such as rights of the working man, poverty, the liquor trade, slum housing and racial bitterness, all arising from the impulse of the Mid-Century Awakening. Out of this evangelical concern grew a liberal social gospel whose advocates became increasingly indifferent to the dynamic of the Christian gospel, the transforming of individual lives by the power of Jesus Christ, evangelism before reform.

5. THE FIFTH WAVE

Prayer meetings were held in the Moody Bible Institute and elsewhere at the turn of the twentieth century for another awakening. Traceable to this intercession were the Welsh and other Revivals in 1904-1905 onwards, as well as the world-girdling evangelistic campaigns of Torrey and Alexander and Chapman, who succeeded D. L. Moody in mass evangelism.

A 26-year old student, Evan Roberts, was the chief instrument in a remarkable outpouring of the Spirit upon the Churches of Wales in 1904, in which fully 100,000 were converted. There was a similar awakening in Scandinavia in 1905, and repercussions in Germany and Russia. In Boer prisoner-of-war camps, a revival of evangelical fervor communicated itself to the home churches.

Awakenings were reported from 1905 onwards in Madagascar, Assam and all parts of India, Korea, Manchuria and parts of China, Chile and parts of Latin America. The Chilean movement brought forth glossolalic manifestations and gave rise to an indigenous Pentecostal denomination which soon became the dominant force in the evangelical life of that republic.

In the early 1900's and even before, there were glossolalic utterances reported in the United States. From one of these in Los Angeles in 1906 grew the modern Pentecostal movement. Converts of the Welsh and Scandinavian Awakenings came in touch with this interest, giving rise to very vigorous Pentecostal denominations in British and Scandinavian countries, while similar fellowships such as the Assemblies of God arose in the United States and elsewhere. There was widespread opposition to the movement, especially in the historic evangelical constituency, but the new effluence of evangelical Christianity outlived its initial extravagances and became evangelistic.

The Pax Britannica, from Waterloo in 1815 till the first World War in 1914, coincided with this "great century" of evangelical renewal and advance. It was the period in which Great Britain led the world in industrialization, when British commerce penetrated the seven seas, when the royal navy was supreme, and when the British Empire outgrew all its predecessors in an imperialism whose benefits outweighed its injustices. It is impossible to escape the conclusion that this imperialism facilitated the growth of missions in its territories and in the territories of neighbors. This factor, together with the independence of the United States and its Monroe Doctrine, led to the remarkable growth of evangelical Christianity in the Americas. Likewise, the building of schools and hospitals concurrent with missionary penetration of Africa followed imperialism. Even the Opium Wars in China which the missionaries opposed, led to the opening of China to the gospel and the founding of schools, orphanages, leprosaria, hospitals, and universities.

From 1858 till 1908, evangelical awakenings had raised up men to preach the Word and practice the unity of the Spirit. Thereafter, in the United States, reaction set in and it was not till 1948 that a worldwide evangelical resurgence was seen. Politically, this was a period of revolution to be compared with that which began in 1775 and ended in 1815. It included the First World War of stalemate and bloody slaughter, a worldwide economic depression, and the Second World War.

The years of decline were marked by division and polarization in Protestantism. Modernism grew out of the Enlightenment in Germany, with a period of incubation roughly coterminous with the "great century" of evangelical advance, but it dominated Protestant thinking in the decades of war and depression. To counter it, a movement arose in evangelical Christianity, first a protest for the fundamentals of the faith but afterwards a factious fundamentalism which denied the unity of the body of Christ as taught and practiced earlier. The polarization was manifest in the modernist denial of the authority of Scripture but support of interdenominational cooperation, whereas the fundamentalist (of the factious type) supported the authority of Scripture but obstructed interdenominational cooperation. The modernist opposed evangelism but promoted social reform, whereas the fundamentalist practiced evangelism but neglected the social implications of the gospel.

Evangelism in the United States suffered much in the second, third, and fourth decades of the new century through the commercialism, sensationalism, and irresponsibility of free-lance evangelists who lacked loyalty to an organization, or discipline. The leading evangelist, Billy Sunday, was less widely accepted than Moody, Chapman, or Torrey on account of alleged commercialism and undoubted sensationalism, although there were lasting fruits of his campaigns. Most of the more than 600 active professional evangelists counted in 1911 copied Billy Sunday in style. Sunday built temporary tabernacles, working with sponsoring committees of ministers and laymen. Imitators found the device of a tabernacle enabled them to work independently, divisively, and commercially.

A movement rose in Britain which helped keep its evangelism wholesome. Out of the successful campaigns of the brothers Arthur and Frederick Wood grew their National Young Life Campaign. Older societies continued to provide sponsorship, responsibility, and discipline for evangelists.

In the 1930's, there was an evangelistic stir of sorts, thrusting forth evangelists who gained worldwide usefulness — Joe Blinco, Bryan S. Green, Roy Hession, J. Edwin Orr, T. B. Rees, and Ian Thomas. The outstanding evangelist of the between-Wars period was Lionel B. Fletcher, who campaigned in the great cities of the British Commonwealth as the "Empire Evangelist" of the Milday group. Gipsy Smith, born in 1860, continued to conduct campaigns in Britain and the States, with slackening response. Oswald Smith of Toronto first a missionary promoter, became a widely accepted evangelist on every continent. J. C. Massee, Paul Rader, Walter Kallenbach, Hyman Appelman, and other evangelists labored in the United States.

In these decades of spiritual decline there were few movements that could be considered as true revivals, but enough to maintain godly hopes. There were a few localized awakenings in Great Britain in the 1920s (a revival among fisher folk in northeast Scotland led by Jock Troup, another in East Anglia led by Dr. Douglas Brown). The strongly evangelical province of Ulster (Northern Ireland) became a source of evangelical strength because of the lingering effects of the '59 Revival and the post-Irish Civil War revival of the 1920's.

When the Irish "troubles" were at their worst, evangelical Christians prayed for an awakening which came through an Irish-American, William P. Nicholson. In 1920, news of blessing in Bangor opened the doors to service in other districts — and Ballymena, Londonderry, Lisburn, Lurgan, Newtownards and Portadown were the scenes of movements of the Holy Spirit, with converts by the thousands, chiefly among grown men moved by Nicholson's rough and manly preaching.

In 1922, Nicholson visited Belfast during the worst political strife. The response was unusual, shipyard workers marching thousands strong to meetings, tens of thousands of people converted, the movement going on for years, though later visits to his native land won neither the results nor the acceptance of the times of Revival, due in part to the lash of the evangelist's tongue.

In the 1930's, there were successive revivals in the Baltic States of Estonia and Latvia. Fetler, driven out from a great work in Petrograd, had established a capacious tabernacle in Riga. The movements lasted seven years, but were crushed by war and the Soviet occupation.

The lay evangelist James Stewart commenced remarkable work in the Hungarian capital in 1937. Enjoying the support of Lutheran, Reformed, and Free Church ministers, he preached in cathedrals, theaters, ice-skating rinks, and churches with a huge attendance. Many formalistic pastors were converted with tens of thousands of members. He extended his work into many European countries, launching the European Evangelistic Crusade.

In the 1930's, there were awakenings in the Scandinavian countries. The ministry of Frank Mangs in Finland, Sweden, Denmark, and Norway reached its climax in a great movement in Oslo. The Oxford Group followed up the opportunities. Churches were crowded and conversions were common. The participation of Armin Gesswein and J. Edwin Orr in the awakening deepened their interest in revival as distinct from evangelism.

Gesswein returned to the United States to promote a prayer interest among ministers in revival, a work that bore fruit later, while Orr toured the English-speaking countries with a message of revival, witnessing local stirrings in 1935 and 1936 in Canada, the United States, New Zealand, Australia, and South Africa.

By far the greatest awakening of the between-Wars period was the revival in China, starting in 1925 during a great anti-missionary uproar. Missionary prayer meetings in Shanghai led to a great awakening among Chinese, producing a group of outstanding evangelists such as John Sung and Andrew Gih. A Norwegian, Miss Marie Monsen, led a movement which became known as the Shantung Revival. The Bethel Bands led by Andrew Gih witnessed great awakenings all over China. The awakening in China continued through all the turmoil but came to an end in the Sino-Japanese War of 1938, and was blotted out finally in the Communist takeover.

The 1930's brought awakenings to sections of Africa. Andrew MacBeath reported an unusual revival in Balobo country in the Congo in 1937. There were evangelical revivals in West Africa.

In 1927, a week of prayer was held in church missionary stations in Ruanda, East Africa. Rising interest reached its climax in 1932 at Gahini, and an amazing movement developed among the Africans, manifesting the phenomena of revival, conviction, confession, conversion, and witness. In 1936, the movement was renewed and teams of Africans with missionary assistance visited the Sudan, Uganda, Kenya, Tanganyika, and the Congo. There was considerable opposition to the unconventional methods of the revivalists, not without any justification, but the movement continued for a generation and survived the Mau Mau terror in Kenya with lasting credit.

Between 1927 and 1936, a third major revival in Madagascar ran its course. It began as before in Norwegian mission fields in the middle south. Its greatest leader was Rajaofera.

Prior to the Second World War, the Child Evangelism Fellowship was begun. Young Life Campaign was started by Jim Rayburn to reach teen-agers. The Inter-Varsity Christian Fellowship moved onto the campuses of American universities to fill a vacuum caused by the liberalizing of other student organizations. Christian Businessmen's Committees multiplied.

In the war years, Youth for Christ rallies on Saturday nights sprang up in the major cities, a central organization being formed under leadership of Torrey M. Johnson and his associates. Billy Graham soon emerged as their outstanding evangelist. The method was popular evangelism, combining simple gospel preaching with entertainment of a religious kind. The movement expanded rapidly overseas, in the cities of Britain and other English-speaking countries and around the world, raising up a phalanx of evangelists.

6. THE SIXTH WAVE

The First World War (1914-1918) did not bring about a revival of New Testament Christianity, nor did the world economic depression (1929-1935); nor did the Second World War (1939-1945). Political and economic distress does not always drive people to prayer and repentance. The next worldwide movement came with prosperity.

The general awakening of the mid-twentieth century showed by its spontaneous and simultaneous nature the marks of a simple outpouring of the Holy Spirit. Evangelical revival was reported from places as far apart as Madagascar, the Hebrides, Korea and Brazil, and in each of these places there had been the preparation of intercessory prayer — as, for example, in 1947 Christians in North

Korea secured a permit to hold an early morning prayer meeting in Pyungyang to commemorate the outbreak of revival forty years before, and ten thousand attended.

In Korea, the mass meetings of prayer for a revival were followed by a general awakening just before the outbreak of the Korean War in 1950. Early morning prayer meetings attracted their thousands and evangelistic meetings produced thousands of conversions. The awakening continued through the War and receded only when fundamentalists introduced bitter disputes.

In 1946, a fourth major awakening broke out in Madagascar, manifesting prayer, confession of sins, exorcis mof evil spirits and restitution. Its leader, Rakotozandry, who had addressed crowds of 25,000, died of tuberculosis.

In 1949, a grass roots movement of ministers seeking to pray together appeared in Los Angeles, Minneapolis, and other cities, spreading throughout the country, Armin Gesswein a director.

In 1949, a series of extraordinary revivals of religion occurred in many Christian colleges and universities, bringing the normal life of several to a halt. About the same time, the students of many secular colleges and universities showed unusual interest in things spiritual. This college awakening was a grass roots movement, though not without human leadership and direction. Its first manifestation occurred at Bethel College in Minnesota, but the movement won national attention in newspapers and news magazines after a revival at Wheaton College filled the chapel for thirty-eight hours. Most significant was a revival at Forest Home.

In 1949, Christian entertainers in Hollywood began to pray for a spiritual awakening in the entertainment world long neglected by churches. This was followed by conversion of outstanding celebrities, foundation of the Hollywood Christian Group by Henrietta Mears and Edwin Orr, and conversion of scores of stars and starlets of radio, television, stage, and screen. About the same time numerous entertainers in other parts of the country were spontaneously converted, many entering full-time Christian service.

In 1949, an extraordinary revival began in the Gaelic-speaking Hebrides of Scotland under the ministry of Duncan Campbell. The movement was marked by the phenomena of visions, conviction of sin, attendance at prayer meetings exceeding normal church attendance.

In 1949, mass evangelism – after being treated with contempt by most laymen and many pastors – received both a cleaning and refreshing. Billy Graham (who had experienced personal renewal at a student conference at Forest Home, California) became a national figure. He and other evangelists found themselves preaching to ten thousand per night, with extraordinary results in numbers and in quality. The movement increased for years.

The Los Angeles Crusade held in the autumn of 1949 by the Graham Team was followed by a series of campaigns in strategic cities in North America, success following success whether in the West, the East, the Middle West, or the South. Graham received wider and wider support from the Councils of Churches. Methods used by the founder of a Bible memorization organization, Dawson Trotman, were used by his Navigators to create a follow-up organization for the Graham converts unknown before in mass evangelism.

The honeymoon period of support ended when Billy Graham campaigned in New York in 1957, his ministry being attacked by critics of the left and right. Meanwhile, in the spring of 1954, he commenced a crusade in Harringay Arena in London which confounded his detractors, a final meeting bringing 100,000 people who heard the Archbishop of Canterbury offer closing prayer. In 1955, Graham tackled Glasgow in Scotland, and followed up with a shorter series in Euopean cities. In 1956, he preached to vast crowds in Asian cities, beginning with India. In 1959, he embarked upon extraordinary crusades in cities in Australia and New Zealand. Attendances were huge, up to 50,000 a service. In 1960, Graham campaigned in African countries, omitting South Africa, although other evangelists later held unsegregated meetings in that racially tense land. Then followed campaigns in Latin America.

There were awakenings in India from 1951 onwards, deep revival in the national churches and successful evangelism in the cities by nationals and by foreign visitors.

In 1951, there were signs of an awakening in Brazil and in 1952 the visit of J. Edwin

Orr with the support of churches of every denomination coincided with a general awakening, the Bible Societies and other observers declaring it "a year of triumph" in which Brazil was shaken by winds of the Spirit. The movement continued for years, and the expansion of the evangelical constituency was greater than that of the population.

In 1954, a Pentecostal evangelist Tommy Hicks held sixty meetings in Buenos Aires that brought a total of three million to the stadiums. There was controversy during the campaign and a reaction afterwards. In other Latin countries the evangelism-in-depth directed by Kenneth A. Strachan reaped great results.

In all his work Billy Graham was assisted by a talented team, and by an organization without precedent in the history of evangelism. Leighton Ford and other Graham associates engaged in a great Crusade in Canada in the 1960s.

In the 1950's in Britain, a number of church-related evangelists accomplished a great work – Bryan Green, Anglican, Tom Allan, Presbyterian, and others besides interdenominational leaders such as T. B. Rees and Eric Hutchings. There was little accompanying revival. A resurgence of evangelism was reported in New Zealand and Australia and South Africa through overseas teams and national missioners.

In 1935, Abraham Vereide began a specialized evangelism of leaders in government, industry and business, out of which arose the International Christian Leadership movement, whose prayer-breakfasts in Washington annually attracted the leading figures of government, including successive Presidents of the United States.

Robert Pierce, involved in the movement of the Spirit in California and Korea, was stirred further by the appalling need of war-torn Korea and the Orient to begin a mission of emergency help, World Vision. It promoted many pastors' conferences in countries of younger churches, Paul S. Rees and Richard C. Halverson helping while Pierce with others engaged in crusades.

During the period of the mid-Twentieth Century Awakening, there was a resurgence of evangelical conviction as well as evangelism, and a survey promoted by a dynamic new magazine of evangelical theology, *Christianity Today* edited by Carl F. H. Henry, showed that approximately seventy-four per cent of American ministers adhered to an evangelical theology (fundamentalist or conservative).

The awakening in the United States reached its climax within ten years, when church attendance claimed approximately fifty per cent of the adult population and membership rose steadily. In the 1960's, attendance began to decline concurrently with the rise of a "new morality" and pantheistic theology among philosophers.

BIBLIOGRAPHY

Beardsley, F. G., *A History of American Revivals,* New York: American Tract Society, 1904.

Balleine, C. R., *History of the Evangelical Party in the Church of England,* London, 1908.

Bready, J. W., *England: Before and after Wesley,* London: Hodder & Stoughton, 1938.

Finney, C. G., *Autobiography of the Rev. C. G. Finney.* New York: Fleming H. Revell Co., 1876.

Latourette, K. S., *History of the Expansion of Christianity,* Vols. 1-7. New York: Harper & Brothers, 1938-1945.

Moody, W. R., *Life of D. L. Moody.* New York: Fleming H. Revell Co., 1900.

Orr, J. Edwin, *The Second Evangelical Awakening in Britain.* London: Marshall, Morgan & Scott, 1949.

———, *The Light of the Nations.* Grand Rapids: Wm. B. Eerdmans Publishing Co., 1966.

Pollock, J. C., *The Keswick Story.* London: Hodder & Stoughton, 1964.

———, *Billy Graham.* New York: McGraw-Hill, 1966.

The Pastor an Evangelist

1. THE PASTOR AS HERALD

The gospel is good news, ***euangelion.*** Paul said, "Moreover, brethren, I declare unto you the gospel which I preached unto you, which also ye have received, and wherein ye stand" (I Cor. 15:1). Preaching, as stated in the word declare, *gnoridzo,* is "to make known, to declare, to publish" the gospel. Preaching is given prominent emphasis in the New Testament: "Jesus came preaching." Jesus went about the villages of Galilee "teaching in their synagogues, and preaching the Gospel of the kingdom" (Matt. 9:35).

Preaching may be defined as declaring news, as publishing a message. In Romans 10:15, we read, "How beautiful are the feet of those who publish the news of good things." The best manuscript attestation causes us to omit the words "peace" and "bring glad tidings." They comprise the commendation by God's Word of all those engaged in publishing the good news. The word "beautiful," *horaioi*, first means "seasonable" then "ripe." It is used in Genesis 2:9 to describe the trees which God created in the Garden of Eden. From this it goes on to mean fair, lovely or pleasant. It may be applied to people or things, such as God's evaluation of the herald of truth.

"To proclaim" or "to preach," *euangelidzo*, is to publish or to proclaim or to preach the message of salvation, the messianic proclamation. In colloquial language it could be "to good news the glad tidings." Since the word is in the middle voice, it has the intention of including the thing proclaimed as well as the person who receives the message (cf. Arndt and Gingrich).

"Good things," *agatha*, refers to things of the highest order of possessions. Here the things of salvation, of eternal life, of God, of the messianic era for Israel are declared. These form the content of the gospel which Paul preached and consisted of glad tidings.

The word "declare," *gnoridso*, is used by St. Paul not only in I Corinthians 15:1, but also in Galatians 1:11 with the sense of certifying and means "I make known emphatically." As used in this text, it emphasizes that what is now declared is what he had declared to them and what he will always declare, namely the gospel, regardless of what may be adduced against it or may be in conflict with it. In Galatians he uses the word in connection with the error which had arisen among the Galatians, stemming from Judaism.

Preaching, proclaiming the gospel, is making known what otherwise is hidden. Thus, Jesus used the word to described his making known the Father (John 17:26), and to describe his making known the truths which he had heard from the Father (John 15:15). Thus the ministry of preaching is the making known of what men would not otherwise surmise or discover, namely the mysteries of God (I Cor. 4:1), the revealed truths of God. Expository preaching is the unfolding of the meaning of God's revelation concerning Himself, Christ, the Spirit, salvation, effectual calling, and destiny.

Preaching is declared to be the instrument of salvation (I Cor. 1:21). This must be understood, however, not as the act of preaching but as the content of preaching joined with preaching, or the *kerugma*. When thus considered, there is a glory to preaching. No one can read of the eloquent ministry of John Chrysostom, the thundering denunciations of G. Savonarola, the argumentative preaching of Martin Luther, the persuasive reasoning of George Whitefield, or the sweet reasonableness of John Wesley by which minds were convinced, hearts were swayed, and wills were moved so as to embrace Jesus Christ as Saviour, without seeing something of the glory of preaching. This ability to "prophecy," understood in the framework of the proclamation of the gospel, is a gift of the Holy Spirit to choice individuals (I Cor. 12:10). While every Christian is a witness and must bear testimony to the truth, the gift of proclaiming the gospel publicly is solemnly bestowed by God's Holy Spirit. Preaching in the sense of "the thing preached," is the ground of salvation. The grace of God is mediated to souls through the preaching of the gospel. There is no higher activity in which man can be engaged than in the sincere, effective, and faithful proclamation of the gospel.

That which Paul declared was the *euangelion*, or the gospel (I Cor. 15:1). The content of this gospel is called the *kerugma*. That means "that which is promulgated by a herald or a public crier. . . the message proclaimed by the heralds of Christ." This *kerugma* is declared by C. H. Dodd to consist of certain historical events. These events were the core of the New Testament gospel. They included the incarnation of the Word of God in the person of Jesus Christ, the death of Jesus Christ as an atonement upon the cross, the bodily resurrection of Christ from the dead, and the ascension of Christ into heaven. These historic events formed the content of the early Christian message.

The meaning of these events is the revelation communicated to the New Testament apostles. Because this came by revelation, there is a unanimity of conviction and teaching by the apostles as to the content of the gospel. We do not find several gospels of the New Testament but only one. It is the gospel of a federal representative, the last Adam. who made a satisfaction upon the cross for our sins, vicariously dying for us and rising again to begin a life as the head of his renewed people. This interpretation of the events was given by Jesus Christ to his apostles after his resurrection (Acts 1:3). Paul received his information concerning it by revelation (Gal. 1:12). The reason for Jesus tarrying for forty days after his resurrection was to instill the understanding of this content of the gospel into his apostles. As a result, there is no conflict in their presentation of the *kerugma*, there is no change in this gospel today. It is the same as that committed unto the apostles by the resurrected Christ.

Intrinsic to the proclamation of the gospel is the call. *Kerugma* goes beyond content to a summons, a challenge, a call by a herald. This implies the person of the herald, or the *kerux*, who is the one who proclaims, a messenger vested with public authority. The *kerux* had the following qualifications: An appointment to his office, fidelity to his responsibility, understanding of his message, ability to communicate, and authority to summon. Thus, when Paul spoke of his preaching, it was as being entrusted with the *kerugma* (Titus 1:3). The gospel thus consisted of a proclamation by a herald sent by God. His message is the *kerugma iesou chistou.* It centers in the person and work of Christ. There is a difference between *kerugma* and *didache.* One is the historic content of the gospel summoning men to a response, the other is the teaching, or elaboration of the message. A crisis is brought about by confrontation with the gospel or the summons of the herald. To be a bona fide message, there is the necessity of mental comprehension of the message. This involves the duty of presenting it with utmost clarity. Once comprehended, it is impossible for the one summoned to be neutral, indifferent or uncommitted. He must either accept or reject the message. He must be for or against the summons. The responsibility for this decision of faith or unbelief, of acceptance or rejection, lies with the one who hears the message of the gospel.

2. THE PASTOR AS AMBASSADOR

When the call to preach (I Cor. 9:16), has been received by the individual he becomes an ambassador of the Lord Jesus Christ (II Cor. 5:20). Webster says, "An ambassador is a minister of the highest rank accredited to a foreign port to reside there and represent his sovereign and country." An ambassador has dignity. The word is derived from the root, *presbus,* meaning old or experienced. The words presbyter, or elder, in the New Testament church comes from the same root. Usually ambassadors are men tried and proved in responsible positions. His is an exalted position climaxing a career and marking a high honor. His dignity is equal to that of the state which he represents.

An ambassador is an agent. He has authority to speak and act for his government. His own words and thoughts, promises and demands, person and attainments are of little weight. He must be the mouthpiece of his government. Because he is this, his person is inviolable and not subject to local powers. An ambassador is a minister of his country and his embassy service has been called a ministry. His ministry must be that of service to his government. His minstry may be that of representation, or of reconciliation, or of transmitting a message, but always it is a ministry of an ambassador.

Our appointment as ambassadors is in the kingdom of God. Our citizenship is in heaven (Phil. 3:20). We have entered this through the new birth and are constituted a new creation with a new standing before God. Only when we reach a degree of maturity do we become ambassadors for Jesus Christ. We must first have instruction, experience, and strengthening so that we may adequately represent the kingdom of God.

Moreover, it is necessary to be called to this ministry so that the interests of our lives are identified with the interests of the kingdom. Such ambassadors can no longer live unto themselves. The slightest offense or hurt can bring blame on the ministry and great harm can be done by this. Paul himself was a perfect illustration of an ambassador of Jesus Christ. In II Corinthians 5:20-6:10, Paul describes his own life as an ambassador, under the divisions of the personal life of the minister, the position in which the minister finds himself, and the paradoxes of the ministry.

Paul conceived of our message as ambassadors being that of the "word of reconciliation" (II Cor. 5:19). He declared that "God hath reconciled us to himself." This presupposes an estrangement which needs reconciliation. Sin affected the nature of God so that he was estranged from man and had to be dealt with before there could be reconciliation. That was completed in the death of Christ on the cross so that enmity now is wholly on man's side. God is propitiated, or expiated, by what he did for us on the cross and is favorably disposed, ready to forgive, and ready to reinstate man. What remains to be done in the matter of salvation is the reconciliation of man. Thus it is the preaching of the gospel centered in the cross and attended by the Holy Spirit which persuades men to be reconciled to God. Thus preachers are ambassadors of peace, or reconciliation, of good news, of an accomplished redemption.

Paul also described himself as engaged in the present process of reconciling the world, declaring that God had committed unto him "the word of reconciliation." In this he represented the minister as an ambassador. By bringing the message of objective reconciliation to the world, the minister is engaged in reconciling the world to God. Therefore he can emphasize his mission by declaring "be ye reconciled to God." This becomes the hortatory part, the unsettled aspect of reconciliation, the plea of the representative of God.

The pastor should master the Biblical teaching on formulas which work in the achieving of certain objectives. As we study the Bible, we find that there is a formula which, if followed, will result in a man's salvation. And there are formulas for the Spirit-filled life, for prayer, for God's blessing upon the local church, and for bringing about a revival. There are four elements in the process of salvation which, if a seeker sincerely performs, will result in that blessing for him. The first is repentance, or the change of mind on the subject of God, Christ, self, sin, and salvation. This is the result of persuasion but it is within the power of the individual to exercise. Repentance is usually used in the active tense in the New Testament. The second element is conversion, or the turning about from our sins by means of a clean breach and the turning unto Jesus Christ. This likewise is within the seekers' power. He cannot save himself but he can expose himself unto the source of salvation. The third element is confession which means "to speak the same thing." When we confess what God is saying about us as sinners and in need of salvation, and when we confess what he is saying about Jesus Christ as the Saviour, we definitely are confessing. The fourth element is committal, or faith. This is not historic faith or academic faith, or volitional faith, but is saving faith. It is the kind that eventuates in justification, forgiveness and regeneration. Such faith may best be illustrated as trust. Whenever an individual applies this formula sincerely, he certainly will be saved. We do not infer that salvation is the work of any man but these are Biblical prerequisites to the experience thereof.

There is a formula which will get a man filled with the Spirit, which will terminate the divided state of the Christian life, and which will enable him to enter into that higher condition of Christian experience. Without expounding these in detail, they are: confession of living in a carnal state, consecration of everything to Jesus Christ, prayer for the Spirit-filled life, faith that God has promised us this Spirit-filled life, and finally, obedience to the directions of the Holy Spirit. Whosoever will obey these prerequisites may have a Spirit-filled life and will have it in the proportion that he fulfills the conditions.

3. THE PASTOR AS MESSENGER

It follows that the pastor as messenger has committed to him what he is to proclaim as a herald and to transmit as an ambassador. This raises the question of what is the message we are to proclaim. There is a vast difference between a message from God and a mere Bible reading in which we put together certain self-evident truths of Scripture in either essay or homiletic form. A message must be concerned with one element of God's revealed truth which he has appointed his messenger to proclaim. It is a given consisting of propositional truth made known by God. Only when this truth is communicated to the messenger, or herald, is he capable of proclaiming it. It must be with a sense of burden to transmit the message, to communicate it in intelligible terms, to be faithful to its content, and to seek for a response, that the messenger does his work.

How then does the pastor get his topics for his messages? These may come from many stimuli but they must center in content of the revealed Word of God. This burden may concern a doctrine, a phase of spiritual experience, an ethical principle, a truth illustrated by biography, a prophetic interpretation of current events, or any other element of Biblical truth which impresses itself upon him. For it he must have a burden. This may be obtained in his Bible reading, in his prayer life, in his observance of the spiritual condition and needs of his people in the current events of the day, or in crises which come to pass in human history. But the message must be derived from God's propositional revelation. Having this, the pastor must prepare it for delivery according to sound principles of sermon preparation (see section on Homiletics).

How should that sermon be preached? If the work of preparation has been adequate so that the structure is logical, it can easily be remembered. Saturday night should be devoted by the pastor to getting in mind the outlines of his sermons for the following day. Jesus has promised "to bring all things to your remembrance." But if we have not memorized it or known it, we have no right to expect Him to bring it to our remembrance. Personally, I have always memorized my outline and then have trusted the Holy Spirit to bring what I have already known to my mind when I preach. Do not be afraid to trust your memory. Devote adequate time to getting your message in mind, then believe that God will bring it to your remembrance by the Power of His Holy Spirit.

On what kind of preaching should the pastor major? Although all kinds of preaching from the Bible are valuable, the most useful for edifying people in the faith is expository preaching. Whoever would stay for a long ministry in a church should develop his ability to prepare expository sermons. Ulrich Zwingli, in the cathedral at Zurich, began with the first verse of Matthew to expound the entire New Testament to his congregation. As he preached along through the Bible he preached himself into the Reformation. G. Campbell Morgan also followed this method and would read a book fifty times before beginning to teach it. I have tried to follow this method and also to read the book in the Greek before beginning to preach on it. Then I outline the entire book so that each division is a unit which stands alone. Such a division, no matter how small, can be the object of a sermon. People who come to church for that one Sunday only will hear a complete dissertation totally independent of other dissertations and yet one which builds upon a structure which maintains the interest of those who come faithfully. Each division is worthy of a sermon. The advantage of this kind of preaching is that there is progression of truth. Moreover, the preacher is never at a loss to know what his next text and topic will be. The reading which he does for one sermon contributes to all the sermons. The successive treatment of the divisions of the books of Scripture have a cumulative effect upon the hearer. No other kind of preaching can compare to exposition.

The second type of preaching is doctrinal. Here the preacher makes use of a series of subjects. For illustration, I have a series of sixteen sermons on Christ, fourteen sermons on the Holy Spirit, ten sermons on the steps of salvation, seven sermons on the second coming, twelve sermons on the Apostles' Creed, seven on the Lord's Prayer, and several dozen on the deeper life. Every doctrine is worthy of serious and extended treatment and can become a source of edification to believers. One of the great lacks in the modern church is the failure to present the truths of Scripture in a connected and understandable form.

Another type of sermon is biographical. In this the Bible is inexhaustible. He who reads the Bible for his own inspiration will find light constantly breaking upon the characters of Scripture. Personally, some character will suddenly stand out as exemplifying either an experience, a virtue, a decision, a testing, or a victory which may be pertinent to the lives of believers and then I preach upon that character. One way to present the doctrine of Pentecost is through centering upon the personalities in the New Testament who entered into deeper experience and thus become illustrations or examples for the believer. Every character of

Scripture is worthy of at least one message and it is our privilege to bring such a character up-to-date so that he may be understood by the people.

Then there are topical sermons. These may be moral, political, economic, social, missionary, or experiential. Very necessary for understanding today is the contrast of Communism and the Christian faith, the doctrine of God, the doctrine of man, the doctrine of the state, and all that derives from these doctrines. There is a vast field for preaching in the area of morality. In a day when the new morality is being emphasized, it is necessary for preachers of the gospel to go back to the Ten Commandments and to the absolutes of God. The field of missions offers a perennial source of topical sermons as does also evangelism. In the area of sociology, the quarterly of the Academy of Political Sciences treats of subjects which are also treated by the Bible. We should not fear to apply all the teaching which Christ has given to us to all the fields of life.

Polemic sermons must from time to time be preached. These must deal with matters like the ecumenical movement, the Vatican Council, the teachings of Roman Catholicism, the differences between modernism and orthodoxy, the sects which have become so powerful in our day, and the heresies which from time to time appear in the history of the church. If the believer cannot look to the minister for guidance on these subjects, whither shall he turn. It is our responsibility to handle these in the light of God's revelation, church history, and the exigency of the moment.

Another very profitable field is that of human experience. It is possible to take a phrase or a clause of a conversation which one has overheard, or read, and then to develop from this one of the great truths of Scripture.

Whether evangelistic, polemic, experiential, biographical, doctrinal, or expository, our preaching should aim at decisions for Christ and the edification of believers. There should be a throb in every sermon which causes the hearer to catch his breath in awe. There should be a sense of unction and power in our sermons which will communicate the urgency of the message. Thus the pastor becomes a preacher of the Word.

4. THE PASTOR AS MISSIONARY

The missionary interest of the pastor will depend upon his own conviction of the authority of the Word of God. If he accepts the Bible as the infallible rule of faith and practice, by the inspiration of the Holy Spirit, he then will take seriously the post-resurrection commandments of the Lord Jesus Christ. The resurrected Christ remained upon earth forty days speaking things pertaining to the kingdom of God. He did not immediately ascend to the Father and terminate his work upon earth because the apostles and disciples needed that forty day ministry to have instruction in reference to the content of the gospel, to the program of the church in this age, and to the power or efficiency to achieve that program. An analysis of the resurrection teachings of our Lord Jesus Christ reveal that he placed the worldwide evangelistic activity first. Each form of the Great Commission recorded gives unto us this emphasis. Though the pastor himself is not a missionary in the technical sense of that word, missions should be first in his emphasis. His own example in interest, in burden of teaching, and his personal giving will count more than any other influence to advance the missionary interests of his church. Although there is no qualitative distinction between evangelism at home and missions abroad, it is certain that the people in America can hear the gospel if they wish to hear it; whereas, there are, according to Frank Laubach, eleven hundred million people in the world who have never heard the name of Jesus and thus could not believe if they wanted to believe. Thus there is a primacy of responsibility in reference to the world evangelistic task. However, the church which is missionary will also be evangelistic at home. We cannot ask our sons and daughters to go to foreign parts to proclaim the gospel as heralds if we are not willing to proclaim that gospel at home. The program then involves teaching all things whatsoever the Lord has commanded us. This means the application of his truth to all areas and phases of life. We do not live in a vacuum and we are to preach the gospel in the educational, economic, industrial, political, and social world in which we live. This is the great educational task of the church. Join with these the humanitarian interests of the church so often emphasized by our Lord

Jesus Christ, and we have a program which will adequately challenge the people of God in the age in which we live. Thus our Lord gave unto us the gospel which we are to preach, namely his own interpretation of his incarnation, life, death and resurrection, a program to follow, and the power of the Holy Spirit in Pentecostal presence to effectuate this mission.

A practical methodology to advance this in the local congregation is to use the missionary conference, so for over twenty-five years I have practiced this methodology in connection with my own congregation. Phenomenal results have come from a ten-day period of listening to missionaries, facing candidates, visiting exhibits, and hearing missionary messages. In one twenty-five year period in Park Street Church, Boston, our giving to missions went from $2000 a year to $333,000 a year and a total over the period of $4,500,000 for missions. There is nothing unusual about this method and where it is adopted it will work in every case.

5. THE PASTOR AS APOSTLE

The word apostle means "sent one." The pastor should have the authority of being sent. The New Testament emphasizes the fact that there are different callings and ministries and offices. The Holy Spirit bestows upon different individuals different gifts and callings for the good of the church. There are some apostles, some prophets, some teachers and pastors, some with gifts of healings, some with the ability to help, some with ability to govern, etc. We are to accept our gift according to the measure of our faith (Rom. 12:3). Once this gift has been made in accordance with our faith, we are then to exercise it with authority.

Jesus said, "As the Father hath sent me, so send I you." There is an analogy between his being sent forth by the Father and his sending us forth as his servants. He gave a strict assignment unto the church by saying, "As ye go, preach the gospel, heal the sick, cleanse the lepers, raise the dead, exorcise demons, freely ye have received, freely give." This is what the church has been doing to its apostles throughout the world. Among the sent ones are doctors who are healing the sick and nurses who are treating astronomic numbers of patients; there are leprosariums, hospitals, schools, exemplary farms, and all manner of work among peoples all over the world. The sent ones are doing the work.

The appointment we receive as apostles depends upon the will of the Holy Spirit. We ask the question, Where shall I labor, at home or abroad? The answer to this must come from the will of God mediated by his Holy Spirit. To know the need and to have the ability to meet that need is not enough. The appointment must be made by the internal direction of the Spirit. The question of how long shall one stay in a particular field must again be answered, not by the elements of reason alone although these are important, but by the guidance of the Holy Spirit. Is my service more valuable in this place of labor or in another? How shall I most advance the kingdom of God? In such service sacrifice will be pre-eminent. Often an apostle must serve without honorarium or recognition. His is the greatest service for the love of the Lord Jesus Christ. A good rule to remember is not to discuss money in reference to the preaching of the gospel. Make your decisions independent of the remuneration or the honorariums involved. Do all for the glory of God because we are his apostles sent forth by the Lord Jesus Christ.

BIBLIOGRAPHY

Allen, Roland, *Missionary Methods — St. Paul's or Ours?* Grand Rapids: Wm. B. Eerdmans Publishing Co.

————————, *The Spontaneous Expansion of the Church.* Grand Rapids: Wm. B. Eerdmans Publishing Co.

Allan, Tom, *The Face of My Parish.* New York: Harpers.

Chafer, Lewis Sperry, *True Evangelism.* Findlay, Ohio: Dunham.

Colquhoun, Frank, *Christ's Ministry.* London: Hoddard & Stoughton.

Green, Michael, *The Meaning of Salvation.* London: Hoddard & Stoughton.

Kuiper, R. B., *God-Centered Evangelism.* Grand Rapids: Baker Book House.

Packer, J. I., *Evangelism and the Sovereignty of God.* Chicago: Intervarsity Press.

Stott, John R. W., *Motives and Methods in Evangelism.* Chicago: Intervarsity Press.

Winter, David, *The Old Faith in a New World.* London: Hodder & Stoughton.

Wood, A. Skevington, *Evangelism and Theology in Practice.* Grand Rapids: Zondervan Publishing House.

Wood, Maurice, *Like a Mighty Army.* London: Hodder & Stoughton.

Evangelism in the Home Church

The church exists to convey to all men the message of Christ. Early apostolic Christians did not think of the church as merely a place for the shepherding of believers. While the flock of God is to be fed and nourished and trained and built up within the fellowship of the church these graces are for the strengthening of the saints for battle. The church is therefore not an end but a means. Emil Brunner says, "The Church exists by mission as fire exists by burning." Its success or failure is determined not by the state of its buildings or the size of its membership, but solely by what it is doing to reach the untouched. This is evangelism, and the New Testament knows nothing of evangelism apart from the church. Everything emanates from the church and feeds back into the church. Thus the church functions not only as the center of worship, Bible study, fellowship and social service, but as the center of evangelism with the membership and the clergy participating together in this great task. The minister is but one. His contacts are limited. But the lay members of any church are in touch with scores of people every week. It is the man in the pew who must assume evangelistic responsibility as did his first century brother.

George Sweazey says, "Evangelism is a connected series of four steps – contact, cultivation, commitment, conservation – each depending on the others." This view of evangelism makes it plain that it must be the work of the whole church. Evangelism fails when it comes to be regarded as a special activity for special people at special times. It succeeds when it is made a normal activity for all the church people all the time. Evangelism must be a regular part of the church program. No follower of the Saviour can dismiss it as someone else's duty. To quote Sweazey again, "There are no closed seasons for the fishers of men."

The word "evangelism" has been spoiled for many church people. They associate it with the shouting zealot who demands, "Brother are you saved?" It is suspect because of extremes and excesses often connected with revivalism – extremes of emotionalism, high pressure, arrogant Bible pounding, and exaggerated statistics.

But the word is really one of the most beautiful and meaningful in the entire Christian vocabulary. "Evangelism," says William Temple "is the presenting of Jesus Christ so that, by the power of the Holy Spirit, men shall come to put their trust in God through Him, to accept Him as their Savior from the guilt and power of sin, to serve Him in the fellowship of the church, and to follow Him in the vocations of the common life." Man is estranged from God. In Christ there is reconciliation. It is to his church that he has committed the ministry of reconciliation. This is evangelism.

Frederick Taylor says that the ideal in parish evangelism is "a church which from pulpit to primary department is permeated by a desire to see a constant flow of people who have come to know Christ as Savior, and who in turn are seeking to lead others to the same experience." But such a church does not emerge by assuming the attitude, "Why, everything we do is evangelism," or "a good Christian life is the best evangelism." These are what Bryan Green would call pre-evangelism. For Christianity cannot be radiated. Truths about God and his Son have to be communicated and accepted. Sweazey says, "A church's good influence in a community will produce well-disposed outsiders who will remain outsiders until someone says 'This is for you.' "

There are many approaches to evangelism within the local church, and each specific mode or method is a reminder that all preaching, all visiting, in fact all of one's Christian life should be primarily evangelistic.

1. PASTORAL EVANGELISM

A church always tends to drift away from evangelism, never toward it. A pastor never finds time to do all he should be doing for the members he already has. Therefore the tendency, as one has said, is to put evangelism in a file marked "Important . . . for the first free moment" – a moment which in church life so seldom comes. Yet the pastor should be leading his church in a perennial program of evangelism. He is the key. What he is his congregation becomes. Without evangelism in the pulpit there will be none in the pew. When what Jowett called "the passion for souls" grips the mind and heart of a minister so that in all his ministry there is displayed a deep, genuine love for people, the fires of spontaneous evangelism begin to burn.

2. CRUSADE EVANGELISM

In the strictest sense there can be no such thing as mass evangelism. The gospel can be proclaimed to the masses but people can only be won for Christ individually. One by one they meet the Saviour and pass from death unto life. An evangelistic crusade to be successful must be undertaken at the right time, in the right place, and when there is the movement of the Holy Spirit confirming that this is the course to take. Such crusades must always be regarded as an addition to, and not a substitute for, the continuous evangelistic activity within the local church. Part of the danger connected with this type of evangelism revolves around the evangelist himself. In a day of easy travel there are many in the ministry of evangelism who move rapidly from one place to another. Sometimes such evangelistic activity is on a hit-and-run basis. An evangelist comes to town. There is what has been called "a spectacular spiritual bang followed by an anemic splutter as he departs, leaving the church with an impressive legacy of spiritual shipwrecks." Further problems are created when independent campaigns are conducted having little to no connection with the local established church. A man who operates on such a basis is dangerously deficient in his concept of the body of Christ. What then is the relationship between the ministry of the local church and that of the itinerant? They complement each other. The local church must recognize the evangelist's gift, his call, and his place in the body. The evangelist in turn has to recognize these same factors plus the authority and integrity of the local church. The evangelist is dependent on the favor, invitation, and support of the local church and he comes humbly as a servant of the church. Thus all members of the one body work in harmony together.

3. FRIENDSHIP EVANGELISM

When evangelism becomes merely a matter of well-polished methods it is finished. Prayer is really the basic evangelistic method, and a close second is friendship. It can almost be said that no person was ever brought to Christ save through another person. Those who would talk to their friends about their Christian faith have to learn how to bring it into their conversation. Everyone is talking about race relationships, war, the atom bomb, industrial strife, and all the current social predicaments. It is not hard to turn the talk around to how Christians look at these things and then go straight to one's personal word of witness for Christ. Ofttimes a book or pamphlet can be given to a friend with the request for an opinion of it after it has been read. Indiscriminate tract distribution among friends may not be the thing but a good piece of literature will frequently open the way to future conversations which may result in conversion. There are times when asking a person where he goes to church, or inviting him to a church service, or better yet to one's home for an evening can be the means of eventually leading a friend to Christ. The best argument for Christianity is a Christian, and if a person is liked others will take seriously what he says.

4. PERSONAL EVANGELISM

There are really only two kinds of evangelism: personal and impersonal. Preaching is impersonal. All mass evangelism, if it stops there, is impersonal. Film, literature, radio, television — all these are completely impersonal to both speaker and hearer. Enlistment evangelism, if it is merely an abstract relation of teacher to pupils, is impersonal. This means that much of today's evangelism is impersonal. There is so little real personal contact. And yet Christianity is personal. It is one person meeting and getting to know another person, Christ. How can one prove his love while standing in a pulpit preaching "at" a man sitting thirty yards away? How can real love and concern be conveyed unless it is done person to person? And yet, as with all evangelism, personal evangelism needs to be anchored in the local church. But the plain fact is that the average churchgoer seldom appears to sieze the casual conversation and the daily contacts in his office, factory or social life as opportunities for witness.

Every Christian carries the responsibility of priesthood. The priest is one who "stands on the God-ward side of man." His function is to lift men up to God in intercession, then to take the message of the gospel and proclaim it to them. To this responsibility Christians need to be awakened, but more than this, they need to be trained. To bring home to a person the good news of the love of God so that his soul may find its true fulfillment by responding to that love is the greatest privilege one can ever have. Such a conveying of the love of God is not accomplished by a domineering statement or a ruthless probing into a man's private life. It is effected by the life and words of a man in Christ whose being is dedicated to and permeated by the love of God. Such a man is bound to find himself engaged in personal evangelism. It is heartening to know the Lord Jesus did not command his disciples to be fishers of men. He said, "Follow me and *I will make* you fishers of men." As someone has said, "Responsibility – the response is to come from us, and the ability will come from Him." This, like every other form of evangelism, is best pursued under the leadership and sponsorship of the local church. But the church, as such, is not an end. It is the means the Holy Spirit uses to bring men to faith in Christ and to maturity in him. Whenever the church fails here it is not the body of Christ, whatever title it may claim.

5. SMALL GROUP EVANGELISM

The cell movement is perhaps one of the most significant trends in the church today. Many pastors are discovering that they can present Christ in a peculiarly forceful way to some who as yet have no interest in the Christian faith, but who are seeking to discover within their own situation a meaning and purpose for life. The genius of the cell is its spontaneity and lack of organization. The freer and more unstructured all such groups are the better will be the results. Some cells consist only of convinced Christians who meet for Bible study, prayer, and fellowship. With others the main purpose is to train and encourage one another in witness. A third type is the mixed cell of Christians and non-Christians. All have their place in the life of the church, but from the standpoint of evangelism, it is the mixed cell where many whom nothing else can reach are won. It is far more personal than ordinary church evangelism and can therefore make a more direct and thorough appeal for faith. When many who are spiritually hungry and confused stay aloof from the church they will never be won by preaching, for frequently they are prejudiced against the church and skeptical. But intellectual curiosity and restlessness often make them glad to attend a group where beliefs are discussed in an informal, open way. Doubters must be able to discuss their doubts without feeling out of place. In these groups non-Christians frequently outnumber the Christians. Prayer at the meeting may seem out of place at the start, but will grow more appropriate as intimacy and spiritual interest develop. Some of the best groups are started by lay members. There seems to be an advantage when a group invites the pastor to be with them rather than the pastor inviting the group, even though the idea may have come originally from the pastor as he meets regularly with a few of his dedicated men, sharing with them everything he has and knows and feels. This was Christ's own method of evangelism. He spent most of his time with individuals or small groups. In fact so often when he had a great crowd it seems the results were small. He built his church in this way and any local church which follows his plan will grow and prosper.

6. SUNDAY SCHOOL EVANGELISM

Education evangelism or enlistment evangelism as it is called in some denominations has developed into the most exact science within the church. The Church School or Bible School are synonymous terms in other communions. More books have been written and more programs worked out in this field than in all other forms of evangelism. This is only natural since seventy-five per cent of those the Protestant church receives on profession of faith come through the Sunday School. This gives the Sunday School a paramount place in evangelism. Under the leadership of spiritually knowledgeable teachers and officers the Sunday School should be held in perpetual sacredness as an opportunity to win both the young and old to saving decisions for Christ. While the status and level of Sunday School teaching is being constantly raised through the better training of teachers, and the provision of better methods, material and equipment, it does need to be stressed that teachers may be up-to-date in their methods, but fail because they regard their sole business as the imparting of knowledge. The Sunday School is never the place for unregenerate teachers to present nature studies and perform dramatic acts with never a thought of leading their pupils to a personal confession of Jesus Christ as Savior and Lord. The old-fashioned teachers may have had poorer methods and inferior equipment but they did very often keep a prayer list. Every day they prayed for each member of their class by name, earnestly desiring that each should personally come to know and love and follow the Saviour. Without this emphasis the Sunday School cannot help to fill the place it should in evangelism within the local church.

7. VISITATION EVANGELISM

In visitation evangelism the "professional evangelist" is replaced by the "evangelist in the pew," whose role in evangelism is too often overlooked or underestimated. How will the church ever fulfill its commission to be "witnesses in Jerusalem, Judea, Samaria, and unto the uttermost part" without returning to the New Testament pattern which calls for the propagating ("gossiping") of the gospel by the total membership of each local church! It must be realized that evangelism was never intended by the Holy Spirit to be centered in a church building. It is to be centered outside the church. The church is not a place into which to bring lost and bewildered people to convert them. Modern preachers have very little opportunity to reach the unconverted. The church must be viewed as a battle station — a training center — out from which Christians go in their witness for Christ. Ask Aquila in the early church at Ephesus how that city — in fact all of Asia Minor — was evangelized and he would say, "we simply visited every home in the city. That's the way the church in Jerusalem first evangelized that city (Acts 5:42), and they did it in a very short time. All our churches in Asia Minor have followed that example."

Books and helps in visitation evangelism are in abundance. Some are criticized as being too "membership conscious," i.e., churches sending members out simply to gain more members. In this connection Paul Rees comments that "of all pathetic and abortive performances in the church that bears Christ's Name just about the saddest is this: a group of members who have never been converted going out as visitation workers to bring into the church more of the same kind of people who are already there in numbers alarmingly too large!" But this is by no means intended to cancel out visitation evangelism as a mighty force of Christian witness and outreach. Today more and more churches are promoting some plan of systemtic visitation evangelism, adopting whatever approach is suitable to the respective community be it urban, suburban, or rural. Christianity void of a spirit and method of constantly winning new followers to Jesus Christ is not Christianity at all.

8. RETREAT AND CAMP EVANGELISM

When one is tempted to bemoan the decline of some of the older evangelistic methods, the church can point with delight to the rise of its camping and conference program as a new method which may prove to be more effective than any which have been lost. Such retreats and conferences, when well conducted, are unsurpassed as means of bringing people into direct confrontation with Christ and the gospel. Three classes of people, as a rule, are present at such camps or conferences. There are (a) the converted — the faithful, practicing Christian; (b) the nominal churchgoer, and people who are on the fringe of the Christian faith, who come to church occasionally, are not hostile nor completely indifferent to Christianity, but are simply careless about it; and (c) the outsiders. They are uncommitted to the Christian message and for the most part illiterate in it. But frequently in a non-church situation they are stabbed, awakened, convicted, and converted. A strange dynamic occurs during a retreat. When an individual is removed from the rut of his day-to-day environment he is much more open to new ideas and influences. Released from his routine commitments he is free to consider issues which are normally crowded out of his life. Many who specialize in the retreat or camp type of ministry testify to the fact that in certain cases more direct evangelism can be achieved in a week than in months of regular church life. And this is not to mention the tremendous potential and power for follow-up in evangelism which these camps and conferences afford. Every local church would be wise to investigate and study all the denominational and inter-denominational camp conference and retreat centers and programs available to its membership, and to evangelistic goals.

9. OPEN AIR EVANGELISM

Bryan Green states the case well when he says, "at a time when political programs, a thousand 'isms,' and every other form of human philosophy are taken out into the open air by their devotees the Christian Church cannot accept the dictum that open air work is ineffective." The question, in fact, is not whether the church should go out into the open air with its message, but rather in what sort of way should she go. How can the message be brought and a hearing for it be gained? The old-fashioned, mission-type open air meeting where hymns are sung, testimonies given, and a good indoor sermon delivered out-of-doors has little attracting power to this sophisticated generation and not much evangelistic value. On the other hand, when Inter-Varsity Christian Fellowship goes onto the beaches and sets up its umbrella and posts its announcement for a discussion meeting to be held at 2:00 P.M. this makes an appeal and the gospel wins a hearing. Or, when Campus Crusade likewise takes to the beaches with its "religious survey" and its every-hour-on-the-hour tent service from 7:00 P.M. to midnight people are attracted and many are won. Or, when Open-Air Campaigners parks one of its modern well-equipped vans on some busy downtown street and a competent evangelist begins to use his sketch board and speak in a language people can understand, the Christian message is commended and if there is offense it is the "offense of the cross," not offense caused by the cross bearer. The local church can well afford to examine all such movements as these and to seek to interest and involve its people in evangelism along these lines.

10. YOUTH EVANGELISM

The evangelism of young people in their adolescent years presents peculiar problems. They are shy and self-conscious. They are suspicious of organized religion. They hate to be cornered or "got at." About the only way to win them is through sustained, proven friendship. This requires patience, ofttimes suffering, and much prayer. Real friendship is an incarnation. One lives again in the life of another. This is costly. It is precisely because they have this attitude of friendship that we see some rather unlikely persons amazingly successful in working with youth. Their technique may be faulty; their methods unorthodox; their theological views peculiar to us; their personality unattractive, but so utterly do they devote their time and energy to their young friends that they are given in return a confidence and loyalty which create opportunities to win many to Jesus Christ. The particular organization – be it Young Life, Youth For Christ, or any one of the dozen or more church related youth movements – in which this redemptive friendship may be exercised and in which conversion takes place is not so important. What is important is that the church not think of its young people as a "problem." That the hackneyed question, How can we hold our dear young people? be no longer asked. Andrew Blackwood is right when he says in the chapter on Parish Evangelism in his book *Evangelism in the Home Church,* "Don't try to hold them! Let them go! . . . Treat them as people. . . . Love them. Believe in them. . . . Treat them as partners in the home and in the church. Fortunate is the church with one or more people in it who know how to befriend young people and lead them to Christ who is the Friend of friends.

11. VOCATIONAL EVANGELISM

Vocational evangelism has been defined as "evangelism, with all its component elements of witness and invitation, reconciliation and sharing in the turmoil of the world, *within* the structures of the world." This means within one's role as a Christian citizen, parent, worker, consumer, employer, organization member, community resident, etc. This vocational evangelism is not to be thought of as a method so much as it is a broad undergirding base for all the various elements and facets of evangelism. A church where the laity are wisely instructed in the Biblical principles of vocational evangelism recognizes that to get people into the church is *not* to get them *out* of the world, but to make them part of a living fellowship which is called by God to be *in* the world in a *new* way. It is within the everyday relationships that evangelism, including witness, fellowship and service, is to be exercised. Vocational evangelism properly understood puts evangelism at the center and core of all the church's life and activity. It is a reminder that all preaching, all visiting, in fact all of Christian living should be primarily evangelistic, and that any particular method of evangelism is suspect only if thought of in itself as comprising the whole of evangelism. Vocational evangelism requires Christians who are sensitive to God's presence and activity in the "secular" world. In training for this type of evangelism no special variety of techniques or approaches is required or developed. It is rather a matter of Christians discovering, through Bible study and involvement in the world, what God is doing now in human history and then committing themselves to the communication of their faith to their fellows, remembering that the quality of one's life alone is never a complete witness. Christianity, unlike mystical religions, demands articulation and verbal confession. Without this verbal confession of Christ evangelism is short circuited. Those who respond to Christ are brought into the fellowship of his church. but vocational evangelism does not equate a name on a church roll with membership in the body of Christ.

12. COMMUNICATIONS EVANGELISM: LITERATURE, FILMS, RADIO, TELEVISION

By far the best way for a Christian to help others accept what he believes is for him to tell about it in his own words. Handing out tracts is no substitute. Nevertheless a printed message can be a valuable supplement to what is said. A vast amount of excellent material is available and a minister will do well to examine what is offered by a variety of publishers. Then he must see that it is made accessible to his people and they are instructed in its use. A pamphlet or tract may say just what someone has been wishing to tell a friend. To discuss a piece of literature may be the easiest and best way to open a conversation which will lead into a witness for Christ. But rather than abruptly shoving it into a person's hand one might say, "Here's something I should like you to read. It's well worth a thinking person's time. After you have had a chance to read it I should like to know what you think of it." A literature rack will serve a church's ministry of evangelism provided it is kept well supplied and carefully attended. Some churches make a nominal charge for their literature, not only to take a burden from the church budget, but because they believe it makes the material seem more respectable and therefore more likely to be read. What is given away is easily thrown away.

Films and other visual aids have become a strong tool for evangelism. However a good deal of research work is necessary to assure that these modern means of proclaiming the gospel are put to their greatest use. One difficulty is in producing films which convey with force and dignity the vital truths of the Christian faith. Another area of concern is how to properly conserve, following the film showing, what the Holy Spirit was seeking to accomplish in the hearts of the unconverted while they were watching the picture. All this needs discussing and teaching within the church if this medium is to become more and more an effective agent in winning men for Christ.

Radio and television are both mighty instruments for mass communication. Never before has the church had access behind closed doors to the people the air waves reach. People to whom the inside of a church is as unfamiliar as the North Pole now sit before their television set and watch the preacher behind the pulpit, and if his vocabulary and ideas are somewhat within their range of understanding they may listen to his message. A common failure in the church's use of broadcasting is that it so often leads to nothing. Ministers on radio and television seldom give the slightest hint that anything more than radio religion is necessary. Every minister on the air should tell about his church and the benefits of Christian fellowship which it affords. What a preacher can effect in those few minutes may be small, but what he can commence is great.

13. HOME EVANGELISM

The Christian home should be and can be one of the greatest evangelistic agencies the church has. Every pastor should seek to impart to his people the concept of the home as a place which is always open to anyone to come in, a place where the grace of hospitality reigns, where quietness and peace prevail, and where husband and wife play their part in interpreting the gospel so that the stranger may meet the Saviour there. This unit in evangelism needs neither learning nor wealth, only love. This quality of home contains the richest thing the church has to offer the world for therein Christ becomes, as it were, incarnate and can reach out and win those who come within its influence. More teaching needs to be given to church people, particularly to young people, about the witness of a Christian home and its power for evangelism within the local church.

The spirit of the apostle Paul breathed into a church or an individual by the Holy Spirit is the only spirit that will make a church evangelistic or a man an evangelist. "We persuade men"; "We are ambassadors for Christ"; "If by any means I may save some"; "In labors unceasing"; "The love of Christ constraineth me"; – here is urgency; here is the compulsion of constraining love, a love that goes with a man *through* difficulty rather than exempting him always *from* it. This passion for the gospel and this zeal for its proclamation cannot be organized. It is the gift of God when "the love of God is shed abroad in our hearts by the Holy Spirit." Evangelism, by its very nature signifies that "the Gospel wants wings." It wants out. It is itinerant, outreaching, outgoing, bound for the open, restlessly reaching for the lost, the least and the last. Witnesses and wings – that is what the gospel wants, and a worthy well-rounded program of evangelism in the home church will give it what it must have.

BIBLIOGRAPHY

Allan, Tom, *The Face of My Parish.*

Archibald, Arthur C., *New Testament Evangelism.*

Bayly, Joseph, *The Gospel Blimp.*

Blackwood, Andrew W., *Evangelism in the Home Church.*

Bright, William R., *Ye Shall Receive Power.*

Bryan, Dawson, *A Workable Plan of Evangelism.*

Cailliet, Emile, *Young Life.*

Cassidy, Michael, *A Philosophy of Evangelism.*

Casteel, John, *Spiritual Renewal Through Personal Groups.*

Coleman, Lyman, *Growth by Groups.*

Coleman, Robert E., *The Master Plan of Evangelism.*

Conant, J. E., *Every Member Evangelism.*

Dobbins, Gaines, *Evangelism According to Christ.*

Edwards, Gene, *How to Have a Soul Winning Church.*

Faith at Work, *Groups that Work.*

Green, Bryan, *The Practice of Evangelism.*

Homrighausen, Elmer G., *Choose Ye This Day.*

Krupp, Nate, *You Can Be a Soul Winner.*

Lovett, C. S., *Soul Winning Made Easy.*

Miller, Paul, *Group Dynamics in Evangelism.*

Niles, Daniel T., *That They May Have Life.*

O'Connor, Elizabeth, *Call to Commitment.*

Olford, Stephen, *The Secret of Soul Winning.*

Packer, James I., *Evangelism and the Sovereignty of God.*

Powell, Sidney, *Where Are the People.*

Raines, Robert A., *New Life in the Church.*

Rees, Paul S., *Stir Up the Gift.*

Rinker, Rosalind, *You Can Witness with Confidence.*

Sangster, W. E., *Let Me Commend.*

Sanny, Lorne, *The Art of Personal Witnessing.*

Shoemaker, Sam, *With the Holy Spirit and with Fire.*

Stott, John R. W., *Fundamentalism and Evangelism.*

Sweazey, George E., *Effective Evangelism.*

Taylor, Frederick E., *The Evangelistic Church.*

Trotman, Dawson, *Born to Reproduce.*

Trueblood, Elton, *The Company of the Committed.*

Webber, George E., *The Congregation in Mission.*

Modern Protestant Missions

Modern missions is usually dated from William Carey who went to India in 1793. It is well to realize, however, that this is not a sudden breakthrough within history of forces thus far hidden from men. There is a chain of historical events behind the event which finally brought forth modern missions. Historical continuity is clearly traceable in the making of modern missions. A number of factors, movements and men, worked providentially in the direction of missions. Finally, the various streams combined and became embodied in William Carey and thus modern missions was born. To acquaint ourselves with the creative forces, we trace them briefly in history.

1. THE MAKING OF MODERN MISSIONS

Protestantism was not born as a missionary religion and the great reformers — Luther, Zwingli, Calvin, Knox — did not make direct contributions to world missions. The message, however which they discovered in the Bible could not but produce a mission consciousness, which under favorable circumstances would break forth in a vital and effective world mission movement. This became a reality less than two hundred years after the Reformation. We group the factors which led to the breakthrough into general and specific factors.

a. *General Factors*

Under general factors we list such as (1) the influence of world exploration which acquainted the Christians with hitherto unknown people in need of the Christian message; (2) the development of world trade with the resultant "companies" who obtained land and possessions overseas. Small colonies of Europeans sprang up in various sections of the world who called for overseas spiritual ministries, some of them expanding into mission outreaches; (3) the spread of learning and the broadening of knowledge among the common people created attitudes favorable to missions and developed leaders among Christians with a world vision; (4) the humanitarianism in France which spread to England and aroused the Christians of that land to their responsibility for giving the best they have for the enriching of the life of others.

b. *Specific Factors*

Under specific factors we refer to:

(1) *Noteworthy forerunners.* Here we list Adrian Saravia (1531-1613) a Dutch Reformed pastor, and Justinian von Weltz (1621-1668), an Austrian baron and a member of the Lutheran Church. Here also Roger Williams, John Elliot, the Apostle to the American Indians, the five generations of Mayhews, and David Brainerd need to be mentioned. All made their contribution to the awakening of the mission consciousness. On the continent no man towers above August Herman Franke and next to him Nicolaus Ludwig, Count von Zinzendorf whose significance we shall emphasize somewhat later.

(2) *Noteworthy movements.* Of the noteworthy movements we refer only to several companies whose charters obligated them by their respective governments to undertake Christian ministries not only to the people in their immediate employment but also to the neighboring non-Christian peoples. Such companies were the Dutch East India Company (1602), the Dutch West India Company (1621), the Virginia Company (1606), the Massachusettes Company (1602), the Danish East India Company (1602), and others.

(3) *Noteworthy Mission Societies.* Mission societies which directed the thinking towards missions were the Society for the Propagation of the Gospel in New England (1648), Society for Promoting Christian Knowledge (1698), Society for the Propagation of the Gospel in Foreign Parts (1701), and the Scottish Society for Propagating Christian Knowledge (1709). On the continent the Danish-Halle Mission (1705), and the Moravian Mission Society (1728) pioneered mission interest.

2. THE BIRTH OF MODERN MISSIONS

The foregoing records bring us to the dawn of modern missions. The nineteenth century is, indeed, the "Great Century" in relation to world evangelization. A general stirring took place in the Christian world and much prayer was being made for the conversion of the heathen. The reports of Captain James Cook on his travels in the South Pacific and a sermon by Jonathan Edwards stirred the heart of William Carey profoundly and molded him into a vessel fit for the Master's use.

a. *The Rise of the Early Denominational Mission Societies*

(1) *In Great Britain.* The first was the particular Baptist Society for Propagating the Gospel among the Heathen. Already since 1784 the first missionary prayer meet-

ings had been held in a little circle of devout Baptists under the guidance of the Reverend Andrew Fuller. The impulse to these was given through the reading of a little tract by Jonathan Edwards published in 1747: "An humble attempt to promote an explicit agreement and visible union of God's people for the revival and the advancement of Christ's kingdom in the earth." In 1792 William Carey published the epochal treatise: *An inquiry into the obligation of Christians to use means for the conversion of heathen in which the religious state of the different nations of the world, the success of former undertakings and the practicability of further undertakings are considered.*

At Nottingham, on May 31, 1792 Carey preached the decisive message on Isaiah 54: 2-3 on the subject, "Expect Great Things from God and Attempt Great Things for God." The impression was profound. On October 2, 1792, the Particular Baptist Society for Propagating the Gospel among the Heathen was organized with twelve or thirteen ministers being present. Carey became its first missionary, leaving England June 13, 1793, and arriving in Calcutta November 10 of that same year. Thus the "Age of William Carey" was born and a new epoch in foreign missions was ushered in.

The Baptist Society was followed by the London Missionary Society (1795), at first an interdenominational sending agency and later the board of the Congregational Churches. The Glasgow and Edinburgh Missionary Societies (Presbyterian) was organized in 1796, to be followed by The Church Missionary Society (1799).

(2) *In Germany.* Pietism more than anything else had prepared the soil for mission activities. At first numerous missionary associations were formed to support the missionary advances from Great Britain. Both finances and personnel were channeled through the British societies. However, in 1861 the Basel Missionary Society was organized into an independent sending agency. Several other societies followed in rapid succession. The Berlin Missionary Society (1824) sought to become central in Germany but it never superceded Basel.

(3) *In France.* The Paris Evangelical Society was organized as a sending agency in 1822 and developed into a strong arm of French Protestantism operating overseas.

(4) *In Holland.* A free, adventurous, and missionary spirit had lived here for some time. The development of the organizational aspect was not, however, as normal as in some other countries. Already in 1797 the Netherlands Missionary Society had been instituted. At first this organization served more as an arm of the London Missionary Society, contributing men and finances to this agency. In 1816 it opened its own seminary for the training of missionaries and soon developed into an independent sending agency. After the middle of the century internal disruptive forces set in and the society split into four separate societies.

(5) *In the Scandinavian Countries: Sweden, Norway, Denmark, Finland.*

All of these countries organized their own sending agencies in the following order: Danish Missionary Society (1821); Swedish Missionary Society (1835); Norwegian Missionary Society (1842); and the Finland Missionary Society (1859).

Thus within half a century from 1792 every one of the continental Protestant countries and France, except Finland which followed some years later, had organized their own sending agencies and were seeking to advance the missionary cause.

(6) *In America.* Here things were also moving beyond the evangelization of the Indians and the Frontier Missions. At Williams College under the leadership of Samuel J. Mills a student mission prayer circle was formed which will remain known for the "Haystack Prayer Meeting" where modern American foreign missions was born. Coming next to Andover Seminary, Mills became instrumental in arousing missionary interest, and upon the instigation of a group of students in 1810 the American Board of Commissioners for Foreign Missions came into being.

Due to peculiar circumstances the America Baptist Foreign Missionary Union was organized in 1814. Soon all major denominations established their own Boards. Some at first cooperated with British or continental societies. Sooner or later, however, they became independent sending agencies. Thus the home base was at least organizationally ready for an aggressive enterprise.

b. *The Rise of the Interdenominational Missionary Societies*

The rise of the interdenominational missionary societies in the latter part of the nineteenth century is due to a number of factors, some obvious, some mysterious. whatever these factors may be and however we may evaluate them, the Lord's blessing has been upon these agencies. He has prospered them with finances, missionary candidates, converts, great movements, strong indigenous churches, and some fine institutions. While this cannot be said of all, it is true of many of them. Some are today among the major sending agencies of the Christian church.

The beginning of this movement was made by James Hudson Taylor, who in 1865 against his own desires, but driven by a deep and abiding burden of responsibility for inland China, organized the China Inland Mission. Bishop Stephen Neill summarizes the distinguishing principles of this mission from the principles currently in vogue in other missions and churches of the Protestant world:

(1) The mission was to be interdenominational. Conservative in theology, it would accept as missionaries any convinced Christians of whatever denomination, if they could sign its simple doctrinal declaration.

(2) A door was opened for those of little formal education. This was of great importance; missions were tending to become professional, and to have less place for pioneers of the type of Robert Moffatt.

(3) The direction of the mission would be in China, not in England, a change of far-reaching significance. And the director would have full authority to direct.

(4) Missionaries would wear Chinese dress and as far as possible identify themselves with the Chinese people.

(5) The primary aim of the mission was always to be widespread evangelism. The shepherding of the churches and education could be undertaken, but not to such an extent as to hide or hinder the one central and commanding purpose (*History of Christain Missions,* pp. 333, 334).

The evident blessing of God upon the mission inspired other pioneers, and soon other and similar organizations followed. Some fifteen such missions had been organized before the turn of the century. At present more than one hundred of such agencies are functioning. More than forty-five linked themselves together in the Interdenominational Foreign Missions Association, organized March 31, 1917 in Philadelphia, Pennsylvania, U.S.A.

3. THE MARCH OF MODERN MISSIONS

The occupation of the large mission fields did not proceed as rapidly and as smoothly as it may appear from some records. There were numerous and formidable obstacles to be overcome. The limited vision of the home constituency, the small number of volunteers, the difficulties of securing the necessary finances, the problems of entering foreign lands, the non-cooperation and at times active opposition of the large trading companies, the hostile attitude of the subjugated people, the natural barriers – uncharitable climate, infectious diseases, etc., were some of the difficulties that had to be overcome.

Undaunted faith and indomitable courage, however, pressed forward and the unfolding story constitutes a most stirring and fascinating chapter of human history. We turn our attention to Asia, for here modern missions begins. Then, after a brief summary of Oceania, we will see missions penetrating Africa, knocking at the gates of the Muslim countries, and lastly, expanding into Latin America.

a. *Asia*

(1) *India* constituted the first great mission field. While Christianity had existed in this land for many centuries, perhaps from the first century of the Christian era, and later in the eighteenth century the Danish-Halle Mission had planted evangelical Christianity firmly in South India, the progressive evangelization of India begins with the arrival of William Carey in November of 1793. The "Serampore Triad" – Carey, Marshman and Ward (1799) – will remain the famous pioneers of India.

It was not long before Carey was joined by such famous men as Nathaniel Forsyth (1798), Henry Martin (1806), Reginald Heber (1822), and Alexander Duff (1829). Soon the major missionary societies spread over large sections of India, fanning out from various centers such as Calcutta, Madras, Tinneyvelly, Bombay, and Cochin. They followed the Ganges River northwest to New Delhi and entered other inland cities. By 1857, the year of the Sepoy Mutiny and the assumption of political control by the British government of India, British, Continental, and American societies were at work with practically every major city having some Christian witness. From here on the evangelization of India has proceeded at a rapid pace without any major difficulties or serious disruption. Today a living Christian community of some 10 to 11 million Indian people witnesses to the fact, that Christianity is a living religion also in India. From India missions traveled east and north.

(2) *Ceylon* was first reached by representatives of the London Missionary Society in 1804. The English Baptists arrived in 1812, to be followed by English Methodists (1814), the American Board of Commissioners (1815) and the Church Missionary Society in 1818. The latter has become the largest Protestant Church in the country.

(3) *China* opened its doors to the gospel and foreigners only gradually and by a series of treaties which the Western powers forced upon the land much to the resentment of the people and the government. Robert Morrison of the London Missionary Society is the pioneer of Protestantism in this vast land. He came to China in 1807. The Netherlands Missionary Society, the American Board of Commissioners (1830), and the Protestant Episcopal Church of America (1835) sought to establish beach heads in these risky pioneer years with rather limited success.

The Treaties of Nanking (1842) and Tientsin (1860) opened the cities and the land to foreigners and missions. By 1859 twelve additional societies had come to China for mission Work. In 1865 the China Inland Mission began its heroic penetration of the interior of China which stands unparalled in the history of missions.

By the end of the century large advances, geographically as well as spiritually, were registered. The gospel was beginning to penetrate the soil and the soul of China, making itself felt in the web of life. However, since the 1890's China has been ravaged by wars and revolutions. Though Christianity made considerable progress, difficulties were serious and interruptions were numerous. Since the Communist takeover in 1951, all mission work has discontinued, though Christainity is surviving.

(4) *Burma* received the first missionaries in the persons of Adoniram and Ann Judson of America, representing the American Baptist Missionary Union. Eventually the Baptists found their most fruitful field among the Karen tribes, where at present one of the largest Baptist Conventions in the lands of the younger churches may be found. Besides the Baptists, the Anglicans and Methodists are represented among the pioneer missions in Burma.

(5) *Thailand* became in the main a Presbyterian mission field, though the Netherlands Missionary Society sent its representative Kark Gutzlaff here in 1828 and the Congregationalists came in 1831. Neither society remained in the land. The Baptists, who came to Thailand in 1833 succeeded in organizing the Maitri Chit Baptist Church in 1837. The church has continued till the present and is the world's first and oldest Chinese Christian Church. The Presbyterians (American, North) entered the field in 1840 and established themselves in Bangkok and Cheingmai. They have gained considerable numbers of converts from among the Lao people of northern Thailand. In 1903 the Anglicans and the British "Churches of Christ" also entered Thailand for mission work. The Christian and Missionary Alliance (1929), and the Overseas Missionary Fellowship (1951) have a considerable mission force in the land. The Church of Christ in Thailand integrates most of the demonimational work and churches into one united body.

(6) *Vietnam, Laos, and Cambodia,* former French Indo-China, remained closed to Protestant mission work until the beginning of this century. In 1902 the Swiss Brethren were permitted to establish a work in Laos. The Christian and Missionary Alliance secured permission to enter Vietnam in 1911 and Cambodia in 1922. Several tribal movements have yielded a considerable following of Christianity.

(7) The beginning of mission work in *Malaya and Singapore* is difficult to date.

Due to a heavy influx of Europeans and immigrants from India Christian churches sprang up among these groups. Some work was also done among the Chinese people which later was transferred to China. Before the middle of the nineteenth century, how ever, the Anglicans, Methodists, and Presbyterians had established some work among the various peoples. The original inhabitants, being in the main Muslims, were practically untouched with the gospel at the beginning of this century. At present the Overseas Missionary Fellowship has its headquarters in Singapore and a large staff operating inland.

(8) *Indonesia,* being governed by Holland, received its first missionaries from that country. The regular missionary societies were preceded by Company chaplains who had developed some missionary work. Four missionary societies pioneered much of the work with considerable success. The first to enter was the Netherlands Missionary Society, beginning work in the first decade of the nineteenth century. It was soon followed by the Basel and Rhenish Missionary Societies. The latter society established itself on Sumatra and developed a prosperous work among the Batak people. The American Methodists also entered the field quite early with Batavia as the main center. All four missions fanned out to the animistic people of the numerous islands and reaped marvelous results from their labors. The mission to the Muslims of Indonesia has borne more fruit than in any other Muslim country.

(9) Protestant work in the *Philippines* became a possibility when Portuguese power over these islands was broken and the United States assumed the protectorate in 1898. The American Presbyterian Board responded to this open door in 1899, to be followed by the Baptists and Methodists in 1900. In rapid succession the major American Boards established themselves in the Philippines with good response in most areas.

(10) *Japan,* the land of the rising sun, remained long in the shadow due to its rigid policy of isolation. It opened its door to foreigners only after serious pressure by the American Navy. The ratification of a treaty in 1858 opened some ports to foreigners, and finally Japan veered from the path of isolationism. The Protestant Episcopal Church, the American Presbyterian Board and the Reformed Church of America sent their missionaries to Japan in 1859. In a decade and a half the major denominations were represented with the exception of the Lutherans who were to arrive considerably later. Though not without difficulties, the work continued without too serious interruptions until 1941, when Japan became involved in the Second World War. A new epoch in the evangelization came with the defeat of Japan and the influx of numerous inter-denominational and evangelical missions. The prospects of Christianity in this modern and aggressive land are good. The national leadership is strong and the evangelistic fervor is encouraging.

(11) *Korea* remained closed to the gospel and foreigners until 1882 when the United States signed a treaty with Korea, which enabled missionaries to enter the land of the morning calm. The first ordained missionaries, Horace G. Underwood and Henry G. Appenzeller, representing the American Presbyterian and Methodists respectively, arrived on Easter Sunday, April 5, 1885. Though other missions have come to Korea, the Presbyterian movement has dominated the Christian church of that land. Korea has been visited by tremendous waves of revival and the church has grown more rapidly than in most mission fields, the Christian Community edging up close to ten per cent of the population.

b. *Oceania*

In the vast expanse of the Pacific Ocean are scattered some thirty main groups of islands, and many lesser clusters and separate units. Their total number is estimated at 1500. The 4,0000,000 people who inhabit these beautiful islands are a heterogeneous multitude, but may roughly be classified as Polynesians and Papuans. The evangelization of this area constitutes one of the greatest triumphs of the gospel in the nineteenth century, while at the same time reporting some of the most savage-like atrocities committed against Christian missionaries.

The first party of missionaries was sent out by the London Missionary Society, departing from England in September, 1796 for Tahiti and Tonga. All experienced indescribable hardships and the Tonga party was not able to maintain itself. Conditions changed in Tahiti when King Pomare in 1812 decided to become a Christian. Seven years later, in 1819, he was baptized in a large church, which he himself had constructed in the presence of 4000 of his subjects. Now paganism gradually gave way to civility and Christianity.

The most famous of all South Seas pioneers was the Congregationalist John Williams of the London Missionary Society who was assigned to the Society Island where he arrived in 1817. From here he evangelized numerous islands with the assistance of native Christians. By 1834 he was able to report that "no group of islands, nor single island of importance, within 2,000 miles of Tahiti had been left unvisited."

The Methodists, Anglicans (C.M.A.), American Congregationalists, and the Reformed Presbyterian Church of Scotland also became active in the various islands. Of all the islands of the Pacific, New Hebrides and Solomon have proved the most resistant to Christian influences, though the Lutheran work begun in 1886 has prospered and constitutes a community of more than 200,000 numbers. Also some per cent of the population of Papua, southeastern New Guinea, professes Christianity. The interior of New Guinea remained neglected until more recent decades. John Paton and New Guinea will remain associated in our minds.

The pattern of evangelization on numerous islands was very similar. At first there was fierce resistance. Gradually the atmosphere changed and the chief or king was won to Christianity. Upon his baptism mass movements became the order of the day and large accessions to the church were reported. Today most of the inhabitants consider themselves Christians and some are most active in mission activities.

c. *Africa*

The vast continent of Africa (11,500,000 square miles) is populated by some 275 million people, belonging to several races, speaking some 523 distinct languages and more than 300 dialects. It is divided into a number of independent nations with large territories still under European administration.

It has become common practice among writers to divide Africa into five major areas and think of a five-pronged thrust in the evangelization of Africa – West, South, North, East, and Congo River areas.

(1) *Thrust from the West*

The Church Missionary Society was the first to establish a permanent work on the west coast in 1804. Back of it lay the attempts of the Baptist and the Glasgow and Edinburgh societies, who entered the field in 1795 and 1797 respectively.

Sierra Leone naturally attracted the British societies, since it was a colony established by a British group for repatriating freed slaves. The English Methodists came to the colony in 1811. Though several other societies later began work in this area, the Anglicans and Methodists have remained by far the strongest through the years with the latter being in the lead.

From Sierra Leone the various missions followed the coast line east and south, never penetrating too far interior due to the extremely unhealthy climate, though serious attempts were made to follow the Niger River inland. In the last decade of the past century the Sudan United Mission and the Sudan Interior Mission, the former British, the latter Canadian, began in all seriousness and under tremendous difficulties an extensive inland mission program in Nigeria and the Sudan. Both missions entered the field through Nigeria and expanded to the north and to the east.

(2) *Thrust from the South*

As early as 1737 the Moravian George Schmidt was sent out from Herrnhut to begin work among the Hottentots in South Africa. The Dutch settlers, however, opposed him and Schmidt was ordered out of the country by the authorities. Only in 1792 were the Moravians permitted to resume the work which is being carried on to the present times. The more significant pioneer work was done by the London Missionary Society. The three stars, John Theodore Vanderkamp, (1799), Robert Moffatt (1817), and David Livingstone (1840) will ever adorn the London Missionary Society's work in Africa. Though the London Missionary Society was followed by a host of other societies, the Congregationalists remained dominant in the South African mission thrust.

(3) *Thrust from the North*

The once Christian North Africa became Muslim in the seventh and eighth centuries. The late occupation of the south Mediterranean coast line is one of the strange anomalies of history. Actually it was one of the last areas to draw the missionary societies to itself. Missionary efforts in North Africa began in Egypt. In 1818 the Church Missionary Society sent a group of five missionaries for the purpose of assisting the Coptic Church in Egypt and Ethiopia. In 1854 the United Presbyterians launched an aggressive program in Egypt and expanded it later into Ethiopia. The Swedish Evangelical Society entered Ethiopia in 1866 and developed a considerable work. The Egypt General Mission, an independent faith work of British origin, began evangelistic work in Alexandria in 1898 while the North Africa Mission, also an independent faith mission, became the pioneering society in the several Barbary States along the Mediterranean coast. The work has been grinding and unrewarding.

(4) *Thrust from the East*

The Church Missionary Society workers, who had entered Ethiopia from Egypt were forced out of the country in 1838. Johann Ludwig Krapf, a German missionary, found his way to Zanzibar and from here began his eastern explorations and mission operations. He established himself at Mombasa on the east coast. Zanzibar and Mombasa became the points of departure into the well-responding mission areas of Kenya and Uganda as well as for a thrust to the southeast. The Church Missionary Society remained in the lead in this mission area, though a number, especially German societies, worked successfully along the east coast and from there inland.

(5) *Thrust into the Congo area*

After Henry M. Stanley, the great explorer and successor to David Livingston, had laid open the Congo territory to the world, the missionary societies were not slow in entering this jungle area. First in the field were the English Baptists who transferred the famous George Grenfell and his companion Thomas Comber from the Cameroons to the Congo in 1878. The American Baptists followed in 1884, absorbing the work of the independent Livingstone Inland Mission. Other societies, American, British, and Continental soon entered, and the Congo became one of the best staffed mission areas, divided between a legion of mission organizations, both denominational and interdenominational.

d. *The Muslim World*

Islam stretches its arms over thousands of miles from the west coast of North Africa to the islands of Indonesia and even into the Philippines. Some 450 million people have become followers of the prophet of Mecca. Islam has challenged Christianity more than any other religion and has yielded less to Christianity than any other religion. Here is Christianity's challenge.

The Christian penetration of the lands of Islam (we are not including here Indonesia and Pakistan) has been very slow and difficult. Direct evangelism was an impossibility and the change of religions was illegal and still is in some sections of the world of Islam. Yet the Christian forces dared to enter this world with the hope and anticipation that changes could be effected and that the doors would eventually open to the gospel of God.

In general it may be said that comity arrangements have been observed well. The American Board has worked from Istanbul into Asia Minor. The American Presbyterians (North), with Beirut as the western center have worked from here east into Iran and Iraq. The United Presbyterians occupied Egypt. The Reformed Church of America operated extensively in Arabia. The North Africa Mission labored in the northern states of North Africa along the Mediterranean coast. Other missions have joined in the task, especially the Church Missionary Society and the Christian and Missionary Alliance.

The main approach has been through educational institutions — Roberts College, Istanbul; American University, Beirut; American College for Girls, Istanbul. Other missionary institutions of higher learning are three colleges in Turkey under the American Board and four Presbyterian colleges, two in Egypt, one in Lebanon, and on in Syria. Though these schools are serving well in cultural orientation, they yield few converts. The medical approach is also used extensively. The Reformed Church operates eight hospitals in Arabia. Altogether there are some forty church-related hospitals in the Middle East.

From the very beginning the missions have relied heavily upon literature and of late a powerful radio station has been built in Ethiopia by the Lutheran World Federation to reach all of Africa and the Near East with the radio. The results among the Muslims have been very meager. The main gospel outreach has been among the remnants of the ancient Christian church. Here considerable numbers of converts have been gained and evangelical churches have been founded.

e. *Latin America*

The names of James Thomson (1818), a Scotsman, and founder and promoter of the Lancastrian system of education in a number of Republics, and Allen Gardiner (1844), the heroic Britisher who loved himself to death for South America's Indians, will always be remembered as pioneers of evangelical advance into Latin America.

The progressive evangelical penetration of Latin America began around the middle of the past century. The Presbyterians (North) are credited with much of the pioneer work in this area of mission endeavor. Some of their pioneers were B. H. Pratt (1856), Colombia; and A. G. Simonton (1859), Brazil. Dr. David Trumbull began his work in Chile in 1845 and the Presbyterians assumed full responsibility for the work in 1873. They entered Mexico in 1872, came to Guatemala in 1881, and to Venezuela in 1897. Eventually they spread practically over all of Latin America, and have become a strong and influential church with impressive and well-recognized institutions.

The Presbyterians were followed by the Methodists and in some Republics the latter were the first in the field – Argentina (1836), Uruguay (1839), Chile (1877), and Mexico (1873). The Methodists, too, have spread over almost all the Republics and have numerous and strong churches. The Baptists are third numerically of the denominational missions, and have developed much evangelistic as well as institutional strength, especially in Brazil, Argentina, and Colombia. The Christian and Missionary Alliance have entered with considerable force most of the Spanish speaking Republics, and have established strong evangelistic churches and preaching centers in numerous places. By the end of the past century most American denominational Boards had representation in the lands of their Latin neighbors to the South.

Latin America has also been an open field of activity for inter-denominational missions. Though no one mission has achieved the prominence that the China Inland Mission had in China and the Sudan Interior Mission holds in Africa, the cumulative strength of the interdenominational missionary societies outweighs by far the strength of the denominational movements, except for the large, well-established, and influential institutions. At present the greater part of evangelism is carried forward by these missions.

In addition to this, we must mention the phenomenal progress of Pentecostalism in several countries, especially in Brazil, Argentina, Chile, and El Salvador. In the first three countries they constitute either a majority or close to a majority of all Protestant Christianity. Much of this growth is purely indigenous.

Protestantism is, indeed, on the march in Latin America. In 1900 there were 50,000 Christians in this part of the world; by 1914 the number had risen to 250,000. In 1958 the figure stood at 5,000,000 and in 1965 we may well accept 10,000,000 people as constituting the Protestant community.

4. THE ADVANCE OF MODERN MISSIONS

The progress of missions has differed greatly. In Asia, India leads in the number of Protestant Christians. Here mass movements have greatly augmented the Christian cause and made a people out of some 60 million outcastes. Large and numerous churches adorn the once gospel-destitute land, and Christian education has made its mark upon life and culture. In Korea great waves of revival have visited the churches at several intervals making for astounding progress of the gospel. At present Korea leads the Asiatic countries in the percentage of population adhering to Protestant Christianity. Among the animistic tribes of China, Formosa, and the islands of South East Asia tribal movements have brought large numbers into the Christian fold and transformed whole communities and wide areas. In Africa, south of Sahara the spread of the gospel and the penetration of life and culture by Christianity has been phenomenal. The old tribal life has disintegrated before the march of modern western civilization and prepared multitudes to embrace Christianity which often is merely a transfer to western culture. The sweep has been very extensive in certain areas like Kenya and Uganda. Bishop Stephen Neill optimistically anticipates that if the present pace can be sustained, Africa South of Sahara may be predominantly "Christian" by the end of this century. In Latin America the progress of evangelicalism has been nothing short of miraculous. In one century of mission activities the membership of the Evangelical church has risen to approximately 5 million with a Christian community of some 10 million members. In Chile where the percentage of the Christian community is highest it stands at 9.3% in comparison to 10% of active Roman Catholics. Over all, Latin American evangelicalism grows approximately three times as fast as the population. Thus there is room for optimism.

This optimistic and positive outlook is clouded by several factors. First, though Christianity has won large numbers of followers and has greatly modified the ancient Asiatic systems of religion, it has not succeeded in displacing them anywhere. Thus Hinduism stands erect in India and is asserting itself more than ever before. The renaissance of Hinduism is evident on every hand. Buddhism holds Southeast Asia firmly in control religiously. Confucianism and Buddhism reigned supreme in China until the day of Communism's triumph. Shintoism and Buddhism are firmly entrenched in Japan and show no sign of yielding to Christianity. Islam has proudly defied the march of Christianity and has yielded very few converts outside of Indonesia. Christianity has registered its success not in triumph over these competitive systems, but rather in areas where these systems had not yet penetrated. This is most significant and raises the serious question whether Christianity is powerless against these religious systems and destined to be a minority movement in these vast Asiatic areas.

Secondly, Christianity has drawn to itself numerous adherents in the various countries, and some strong personalities and aggressive leaders have emerged. As a whole, however, missions has brought forth a relatively passive and evangelistically non-agressive church. There is little missionary outreach and not much positive drawing power to attract the immediate community to the groups of professing Christians, nor strong and positive influence issuing forth to transform and mold the non-Christian culture. The heritage of a static culture and the non-missionary nature of most non-Christian religions may afford a rational explanation for the existence of such a situation. Yet the dynamic of Christianity which is personal Christian discipleship and missionary outreach is lacking. And this may be a heritage from the sending churches rather than from a cultural background. Perhaps the words of Stephen Neill are correct when he says, "As we look back over history and consider the enormous difficulties to be overcome, the unwillingness of many great western churches to take part in missionary work at all, the miserable niggardliness with which the work of missions has always been supported, the lack of distinction in some of those who have undertaken this service, the innumerable mistakes in policy and practice that have been made, it seems a sheer miracle that there are any Christians at all in the lands of the younger churches. And yet there they are" (*The Cross Over Asia*, p. 28). We can only thank God for them, as we earnestly intercede that the dynamic of God may fill these churches and create in them a real passion and vision for missionary outreach. Positive signs are appearing on the horizon, though most pioneer mission work is still carried on by westerners. The third factor that clouds missionary progress is the tendency towards religious and theological syncretism on the one hand and separatist movements on the other hand. The former is constantly threatening the gospel in the lands of the great systems of religion and philosophy as we find them in India, China, Japan, and Southeast Asia. Here neither absolute truth nor final authority is welcome. Relativism, accommodation and adaptation, not only in form but in content are natural tendencies. To such mentality the finality, authority, inclusiveness and exclusiveness of Christianity are not acceptable. This mental attitude is reinforced by modern theological liberalism and finds an ally in it. The danger of separatist movements manifests itself more in Africa in the "prophet" movements than anywhere else, though it is entering strongly into some areas in Latin America. Whatever the reasons for such movements may be, they are proving disruptive and paralyzing to the progress of the gospel of Christ.

To these clouds we may add such problems as nationalism, secularism, materialism, and communism. All these constitute formidable obstacles. Yet into such a world Christ speaks his sovereign and omnipotent word, "I will build my church and the gates of hell shall not prevail against it."

Looking over the field that a century and a half ago lay in darkness and without the gospel, we are compelled to exclaim: Behold, What God hath wrought! At present every nation has at least a limited Christian witness, and by means of radio broadcasts the gospel can be heard wherever man is found. Not that the need is not appalling. It certainly is. There is no time to relax. But neither is this the time to dismay. Vast multitudes must be reached, countless villages must hear the gospel, numerous tribes must have the message in their tongue. Every area of the globe must know of Christ and all of life must be claimed for the Lord. There is much land yet to be possessed. But an evangelical community has been raised up. According to the 1962 World Christian Yearbook there may exist a Christian community in Asia, Africa and Latin America of some 50 to 55 million people of whom approximately half live in Asia. A world witness has been established. Christ's promise is being fulfilled. His cause does triumph.

5. ECUMENISM

The word ecumenical is an Anglicized adjective of the Greek noun *oikoumeme*, meaning the inhabited earth. It is also used of the Roman empire, and the world as viewed by the speaker. The word appears some fifteen times in the Greek New Testament. Historically it came to be applied to the great councils of Christendom of the fourth to the eighth centuries which represented the entire Christian church and where doctrinal and other church concerns were debated and agreed upon. It thus signified the universality, catholicity, orthodoxy, and unity of the Christian church. It is well to differentiate between ecumenism as a mood, as a theology, and as an organizational structure. We can consider only the latter aspect.

The World Council of Churches was preceded by a series of international missionary conferences. In 1921 the International Missionary Council was organized as a result of the Edinburgh conference and consequently became the sponsors of the succeeding conferences. In the third decade of our century the Faith and Order Conference and the Life and Work movement had been established. The former concerned itself with doctrine, the latter with social ethics. These movements were augmented by the Y.M.C.A. (1851), Christian Endeavor (1881), the Student Volunteer Movement (1886), and the Student Christian Movement (1895). Here the young men and future leaders in churches and missions had learned to think across denominational, cultural, and national borders and limitations.

The World Council of Churches came into being as a direct result of the several lines of development – the Faith and Order Conference, the Life and Work Movement, the International Missionary Council, and the international Christian youth movements.

The Edinburgh and Oxford Conferences in 1937, on Faith and Order and Life and Work respectively, proposed to unite in the formation of a World Council of Churches. At Utrecht in 1938 under the chairmanship of William Temple, then Archbishop of York, a constitution was drafted for submission to the churches, and a provisional committee was appointed to act for the 'World Council of Churches in process of formation.' Due to the Second World War the actual organization had to be postponed. In 1948, 351 delegates and 238 alternates representing 147 churches in forty-four countries met at Amsterdam to form the World Council of Churches, with headquarters in Geneva, Switzerland.

A second conference was held at Evanston, near Chicago in 1954 and a third in New Delhi, India in 1961. More than 175 churches from more than fifty-five nations are united in this body, forming a gigantic organizational structure with multiple functions. In New Delhi the International Missionary Council merged with the World Council of Churches and its ministry is carried on by the Division of World Missions and Evangelism.

The goals and the theology of the World Council of Churches are not clear. At the present it is "a fellowship of churches which accept our Lord Jesus Christ as God and Savior." This is its theological basis. The goals are undefined and wide open.

The functions of the World Council are stated in its constitution as follows: (1) to carry on the work of the two world movements for "Faith and Order" and for "Life and Work"; (2) to facilitate common action by the churches; (3) to promote cooperation in study; (4) to promote the growth of ecumenical consciousness in the members of all churches; (5) to establish relations with denominational federations of worldwide scope and with other ecumenical movements; (6) to call world conferences on specific subjects as occasion may require, such conferences being empowered to publish their own findings; and (7) to support the churches in their task of evangelism.

For the most part evangelicals have reacted negatively to the ecumenical movement. This has been due to a number of causes, some of which are:

a. *The mixed multitude within the World Council of Churches.* Evangelicals find it rather difficult to disregard their history, theology, ecclesiastical practice, and ethical standards to join in a union movement merely for the sake of union.

b. *The signs of an inclusivistic message and theology.* It is clearly observable that the World Council of Churches is unable and unwilling to deal with theological liberalism and rationalism which have repudiated many cardinal doctrines of historic Christianity nor can it combat successfully religious syncretism. All this is due to the fact that the objective authority of the written Word of God has been forsaken. The love of union can easily crucify the holiness and sternness of truth. Its message, therefore, is weak and its theology diluted.

c. *Fear of an authoritative super-church.* Though such intention has been denied officially and repeatedly, the fear and suspicion persists in the hearts and minds of many evangelicals.

d. *The recent Protestant-Roman dialogue.* With deep anxiety evangelicals have been following the prospects of a future union of these two historic movements, and the readiness to engage in dialogue not for the purpose of conversion but for better understanding and amicable relationships.

e. *The uncertainty of the missionary outreach.* The evangelical has no hesitation in accepting the principle that when a church has matured she should not only be autonomous in directing her own affairs but also the mission to her community. This does not, however, make missionary societies superfluous. It may cast them into a different mold but it does not cast them away. While it sounds very ideal that the church is the mission and the mission is the church, history does not support such an ideal. To the contrary, it has always been a small minority in the church that has carried the burden of world evangelization.

On the positive side it may be said that evangelicals firmly believe in the unity of all believers in Christ and are ready to practice such unity. This is evident from: (1) the great interdenominational Bible institutes, Bible colleges, colleges and seminaries they have established at home; (2) the large Bible conference grounds they have built up for the benefit of all, regardless of denomination; (3) the numerous and strong interdenominational missionary societies they are upholding and the thousands of missionaries they are supporting; (4) the large quantities of evangelical literature that comes from nondenominational publishers to be distributed on an interdenominational basis; (5) the several interdenominational service agencies, serving numerous missionary societies and younger churches regardless of their denominational adherence; (6) the organization of the World Evangelical Fellowship which binds the evangelicals together in fellowship and service as well as in bearing one another's burdens; and (7) numerous cooperative projects at home and abroad such as missionary radio, the World Literature Crusade, the Pocket Testament League, Evangelism in Depth, etc.

The evangelical believes in unity not necessarily in union; in unity by the Spirit not necessarily in structure and organization. But he does believe in the Biblical ideal of the true unity in Christ of all who have been born again by the Spirit and by that same Spirit have been baptized into the body of Christ.

BIBLIOGRAPHY

DuPlessis, J., *The Evangelization of Pagan Africa.* Juta & Co., Ltd.

Firth, C. B., *An Introduction to the Indian Church History.* The Christian Literature Society.

Glover, Robert Hall, *The Progress of World-Wide Missions,* revised by J. Herbert Kane. Harper.

Iglehart, Charles W., *A Century of Christianity in Japan.* Charles E. Tuttle Company.

Latourette, Kenneth Scott, *A History of Expansion of Christianity* (Seven volumes). Harper

Moffett, Samuel Hugh, *The Christians of Korea.* Friendship Press.

Thiessen, John Caldwell, *A Survey of World Missions.* Moody Press.

Warburton, Stacy R., *The Making of Modern Missions.* Fleming H. Revell.

One World and One Church

The world in which we live has become one world. As never before the physical dimension of the globe is shrinking. The process has been quickened in the twentieth century by scientific advances in transportation and communication. Messages by cable and radio can be transmitted anywhere around the world in a matter of seconds. Even television communication via Telestar is no longer a novelty. Aircraft carry men everywhere at an increasing rate of speed and a decreasing time schedule.

The unity of our world has been furthered by international travel. People from every country travel or live in other nations as students, businessmen, statesmen, or tourists. Organizations and agencies that are international in character abound on every hand. The Olympic games bring athletes from many nations together every few years.

There are centripetal forces at work but there are also centrifugal forces that divide and separate one people from another. Opposing ideologies like democracy and communism, new brands of nationalism, the divisive tendency of opposing ideas, and built-in prejudices all operate to intensify conflict in the world. When these forces have been taken into account, however, it is still true that the world is essentially one. From the Christian point of view all men are one in that they come from a common ancestor. All men are bound by the thralldom of sin. All men need the redemption that is to be found in Jesus Christ.

The Christian, conscious of the oneness of the world, also knows that men are divided into two classes: those who are Christians, and those who are not. He realizes that each is part of a world system that is in opposition to the other. There can be no peaceful coexistence between them. Each is out to destroy the other, since the intrinsic nature of each is antithetical to the other. The final victory of one supposes the defeat of the other. The kingdom of this world to which unbelievers belong operates in this world and has neither part nor future in the world to come. The kingdom of God to which believers belong penetrates this present world dominated by the power of evil. It acts as leaven, but its true genius lies in its transcendental character. It exists in this world and it witnesses against, and yet works and lives on behalf of, this world but in its true nature it is not of this world, although it is in it. This is the tension under which the Christian lives for he belongs to two orders of life – the natural order ruled over by the prince of the powers of darkness, and the divine order ruled over by Jesus Christ. The follower of Christ has his citizenship in two kingdoms, although his true allegiance is to the kingdom of God and to his Christ.

Those who belong to God through Jesus Christ are members of a body identified in the Scriptures as the church of Jesus Christ. Of this body, its basic nature, and its form more shall be said shortly. Prior to that, however, we must commence with the realization that the people of God exist in and for the sake of the world. This means that they have an obligation to speak to men about God through the preaching of the gospel of Jesus Christ. This gospel is the message they must bear. They are called upon to spread it everywhere precisely because they are rooted and grounded in God through Jesus Christ. Commanded though they are by the Great Commission to evangelize the world with the gospel, they would be bound to do this even if there were no command. Just as living creatures breathe to live, and sleep when they get tired, so do those who have tasted of the good things of the kingdom of God reflexively speak forth the good news of salvation as a witness to men. They become witnesses precisely because they are rooted in Jesus Christ.

The gospel must be taken to all men everywhere. This means every kindred, tribe, people, and tongue. God knows no color lines. He shows no preference for one over another. There is also a sense of immediacy. Life's span is short and the fields are white to harvest. Laborers are to go into the harvest fields while the ripe grain waits to be plucked. If the harvest is not gathered when it is ripe it will be lost. To this one world, then, this one church takes this one gospel which brings this one salvation. What is the nature and dynamism of this one church of which we speak?

The church of Jesus Christ comprises the elect of all ages: past, present, and future. The identity of the elect is known only to God. Many who are members of visible churches are not included in the invisible church which is known to God alone. Some who are not on the rolls of the visible churches are among the elect. The true church of Jesus Christ knows neither the limitations of time or space. Thus there are saints whose bodies rest in tombs who are members of Christ's body just as much as those who are alive. There are those who are yet unborn whose names and sainthood are known to our omniscient God. Living believers are tied together spiritually even though separated spatially by geography.

The church of Jesus Christ has a given unity. The Scriptures teach that there is one Lord, one faith, one baptism. Whatever differences separate believers one from the other they are still members of the same body and share in its essential unity. This given unity is imperfectly realized in this life and will never be perfectly attained until the church has been glorified. The imperfection of the unity springs from sin. Sin mars concord, affects understanding, and ranges into every area of life. Thus it should occasion no surprise that grave differences of opinion exist about important matters and that these differences divide the visible body of Christ. Division should not be accepted quiescently nor should the desirable objective of the unity of the church be overlooked or forgotten because of differences. Some major doctrines of the faith are accepted by all of the historic churches and over them there is no continuing dispute. The divisions arise over others about which there are profound differences of opinion. Since true unity must be predicated upon a common theological consensus, clearly doctrinal differences must be settled before unity can be attained.

There is a spiritual unity which is not necessarily embodied in concrete empirical or visible form but which is marked by love and characterized by fraternal relations despite the continuing differences. While this spiritual unity exists, dialogue can be continued to determine exactly what, and how deep, the differences are that divide. It is painfully obvious that when one group insists upon its own interpretation of the faith in a way that differs from the interpretation of others, and so long as the differing parties refuse to make vital concessions there can be no visible unity. Thus when the Baptists insist upon immersion as the only acceptable mode of baptism and when the Anglicans insist upon apostolic succession there is neither any base for, nor any hope of, visible unity. This means that if there is to be any visible unity in the future among those who are basically in disagreement one or the other of the differing parties must sacrifice something which it presently believes to be essential. If such concessions are not made any visible unity built upon conflicting viewpoints that annul each other would not result in real unity but would undoubtedly create tensions and conflicts far worse than the divisions which now exist.

In our day there are sincere differences of opinion as to what form the visible unity of the church should take. Some hold that denominationalism is sinful and wish to demolish all denominations and bring the church under one roof. Others feel that denominations can be retained and their autonomy insured without impairing the visible unity of the church. The problem is materially increased by the ecclesiology of those who believe the local church is a full, complete and true organism demanding total local autonomy. This hardly allows for the possibility that there can be one church in an organic sense. Since those who hold to congregationalism in church polity are numerous, it remains for this vexing problem of ecclesiology to be worked out in the decades ahead.

The group that most strongly endorses organic union of the divided churches is the Ecumenical Movement. It has already brought into its organization complex the World Council of Churches, and the Greek and Russian Orthodox Churches. It has expressed great interest in carrying on conversations with Rome looking to some form of rapprochement with that communion. While it would be technically incorrect to speak of the World Council of Churches as a superchurch it would be equally wrong to deny the appellation since key leaders of the movement think of the World Council as the vehicle through which the reunion of the churches will be accomplished. At the same time men like Henry Pitney Van Dusen ask why the World Council of Churches should not be called a church itself as he favors calling it.

Standing apart from the World Council of Churches are strong and numerous church groups and agencies who are in disagreement with the idea of a single organically united church. Their objections to one church spring from the conviction that the theology of the Ecumenical Movement is defective and the generally held assumption that theological liberals have just as much right in the movement as those who are theologically conservative. Most of those who reject the World Council of Churches also are opposed to inclusion of the Eastern and Russian Orthodox Churches and are deeply disturbed by efforts to secure rapprochement with Rome. Many of these people see in the movement toward one church an eschatological fulfillment that includes the apostasy of the professing church prior to the second advent of Jesus Christ.

Two dangers arise among those who concern themselves with the nature of the church and its visibility and invisibility. On the one hand there are those who limit the church to what may be seen empirically. Then the organization is exalted and the concrete manifestation takes precedence over all else. On the other hand there are those who so exalt the hiddenness of the church and its invisibility that they have no use for a visible church. Both of these views are defective. Both represent extremes which should be avoided. The church is certainly invisible but it also has visible manifestations. The latter is necessarily true because the church is in the world and has its ministry to the world. Indeed the church is God's witnessing reality through which he operates to work out his plan of salvation. This church has for its marks holiness, catholicity, apostolicity, unity, and perpetuity. It is the church of the apostles. It is evangelical in that it witnesses to the apostolic faith, i.e., the gospel of the Lord Jesus Christ. It is universal in that it exists everywhere. It knows no geographical, racial, class, or other barriers – this is catholicity. It is marked by holiness, a holiness that is positionally the possession of the church in Jesus Christ and which becomes the possession of the church in its experience in the world as it is conformed to the image of its founder. And unity belongs to the inner being of this church.

The unity of the church is a given. This unity is possible because the church has Jesus Christ for its head. He is not divided. Each believer is a member of his body and each part of that body has its peculiar place and function in relation to the whole body. Thus division and disunity are an affront to Jesus Christ, the Head of the church. The given unity of the church is to be preserved. It is not to be broken. The tragic divisions of the church today are an evidence of the brokenness of the church. No one can rejoice in this brokenness. At the same time the healing of the church's brokenness at the expense of truth is no solution to a real problem. It does suggest, however, that earnest efforts should be made to heal the brokenness. Even though such efforts may not succeed yet the very act of seeking to heal the brokenness will do something for the spiritual unity of the church. One of the greatest arguments advanced for the reunion of the churches is the effect that a united witness will have on a world which has little respect for present divisions and which cannot understand them. This is no real argument favoring unity for the real reason favoring unity is that Christ himself desires that unity and cannot look upon a divided church as though it were in accord with the divine will. The Spirit of God is moving in a fresh way among the churches. The intense dissatisfaction with present conditions suggest that changes are imminent. That real renewal may come cannot be denied. Amid the diverse organizational expressions of Christianity are many true believers who, despite their sinfulness, their wrong beliefs about some things, and their inability to adjust their sights to the teachings of Holy Scripture, love God and are members of that invisible body called the church.

Let the church be the church. Let it recognize that it exists in and for the benefit of the world and that its chief business is to preach the gospel of Jesus Christ to every creature. Let it also act as the salt in society, the light that dispels darkness, and the city that is set upon a hill. It is sent by Jesus Christ who in turn was sent by the Father. It experiences both victory and defeat. It knows both nights of darkness and days of light. Its ultimate victory is assured, not because the church *per se* will be victorious, but because Jesus Christ will break into history in his second advent when the triumph of the church will be the triumph of Jesus Christ who comes as King of kings and Lord of lords. And He shall reign forever and ever.

BIBLIOGRAPHY

Beaver, R. Pierce, *Ecumenical Beginnings in the Protestant World Mission: A History of Comity*, New York: Thomas Nelson & Sons, 1962.

Bell, G. K. A., ed., *Documents on Christian Unity*, First Series, 1920-4, London: Oxford University Press, 1924.

————————, *The Kingship of Christ: The Story of the World Council of Churches*, Baltimore: Penguin Book, 1954.

Bridston, Keith R., and Wagoner, Walter D., *Unity in Mid-Career: An Ecumenical Critique*, New York: The Macmillan Co., 1963.

Goodall, Norman, *The Ecumenical Movement: What It Is and What It Does*, London: Oxford University Press, 1961.

Hedegard, David, ed., *Ecumenism and the Bible*, London: The Banner of Truth Trust, 1964.

Hogg, William Richey, *Ecumenical Foundations: A History of the International Missionary Council and Its Nineteenth-Century Background*, New York: Harper & Brothers, 1952.

Mackay, John A., *Ecumenics: The Science of the Church Universal*, Englewood Cliffs, New Jersey: Prentice-Hall, Inc., 1964.

Nelson, J., Robert Nelson, ed., *Christian Unity in North America: A Symposium*, St. Louis: The Bethany Press, 1958.

Nolde, O. Frederick, ed., *Toward World-Wide Christianity*, New York, Harper & Brothers, 1964.

Wedel, Theodore O., *The Coming Great Church: Essays on Church Unity*, New York: The Macmillan Co., 1945.

SECTION 5

COUNSELING

"For I shrank not from declaring unto you the whole counsel of God."
— Acts 20:27

The Minister Meets Personal Problems

1. THE NEED FOR COUNSELING

Counseling, in the sense in which it will be used throughout this section refers to a process of encouraging growth from within, which in the final analysis is the only true growth. It is rooted in a growing awareness of one's self. From this should come a less distorted way of seeing persons and relationships and greater courage to accept one's responsibility to make commitments and decisions. Rollo May once described the goal of psychotherapy as the science and art of helping persons remove blocks to self-awareness and inhibitions of feeling, thought and action so as to enlarge the range of responsible freedom, i.e., to increase possibility. Out of this greater personal wholeness should emerge.

Pastoral counseling represents a fusion of two not altogether discrete sources: pastoral care, i.e., the traditional shepherding function of the Christian minister; and dynamic psychology, which focuses upon the striving aspects of personality as the key to understanding persons. Inasmuch as the latter developed from the work of Sigmund Freud, counseling has seemed to be a concession to the enemy. "Did not Freud," they say, "dismiss religion as the obsessional neurosis of mankind, an expression of his immaturity which man would (hopefully) outgrow?" While this may still be a source of difficulty to some Christian ministers, we seem to have reached a point where we recognize that all truth is God's truth, that God's ways are not our ways, and that the Scriptures abound in examples of unlikely messengers God used to carry out his purposes. Moreover, the validity of many of Freud's insights on personality and on counseling procedures have no necessary connection with his attitudes toward religion. There are psychologists aplenty who feel Freud's valid discoveries are better explained by their own view of man than by his. The Christian who considers thoughtfully the findings of the psychotherapist sees many of the processes associated with the Christian's rebirth and sanctification operating in another context and described in a different vocabulary. Examples of this include confession (progressively laying aside one's self-deceiving and self-distorting ego-protective devices), repentance (acknowledging responsibility for one's impulses, attitudes, goals and relationships together with a determination to see that changes are effected), forgiveness (the sense of being accepted as a person notwithstanding the other's awareness of one's greed, hatred, lust, self-pity, and exploitive demands upon others), and the transforming power of disinterested love. On this basis, then, the thoughtful Christian tends to regard counseling as added equipment made available to help him deal with the peculiar stresses of our time.

What these stress-creating characteristics of life in America today might be has been explored at length by a variety of observers and thinkers. In several studies seeking answers to the apparent rise in the incidence of mental illness, mobility was recognized as a major source of trouble. This includes both geographical mobility and status mobility. This is a day of immense possibility. By leaving one's home town for the city there is the chance of better education, a better job, a promotion, or just a needed new start. Often it works out as the person hopes it will. But there is more to it than this. Not everyone thrives on transplanting, for this puts a premium on shallow roots. To translate this into the sphere of personal relations, being forced to move about at frequent intervals places a premium on the ability to form quick, superficial relations with others. The socially successful learn to sense quickly those social behaviors which gain approval from the desired group. Usually this involves shucking off certain social patterns and acquiring others. However, by putting a premium on adaptability the resulting absence of close friendships can and often does create destructive stresses.

The central stress seems to be loneliness. Not the loneliness of a Wordsworth rejoicing in the beauty of a spring day nor of a Thoreau resourcefully establishing himself in the wilderness. Not the healing balm of solitude but the frightening vulnerability of isolation. Rough and ready personal relations based mainly on charm and the approval of others provide little basis on which to share those aspects of oneself which are troubling rather than amusing. Family, relatives or friends of long standing could help but are seldom near, and one hesitates to presume upon people known only through shallow, pleasant day-to-day contacts. It is easy to feel completely alone, that no one really cares. The overwhelming sense of loneliness likely to follow pushes some into a frantic round of social activity, others to the pursuit of anesthetics ("gorging" on detective adventure or love novels; television, movies, or alcohol, and even sleep), still others into premature, ill-conceived marriages, marriages in which excessive emotional demands are made upon the spouse.

Contemporary social conditions, then, encourage a sense of uprootedness, followed by a sense of estrangement from others, a sense of isolation, and, too often, meaninglessness. The result in many is a vague haunting sense of threat. Many try to ignore or palliate this anxiety. They treat it as the problem instead of coming to terms with the conditions that cause this vague sense of threat. The result is growing personal tension, further retreat from reality, and a crippling of the capacity to come to terms with reality.

Psychotherapeutic procedures have been developed to help persons give up their ego defensive maneuvers, thus enabling them to come to terms with the demands of life and death.

2. COUNSELING AND THE PASTOR

a. *The Pastor's Involvement.* It is not unusual for the pastor to feel ambivalent about this new tool provided him by the psychotherapist. Some, to be sure, have seized upon counseling as a respectable escape from the study or from pastoral calling. But many shy from counseling. It is demanding, soul-wearying work which seldom ends either in quick success or in recognition for his services. It is a crisis ministry. The pastor is plunged into all kinds of distressing situations: serious illness, mental breakdown, alcoholism, marriages on the verge of dissolution, spiritual depression or distress, bereavement – the entire gamut of human problems. Always he is looked to as the source of strength, calm, justice, and wisdom. Small wonder that often he feels inadequate and would prefer not to be involved. One can feel so much more useful and in control of himself and the situation when in the pulpit pronouncing profundities or generalities with a detached, "if the shoe fits, wear it," attitude. But the conscientious pastor is too conscious of our Lord's emphasis upon the obligation of shepherds and his blistering denunciation of faithless hireling shepherds to let himself get by with this detached maker-of-pronouncements role.

Preaching and counseling are neither antithetical nor independent of one another. What a minister preaches about and how he says it do much to determine whether or not he is sought out for counsel. In preaching he bares his fundamental attitudes toward people's weaknesses, their problems, and their sins. Either these attitudes create confidence that the minister is understanding and compassionate or they indicate that he is censorious and given to oversimplification. Fosdick once suggested that a good test of a sermon is the number of people who afterward want to see the minister alone. The pastor does well to ponder this. The counseling ministry, on the other hand, helps keep the individual and his problems real to the minister as he prepares his sermons, and as such they deliver him from the too human propensity to indulge in flights of oratorical generalities. Counseling experience not only produces a healthy respect for the complexity of personality but also a practical wisdom in human affairs which prompts one to eschew platitudes. As Richard Baxter pointed out, it is through faithful shepherding that one learns to become a good shepherd.

b. *The Pastor's Self-Understanding.* Central to all effective shepherding, particularly that aspect we speak of as counseling, is self-knowledge. The Apostle Paul, in his concluding instructions to Timothy, points out that to progress in the ministry one must progress as a person, and to progress personally he does well to "take heed to yourself and to your teaching" (I Tim. 4:16). Self-understanding facilitates one in his understanding of others, for in an existential way it underscores human complexity. Prejudice, oversimplification, and that facile (usually unconscious) but egregious error that the counselor is formed from nobler clay than the counselee fall before the inroads of genuine sell-understanding, for self-confrontation quickly elicits an echo of the words of Barnabas and Paul to the people of Lystra, "We also are men, of like nature with you" (Acts 14:15a). A pervasive sense of his own humanity, with all its complexities and contradictions, helps to immunize the counselor against simplistic and facile responses to human need. Rather the wise counselor learns from the Prophet Ezekiel, who, when commissioned to speak God's message to Israel, sat dumb among the people for seven days; similarly he seeks first to acquaint himself with some thoroughness with those whom he seeks to help.

c. *The Pastor's Relationship to His Family and Others.* The "Fighting Angel" is Pearl Buck's withering description of growing up in a minister's home. Clergymen and their wives, who, being aware of their inadequacies as parents and the competing demands of the congregation with those of the family, cannot dismiss reactions such as Pearl Buck's as mere perversity. The thoughtful pastor recognizes that the Apostle Paul, bachelor though he was, placed a premium on good family life. When discussing fitness for leadership in the church Paul said, "He must manage his own household well . . . for if a man does not know how to manage his own household, how can he care for God's church?" (I Tim. 3:4, 5 RSV).

Wise family nurture avoids both "rule them with an iron hand" and "familism," the idolatrous retreat into the family circle to the neglect of vocational responsibility. Wise family nurture recognizes that effectively disciplined, winsome children are those who identify with a mother and father who are loving, sensitive, empathetic, and able to be firm enough to protect their children from being dominated by their own immature, undisciplined impulses. Such parents are essentially fulfilled people, who find their primary emotional satisfaction in the husband-wife relationship. Few things leave a counselor more vulnerable to possible sexual complications growing out of the counseling relationship than the lack of a satisfactory home life. If a minister cannot enjoy a family outing without feeling guilty that he "ought" to be doing something at the church; if he is usually so preoccupied when at home that little or no meaningful personal interchange takes place between himself and his wife and children; if, out of anxiety or ambition, he feels compelled to maintain a façade of outward perfection which neither allows him nor any member of his household the normal human prerogative of mistakes; or if his wife insists on placing him upon a pedestal so that he cannot relax and be human even at home, he has potentially explosive problems that require immediate attention.

Relationships with one's colleagues may degenerate into a source of chronic personal tensions which have a vitiating effect upon the counseling ministry. Competitiveness, envy, inferiority feelings, and the sense of failure do not cease to plague those who enter the Christian ministry. The minister knows this. Nevertheless he may find it humiliating to discover these in himself and when he does may be too embarrassed to confess them or may not be able to find one whose Christian understanding he trusts with this burden. These feelings then continue to create inner barriers to healing fellowship with his colleagues.

Ambition and the sense of competence are part of our human equipment. Without these, a dull apathy often sets in. And yet in the ministry it is difficult to determine whether or not one is doing well. The temptation to measure one's effort against that of others is great indeed. The pastor needs the constant reminder that God's ways are not our ways, that "the race is not to the swift, nor the battle to the strong." He, too, cannot be told too often that having entered the Christian life by grace he continues in it on the same basis, responsible for doing what he does faithfully, with a sense of wonder and gratitude at being a member of the household of God. To the degree he genuinely grasps this he keeps his perspective clear, is freed for deep friendships among his colleagues, and for far more constructive dealings with his enemies.

3. COUNSELING AND HUMAN BEHAVIOR

a. *The Simplistic Approach to Personality.* The pastor's working view of human behavior has much to do with his effectiveness as a counselor. By "working view" I mean the attitudes which genuinely influence his evaluation and his approach to people; these may or may not be related to his formal (verbalized) view of behavior.

One working view of behavior which exerts widespread, if unconscious, influence upon counseling is based upon the following premises:

1. Man is a rational creature. This means he is fully conscious of his behavior and has the power to assume full control over it if he wishes. Behavior problems are rooted in ignorance, erroneous choices, perverse choices, or weakness.
2. There is a one-to-one relationship between inner personality factors and external acts, i.e., a simple relationship between symptoms and causes.
3. Since symptoms and their causes are not differentiated, treatment aims at the elimination of symptoms, i.e., the offending behavior, for to eliminate the undesirable behavior is to effect a cure.
4. Therapy consists in combining education with exhortation. To bring about constructive change the troubled person first must be convinced that what he is doing is wrong. This accomplished, he must be shown what is right and, if necessary, be convinced that it

> is in fact right. Exhortation to strengthen resolve is of particular importance, since to change one only has to want to badly enough, then follow directions. Hence if a person does not bring his behavior into line with his counselor's exhortation, it is easy to censure him as not serious about his problem.

This view may be described as simplistic, although since it so easily slips into condemnation and scolding it is more often spoken of as moralistic. There is a tendency among those who operate from this perspective to be more concerned with labeling behavior as right or wrong than to discover what is the matter and how to help. Let us, however, be clear about what is being said here. No attempt is being made to minimize the value of earnest resolve nor a sound sense of direction. But these may not be enough. Behavior is incredibly more complex than this essentially Pelagian concept of behavior implies.

b. *The "Depth" Approach.* The pastor does well to bear in mind the words of Samuel, "the Lord sees not as man sees; man looks on the outward appearance, but the Lord looks on the heart" (I Sam. 16:7 RSV). A person's acts may be quite simply motivated, e.g., a man scratches because he is flea bitten. But this same behavior pattern may have an incredibly complex origin, e.g., a man scratches because "insects are crawling beneath his skin." In the latter instance tactile hallucinations are involved. These may result from addiction to sniffing cocaine (the "cocaine bug"). Sometimes, however, it results from lead or other chemical poisoning, a by-product of a man's efforts to support his family rather than his misbehavior. The particular form of expression is a product of the specific cause. the person's history and psychic make up, and, possibly, factors in the immediate environment. Some factors are apparent to the sufferer, others he can bring to mind, but crucial elements may be beyond voluntary recall. His behavior baffles himself as well as others.

A "depth" view of behavior, then, proceeds from the premise that the relationship between a pattern of behavior and its cause may be complex and difficult to understand. It is nevertheless meaningful. Problem behavior usually represents an inept and destructive attempt to express some basic need. Hence the sensitive pastor focuses primarily on *why* he is doing what he is doing. It is not enough to be concerned merely with *what* he is doing. The focus is upon motives, upon the inner life, upon what the person is trying to do. In some measure this includes unconscious fears, hopes, and goals. These must be sufficiently understood to make clear how a person can come to terms with reality in such a way that he feels lovable, able to love others, and able to contribute his part toward the common good.

Much trouble-making behavior, then, represents an effort to manage feelings of anxiety, guilt, loneliness, meaninglessness, or resentment. Men have differed concerning the ultimate source of these, e.g., Freud regarded it as the repression of forbidden but pleasurable impulses; Adler the striving for superiority; and Otto Rank the conflict between the wish to become a distinct individual and the fear of loss of relatedness. More recently O. Hobart Mowrer has argued that guilt over not living up to the best that is in one is the source of trouble, while Viktor Frankl regards its source as the failure to find sufficient meaning for one's life. The Biblical diagnosis is estrangement from God, rising from mistrust of him and his intentions and a false trust in oneself. This attitude introduced a destructive element into human relations and human creativity, grossly complicated man's search for identity, and left him prone to temptations arising from the sense of isolation, of vulnerability, and of meaninglessness.

What these views share is the idea that men are confronted daily with crucial decisions in which there is risk of being hurt. The presence of a crucial risk generates anxiety ranging in intensity from vague uneasiness to terror-stricken panic, a sufficiently uncomfortable experience that it may readily substitute itself for the real problem. One of Sigmund Freud's major contributions to our understanding of behavior problems is that a person's response to an anxiety-laden conflict may be to seek to eliminate the anxiety per se rather than seek a solution for the problem which gives rise to the anxiety. The (often) unconscious "choice" to avoid risk or decision involves psychic maneuvers which distort reality and deceive oneself. These include repression, displacement, rationalization, the development of phobic or compulsive behaviors, and emotional withdrawal.

Many problems brought to the pastor represent this process of defense: alcoholism, drug addiction, depression, marital and family tensions, perhaps even chronic bodily ailments. Some of these defenses are such that they become problems in themselves and must then be dealt with as well as the underlying problem. A case in point is alcoholism, in which the person's problem-drinking must first be stopped, although that alone will not solve the person's problem. The excessive drinking may have begun as a way of solving the problem of shyness or inferiority feelings.

Religious attitudes and practices when used as ego defenses are particularly stubborn. This is not a palatable idea for some ministers, but it is not an idea invented by Freud. The prophets and apostles distinguished between religion of the letter and religion of the spirit. They criticized vigorously the former. Critiques of the religious life issued by twentieth century psychotherapists merely echo the prophets and apostles as they underscore the danger of clothing "an essentially pagan and idolatrous concept of God with Christian symbols," to borrow Rollo May's phrase. There are, then, from the counselor's perspective, two distinct forms of the religious life. The basis for distinction lies not in the central object of worship, nor in differences of doctrinal formulation, nor in the simplicity or complexity of the order of worship. Rather it is based upon attitude: whether the person's religious commitment is being used to retreat from or fight a holding action against life, or whether his faith gives him courage to face life, find strength in adversity and impetus to abandon his self-centeredness in service to God and man. Probably both sets of attitudes exist side by side in every Christian, but one or the other usually gains ascendance. Thus a person's faith may be the springboard to a larger life or it may be an infantilizing securing operation. What makes faith-as-security-operation so difficult a defense to set aside is the ease with which it acquires the cloak of sanctity (obedience, humility, willingness to suffer for Christ's sake).

4. THE CONTRIBUTION OF COUNSELING

Personal difficulties which represent a person's security operation require special handling. Ordinarily when a person refuses to face his problems and employs diversionary measures, we bring him up short. His subterfuges are pointed out to him — not always in loving terms. The more frightened a person is, however, the less such an approach is likely to be helpful. Head on assault tends either to stiffen defenses or to shatter the person. Counseling seeks to bring about healing. Hence its approach is to try to make it safe for the person to drop his guard. What is wanted is not acquiescence based on the counselor's psychological insight or the force of his character. Such surface compliance is not difficult for a minister to procure. What is wanted is singlemindedness, wholehearted openness. To gain this the counselor learns to communicate his love; his respect for the unique qualities, experience and viewpoint of his counselee; and his wish to understand rather than to judge. Hence the emphasis upon the proper understanding of personality must be supplemented by loving concern and respect, for, in the words of Dorothy L. Sayers, "The only way of 'mastering' one's material is to abandon the whole conception of mastering and to cooperate with it in love: whoever will be a lord of life, let him be its servant. If he tries to wrest life out of its true nature, it will revenge itself in judgment, as the work revenges itself upon the domineering artist" (*The Mind of the Maker,* Meridian Books, p. 173). This is the attitude of the good shepherd, who knows his sheep by name and who leads them out of their personal wilderness. His voice gives them confidence. This shepherd of souls creates a sense of community among the members of the flock, so that adversity draws them together rather than scattering them. In this way they discover what it means to be a member of the community of Christ's beloved.

Several subsequent articles will deal with the counseling process. Others will seek to provide understanding of certain recurring pastoral problems. These can provide a useful orientation to the neophyte and review to the veteran pastor. But it is no substitute for a program of supervised training in pastoral care. Such programs are being made more and more available as properly trained chaplain-supervisors are being placed in many of the hospitals in larger cities. The pastor who seeks out such training stands to accrue great benefits on behalf of those to whom he will minister.

BIBLIOGRAPHY

Allport, Gordon, *Becoming: Basic Considerations for a Psychology of Personality.* New Haven: Yale University Press, 1955.

———————, *The Individual and His Religion:* A Psychological Interpretation. New York: Macmillan, 1951.

Arnold, Magda B. and Gasson, John A., *The Human Person:* An Approach to an Integral Theory of Personality. New York: Ronald Press, 1954.

Bugental, J. F. T., *The Search for Authenticity.* Holt, Rinehart & Winstrom, 1965.

Buhler, Charlotte, *Values in Psychotherapy.* Free Press, 1962.

Frankl, Viktor, *Man's Search for Meaning:* An Introduction to Logotherapy. New York: Washington Square Press (W 642), 1963.

Frame, John D., *Personality: Development in the Christian Life.* Moody, 1961.

Glasser, William, *Reality Therapy.* Harper & Row, 1965.

Goldbrunner, Josef, *Cure of Mind and Cure of Soul.* Pantheon, 1955.

Hulme, William E., *Counseling and Theology.* Muhlenberg, 1956.

Laing, R. D., *The Divided Self: A Study of Sanity and Madness.* Chicago: Quadrangle Books, 1960.

———————, *The Self and Others:* Further Studies in Sanity and Madness. Chicago: Quadrangle Books, 1962.

McKenzie, J. G., *Nervous Disorders and Religion.* Allen and Unwin, 1951.

Menninger, Karl, *The Vital Balance:* The Life Process in Mental Health and Illness. New York: Viking Press, 1963.

Oates, Wayne, *Religious Factors in Mental Illness.* Association Press, 1955.

Outler, Albert C., *Psychotherapy and the Christian Message.* Harper, 1954.

Roberts, David, *Psychotherapy and the Christian View of Man.* New York: Scribner's, 1950.

Sullivan, Harry Stack, *The Interpersonal Theory of Psychiatry.* New York: W. W. Norton, 1953.

Tournier, Paul, *The Meaning of Persons.* New York: Harpers, 1957.

————————, *Guilt and Grace.* Harper and Row, 1962.

Walker, Daniel D., *The Human Problems of the Minister.* Harper, 1960.

White, Robert W., *Lives in Progress,* Second Edition. New York: Holt, Rhinehart and Winston, 1966.

Emotional Involvement and Pastoral Care

As we can all easily observe in everyday life, people misinterpret each other and distort ordinary communications in seemingly absurd fashions. But these distortions are no laughing matter when a wife misinterprets why her husband came home late, or when the soprano takes the choir director's suggestions as a personal insult. Such distortions are always present in the personal encounters of pastoral care, particularly so because the pastor is dealing with acute crises and emotionally charged situations.

Recognition and investigation of these distortions began with Freud in his early years of psychoanalytic experience when he found that as the analysis progressed the patient began to treat him as if he were some emotionally important figure from prior life. It appeared that the patient transferred disturbing ideas and feelings onto the figure of the physician which he did "through a false connection." Further experience has demonstrated that this transference is the repetition of memories of the past applied to the current situation, and in addition is an adaptive maneuver, that is, the patient begins to adopt infantile behavior in relation to the therapist. What we have been describing in the patient is *transference neurosis.*

However more general distortions which affect both the therapist and patient are observed in all counseling situations. Harry Stack Sullivan described these distortions quite clearly under the name of *parataxic distortions.* What Sullivan observed was that we often ignore the real characteristics of the other person and behave as if the relationship were quite different from its reality. It is as if *you* and *me* were several different persons during an interpersonal encounter. For example, during a business consultation between a pastor and deacon the relationship might shift between that of father-son, brother-brother, teacher-pupil, bully-coward, God-sinner, mother-infant, boss-worker, and so on. One can observe many examples of parataxic distortions in marriages. One husband was always suspicious of his wife when she talked to other men. It turned out that his mother had carried on illicit love affairs and so he ascribed his mother's attitude to his wife's behavior. In another case the wife became violently angry with her husband when he did not discipline the children. Although he was concerned about the children she mistook his passiveness for the disinterest her own father had displayed.

These parataxic distortions in a counseling relationship can be used to therapeutic advantage by the therapist when they can be pointed out and interpreted to the patient. However, when these distortions are overlooked, accepted as reality, reacted to or mutually reciprocated by the therapist, they may interfere with or even vitiate therapy.

The third and final distortion may be called *chronic personality distortions.* These are the distortions due to fixed habitual patterns of reaction. The always angry, persistently passive, eagerly erotic, habitually humble, or durably dominant, are all types of characters that stand out because they cannot modulate their relationships to others according to the needs of the situation. More commonly such chronic personality distortions are evoked in particular emotional encounters. For example, the pastor who cannot accept his own dependent feelings may react with hostility to the old, the young, the helpless, or any who try to emotionally lean upon him. Or a pastor who fears his own anger may not be able to firmly maintain discipline with the adolescents of his church. Chronic personality distortions reflect unresolved conflicts which have been fixed in the personality and result in stereotyped responses in interpersonal relations such that the person is insensitive to the feelings, reactions, and needs of the other person, and cannot respond in appropriate fashion.

1. TRANSFERENCE IN PASTORAL CARE

By virtue of his ministerial role the pastor is placed in a position of symbolic conflict. In an article "The Minister and Congregation: A study of Ambivalence," Rosenzweig points out that the minister is a father-authority figure who is representative of God. As such, he is the object of the universal ambivalence toward father-authority: on the one hand veneration and respect, on the other hand resentment, rebellion, and hostility. Often this ambivalence is split between members of the congregation or even acted out in church divisions where the positivism leads some to fanatic loyalty to the pastor, while the negativism leads others to form a new church. In lesser form, this same ambivalence feeds much of the petty rivalries that seem to flourish in most churches.

On a more personal level the pastor is personified as God and as such is subject to the distortions made of God. Anyone observing children can readily see their anthropomorphic concepts of God modeled on their own parents. Unfortunately many Christians never give up their anthropomorphic God who remains a distortion of their own mother and father relationships. These infantile God-images ultimately affect the pastoral role. If God is a mean old man, an aloof disinterested father, a violent unpredictable parent, so too may be the pastor in the eyes of his parishioner. The person who sees God as a protective, all-giving, warm mother may expect the pastor to be all-giving and ever-protective, and react with anger if the pastor does not fulfill all these expectations.

These identifications account for many of the guilt feelings the parishioner experiences with his pastor and reacts to with anger. And although the pastor may behave in a quite innocuous fashion he may be treated as if he were vigorously condemning the person. Rebellious members, particularly adolescents, may react to the authority of the pastor-God image by flouting their skepticism or disdaining the conventions of church behavior. On the other hand, those who react to authority with a passive-submissive stance may acquiesce to all suggestions as if they were commands. Or they may react angrily if the pastor does not give them explicit guidance or commands to follow. They demand to be told what to do.

Sexual transferences are likewise common. The woman who overvalued and idealized her father may overestimate the pastor and regard the pastor's wife as a rival. This woman may overpraise the pastor, offer to do extra work, or defend his ideas to all comers. By her actions she hopes to win the pastor's recognition and approval just as she had tried with her father. Unfortunately, this breeds jealousy and anger if the pastor does not give her the rewards she feels she merits. Some people become defensive when their sexual impulses are stimulated and they fear the expression of the impulses. Thus the pastor may provoke negativism to a warm intense personal approach which the parishioner experiences as sexually stimulating. The pastor is well advised to refrain from physical contacts as well as intimate gestures which may provoke unwanted sexual phantasies or frightened withdrawal.

Grief is another setting for frequent distortions. The bereaved person may blame God for sickness or death and project his anger on to the pastor. For example, a young mother lost her eldest son from protracted cancer. The pastor had kept an all-night vigil with the parents, but when the child died the mother screamed in rage, cursed abuses at God, and then turned to beat the pastor with her fists.

Another problematic group are the elderly members of the congregation who may react to the pastor in quite opposite fashions. On the one hand they may resent the young man who is seen as replacing them or challenging their wisdom, while on the hand they may wish to become childishly dependent on the pastor who becomes a type of watchful concerned son for them.

The recognition of transference distortions is necessary for the pastor if he is to avoid accepting them as real and relating to him personally. Some indicators of transference reactions may be noted:

1. Frequent requests for individual attention.
2. An unusually intense emotional reaction to routine situations.
3. A person in a group who reacts differently than the rest to you.
4. Overly positive or overly negative responses to routine pastoral work.
5. Requests for counseling in unusual places, times, or situations.
6. Demands that the pastor resolve personal problems or make personal decisions for a parishioner.
7. Failure to keep appointments or fulfill obligations.
8. Overscrupulous performance of duties, especially if related to the pastor's work.

2. COUNTERTRANSFERENCE IN PASTORAL CARE

The most difficult task to learn in psychotherapy is how to handle one's own reactions to the emotional currents of intense interpersonal relationships. The same problem is not less true for the pastor, particularly because he is socially and emotionally much more intimately involved with the people with whom he works.

The pastor who is afraid of his own aggressive impulses may have difficulty in being firm, or reacting with appropriate anger, or using his authority with judicious restraint but forthright conviction. The pastor who is afraid of his own sexuality may deny his erotic feelings in situations where he should be aware that he is responding in a sexually provocative or reactive fashion. Often pastors find women accusing them of improper advances while the pastor protests his innocence. Had the pastor recognized his own impulses he might have avoided playing into a mutual sexual distortion of the relationship.

Countertransference distortions occur when a pastor attempts to solve his own problems through the problems of the parishioner, or vicariously enjoys behavior in his parishioners which he feels he must deny in himself. For example, a youth pastor encouraged a young girl to extensively discuss her sexual phantasies, while another pastor encouraged a husband to abuse his wife.

Karl Menninger has called attention to a number of practical indications that may alert one to countertransference problems:

1. Carelessness in appointment schedules.
2. Repeated erotic or hostile feeelings.
3. Boredom or inattention during counseling.
4. Permitting or encouraging misbehavior.
5. Trying to impress your parishioners.
6. Arguing.
7. Taking sides in a personal conflict.
8. Premature reassurance to lessen anxiety.
9. Dreaming about a parishioner.
10. Feeling that the parishioner's welfare or solution to a problem lies solely with you.
11. Behavior toward one parishioner in a group differently from other group members.
12. Making unusual appointments or behaving in a manner unusual for you.

Although we have outlined many types of transference distortions it should be apparent that the pastor neither is professionally equipped nor is he in the type of counseling situation where it is appropriate to interpret distortions, even though he observes them. The pastor can best preserve his pastoral role and protect himself and his member from the vicissitudes of transference and countertransference problems by keeping the relationship a pastoral one, and focusing on the realities of the problem situation and the realities of the parishioner's life.

Finally, one of the best methods of maintaining perspective in one's counseling relations is periodical review with a constructive critic. Thus the pastor might systematically share his pastor care experiences with a reliable colleague or in consultation with a professional psychotherapist. Such sharing is vital in maintaining a realistic view of oneself. But even more importantly, an uninvolved third person has a unique vantage point from which to detect distortions of the counseling relationship.

BIBLIOGRAPHY

Clinebell, Howard J. Jr., *Mental Health Through Christian Community.* New York: Abingdon Press, 1965.

Faber, Heije and vander Schoot, Ebel, *The Art of Pastoral Conversation.* New York: Abingdon Press, 1965.

Oates, Wayne E., *Protestant Pastoral Counseling.* Philadelphia: Westminster Press, 1962.

Oates, Wayne E., ed., *The Minister's Own Mental Health.* Great Neck, N. Y.: Channel Press, 1961.

Dynamics and Process of Pastoral Counseling

Pastoral counseling occurs whenever a trinity of persons join to solve a human problem. First, there must be a person or persons with an existential problem. This may vary from the hidden hurts of childhood currently revealed in recurring anxiety or feelings of inadequacy or grief over the loss of a loved one or a temptation to sinful behavior. Then, there must be a pastor, a man of God, trained in the psychological skills that plumb the depths of human emotion and who is involved in an understanding of the needs of a suffering person. Finally, the Holy Spirit is directly and directionally present, initiating the pastor's concern and ministering to the sufferer's pain or conflict.

When a pastor, significantly related to his congregation, confronts a suffering and disturbed person, he brings with him the wealth of both psychological training and spiritual power. Without disputing the essential place of psychiatric specialists in dealing with mental illness in its more virulent and physiological forms, the Christian turns to the pastor for sensitive understanding and the resources of power and resolution that can come primarily from the caring of the church, and the profound concern it holds for the total range of man's existence, i.e., wholeness and holiness.

In this discussion of the process of pastoral counseling we shall assume that everyone understands that the church is first called to serve her Master, Jesus Christ through whom she knows the God who is the creator and concerned Father. Everything that will be said grows out of this primary assumption which claims that our concern for persons is firmly grounded in the love of God for all men everywhere.

It is C. W. Brister, in his *Pastoral Care in the Church,* who describes the cohesiveness of Christian faith and knowledge when he writes, "the pastor's primary clues about God, man, the world, Christian experience, and his vocation are givens of the Christian faith rather than discoveries of empirical knowledge" (p. xix). The pastoral task cannot be wedded to a superficial theology superimposed upon a sterile and technical psychotherapy. The heart of pastoral functioning is never anything less than *theology* rooted deeply in a finality of commitment to the living God and characterized by a tentativeness of our understanding of any part of the universe at any moment in history.

The pastoral counselor does indeed recognize that pastoral counseling is only one of many pastoral tasks. But since it is a strategic responsibility of his ministry, he develops a sense of timing without neglecting his other pastoral tasks so that he is emotionally available at the moment of crisis in any parishioner's need. There is no substitute for assuming full theological and personal responsibility in his ministry. He must indeed know the WHY (theoretical knowledge), the WHAT (theological information), and the HOW (technical skills) of his pastoral role. Here is the focusing of the wisdom of the basic Christian relationship transmitted through the Scriptures and the church, and contemporary clinical insights into human behavior and psychotherapy.

Counseling and psychotherapy may be seen functionally as at opposite ends of a continuum. A friend who hears one's problem, a sensitive teacher, a vocational guidance expert, a choir director who listens, and many others all do counseling. This counseling is focused on this moment's conflictual situation, with a close relationship but little or no reactivating of past meaningful or traumatic experiences between counselor and counselee, and the relationship usually serves its purpose in from one to ten hours.

Psychotherapy, on the other end of the continuum, usually lasts over a longer period (50-600 hours) and uses "transference," in which the patient projects upon the therapist his learned perception of important persons from his infancy and childhood, and results in a major reconstruction of the patient's character structure. It provides an opportunity for the person to relearn his attitudes toward himself and other significant persons in his life.

Since one's conception of man determines the goals and processes of counseling, an understanding of man's nature and need is of crucial importance. Learning theorists, by and large, see man as a mechanical robot with stimuli entering the respondable individual and behavior resulting (the stimulus-response paradigm). Conditioning (learning) occurs when the stimulus or stimulating environment produces a response, the strength of which may be measured. Psychoanalysts, by and large, see man as a bundle of drives, chief of which would be the pleasure principle (sexual in nature) or some mature sublimination of it, which demand fulfillment or balancing (homeostasis) or reduction through expression. These are basically neutral explanations (i.e. common sense) until their proponents seek to force their explanations as the *only* important facts. Neither description of man actually denies the Biblical Model of Man except when they leave no room for it.

Biblically speaking, in addition to the above models, man is created out of the same basic "dust of the earth" as the animals, but also he is created in "God's image" for fellowship with his fellowmen and with God (Gen. 1:26f; 2:7f). The record strongly suggests that the Creator also built in man's responsive ability to personal relations as well as his erotic drives. The Biblical account further states that the Creator designed a man-woman (male-female) relationship for the continuation of the human race and for community (or fellowship) (Gen. 4:1). Man is depicted as being responsible to a God who lives through history and in relationship with men. Man's later rejection, or post-creation rebellion, of God's companionship, implying strongly some element of self-direction, resulted in sin and man's bondage to "inner drives." The Biblical description of man's original nature sounds amazingly like that of the psychoanalyst's description of infantile, narcissistic, and neurotic personalities.

Shame, fear, and hate became part of man's nature after the fall along with purity, courage, and love as basic attitudes in man's behavior. But this fall from the original relationship, while leaving man vulnerable, is not the end of the story, for God through Jesus Christ restores a loving relationship. The aim of counseling (at least symbolically) and of salvation are very close (Eph. 2:

13-16); that is, to resolve hostility, to relieve anxiety, and to reconstruct personality. Two modes of potential personality change, (1) a radical "new birth" resulting in a new pattern of being, and (2) a continuous growth process, a becoming, are possible in man. Counseling and evangelism are both the responsibility of pastoral process with tragedy resulting when either is ignored – a temporary "adjustment" which soon fails, or a "falling-away" or "backsliding."

Pastoral care, in its ultimate definition, is the mutual care and concern of Christians for each other and for all persons for whom Christ lived and died. It locates its foundations in a Biblical theology and functions through the pastor's ability to consciously use himself. As a wise pastor once said, "no pastor can lead any one closer to God than he is himself."

We need to recognize here that European and American pastoral care spring from somewhat differing assumptions. Edward Thurneysen, Theodor Bovet, Ankor Nielson, and others would define pastoral care as the skills by which a pastor brings the Word of God into living touch with the needs of persons. Pastoral diagnosis would identify those things which separate the person from his Christ and would be followed by confession and the relating of the individual to God. European pastoral theologians, by and large, divide the responsibilities of pastors and psychotherapists clearly, one dealing with reconcilation, the other with the treatment of mental illness.

American pastoral theologians, on the other hand, usually fail to see any clear line of demarcation between emotional and spiritual conflicts, in fact see them as inseparably intertwined in mutual complexities. They see the "living documents" of Boisen, persons who sin and hurt, as needing the attention of the "pastoral psychotherapist," which they define as the pastoral counselor. For our purposes, these contrasts may be ignored for they only becloud the issue.

Note, however, that the same strong contrasts occur in strictly psychological theory. The psychological schools that emphasize patient autonomy do little but reflect the patient's feelings (the early Carl R. Rogers "non-directive" counseling). These are usually embedded in a rationalistic, humanistic conception of man. In contrast the behavioral or manipulative schools of therapy describe personality as basically a neurophysiological mechanism and attempt to manipulate it through conditioning techniques. Representative exponents of this school would be B. F. Skinner, Andrew Salter, and Albert Ellis.

Let us trust that time and experience will see that pastoral care and counseling, now split by the extreme of European and American pastoral theology and the contrasting schools of psychological treatment is brought into focus in the pastor who is prepared for every good work. To do so requires that the counselor learn such skills as (1) developing Christian concern that reaches out to the counselee's need without crippling his self-direction, (2) relating in authentic dialogue, and (3) developing an empathetic listening with "third-ear" sensitivity.

This skill in knowing when to do what is largely learned during supervised counseling, where the student-pastoral counselor carries out his task under the direction of an experienced counselor, and often uses tape recording, conferences, written case records, etc. to gain insight into what he is doing and why. This skill also comes out of personal involvement in a therapeutic experience, and in sensitive relationship with one's fellow learners.

Again, the pastor in his day to day visitation, and in his intimate knowledge of his people and in their trust in him, both refines his skills and prepares himself to join in the rest of this counseling trinity, under the direction of the Holy Spirit and in the presence of human need.

BIBLIOGRAPHY

Belgum, David, *Guilt: Where Psychology and Religion meet.* Prentice-Hall, 1963.

Bonhoeffer, Dietrich, *Ethics.* Macmillan, 1955.

Brister, C. W., *Pastoral Care in the Church.* Harper & Row, 1964.

Clebsch, William A. and Charles R. Jaekle, *Pastoral Care in Historical Perspective.* Prentice-Hall, 1964.

Coburn, John B., *Minister-man-in-the-middle.* Macmillan, 1963.

DeWire, Harry A., *The Christian as Communicator.* Westminster, 1961.

Godsey, John D., *The Theology of Dietrich Bonhoeffer.* Westminister, 1960.

Johnson, Paul E., *Psychology of Pastoral Care.* Abingdon, 1953.

Krill, Donald F., "Psychoanalysts, Mowrer and the Existentialists," *Pastoral Psychology,* Oct. 1965, Vol. 16, No. 157, pp. 27-36.

Leslie, Robert C., *Jesus and Logotherapy,* Abingdon, 1965.

Oates, Wayne E., *Religious Dimensions of Personality.* Association Press, 1957.

Pattison, Mansell, "Contemporary Views of Man in Psychology," *Journal of Religion & Health,* IV, 4, July 1965.

Roberts, David E., *Psychotherapy and a Christian View of Man.* Scribners, 1950.

Thurneysen, Eduard, *A Theology of Pastoral Care,* trans. Jack Worthington, John Knox Press, 1962.

The Process of Counseling

In this discussion of pastoral counseling our concern is exclusively with one type of pastoral counseling. We are not concerned with *evangelistic* counseling, a face-to-face encounter which has as its objective the exercise of redemptive faith in Jesus Christ. Nor are we concerned with *didactic* counseling, any attempt to explain doctrine, supply data, or dispense advice. Our sole concern now is with *therapeutic* counseling. This, no doubt, may at times overlap evangelistic and didactic counseling, but its goal, unlike their goals, is the relief of emotional disturbances and the reorientation of maladjusted personalities. Typically, therapeutic counseling occurs during or after a life-crisis, some situation which has placed an individual under such stress that his ordinary coping devices cannot handle it. Because of the restricted nature of pastoral therapy, it seems wise to ignore completely any technical classifications of the so-called neuroses and psychoses. In any event, the common and confusing terminology of technical classifications has been skillfully dissected by Karl Menninger in his *The Vital Balance,* a text which any minister ought to read before he undertakes counseling.

Counseling is a fluid, changing, and dynamic process, impossible of neat schematization. Yet in its ongoing certain phases may be isolated chronologically and logically, somewhat as we can isolate the depth, temperature, color, current, and purity of a river, aware even as we isolate them that they are simply aspects of one indivisible stream.

1. THE PHASE OF PREPARATION

Everything a pastor is and does lays the ground work for his counseling ministry. The whole range of his interpersonal transactions may be properly viewed as a preparation for the practice of spiritual therapy. The motives he discloses, the attitudes he manifests, the opinions he expresses, the doctrines he emphasizes, the values he espouses, his friendliness, his approachability, his understanding, his warmth, his discernment, his empathy, are all factors that induce people to seek a pastor's help. They bring church members to his door without his solicitation; they afford entrance into lives which might otherwise be inaccessibly locked and barred.

Let us assume this foundational relationship of trusted motive, demonstrated concern, and proved understanding. In many cases, nevertheless, before counseling *per se* can begin, need must be discovered and contact made. And in any case before counseling *per se* can begin, a definite appointment must be arranged.

2. THE PHASE OF RELAXATION

Usually a help-seeking individual is unfamiliar with the process of counseling. Beset by worries and sometimes burdened with misgivings and immured behind prejudices, he comes for the purpose of talking with his pastor, an authority figure whom he respects, the flesh-and-blood embodiment of conscience and morality. Often the counselee wishes to expose some skeletons which previously have been locked in the family closet. Several obstacles are therefore commonly encountered at the very outset of this relationship. There may be the reaction of nervousness. Tense and uncomfortable, the client wants to talk frankly, and yet he may be afraid. The disclosure of his serious difficulties may be construed, he thinks, as a reflection on the genuineness of his faith. Or the request for help may contradict his pose of self-sufficiency. Or the counselee may feel that he is virtually impugning the truth and adequacy of God Almighty. So nervousness may be rooted in a compost of anxiety, shame, and guilt. Again, there may be the barrier of hostility.

The counselee is entering into this relationship under duress: he has been compelled by sheer force of circumstances or he has been browbeaten into acquiescence by an individual, maybe his employer or his wife or a parent. He may, consequently, view the pastor as a source of threat rather than a source of help, an enemy rather than a friend. Conversely, there may be a naive attitude of quasi-awe. Lacking any realistic notion of what is going to transpire, the client may consider therapy a species of magic. He may fancy that there is some kind of pill or injection which the pastor can give him. Since his expectations are grossly erroneous, he may perceive the counselor as a supernatural helper. He may not realize that time and effort are involved; he may not realize, either, that the outcome of therapy will depend chiefly on his own cooperation.

Thus it is the counselor's job to modify reactions, correct mistaken notions, dispel illusions, scale down expectations, and break through barriers which impede free communication. He must, in short, establish a working relationship with his counselee. How can this be done?

If the counselee is a person whom the pastor knows, a friendly greeting suffices. If the person is unknown, however, the customary introductions take place as the pastor ushers him into the office or study. For counseling to be effective privacy and quiet are imperative. In addition, a pastor will be wise to protect himself against the hazards of gossip and blackmail. Ordinarily, though, these hazards are not especially serious.

As for the counselor himself, he is relaxed rather than formal. He does not sit down pompously behind his desk. That creates another barrier. He sits near his client, a short distance between them, placing his chair obliquely in order to obviate face-to-face staring. He does not engage in note-taking. Pen and pad may create one more barrier. His undivided attention is fixed on his counselee though not in an eagle-eyed scrutiny.

Sometimes, once an individual has been seated, he plunges without delay or inhibition into a recital of his problems. Such verbal outpouring eliminates, of course, need for any other preliminaries. But with many counselees ice-breaking proves imperative. Perhaps, then, there are a few casual questions about mutual acquaintances or interests. Perhaps prayer is offered, particularly if prayer is expected and the pastor can offer it sincerely. Prayer ought not be offered if it is a mere technique rather than a trustful petition for God's enablement.

In a majority of cases perhaps the best approach is to define the whole situation, explaining in simple terms what the counseling relationship is going to involve. The pastor may remark that the help-seeking individual has come because of a problem which he wants to discuss, but before the counselee even begins talking about his problem, a few things ought to be understood. People have problems of every sort and size; and we have learned, the pastor points out, that if they can talk about their problems in an atmosphere of trust and freedom, often they gain a new perspective, experience a great relief of tension, are able to make decisions more readily, and find themselves initiating changes in their behavior. Odd as it may seem, therefore, the mere talking about a problem can be surprisingly beneficial. The pastor may also point out, reassuringly, that no matter what problem may be bothering the counselee, such problems are by no means uncommon. A minister who has Scripture at his command may quote I Corinthians 10:13.

It may be pointed out, moreover, that the counselor's job is essentially to help the client help himself. The counselor uses no pills, no injections, no incantations. All he does is listen while the counselee talks — and, listening, tries his utmost to grasp what the counselee is really saying and feeling. Sometimes the counselor may break in to ask questions. And then eventually a plan of action can undoubtedly be worked out.

It may be pointed out, still further, that any material divulged in counseling is privileged communication. The counselee may, accordingly, be sure that whatever material he chooses to disclose will not be shared with anybody, including the pastor's wife and the counselee's spouse. Bear in mind, however, that, if the counselor is a chaplain or an administrator, he must avoid a possible conflict between his counseling role and any other role he is playing. To a more limited degree the same holds true with respect to a pastor. Then, too, caution will be needed if the material a counselee divulges proves to involve legal complications. But aside from such qualifications the counselor must guarantee that his counselee's disclosures will be kept in completest confidence. Failure to give such assurance may pollute the psychic atmosphere with suspicion and mistrust.

In defining the relationship between himself and his client, the pastor likewise states his own expectations. What is it that he, as a counselor, expects of his counselee? In short, he expects openness. Admittedly it is hard to be transparently honest with an authority-figure whose respect the counselee desires to keep. Yet the counselee will discover that, as he talks with his pastor in this new relationship, he will gradually be able to discuss troublesome things more and more freely. In later sessions he will probably experience little inhibition in talking about matters which he has hesitated to discuss at the outset.

In this threshold phase of counseling which has *rapport* as its goal, the pastor's attitude is all-important. Is he personally at ease? Is he calm, acceptant, understanding, and unhurried? Does he communicate a spirit of concern and friendliness? Is he the incarnation of a non-judgmental *agape* which breathes compassion rather than condemnation? If so, the tense, nervous, rigid individual may begin to thaw out and a productive relationship can be established.

Elusively mystical though it may sound, the pastor creates psychic atmosphere by what he is more than by what he says and does. All of us know from experience that there are conjunctive personalities with whom it is comparatively easy to establish a relationship. There are, on the other hand, disjunctive individuals with a peculiar genius for generating coldness and distance. Hence the pastor must seek to establish a relationship of freedom and acceptance without abandoning his own moral standards and without somehow suggesting contempt for the ethic and theology to which he is committed personally as well as professionally.

At the conclusion of this initial session the pastor may decide that he has neither the time nor aptitude for ministering therapeutically to this particular help-seeking individual. He may therefore tactfully suggest referral, mentioning the name of a counselor who is better qualified to be of help. He may discuss the possibility of referral, arrange for it, and even introduce his counselee by phone or in person to the new helping-agent.

3. THE PHASE OF EXPLORATION

Counseling is an opportunity for self-diagnosis, self-discernment, and self-discovery with a view to self-decision. We cannot too often remind ourselves that it is a process designed to help the help-seeking individual help himself. Exploration, consequently, is the very heart of this process. In pastoral counseling, however, the exploration is not carried on by free association, hypnosis, or psychodrama. It is carried on by conversation.

As counseling gets under way, the client generally talks about his contemporary problems, those difficulties which are acutely bothering him and of which he is painfully aware. But if counseling continues for a number of sessions, the customary pattern is, then, likely to be this: a session opens with the counselee verbalizing material concerning some immediate and pressing problem; he may then proceed autobiographically to tie the contemporary problem to past experience; after that he may shuttle back and forth between the two. That is why many counselors very flexibly employ the chronology of a counselee's development as a kind of Ariadne's thread: they follow up the sequence of significant episodes through which he has passed since infancy. Harry Stack Sullivan's *The Psychiatric Interview* is a penetrating guide for the pastoral counselor to use; it lists the salient and sensitive subjects which need to be covered in any genetic investigation.

The phase of exploration may be broken down into these factors.

a. *Verbalization.* Counseling essentially is a kind of monologic conversation between two people, one of whom, a help-seeking individual, does the lion's share of the talking while the other, the help-offering individual, listens empathically, occasionally offering a comment or asking a question. It includes, to be sure, all manner of nonverbal communication, but it is substantially a matter of verbal interaction. The counselor's objective is to motivate his client's verbalization of troubling problems. But sometimes that objective is most difficult to achieve, even assuming a high degree of *rapport*. So counseling may require an interrogative pump-priming, a tactful questioning which is the last remove from legal cross-examination.

Suppose, then, that the counselee can be encouraged to verbalize his problem. What is the counselor's function while this verbalization occurs? The counselor listens. His function, a difficult and demanding task, is concentrated listening, listening with his attention undivided. The counselor listens – empathically, permissively, responsively, understandingly, creatively. Yet as he listens he is hearing not primarily the words which are used – their dictionary signification, their logical coherence, or their grammatical structure. Primarily he is feeling the emotions which words as words may fail to convey. He is focusing not on what the person says, but rather on what the person means. Thus he listens, schooling himself to refrain from interruption.

The counselee's verbal flow can be facilitated by a responsive silence, a silence which non-verbally communicates the counselor's presence and receptivity. An inexperienced counselor may at first be disturbed by silence; yet silence can be very empathic, an opportunity for a counselee to collect his thoughts and reflect more deeply on what he has been struggling to communicate. Or the verbal flow may be encouraged by facial expression. It may be encouraged, too, by an occasional remark which signifies nothing except that counselor and counselee are still on the same wave-length. It may also be encouraged by the technique of picking up the end of the sentence and repeating it. Thus listening, empathic listening, is one of the most important tools in the therapeutic kit.

b. *Interrogation.* Some schools of counseling eschew dogmatically the use of questions, but in pastoral counseling inquiry usually proves inescapable. So the counselor, if his client seems to bog down unproductively, may move from contemporary problems to backlying issues, embarking on the genetic or biographical investigation previously mentioned. It must be understood, however, that relentless grilling, a kind of third-degree, is not intended. The pastor's questions are entirely a pump-priming operation. Their function is to induce the client's continued verbalization.

c. *Reflection.* The counselor serves somewhat as a mirror, if that metaphor can be personalized. Verbally he gives back what the client has been saying. He repeats the disclosure, echoing it with virtually no modification. Why? The mere repetition of a statement sometimes enables a person to catch the import of what he has been ambiguously communicating. He hears it re-echoed by the counselor, and the very hearing induces clear perception for the very first time.

d. *Clarification.* This overlaps reflection and springs directly from it. The counselor reformulates in different words what the client has told him. In addition, he puts into words the emotional undertones and nuances of his counselee's disclosure.

e. *Interpretation. As sessions continue the* counselor may begin to venture some possible explanations. He may suggest reasons and causes. These are evaluated by the counselee and discarded if he feels they are inept or erroneous. Hence several things are vitally important. Interpretation requires skill, a sense of timing, an intuitive sensitivity which a counselor gains only by experience. A counselor, accordingly, needs a great measure of self-restraint. Repeatedly he is tempted to offer an insight which strikes him as screamingly obvious. But until the counselee is able to grasp an insight for and by himself, he remains astonishingly impervious to even the most obvious reasons and causes. Furthermore, the counselor must offer interpretation with utmost tentativeness, insisting that the counselee modify or reject it at will. Thus the counselor prefaces any interpretation with a remark like, "I may be a hundred miles off target, but I am wondering whether. . . ." The counselor must not forget that his counselee may be all too ready to accept gullibly the counselor's merest opinion as an authoritative diagnosis, and that such acceptance may nevertheless be wholly superficial.

It is impossible to predict in any specific case the number of sessions which this phase of exploration may occupy. A pastor may counsel with an individual only once on the other hand, he may counsel with an individual for months on end. There are imponderables which differ enormously in every instance. Freud, for example, once suggested that analysis might be interminable. But a pastor will usually settle for short-term therapy of five or six sessions. His aim is not to make the unconscious conscious or to induce any major personality-change unless the Holy Spirit supernaturally induces it. As a rule, the pastor's aim is to help his counselee work out his more disruptive problems and as a result continue to be a functioning member of society.

4. THE PHASE OF EXTERIORIZATION

As a client verbalizes his problems, he does something else simultaneously: he concretizes, objectifies, and exteriorizes those problems. He is managing to get outside what has been disturbing him inside. William James expressed it vividly, "we must exteriorize our rottenness." Rottenness may be too strong a term in all instances, but James was incontestably right. Our problems must be brought out into the open. What happens, then, as they are thus exposed?

a. *Abreaction.* Often a strong outburst of feeling occurs, anger, or grief, or shock. Emotionally the counselee relives some traumatic experiences. They may have been childish, or frustrating, or even terrorizing. Now, perhaps long afterward, their effect is once more experienced, sometimes moderately, sometimes with an almost incredible strength. Tears are by no means infrequent even when men are being counseled.

b. *Catharsis.* The resurrection of past feelings brings about a measure of emotional purgation. Rather literally the counselee gets the burden off his chest and the weight off his shoulders. At this juncture the pastor may urge that his client practice Hebrews 4:15-16, "For we have not a high priest which cannot be touched with the feeling of our infirmities; but was in all points tempted like as we are, yet without sin. Let us therefore come boldly unto the throne of grace, that we may obtain mercy, and find grace to help in time of need." When the writer admonishes his readers to come to the throne of grace boldly, he is literally admonishing them to come without inhibition, spilling everything out, keeping nothing back. Thus even in a Protestant context counseling can be the equivalent of a confessional: divine acceptance is experienced with a consequent sense of cleansing and relief.

Catharsis is a discharge of emotional steam, a desensitizing of psychic inflammation and pain. It is much akin to the lancing of a boil. Emotion is drained out, and quite commonly a feeling of liberation obtained.

c. *Insight.* As the counselee objectifies and exteriorizes his problem, it is almost as though he were getting it out of a dark basement into sunlight where he can actually see it and evaluate it for what it is. Hence another consequence of exteriorization is sharpened perspective, a deepened understanding of what and how and why.

In counseling, moments of illumination may dawn very dramatically: light virtually begins to shine on a person's face. But insight may also be gained between sessions, gropingly and slowly with a gradual dissipation of confusion.

5. THE PHASE OF REORIENTATION

After a sequence of, typically, five or six sessions, the counselor may feel that the phase of investigation has been carried on in sufficient depth. Since he is not engaged in psychoanalytic dredging, the pastor may decide that the time has come for an attempt at reorientation. How is this achieved?

a. *Review.* The counselor may suggest that the counselee summarize the material covered, mentioning any insights which have been gained. Or the counselor may elect to do this himself, using his client's phraseology whenever possible, asking now and then, "Is that what you told me? Wasn't that what we found out? Do I have that straight? Is there anything I have omitted?"

b. *Reconnaisance.* Once the review has been concluded to the mutual satisfaction of both counselee and counselor, a key question can be raised: What are the viable solutions to this situation? Counselor and counselee mention all the possibilities that come to mind. Then each of these is canvassed exhaustively, *pro* and *con*. As this is done several options will loom up as viable while others are discarded as impracticable.

c. *Decision*. After the possibilities have thus been narrowed down, the counselor helps the client elect that course of action which seems most advisable. Here is a delicate maneuver indeed. The choice must be the choice of the counselee. Yet the counselor can scarcely avoid weighing the scales in favor of whatever option impresses him as most advisable. Hence candor, honesty, and straightforwardness are called for. Aware of his self-involvement, the counselor must prevent his own prejudice and desires from controlling the outcome.

d. *Program*. The counselor and counselee must map out step by step the concrete implementation of the decision which has been mutually reached. All too frequently, however, a counselor leaves his counselee floundering with no course of action projected. It seems advisable, therefore, for the counselee to know exactly what he is going to do first after he leaves the office. Suppose, by way of illustration, that there has been an agreement on the need for a deepened relationship to God. Then tomorrow at a certain time prayer is to be offered and the Bible is to be read, perhaps even specific passages assigned. In some cases direct intervention in a client's life-situation seems warranted. Pastoral counseling calls for environmental manipulation as perhaps no other form of counseling does. This is not overly directive, considered in the light of the pastor's role. He is a spiritual advisor, a shepherd who must lead his people.

6. THE PHASE OF TERMINATION

Let us suppose that the client's symptoms have been rather successfully handled. Let us suppose, further, that pastor and counselee together decide nothing of value is to be attained by additional sessions. Then the time for the termination of this relationship has arrived.

In professional counseling there is what Harry Stack Sullivan calls the formal leave-taking. Such a severance of relationship does not occur, however, in pastoral counseling unless the counselee is outside the counselor's church. The termination is much less formal and final. Nevertheless, it may prove to be a minor crisis, causing the counselee to feel both helpless and rejected. The unique relationship which counseling requires cannot be established without the development of friendliness and intimacy. In pastoral counseling, to be sure, the so-called transference is not liable to be experienced as intensely as it is in other types of counseling but the pastor must realize that deep emotions have probably been aroused and that he has become the object of affectional feelings. The dissolution of this unique relationship, a preferential relationship of dependence and pleasure, should then be brought about with a minimum of negative reaction. The pastor can frankly discuss the emotions which have been aroused and which may now be aroused. He can also emphasize that the goal of counseling is autonomy: the individual must learn to stand on his own feet; he must not permit himself to exist as a kind of clinging vine. In fact, if counseling has been at all successful, there ought to be increased freedom. Yet at the same time the pastor may point out the possibilities of future difficulty and make provision for a return visit if that is advisable. Perhaps he may quote Proverbs 24:16, "A just man falleth seven times, and riseth up again." He may use the analogy of climbing a mountain peak. Though the movement is steadily upward, there are times when one goes down into shadowed valleys and stumbles through rocky ravines before it is obvious that he is still gradually ascending.

In this concluding phase of counseling it is certainly appropriate for the pastor to offer prayer if he so desire, committing his counselee to the guidance and enabling of the Holy Spirit.

7. THE PHASE OF HABITUATION

The pre-counseling stage of preparation is paralleled by a post-counseling stage of experimentation as the client struggles to consolidate his gains, readjust his attitudes, and cultivate new modes of behavior. It is only by practice in the context of everyday living that old habits of feeling, thinking, and acting are gradually supplanted; it is only by practice that new habits are gradually strengthened until they become ingrained, forming a kind of second nature. Thus without compromising the counselee's autonomy the pastor may – and very often must – continue to play a supportive role. If the counselee is a member of his church, he can exchange a few words with him after a service or conveniently discover an opportunity for brief conversation. He can make use of the telephone. He can mail a note or a card or a booklet. By one means or another the pastor can nurture and guide and motivate, revealing his continued interest and his steadfast concern. Above all, he can carry on a ministry of intercession. If pastoral counseling is unique in any respect, it ought to be unique in its open acknowledgment that help and healing come ultimately from God. Pastoral counselors ought to confess gratefully that the most skillful of spiritual therapists is simply the agent of a gracious Lord.

BIBLIOGRAPHY

The outline which has been followed comes with modifications, from Wayne E. Oates, *The Christian Pastor,* Rev. ed., Philadelphia: The Westminster Press, 1954, pp. 192-219. My indebtedness to Dr. Oates is gratefully acknowledged.

Other works which may be profitably consulted are the following:

Bergsten, Gote, *Pastoral Psychology.* New York: The Macmillan Company, 1951.

Bonnell, John Sutherland, *Pastoral Psychiatry.* New York: Harper & Brothers Publishers, 1938.

Bovet, Theodor, *That They May Have Life.* London: Darton, Longman & Todd, 1964.

Brister, C. W., *Pastoral Care in the Church.* New York: Harper & Row, Publishers, 1964.

Bruder, Ernest E., *Ministering to Deeply Troubled People.* Englewood Cliffs, N. J.: Prentice-Hall, Inc., 1963.

Doty, James Edward, *The Pastor as Agape Counselor.* Indianapolis, Indiana: John Woolman Press, Inc., 1964.

Drakeford, John W., *Counseling for Church Leaders.* Nashville, Tennessee: Broadman Press, 1961.

Ducker, E. N., *Psychotherapy: A Christian Approach.* London: George Allen & Unwin Ltd., 1964.

Godin, Andre, *The Pastor as Counselor.* New York: Holt, Rinehart and Winston, 1965.

Hiltner, Seward, *The Christian Shepherd.* New York: Abingdon Press, 1959.

———————, *The Counselor in Counseling.* New York: Abingdon-Cokesbury Press, 1952.

———————, *Pastoral Counseling.* New York: Abingdon-Cokesbury Press, 1949.

———————, *Preface to Pastoral Theology.* New York: Abingdon Press, 1958.

Hiltner, Seward and Colston, Lowell G., *The Context of Pastoral Counseling.* New York: Abingdon Press, 1961.

Hulme, William E., *Counseling and Theology.* Philadelphia: Muhlenberg Press, 1956.

Johnson, Paul E., *Psychology of Pastoral Care.* New York: Abingdon-Cokesbury Press, 1953.

Kemp, Charles F., *The Pastor and Vocational Counseling.* St. Louis, Mo.: The Bethany Press, 1961.

Lynch, William F., *Images of Hope.* Baltimore. Helicon, 1965.

Menninger, Karl, et. al., *The Vital Balance.* New York: The Viking Press, 1963.

Moser, Leslie E., *Counseling: A Modern Ephasis in Religion.* Englewood Cliffs, N. J.: Prentice-Hall, Inc., 1962.

Moser, Lesie E. and Ruth Small Moser, *Counseling and Guidance: An Exploration.* Englewood Cliffs, N. J.: Prentice-Hall, Inc., 1963.

Oates, Wayne E., ed., *An Introduction to Pastoral Counseling.* Nashville, Tennessee: Broadman Press, 1959.

Oates, Wayne E., *Protestant Pastoral Counseling.* Philadelphia: The Westminster Press, 1962.

Olsen, Peder, *Pastoral Care and Psychotherapy.* Minneapolis, Minnesota: Augsburg Publishing House, 1961.

Scherzer, Carl J., *Ministering to the Physically Sick.* Englewood Cliffs, N. J.: Prentice-Hall, Inc., 1963.

Schmidt, Lyle D. and McGowan, John F., *Counseling: Reading in Theory and Practice.* New York: Holt Rinehart and Winston, Inc., 1962.

Schofield, William, *Psychotherapy: The Purchase of Friendship.* Englewood Cliffs, N. J.: Prentice-Hall, Inc., 1964.

Sullivan, Harry Stack, *The Psychiatric Interview.* New York: W. W. Norton & Company, Inc., 1962.

Tarachow, Sidney, *An Introduction to Psychotheraphy.* New York: International Universities Press, Inc., 1963.

Thornton, Edward E., *Theology and Pastoral Counseling.* Englewood Cliffs, N. J.: Prentice-Hall, Inc., 1964.

Tournier, Paul, *The Whole Person in a Broken World.* New York: Harper & Row, Publishers, 1964.

Tweedie, Donald F. Jr., *The Christian and the Couch.* Grand Rapids, Michigan: Baker Book House, 1963.

Williams, Daniel Day, *The Minister and the Care of Souls.* New York: Harper & Brothers, Publishers, 1961.

Wurth, G. Brillenburg, *Christian Counseling in the Light of Modern Psychology.* Grand Rapids, Michigan: Baker Book House, 1962.

Using Groups in Counseling

Counseling and psychotherapy have undergone a major revolution since World War II. One of the more prominent aspects of this is group therapy. This is the gathering of a small group of individuals with a trained leader for the purpose of resolving some of the unsatisfactory personal adjustments in the lives of the individuals.

There are differences of opinion as to whether this procedure should be called counseling or psychotherapy. Some reserve "psychotherapy" as a medical term referring to the activity of medically trained psychiatrists. Counseling, from this point of view, is the proper term to be used for such group activities when these are conducted by psychologists, social worker, ministers, or other personnel trained in the behavioral sciences rather than medicine. Another distinction is to refer to counseling as the more superficial, minor personality adjusting process and psychotherapy as a deeper restructuring of the personality. In this discussion the terms will be used more or less interchangeably. Both are descriptive of what transpires in group therapy, where several persons come together to rectify unsatisfactory life patterns with the help of a trained counselor and or therapist.

1. BACKGROUND

Psychological treatment for maladjustment has developed since the turn of the century. The primary model of treatment has been the "one to one" relationship between counselee and counselor. This developed largely from that theory and practice originated by Sigmund Freud and called psychoanalysis. Pressure toward the development of therapy involving groups arose from both theoretical and practical sources. Theoretically, there is widespread and increasing acceptance of the idea that personal maladaptation is to a great extent a function of disturbed interpersonal relationships. Man is a social animal, the argument goes, and emotional disturbances must always be viewed in the light of some social disruption. A small group context, therefore, provides an arena in which an individual may resolve and heal his social wounds. Practicality has also stimulated the use of groups in counseling. The small number of trained therapists when compared with the increasing demand for therapeutic services forced the growth of group therapy. This has afforded an increased economy in the use of trained professionals and has made services available to a greater number of people.

2. SELECTING THE GROUP

Selection of a group for counseling depends somewhat upon the preference of counselor for homogeneous or heterogeneous groups. Homogeneous groups are those selected in terms of one or more basic similarities of the individuals making up the group. Factors frequently serving as criteria for selection are sex, age, symptoms, socioeconomics status, educational background, and marital status. It is assumed that the more similar the personal and social history of members of the group, the more quickly they will gain rapport and understanding of each other and their mutual problems.

Some counselors, however, prefer heterogeneous (mixed) groups. They aver that this makes a better and more realistic social sample, being a cross section for society, and hence an easier group to establish. The sole criterion for a truly heterogeneous group would be the felt need for help with a personal problem from a professional counselor. However, even the most radical of mixed groups ordinarily excludes certain types of personalities, such as the very young, the very old, or those with character traits which would tend to disintegrate the group. These might include very aggressive disturbed persons or those sociopathic individuals who are more highly motivated to disrupt a group then to be healed through it. It is hoped that the mixed group, being a better cross section of social reality, will avoid the artificiality of homogeneity, and will better prepare individuals for personal and social interrelationship outside the group context.

The development of counseling with groups has resulted in a variety of special homogeneous groups. There are age selected groups such as adolescent and child, groups based upon specific similar symptons such as alcoholics, homosexuals, or various psychoneurotic categories, and also a trend toward group therapy with that most basic of social units, the family.

It was thought at first that the success of group counseling depended upon composing the group with individuals who had no social contact apart from the group, since thus they should better be able to express their personal problems in a context of social anonymity. It was assumed further that since the family was the primary ground of the maladjustive development, the best way to evaluate and to ameliorate was to do so apart from the family situation. However, there is presently a good deal of literature describing family group therapy, in which the whole family participates, and also therapeutic groups which involve married couples who join groups to find solutions for marital or parental disturbances.

3. THE LEADER

The role of the group counselor also varies. Some leaders are directors and guides of the group. These tend to take on the stance of an authoritative teacher and utilize a didactic method. A series of lectures may be presented in which the leader-therapist may be quite directive in his approach. Although this tends to run counter to contemporary psychological and psychotherapeutic theory in general, there are reports of success from this kind of counseling. It is assumed that the members of the group are prevented from meaningful and effective living due to unstructured or unwise behavior patterns and that they need to be educated to more effective ways of coping with the world.

Other leaders assume the role of observer-recorder. This person is construed as a social catalyst who is both the occasion for the group meeting and serves as an occasional stimulant for group activity. His function, when active, is to reflect the emotions and actions of the group, not his own. He is an accepting, nondirective focus for the group.

A third, and contemporarily more popular, type of group therapist is the participant-observer. This leader becomes a bona fide member of the group who nevertheless bears chief responsibility for the group. In a sense he becomes a benevolent father figure for this new family, the therapeutic group.

The various therapist stances detailed here should be construed as attempts to define the general relationship of the therapist to the group rather than as any technical-theoretical categories.

4. GROUP CHARACTERISTICS

Some of the characteristics of the therapeutic group are as follows. A group ordinarily consists of about eight individuals or four or five couples. As a rule of thumb, I start a therapeutic group when I have four members and permit more than eight only under unusual circumstances. These numerical limits allow for sufficient social interaction, while leaving optimum for individual responsiveness from each member.

Also decision has to be made concerning whether the group will be an open or closed one. The closed group does not admit additional members once it has started. The open, on the other hand, maintains its numerical strength by adding additional members when dropouts occur. Whether a group is open or closed may depend upon whether it is a term or a continuous group. Some groups are organized with a specific time limit set for the number of meetings or number of months the group will function. A continuous group carries no time limits and replenishes its members as others leave the group.

Groups are also differentiated as to frequency of meetings. A modal sequence of meetings, and one to which I adhere generally, is a weekly meeting of about an hour and a half. I also like to see each group member individually once a month.

I should perhaps mention that while the foregoing factors are commonalities that have developed out of group therapy research, there are many exceptions to them. There has been, for instance, recent reports of effective therapeutic results from intensive groups maintained continuously through a period of several days, Dr. George

Bach, one of the leaders in the field of group therapy, reports signal success in "weekend therapeutic groups." In such experience the groups meet continuously for forty-eight hours or more, leaving the group only for food and rest breaks. Fatigue and sleepiness are resolved by the group members dozing on the floor or on the sofa during the group meeting. This and other innovations add important new possibilities in utilizing therapeutic groups.

The basic nature of the group is an interesting theoretical problem. There are those who believe that a group is nothing more than a conglomerate of individuals, each with his special personal problem, gathered for common purpose. Other investigators regard the group as an individual in itself, with a "group mind" and a special intra-personal movement that is not understandable with reference to any cumulative or additive function of the group members. It seems to me that there are certain senses in which both of these theories are descriptive of the group and both must be kept in mind. It is very imporant to treat the group as an organic whole and to keep the members of the group as "transparent" to each other as possible. Inevitably the distinctiveness of individual problems will become apparent, for these resist attempts at becoming encapsulated within the therapeutic group.

5. GROUP PROCESS

The group process is somewhat amorphous. Attempts to outline and categorize it seem both artificial and misleading. However, for purposes of explanation it is sometimes necessary to note tentative structural components. I present the following in this tentative mood. It should also be noted that, the steps listed are much more logical than chronological, and do not necessarily indicate the order of growth and maturation of a therapeutic group, particularly if it is a continuous group.

The first phase following the practical steps in organizing the group is the period of leader testing. This is the time, characteristically, when the group attempts to establish the therapist as an authority figure, one who is there to tell them how they are to live. Comments of members of the group usually are directed toward the therapist and he in turn is expected to respond to them in a personal way. This testing refers to his relationship to the group as well as to individual members. This is, in effect, an attempt to establish a special relationship with the leader. This is frequently done through references to special information shared by the leader and individual group members that may have come out in individual sessions. Many groups are extremely resistant to establishing their own patterns and limits, and spend a good deal of time in testing the therapist.

A second and overlapping phase is the testing of the group. This is similar to the testing of the therapist in that it consists in the attempt to make special alliances within the group. Some therapists do not permit social contacts among group members outside of therapy setting, believing that it may disrupt the therapeutic process. In the groups which I conduct, this is permitted so long as it is not a secret from the rest of the group and the motivation underlying the contact is discussed within the group. Upon successfully working through these two phases the group becomes a functioning organism with the flexibility to open up to the needs of the several members.

The third and general phase of group counseling is the group interactive process. During this time the members may report significant experiences that happened during the interval between meetings or within the group. Problem decisions are presented for group resolution. The therapist stimulates and guides the group as together they reflect upon present experiences, thus maintaining awareness of the purpose for its existence.

The layman may assume that this may be a "Quaker meeting" phase, and that persons are unlikely to reveal their innermost thoughts and feelings in so threatening an atmosphere. However, universal group experience is that the contrary is more likely to be true, that persons will reveal themselves too quickly, then feel threatened over having been too much "themselves." A social façade is difficult to maintain in group interaction.

The final phase in group counseling is the weaning away of group members from the counselor and from the group. This occurs when members believe they have matured sufficiently to cope with their life problems on their own. This depends on the initiative of the individual member and, while voluntary, it is nevertheless a matter to be worked through in the group setting. Members of my groups are required to spend a minimum of two months in the group before they are permitted to leave. This is a condition for enrolling in the group. The length of time necessary in the group for maturing personal growth is much more a function of the person's involvement, his openness to the group, and his willingness to profit from the group than it is a calendar time. Some people remain in the group longer than they feel necessary in order to help other members of the group. When this is an expression of mature caring and not a neurotic need it is an encouraging indication of mental health.

6. GROUPS AND THE CHURCH

The movement toward the use of groups in counseling has not only become a well developed phenomenon in psychotherapeutic circles but also has become related to the life of the church. A growing interest among pastors and church workers for a better understanding and helping relationship to the mentally and emotionally disturbed has developed. However, group therapy has not been merely an external source opportunity for the church but has also developed as a process within the church. Whether this ought to be referred to as group therapy or not is a moot question. Nonetheless the whole history of the care of souls has been a healing ministry in its total context and the concepts of healing, health, and holiness have grown out of the same root source both etymologically and functionally.

One of the significant contributors to research and theory in this area is Dr. Robert Leslie whose doctoral dissertation "Group Therapy as a Method for Church Work" investigates and encourages group counseling in a church setting. The interested pastor will find helpful bibliography of the area in the January, 1955, issue of *Pastoral Psychology*. A more recent edition of the same journal is entirely devoted to the topic "small groups in the church" and Dr. Leslie is the guest editor of this issue.

In addition to groups organized primarily for personal adjustment and growth there are opportunities for developing prayer groups, task-centered groups, and Biblical or theological study groups in the church.

In the early 1950's Dr. Clifton Kew, head psychologist of the counseling service of Marble Collegiate Church in New York City, and his brother, Dr. Clinton Kew, an Episcopal rector, reported successful attempts at group therapy in a church setting. They stated that therapy in such a setting has definite merit over other group therapy conducted on other contexts, for it aids the therapist in his role as a good authority figure. Transference is also supported in a positive way in the familiar atmosphere of protection, love, and forgiveness of the church. In addition, the parishioner patients are reassured that therapy is not for just the insane or the abnormal. The Kews also felt that the church tended to unite the group, which enabled the mutually helpful therapeutic functions of both religion and psychiatry to be utilized. This work is presented in a helpful volume, *You Can Be Healed* (Prentice Hall, 1953).

Dr. Phillip Anderson has also done some intensive work in the establishing of dynamic groups in local church activities. These are both therapeutic groups and general fellowship groups. In such groups the minister is a participant member of the groups, and the resource person rather than the primary worker in the church. "Working *with* people rather than *for* them makes the life and vigor of the church depend on the people rather than the minister." After more than a decade of research in such church-centered group programs Dr. Anderson reports in *Pastoral Psychology* (June 1964) that persons who are involved in well conducted church groups should find personal growth and movement in nine ways:

1. From self-centeredness to care for others.
2. From doubt about self to trust of self.
3. From irresponsibility to a sense of responsibility for self and others.
4. From secrecy to sharing.
5. From unfreedom to freedom.
6. From mistrust to trust.
7. From the need to receive ministry to the ability to give it also.

8. From a closed mind to a mind open to learning.
9. From fear of self, neighbor, and God to a love of self, neighbor, and God.

It should perhaps also be noted that while these trends were observed in research on church groups, they are not dissimilar to those observed in successful non-church therapeutic relationships, whether group or individual. In the church setting the productive group is one which is goal-oriented, task-centered, and God-related. This is also true of the productive individual.

In the editorial in the above mentioned special issue of *Pastoral Psychology,* Dr. Leslie comments that the church group is a group with a higher loyalty than the therapeutic group outside the church context because it is gathered "in my name" (Matt. 18:20). "What the proponents of group dynamics often fail to see is that groups, no matter how personally therapeutic, can easily become delinquent groups when no external criteria for judgment is provided" p. 37). In order to insure this higher loyalty, efforts should be made to distinguish the Christian-oriented therapeutic group from its secular counterpart.

BIBLIOGRAPHY

Durkin, Helen, *The Group in Depth.* New York: International University Press, 1964.

Johnson, James, *Group Therapy.* New York: McGraw-Hill, 1963.

Leslie, Robert (Ed.), *Pastoral Psychology,* Vol. 15, No. 145. New York: June, 1964.

Mowrer, O. H., *The New Group Therapy.* New York: Von Nostrand Press, 1964.

Rosenbaum, Max, and Berger, Milton, *Group Psychotherapy and Group Function.* New York: Basic Books, Inc., 1963.

Tweedie, Donald F., *Logotherapy and the Christian Faith.* Grand Rapids: Baker Book House, 1965.

The Use of Prayer, the Scriptures, and Hymns in Pastoral Counseling

Ministers have traditionally used the means of grace in their ministry of pastoral care. These same resources can also be used effectively in pastoral counseling.

There is currently a new appreciation of the significant religious resources which pastors can utilize in counseling. Leaders in the field of mental health rightly expect pastoral counseling to be different from the psychotherapy of secular psychiatry. In contrasting the clergymen's approach with that of the psychiatrist, Dr. Stanley F. Yolles, Director of the National Institute of Mental Health says, "The priest, minister or rabbi . . . cannot remain neutral and remain true to his religious calling. Whatever his personal inclinations may be, he remains the symbol of commitment and involvement" (*Academy Reporter,* April, 1965).

1. PRAYER

The pastor's use of prayer in pastoral counseling must be relevant to the experience of the interview. The counselee should be asked if he wishes prayer, otherwise it may be perceived as coercion from an authority figure to enforce abject surrender. If the counselee refuses prayer the counselor can engage in prayer for the counselee in the privacy of his study.

Prayer should never be used authoritatively to consolidate the pastor's point of view, and as a last attempt to coerce the counselee into changing his attitude. Prayer is also abused when its performance is a mechanical religious substitute for saying, "the hour is finished." When two persons have experienced an interpersonal relationship in depth in which there is a common desire to talk with God, then the required mutuality in prayer is present.

Some pastors prefer to pray at the beginning of the pastoral consultation in order to structure the interview as distinctively pastoral. However it is possible that this gain is offset by probable effect of silencing or restricting negative verbal expressions by the counselee. Each pastor must do that which is both natural and intelligent to him, as well as that which is relevant to the counselee. One must recognize that a spiritual encounter can occur in pastoral counseling without the use of prayer. It is also true that the mere parroting of trite religious phrases does not constitute a spiritual ministry to a person in need.

Prayer can be used effectively in pastoral counseling if it is relevant, timely, and mutual. In appropriate settings and contexts the use of liturgical prayers can be helpful.

In addition to the therapeutic gain which occurs to the client, true prayer always honors God and pleases Jesus Christ, the shepherd of souls. This is the higher goal which makes all human endeavors significant.

2. SCRIPTURE

The Scriptures are able to make men wise unto salvation through faith which is in Christ Jesus. The Word of God is "profitable for doctrine, for reproof, for correction, for instruction in righteousness" (II Tim. 3: 16).

The main problem in the use of the Scriptures in pastoral counseling is the method in which they are employed. The Scriptures ought not to be used merely to conform to social expectations. The Word of God should be allowed to carry its own authority with the promised expected accompaniment of the Holy Spirit, and without the dubious aid of cold authoritarian preachment from the counselor.

Inasmuch as the counselor cannot infallibly judge the spiritual condition of the counselee, it would seem to be more prudent to suggest the possible applicability of a specific passage or theme, rather than to arbitrarily make the connection between Scripture and client.

If the counselor judges that the reading of the Bible might be perceived as threatening to the client, he may be more effective in quoting a brief passage from memory.

A majority of clients who seek pastoral counseling manifest anxiety. Pastors should resist the temptation to give the reassurances of the Scriptures prematurely. The promises of the Word of God can be more effectively applied after the person has had the opportunity fully to verbalize the turmoil which initially caused him to seek help.

Those clients who manifest no anxiety or guilt in relation to sinful attitudes or actions are persons for whom the admonitions of the Scriptures are pertinent. This procedure would be proper only if the counselor judged that the careless attitude manifested by the counselee was not a façade to hide deep underlying concern. The admonition of the Scriptures must always be immersed in love, even as they were in their original historical context.

Every use of the Scriptures must be done prayerfully. Personal meditation upon the Scriptures best qualify the pastoral counselor freely to use the Scriptures appropriately.

Clients can also become participants in God's healing program by daily meditation upon brief selections of the Scriptures which relate to their basic problems. This procedure has been called "homework" to be done between pastoral counseling contacts.

Pastors may find a Biblical directory helpful in appriasing significant choices of Scripture for particular counseling situations. A convenient directory is given by Dr. Wm. E. Hulme in *Counseling and Theology* (p. 209). The following directory is taken from the "Order for the Visitation of the Sick" of the Reformed Church in America.

SUGGESTED SCRIPTURE PASSAGES

Before an Operation: I Tim. 1:12; Phil. 4:13; Ps. 91:1, 11; Isa. 30:15b; Matt. 28:20; Ps. 46:1.

Confidence in God: Ps. 23; Ps. 46:1; Ps. 27:1-3; Eph. 3:20; Rom. 8:38-39; Heb. 13:5b.

The Purpose of Suffering: John 9:1-3; John 11:3, 4; Ps. 66:10; Heb. 12:6, 11; Job 1:8-12; 42:5-6; II Cor. 1:3-5.

Sense of Guilt or Failure: Ps. 51:1, 7-10; Isa. 1:18; Ps. 103:8; John 6:37; Luke 15:7; I John 1:9.

Anxiety: Ps. 263; Isa. 30:15; Phil. 4:7-8; Matt. 6:34; Ps. 42:1-5.

Patience: Rom. 5:3-4; Ps. 46:10a; Job 42:10; James 5:10-11; Phil. 4:13.

Discouragement and Disappointment: Ps. 37:7; Ps. 138:8; Matt. 11:28; Rom. 8:28; Isa. 40:31; Ps. 6.

Aged Persons: Ps. 16:5-11; Ps. 71:16-24; Luke 2:29-32; II Tim. 4:7-8.

Sleeplessness: Ps. 4:8; Ps. 30:5b; Ps. 46:10a; I Peter 5:7; I John 4:18.

Fear of Death: Ps. 23:4; Rom. 8:37-39; John 14:1ff; Isa. 12:2; Ps. 46:1-4; Isa. 41:10.

Hope at the Time of Death: Ps. 23; John 14: 1-3; II Cor. 5:1; I Cor. 15:57; Rev. 21:4-5; 22:3-5.

Thanksgiving: Ps. 103:1-4; Ps. 118:5, 17-18; Ps. 138:1-3; Ps. 22:23-25; Ps. 28:7; Ps. 40:2-5.

Childbirth: Ps. 116:1 5; Ps. 127:3-5a; John 16: 21-22; James 1:17; Mark 10:14-16; Deut. 6:7; Prov. 22:6; II Cor. 12:9a.

3. HYMNS

Persons in crisis situations cling to persons and things that are familiar. Familiar hymns can be used to communicate hope in pastoral conversations with those who are critically ill and with the bereaved. Many hymns incorporate the words and message of the gospel in significant ways. A judicious use of hymns can effectively enhance therapeutic pastoral counseling. Some suggested hymns are "Blessed Assurance," "Rock of Ages," "Standing on the Promises," "A Wonderful Savior Is Jesus My Lord," "Jesus, Lover of my Soul," "O Love That Wilt Not Let Me Go," and "What a Friend We Have in Jesus."

BIBLIOGRAPHY

Goulooze, William, *The Christian Worker's Handbook.* Grand Rapids: Baker Book House. 1953.

Heynen, Ralph, *Building Your Spiritual Strength.* Grand Rapids: Baker Book House, 1965.

Hulme, William E., *Counseling and Theology.* Philadelphia: Westminster Press, 1963.

Oates, Wayne E., *The Bible in Pastoral Care.* Phildelphia: Westminster Press, 1963.

Family Tensions

Marriage and the family are social institutions which our society both praises and derides. They provide the most intimate of human relationships and can bring either meaningful fulfillment or despairing agony. In less complex societies marital and family relationships are well defined and afford the major context for work and play. However in American society they no longer dominate our social structure, nor are marital and family relationships as clearly defined. As a result, we see a wide variety of experimental family roles being tried out in a society where new social behavior is required, and where the former reliable guidelines are no longer adequate to the demands of our complex society.

Since marriage is now a less predictable relationship, there is a compensatory false idealization of marriage into a stereotyped model. The romantic idea of falling in love as solely an emotional experience obscures the realistic need to choose a partner appropriate to one's own life situation, personal expectations, and mutual goals. In contrast to romantic infatuation, mature love is a relationship in depth between persons who know each other intimately as persons. In a mature love relationship, both partners accept the liabilities of each and appreciate the particular assets that each contributes to the other. The virtue of monogamy is the opportunity to share oneself — to know and be known as a person in an intimate depth impossible in other human relations. For only within the security of a known marital commitment is it possible to risk exposure of the intimacies of self to another. Unfortunately, many marriages remain superficial social alliances, for partners find it difficult to commit themselves to each other or learn to explore the depth of personhood with each other.

Marriage is one of a series of life phases, each of which presents particular adjustment problems. During adolescence one faces the development of a stable self-identity and the determination of one's role vocationally, socially, and sexually. American society prolongs this adolescent phase with its partial dependency and uncertain roles into the mid-twenties. Hence our youth often marry before they are financially independent or have a stable self-concept and life role.

Marriage presents the problem of learning to achieve true personal intimacy with another immediately after facing the adolescent problem of becoming an autonomous self-reliant person. If the adolescent phase has not been resolved, a young couple may find it difficult to learn to give up their new autonomy in the process of sharing oneself with another in marriage.

Pregnancy and children usher in the next phase. Whatever balance was struck between partners is now upset by the wife's restrictions and the husband's responsibilities. The infant is another person who claims time, attention, and affection. Children may be resented by a spouse as an interference in the marriage, or involvement with the children may be an escape from the problems of marriage. A new balance between three or more people must be developed. This balance may bring satisfactions to each member, or a lopsided affair may develop to the neurotic advantage of only part of the family.

In the mid-life phase comes the problem of continued productivity versus stagnation. When all the children enter school, the wife is left with whole days free, while the husband can now see where his job will lead him in life. The busy expectant years of early marriage merge into a rather predictable routine. This time may hold dissatisfaction for both husband and wife in terms of fulfillment and the realization that earlier goals may now need re-evaluation.

In the late adulthood phase when the children all leave home, the couple are again left alone with each other. A whole new adjustment presents itself. In addition to the problems of aging and familiarity, unresolved aspects of the relationship in early marriage, diverted by the presence of children, again emerge into the marital relationship. This phase places particular stress on the marriage, and it is here that marital quarrels, separations, and divorce may frequently occur.

Finally, with retirement and physical aging come the problems of senescence. Grandparents are usually separated from their families and have few deep community ties in large urban societies. Our culture has moved to a focus on youth and we do not have adequate cultural roles or social uses for our aging population, nor do we have appropriate means for caring for our aged as debility increases. Ultimately comes death, which in our culture has become taboo and feared instead of being a culmination of the process of life. In some societies death is the most important event in one's life, but in our society we are in conflict over even funeral arrangements. Old age and death, however, can be important and meaningful.

Now it can be seen that marital and family tensions do not stem from some specific problem. There is a sequence of life situations which are stressful and must be resolved. If the problems of one life phase are not solved successfully, it may compound the problems of succeeding phases. Each family is faced with these situations and the outcome will depend on the mental health of each member and mental health of the family as a unit.

Another aspect of these life phases is that these are real life problems, or perhaps better, life situations. These are not neurotic problems, although the personal and family solutions can be neurotic. It is important to emphasize that normal families do not avoid problems or stresses. The healthy family is the one that has developed effective personal and family methods for solving crises and life situations. At the onset of marriage a couple must experiment with methods for dealing with situational stresses. If they develop neurotic problem solving methods this will influence the entire life course of the family. Whereas if the couple develops effective methods, they will have laid a solid foundation for family growth.

To summarize, the marital partners may be relatively effective, healthy, individuals as such, but may have never developed the capacity to share the intimacy of a love relationship, or never developed effective family problem solving approaches to the various phases of family life. They have not learned to communicate or collaborate in the task of living a marriage.

Other marital problems stem from personality problems in the partners. If marriage occurs before a firm role and identity has been established, a person may move from dependence on parents to dependence on the spouse. The spouse is not seen as his or her true self, but rather with many attributes of the parent. The spouse becomes the object of the demands made of the parent and the fears and rebellion toward the parent. Marriage then becomes a mutual distortion with both partners perceiving and reacting to each other on the basis of earlier child-parent relationships. Instead of a mutual willful dependence shared by two autonomous adults, there is a mutual ambivalent dependence based on childish demands and fears. If parents continue to act out their own childhood conflicts with each other it will involve their own children, leading to problems in child-rearing because the parents still play child-roles instead of mature adult-parent roles.

Sexual relations are another source of tensions. Despite the current American preoccupation with sex, there is widespread misinformation about sexuality among both professionals and laity. Sexuality is often reduced to the nature of a physical act, which alone is a meaningless biological mechanism. Whereas the significance of sexuality is its intimacy between two people who emotionally and physically explore each other's persons, an intimacy requiring the security that comes with responsible, public commitment to lifelong, mutual fidelity. Physical abnormalities play a minor role in most problems of sexual adjustment, although physical sexual complaints are often the presenting symptom of an interpersonal problem. Couples often try to use sexual relations to solve personal problems between them, to bargain with each other, to punish each other, or to control each other. In these instances sexuality becomes a disguise for problems in the relationship. Meaningful sexual relations are the consequence, not the source, of a satisfying personal relationship between partners.

Theology has been slow to develop an adequate appreciation of the body as part of personality, and ascetic degradation of the body persists in church teachings. However the Biblical concept of man is that of a unitary personality, of which body, mind, and spirit are not separate entities but reflections of an integral self. Asceticism denigrates the body, hedonism exalts the body, while Christianity affirms that the body is an essential part of self. Surveys among pastors and church teachers reveal that many believe that sexuality even within marriage is sinful. Even if accepted as proper, anxiety about being free and open about sexuality within marriage continues to be a serious problem for the church. In Europe the problems of sexual frigidity, impotence, and perversion among conservative Protestant church members has been significant enough to merit the name "ecclesiogenic neurosis." A most important task for the pastor and the church is to provide instruction in a wholesome Christian perspective on the body as part of self and sexuality as part of the sharing of self within marriage.

Since our society now less clearly defines the roles of husband, wife, and children, each marriage and family tend to develop their own unique configuration. Although there are national stereotypes, these are ill-suited to the actual situations of families. Hence there may be difficulty, anxiety, guilt, or shame about assuming unorthodox or unfamiliar roles. Or tensions may arise from competing or overlapping roles. Some examples: both parents may work and compete for the most prestigious job and money, or a husband may wish to play a passive role while the wife wants him to be more active, or a woman may be expected to fill multiple roles of full time employee, meticulous housekeeper, solicitous mother, and sophisticated hostess, all at the same time.

Then there is the question of leadership. Overconcern with the idea of equality may lead to a marital stalemate when leadership is confused with superiority or dominance. There is a natural balance between partners, and the dominant one, whether man or woman, may or may not be the defined leader of the home. It makes little difference so long as both partners can agree and collaborate in leadership responsibilities. Otherwise there is either convert and overt competition, or mutual deference with the frustrating failure of either one to make even everyday decisions.

Each family is also unique in its own system of communication. If early in marriage husband and wife do not learn to communicate clearly in words, they will meet problems in marriage for they will resort to communication via actions instead of words. Frustration follows, for they cannot understand each other when they do talk together and their communication in action remains obscure, contradictory, and usually fruitless. The ability to openly and fully express one's ideas and feelings to one's spouse and children is perhaps crucial to resolving family tensions and the key to restoration of family health.

Marital and family problems are among those most commonly brought to the pastor. In his role of pastoral care he possesses unique advantages for dealing with families, although he is also faced with particular pitfalls.

First, the pastor has an advantage in usually knowing all the family members. The member with the defined problem usually is not the sole problem, but is symptomatic of the family and its problems. The pastor's job is not to determine who is the culprit in the family, but rather to determine how each member of the family interacts in creating the particular problem of which the one member is the symptom.

Secondly, the pastor should remain alert to the bias presented by a single family member. In most marital problems, the partners are relatively healthy and effective people by themselves. The problems arise in the marital relationship between each other. The pastor should avoid getting caught between the partners or taking sides. Rather he should help each to see their own contribution to the problem and responsibility for its resolution. It is well to see family members separately and then together to obtain an overall picture and then help the family to see their overall problem.

Thirdly, the solution to marital and family tensions rests upon changes in the interaction between family members. What works for one family may be inappropriate for another. There are no specific answers to family situations, but rather each family must work out its own specific answer. Likewise, the pastor must be alert to his own marriage and family situation, so that he will not copy from his own life as the basis for helping others.

Fourthly, the pastor can offer reassurance to the family while he explores the source of their problems, and guides the family or members to further help, if necessary, from a family service agency, marriage counseling service, child guidance clinic, or psychiatric clinic.

Fifthly, the pastor is not a therapist but he can be therapeutic. Families often look to the pastor for reinforcement of their standards and behavior in terms of the teachings of their church. The pastor should feel confident in counseling within the standards of his church, helping its families to live according to its established precepts. This, of course, implies that the teaching and life of the church should be carefully reviewed so that it will foster healthy patterns of family relations.

BIBLIOGRAPHY

Berne, E., *Games People Play, the Psychology of Human Relationships.* New York: Grove Press, 1964.

Hulme, Wm. E., *The Pastoral Care of Families.* New York: Abingdon, 1962.

Klemer, R. H. (ed), *Counseling in Marital and Sexual Problems.* Baltimore: Williams & Wilkins, 1965.

Thielicke, H., *The Ethics of Sex.* New York: Harper & Row, 1964.

Divorce and Remarriage

Church and community are concerned with the stability of family life. Family instability contributes inordinately to human suffering "unto the third and fourth generation." Children need two actively involved parents who love each other and them if they are to be emotionally prepared for deep personal relations and making of a good marriage. Divorce represents a kind of bereavement, for out of it comes severe damage to or destruction of important personal relations. It is an experience which is in important respects more difficult emotionally than bereavement through death. In comparison, bereavement through death may be likened to a wound from surgery while divorce represents a deep jagged tearing of tissue which heals with far greater difficulty. Out of it come such problems as deep mistrust of others, the fear of close relations and the fear of desertion, so that a person hesitates to commit himself to another. The capacity for friendship and for happy marriage is radically damaged. A second kind of problem is referred to by the social psychologist as difficulty in effecting a strong role identity. This means that boys from broken homes may have greater than usual difficulty understanding on the emotional level what it means to be a man, and developing confidence in one's adequacy as a man. So also with girls and the feminine role. This aspect of maturing is complicated by the loss of the like sexed parent from the home. In our urban small family pattern this becomes exaggerated by the scarcity of concerned parent surrogates. This has been invoked as one important factor in the apparent sharp rise in incidence of male homosexuality. All of which underscores the point that divorce is not an experience from which a sensitive person easily recovers. Residual emotional scars may be lifelong and contribute to emotional warping in the next generation.

There is a note of cheer for us in the decrease in divorce rate. From a peak of 17.9 per thousand married women in 1947, sparked by hasty, ill-conceived war marriages, it dropped to 9.2 per thousand married women in 1964. (This compared with 10.3 per thousand married women in 1950. See Wattenberg and Scammon, *This U.S.A.*, 1965.) Nevertheless the rapid population increase these past twenty years has kept the absolute number of newly divorced persons each year a large one. What is the pastor to do as he is faced with a growing number of personal tragedies arising from homes broken by divorce?

First, he must clarify his feelings toward

divorce, for those often set the tone for his feelings toward divorcees. The Christian pastor knows that God's ideal for marriage is that it be permanent. "What therefore God has joined, let not man put asunder" (Matt. 19:7). This principle of the indissolubility of marriage has had difficult going. Divorce regulations were included in the Mosaic Civil Code. When confronted with this Christ does not condemn Moses. Instead he points out that Moses as a civil legislator was obliged to deal with men as he found them, and that man's "hardness of heart" necessitated what ideally was never intended. Moses provided divorce regulations in order to prevent the greater evils brought about by an absolute prohibition of divorce. This is abundantly illustrated by the experience of the Roman Catholic Church. Despite both its determination to absolutize the principle of indissolubility and its immense authority, it took almost eleven centuries to impress it upon the Western world (D. S. Bailey, *The Mystery of Love and Marriage.*) Protestantism has taken three directions. Some have pointed to Christ's words "except for adultery" (Matt. 5:31, 32; 19:9), and regarded adultery as the sole ground for divorce.

Others question whether Christ intended a definitive pronouncement concerning permissible grounds for divorce, or whether he was merely addressing himself to the practices current among the Jews of his day, that is, that he was speaking illustratively rather than definitively. There is ground for such a viewpoint in the fact that the apostle Paul said, "If the unbelieving partner desires to separate, let it be so; in such a case the brother or sister is not bound. For God has called us to peace." (I Cor. 7:15 RSV) In interpreting this passage John Murray maintains that the word "separate" together with the phrase "is not bound" clearly intends permanent severance of the marriage bond, so that remarriage is a possibility (*Divorce*, rev. ed., 1961, pp. 67-68). How can this be in view of the statements of Christ? Murray observes that Paul dealt with cases peculiar to a religiously mixed society, hence with cases that did not come within the purview of Christ's teaching. The Reformed churches dealt with this passage additively and regard adultery and desertion as providing proper ground for divorce. But this begs the question. If Christ intended to be definitive it is difficult to conceive by what authority Paul added desertion to legitimate grounds for divorce. If he was illustrating, then it is possible the apostle Paul was too. If so, what were they illustrating? Acts of adultery or desertion may but do not inevitably destroy a marriage. Instances abound of forgiveness and reconciliation after adultery or prolonged desertion. Hence it does not seem to be these acts themselves but some deeper factor which determines whether or not a marriage is destroyed or can be revivified. What might this deeper principle be? The Bible repeatedly defines marriage as "one flesh" — organic union grounded in a mutual pledge of lifelong love and faithfulness. It may be that the fundamental issue of divorce is whether or not the "one flesh" relationship is destroyed or merely damaged.

The "one flesh" relationship involves an institutional aspect, the contract, and an ontological aspect, the couple's mutual commitment to loving faithfulness to one another. Both are necessary, for marriage never is solely a private matter. This relationship may be voluntarily broken, as when one takes initiative to commit adultery or desert one's spouse. It may be involuntarily broken, as when one's spouse does these things. Christ admonished against voluntary breach of the marriage relationship. His hearers were perfectly aware that the sex relationship represents the outward and physical expression of an inner and spiritual truth: the organic unity of husband and wife, a fact which has moved some to speak of sex as "the sacramental expression of the 'one flesh' relationship." In this reference to adultery Christ was telling these people as pointedly as possible that they were to do nothing that threatened to destroy the marriage tie.

The "Pauline privilege" situation (I Cor. 7:15) is of a different order. It represents an involuntary breach of the marriage tie. In such situations the "innocent party" is given explicit permission to dissolve the marriage. This raises the following considerations: if adultery and desertion are intended to be illustrative rather than definitive, are there other situations peculiar to our society and times which point equally to the destruction of the one flesh relationship? Are there, Albertus Pieters inquires, cases in which perpetuation of the marriage relationship involves the greatest cruelty to one or another of the participants and to children as yet unborn? "If such cases as these can be identified," he goes on, "would this be a place to apply our Lord's principle that the law of mercy takes precedence over the law contained in the ordinances? That, to paraphrase, man was not made for marriage, but marriage for man?" ("Christian View of Marriage and Divorce," a paper read before the Western (Michigan) Social Conference, Allendale, Michigan, December 10, 1930).

Today one hesitates a bit to raise the questions discussed in the preceding paragraphs. This is a day of easy divorce. Many people enter marriage in an "escape hatch" frame of mind — "if this doesn't work out we can always call it off and try again." Hence one hesitates to seem to be building a case for a more cavalier view of divorce within the church. This is not intended. Divorce involves sin. God's intention for marriage is loving faithfulness "so long as the two shall live." What is intended is that the church not merely react to the constant attack on indissolubility with an unbalanced emphasis on the institutional over the ontological aspect of marriage, thus finding herself in a legalistic straitjacket. Let it quickly be pointed out, however, that wholly to set aside institutional considerations in the interest of individual welfare may result in maudlin and ineffectual sentimentality. Institutional and personal considerations must be weighed in each case. This is often knotty. Much of the time one must choose the lesser evil. But it seems a sound application of the Biblical principle of *agápe* that in such dilemmas it is better to err on the side of grace. In this way the church is in a stronger position to extend her ministry of forgiveness and healing.

A comment on the idea of "the innocent party" seems in order. Any experienced pastor knows that it is rare that such a term is more than relative. Married life is an intricate tapestry of interwoven actions and reactions. Both parties usually contribute to misunderstanding, each in his own way. Silence may be golden, but it may also be more destructive to a relationship than a verbal blistering. Hence the pastor is well advised to listen long and carefully and be slow to apportion blame. The more obvious offense is not necessarily the greater.

But what of remarriage? Among some Christian groups there is a conviction that remarriage is forbidden in the Scriptures so long as one's spouse is alive. Others, with the so-called "Pauline privilege" in mind (I Cor. 7:15), may have their reservations, but do not feel justified in taking the first view. Some remember Paul's words to young widows, "I would have younger widows marry, bear children, rule their households . . ." (I Tim. 5:14) and ask whether it was not their vulnerability to emotional and financial exploitation and their potentiality as home wreckers that Paul had in mind as he encouraged remarriage? If this is as correct as it is plausible, then we do well to remember that these reasons are likely to apply in greater measure to many divorced persons. Characteristically divorcees are less emotionally mature and less likely to have helpful family relations hence, correlatively, more likely to exploitation and less capable of providing alone a proper home for their children; especially so in the unstable social conditions found in our large metropolitan centers.

Let it be said, however, that remarriage *per se* is no solution to a divorcee's situation. It may only aggravate things. Edmund Bergler's thesis is a telling one (*Divorce Won't Help*, Harper, 1947). Some people fail in marriage because of their deep-rooted emotional immaturities. These immaturities encourage the selection of a particular type of marriage partner whose immaturities in turn guarantee marital difficulty. Thus to divorce this partner, argues Bergler, only results in picking another with the same qualities. Thus another marriage another marital failure. This is too cut and dried to apply universally. Our times do encourage hasty marriages among teen-agers. Many of these fail. But a study of remarriages by such persons indicates that at least eighty-five per cent make fine marriages the second time. Apparently this kind of bitter experience can produce growth in many.

It appears that there are two constructive things the church can do in these situations. First, provide support and help during time of marital upheaval and especially during the period of rebuilding which follows divorce action. To be a kind of family to these persons, providing them with encouragement, companionship, a place to contribute to the lives of others and to clarify their life commitment is to help immunize them against the sudden, rash remarriages which are so often a fruit of an aching loneliness and the need to reassure oneself he is still lovable. For divorce frequently shakes a person at the root of his being. The bitter accusations of an angered spouse are rejected in the heat of battle, but they return to haunt during the endless lonely hours following divorce. Thus in providing affectionate companionship and a sense of usefulness, the church as beloved community prevents another foolish marriage while making healing and growth possible. But among evangelical churches divorcees far more often meet suspicion and censure and feel kept at arms length!

The church can also establish a sound policy governing the pastor's officiating at a wedding involving remarriage of divorced persons. Here I commend to you the policy adopted by the Moravian Church at its Twenty-ninth Synod (1961). It states:

A pastor can in good conscience officiate in the remarriage of divorced persons if in his judgment, and the judgment of the congregation's board of elders, the persons have met the following requirements:

1. Recognition of personal responsibility for the failure of the former marriage.
2. Penitence, and an effort to overcome limitations and failures.
3. Forgiveness of the former partner.
4. Fulfillment of obligations involved in the former marriage.
5. Willingness to make the new marriage a Christian one by dependence on Christ and particpation in his church.

This is a tough, realistic policy. It seeks to ensure that those attitudes which would threaten a new marriage have been properly worked through. This is neither quick nor easy. It is difficult to see how these could be sufficiently accomplished in much less than two years, although legalistic imposition of some arbitrary period of time is not called for. This too quickly takes on magical import and becomes a mechanically applied substitute for the difficult task of ascertaining whether the necessary inner changes have taken place.

Indissolubility "so long as ye both shall live" is the ideal we seek to instill. But "hardness of heart" is still part of the human condition. The church, through her pastors, has an extraordinary opportunity to demonstrate the relevance and healing power of the gospel in dealing with divorced persons, if only they see these people as needy people and reach out to them in wisdom and loving concern.

BIBLIOGRAPHY

Bailey, D. S., *The Ministry of Love and Marriage:* A Study in the Theology of Sex Relation. New York: Harpers, 1952.

Bergler, Edmund, *Divorce Won't Help.* New York: Harpers, 1948.

Despert, Louise, *Children of Divorce.* New York: Doubleday, 1953.

Fairchild, Roy W., *Christians in Families*: An Inquiry into the Nature and Mission of the Christian Family. Richmond, Virginia: Covenant Life Curriculum Press, 1964.

Howe, Reuel, *The Creative Years.* Greenwich, Connecticut: Seabury, 1959.

Murray, John, *Divorce.* Philadelphia: Presbyterian and Reformed Publishing Company, 1961.

Piper, Otto A., *The Biblical View of Sex and Marriage.* New York: Scribner's, 1960.

Ploscowe, Morris, *The Truth about Divorce.* New York: Hawthorn Books, 1955.

Wynn, John Charles, ed., *Sex, Family and Society in Theological Focus.* New York: Association Press, 1966.

Problems of Addiction

Drug addiction is increasingly a problem. Particularly so with alcohol which today is the fourth leading public health problem. The abuse of other drugs is less widespread, but the use of narcotics is a particular problem among the youth in our larger urban areas. Although not so obviously visible, alcohol and narcotic problems do exist in suburbia and its religious groups.

Parenthetically, the use of hallucinogenic drugs to induce mystical experiences is receiving wide attention in some religious circles. The transcendental states of consciousness produced by these drugs are sought by those who define religion as a mystical experience, although such experiences are not related to any theological concepts. The indiscriminate use of such drugs by nonprofessionals can result in subsequent serious emotional disturbances.

The person addicted to narcotics often has been despised as a morally reprehensible, psychologically inferior, and physically dissolute character. Actually it is easy for anyone to become addicted to narcotics during prolonged periods of illness; and many of the new common sleeping medicines can easily lead to addiction. So the pastor may well discover addictive problems among his parishoners. His role in such cases may be to help the person obtain the appropriate medical help; and assist the person in handling the tremendous guilt and social disapproval which usually accompany such addictive problems.

The alcoholic has often been caricatured as a skid-row bum. Factually, less than ten per cent of alcoholics are found on skid-row, and most of the skid-row habitues are not alcoholics but inept derelict personalities existing on the margin of society. The real service of the church to the problem of alcoholism does not lie in skid-row mission projects, but rather to the large number of alcoholics who live within society and the church. The typical alcoholic may be discribed as a middle-aged man with a good job, married with children, a member of a church, and a likable personality. When such a person develops an alcoholic problem we lose a good worker, husband, father, and valuable member of the church and society. Also an increasing number of suburban women are developing alcoholism problems.

Rather than attempting to arbitrarily define who is an alcoholic, I find it more helpful to define *what problems a person has with alcohol.* Some cannot drink without getting intoxicated, while others never get drunk but rely on drinking heavily and continuously. Some drink in sporadic binges, while others spend meager earnings in small amounts of regular drinking. Some drink just enough to reduce themselves to marginal effectiveness, while others cannot function effectively without a certain amount of alcohol. Some become boisterous and abusive while drinking and others become moody and withdrawn. Thus there are many problem patterns of drinking. A problem with alcohol may be defined as that drinking which disrupts the effective function of one's personality, with one's family, or in one's social and vocational life.

There is no one cause of alcoholism. It is the consequence of physical, psychological, social, and cultural factors. Physical dependence on alcohol plays a necessary, but only a secondary role, in the genesis of alcoholism. It is not a physical allergy as some assert. More important is the psychological dependence on alcohol to reduce anxiety, relieve feelings of inadequacy and dependence, and escape from difficult life situations.

While certain cultures like the Italians drink heavily they have a low rate of alcoholism, whereas the Irish drink as heavily and have a high rate of alcoholism. Among orthodox Jews where all drink wines from childhood on there is virtually no alcoholism, while in some Protestant groups which practice abstinence there is a very high rate of alcoholism among those who do drink. The point is that the prevalence or amount of alcohol consumption does not determine the incidence of alcoholism. Rather, the crucial factor is the *social and personal meaning* of drinking alcohol.

The ascetic trends in Christianity have perpetuated an unnecessary tension between mind and body. There is persistent distrust and guilt about personal and physical satisfaction. So the use of alcohol is suspect and attended by both group and personal feelings of guilt about such self-gratification. Our American culture tends to define drinking as a mark of maturity, thus making it a prestige factor for young people. And we tend to use alcohol as a social defense, as a justification and opportunity for social misbehavior (a use not condoned or allowed in many other societies). In socio-cultural settings where alcohol is used like a food, used primarily in the home, and used in moderate quantities, there are low rates of alcoholism.

The treatment of alcoholism, then, at the first level must deal with social and cultural uses and attitudes. The pastor and the church can contribute through the education of youth on a healthy attitude toward the self, the proper uses of alcohol, and the dangers and abuses of alcohol. Further there is a signal need to influence community attitudes and behavior toward a revision of the socio-cultural role of alcohol in our society.

Although the concept of alcoholism as a health problem has been accepted officially by all major health, social, and religious agencies, there is still widespread prejudice against alcoholics making it difficult to develop community support for treatment and rehabilitation facilities. Although persons with alcohol problems can be problem patients, treatment in carefully planned programs is often successful.

The concept of abstinence also needs reevaluation. Most of the pioneer treatment programs dealt only with chronic addictive alcoholics for whom life-long abstinence was the only answer to rehabilitation. These alcoholics traded the daily pursuit of alcohol for the daily pursuit of sobriety. More recent experience indicates that for other types of alcoholics abstinence may neither be feasible nor necessary as a condition of treatment or as a goal of rehabilitation. Although this is controversial to those who view abstinence as a moral virtue, abstinence versus social drinking as a moral position must be decided apart from the scientific evaluation of treatment possibilities.

The second level of treatment involves the earlier and more effective detection of alcoholism problems before the person has gotten into serious trouble leading to irreparable social and personal damage. There is no need to await flagrant alcoholism with the loss of wife, family, and job, before help is offered. The pastor can help by providing acceptance to and guidance for the person in the early stages of alcoholism. The person in difficulty with himself, his family, or on the job, because of drinking may be helped to see his problem with alcohol. While he is not yet an alcoholic, help at this stage may avert alcoholism.

Finally, the third level of treatment is aimed at the rehabilitation of the obvious alcoholic. Sometimes alcoholism is considered to be solely a moral problem stemming from the lack of will power or moral concern. Such attitudes overlook the real human needs of the alcoholic. Further, it is an erroneous concept of responsibility. Our lives are more determined than we realize, although we have more responsibility than we wish to assume. The alcoholic is in trouble and needs realistic help, not encouragement, advice, or moralisms.

The first step is *not* to accept the responsibility for the alcoholic's life and behavior, but rather to help him to see the reality of his particular problem with alcohol and motivate his interest in rehabilitation. The second step is *not* to get involved as an intermediary in the family. The spouse may attempt to get the pastor to take sides in family disagreement, or handle communication between husband and wife which has broken down. Rather, the pastor should assist the family members in seeing their own roles in the reaction to or perpetuation of the alcohol problem in the home, and assist the family in developing a therapeutic attitude. Many treatment programs now provide ancillary services for the wives of alcoholics, either individually, in groups, or in conjunction with the husband. And in collaboration with Alcoholics Anonymous there is the Alanon program for wives, and the Alateen program for children.

Finally, the pastor should assess with the alcoholic and his family what type of community treatment resource will most appropriately meet their needs. Most communities now have a Council on Alcoholism which provides treatment information and coordinates treatment resources. In many areas there are family service agencies, alcoholism clinics, and Alcoholics Anonymous groups. Each offers specific services appropriate for different types of alcoholism problems. In the past Alcoholics Anonymous was the only help available, and it will remain a major resource. But the A.A. approach is limited to those with chronic addictive alcoholism, whereas many other alcohol problems require a different approach. A.A. has appealed to religious groups because of its broad religious overtones, although there is nothing theologically specific about A.A., nor does its effectiveness stem from this religiosity. The church can be of fundamental value to the alcoholic by providing acceptance and sustenance during the period of rehabilitation, and the pastor can be a primary agent in the detection, evaluation, and guidance of the alcoholic on the path to recovery.

BIBLIOGRAPHY

Bier, W. C. (ed.), *Problems in Addiction: Alcoholism and Narcotics.* New York: Fordham Univ. Press, 1962.

Chafetz, M. E. and Demone, H. W., Jr., *Alcoholism and Society.* New York: Oxford Univ. Press 1962.

Clinebell, H. J., Jr., *Understanding and Counseling the Alcoholic Through Religion and Psychology.* New York: Abingdon, 1956.

Shipp, T. J., *Helping the Alcoholic and His Family.* Englewood Cliffs, New Jersey: Prentice-Hall, 1965.

Counseling the Bereaved

Crisis is the stuff of a pastor's ministry. Week after week, morning, noon, and night, a pastor is called upon to help in situations of maximum stress and distress. One such situation is bereavement as people face the crisis of irreparable separation and heart-rending sorrow. Certain principles can be suggested for a clergyman to follow as he seeks to fulfill his shepherd-function within the context of this life-disrupting experience.

1. BASIC ESSENTIALS

a. The pastor must understand the nature of death. Biblical faith may beget an attitude which belittles death, reducing it to a trifling incident; and the narcotizing effect of faith may be abetted by the clergyman's professional familiarity with an experience that to nonprofessionals is disturbingly unfamiliar. Hence a pastor may be hard put to understand what death means. It is an irremediable loss (at least from the perspective of existence within this world), the shattering of a significant relationship, a feeling of emptiness inside, a collapse of plans, a shrivelling of hope, and sometimes a radical restructuring of life when there is no strength or desire to undertake the task. In some cases, of course, death comes as a relief; in many cases, however, it is an unmitigated horror, a tragedy which punctures the shell of professional familiarity. But in every case, if one accepts the Biblical view, death is a horrendous abnormality, a grotesque perversion of a God-created order, a violent ripping of what ought to be a seamless fabric. The pastor should be aware of all this, not morbidly but empathically. He should not maintain an objective, scientific stance, insisting that this particular death is simply one more illustration of the natural law of mortality. And he should keep himself open and responsive to the meaning of death in general and this death in particular.

b. The pastor must understand that his ability to help members of his own congregation in time of bereavement (the case with strangers is somewhat different) depends largely on the quality of his total relationship with his people. He may not be characterized by concern, sympathy, availability, compassion, and faithfulness. His people may not call upon him in their penultimate crises because they are not sure he cares genuinely or feels profoundly. They may regard him as distant, indifferent, and perfunctory. If so, then in the ultimate crisis of bereavement they may request him to officiate; but it is highly improbable that he will be able to minister in any depth to their needs. Confidence, trust, and rapport are not magically produced by emergency, and without these factors, the fruit of a sustained and agapaic relationship, no clergyman is ever very successful in mediating the grace of God to his people.

c. The pastor must understand that bereavement, whether expected or unexpected, whether brought about by sudden tragedy or lingering illness, often is a sort of emotional earthquake. It can produce psychic pain of severest intensity, to say nothing of physical reactions. It may trigger virtually any pattern of behavior – agitation, hysteria, shock, bitterness, withdrawal, bewilderment, apathy, mild sadness, prolonged melancholia, even suicidal despair. A minister, consequently, must be prepared for unpredictable effects and affects – a once serene believer, for example, may become a belligerent agnostic. Remember the experience of Joseph Parker, the pulpiteer who made London's City Temple world famous. He had publicly declared that doubt never bothered him; then his beloved wife died, and Parker afterward wrote:

> In that dark hour I became almost an atheist. How could I be otherwise – my chief joy taken from me – my only joy – the joy that gave gladness to everything else – the joy that made holy work a holy sacrament? O the Gethsemane bitter-

ness! the Calvary solitude! I had secretly prayed God to pity me by sparing her, yet he set his foot upon my prayers, and treated my petitions with contempt. If I had seen a dog in such agony as mine I would have pitied and helped the dumb beast; yet God spat upon me and cast me out as an offence, — out into the waste wilderness and the night black and starless. My feet had wellnigh slipped. Then a cruel voice said: "Renounce him! Defy him! He forsook his own Son on the Cross. Hate him, and join us, whom he derides and torments as devils!" My soul was exceeding sorrowful even unto death (*Pathways to Happiness*, pp. 35, 36).

The minister should be prepared for such reactions. He must accept them quietly, non-judgmentally, reassuringly.

d. The minister must understand that his most important function is just to be there with his people, not compulsively talking but helpfully caring and sharing by being there. Certainly words have a vital part in the ministry of comfort; yet words, even Biblical quotations, may fail to register. Presence, however, the literal presence of the pastor, serves as a source of strength. He is the flesh-and-blood symbol of God's resources, the embodiment of invisible realities. When he moves into a situation of bereavement, his very presence recalls the promise, "Lo, I am with you always." And, in addition to restrained speaking, the clergyman ministers by listening prayerfully. Sometimes, in fact, the eloquence of nonverbal communication proves more consoling than verbal eloquence.

e. The pastor must understand that there are occasions when holy reticence is more in order than easy explanations which fail either to convince or to console. Assuredly, a clergyman has his faith. And faith, especially evangelicalism, possesses its luminous certainties which cry out for affirmation. The minister is to be pitied who really cannot minister because he has no faith to affirm. Thus the knowledge of Scripture is a prerequisite, a *repertoire* of appropriate texts which can be used meaningfully with tact and discretion. But when ministering to sorrowing people, and particularly people shocked by grotesque and unexpected bereavement, the pastor must avoid clichés, however true and pious they may be; he must avoid learned disquisitions; and he must avoid a mechanical, parrotlike repetition of texts.

Something else needs to be emphasized. The ministerial task is prophetically to afflict the comfortable and pastorally to comfort the afflicted. But in the crisis of bereavement only a calloused pastor insists on discharging the role of prophet. Loyal to his convictions, he will refuse to intimate a bland universalism; yet at the same time he will remember that God alone is the judge and determiner of destiny; and he will, accordingly, eschew severity. Like his Lord he will refuse to break the bruised reed of a human heart.

f. The pastor must understand the central importance of the funeral. He will therefore give careful attention to all its details — hymns, prayers, music, Scripture, sermon, and committal. He must realize that here is a rare opportunity to minister comfort, to magnify God's sufficiency, and to reaffirm the great truths of Christian faith and hope.

g. The pastor must understand that he is only one member of the team which is helping his people meet the crisis of bereavement. He must realize that the mortician is his colleague, not his competitor. He must likewise see to it that all community and church agencies are coordinated to provide a supportive framework for mourners.

2. PIVOTAL PRINCIPLES

Following such guidelines as these, what can the pastor say to his parishioners as they encounter the crisis of bereavement? Bearing in mind that every situation is unique, he may offer such counsel as this:

a. Don't suppress your emotions; express them. If "Jesus wept," there is nothing particularly Christian about dry-eyed courage. An imperturbable self-control is a stoical ideal without New Testament warrant. Genuineness is what God approves rather than a hypocritical façade inspired by the ambition of being outwardly submissive to the divine will when a spirit of angry rebellion seethes within. A measure of self-control is imperative; but an honest expression of emotion is more in keeping with the gospel than a rigorous suppression of emotions.

b. Don't deny your need for help. Far from teaching unaided self-sufficiency, the New Testament teaches loving mutuality. In I Corinthians 12 Paul compares the church to a body, reminding us of our interdependence and rebuking the spirit of people who assert, "I have no need of my fellow-Christians." We are, Paul asserts, a fellowship of weak, inadequate sinners who ought thankfully to lay hold on the grace which comes through the community of the saints. And, helped now, you in the future will be God's means of helping some other mourner.

c. Don't retreat and withdraw. You may be tempted to take refuge in privacy, nursing your hurt and prolonging your sorrow. But this is a temptation which must be resolutely denied. Compel yourself to be with people even if they seem callously preoccupied with ordinary pursuits. They constitute your ties with the world to which you must return.

d. Don't refuse to talk. It may be a struggle to start putting your chaotic feelings in words. But keep up the struggle, and do it from the very onset of bereavement. Relive the whole sequence of events. Rehearse the details out loud and repeatedly. Talking about the experience enables you to desensitize and accept it. Free and uninhibited verbalizing acts as an emotional catharsis.

e. Don't hesitate to avail yourself of Christian resources even though you may have been only an indifferent church member previously. Now is your opportunity to discover how meaningful faith can be. Now is your opportunity to learn that prayer and the Bible and spiritual fellowship are reservoirs of grace and help. Now is your opportunity to realize that in Jesus Christ we can have possessions which are immune to change and decay.

f. Don't indulge in self-condemnation. This is an enervating practice which can be emotionally harmful. Deliberate neglect and malicious harm are a whole dimension removed from innocent error and faulty judgment. Suppose there was innocent error or faulty judgment. Remember that no human being is either omniscient or infallible. One does the best he can in any situation and then blankets his less-than-perfect efforts under the all-forgiving grace of God. With the apostle Paul one must resolutely and emphatically resolve, "Forgetting those things which are behind, I press on" (Phil. 3:18).

g. Don't stay inactive, brooding in idleness. Carry on a routine which is as normal as the abnormal circumstances allow. Get busy once the funeral is over. Launch new projects and begin new activities. Perhaps there are ways in which you can continue some of the purposes and conserve some of the values to which the person you are mourning was committed.

h. Don't make hasty decisions. This principle obviously counterbalances the preceding principle. Refrain from any far-reaching changes until you have regained perspective.

i. Don't undervalue the healing power of time. In the early stages of grief you may imagine the pain will never subside, the great emptiness will never be filled in. But hold on! In time the deepest snowpack melts in the mountains, the broken bones knit, the wound becomes a faint scar. And in time the ache of bereavement dulls and disappears somewhat like the haunting horror of a bad dream.

j. Don't ignore the fundamental fact which bereavement italicizes — your own mortality. Let death motivate reflection on that inescapable encounter of which the Bible speaks in Hebrews 9:27, "It is appointed unto man once to die." Modern psychology unites with Biblical theology in affirming that only the person who has come to terms with the reality of his own death can live out his life authentically.

BIBLIOGRAPHY

There is an ever-increasing amount of literature on this subject, much of it very helpful. A busy pastor may find the following books of value:

Bachmann, C. Charles, *Ministering to the Grief Sufferer.* Englewood Cliffs, N. J., Prentice-Hall, Inc., 1964.

Bowers, Margaretta K., et. al., *Counseling the Dying.* New York: Thomas Nelson & Sons, 1964.

Clerk, N. W., *A Grief Observed.* Greenwich, Connecticut: The Seabury Press, 1963.

Feifel, Herman, ed., *The Meaning of Death.* New York: McGraw-Hill Book Company, Inc., 1959.

Fulton, Robert, ed., *Death & Identity.* New York: John Wiley & Sons, Inc., 1965.

Hoffman, Frederick J., *The Mortal No.* Princeton, New Jersey: Princeton University Press, 1964.

Jackson, Edgar N., *Understanding Grief* New York: Abingdon Press, 1957.

————, *You and Your Grief.* Manhasset, New York: Channel Press, Inc., 1962.

Lyman, Mary Ely, *Death and the Christian Answer.* Lebanon, Pa.: Sowers Printing Company, 1960.

Marshall, Catherine, *To Live Again.* New York: McGraw-Hill Book Company, Inc., 1957.

Pelikan, Jaroslav, *The Shape of Death.* New York: Abingdon Press, 1961.

Rogers, William F., *Ye Shall Be Comforted.* Philadelphia: The Westminster Press, 1950.

Scherzer, Carl J., *Ministering to the Dying.* Englewood Cliffs, N. J.: Prentice-Hall, Inc., 1963.

Ulanov, Barry, *Death: A Book of Preparation & Consolation.* New York: Sheed and Ward, 1959

The Hospital Ministry

Pastors are expected to perform a pastoral ministry to the sick at home and in the hospital. There is growing awareness among ministers that an effective ministry to hospitalized parishioners requires considerable time, effort, and skill. At the present pastors are most interested in becoming more effective in their ministry to the sick.

In the development of modern pastoral counseling pastors were first concerned about "What shall I say?" later, "What shall I do?" and now, "What shall I be?" The recent emphasis is correct. If pastors have acquired spiritual and emotional health it is probable that they will say and do the right things. The best therapeutic skills and techniques are rendered ineffective if the person using them lacks spiritual vitality and emotional maturity.

The pastor's hospital ministry can be made more effective by cooperation with nurses and physicians, the other professional persons who have close contact with the patient. A majority of nurses and physicians have a cordial attitude toward clergymen because of the contribution they make to the health of the hospitalized person. Dr. Paul B. McCleave, Director of the Department of Medicine and Religion of the American Medical Association reveals this cooperative spirit when he writes, "In dealing with the total care and treatment of man for full health we are treating more than a diseased part" (*Journal of Religion and Health,* April, 1963, p. 242). Due in part to the advances in psychosomatic medicine, physicians are increasingly interested in problems of ethics and values, and consequently are seeking guidance from an informed clergy.

The pastor should introduce himself to the head nurse at the hospital as he makes a general inquiry about his parishioner. He should also speak to the head nurse and report on his visit before he leaves. This procedure will give proper recognition to the importance of the nurse and also probably facilitate a pastoral visit by reducing unnecessary interruptions. It is also good etiquette. Nurses will be more hospitable toward visiting pastors if they observe hospital regulations and try to avoid visiting at hours of the day when patients receive care or food.

1. SUGGESTIONS

A therapeutic pastoral ministry to hospitalized parishioners requires that the pastor try to understand the sick person in relation to his illness and environment. Some specific suggestions are:

a. *Be natural.* Do not convey indifference or fear by an air of professionalism.

b. *Be brief.* Persons suffering from pain, fatigue, or fever cannot endure lengthy visits. A 10 minute visit will probably be more helpful than one of 30 minutes.

c. *Do not hurry.* Sit down on a chair (not too close to the person) so that you really give of yourself to the patient. Standing creates the impression that you are anxious to leave.

d. *Do not talk about yourself.*

e. *Do not make jovial remarks or flippant comments* about the body, for example, as, referring to the urinary tract as the "plumbing system."

f. *Do not approach the subject of sickness too soon.* Allow the patient the opportunity and responsibility of telling you about his illness. This can be facilitated by asking the deliberately vague question, "How are you doing today?"

g. *Do not avoid serious conversation when it is initiated by the patient.* He may have spent many hours in making a decision to talk about a difficult subject.

h. *Do not talk about the sick person to others in his presence* otherwise the person is made to feel as an object or thing.

2. CAUTIONS

Some cautions should be noted in dealing with various emotional reactions of hospitalized patients.

a. *The resigned patient.* Some patients may have the fatalistic peaceful resignation of a stoic and consider this attitude to be evidence of superior Christianity.

b. *The rebellious patient.* Patients who feel powerless over against God and the adverse circumstances in their lives may become bitter and rebellious. They may be preoccupied with their exemplary past performances in life and be most concerned with their deserved right to health as God's obligation to them. Such patients ought neither to be rebuked nor comforted. In compassionate love, the pastor must reflect the patient's negative feelings as a necessary beginning to working through the difficulty, with the expectation that the patient will achieve insight in order to correct his perceptions of God and self.

c. *The dependent patient.* Patients may become overly dependent upon pastors and avoid participation in the healing process by regressive behavior. Such patients may derive much secondary gain from their illness and dependency. Naive pastors are frequently party to reenforcing this secondary gain by responding with increasing pastoral attention to those who find their ministry "so helpful."

d. *The manipulative patient.* Some patients may endeavor to have the pastor take a position with him against the physican or family. The pastor should not allow the social prestige of his ministerial office to be used as a tool by the manipulative patient to "play one authority against another" for the patient's own supposed advantage.

3. GUIDELINES

Different kinds of illness produce varied emotional reactions in individuals. The acutely ill person suffers from shock and pain. He needs frequent, brief pastoral visits which provide emotional and spiritual support. The chronically ill person often feels discouraged. He must be helped to verbalize his feelings and work through his problems with the pastor. The critically ill may be argumentative, irritable, pessimistic, or euphoric.

The sick person must be allowed to express negative feelings without either experiencing rejection by the pastor, or being silenced by premature Scripture quotations designed to induce gratitude or get the patient to "look on the bright side." It is as the patient is unconditionally accepted with positive regard by the pastor that he can make progress in achieving a healthy, constructive, attitude toward his illness and hospitalization. This involves both a verbal and attitudinal communication of Christian hope, an essential in the pastor's hospital ministry. Hope makes possible the acceptance of crisis situations with its attendant suffering and pain. Christian hope proffered one person by another provides strength for endurance in rehabilitation and redemption.

Many persons are threatened by the thought of facing surgery. Pastors best support the preoperative patient by dealing with his fears. Surgical patients will express their fears if the pastor offers both a warm, accepting relationship and too much respect for the person to offer false cheer or cheap reassurance. The pastor can strengthen the patient's will to live as he embodies faith, hope, and love and makes a wise use of Scripture, prayer, and hymns.

The convalescent in the hospital or at home is easily ignored. Yet loneliness and boredom opens a convalescent patient most appreciatively to a concerned pastoral ministry. Thanksgiving should be the dominant theme in the pastor's conversation as well as in his use of Scripture and prayer. Some convalescents may wish to ignore the dark days of crisis. Wise spiritual guidance aims to lead the parishioner to a serious recollection of his crisis and consequent deliverance, for the experience of gratitude toward God is an antidote to his loneliness and boredom.

Other convalescents may be depressed because their health is not now as good as it was before illness. These patients need encouragement and guidance in achieving a new sense of the possibilities in Christian living. Some convalescents may disguise their depressive feelings by a hyper-spirituality in which they are morbidly preoccupied with their preference for death rather than life. Spiritual guidance which reveals the Christian obligation to serve God here and now as well as later, may be a profitable prescription.

New mothers and babies unfortunately, are sometimes considered routine and therefore not in need of pastoral concern. New mothers appreciate a call from the pastor while in the hospital. Here the church, a fellowship of the concerned, can enter into the parents' joy and reaffirm with them that every birth, however routine, represents a gift and miracle of God. The hospital call should be followed by a family call at home. Especially so if this is the first child and the parents are somewhat bewildered by and fearful of parenthood.

Pastors should try to be aware of the personality of each patient. This implies sensitivity to the possible false bravado in the emotionally unstable patient who says, "You know me pastor, my faith is strong and I'm always ready for all news – good or bad." Behind these brave words may be a strong fear. In Christian charity the pastor must react to the unspoken truth rather than to the "brave words." But a pastor cannot depend on some inherent sensitivity to accomplish this. He lays the groundwork for such discernment in all efforts designed to get to know his people well.

The pastor need not feel obligated to initiate the topic of death with all those who are critically ill. Certainly he should not plunge into it thoughtlessly or with compulsive urgency. Consultation with the physician and family should precede any such discussion with the patient. Human judgments are not always valid in predicting the course of disease. Patients have a right to know the truth, but they are not always the best judges as to the choice of proper time to receive this information. Inasmuch as God hides the future from us in mercy in order that we might have strength for each day, it would seem proper that we should not presume to reveal quickly what we think the future will be. This is neither to be considered giving false comfort nor lying, but merely a humble awareness that we do not know, and are enjoined to act in love.

Pastors can be helpful to the dying by recognizing that the patient probably considers death an enemy which cuts human bonds of love and attacks the unity of his body and soul. In this circumstance it is important to reaffirm the promises of the gospel, especially the truth that death cannot separate from God. The use of prayer, Scripture and hymns are most appropriate in a pastoral ministry to the dying.

The subject of death and the life to come may be gently initiated in pastoral conversations with those aged who are excessively concerned about the problems of this life. The pastor should also be alert to the spiritual needs of patients who want to die in order to be relieved of pain, but who ignore the act of faith in giving the heart to Christ. The Father's house is open to those who are and want to be children of God.

BIBLIOGRAPHY

Westberg, Granger E., *Minister and Doctor Meet.* New York: Harper & Brothers, 1961.

Wurth, G. Brillenburg, *Christian Counseling.* Grand Rapids: Baker Book House, 1962.

Young, Richard K., *The Pastor's Hospital Ministry.* Nashville: Broadman Press, 1964.

Young, Richard K. and Meiburg, Albert L., *Spiritual Therapy.* New York: Harper & Brothers, 1960.

Dealing with Illegitimacy

The number of registered out-of-wedlock births in the United States each year has increased to the staggering figure of about 250,000. Annually, this represents about one out of every nineteen births in the nation. This problem spans an age range of about eleven years to the early forties, with the greatest number occurring in persons from seventeen to twenty-five years of age.

The problem is no respecter of race, intellect, educational achievement, social status, economics, vocation or religion.

Local, state and national groups – both

privately sponsored and governmental agencies – have been much involved seeking ways and means of meeting this ever-increasing problem.

The problem has also very seriously invaded the Christian community. Maternity homes and adoption agencies are reporting a constant increase in the number of unwed mother referrals from pastors.

1. THE PASTOR'S ROLE

Thus the local pastor is now, and will be increasingly, involved in this problem at the grass roots level. I feel this is good because it presupposes an image of the pastor as one who understands life's problems and one to whom a distraught soul can go in times of serious personal difficulties.

Because pastors are increasingly confronted with this problem, it is important that they examine their own feelings and philosophies about illegitimate pregnancy, that they understand some of the underlying causes and effects of illegitimacy, and that they be aware of the community resources that can be of assistance.

The moment of discovery of an unwed pregnancy is usually a moment of shocked disbelief, of panic, and of serious emotional trauma. By the time the girl has marshaled her courage to inform her pastor, she has already recognized the wrong in her situation. Thus we do not feel that the traditional Victorian concept which cries, "Let us make her suffer for her misdeeds" is appropriate.

One of the most frequent comments by pastors referring an unwed mother to a Christian adoption agency is this: "I don't know how this could have happened to a girl from such a wonderful, Christian home." The clinical experience of Christian adoption agencies, however, has highlighted the fact that the underlying causes of illegitimacy are usually the same for the Christian as for the non-Christian girl or boy. (Studies reveal that the same basic factors which propel a girl into unwed motherhood also propel a boy into unwed fatherhood.)

2. POSSIBLE ALTERNATIVES

When a pastor is confronted with this problem it is usually with the understanding – either by the girl or boy or their parents or both – that he will be able to offer wise counsel. The immediate questions which need to be answered are essentially these: (1) Should I, their pastor, encourage the young couple to marry? (2) Should I advise against marriage? And, if so, under what circumstances? (3) Should I encourage the girl to keep her baby even if marriage is not possible? (4) Or should I refer her to an adoption agency?

These are very difficult questions. The appropriate answers will result from an understanding of the basic psychodynamics involved in out-of-wedlock pregnancies and the peculiar circumstances of each such situation presented.

Let us begin with marriage as the alternative. Is this the better answer? Not if pregnancy is the only motivation for the marriage. Two wrongs do not make a right. They only serve to compound an already complex situation. A forced marriage is nearly always an unhappy marriage of two bitter people who feel trapped and resentful. The child will be a constant reminder to them of the act which precipitated the unhappy union – if indeed it remains a union very long.

Some will argue that a short, platonic marriage will give the child a name and this is preferred to permitting the child to be born illegitimately. This is not so, for at least three reasons. God never intended marriage to be used in this fashion; divorce is never an easy out; and it is erroneous to assume that every girl bearing a child out-of-wedlock, no matter what her age may be, really wants to be a mother, or is emotionally fit for motherhood.

Another frequently heard alternative dictates that since the girl was adult enough to produce a child she should be made to keep and care for her child because she needs to learn to be responsible for her own actions. The fallacy in this statement is that it discounts the underlying psychodynamics in illegitimacy. It usually compels the child to suffer for the irresponsibility of his mother. It also erroneously presupposes that every girl who bears a child out of wedlock is able to assume the responsibility of motherhood.

The other alternative is one that many pastors have come to realize and to utilize with increasing frequency. This involves the referral of the girl to a licensed adoption agency. Here she encounters professionally trained people who will accept her status of impending motherhood – not condoning her illicit sex relationship but recognizing the reality of its motivation and consequences. She will be assisted in arriving at a meaningful and realistic decision with regard to the baby of the application of the therapeutic counseling and the exploration of alternatives.

We have mentioned the psychodynamics of illegitimacy several times, and have intimated that an understanding of the underlying causes of illegitimacy will usually point to adoption as the better answer. This is true, because we find that in these situations the child is not usually desired for himself but rather is a symbol or a means to an end. In most instances there is an unconscious motivation for the pregnancy which, with professional help, can be discerned. Some frequent motivations are a need to prove femininity, a desire for marriage, retaliation against an unloving, neglectful or abandoning parent (a situation real or imagined), or a need to prove creative ability to parents.

Most unwed mothers are victims of their parents' problems and come from homes dominated by one parent – usually the mother. Here the mother is reluctant to accept her femininity; she resents and often despises her weak, ineffectual husband. In homes where the father is dominant, clinical observation reveals him to be an abusive, unreasonable tyrant. The mother is also afraid of him and becomes more of a big sister than a mother to her daughter. The girl unconsciously resents her mother for this and is more dependent on her father than she realizes. In both of these situations the girl is deprived of a right relationship with either parent.

In these instances the sexual involvement on the part of the girl is almost incidental. The basic need for which she sought gratification was emotional. She had need to feel loved, to be needed, and wanted and useful. This girl is easy prey for sex involvement because of her desire to please.

With this information as background, I feel pastors are in a unique situation to do some preventive work in this area. Obviously the key here is the relationship between mother and father. If a woman is to be a good mother she must first be a good wife; if a man is to be a good father he must first be a good husband.

Wholesome marriage and parent-child relationships based on Scriptural patterns and a dedication of the body to the Lord are the best preventive measures in existence today – as indeed they have always been throughout the history of human relationships.

BIBLIOGRAPHY

Vincent, Clark E., *Unmarried Mothers.* Glencoe, Ill: Free Press, 1961.

Young, Leontine, *Out of Wedlock.* New York: McGraw-Hill, 1954.

Hawes, Sheilah James, "Pregancy out of Wedlock," *Journal of Pastoral Care,* XIX, pp. 154-163, Fall, 1965.

The Mentally Ill and Their Families

The pastor in his ministry to the mentally ill must have a determinative principle to know what he is doing. The determinative New Testament pastoral principle is the obligation to bind people to Christ and to keep up that relationship of faith in the people who are bound to Christ through the aid of the Holy Spirit. Adherence to this Biblical perspective will keep pastors from entering upon the respective roles of the psychiatrist and psychologist.

1. IMPORTANCE OF WORKING WITH THE FAMILY

An important aspect of the pastor's ministry to the mentally ill is related to the families of the mentally ill and the pastoral care they desire and should receive. There are many emergency needs in connection with mental illness. This is particularly true in connection with attacks of serious mental illness such as the involutional psychotic reactions, the depressions of various types, and the acute schizophrenic reactions. Parishioners have confidence in their pastor's willingness and ability to help them in meeting crises in connection with the onset of disturbed behavior related to mental illness. The minister's role and performance in an emergency situation is affected by his relationship with psychiatrists, psychologists, and physicians. The pastor should have accurate information about mental health resources available for referral.

Families of the mentally ill frequently need pastoral assistance in deciding what professional assistance will be most helpful to the emotionally disturbed person. Pastoral support and assistance is needed in seeking good answers to such pressing questions as: Is hospitalization necessary? Acutely disturbed behavior and symptoms such as agressiveness or withdrawal suggest the need for hospitalization. In the event that the mentally ill person has no insight into his need for assistance, it may be necessary for his protection and that of society that the family use the process of legal commitment to a psychiatric hospital. The pastor must not make this decision because he will lose his important religious and pastoral role. However the pastor should provide emotional support to the family in their considered decision to effect legal commitment when the prospective patient cannot or will not agree to a voluntary hospitalization. If the pastor is in doubt about the necessity of hospitalization he should consult with the family physician or a psychiatrist. He may also consider arranging for a psychiatric interview and evaluation at a hospital with a view to possible admission.

2. SELECTING A HOSPITAL

If hospitalization is necessary, to which hospital should the mentally ill person be referred? Only three per cent of the psychiatric hospitals in the United States are nongovernmental and most of these are private institutions. There is now an increasing trend for the general hospitals to operate a psychiatric unit. Many families now have hospitalization insurance but some insurance plans give less assistance to patients in a psychiatric hospital than they do to those in psychiatric units of general hospitals. Families should be discouraged from accumulating great indebtedness through extended hospitalization in a private institution operated for a profit. In many cases churches can give financial support to the families of the mentally ill for the care and treatment of the sick person. The Biblical principle of bearing one another's burdens for the fulfillment of the law of love comes into the picture here (Gal. 6:2).

The pastor should assist the family in selecting a hospital that offers an active treatment program supervised by a qualified professional staff. This will facilitate early treatment and consequent earlier recovery. The hospital of choice may be determined by finances, the hospital's past record in treating troubled persons, and, other things being equal, geography. If the mentally ill person is hospitalized near his home he will have the advantage of having frequent visitors and will not feel as hopelessly cut off from his friends and family.

If a decision is made by the family to use the facilities of a state mental hospital they may need help with the idea of chronicity and hopelessness associated with these. The pastor should be aware of the many fine improvements recently made in the operation of these governmental institutions, and the constant attempts of administrators to effect additional improvements in the psychiatric services rendered.

The author would like to suggest that churches, pastors, and the families of the mentally ill give serious consideration to the establishment and utilization of Christian mental hospitals. The properly accredited Christian mental hospital with an adequately trained professional staff is best qualified to help the mentally ill because mental illness, whatever else it may be, is basically a religious problem because it cannot be understood apart from that which gives meaning to our living: our values, sense of destiny, commitments, communion, and convictions. The mentally ill person has been hurt in his interpersonal relationships and it is love which is the most dynamic healing force. This love, joined with faith and hope, is the motivating force in a wise and compassionate care and treatment of the mentally ill.

The Christian mental hospital believes that religion is not a necessary corrective to be added as a complement to other disciplines, but that it is a central unity to be integrated with science in order to give proper dimensions to all of life. Secular healing renders obeisance to the principle of reverence for life. The Christian hospital worships the Holy Spirit (the source of life) as the divine person who saves and heals today. In faithful dependence upon the Holy Spirit, the Christian hospital fulfills its mission of mercy and healing in quiet confidence that a sovereign God has made available since Pentecost an eternal Spirit whose healing potential we have not yet fully realized. The recognition and dependence upon the Holy Spirit undoubtedly is the most unique feature and significant resource of the Christian mental hospital. This resource may be quite intangible, but it is everlastingly real.

The Protestant denominations which have taken an interest in the establishment of church-related mental hospitals in the United States are the Society of Friends, the Presbyterian, the Lutheran, the Mennonite, and the Seventh-day Adventist churches. In addition there is the cooperative work of the Reformed Church in America and the Christian Reformed Church in the maintenance of Christian psychiatric hospitals at Wyckoff, New Jersey, Grand Rapids, Michigan, and Denver, Colorado.

Hospitalization is not always necessary. Pastors who have had supervised clinical pastoral training may be able to provide adequate help to the mildly neurotically disturbed parishioner by means of pastoral counseling. Many persons suffering from a more serious neurotic difficulty can receive successful therapy from psychiatrists and psychologists on an out-patient basis. The new community mental health centers may also be able to provide therapy for people whose emotional disturbances are related to life situation adjustment reactions.

3. SELECTING A THERAPIST

The pastor should be aware of the value system of the therapist whom he recommends to the mentally ill and their families. Every therapist has a value system which includes negative and positive relationships to God. He cannot free himself from the totality of his personality with its background material of faith or unbelief regarding God. This position is supported by Dr. Richard P. Vaughan who makes the observation in the *Journal of Religion and Health*. "Although he [the therapist] may make every effort, he will never be able to obliterate completely the influence of religion on his attitudes and views. These influences are sometimes reflected in seemingly innocuous responses and reactions to the patients statements. Consciously or unconsciously, he gives an indication of approval or disapproval through the medium of words or gestures. If the therapist is honest with himself and takes the time to reflect, he will see that a number of his responses are based upon his own religious and moral convictions" (Vol. 2, No. 3, p. 201).

The pastor should not recommend to a Christian in need of psychiatric care a therapist who is known to be hostile toward the Christian faith. It is also important to recognize that it would be preferable to refer to a non-Christian therapist who would be tolerant of Christianity than to refer to a professing Christian therapist who was known to be psychiatrically or psychologically incompetent.

The professionally competent Christian therapist should be the referral of choice since the Christian patient may expect to receive more understanding and help from a therapist who has a similar value system. The non-Christian patient may also expect the Christian therapist to provide maximum therapeutic help as he is perceived as a creation of God with individual potentiality for self-actualization. Names and addresses of practicing psychiatrists and psychologists who are professing Christians (it is not to be inferred that all Christian therapists are members of the listed organizations) may be obtained by correspondence with: The Christian Medical Society, 1122 Westgate, Oak Park, Illinois, and Christian Association for Psychological Studies, 6850 S. Division Avenue, Grand Rapids, Michigan 49508.

4. VARIOUS RESPONSIBILITIES AND SERVICES

In the pastor's ministry to the families of the mentally ill, he is often called upon to be an interpreter of mental illness. Families find it difficult to understand the bizarre behavior of a loved one, particularly when the person has turned against one or all of them. It is helpful if the pastor in his ministry to the families of the mentally ill can provide necessary information concerning the various forms of treatment that are available for the benefit of the mentally ill and the emotionally disturbed. There are still too many people who lack elementary information about mental illness. The pastor should have available for distribution copies of *Mental Illness: A Guide for the*

Family, by Edith M. Stern which gives important information in plain language. In all his interpretation the pastor should convey genuine optimism about the possibility of recovery without minimizing the seriousness of the problem.

The pastor in his ministry to the family must be aware of the emotional needs of the family. He must be alert to the probability of panic reactions in the family because of the sudden onset of some forms of mental illness. He must be sensitive to the fact that there is a likelihood that there will be feelings of hopelessness, helplessness, loneliness, and anxiety. There is a possibility that the wife will be concerned about the threat of possible divorce as a result of chronic mental illness. An adolescent might interpret mental illness to be synonymous with death. Pastors ought to be aware of these and other tensions in the family which are precipitated by mental illness. Dr. Samuel Southard writes about the tensions in the family to which the pastor ought to be alerted. He says in *The Family and Mental Illness*, "The National Institutes of Health discover that when a husband is hospitalized there is likely to be much tension between the wife and her in-laws. Before hospitalization, the wife tends to turn toward her husband's relatives for support and assistance. There is a good deal of hostility running through this; the wife may tend to blame the husband's parents for causing the illness, the parents blame the wife for the same thing. Once the husband is in the hospital, the wife tends to look to her own family for help; they now offer financial assistance, and help to care for the children. Husband's families are more frequent in their visits to the hospital, but neither side of the house does much consistent visiting. The wife seems to understand this, and makes little complaint" (p. 86).

The pastor is often called upon to serve as a pastoral guide in dealing with ethical matters — shall the patient know the truth, and who shall inform him of his present condition, etc. The pastor may also function as a pastoral director as he alerts the diaconate and the district elder concerning the needs of the family so that the church may demonstrate love as a fellowship of the concerned. The families of the mentally ill have great needs, some are met by the social worker, some are met by the psychiatrist, but the pastor also has a role in which he tends the sheep who are in need of the undershepherd. He needs to provide understanding, support, direction, comfort, and consolation.

Pastors can perform an expected and a necessary service to the mentally ill before hospitalization because many parishioners will consult a psychologist or psychiatrist or visit the out-patient department of a psychiatric hospital upon the recommendation, and with the encouragement of the pastor. In this way the pastor can exercise a supportive role prior to and during hospitalization. Patients affirm that this supportive relationship is very important to them because of their real need for emotional support and religious comfort.

There should be a pastoral ministry to the mentally ill during hospitalization. It is important to the patient to have his pastor visit him soon after hospitalization, especially if the pastor did not see the patient prior to hospitalization. The pastor represents the Christian community and is an important person in the life of the person who is sick. A pastoral visit means that a representative of the church is concerned about him. The pastor's visit is also an indication of the interest of Jesus Christ, the Chief Shepherd. There is a symbolical connection in the minds of patients between their pastor and Christ, the compassionate High Priest.

Pastors who have some understanding of mental illness will not naively debate delusions or directly and persistently challenge hallucinations. A listening ministry and responsive counseling joined with a patient searching for the meaningful specific spiritual prescription is to be preferred. This kind of counseling with the mentally ill proceeds from a theological orientation which utilizes the Word of God and prayer plus psychotherapeutic techniques in order to promote spiritual health and indirectly psychic health.

Pastors do not always need a diagnosis before they can help. Pastors who have some knowledge and training can be trusted by therapists to utilize caution so that they do not merely give easy assurances which unintentionally seek to minimize deep depressions (and actually aggravate them). Neither will they want to encourage over-dependency in severe neurotics who need professional psychiatric care.

The pastor can be most effective in his ministry to the mentally ill when they return to home and church after a period of hospitalization. The pastor should maintain close ties and be readily available for counseling during the adjustment period following treatment. The understanding pastor also can help the convalescent to become reintegrated into the life of the church and community by enabling the person to take on small responsibilities in order to regain self-confidence. A prominent European psychiatrist, Dr. Andre Liengme, has written that that which afflicts the mentally ill more than anything else is a lack of confidence. Pastors can also educate their parishioners to demonstrate Christian love and acceptance to the convalescent in order to facilitate his rehabilitation.

One of the greatest contributions that the pastor can make is of a preventative nature. By means of an effective preaching, teaching, and counseling ministry, the minister can promote healthy relationships for persons with themselves, with God, and with their fellow men. This program will help build a reservoir of strength which shall enable people to more effectively persevere in the crises of life.

In the process of developing an effective program of pastoral counseling to the mentally ill and their families, the pastors must resist the secularistic pressure to bypass Jesus Christ in favor of a complete subservience to the latest psychological and sociological theories concerning personality. They must also resist the unhealthy religious pressure to bypass all interest in the areas of psychiatry and psychology in favor of an other-worldliness which is unrealistic in its attitude toward mental illness. Pastors must be willing and able to join other interested persons in accepting the challenge courageously to investigate the dynamic interrelationships of spiritual health and psychic health in order that they and those to whom they minister may truly participate in a more abundant life in and by Jesus Christ (John 10:10).

BIBLIOGRAPHY

Clinebell, Howard J., Jr. *Mental Health Through Christian Community.* Nashville: Abingdon Press, 1965.

Kemp, Charles F. *The Church: The Gifted and the Retarded Child.* St. Louis: Bethany Press, 1957.

Laycock, Samuel R., *Pastoral Counseling for Mental Health.* Nashville: Abingdon Press, 1961.

National Association for Mental Health, 10 Columbus Circle, New York 19, New York.
Stern, Edith, *Mental Illness: A Guide for the Family.*
Clergyman's Guide to Recognizing Serious Mental Illness.
Ministering to the Families of the Mentally Ill.
Milt, Harry, *Basic Facts About Mental Illness.*

Oates, Wayne E., *Religious Factors in Mental Illness.* New York: Association Press, 1955.

Southard, Samuel, *The Family and Mental Health.* Nashville: Abingdon Press, 1961.

Counseling in Sexual Deviation

Abnormal sexual behavior among members of his congregation or parish at times requires the attention of the minister. Perhaps the one who indulges in this activity himself seeks counsel. This may be because of his own distress at his actions or upon the request of his family. Not infrequently the pastor finds himself called upon to render assistance to someone who has brought upon himself police or court action. On occasion he may be asked to advise as to the permissibility of some form of sexual behavior. For these reasons he must be aware of the existence of sexual deviation, and in a general way, of its causes.

Sexual deviation must be considered any pattern of sexual behavior serving as a major source of sexual gratification in itself, rather than being a part of or leading to normal affectionate sexual relations.

1. TYPES OF PERVERSION

Among common perversions (sometimes known as paraphilia) which may come to the attention of the pastor are:

(a) *Overt homosexuality,* the choice of a sexual object of the same sex. Homosexuality among females is often known as Lesbianism.

(b) *Pedophilia,* the choice of a sexually immature object for sexual activity, such as the molestation of children.

(c) *Exhibitionism,* the exhibition of the genital organs for the purpose of obtaining sexual gratification.

(d) *Voyeurism,* obtaining sexual gratification in looking at the sexual organs or activities of others.

(e) *Sadomasochism,* requiring the infliction or suffering of pain as the prerequisite of sexual gratification.

(f) *Compulsive masturbation,* the preference of self-stimulation to a sexual relationship with another person.

(g) *Nymphomania,* the compulsive desire for sexual relation, with no true affection, and no real satisfaction.

Less commonly the pastor may be faced in his parish with *transvestism* (the desire to wear the clothes of the opposite sex), *fetishism* (sexual gratification through a part of the clothing of the opposite sex), *zoophilism* (often called sodomy, sexual love for animals), and lust murder. At the other extreme, *obscenity* (obsession with dirty words) and *pornography* (the interest in erotic literature) may be so common that he may not recognize them as often being perversions, more of a source of sexual gratification than is a relationship with a real person.

2. PROPER PROCEDURE

To be able to counsel with those afflicted with these aberrations the minister may first need to rid himself of the revulsion or horror that society feels toward them. Though he may consider them sins, understanding, compassion, and concern will be far more effective than disgust as tools in his dealing with the deviant who is truly a victim of his deviations.

For, in fact, each of these people has either never developed beyond certain immature stages of sexual interest known in childhood, or under certain circumstances has returned to immature attitudes and ways of sexual gratification. The person subject to these means of sexual pleasure has not "grown up" to be able to find an adult relationship with another adult. Each of these represents some deviation from the practice of a normal adult relationship.

This fact leads to another, that the impulses to perform these acts are beyond ordinary methods of control. Counseling a person to use more self-control is usually wasted advice. The one who performs the acts mentioned is himself helpless to prevent his impulses. His coming to a pastor for help indicates his need.

When the pastor is counseling such a one, he should first listen patiently and without shock to what the other has to say. If the person before him is full of the agony of remorse, there is no need for a lecture on the enormity of what is being done. At times the person seeking counsel may really want justification of his acts. The pastor may point out that certain of these perversions are specifically mentioned as sins in the Bible (homosexuality, zoophilia – Lev. 20: 15, 16, 23; Exod. 22:19), that others are more generally sinful in that children are damaged, that the person is not truly being what God made him to be and the like. Some homosexuals condone their activity by protesting that this is less sinful than fornication; this type of "moral" appeal should always be rejected firmly; its seeming religiosity is simply a cloak for the psychiatric problem recognized by every one versed in the psychological development of homosexuality.

After he has listened, the pastor may try by questioning to discover what steps the person has taken to avoid carrying out his impulse. It may be important to point out to this person that at times carrying out the impulse may be controlled, just as the average man does not always give way to his impulses toward a woman. However, control in these diviations is usually far more difficult than in the care of normal sexuality. The person may need to regulate his life so as to avoid opportunities for temptation – a homosexual or pedophiliac should ordinarily avoid working with children or young people, etc. A painful experience is that of helping an older and often faithful member of the church when he has begun to expose the sexual organs of children, or show his own to them. It is in these cases that tactful discussion with the family may be most useful in the prevention of occasions for such behavior, so that confinement in an institution can be foregone.

Many of these people refuse to seek full psychiatric help, even though it may correct or at least ameliorate their problem. The pastor, through emphasizing the fact that these practices cannot be condoned, may encourage the one practicing them to seek the help he needs. The homosexual in particular is likely to refuse help by self-justifying excuses. He is likely to profess satisfaction in his mode of behavior, and to complain that he is being persecuted for his preference for men. It may be useful to listen to his complaints, his stories of the unfaithfulness of his friends, both normal and homosexual, and then point out that his inability to make lasting friendships (a notorious fact which even he may admit) indicates as much as his abnormal sexual behavior that he suffers from a profound personality disorder.

Above all, the pastor needs to assure sexual deviates that the love of God does not fall short of them, that they are not beyond his grace. The fact that they are still deviates (and perhaps always will be) should lead them to an increasing recognition of their need for God's grace. An excessively judgmental and censorious attitude will likely drive the deviate to such despair, particularly if he is indeed deviant, that all the joy of his salvation (and he needs joy more than most of us) will be lost.

It is important for the minister to recognize what is not a sexual perversion. For instance, he may be told by a married woman that her husband practices unnatural sex acts. Rather than assume that this is so, he should recall that a sexually disturbed person may consider many of the caresses of normal love-making as sinful or beastly. It may not be advisable to insist that she tell what disturbs her, for her own problem may be too serious to be dealt with except by a well-trained professional therapist, but if she seems reasonable, it may be possible to point out to her that there is a wide variety in normal sexual behavior. Her own distaste for some particular form does not necessarily indicate that her husband is perverted.

Most sexual deviations indicate severe psychological disorders, and should be referred to the specialist – the psychiatrist or clinical psychologist. The minister, however, may be a strong friend to the sexual deviant, reminding him of the normal Christain standard of behavior and of God's forgiveness and grace as well. The pastor counseling with sexual deviates will often find himself sorely tried, but will gain satisfactions in finding that he has restored more than one drifting person to full fellowship with his Lord.

BIBLIOGRAPHY

Arieti, Sylvana, ed., *American Handbook of Psychiatry*, 2 vols. New York: Basic Books, Inc., 1959.

Abse, D. Wilfred, "Sexual Disorders and Marriage" in *Marriage Counseling in Medical Practice.* Chapel Hill, N. C.: University of North Carolina Press, 1964.

Bergler, Edmund, *Homosexuality: Disease or Way of Life.* New York: Collier Books, 1962.

Eisenstein, Victor W., ed., *Neurotic Interactions in Marriage.* New York: Basic Books, Inc., 1956.

Hampton, Wate T., *The Sexual Psychopath.* Los Angeles: Medco Books, 1965.

Noyes, Arthur P., and Kolbe, Lawrence C., *Modern Clinical Psychiatry*, 6th ed. Philadelphia: W. B. Saunders Co., 1963.

Piper, Otto, *A Biblical View of Sex and Marriage.* New York: Charles Scribner's Sons, n.d.

Counseling the Aged

The pastor who is counseling with the aged is likely to discover that they, like the poor, require much help in the solution of practical details of living.

This need for material help arises from the generally lowered income, the loss of family on which he may have been dependent, the need for a change in his home. The aged person is particularly vulnerable to these vicissitudes. These all occur at a time of life when waning physical power and at times emotional limitations render him less capable than formerly of making the decisions and adjustments that his life requires. For example, he is likely to need advice as to housing and medical and nursing care. The lack of a housekeeper may seriously handicap an aged woman caring for her infirm husband; she may not even know how to go about finding such assistance, even if she is willing and able to afford such help.

The older person faces the problem of housing because of varying circumstances. His home may be destroyed in an urban renewal program, or it may be too large for him to maintain once the family has gone. Perhaps he is no longer able to care for himself adequately. Under these or other circumstances he needs assistance in deciding where to live. The pastor may not feel qualified to give advice and under these circumstances can refer his parishioner to some sort of social service agency offering services for the aged. At the same time, it is of utmost importance for him to guide the older one who is unwilling to consider some of the choices of a place to live that would suit him best. Among the possibilities to be considered are communities for the aged, often known as retirement villages, residential hotels, rooming houses, nursing homes. Often the aged have prejudices against these that must be overcome. If the minister becomes aware of the facilities near by he can be of immeasurable value by his personal evaluation of their quality. Of course, at times it is possible to continue living in the old house with some assistance from the outside – a younger family may be happy to take over many of the chores of the household in return for good housing for themselves. It still is best at times to encourage the oldster to live with his children, though modern living conditions with the increased concentration in small homes or apartments in the city makes this generally less frequently feasible. Counseling may be needed to help overcome some of the problems raised by these arrangements.

It is good for the pastor to know a physician to whom he can refer the aged, one who is particularly interested in their needs. Such a referral may lead to the alleviation of many minor annoyances of the later years, as well as encourage proper attention to treatment of more serious conditions.

Counseling in the areas of less material aspects of life cannot be ignored. Each of us needs some sense of significance, and the old man and woman are not exempt from this need. No longer the breadwinner or the nurturer, the aged one feels useless and life is likely to seem a heavy and sad burden to him. In fact, the roles of the earlier years may have been reversed so that a parent finds himself now being almost the ward of the children he previously directed and supported.

It has been found that one of the important factors in keeping the aged in good physical and mental health is the presence of some purpose for their lives. These purposes may seem trivial to outsiders, but important to them. If he lives with his family, the old man may find importance in walking the grandchildren to school, or doing some of the shopping. Often the family must be counseled not to become too solicitous or protective. In the church, there are definite tasks for some – church visitor, adult (or even young people's) Bible school teacher, part-time helper in the church office when mailings are to be sent out, or sexton. The filling of these positions and others not only helps the older person but also fills in gaps of the church program. Clubs for older people are increasing. Some have programs that do not appeal to church people, but others afford opportunities for the development of artistic talents, mechanical skills, socializing and education. At times the aged man or woman can be encouraged to develop some interest in a part-time occupation.

Within the last twenty years it has been found that much of the mental and emotional problems of old age are due to the same processes that effect the younger. It was formerly felt that the "queerness" of old people was due to hardening of the arteries of the brain, or degeneration of brain tissue. However, it is now known that this is only a part of the problem, perhaps only a small part. Frustration at being unable to perform as well as before, loneliness as contemporaries die or move away, anxiety about financial security and health, unhappiness with a circumscribed life – these are the factors that counselors will listen for, knowing that they lead to most of the mental deterioration of old age.

The counselor is at times startled to discover that a couple long married approaches him because of marital conflict. During the early years of the marriage, the relationship between the man and woman was held together by the needs of the children rather than by the mutual bonds between the two. Now that the children no longer need them, the relationship between the two older people may prove so destructive and disturbing that they can no longer tolerate each other's presence. The mere fact that they have lived together many years does not make the aged couple better suited to continue in the marriage. The fact that the man is at home more than formerly may increase tensions which were previously controlled. Contrary to the general opinion, sexual feeling does not disappear with advancing years, and frustration in this area of life may prove even more disturbing as life draws to an end and the person who has found difficulty in sexual expression becomes anxious that he will never receive what he has been looking for.

Spiritual counseling in this era of life is as important as ever. If the older person has been a Christian for many years, his earlier experience of faith may sustain him and the pastor finds himself blessed, receiving rather than giving. However, even this type of a saint appreciates the opportunity for fellowship with a fellow believer, particularly if he is shut-in, and his faith may be warmed by the pastor's concern for his needs. There are others whose faith has waivered under the stress of bereavement, or who have grown cold through the years. Still others may be ready now for the first time to face the issues of their relationship to God through Jesus Christ, the whole matter of salvation. And, then, the possibility of death becomes much more immediate as one grows older.

The person who comes for counseling has a need; the pastor may discover that the expressed problem disguises a more profound one. Evangelism in the later years of life seems difficult. Rather moralistically, some people feel that too much time has been lost for effective service, that it is better to work with young people. On the other hand, the old stand in the need of grace as well as the young. The Lord Jesus Christ spoke of the employer who paid his workers the same wages whether they had worked one hour, or all day – their needs determined their pay.

Whether encouraging a person to accept salvation for the first time, or encouraging rededication in the one whose faith has grown dim, counseling in spiritual matters affords not only an opportunity for a closer walk with God, but also a means of finding satisfactions, joy, companionship, and meaning in whatever state a man lives. However, the counselor may need to demonstrate the sincerity of his interest by attention to the problems that brought the aged to him. Genuine friendliness is probably the first step in evangelism.

As for the fear of death, this is present even among many Christians. The assurance of God's love and protection, the evidence of Christ's resurrection, the promise of eternal life, rather than scolding weak faith help in the development of a clam willingness for death when it comes. The fact that dying is a part of living may seem strange but it is a fact nonetheless. One of the greatest obstacles in counseling in the face of death is that the counselor himself has not faced up to the fact of death. Too often his own anxiety or denial makes his help inadequate.

Counseling of the aged demands knowledge of their needs and of the resources available to meet them, awareness of the special problems and limitations of the old, and patience in dealing with them. It offers at the same time definite satisfactions in bringing usefulness, enrichment, and joy into the lives of people facing increasing constriction in many aspects of life.

BIBLIOGRAPHY

Blanchard, Fessenden S., *Make the Most of Your Retirement.* Garden City, N. Y.: Doubleday & Co., 1963.

Donahue, Wilma T. and Tibbits, Clark, *New Frontiers of Aging.* Ann Arbor: University of Michigan, 1957.

Lally, James J., *The Over-50 Health Manual.* Englewood Cliffs, N. J.: Prentice-Hall, Inc., 1961.

Smith, Horace Grady, *Don't Retire from Life.* Chicago: Rand, McNally & Co., 1965.

Stern, Edith M., *You and Your Aging Parents.* New York: Harper and Row, 1965.

Tibbitts, Clark and Donahue, Wilma, *Aging in Today's Society.* Englewood, N. J.: Prentice-Hall, Inc., n.d.

Tournier, Paul, *The Seasons of Life.* Richmond: John Knox, 1963.

DIRECTORIES

Directory of Member Agencies
Family Service Agency of America
44 East 23 Street
New York, New York 10010

Directory of U. S. and Canadian Hospitals
American Hospital Association
840 North Lakeshore Drive
Chicago, Illinois 60611

National Directory of Homes for Older People
National Council on the Ageing
49 West 45 Street
New York, New York 10036

SECTION 6

ADMINISTRATION

"Tend the flock of God which is among you, exercising the oversight . . . neither as lording it over the charge allotted to you, but making yourselves ensamples to the flock."

— I Peter 5:2, 3

Church Organization: Its Development and Forms

There is some uncertainty, and therefore some dispute, concerning the manner in which the Christian church was organized during the early years of its separate existence. But it seems likely that in the churches of the New Testament no one pattern of government prevailed universally. The well-known Anglican scholar, the late Burnett H. Streeter, states the matter thus, "There is no one form of church order which alone is primitive, and which therefore possesses the sanction of apostolic precedent" (*The Primitive Church*, pp. 261, 262). A more recent Episcopalian scholar, Frederick C. Grant, says, "There is variety in the forms of organization, in the ministry, and in worship as reflected in the New Testament. The late Canon Streeter was certainly right in the main theses of his book, *The Primitive Church*. Instead of one universally recognized type of organization, instead of one most primitive type from which the rest were derived, what we see in the church in the first century, say from A.D. 30 to 130, is a number of quite different types — all the way from the primitive Palestinian, modelled probably on the Synagogue or Jewish community organization, to the Hellenistic religious society in Corinth and other cities of the Aegean basin" (*An Introduction to the New Testament Thought*, p. 38).

The New Testament mentions three chief classes of men who may be considered as officials of the local church, bishops, presbyters, and deacons. The deacons took care of the material and financial side of the church's program, for example, the collection and distribution of relief. The bishops and presbyters regulated the spiritual side of the church's work, its worship and discipline. Exactly how these two classes of officials, bishops and presbyters, were related to each other is a question to which no unanimous answer has been given. For example, Walter Lowrie says, "It is not evident that in the earliest stadium the elders (*presbyteroi*) held a definite 'voice' in the church or were regarded as an 'order' of the ministry. They seem rather to have been at first an indefinite class of older disciples who had a place at the Lord's table" (*Ministers of Christ*, p. 79). But the more generally accepted view is that these two names refer to the same church officials. This viewpoint was impressively set forth by the Anglican scholar, Bishop J. B. Lightfoot in his *Commentary on Paul's Epistle to the Philippians*. It has more recently been reaffirmed and restated by another Episcopalian, Dr. Leon M. Morris, in his book, *Ministers of God* (pp. 72, 73). Dr. Morris summarizes the evidence for this viewpoint thus: (a) In Acts 20:17 Paul summons the presbyters of Ephesus to come and meet him. But when they come he calls them "bishops" (verse 28). (b) In Philippians 1:1 the address is "to all the saints in Christ Jesus which are at Philippi, with the bishops and deacons." Since this is a formal salutation in an official letter, it would seem incredible that the order of presbyters should be passed over, since this order formed the backbone of local organization. (c) The qualifications of bishops and deacons were given in I Timothy 3; and in this passage the writer passes without a break from the qualities needed in bishops to those needed in deacons. He does not mention any intermediate order. But he definitely knows about presbyters (I Tim. 5:17-19), and the functions which he ascribes to them are similar to those discharged by bishops (cf. 5:17 with 3:4ff.). (d) The identification between bishops and presbyters seems very plain in the opening chapters of Titus. Here Paul reminds Titus that he had left him in Crete "that you might . . . appoint elders in every town as I directed you, men who are blameless . . . for a bishop, as God's steward, must be blameless" (Titus 1:5-7 RSV). This passage is difficult to interpret except on the assumption that the office of bishop is identical with that of elder or presbyter.

The second century, however, saw the rise of what the late bishop Charles Gore called "monepiscopacy," i.e., the rule of one bishop in each congregation. Just why this development should have taken place is not known exactly. But doubtless Hans Lietzmann was correct when he said that "If we inquire the reason of the change, the simplest answer would probably be the most appropriate; it was recognized that in difficult times . . . the concentration of power in the hands of a single person offered the sure guarantee of good leadership" (*The Founding of the Church Universal*, p. 58). But as to how this development came about, Dr. L. E. Elliott-Binns rightly says that "The process by which the bishop came to be distinguished from his fellow presbyters, and at last to occupy a position of authority over them and the Church, can no longer be traced" (*The Beginnings of Western Christendom*, p. 318).

The beginnings of this movement towards the rule of a single bishop are reflected in the Epistles of Ignatius of Antioch, whose writings probably date from the second decade of the second century. On this F. C. Grant has the following comment to make: "In the Epistles of Ignatius the 'monarchial' bishop makes his appearance; Ignatius is so ardent and indefatigable in urging his rights and claims that we suspect he cannot have been very long established in his supreme position of authority, even in his own church at Antioch" (*ibid.*, p. 38).

This movement towards "monepiscopacy" gathered momentum so rapidly that by the end of the second century it was the standard pattern of church government throughout Christendom. That is to say, each congregation was governed by a bishop, a body of presbyters, and a board of deacons. In the latter part of the third century a development began whereby the bishop of the chief city in any province tended to become the principal bishop – metropolitan or archbishop – of that province. And in the sixth century the bishops of the five chief sees of Christendom – Jerusalem, Antioch, Alexandria, Constantinople, and Rome – were accorded the title of patriarch. Their jurisdiction extended over the adjacent territories, and included the right of ordaining the metropolitans under them, of trying these metropolitans when they were accused, and of hearing appeals from their judgments. This means that the church was becoming organized on hierarchical lines.

Of these five patriarchs the two chief were those of Rome and Constantinople. The bishop of Constantinople derived importance from the fact that his see was the capitol of the Roman Empire, the only such capital city after the downfall of the Roman Empire in the West in 476. Rome was important, from the Christian point of view, because it was the only church in the West of undoubted apostolic origin, because it was associated with Peter and Paul, and because its bishops were usually found, in theological disputes, on that side which finally won acceptance as orthodox. Strenuous rivalry between the patriarchs of Rome and Constantinople came out into the open during the reign of Pope Gregory I, 590-604, who objected to Bishop John of Constantinople describing himself as "Ecumenical Patriarch." This rivalry between the bishops of Rome and Constantinople was the main, though not the only, reason for the separation between the Western Church and the Eastern Churches which is usually dated from 1054, and which has continued ever since. These Eastern Churches, called Orthodox, are episcopally governed, and accord to the patriarch of Constantinople a primacy of respect and honor, but not of jurisdiction.

After this final separation between East and West the Roman bishop was able to make good his supremacy over the churches of western Christendom. During the fifteenth century the leaders of the so-called Conciliar movement sought to assert the priority of a General Council of the church over the Roman pope. But the victory which this viewpoint achieved at the Council of Constance (1414-1418) was only temporary; and by the time of the Reformation the Pope of Rome was the acknowledged ruler of western Christendom. Since then, the Vatican Council of 1870 has decreed that the Pope, when speaking *ex cathedra,* i.e., in his official capacity, on questions of faith and morals, has the divinely given attribute of infallibility. Vatican Council II (1962-1965) has affirmed the doctrine of "collegiality" by which the bishops of the Roman church share in the Pope's governmental responsibilities; but it remains to be seen how much this decree means in practice in Roman Catholicism, at the decision-making level.

The Protestant churches which renounced allegiance to the Pope and set up ecclesiastical housekeeping on their own following the sixteenth century Reformation, developed three main types of church government.

1. Congregationalism, or Independency. In this pattern of government each local congregation is autonomous in the sense that it governs its own affairs – for example, calling and dismissing its ministers, regulating its finances and disciplining its members – without any outside interference. This form of government was adopted by such Protestant groups as the Anabaptists on the continent of Europe, and the Independents, or Congregationalists, in England.

2. Presbyterianism. This kind of church government consists in a series of graded courts, the Kirk Session for the local congregation, the Presbytery at the regional level, the Synod at the provincial level, and the General Assembly at the national level. In each of these courts ministers and laymen have equal representation, and all members, ministerial and lay, are equal in status. The basic court in this system is the presbytery, since it alone has the responsibility of ordaining to the Christian ministry and deposing from it.

This type of government was started by John Calvin in Geneva, where he was the chief minister from 1541-1564. In Calvin's Geneva the Consistory, or Kirk Session, was the governing church body for the administration of ecclesiastical discipline. Since the church in Geneva was only city wide, no higher court than this Consistory developed there. The higher courts, Presbytery, Synod, and General Assembly, were developed on a nationwide basis in France and Scotland during the later sixteenth century. This Presbyterian pattern of government is characteristic of all the churches which derived from John Calvin and are popularly known as Reformed.

3. Episcopacy. In this type of church government the key figure is the bishop, since he alone has the power to confirm catechumens in full communicant church membership, and likewise to ordain men to the Christian ministry or priesthood. In certain cases the bishop also has power to appoint

to some lower church offices, and to recommend for others. Episcopacy is the form of government which, after the Reformation, prevailed in the Church of England, and in churches derived from it as the Protestant Episcopal Church in the United States.

For some time after the Reformation each of these three systems of church government thought that it was under obligation to prove that it alone was to be found in Scripture. For example, in England, during the latter sixteenth century, John Whitgift, the Anglican, argued with Thomas Cartwright, the Presbyterian, on this very issue. In Scotland in the mid-seventeenth century, the defense of Presbyterianism against Episcopacy and Congregationalism was undertaken by David Calderwood, Robert Baillie, and Alexander Henderson. Though this dispute died down after the restoration of Episcopal government in the 1660's, it was revived after the Revolution Settlement of 1690.

There is, however, little or nothing in the official documents of any large scale Protestant church to suggest that its particular form of church government is of divine right. For example, Article XIX of the Thirty-nine Articles of the Church of England deals with the Church, but without saying anything about its government. And all that the preface to the Ordinal of the Church of England says about the matter is that "It is evident unto all men diligently reading Holy Scripture and ancient authors, that from the Apostles' time there have been these orders of ministers in Christ's Church; Bishops, Priests, and Deacons. Which offices were evermore had in such reverend estimation, that no man might presume to execute any of them, except he were first called, tried, examined, and known to have such qualities as are requisite for the same; and also by public prayer with impositions of hands, were approved and admitted thereunto by lawful authority." Nothing is said about the divine right of episcopacy. Again, the form of presbyterial church government drawn up at the Westminster Assembly and approved by the General Assembly of the Church of Scotland in 1645, under the heading "Of Church Government, and the several sorts of assemblies for the same," says that: "Christ hath instituted a government, and governors ecclesiastical in the Church: to that purpose the Apostles did immediately receive the keys from the hand of Jesus Christ, and did use and exercise them in all the churches of the world upon all occasions. And Christ hath since continually furnished some in His Church with gifts of government, with commission to execute the same, when called thereunto. It is lawful, and agreeable to the Word of God, that the Church be governed by several sorts of assemblies, which are congregational, classical, and synodical." In all this no exclusive claim is made for the presbyterian form of church government.

Today spokesmen for these forms of church government do not usually claim exclusive New Testament sanction for them. It would be agreed by most authorities that, as the Anglican Bishop Arthur C. Headlam once acknowledged, "Christ left the Church to organize its own form and order" (*The Church of England*, p. 13, Quoted in J. M. Shaw, "Christian Doctrine," p. 269). What is usually claimed for any form of church government is that it is in accord with the mind of Christ, and helpful in enabling the church to carry out its distinctive functions of worship, evangelism, and Christian education. The only exception to this would seem to be those "High Church" Episcopalians who still seek to assert that government by bishops goes back in a direct line of apostolic succession to Jesus Christ, and that episcopacy therefore belongs to the essence of the church (cf. K. E. Kirk, *The Apostolic Ministry*, 1946, and the reply of T. W. Manson, *The Church's Ministry*, 1948).

Recent commentators have noted a growing similarity among those three forms of church government. Robert Lee, in, *The Social Sources of Church Unity*, pp. 93, 94, quotes Walter Rauschenbusch as saying that "the divergent types of church government which separated these bodies (Methodist, Baptist, Presbyterian, Disciples, Congregationalists, German and Dutch Reformed) have been worn down by generations of practical experience and they have gravitated toward the same methods of work and life. The Presbyterian type has become more Congregational, and the Congregational type has become more Presbyterian and representative. . . . The most decisive fact for the essential unity of these great bodies is that they have all thoroughly assimilated the principle of democracy and are allowing any *jure divino* theories to fall into oblivion."

And Lee also quotes the conclusion of the New York Study Group preparing for the Oberlin Conference of 1957, to this effect, that church governments, whether Episcopal, Presbyterian, or Congregational in form, are similar in function and power structure. "Theories and practices of church government, which to an external view seem widely divergent and even divisive, disclose, to a more interior examination many striking correspondencies and similarities." At least in the United States this is certainly true.

BIBLIOGRAPHY

Kirk, Kenneth E., (ed.), *The Apostolic Ministry,* 1946.

Lightfoot, Joseph B., "The Christian Ministry," *St. Paul's Epistle to the Philippians,* 1878.

Manson, Thomas W., *The Church's Ministry,* 1948.

Morris, Leon M., *Ministers of God,* 1964.

Streeter, Burnett H., *The Primitive Church,* 1929.

Telfer, William, *The Office of a Bishop,* 1962.

Wedel, Theodore O., ed., *Ministers of Christ,* 1964.

The Presbyterian Church

Administration is working with and through people to get things done. The English word developed from a Latin verb meaning "to serve." The New Testament Greek word is a term which means "servant" or "waiter." It is frequently translated "minister" and has come into our language as "deacon." On at least two occasions it is used in the Pauline letters with a clearly executive or managerial intent.

The early church assumed that some persons must devote time and energy to administration if there was to be effective group activity. Life together required planning, organization, program, the discovery and training of leaders and workers, the guidance of group activity, and the exercise of discipline. The risen Lord provided these necessities himself, in order that a collection of very different persons might function as his body, the church. He did not provide them by appearing repeatedly in the flesh, but by endowing certain persons with the requisite gifts and enabling the church to recognize them as qualified for leadership. The same Spirit who gave them new life and incorporated them in the church endowed members with administrative gifts and enabled the whole group to recognize and use the gifted persons.

Presbyterians take their name from the method by which their common life is ordered or administered. "Presbyter" was the Greek word for "elder," the spiritual leader and administrator of the synagogue in the time of Jesus. It was the opinion of John Calvin, who laid the foundations of the Presbyterian Church, and of the Westminster divines who gave its English speaking adherents a constitution, that the members of the early church elected as elders those whom they regarded as particularly endowed by Christ for teaching and governing. They believed that, as in the synagogue, it was recognized in the church from the beginning that these officers were administrators, not sovereigns, that they performed their administrative functions as a group, and when they functioned individually it was at the direction of the group. The founders of the Presbyterian Church were convinced that it was in accordance with Biblical practice, and therefore acceptable to Christ, for elders meeting in groups to care for administration in the church. They therefore provided for a group of elders known as a "session" to be elected by each congregation for the ordering of its life, for sessions to elect elders to represent congregations in a larger body of elders known as the "presbytery," and for the presbytery to elect representatives to an even more widely representative body, the synod or general assembly.

It should be noticed that American Presbyterians in drawing up "Preliminary Principles" to be affixed to "The Form of Government" in the Church's "Constitution," preparatory to the establishment of the General Assembly in 1789, stressed that, while church officers are called by Christ, "the election of the persons to exercise this authority, in any particular society, is in that society." Five years later the General Assembly adopted a further statement and made it a part of the constitution, saying, "The radical principles of Presbyterian church government are: That the several different congregations of believers, taken collectively, constitute one Church of Christ, called emphatically, the Church; that a larger part of the Church, or a representative of it, should govern a smaller, or determine matters of controversy which arise therein; that, in like manner, a representative of the whole should govern and determine in regard to every part, and to all the parts united: that is, that a majority shall govern; and consequently that appeals may be carried from lower to higher judicatories, till they finally be decided by the collected wisdom and united voice of the whole Church."

Presbyterians, while influential, were comparatively few at this time; their churches were small and limited in number. It is obvious that while their officers led them in planning, organizing, programming, recruiting and training leaders, the guidance of group activity, and discipline, it was discipline which occupied the large place in their thinking about administration and took many hours in their meetings. The growth of church membership to the point that one Presbyterian communion has more churches and members than ever before functioned under Presbyterian administration, and the increasing complexity of life in and around the church, together with new views of the functions of the church and wider participation by its members, have resulted in a greater awareness of the importance of administrative activity and growth in the number of persons administratively employed. Many administrative structures have developed to meet particular needs, only gradually finding a place in the total program, and often unmentioned for years in the church's constitution. This has been the story of such varied things as Sunday schools, youth groups, publication societies, mission boards, and seminaries.

1. THE SESSION

Presbyterian church administration in the particular church begins with the session, composed of ruling elders elected by the congregation and moderated by the teaching elder, or pastor. A board of trustees (deacons in some communions) may hold property for the congregation under provisions of state law, and, subject to the authority of the session, may deal with matters of property and finance. In an increasing minority of churches there is no board of trustees, and the session cares for the trustee functions. A board of deacons may be elected to assist the session in assuring pastoral care for the congregation and community, or this may be the responsibility of a committee of the session. The session has the basic administrative functions: planning, organization, program, personnel, and guidance of group activities and discipline. In planning, it must agree upon the church's purpose, analyze the situation with its possibilities and needs, devise alternative programs and choose the best one. It must then work out a detailed program, develop a plan of organization relating individuals, establishing and relating groups, and providing for their guidance. It must recruit and educate leaders and workers, and provide discipline. In a small church this may be done very simply with the little group of elders acting as a committee of the whole. In larger congregations, the session will probably have committees on worship, Christian education, pastoral care, evangelism, social action and stewardship. In most places, church schools, youth groups, and adult activities will be a carefully planned part of an overall program and will be administered by the session through a committee which is also responsible for leadership education, the church library and visual aids, and may be known as the Board of Christian Education. In most congregations, the session expects the pastor to perform the executive function and to serve as supervisor of other employees.

Special ministries have developed in response to needs and circumstances in particular areas. These may be store-front missions, neighborhood houses, community centers, youth canteens, counseling centers, coffee shops, chaplaincies in hospitals, industries, or state institutions, campus ministries, homes for the aging or for handicapped or delinquent children or unmarried mothers, hospitals, or agencies for deploying pastors or community workers where they reach the unreached. These ministries, like the particular churches, are usually under the administrative oversight of a presbytery, but unlike the congregation, the special ministry is without a session. It may be administered by those who volunteered for the work or by a board self-appointed and self-perpetuating, or elected by neighbors or by presbytery, or it may be directed by a presbytery committee which sometimes functions through a paid executive. With these ministries increasing to the point that in some presbyteries they may be as numerous as congregations, Presbyterians are studying methods of keeping their representative structure, possibly through the establishment in each agency of something like the session.

2. THE PRESBYTERY

The presbytery performs administrative functions for a group of particular churches and special ministries. It plans, organizes, and develops programs for an area. It provides an ordained ministry, supervises sessions, and assures discipline. This is done by actions at regular meetings where membership is limited to the ministers of the area and elders representing the congregations, and through committee activities. Increasingly, presbyteries are supplementing a traditional annual review of session minutes with yearly visitations of each session by a committee of presbytery, in order to assure adequate guidance for the congregation. A committee supervises candidates for the ministry, conducts examinations, and recommends persons for ordination. Another committee usually screens the names submitted to a congregation's pulpit committee, interviews the candidate favored by the committee before he is recommended to the congregation, and either recommends to presbytery approval of a call issued by the congregation, or indicates reasons for caution. The presbytery has authority to install pastors and to dissolve pastoral relationships, but seeks to preserve the right of a people to choose their pastor, and the freedom of a minister to respond to a call or refuse it. Pastoral relations are ordinarily dissolved by presbytery upon the mutual request of a pastor and congregation. When problems arise in established pastorates, a committee of presbytery may seek to resolve differences in conferences, may arrange treatment occasionally needed by a pastor, and in extreme cases may recommend to him that he seek another place. Recommendations to presbytery for the involuntary dissolution of a pastorate may not come from this committee, but must be proposed for only the gravest reasons by a commission elected to study the affairs of the church and make recommendations. It may be observed that the obvious virtues of these personnel practices are counterweighted by certain disadvantages: (1) churches frequently face long interim periods without a pastor while pulpit committees examine the qualifications of the ministers available; (2) pulpit committees often have a limited vision of the mission of their congregation or lack experience in judging qualifications for effective ministry; (3) the system precludes the possibility of a personnel policy which (a) assures gifted men of a variety of experience before imposing burdens which may stunt growth, (b) takes advantage of the limited talents of other men in periodic assignments, and (c) generally encourages development with opportunity; (4) a minister may remain with a congregation for years in a relationship which is frustrating to both because he cannot find another place. Presbyterians are feeling the need to devote more attention to this area, and presbyteries are using more of their authority in the area of ministerial relations. Some presbyteries have begun to recommend candidates for particular churches, a step which opens the way for a reasoned personnel policy. Presbyteries vary in size from a handful of churches to more than two hundred, and the larger ones may employ an executive and in some cases supply him with several associates to provide staff services to committees and to assist the judicatory in the effective performance of its administrative task. Presbyterians are aware that some functions may be more efficiently performed by an individual than by a committee. They are also alert to the abuses of power to which an individual is always subject. Therefore, when one person, volunteer or employee, is assigned responsibility he has authority only insofar as it is delegated to him by a presbytery or a presbytery committee and he works under committee direction. The number of persons employed in presbytery administrative positions is steadily increasing.

3. THE SYNOD

An alternative is the development of a larger employed staff for the synod, which administers an area including a number of presbyteries. Synods usually meet annually and are composed of an equal number of ministers and ruling elders elected by the presbyteries, or of all the ministers and at least one ruling elder representative of each church in the area. In many instances, the synod's chief functions are the supervision of procedures in presbyteries and the hearing of appeals, the oversight of special ministries within their bounds which are functioning in more than one presbytery, and the coordination of presbytery activities through a committee structure which roughly parallels that of the presbyteries. However, a number of synods have undertaken the primary administrative functions of planning, organization, and program, leaving to the presbyteries major responsibilities in the areas of personnel, guidance of groups, and discipline. This frees the presbyteries to devote more time to nonadministrative responsibilities such as doctrinal development, and to administer more effectively in the personnel or ministerial relations area, and the group guidance or session visitation program. It enables Presbyterians to view a larger area in strategic planning and to employ wider resources in meeting needs. It uses employees efficiently and provides for the coordination of their efforts in the area. It also involves a certain concentration of individual authority since, under this plan, executives working at the presbytery level are asssociates on the staff of the synod executive. Since they are represented in meetings and on committees of synod, many Presbyterians are satisfied with this development while others prefer an arrangement which keeps primary administrative responsibility at the presbytery level, where they feel it will be more responsive to local needs. Some who are satisfied with the division of administrative tasks between synod and presbytery are seeking a way by which presbytery committees supervising sessions, developing ministerial candidates, and handling ministerial relations with churches, may have the staff help of a gifted pastor and administrator who is definitely not a part of the synod staff.

4. GENERAL ASSEMBLY

The general adminstration of the affairs of the Presbyterian Church is by the General Assembly, which meets annually and consists of an equal number of ministers and ruling elders elected by the presbyteries. Most of its business is carried on with the aid of three kinds of committees: (1) There are permanent boards, commissions, and committees elected by the Assembly to administer programs in such areas as Christian education, ecumenical mission and church relations, national missions, pensions, evangelism, social action, women's organizations, men's organizations, ministerial relations, judicial business, and periodical publication. (2) There are standing committees which are in being only during the Assembly period and are composed of commissioners elected on the first day of each Assembly. They prepare business for meetings of the Assembly and survey and make recommendations regarding the work of the permanent groups. (3) There are special committees with membership from the church at large, appointed by the Moderator of General Assembly, upon authorization of the Assembly, for specific tasks. Their tenure is for one year, though subsequent Assemblies usually extend the life of a special committee until its task is completed. Budget making and long range planning for the whole church, as well as coordination of program activity is carried on through a General Council composed of members at large and representatives of the permanent agencies, elected by Assembly.

The Stated Clerk of General Assembly is the chief administrative officer of the church. Elected for five year terms by Assembly, he exercises his function through acting as resource person for the Assembly and its committees, and through public statements which have weight because of his position. The Secretary of the General Council carries a coordinating ministry and works closely with those responsible for planning. The permanent agencies have many employees engaged in administrative activity, always subject to direction and review by elected committees or boards. Some of these agencies are incorporated and hold in trust very large resources.

It will be noticed that Presbyterian church administration involves a balance of widely divergent interests to the end of justice for all, uses an effective blend of group activity and individual enterprise, and is proving flexible in the face of needs for change.

BIBLIOGRAPHY

Adams, Arthur M., *Pastoral Administration.* Philadelphia: Westminster

Loetscher, Lefferts A., *A Brief History of the Presbyterians.* Philadelphia: Westminster.

The Constitution of the United Presbyterian Church in the U. S. A.

The Handbook for Presbyterians.

The Presbyterian Constitution and Digest, 2 vols. with annual supplements.

The Congregational Churches

A generation ago, Canon Streeter, of The Church of England, wrote that there were to be found in the historical development of the Christian churches in the first three centuries three forms of church association and government. These were the congregational, the association of autonomous churches; the presbyterial, the direction by presbyters; and the episcopal, the direction by bishops, with a hierarchy of the clergy leading up to that office. These three forms have remained present and active down to the present day.

There are two problems in describing what has been known in church history as the Congregational Churches. The first is that the present day churches which use the name of The Congregational Churches are most certainly not the only churches using congregational polity as their form of church order. Actually, one of the others, the Baptist churches, have a total membership which is the largest of all the denominational bodies of Protestantism. Besides these two, there are the Disciples of Christ (the Christian Churches); the Unitarian Universalist Churches; The Society of Friends (Quakers); the Nazarenes; The Church of God; and many other smaller sects.

The second is that a major historical transformation of the Congregational churches which constituted The General Council of the Congregational Christian Churches in the United States, occurred in 1960 when those churches were united with the Synod of the Evangelical and Reformed Church into a new denomination declared to be The United Church of Christ, whose governing body is its General Synod.

By an understanding of the first consideration, and by an inevitable acceptance of the second, there remains only one group of churches which are now constituted solely under the title of Congregationalism. It consists of those churches which refused to become members of The United Church of Christ and then formed themselves, as continuing Congregational churches, into the National Association of Congregational Christian Churches. They are best described as churches which are amenable to no ecclesiastical judicatory.

These churches are inclusive in spirit and character for these Congregationalists, who have inherited the validity of their order from Christian history, tradition, and religious experience, realize that the presbyterial and episcopal orders of church life are just as valid as theirs. They reach out for association with followers of Christ among the people of all the churches, insofar as that association does not rest upon any coercion or authority of any ecclesiastical or civil nature, but resides only in the spiritual.

The source and nature of the polity and order under which these continuing Congregational churches live and witness has been, and may be, described in the following manner.

1. THE SPIRITUAL AND THEOLOGICAL BASIS OF CONGREGATIONAL POLITY

The essence of congregationalism cannot be found adequately in documents, even in its own documents. Rather it is to be found and seen most clearly in the direction and quality and character of its spirit. Congregationalism is a definite type of Christian experience, finding visible practical expression in the churches and its polity. Thus the church life, the polity, and the organizational structure are finally not of codification, but they are of the spirit.

As the surrounding secular life becomes highly organized so that there are strong institutional pressures in politics and in religion, the spiritual freedom of uncodified congregationalism appears to be at a disadvantage. Actually its lack of rigidity and codification, and its freedom from ecclesiastical centralization are among its greatest strengths. Congregationalism is not the helpless prisoner of its form of polity. Rather because of freedom and lack of rigidity it can ever be ready for frontier adventures in Christian fellowship and in making a Christian impact on the surrounding society.

For Christian people the primary relationship is to God in Christ, for it is in that relationship that we are saved. It is because of this relationship that they are part of Christ's church, and not vice versa. Their first and final loyalty is to God in Christ, the Christ who is the head of the church. Their final authority is in him, and he is always their final court of appeal beyond clergy or ecclesiastical judgment or legal compulsion.

Thus congregationalism as a pattern of Christian life and experience, in the churches and for the individual, centers in their relation to Christ as the head of the church, in their acceptance of the Holy Spirit as guide and source of power and in their belief in the priesthood of all believers.

We believe that such a gathered group, gathered around the Christ who said "wherever two or three are gathered together in my name, there am I in the midst," has an essential completeness about it, so that the local church is the church universal, visible before men at a particular time and at a particular place. Thus the church is not present, nor does it come into being, because there is a minister, or a building, or a bishop, or an ecclesiastical adminstrative office. The church is where two or three are gathered together in his name.

Congregationalism believes that the church is both local and universal. While the one aspect is not to be stressed at the expense of the other, congregationalism has always been sensitively aware of the danger of losing sight of the completeness of the local church, which within itself compasses both the local and the universal. For that reason, while we have emphasized the fellowship, we have insisted on the fact of the autonomy of the local church. This complete autonomy is not a secular permit "to do as we please." This autonomy rests upon a specific binding religious experience, a seeking of and a following of the guidance of the Holy Spirit by the people of this gathered church.

Congregational Christians do not set a doctrinal test as a condition of admission to the covenanting church. They believe that no Christian has the right, under God, to exclude another Christian from the church because in his devotion to Christ and in his experience of Christ there are differences in the expression of that experience and devotion. The Congregational Christian churches have felt that to impose such a test is to distort the relationship between a man and his God made known in Christ. But always the relation between the believers is the binding relationship of having covenanted together in Christ to be Christ's men and women.

Congregationalism acknowledges that its experience and practice are one among many, for among the redeemed followers of Christ there are variants and variations in Christian experience and practice. Congregationalism does not deny the reality of any man's claim for his Christian experience, nor the reality of any church's claim for its Christian experience and practice, if the fruits of Christian deed and character mark them, and if these claims are not exclusive in character implying that they shut other believers off from some essential phase of God's grace and blessing. Congregationalism believes that all Christians have the same Lord, living, crucified and reigning eternally, the same baptism, the same faith, the same Word, the same forgiveness, the same promise of salvation for this life and the next. Congregationalism does not find in the New Testament any divine command about exclusiveness or uniformity of experience and of practice when Christ's brethren gather together; but it does acknowledge the validity of variances, and finds an assurance of strength in the variance, if the units of gathered Christians are directed by a genuine desire for the fulfillment of Christ's purpose. For the units (varying in experience and in practice) are the acknowledged parts of his body, without the parts being able to claim Christian preference for themselves. Congregational Christians believe in the equality of the churches.

The belief of congregational churches has been that the gathered church could choose and set aside its own leadership. The man who was consecrated and set aside for this leadership was one who believed that he had been called by God, and in his own living had given evidence of that fact. In setting him aside the gathered church asked for him a special endownment of God's grace. At the same time he was not regarded as being set aside in a special order called "the clergy" so that he differed in character from the so-called "laity." Even though this pattern is now modified by calling in the association of churches, the root of the authenticity of our ordination is the power of the local church thus to set a man aside. And today the ecclesiastical standing which the ordained receive are recognitions, not spiritual power-giving relationships. The authority which this man has in the church is the authority which the people give to him freely because of the Christian character and quality of his leadership among them.

That which is "sacrosanct about the autonomy of the local congregation" comes in the fact that this self-governance arises out of the primary relation of the people with Jesus Christ, and in their insistence that they as a church, are representative in time and place of the universal church of Jesus Christ. Therefore those who are of this local fellowship insist that in matters of faith and order and final administrative procedure there is no council or other body or person with the ecclesiastical or legal right of compulsive authority over them. Such authority as exists within the congregational order is the authority of persuasion, suggestion, advice and willing cooperation, which come as the churches in fellowship work and plan together on association, state, and national levels, seeking a more effective Christian witness and a more enriched Christian experience.

2. THE LOCAL CONGREGATIONAL CHURCH

a. A church originates as a body of Christians in a particular community. It writes or chooses its own statement of purpose, belief, covenant, or creed, adopts its own constitution, or other governing rules, and is subject to no external ecclesiastical authority for the substance of them. In practice there is often consultation with representative Congregational Christian individuals or organizations. Provisions for extending fellowship to a church by an association vary, but in no instance do they or can they prevent a church from governing itself according to its own desires. "Recognition" is recognition of a church that already exists; it is not the "creating" or "constituting" of a church which had no prior existence. But recognition by other Congregational Christian churches is a prerequisite of denominational standing.

b. A church sets its own standards for membership. These may or may not require baptism or assent to a creed. Many churches have adopted the Kansas City Statement of Faith as formulated by the National Council of 1913. Reception of members is by confession of faith, by letter of transfer from other Chrisitan churches, or by reaffirmation of faith, but each church exercies the right to set forth the specific meaning of these three modes of reception.

c. A church orders its worship as it believes to be most fitting. In actual practice the individual minister leads the regular Sunday services, and is expected to win the approval of the members when significant changes are to be made in the order of worship. Normally, the board of deacons or similar committee is charged with concern for the worship of the church.

d. A church administers the sacraments and holy rites on conditions and after such manner as it chooses so to do. Although laymen may preside at the Lord's Table, the sacraments are customarily adminstered by ministers. The right to administer the sacraments may be granted to a student-pastor or lay reader by vote of the individual church.

e. A church is free to adopt and follow its own program of education, fellowship, community service, missionary action, music, pastoral work, and kindred religious and civic activities.

f. A church calls its minister, sets his compensation and tenure, and makes all other business arrangements. Some parishes still maintain an ecclesiastical society which performs some of these functions.

g. A church may request that a council (association or vicinage) either "install" or "recognize" its minister. The council may withhold "recognition" or "installation" or may give counsel, but the final decision as to whether or not the candidate will be its minister rests with the local church. The holding of a council (if any) is at the request of the church. The minister may exercise his ministerial duties whether or not he is "installed" or "recognized."

h. While a local church, in its own right and by itself, may license and ordain candidates for its own Christian ministry, such licensure or ordination need not be accepted as valid by an association (or conference, where conference is the body in which ministerial standing is held).

i. A church or "ecclesiastical society" holds title to property in its own right. When title is held by a conference or board because of gifts or loans, it is assumed that the local church will gain title at the earliest possible moment, and will, in the interim, be free to conduct its business affairs according to the dictates of its members. In some instances local church property is held in trust by the conference, on request of the church.

j. A church expresses concern for Christian outreach by voluntary acceptance of responsibilities in associations, conferences, boards, councils of churches, and other organizations.

3. THE NATIONAL ASSOCIATION OF CONGREGATIONAL CHRISTIAN CHURCHES OF THE UNITED STATES

It has been considered desirable that Congregational Christian Churches should have an organization embracing the entire nation, of which the members shall be churches, and through which they may take counsel and may realize their common purposes, and advance God's Kingdom. The name of this association is the National Association of Congregational Christian Churches of the United States.

The purposes of this Association are:

a. To provide a means by which Congregational Christian Churches of this nation may, without in any wise disturbing or altering their present associations and affiliations, consult and advise together as churches upon matters of common concern to them, both temporal and spiritual.

b. To provide this closer fellowship and unity in all spiritual matters among Congregation Christian Churches.

c. To aid, in such ways as may from time to time be appropriate and proper, the continuance and growth of those Christian purposes and practices which have been the historic and accepted characteristics of Congregational Christian Churches.

d. In cases of necessity to do and perform any and all functions ordinarily and customarily performed by Congregational Christian associations.

e. To promote, carry on and supervise such co-operative activities among member Churches as to them from time to time may seem wise and expedient.

f. Upon application therefore by member churches, to provide for them such assistance, whether financial or through advice and consultation or otherwise, as may be proper and expedient.

BIBLIOGRAPHY

Atkins, Gaius G., and Fagley, Frederick L., *History of American Congregationalism.* Boston: Pilgrim Press, 1942.

Hooker, Thomas, *A Survey of the Summe of Church-Discipline. Wherein the Way of the Churches of New-England is Warranted out of the Word.* London: Printed by A. M. for John Bellamy, 1648.

Horton, Douglas, *Congregationalism; A Study in Church Polity.* London: Independent Press, 1952.

Mather, Richard, *A Platform of Church Discipline Gathered Out of the Word of God: And Agreed Upon by the Elders: And Messengers of the Churches Assembled in the Synod at Cambridge in New England.* Printed by S G at Cambridge in New England, 1649.

Miller, Perry, *The New England Mind; from Colony to Province.* Cambridge, Mass.: Harvard University Press, 1953.

Walker, Williston, *A History of the Congregational Churches in the United States.* Vol. III of the "American Church History Series." New York: Christian Literature Co., 1894.

The Lutheran Church

The polity and administrative practices of the Lutheran Church in America have been forged from basic theological doctrines, shaped by cultural and sociological climate, and tempered by an existential milieu.

Of central significance in the story of American Lutheranism is the fact that the Lutheran confessions have gradually been adopted by practically all Lutherans as the basis and constitution of the Lutheran church. It is a confessional church, as is evident from:

> Art. II, Sect. 4 This church accepts the Apostles', the Nicene, and the Athanasian creeds as true declarations of the faith of the Church.

Art. II, Sect. 5 This church accepts the Unaltered Augsburg Confession and Luther's Small Catechism as true witnesses to the Gospel, and acknowledges as one with it in faith and doctrine all churches that likewise accept the teachings of these symbols.

Art. II, Sect. 6 This church accepts the other symbolical books of the evangelical Lutheran church, the Apology of the Augsburg Confession, the Salcald Articles, Luther's Large Catechism, and the Formula of Concord as further valid interpretations of the confession of the Church.

Art. II, Sect. 7 This church affirms that the Gospel transmitted by the Holy Scriptures, to which the creeds and confessions bear witness, is the true treasure of the Church, the substance of its proclamation, and the basis of its unity and continuity. The Holy Spirit uses the proclamation of the Gospel and the administration of the Sacraments to create and sustain Christian faith and fellowship. As this occurs, the Church fulfills its divine mission and purpose.

The process by which this unity has been achieved was a long and difficult one. The transplantation of the European church by Dutch, Swedish, and German immigrants was a natural first step. Various reactions to the churches which surrounded them on the American scene followed. There was also a period of conflict between the older and newer immigrant churches of the Lutheran group, precipitated by cultural, nationalistic, and linguistic differences. Out of these extra-Lutheran and intra-Lutheran struggles there has emerged not so much a unique concept of polity nor even a highly organized methodology of administration, but a unity of faith based on the confessions of the Lutheran church.

Pressures hostile to this confessional unity and loyalty appeared in profusion: from Europe in the forms of pietism and rationalism; from the American environment by way of unionism, unitarianism, revivalism, and social reform. It is not difficult to understand the role played by nationalistic backgrounds, language, liturgical interest, and concepts of the ministry and the church in the problems engendered by these pressures.

In 1817 Lutheranism in America was weak and uncertain. By 1917 the strong effort to "Americanize" the church had not only been disavowed, but Lutheran doctrine and practice had become firmly entrenced in American Protestantism. In the course of that hundred years, the emphasis on revivals had yielded to insistence on child baptism and confirmation. Itinerant ministries and periodic emotional excitements succumbed to orderly church life. *Ecclesia plantanda,* i.e. the church must be planted, became the underlying principle of the mission enterprise. A definite faith was being preached, a discipline in obedience to that faith was being exercised, and the Lord's Supper was a sacrament whose use identified the congregation as Lutheran. In this present century, the structural unity of the Lutheran church is proceeding dramatically, largely because in every instance, reorganized and merged bodies have adopted the confessions as the constitution of the church. The constitution of the church in America is a declaration of faith drawn from the Bible, explained in the catechism, set forth in the Book of Concord, and exemplified in Lutheran hymns, liturgy, devotional writings and in the use of the sacraments.

The basic structure of the organized Lutheran will be considered from the viewpoints of the office of the ministry, the structure of the congregation, the function of the synod, and the whole church.

1. THE OFFICE OF THE MINISTRY

No single form of ministry was prescribed by the Reformation church. In Germany, a consistory of state officials cooperated with officers of the church; in Scandinavia the king was the head of the church and clergy were civil officers; in Holland the Lutheran church had a position of privilege. As a result, the sending of clergy to America was never carried out by the church (except in the case of colonies) but by interested nongovernmental societies. The importance of establishing an indigenous ministry was singularly understood, but the efforts to implement it were uncoordinated. Catechets (exhorters) were licensed; students attached themselves to ordained clergymen for instruction; imposters intruded themselves; and candidates for the ministry under the pressure of circumstance often exercised privileges usually accorded only ordained clergy. Thus impetus was given to academic concerns. Newly established seminaries soon found themselves deeply involved in both preparation for the ministry and strengthening the significance of ordination. At the same time divergent views concerning the ministry were competing with each other. One group held that only pastors could decide on doctrines of the church since they alone, as pastors, had the office of the keys. Another contended that little attention had to be given to a trained priesthood, for each congregation could call from its own membership those who could preach. The power of the keys should be exercised by each Christian. The struggle then between these two schools of thought was whether the ministry should be a particular order apart from the congregation, or a function within the congregation. History provided a compromise between these two concepts of the ministry, even as it presented three types of church polity. The episcopal view is most fully represented by the Church of Sweden (but never in the Roman or Anglican sense as involving apostolic succession); the congregational view is found among all Lutheran bodies but especially in the Missouri Synod; while the Presbyterian view is found among all Lutheran bodies except Missouri, where a "ministerium" (clergy only) exercises authority in the realm of examination, licensure, and ordination of candidates for the ministry. All three forms of church polity (especially as they relate to the office of the ministry) are to be found in Europe and all three justified in terms of the Augsburg Confession. Today, in America, the concept of the episcopacy has been disavowed, and even the "ministerium" principle has been largely abrogated. Democracy has had its influence, and a congregational polity prevails.

2. THE CONGREGATION

When European Lutheranism sought to establish itself in America, its greatest problem of adjustment was in the concept of the congregation and its structure. In this process, as might be expected, doctrine and prevailing practice met head on. Not only did the lack of government support and control raise the question to a prominent position, but the emphasis on "revivalism" with its aim of adult conversion kept it in the foreground. This has an important bearing on the idea of the congregation inasmuch as an unequivocal answer had to be found to the question, "How does one become a member of the church?" Is there in baptism a new birth which engrafts a person into the community of believers, or must one go through an experience of adult conversion in order to be one of the company of true saints? The outcome of this argument, as well as those which were born of the "holiness" concepts (drink, the use of the Sabbath, and secretism), was ultimately a return to the traditional Lutheran liturgical use of the sacraments and the Word. But the way was not easy. Colonial architecture, itself conditioned by an itinerant ministry, was not conducive to liturgical practices, and the linguistic heritage further complicated efforts to define the practices and policies of church administration.

In structure, the legal status of the congregation in America was totally different from that which prevailed in Europe. It was necessary to fashion a congregational structure adapted to a land where church and state were separate, and to adjust to a voluntary system of church support.

Authority in the congregation can be traced from the beginning when European structures were copied to the present when the Lutheran Church exhibits itself as a democratic organization, ruled by officials elected by the congregation and responsible to it. Necessity and expediency dictated that the duties of one class of officers was to be mainly material or financial, while the other class was to be more concerned with the educational and spiritual tasks of the congregation. Thus the rather clear distinction between the trustees and deacons of the usual church council or board. While American Lutherans have made no distinctively new contribution in the area of congregational structure, they have provided an illustration of the shift from governmental support and partial control to a genuinely democratic structure supported by freewill gifts and at the same time retaining the core function of preaching the Word and administering the sacraments.

Membership in the congregation, the governing structure of the congregation, and the relationship of the congregation to the community in which it finds itself, are the three basic problems on this level of church life. The retention of purity of doctrine and the development of democratic practice have been effective in handling the first two matters but the price has been a type of isolation from the tasks of communal life. Fortunately, in recent years, the necessity for a vocational witness to the faith as a legitimate and essential counterpart for the spiritual fellowship has been recognized, both by secular pressure from without and a responsible conscience from within.

3. THE SYNOD

The synodical development of the Lutheran church in America can be mapped in four stages: (1) the period of "individualism" in congregations, often a rejection of any relationship to another congregation; (2) the period of ministerial conferences which grew out of a need for mutual enlightenment and counsel; (3) the period of synods involving both lay and clerical delegates appointed to carry on larger enterprises than the local churches could handle; and (4) the period in which the synods work together in a "general" synod or national body. This progressive course was not automatic; in fact the stumbling blocks of hierarchical fear imported from abroad and the domestic concern for equality generated by the Revolution, frequently threatened the organized life of the church. Even when it was generally agreed that synodical functions should be to conserve the unity of the faith, to protect pastors and congregations in their rights, to provide a reasonable uniformity in congregational affairs and liturgical practice, and to unite efforts in the fields of education, missions, and publication, only an "advisory" power was given to the synods.

In the case of synods, as in the concepts of the ministry and structure of the congregation the heritage of a Continental church, the feeling of being foreigners, the high regard for education, the varied languages, the concern for liturgy, and the emphasis on the Confessions, made the problems more difficult, but in the end made the victory sweeter. In the story of the synods is the heart of the Lutheran work in America.

4. THE CHURCH AS A WHOLE

Without yielding its basic autonomy the congregation has merged something of itself into a synod, and a synod without giving up the functions granted it by its congregations, has merged something of itself into a "general" body. Synods grew large and began to subdivide. Synods tended to be individualistic. Many tasks were too large to be handled by a synod. There was never much question about the need for the larger unit, but there was serious concern about authority and about the basis of unity.

Constituent synods, operating through a convention (usually biennial) find their focus in an executive board with ad interim responsibility, and a juridical court with an interpretive function, yet are responsible for all elective boards and agencies, all standing and special committees and commissions, and all auxiliaries. These in turn are answerable to the constituent synods in convention assembled. Individual synods, on the basis of constitutions approved by the general body, function generally in the same manner.

Local congregations are also governed by constitutions brought in line with that of the synod and approved by that body. All committees receive their authority from the church board elected by the congregation, and are answerable to the board which in turn reports to and takes its direction from the congregation. Thus even the traditional practice of the pastor in acting as President of the board, has been largely discontinued.

BIBLIOGRAPHY

Bergendoff, Conrad, *The Doctrine of the Church in American Lutheranism.* Philadelphia: Muhlenberg Press, 1956.

Distinctive Doctrines and Usages of the General Bodies of the Evangelical Lutheran Church in the United States, The. Philadelphia, 1893.

Fortenbaugh, Robert, *The Development of the Synodical Polity of the Lutheran Church in America, to 1829* (Doctoral Thesis). Philadelphia: 1926.

History of the United Lutheran Synod of New York and New England I: 1786-1860. Philadelphia, 1954.

Jacobs, Henry Eyster, *A History of the Evangelical Lutheran Church in the United States.* New York, 1899.

Neve, J. L., *A Brief History of the Lutheran Church in America.* Burlington, Iowa, 1916.

Wentz, A. R., *The Lutheran Church in American History.* Philadelphia: United Lutheran Publication House, 1933.

The Protestant Episcopal Church in the United States of America

The Protestant Episcopal Church in the United States of America, commonly called "The Episcopal Church" or the "American Espicopal Church," is a self-governing branch of the Anglican Communion, which the Lambeth Conference of 1930 defined as a "Fellowship within the One, Holy Catholic, and Apostolic Church, of those duly constituted Dioceses, Provinces, or Regional Churches in communion with the see of Canterbury."

The nineteen autonomous churches, which currently comprise the Anglican Communion throughout the world, are bound together, not by a central legislative or executive authority, but by voluntary allegiance to a common faith and order as set forth in the *Book of Common Prayer,* under the primacy of the Archbishop of Canterbury.

Each national church can revise or adapt the Prayer Book to meet its own needs, particularly in the spheres of discipline and worship, provided the substance of faith and order "be kept entire."

The Archbishop of Canterbury is *first among equals* — the meaning of primacy — and has no pretensions to spiritual supremacy, temporal supremacy, or infallibility; and no such claims are acknowledged by the autonomous churches.

In the expansion of the Anglican Church into a worldwide communion of some forty million members, the American Episcopal Church has been the trail blazer: (1) It was the first autonomous church to be organized outside the British Isles; (2) it was the first to have a valid, free, democratic, and purely ecclesiastical episcopate, that is, an episcopate both free of state control and free from civil functions or powers; (3) it was the first to prove that a church of Anglican origin could not only survive but thrive without being established or supported by the state; and (4) it was the first to introduce into the government of the Anglican churches the direct representation of the laity.

1. THE MOTHER CHURCH

Christianity reached the island of Britain in the third century, and early in the fourth century bishops of the British church attended councils on the European continent. When the Roman legions were withdrawn about A.D. 410, pagan Angles and Saxons conquered what is now England, and drove surviving Christians into western England and Wales.

The first efforts for the reconversion of what is now England came from the west and north, especially from the Celtic monks whose propagating center was the famous monastery at Iona, founded in 563 by St. Columba off the west coast of Scotland.

In the meantime, Gregory the Great, Bishop of Rome, had become interested in the conversion of the Angles and Saxons. He sent St. Augustine and forty monks, and thus was founded in 597 the see of Canterbury, the mother church of the Anglican Communion.

The fusion of the Roman and Celtic missions began to be effective following the Councils of Whitby (664) and Hertford (673), resulting eventually in the acceptance of Roman customs and usages, including papal claims to spiritual supremacy over the Church of England and temporal supremacy over the state.

The Reformation in England, in contrast to that on the continent of Europe, was a constitutional reformation before it was a doctrinal reformation. The former was effected in the reign of Henry VIII on the principle that "The Bishop of Rome hath no more authority in the Church of England than any other foreign Bishop." This principle was maintained under Edward VI, rejected under Mary, and finally regained under Elizabeth I.

The doctrinal reformation, from the beginning, was an appeal to the faith and order of the primitive church, and the basic beliefs of the reformed Church may be summarized as follows:

1. Holy Scripture contains "all things necessary to salvation," and whatsoever cannot "be proved thereby," is not to be "required of any man . . . as necessary to salvation."
2. The Nicene and Apostles' Creeds, as statements of the Christian Faith, "ought throughly to be received and believed: for they may be proved by most certain warrants of Holy Scriptures."
3. The historic ministry of bishops, priests, and deacons, having been the "Orders of

Ministers in Christ's Church" "from the Apostles' time," was retained.

4. Among the seven sacraments of the Medieval Church, Baptism and the Eucharist (i.e. the Holy Communion) retained their pre-eminence as the only "Sacraments of the Gospel." The other five rites—Confirmation, Penance, Orders, Matrimony, and Unction—took rank as sacraments, but not of the same authority as the first two.

One of the most positive of Anglican principles is that both the services of the church and the Holy Scriptures should be in a "language understood by the people." In 1549, the Anglican Church gave to the Christian world in English the *Book of Common Prayer,* and in 1611, the King James or Authorized Version of the Bible, which was destined to be the most influential single book in the English-speaking world for the next three centuries.

The expansion of the Anglican Church outside the British Isles began in 1607 with the settlement of Jamestown, Virginia, the ministers of which were Anglican. The Church was "established," i.e., supported by taxation, in Virginia first; later in Maryland, and partially in the Carolinas. But up to 1700, its condition in the colonies generally was pathetically weak. The missionary work of the church in England became more aggressive with the establishment of two great societies, which still exist and function effectively all over the world: The Society for Promoting Christian Knowledge (1699), and the Society for the Propagation of the Gospel in Foreign Parts (1701). The latter aggressively pushed the founding of churches in the Northern colonies and in the Carolinas. But for one and three-quarters centuries, 1607-1785, the Anglican Church in America had no bishop.

The Revolutionary War broke the tenuous connection of the American churches with the Bishop of London, and left, not an Episcopal Church, but an aggregation of separate congregations, with no bishop, no constitution, no diocesan or national organization.

A series of General Conventions, with representatives of both clergy and laity, beginning in 1785 and 1786, and culminating in 1789, brought about the organization of an autonomous church: (1) Four American bishops were consecrated abroad — Samuel Seabury by bishops of the Scottish Episcopal Church (1784); William White, Samuel Provost, and James Madison by the English bishops (1787); (2) a constitution was adopted; (3) the Book of Common Prayer was revised and adapted to American needs (1789); and (4) the unity of the church, both north and south, was achieved. The Prayer Book has been twice revised since 1789: in 1892 and 1928.

2. THE GENERAL CONVENTION

The General Convention is the supreme legislative, executive, and judicial governing body of the Protestant Episcopal Church in the United States of America. It meets triennially. It is bicameral, consisting of the House of Bishops and the House of Deputies. The vote of both houses is required for the adoption of legislation.

a. *The House of Bishops.* Each Bishop has jurisdiction (i.e., the head of a diocese or missionary district), every Bishop Coadjutor, and every Suffragan Bishop has a seat and vote in the House of Bishops. A Bishop Coadjutor is an assisting bishop in a diocese, but with a specified independent jurisdiction, such as being in charge of diocesan missions; also, he automatically succeeds the bishop upon the death or resignation of the latter. A Suffragan Bishop is an assisting bishop, without independent jurisdiction and without right of succession, except by special election of the diocesan convention.

All bishops of dioceses are elected by the clergy and lay representatives of the parishes and missions in diocesan conventions. Bishops of Missionary Districts (i.e., not self-supporting jurisdictions) are elected by the House of Bishops, subject to confirmation by the House of Deputies when General Convention is in session, and at other times by a majority of the Standing Committees of the several dioceses.

b. *The Presiding Bishop.* He presides over the House of Bishops, takes order for the consecration of bishops, and is the consecrator of each new bishop unless he designates some other bishop as such. As president of the Executive Council of the Church, he heads up the missionary work, Christian education, and Christian social relations of the church's executive agency.

Before a Presiding Bishop is elected, a

joint committee of the two houses of the General Convention presents to the House of Bishops the names of three of its members for its consideration. The person elected must be confirmed by the House of Deputies. When elected, the Presiding Bishop must resign his diocesan jurisdiction. He serves until he reaches the age of sixty-eight. In other Anglican Churches, he would be called "the Primate of the Church," i.e., "first among equals."

c. *The House of Deputies.* This house is composed of four presbyters and four laymen from each diocese in union with General Convention, and one presbyter and one layman from each missionary district. At the present time, seventy-nine dioceses and twenty-two missionary districts are represented in General Convention. In 1964, the three missionary districts in Brazil were erected into an autonomous church, the nineteenth in the Anglican Communion, but financial support is still received from the American Church.

The House elects its own officers: President, Vice-President, and Secretary. Lay as well as clerical deputies can be elected to any office, but in its one hundred and eighty years of history (1785-1965) this house has had but two laymen as its President.

The power of each order — clerical and lay — is very real. While, normally, the vote of a majority of the deputies on any question shall suffice, when the constitution or the Prayer Book is under revision, the vote must be by orders; that is, the orders vote separately, each diocese having one vote in the clerical order and one vote in the lay order; "and the concurrence of the votes of the two orders shall be necessary to constitute a vote of the House."

Moreover, on any question, either the clerical or the lay representation from any diocese can demand a vote by orders. While this latter privilege is sometimes abused by calling for a vote by orders on matters of secondary importance, it is, on the whole, a salutary protection of each order against domination by the other.

d. *Officers of the Convention.* In addition to the Presiding Bishop, certain other officers of the General Convention, as distinct from the officers of each House, are elected by joint action of both Houses:

Secretary of the Convention. He is now also Secretary of the House of Deputies, and is responsible for printing the Journal of General Convention. He is usually a presbyter of the church.

Treasurer of the General Convention. The holder of this office has always been a layman during the last one hundred and eighty years, but there is no canonical requirement that he be such.

Custodian of the Standard Book of Common Prayer. His certificate is necessary for any "copy, translation, or edition of the Book of Common Prayer" . . . "to be of authority in this Church."

Custodian of the Archives is the Church Historical Society, Austin, Texas, an official agency of the General Convention since 1940.

Recorder of Ordinations is now a corporate person — the Church Pension Fund of New York City, established in 1917.

The Historiographer of the church is elected every three years, but his duties are not defined by the canons.

The Registrar is charged with caring for "the manuscript minutes of the proceedings of both Houses, together with the Journals, files, papers, reports, and all other documents of either House." After a specified time, they are deposited with the Custodian of the Archives, as named above.

e. *Joint Committees and Commissions.* The executive functions of General Convention are delegated to the Executive Council, discussed below, but the preparatory studies for legislation are done between sessions of the General Convention by joint committees and commissions.

A joint committee is one composed exclusively of members of the two houses. A joint commission includes not only members of the two houses, but members chosen at large.

The work of these committees and commissions is very important. Some of their titles indicate the nature of their importance: Eastern Churches; Ecumenical Relations; Evangelism; Education for Holy Orders; Standing Liturgical Commission; Music; Mutual Responsibility and Interdependence; Program and Budget; State of the Church.

f. *The Judicial System of General Convention.* The judicial system of General Convention is set forth in Part IV., Ecclesiastical Discipline of the Canons, as adopted by it. The basic legal principle involved is that a bishop, presbyter, or deacon, presented for trial, shall be tried by his peers. Bishops are tried by their peers in the House of Bishops, and not by the dioceses over which they exercise jurisdiction.

For the trial of a presbyter or deacon, each diocese or missionary district is required to provide by diocesan canon for the establishment of an ecclesiastical court, but such canon must be in conformity with the provisions of all General Convention canons on the subject.

In case of conviction of a presbyter or deacon by the diocesan court, appeal can be made to a court of review in the province to which the diocese belongs. In case of conviction of a bishop, he may appeal to the court of review of the House of Bishops, said court to be composed of bishops only. The most severe sentence which can be inflicted upon a convicted bishop, priest, or deacon is deposition from the ministry of the church.

g. *The Executive Council.* It is generally agreed among the historians of the church that the General Convention of 1919 was a turning point in the history of the Episcopal Church because of its revolutionary reorganization of its executive agency. Before that date, executive functions were exercised by the Domestic and Foreign Missionary Society, and by an independent Board of Religious Education, Board of Social Service, and such like.

In 1919, the National Council (as it was then called) was set up by canon, the Missionary Society became virtually a department of the Council, as did the other formerly separate boards. In 1964, the name of the National Council was changed to "The Executive Council" in order that there should be no confusion with the National Council of the Churches of Christ in America.

The Executive Council today has the following departments: Overseas; Home; Christian Education; Christian Social Relations; Promotion; Finance; Laymen's Work; Women's Work; Research and Field Study; and The Seabury Press. The Executive Council has no control, through its Home Department, for example, over the missionary work within a diocese, except possibly to make a special appropriation to a few special projects such as Indian work, Negro work, etc.

The Executive Council is composed of twenty-two members elected by the General Convention, of whom six are bishops, six are presbyters, and ten are laymen; plus six women nominated by the Triennial Meeting of the Women of the Church. In addition, each Province elects one member to represent it, making a total of thirty-seven members, plus the Presiding Bishop, the Vice-President, and the Treasurer.

A major part of the revolution effected by the General Convention of 1919 concerned the office of Presiding Bishop. Up to that time, the Presiding Bishop was the senior bishop of the church in point of consecration. No election was involved, opening the possibility that the senior bishop might be incapable of functioning effectively. Henceforth, following the death of the then Presiding Bishop, his successor has been elected by the House of Bishops, subject to confirmation by the House of Deputies. The Presiding Bishop was made the head of the Executive Council, is compelled to resign his diocese in order that he may devote all his time and energies to that task, and, therefore, must necessarily be nearer the prime of life when elected than his predecessors of half a century and more ago. As a consequence, the leadership of the Presiding Bishop today is much more forceful than it ever could be under the old seniority system.

3. THE PROVINCES

In 1913, the General Convention set up the provincial system of the church, in order that the church's work might be more effectively done thereby. On the whole, this has not ensued, largely because General Convention has not delegated sufficient powers to the provinces to make them effective. The provinces are as follows:

I. The Province of New England (seven dioceses).

II. The Province of New York and New Jersey (eight dioceses).

III. The Province of Washington (thirteen dioceses in the States of Pennsylvania, Delaware, Maryland, Virginia, West Virginia, and the District of Columbia).

IV. The Province of Sewanee (fifteen dioceses in the States of North Carolina, South Carolina, Georgia, Florida, Alabama, Mississippi, Louisiana, Tennessee, and Kentucky).

V. The Province of the Mid-West (thirteen dioceses in the States of Ohio, Indiana, Illinois, Michigan, and Wisconsin).

VI. The Province of the Northwest (five dioceses in the states of Minnesota, Iowa, Nebraska, Montana, and Colorado, and three missionary districts in the States of North Dakota, South Dakota, and Wyoming).

VII. The Province of the Southwest (ten dioceses and one missionary district in the States of Missouri, Arkansas, Texas, Kansas, Oklahoma, and New Mexico).

VIII. The Province of the Pacific (eight dioceses and six missionary districts in the States of Idaho, Utah, Washington, Oregon, Nevada, California, Arizona, Alaska, and Hawaii; and the missionary districts in the Philippines and Taiwan).

IX. The Province of the Caribbean (eight missionary districts in Central America, Columbia, Cuba, the Dominican Republic, Mexico, the Panama Canal Zone, Puerto Rico, and the Virgin Islands).

4. THE DIOCESE

In the American Episcopal Church, there could not be a national, self-governing church until there were dioceses to organize it. It so happens that the eleven dioceses which adopted the original constitution of the church were all organized in 1784-1785, only four or five years before the completion of the national organization in 1789.

The diocese is the working unit of the church. It is composed of the bishop or bishops and not less than six parishes. There can be but one diocesan bishop, but in addition a diocese may have one bishop coadjutor and not more than two suffragan bishops.

a. *The Bishop.* He is a priest in good standing in some diocese of the American Episcopal Church. He is elected by the diocesan convention by concurrent action of both orders, clerical and lay, subject to the approval of a majority of the bishops of the church exercising jurisdiction, and the approval of a majority of the standing committees of all the dioceses. He is consecrated by three bishops – one consecrator and two co-consecrators.

The bishop is president of the diocesan convention, head of all diocesan agencies, and chief pastor of the diocese. He must make an official visitation to every parish and mission at least once in three years and administer confirmation; and he must ordain candidates for the diaconate and priesthood who are approved by himself, his examining chaplains, and the standing committee of the diocese.

b. *The Diocesan Convention.* This is the legislative body of the diocese, meets annually, and is composed of all the clergy and of the lay representatives of the parishes and missions thereof. It hears reports of the various officers, agencies and institutions of the diocese, adopts or amends the constitution and canons of the diocese, and adopts the budgets by which the diocese and its officers operate. It also elects every three years the four presbyters and four laymen who shall represent the diocese in the ensuing General Convention.

c. *The Standing Committee.* It is a unique institution among the churches of the Anglican communion, and is found only in the American church. It is a heritage from the colonial church, which had no resident bishop. Clergy conventions were voluntary affairs, and a standing committee was elected by each to act for it between sessions of the convention.

It is composed of four priests and four laymen, elected by the diocesan convention. The committee elects its own president and secretary, and reports its actions to the diocesan convention.

It has considerable powers. It is a council of advice to the bishop, and when there is no bishop, bishop coadjutor or suffragan bishop, it is the ecclesiastical ordinary of the diocese.

No person may be admitted as a candidate for Holy Orders without its consent; no one may be ordained deacon or priest without its approval; and every bishop-elect, no matter of what diocese in the American church, must win the consent of a majority of all the standing committees before his consecration can proceed. No parish can morgage its property without its consent, and the bishop can dissolve the pastoral relationship of rector and parish only with its advice and consent. The advice and consent of two-thirds of all the members of the standing committee are required before a bishop may remit and terminate any sentence of deposition pronounced in his juridication upon a minister.

d. *The Executive Council.* In the diocese it is the counterpart to the executive council of the national church, and may be known by other names such as Diocesan Foundation, Bishop and Directorate, etc. As its name indicates, it is the executive agency of the diocese, and functions through divisions such as Missions, Christian Education, Christian Social Relations, and Field and Publicity. All members, except the bishop and executive officers, are elected by the Diocesan Convention. The bishop is the head of the council and of all its departments. All congregations financially assisted by the diocese, most of which are called "missions," are under the jurisdiction of the bishop and the executive council, which votes the appropriations.

e. *The Cathedral.* Not every diocese has one, but more and more are desirous of having one. A cathedral is where the bishop officially has his chair, and more often than not it is a parish church which has entered into a special legal relationship whereby the bishop has some control over its operation. It is the bishop's church, and is supposed to be the center of the diocesan family, where the annual diocesan convention convenes, where the bishop can ordain his candidates for holy orders, and where special diocesan services can be held.

The Cathedral of St. John the Divine, New York City, and Washington Cathedral in the nation's capital, are cathedrals in the fullest sense of the word in that they have no parish lists. Washington Cathedral has the parish of St. Alban's right on its grounds.

f. *The Chancellor.* He is the legal counsel to the bishop, and is invariably a lawyer by profession, and should be learned in both the canon and the civil law.

g. *Diocesan Institutions.* These may be few or many, depending upon the size and wealth of the diocese. They include hospitals, schools, and social agencies, and were generally started because of an acute need in the community which was not being met by the secular government.

5. THE PARISH

The parish is the worshipping unit of the church, and is its principal source of people and money. Yet it is not independent of the other units of the church, for the parish depends upon the bishop to confirm its members and to ordain its priests, and must use a Prayer Book authorized only by General Convention. It may not mortgage or sell its property except with the consent of the bishop and the standing committee of the diocese.

a. *The Rector.* He must be a priest, is the spiritual leader and presiding officer of the parish. He is called for life, and cannot be removed by vestry or bishop, or both, except on doctrinal or moral grounds, or by the bishop acting upon a formal resolution of the vestry requesting a dissolution of the pastoral relationship.

The church building and parish house must be under his "use and control" "at all times." The control of the worship and the spiritual jurisdiction of the parish are vested in the rector, and there can be but one rector in a parish; all other ministers are under his authority. The rector, when present, "shall preside in all meetings of the vestry."

b. *Wardens and Vestrymen.* Every parish has a senior warden or a rector's warden, and a junior warden or a people's warden. If a parish has a rector's warden specified in the charter, he is appointed by the rector; otherwise, as is the junior warden, he is elected by the congregation in annual meeting assembled. The number of vestrymen depends upon diocesan canon or civil law, but usually not less than six nor more than twelve or fourteen. All are elected by the congregation.

The vestry (including both wardens and vestrymen) extends the call to a rector, when the parish is vacant, fixes all salaries, has authority over all finances, and is responsible for the upkeep of the parish property. It elects its own clerk or secretary, the parish treasurer, and the sexton, and its minutes are a principal source for the history of a parish.

c. *The Parish Meeting.* This is convened at least once a year, elects all wardens and vestrymen (except the rector's warden), an all lay delegates to the diocesan convention, the number of which varies in the several dioceses and is fixed by diocesan canon.

d. *Parish Organizations.* These are under the direction and leadership of the rector, and none can be established without his approval. Every parish is expected to have an Altar Guild, the president and members of which are appointed by the rector. Its functions are to take care of the altar and all its appointments for divine worship on Sundays and week days.

e. *Episcopal Churchwomen.* They were formerly known as the Women's Auxiliary, are organized on a national, provincial, diocesan, and parochial level. They are concerned with the church's work in all spheres of its life as enumerated above, plus the community and international levels. Annually, they raise millions of dollars, the most dramatic instance of which is the presentation every three years at each General Convention of their United Thank Offering – the fruit of daily contributions of their famous Blue Box in thanksgiving for divine blessings received.

6. DIOCESAN AND PAROCHIAL MISSIONS

These are congregations which are not self-supporting, are not incorporated under the civil law, and therefore do not have the status and privileges of parishes. The bishop is rector of all missions (except parochial missions, which are under rectors of parishes), and his representative in the administration of a mission is called a Vicar. He has no tenure of office, and is appointed by the bishop and may be removed by the bishop at will. Title to its property is held by the bishop or the diocese.

If and when a mission grows in numbers and financial resources sufficiently to be self-supporting, it can then appeal to the diocesan convention for admission as a parish. If permission is granted, the congregation enters into union with the convention as a parish and usually is incorporated as a parish under the civil law.

Every organized mission has a bishop committee, appointed by the bishop, one of whom is the bishop's warden.

7. THEOLOGICAL SEMINARIES

The Episcopal Church in America did not begin to grow at any satisfactory rate until theological schools were established. In spite of the fact that they are indispensable to its life and growth, they have never, until very recently, received financial support from the national church. Only one is an *official* seminary of the General Convention, namely, the General Theological Seminary, and it has never received any support from its founder. Financial income comes from endowments, alumni and parish offerings.

Of the eleven accredited seminaries, ten are regional seminaries, sponsored by a varying number of dioceses, and sometimes by provinces. They are: The General Theological Seminary, New York, N.Y; Bexley Hall, the Divinity School of Kenyon College, Gambier, Ohio; The Protestant Episcopal Theological Seminary in Virginia (commonly called "The Virginia Theological Seminary"), Alexandria, Va; Nashotah House, Nashotah, Wisconsin; Berkeley Divinity School, New Haven, Connecticut; The Divinity School in Philadelphia; Seabury-Western Theological Seminary, Evanston, Illinois; Episcopal Theological School, Cambridge, Massachusetts; The School of Theology of the University of the South, Sewanee, Tennessee; Church Divinity School of the Pacific, Berkeley, California; and The Episcopal Theological Seminary of the Southwest, Austin, Texas.

Three diocesan theological schools, for the most part established for older men, to whom the call to the ministry has come later than usual, are: The Episcopal Theological Seminary in Kentucky, owned by the Diocese of Lexington; School of Theology of the Diocese of Long Island (N.Y.), was established in 1955; and Bloy House Theological Training School, Los Angeles, California.

BIBLIOGRAPHY

Addison, J. Thayer, *The Episcopal Church in the United States, 1789-1931.* New York: Charles Scribner's Sons, 1951.

Barnes, C. Rankin, *The General Convention,*

Offices and Officers, 1785-1950. Philadelphia: Church Historical Society, 1951.

Chorley, E. Clowes, *Men and Movements in the American Episcopal Church,* New York: Charles Scribner's Sons, 1946.

General Convention of the Protestant Episcopal Church, Journals of . . ., 1785-1964. New York.

Historical Magazine of the Protestant Episcopal Church, 1932 to date. Austin, Texas.

Manross, William Wilson, *A History of the American Episcopal Church.* New York: Morehouse-Barlso Co., 2nd ed., 1950.

White, Edwin A. and Dykman, Jackson A., *Annotated Constitution and Canons for the Government of the Protestant Episcopal Church in the U.S.A., 1789-1952,* Vol. I, II. Greenwich, Conn.: Seabury Press, 1954.

The Roman Catholic Church

The polity of the Roman Catholic Church encompasses the papacy, hierarchy and laity joined together to bring the message of Christ to those who do not know him, to share Christ with the faithful and to celebrate the sacraments. It is in this role as a means of expressing and conveying Christ's blessings and message that the polity of the church may be seen.

Roman Catholicism should properly be viewed as a worldwide society rather than as a "state," with all the modern implications of that policitical term, and despite the existence of sovereign qualities in the *Stato della Citta del Vaticano.* The 108.7 acres of the Vatican City contain little more than St. Peter's Basilica, an astronomical observatory and libraries as well as a museum including the Sistine Chapel, a spacious garden, and a residence and offices for the pope and his immediate aides.

1. THE PAPACY

The pope is recognized by Catholics as vicar of Christ on earth, an ordained priest, but still a bishop possessing no more sacramental power than do his fellow bishops. It is in his office as Bishop of Rome that he succeeds to all the authority and respect which Catholics assign to the holder of the See of St. Peter. In this office the pope has universal jurisdiction over all matters proper to the church and is set apart from the hierarchy by this jurisdiction and by the doctrine of papal infallibility. This latter tenet insists that on those rare occasions when he speaks *ex cathedra* on matters of faith and morals the pope's definitions will necessarily remain free of error. Catholic faith in this aspect of papal dignity is drawn from the traditional teachings of the church and Christ's Scriptural affirmation "That thou art Peter; and upon this rock I will build my church . . ." (Matt. 16:13-19). Catholics believe that with these words Christ announced the foundation of a permanent church and do not doubt that the legislative and judicial powers thus conferred upon Peter were to be transmitted undiminished to his successors. It should be noted that the papal role in defining the precise content of the faith makes the pope the supreme teacher in the church but implies no superhuman abilities. Infallibility is strictly a limited gift, under the agency of the Holy Spirit, and logically restricted to fundamental pronouncements which are usually preceded by comprehensive investigation, consultation and, in some cases, centuries of examination and debate.

The papal activities are primarily dedicated to the establishment and advancement of the church around the world and the preservation of purity in the forms of religious worship. The pope approaches his objectives via the executive, legislative, and judicial authority invested in him.

His executive competence includes, among other things, the establishment, supervision and dissolution of religious orders, control over the material goods of church foundations, the guidance of those missionary activities specifically under his control, the foundation and direction of such papal universities as the Catholic University of America in Washington, D.C., the canonization of saints, and the initiation and supervision of bishoprics. For the latter, he may appoint coadjuter or auxiliary bishops to a diocese wherein the incumbent bishop requires assistance for any reason.

The pope's competence in legislative concerns includes the aforementioned *ex cathedra* statements on matters of faith, the restraint of heresy, clarification of church law, definition of special fast days and feasts, the review of synodical decrees, changes in ritual and the right to preside over general ecumenical councils which he both calls and adjourns.

In his judicial competence the pope may preside over a court of the first instance or a court of appeal, absolve from any punishment due to sin (particularly in those cases reserved to the Holy See), organize clerical courts and appoint judges in the Roman diocese, review and dispense from vows and oaths for grave cause, and make prudential dispensations in matrimonial cases where church-instituted impediments exist. All of the resources of the Holy See, including the agencies of the Roman Curia and hierarchy may be employed by the pope to assist him in the execution of his duties.

The papal acts and communications employ a number of different documents. Among these are Instructions, which are doctrinal explanations and recommendations made without the force of law unless including a specific intention of doing so; Declarations, which are usually interpretations of existing laws; and the Edicts which customarily dealt with temporal concerns in the papal states and which are, consequent to the loss of those states with the emergence of modern Italy, rare since 1870. Because of their special familiarity, two types of Apostolic and Pontifical Letters can be noted. The first of these, the Papal Bull, is an apostolic letter issued in the form *Litterae Apostolicae sub plumbo*. It always deals with grave matters and usually carries the leaden *bulla* or seal from which the name derives, although a proper bull may carry only a red ink imprint of the seal showing a representation of Peter and Paul and a reverse carrying the name of the reigning pope. The well-known encyclical form is a Pontifical Letter and may be a specific encyclical epistle regarding a particular event or the more famous encyclical letter form addressed to all bishops and ordinaries (those upon whom Holy Orders have been conferred) on doctrinal and social matters of great consequence, e.g., *Rerum Novarum* (On the Condition of the Working Classes), Leo XIII, May 15, 1891.

2. CARDINALS AND THE CURIA

There are between seventy and eighty cardinals, priests of extraordinary judgment, piety, and learning. They are nominated by the pope who chooses them as his chief assistants and advisors and are consecrated to the Sacred College of Cardinals for life. The rank of cardinal dates from early times and was originally associated with capable assistants in the curia, the pastors of some of the great Roman parish churches and the personnel administering the papal charities. The college received its present form in the twelfth century and the selection of cardinals was reserved to the pope himself after 1179.

The six Cardinal Bishops hold the suburban sees around Rome. Cardinal Priests represent churches in Rome and dioceses from beyond the city. They differ only technically from the Cardinal Deacons who are assigned to duties at the Vatican. All are ordained priests and in April, 1962, John XXIII announced that in the future all raised to the rank of cardinal would receive episcopal consecration.

The cardinals' duties require a fluent knowledge of Latin and Italian and a majority of them have been Italian. This Italian domination in the college has led to an Italian domination of the papacy and the last "foreign" pope was Adrian VI, born in Utrecht, who served over four hundred years ago. The modern growth of the church in England, the Americas, and other areas has resulted in a manifest feeling that more non-Italian cardinals should be nominated. Such has been the case in recent years and members now come from thirty-one countries including Armenia, Japan, Tanganyika, Syria and Peru as well as from the traditional areas.

The early structure of the curia, in which the cardinals function, is not known to us. There is not sufficient historical information to permit a clear presentation of the development of the curia as the church's central administrative machinery. The concept of the Roman Curia, as with several administrative terms and practices within the church, arose from Roman usage. The term "curia" denoted those centers where the civil administration might meet or where convocations concerned with public affairs might be held. Ecclesiastical records indicate that the Roman bishop was very early obliged to seek assistance in dealing with the numerous matters referred to his decision. By the time of Constantine and the year A.D. 313, a permanent synod or minor council of priests from the Roman area was employed in aiding the pope in the dispatch of his responsibilities. By the fifth century, the *presbyteri cardinales* (*carde*; hinge or pivotal), an assembly of elder priests from the diocese, had evolved and these cardinals gradually enjoyed an ever-widening circle of privileges and responsibilities. Their exclusive right to elect the pope was confirmed by Alexander III at the Third Lateran Council in 1179 and they slowly achieved recognition as the official senate of the church, the chief advisors and assistants to the pope.

The major structure of the curia is threefold. Under the control of the pope, the curia has twelve congregations exercising administrative and executive powers, six offices for ministerial duties, and three tribunals charged with judicial responsibilities.

Not often changed, some of the congregations are permanent and others temporary. However, work, personnel, and responsibilities may be transferred from one congregation to another to meet the needs of the times. The identity of the oldest is traceable to 1587 and the Bull *Immensa Seterna Dei* of Sixtus V. Each congregation supervises special areas of activity which, with the exception of the congregation charged with the maintenance of St. Peter's Basilica, are almost invariably spiritual rather than materail in nature. The Sacred Consistorial Congregation founds, administers, and preserves all dioceses not directly under the Sacred Congregation for the Oriental Church or that for the Propagation of the Faith (*Congregation de Popaganda Fide.*)

The Sacred Congregation for the Oriental Church was founded by Pius IX in 1862 although Roman concern for the Oriental Rites dates from a much earlier era. John XXIII appointed five Eastern Rite and one Latin Rite patriarchs to join with the cardinals who make up this congregation and in November, 1963, Paul VI nominated representatives from all the Eastern Rites to act as consultors to the congregation. The Oriental Church embraces over eight million "Eastern" Catholics who are in communion with Rome but enjoy their own traditions, languages of worship and rites in such widely diverse places as Egypt, Bulgaria, Syria, Sinai, and Afghanistan.

The Sacred Congregation for the Propagation of the Faith was erected as a stable congregation in 1622 and is competent in most matters of missionary activity. Other congregations include those for the administration of Rites, Seminaries Sacraments, Extraordinary Ecclesiastical Affairs, Ceremonies and the Sacred Congregation of the Council which supervises catechetical instruction, reviews the acts of episcopal conference, and is charged with the general care and discipline of the clergy and the faithful. Finally, there is the Supreme Sacred Congregation of the Holy Office, competent to guard Catholic doctrine in faith and morals and to judge heresy, schism, and all questions surrounding new prayers and devotions.

Each of the sacred congregations is under the chairmanship of a Cardinal Prefect and is composed of those named to work under the prefect together with their expert advisors and consultors. Three of the congregations of greatest moment (Holy Office, Consistorial and Oriental Church) have the pope himself as prefect. Each prefect is assisted by a Cardinal Secretary who is, in usual practice, charged with the actual direction of the congregational affairs. In any case, the cardinal secretary assumes the greater burden of the executive work of the congregation, prepares all the materials which will eventually be submitted for the pope's consideration and is, in general, the congregation's central figure.

The curial administrative functions are complimented by three judicial tribunals under Canon 258. The first of these, the Sacred Apostolic Penitentiary, dates from the twelfth century and achieved its contemporary structure under Pius V in 1569. Its competency includes dispensations, absolutions, questions of conscience and supervision of all matters of indulgences not directly involving questions of faith. All grants of powers, rights and privileges, such as the saying of mass, hearing of confession, are termed Faculties and these are under the penitentiary. A familiar tribunal is that of the Sacred Roman Rota, dating from the early thirteenth century and originally a part of the Apostolic Chancery. The rota received a special constitution under John XXII in 1331 by which a board of formally designated judges replaced the unorganized body of ecclesiastical officials who had previously dealt with the myriad cases submitted to the review and judgment of the Holy

See. The rota gradually acquired jurisdiction over the civil as well as ecclesiastical trials in the papal areas but found its activities curtailed after 1870. Its competency was redefined under Pius X in 1908 and Pius XI in 1934. The ten judges function under a Dean who is first among equals and apportions and coordinates the work of the court. Customarily, judges of the rota meet in groups of three to hear cases although special instances of courts impaneling five or seven judges do occur and, once in a great while, the entire Sacred Roman Rota will set in *videntibus omnibus* to render judgment. The decisions, which may be on any disputed point of ecclesiastical law, are usually considered as final. However, the Supreme Tribunal of the Apostolic Signatura allots jurisdiction among the lower tribunals, considers legal problems involving the Vatican City, and in some rare instances, may annul a decision of the rota.

Six Offices, dating largely from the middle ages and the renaissance, comprise the third branch of the papal staff. The Apostolic Camera cares for the temporal possessions of the Holy See. The Chancery draws up pontifical acts and keep the archives. The Office of Latin Letters inscribes the less formal missives, while encyclicals and other major documents together with letters for heads of states, come from the Secretariat of Briefs to Princes. The Apostolic Datary officially confirms the dating, signature, and identification of papal documents. The Secretariat of State conducts relations between the Vatican and civil organizations and oversees the Pontifical Commission for Media of Social Communication. This latter concerns itself with printed materials, radio, television and motion pictures.

The Commission for Media is one of several, not properly part of the Roman Curia, charged with special tasks by the pope. The commissions, of varying number and limited terms, are *ad hoc* bodies of experts working in such areas as canon law, Biblical studies, historical sciences and the revision and emendation of the Vulgate. The proper business addresses of the offices, tribunals, and congregations together with those of the ranking hierarchy in the United States may be obtained from the *National Catholic Almanac* (Doubleday and Company.)

In popular usage the term hierarchy simply refers to the officials and offices of the church's administration taken together with the pope and his ordained fellow ecclesiastics in the cardinalate and the episcopacy. A precise definition of powers and a clear statement of responsibility require a delineation between the two hierarchical powers of order and of jurisdiction. The power of Order flows from the sacrament of ordination, takes its intrinsic qualities from it, and is supernatural and irrevocable in nature. The power of Jurisdiction derives from an appointive or elective office held and, being contingent upon possession of a properly assigned ecclesiastical office, is subject to change.

3. THE EPISCOPACY

Throughout the church, the organization, distinctions and definitions of authority are only instruments helping to manifest Christ to those who do not yet know him and to the faithful. All the powers and processes of the papacy, the hierarchy and the priesthood exist to lead men to Christianity and to sancify them in him via the sacraments. It is usually in his associations with the bishops, parochial priests and members of the religious orders that the polity of the church assumes a personal and immediate identity for the Roman Catholic. A bishop is named to a specific diocese, the limits of which are clearly defined by ecclesiastical law. He may be consecrated only by another bishop, holds the powers to teach, preach and celebrate the sacraments, and is revered by Catholics as a successor to the apostles.

The bishop shares with the rest of the hierarchy the kerygmatic responsibility to proclaim Christ. For the world at large, the pope and curia give overall direction to the missionary societies, seminaries, universities, and establish precepts for the teaching of the Word and the celebration of the sacraments. Within his own jurisdiction the bishop directs his diocesan clergy and visiting priests (such as missionaries under the aegis of the Society for the Propagation of the Faith) in teaching, preaching, and the sacramental life. He does this, among other ways, by furnishing good example to his people, by pastoral instruction in matters of faith and morals, by sponsoring diocesan seminaries and encouraging universities, parochial schools, discussion groups and organizations devoted to the spiritual welfare of the Catholic laity.

The episcopal powers of order and jurisdiction require the bishop to furnish an adequate administration of the diocese, guide and guard the morals of his flock and pray for their spiritual welfare. He consecrates new altars, dedicates all new churches in his diocese, administers the sacrament of confirmation and ordains new priests from his area. Either he or his special representative visits throughout the diocese each year and he is encouraged to hold annual synods of his clergy. The bishop's own preparations for these privileges and responsibilities usually demand that he be at least thirty years of age, more than six months in major holy orders, of good reputation and sound judgment, and hold the licentiate or doctorate in canon law or theology. He cannot, of course, prescribe any course *contra jus commune*, i.e., against the general law of the church, and the legislative, executive, and judicial authority commensurate with his consecration is always subject to Rome. Appeals from cases proceeding before him may be made to the Holy See at any time. In the United States and Latin America the bishop is advised by four to six priests acting as diocesan consultors for three-year terms.

Diocesan boundaries are usually drawn with due regard for the borders and sovereignty of national states as an aid to administration. There have been changes made to coincide with changes in territorial sovereignty among temporal states, as for example, when Spanish bishops replaced the French in Louisiana Territory after control there passed to Spanish civil authorities with the Treaty of Paris in 1763. Although there are national episcopal councils, they are only informally convened in order to discuss some matter common to all and do not represent a permanent national legislative body.

4. THE PARISH PRIEST

To the laity the fundamental agent of the hierarchy and the immediate bridge to the polity of Roman Catholicism is the parish priest. Ordained by his bishop as "a priest forever," he has solemn powers and responsibilities in the community of Christ. He continually expresses his love for God and his pastoral concern for his parishioners by attempting to emulate the life of Christ in bearing the message of salvation. His ordination carries with it perpetual obedience and he henceforth dedicates his every faculty to Christ and to his flock. His day usually begins with the sacrifice of the Mass. By virtue of his ordination, he also hears confessions, grants absolution and administers the sacraments to the gravely ill. Catholics revere him as the direct representative of the bishop in the sanctification of the faithful and the administration of the parish. He assumes all his duties in obedience to the will of his superiors, and ideally his obedience is matched with an increasing depth of wisdom and an ever-growing comprehension and compassion in his ministry.

He joins with the laity in the Liturgy, the official public prayer of the church, in such forms as the Mass and the sacraments. He also reads the Divine Office, a series of daily prayers offered for all the Christian community. In all of these activities he carefully observes the Rites, the ceremonial aspects of the forms of public worship assumed by the Liturgy.

The parish priest fulfills his teaching and preaching responsibilities in many ways. He reads and comments upon episcopal letters to the faithful, illuminates the truths of the Testament in sermons and conferences and clarifies issues of faith and morals. He may be assisted in this regard by visiting members of the diocesan clergy or guest from the missionary and preaching orders invited to share his pulpit at Sunday Mass or in special weekday activities. In his own preaching, his sermons and homilies may be given to a massed congregation but are always addressed to the individual human soul in keeping with his mission to bring Christ to every man. The pastor also explains Catholic doctrine to interested non-Catholics, usually acts as business manager of the parish, directs the building and maintenance of parish structures and supervises the faculty, staff and academic and administrative details of any parish schools.

5. CANON LAW

In all of their ecclesiastical activities, the clergy and faithful in the Latin Rite are guided by the disciplinary legislation known as the Canon Law (*Codex Juris Canonici*).

Here it should be noted that Oriental Rite Catholics share in all those aspects of dogma and canon law which are intrinsic to the entire Catholic Church but that there are some special regulations regarding such matters as marriage in the Oriental Rite. Drawn from informal summaries of *ad hoc* rules, an organization of the scattered canons was made by the Benedictine monk Gratian about 1150. His famous *Concordia discondantium Canonium* (or *Decretum*) was widely used and affords much information about ecclesiastical practice in the middle ages but was never formally sanctioned by the church. Gregory IX issued a five volume series of *Decretals* in 1234 and successive popes extended this work down to 1598 and the time of Clement VIII. Pius X made a special point of initiating the first complete formal codification shortly after his election in 1903 and, after fourteen years of work, the Code of Canon Law was promulgated by Benedict XV in 1917. Its 2414 canons cover the application of the code and pertinent guides for all the operations of the church in every phase of its polity, helping to achieve the unity demanded in the fundamental purpose of its existence.

That fundamental purpose is to bring Christ to every man and thus to raise him from a natural level of life to an active, fully Christian awareness of his place and duties as a child of God. The church exists to help man realize salvation and reminds the Roman Catholic that he cannot allow himself to be separated from the Christian life. The polity of the church thus extends beyond the clergy to all the laity living the secular life and reminds them that they have a special vocation to hear Christ's message and to follow him to salvation. This, to the Roman Catholic, is the fundamental goal of the polity of the church, the mystical body of Christ seen in its ultimate intent.

BIBLIOGRAPHY

National Catholic Almanac, St. Anthony's Guild. Paterson, N. J.: Doubleday & Co., Inc.

Twentieth Century Encyclopedia of Catholicism. New York: Rene Metz, 1960.

Corbishley, Thomas, *Roman Catholicism.* Harper Torchbooks, 1964.

De La Bedoyere, Michael, *The Layman in the Church.* London, 1954.

Ellis, John T., *American Catholicism.* Chicago: Univ. of Chicago Press, 1956.

Heston, Edward, *The Holy See at Work.* Milwaukee: Bruce Publishing Co., 1950.

Knox, Ronald, *The Priestly Life.* Sheed and Ward, 1958.

Lynskey, E., *The Government of the Catholic Church.* New York, 1952.

Magner, J., *The Catholic Priest in the Modern World.* Milwaukee: Bruce Publishing Co., 1957

Masure, Eugene, *Parish Priest.* A Bouchard, translator. Chicago: Fides Publishers, 1955.

Michonneau, G. and Meurice R., *Catholic Action and the Parish.* Newman Press, 1955.

Neill, T. P. and Schmandt, R. H., *History of the Catholic Church.* Bruce Publishing Co., 1957.

Scharp, Heinrich, *How the Catholic Church Is Governed.* New York: Paulist Press, 1962.

Woywod, S. and Smith, C., *A Practical Commentary on the Code of Canon Law.* New York: J. F. Wagner, Inc., 1929, 1957.

The Methodist Church

The Methodist Church is one of the largest and most evenly distributed Protestant ecclesiastical organizations in the United States. It represents a continuation and expansion of the Wesleyan revival begun in England in the eighteenth century by John and Charles Wesley and George Whitefield. John Wesley is usually acknowledged to be "under God, the Founder of Methodism." "Methodism" is the term commonly applied in a broad way to the whole scope and comprehensiveness of Methodist life, doctrine, discipline, and polity.

1. DEVELOPMENT

Historically, the Methodist Church in America was formally organized in 1784. Previous to that date the Methodist movement, which had spread to America in the 1760's had been growing rapidly. It was, however, not a church but a "connexion," composed of Methodist "Societies." These societies kept a close relationship with each other through preachers who traveled about between them, and all looked to John Wesley in England, as their leader and guide. Wesley, in time, sent certain of his preachers – unordained men – to be his "assistants" in the colonies. In 1771 Wesley sent Francis Asbury to America, and within a few years Asbury became Wesley's chief assistant and continued to be such through the Revolutionary War.

The sweeping away by the American Revolution of any authority which the Church of England might possess in the colonies changed everything for the Methodists in America. There was no longer any church to which they could turn for the sacraments and it was clear there never would be again an English church on these shores. But the American Methodists were anxious that they might have the sacraments "according to the Use of the Church of England" in which they had been brought up. So they besought Mr. Wesley to send them ministers empowered to administer the ordinances, since their own preachers, not being ordained men, could not do this.

Wesley attempted to get certain of the English bishops to ordain some of his Methodist preachers that he might send them to America as Priests of the church who could administer the ordinances. The English bishops refused. John Wesley then took the momentous step of ordaining certain men himself, and sending them to America to be "Elders" – a term he liked better than "Priests," as the Church of England terms this higher order. Wesley did however, ordain these men by the form "For the Ordaining of a Priest" as it is in the Ordinal of the Church of England.

At the same time, September, 1784, Wesley ordained and consecrated Dr. Thomas Coke, to be a "Superintendent" for the Methodists in America, and directed him to proceed to the newly freed colonies and ordain Francis Asbury, also, to be a superintendent. Wesley carefully chose the word "Superintendent" rather than "Bishop," for Coke and Asbury, though the ordination service through which these men were inducted into the superintendency is exactly that for the "Ordaining and Consecrating of a Bishop or Archbishop" in the Church of England.

Coke and his two accompanying Elders, Richard Whatcoat and Thomas Vasey, ordained by Wesley, proceeded to America and duly notified Mr. Asbury of Mr. Wesley's desire that he also should be ordained a Superintendent. Francis Asbury demurred at this pre-emptory direction, and stated that that he would only accept the superintendency if the American preachers in conference would elect him to such a position.

Coke agreed with Asbury to call a conference of the preachers to pass upon this matter. The conference met in Baltimore on the 24th of December, 1784 – hence became known as the "Christmas Conference" – with about sixty or more preachers present. The conference agreed to form a "Methodist Episcopal Church in America"; to elect Francis Asbury as Superintendent; to accept Coke also as Superintendent; to adopt a Liturgy, which John Wesley had prepared, which was an abridgement of the Book of Common Prayer of the Church of England; and to receive Whatcoat and Vasey as elders; and to ordain as elders for the new church, twelve of their own men.

The Methodist Episcopal Church grew rapidly in the United States. The Prayer Book which Mr. Wesley had sent over, however, did not prove at all suitable to the American scene. In short order Mr. Wesley's Prayer Book, called The Sunday Service, was discarded, and American Methodism created a book of it's own, which it calls not inappropriately "The Discipline" – not ordered *worship* so much as *ordered life and activity*. Known officially as "The Doctrines and Discipline of the Methodist Church" this book has been reissued every four years following each successive General Conference. It embodies not only the organizational structure of the church and all constitutional provisions, but publishes all new laws and regulations that each General Conference sees fit to enact.

2. DIVISIONS

In the development of American Methodism, two notable divisions occurred. In 1828 a group of Methodists in the states along the eastern seaboard, objecting bitterly to the fact that there was no lay representation in the General Conference, or in the Annual Conferences of the church, seceded and formed the Methodist Protestant Church. This church had no bishops and no district superintendents, each Annual Conference, where laymen were fully represented, managing its own affairs. The Methodist Protestants did, however, carry on Methodist itinerancy, their preachers being "stationed" by a "stationing committee" which each Annual Conference was empowered to elect.

A more momentous division occurred in 1844 when the Methodist Episcopal Church split over the tense issue of slavery, as that intruded itself into the actions of the General Conference. A Southern Bishop, James A. Andrew of Georgia, owned slaves, albeit unwillingly, as he had married a lady who owned them, and a Negro boy slave had been bequeathed him by will. The General Conference meeting in New York, by a majority vote, with the North against the South, passed a resolution that Bishop Andrew should "desist from exercising his Episcopal powers so long as this impediment (slave holding) remains." Though the southerners objected that a constitutional issue was involved; that no General Conference had a right to depose a bishop once he had been elected and consecrated, unless and until some moral or official fault could be charged against him, the deposition stood. Because of the great cleavage that resulted, the Conference adopted a "Plan of Separation, under which the Southern Conferences might be allowed to set up a separate ecclesiasticism if they so chose. Within two years time the Southern Conferences did, under the Plan of Separation, create the Methodist Episcopal Church, South. These two branches carried on their work along separate but parallel lines from 1844 until 1939, when, under a Plan of Union adopted by commissioners from the respective churches, the Methodist Episcopal, Methodist Episcopal Church, South, and Methodist Protestant church joined to form the Methodist Church.

3. DOCTRINE

Doctrinally, Methodism can be said to be mid-stream in Protestantism, as while it emphasizes heavily certain doctrines, such as repentance, justification by faith, regeneration, and the witness of the Spirit, these emphases have not been at all new in the development of classic Chrisitanity. Officially the Methodist Church claims to hold as "Standards of Doctrine" the twenty-five Articles of Religion (abridged from the thirty-nine Articles of the Church of Engand by Wesley and sent to America in 1784). Methodist doctrine is also held to inhere in a certain number of John Wesley's sermons; and also in his "Notes on the New Testament." However, interpretations of Wesley's theology have always differed in certain respects, and Methodists feel free to let their own consciences be their guide in moot matters of faith. The formal Articles of Religion, however, as these are published in the Book of Discipline, and fixed in the Constitution of the church, cannot be changed in any respect, even by the General Conference. They might possibly be changed by the whole church, should it decide to do so, through the constitutional processes provided for such change.

Methodists take exception to the allegation often brought against them that they have no definite doctrine. They admit that their church is much more concerned with life and zeal than with intellectual concepts. They also admit that John Wesley "shifted the center from tradition to experience," in the words of Bishop Paul B. Kern and agree with Dr. George A. Gordon who said that "Wesley brought the whole Christian world back to religion as *experience* in the face of a dead theology and of a dead ceremony. He made religion a living, creative, glorious reality, and the thought and determination and affirmation of Wesley have gone around the world" (*The Rediscovery of John Wesley*; by George C. Cell, p. 73). Methodists do "lead with their hearts, rather than their heads," but no church and no Christian group can carry on long without having as the core and center of all moves the absolute basic convictions, tenets, and faith of Christ's gospel. Methodists with all Christians recognize this fact.

One new doctrine taught by Wesley and specifically emphasized by early Methodists was "the possibility of final perfection" in this life. Christian perfection called by Wesley "Perfect Love" was heavily emphasized in pristine Methodist preaching, and the state of "perfect love" was one held out as being possible in this life. John Wesley himself never claimed to have been so made perfect, but some of his followers did, and insisted that Christian perfection must be sought by all. In Methodism itself, there came about, in its later years, a greatly divided mind over the whole matter of the search for perfection. That all Christians ought to seek for holiness and that continually, is undenied, but that there is a possibility of a second work of grace in this world has not been made clear, and has not been continually championed in Methodism itself. In time, certain groups, as the Free Methodists, The Wesleyan Methodists, the Nazarenes, and certain

Pentecostal elements withdrew from the old line Methodist churches largely because these churches had ceased to emphasize Christian perfection as had the earlier Methodist fathers. The Methodist Church today, while it holds to the idea in a traditional way and with a sort of nostalgic hopefulness, does not preach it with anything like its former enthusiasm. Methodists, do, however, continue to stress the need to live sinless lives, and to keep God's "holy will and commandments," and to aim toward perfection. Methodists still maintain that it is possible, by God's grace, to live lives that shall be "void of offense" both to God and man.

4. DISCIPLINE

While Methodist doctrine has been broad and all encompassing, Methodist discipline has from the beginning been strict and demanding. Methodists early earned the reputation of being "narrow minded," not because of their doctrine, but because of their rules for life. John Wesley himself, at the very beginning of the Methodist movement, laid down certain "general rules," which rules are now embodied in the Constitution of the Methodist Church. In the United Societies, to which these rules were first given, every Methodist was expected to obey them or be excluded from the Society itself. When these societies later became a church in the United States, the General Rules were adopted as part of its formal ecclesiastical regimen and for the first three-quarters of the nineteenth century were so rigidly observed that the very name *Methodist* became a synonym for a strict and unyielding type of iron-clad discipline.

It was found however, perhaps inevitably, that in the development of a Church as over against a Society within the church there had to be a certain yielding for the sake of the larger structural life which a vast ecclesiasticism must provide. Whatever be the reason, in the ongoing and growth of Methodist ecclesiastical life there has been a gradual letting down of the primal Methodist discipline as that once was, and there has come about unmistakably an accomodation to the mores of the surrounding world. Nevertheless, the old ideal of a spiritual people who must individually and collectively seek holiness "without which no man shall see the Lord," and who must show their faith by their works is still present in Methodism.

5. ORGANIZATION

Methodist organization, while highly complex in the intricate involvment of its separate components — Bishops, Conferences, judicial procedures, and local church powers — has proved both authoriative and flexible in many matters of individual and congregational rights and privileges. In polity the Methodist Church has always declared itself "episcopal" because of the highly significant role the bishops occupy in the overall administrative direction.

There are, however, significant presbyterial powers involved in Methodism by reason of the enormous sovereignty exercised by the body of "Elders" who form the permanent membership of each of the Annual Conferences. These elders, who are held to belong to the higher order in the Methodist Church (Elders and Deacons — the Bishop is held to be simply an Elder who has been set apart for a special work) elect from among themselves half the membership of the all powerful General Conference; and also have the right in their own conferences to vote upon any proposed constitutional change which may be referred to the Annual Conferences by the General Conference itself. Elders hold conference membership for life and are the nucleus and controlling body in any Annual Conference.

Congregational powers are also exercised to a high degree in the Methodist Church by each local church or charge. Each local congregation has the right to control its own property in the matter of buying or improving same; of electing its lay delegates to the District and Annual Conferences; and of passing upon all matters which have to do with the management of the local church, including fixing the salary of the pastor. The right of the local church to select its own pastor, however, according to the time-test and ironclad polity of Methodism, has been given over to the General Church, which in turn puts this in the hands of the bishop.

It can be seen, therefore, that Methodist organizational life is an unusual accommodation of episcopal, presbyterial, and congregational powers. One marked feature of Methodist polity which infuses and influences the whole system in every way is itinerancy. This means that the ministers of the church are expected to travel about from place to place under the appointment of a bishop, whose duty at the Annual Conference is to "station" each preacher formally for a year. At the same time, as part of the itinerant plan, each local church must be assigned a pastor. This system calls for a minister to surrender his right to choose his place of work and the people whom he will serve; and calls for an equal surrender on the part of the local churches of their right to select their own minister.

The power of Methodist bishops to station preachers has been a feature of Methodism since its origin. This power has been under ceaseless attack from 1784 to the present day, and has been modified quite definitely under the pressures that have come from successive generations. In time a "cabinet" of district superintendents became established in each Annual Conference, with each district superintendent assisting the bishop in making appointments. Since the bishop cannot know all local churches and all preachers, nor their special situations, he must depend upon the cabinet for its nominations and advice.

Methodist episcopacy as represented by its bishops is *sui generis.* Each bishop is a "General Superintendent" of the whole church, and the constitution of the Methodist Church establishes a Council of Bishops which has the mandate to oversee all the affairs of the whole church. But the bishop in Methodism is not regarded as belonging to a "third order," as is the episcopacy of the Protestant Episcopal Church or of the Church of England. He is an elder who has been separated and consecrated for a specific administrative position and at best is simply *primus inter pares.* The enormous prestige he enjoys comes not from a traditional ecclesiastical rating, but from his very real power to station preachers and oversee the work.

Bishops, beside making appointments, must preside over each of the Annual Conferences assigned them; rule upon decisions of law, which in turn must be passed upon by the Judicial Council before they can have permanent effect; head up a general program for the church in their respective areas; act as over-pastors to their ministers and laymen; and give leadership in many matters having to do with the temporal as well as spiritual affairs of the churches. Methodist bishops also have the ordaining power, but this cannot be used until an Annual Conference has voted "orders" to deacons-elect and elders-elect. No other person in the Methodist Church, other than a bishop, has a right to ordain.

6. THE CONFERENCES

Administratively and legislatively the Methodist Church is also governed by a series of conferences, each of which has definite powers with regard to the churches and persons under its control. Conferences have their own rights guaranteed them by the constitution of the church, and these cannot be infringed upon by bishops, or other conferences. Each conference, as a general thing, covers a geographic division of Methodist Church territory.

The Quarterly Conference is the authoratative and controlling body of each local church or "charge" in Methodism. A "charge" may consist of one church, termed a "station"; or a group of churches, termed a "circuit." The Quarterly Conference meets four times a year, or twice a year if this proves sufficient. The Quarterly Conference is presided over by the District Superintendent, who does not belong to Quarterly Conference, and cannot vote, but acts as moderator and must call a series of questions at each conference. These are carefully specified in the Book of Discipline and have to do with the general administration of the local church and its work.

The pastor(s), stewards, trustees, and other elected officials of the local church comprise the Quarterly Conference, which has full control of property rights, finances, and all manner of local interests. The Quarterly Conference creates, among other, a Committee on Pastoral Relations which is empowered to represent the church to the pastor and the pastor to the church; and when any change in appointments is impending or desired, it consults with the district superintendent, and possibly the bishop about such change. This Quarterly Conference also elects the lay delegates of the church to the Annual and District conferences.

The Annual Conference is administratively the most potent organizational body in Methodism with the exception of the General Conference. Each Annual Conference is composed of the ministers serving the churches in a definite region, and also, of one layman, sometimes two or three, from each pastoral charge within its bounds.

The Annual Conference has historically been the preachers' conference. Its pattern as such was set long before laymen were admitted to its membership. Preachers come to its sessions to make their reports, have their own personal character "examined and passed," vote on all matters of ministerial membership, such as those who are to be admitted to the conference, those to be retired, and those to be ordained. Each Annual Conference completely controls its own ministerial membership. No lay member of the Annual Conference has a right to vote upon the character or qualifications of any minister; the acceptance, rejection, or censure of any ministerial member is entirely in the hands of his conference brethren.

The Annual Conference may by vote "locate" a minister who may not prove acceptable in the traveling connection or who, for good reasons, may ask "location." Location means that he ceases to be a traveling preacher. If located he retains his standing as a minister and his ordination rights, but is no longer under the appointment of a bishop to any "charge." Sometimes a minster is located against his will by majority vote of the conference, if his brethren deem that he is not suited to serving any appointment in the traveling connection. The last question which must be called at each Annual Conference is: "Where shall the preachers be stationed for the ensuing year?" The bishop then proceeds to answer this question by "reading the appointments" and giving the men and the churches their assignments for the coming twelve months.

The constitution of the Methodist Church states that the Annual Conference is the basic body in the church and as such, "has reserved to it all rights not given to the General Conference." This is a sweeping reservation of powers, and the Annual Conferences carefully guard their rights in this regard.

The Jurisdictional Conference is a comparatively new feature in the Methodist Church, coming into being under the plan of union adopted in 1939. For administrative purposes the Annual Conferences within the United States are grouped into five geographic and one racial jurisdiction. These consist of the Northeastern (roughly the Annual Conferences above the Potomac River and east of the Ohio State line); the Southeastern – (the conferences below the Potomac and east of the Mississippi); the North Central Conference (above the Ohio and extending out through Kansas and Nebraska and above the Missouri line); the South Central (those Conferences west of the Mississippi and under the Missouri line); and the Western Jurisdiction (those Conferences including Colorado and all west of the Rockies). The Central Jurisdiction is composed of the Negro Annual Conferences which were in the Methodist Episcopal Church at the time of union. This Jurisdiction is presently being absorbed into the five geographic ones. Each Jurisdictional Conference meets once in four years and has the prime duty of electing bishops, and of electing representatives to the various boards, commissions, and agencies of the Methodist Church. It also administratively provides for the carrying forward of the work of the general church, within its own region.

The General Conference of the Methodist Church meets once every four years and has full authority over all connectional or federal matters. Each Annual Conference is represented in the General Conference by an equal number of ministers and laymen. The clerical delegates are elected by the ministers of each respective Annual Conference, with one delegate allowed for every seventy ministers. An "equal number of laymen" are elected by the lay delegates of each conference voting by themselves. The General Conference is empowered to define and fix the conditions, privileges and duties of church membership, of the ministry, and of the conferences – Annual, Mission, District, Quarterly, and local church. It may also define and fix the powers, duties and privileges of the episcopacy, though it may not "do away Episcopacy, or alter the plan of our itinerant general superintendency." It must provide for and revise the hymnal and ritual of the church, must provide a judicial system, and set up methods of judicial procedure. It has general control over all connectional enterprises such as the publishing, evangelistic, educational, missionary, and benevolent work of the church, and provides boards and agencies to direct these causes. It must fix a uniform basis upon which the bishops shall be elected by the Jurisdictional Conferences, and determine the number of bishops to be elected by the Central Conferences. The constitution of the church, while granting these sweeping powers to the General Conference, denies it the right to change any Articles of Religion, or to "establish any new standards or rules of doctrine contrary to the existing ones." It may not alter the plan of episcopal supervision or itinerancy, which has been in effect from the beginning. It cannot do away with the privileges of ministers or members from having a proper trial if their characters are formally called in question. It cannot change the old Wesleyan rules for proper conduct. The constitution however, does provide that the General Conference may propose an amendment to the constitution of the church by two-thirds vote, which then to take effect must be approved by two-thirds of all the Annual Conference members present and voting. It would take a three-fourths vote to change any doctrinal standard.

Each General Conference starts off a new "quadrennium," and makes plans and adopts a program for the coming four years. It also provides a general budget for the church, sees that this is properly allocated, and controls largely the life of the entire church.

7. JUDICIAL PROCEDURES

The Methodist Church provides a judicial system for the proper evaluation of its own processes, and for the administration of discipline throughout the whole connection. Methodist law is largely administrative, with all the various regulations having to do with the rights, privileges, and duties of clergy and people, conferences and local churches, etc., carefully outlined and provided for. Also, there is a system of trial law by which an offense against the church's own regulations or against the moral law of Christian conduct may be properly looked into, and, if necessary, acted upon. The Book of Discipline sets forth in great detail all these processes.

A high tribunal, called the Judicial Council, composed of five ministers and four laymen, all elected by the General Conference, is empowered to pass upon matters of the constitutional law, and upon all the judicial rulings of the bishops. The Judical Council, sometimes called the "Supreme Court" by Methodists, must meet twice a year and always sits at the time of the General Conference, when it has the duty to pass at once upon the constitutionality of any action of that body which may be challenged.

8. ECUMENICAL MOVES

The Methodist Church has been in the forefront of all moves for and toward the union of all Christian bodies. A Methodist Bishop, Eugene R. Hendrix, was the first president of the former Federal Council of Churches. The Methodist Church is a member of the World Council of Churches, and of the National Council of the Churches of Christ in America and provides more heavily than perhaps any other church for their financial support. It elects at each General Conference a commission, presently called the Commission on Ecumenical Affairs, which is empowered to represent it in every promising move toward church union, and to "explore, receive, study and recommend action on proposals for union of the Methodist Church with other denominations."

BIBLIOGRAPHY

Anderson, William K., ed. *Methodism.* Nashville: The Methodist Publishing House, 1947.

Asbury, Francis, *The Journal and Letters of Francis Asbury,* ed. Elmer T. Clark, J. Manning Potts, and Jacob S. Payton. 3 vols. Nashville, Abingdon Press, 1958.

Barclay, Wade Crawford. *The History of Methodist Missions.* New York: The Board of Missions of The Methodist Church, Vol. I, 1949; Vol. II, 1950; Vol. III, 1957.

Batten, J. Minton, *The History of the Methodist Publishing House.* Nashville: Personnel and Public Relations Division of the Methodist Publishing House, 1954.

Gross, John O. *Methodist Beginnings in Higher Education.* Nashville: Board of Education of The Methodist Church, 1959.

Harmon, Nolan B. *The Organization of The Methodist Church.* 2nd rev. ed. Nashville: The Methodist Publishing House, 1962.

Holt, Ivan Lee, and Clark, Elmer T. *The World Methodist Movement.* Nashville: The Upper Room, 1956.

Knudson, Albert C. *The Doctrine of God.* New York: The Abingdon Press, 1930.

McCutchan, Robert Guy. *Our Hymnody: A Manual of the Methodist Hymnal.* 2nd ed. Nashville: Abingdon Press, 1937.

Schilling, S. Paul. *Methodism and Society in Theological Perspective.* Nashville: Abingdon Press, 1960.

The History of American Methodism, 3 vols., ed. Emory Stevens Bucke. Abingdon Press, 1964.

Wesley, John. *The Letters of Rev. John Wesley, A.M.*, ed. John Telford. Standard Edition. 8 vols. London: Epworth Press, 1931.

Christian Creeds and Confessions

From its very beginnings, the Christian religion was recognized as including a creed as well as a code and a cult. It found expression, not only in worship and in conduct, but in "things most surely believed," particularly with respect to Jesus Christ, its divine founder. In the New Testament no developed or formal "creed" is to be found. But a common corpus of doctrine is present throughout; and summaries of basic Christian belief appear in many places. Sometimes these doctrinal formulae take the form of a one-clause Christian statement, for example, "Jesus is Lord" (I Cor. 12:3, cf. Rom. 10:9). Sometimes they have a two-part structure, including God the Father as well as Jesus Christ the Son (I Cor. 8:6). Occasionally a trinitarian confession occurs (II Cor. 13:14). Says J. N. D. Kelly, "It cannot be too often repeated that, in the proper sense of the terms, no creed, confession or formula of faith can be discovered in the New Testament, with the possible exception of such curt slogans as *Kurios Jesous.* What is manifest on every page is a common body of doctrine, definite in outline and regarded by everyone as the possession of no individual, but of the church as a whole. At the New Testament stage this corpus of teaching was beginning to crystallize into more or less conventional patterns and forms, and sometimes set types of verbal expression were becoming current" (*Early Christian Creeds,* pp. 23, 24).

1. EARLY CHURCH CREEDS

In the ancient church there emerged three formal creeds, The Apostles', the Nicene, and the Athanasian.

a. *The Apostles' Creed.* In the early church each local Christian community tended to adopt a statement of the essentials of the Christian faith for use in the instruction of catechumens (i.e., prospective church members), as well as at the sacrament of baptism at which they were received into full membership. Such creeds might consist either in an affirmative statement to be made by the catechumen, or a reply by him to questions put to him by the officiating clergyman. The church of Rome, the oldest and wealthiest church in the West, had such a formal confession whose existence, at least in its basic structure, can be traced back to the second century. This Roman confession naturally influenced the form of such doctrinal statements in other western churches. It was this confession which provided the pattern for the Apostles' Creed, in its present developed form first appearing in a treatise by a Benedictine monk, Priminius, between 710 and 724. Thereafter it proceeded to take rank as the standard creed of the Western Church, partly at least through the efforts of the Holy Roman Emperor Charlemagne (771-814) who sought to impose liturgical uniformity through his vast domains. This Apostles' Creed, however, was accepted only in the West; at the Council of Florence in 1339 the delegates from the Eastern churches declared that they knew nothing about it.

The Apostles' Creed was designed not only to present a compact yet comprehensive summary of the essentials of the Christian faith; it was also so drawn up as to exclude heresy. The particular heresy against which it was directed was what is called Gnosticism, a complex religious movement originating outside of Christianity but seeking to infiltrate and dominate it. Gnosticism, for example, did not acknowledge God to be "the Father Almighty," nor did it regard Jesus Christ as "His only Son our Lord."

b. *The Nicene Creed.* This desire to protect the church against heresy was the primary motive in drawing up the Nicene Creed, the second of the great traditional Christian symbols. In the early years of the fourth century Arius, a presbyter of Alexandria in Egypt, in the interest of the doctrine of the unity of God, propounded the view that Jesus Christ, the Son, was only a creature, an intermediary between God and man. He thus denied Jesus Christ's full and essential deity. In order to settle the dispute which this Arian Christology produced in the church, the Emperor Constantine summoned the first Ecumenical Council to meet at Nicaea in 325. This council drew up a creed which expressly condemned Arianism as heretical, and asserted that Jesus Christ was "of one essence with the Father." Even this official declaration by the Council of Nicaea did not end the Arian controversy, which continued for another half century or so. But in 381 the second Ecumenical Council, held at Constantinople, reaffirmed the Nicene position with respect to the essential deity of Jesus Christ, and at the same time added that the Holy Spirit, the third person of the Trinity, was equally divine with the Father and the Son. In 589 a Western Church Council at Toledo, in Spain, added a phrase to the Nicene-Constantinopolitan Creed to the effect that the Holy Spirit proceeded "from the Father and from the Son" (filioque). Though this addition was not accepted by the Eastern Church, and indeed was advanced as one reason for the separation of the Eastern Church from the West in 1054, it may be claimed that the Nicene-Constantinopolitan Creed is the only truly ecumenical Christian confession, since (with the above exception) it is accepted and recited by virtually all Christian churches — Western Orthodox, Roman Catholic, and most major Protestant communions.

c. *The Athanasian Creed.* There is a well-known epigram which states that the only two things which are certain about the Athanasian Creed — called the Quicunque Vult, from its opening Latin words — are that it was not by Athanasius and that it is not a creed. Since at least the seventeenth century it has been recognized by scholars that Athanasius was not its author. It would appear to have been composed toward the end of the fifth century or the beginning of the sixth, probably in South Gaul, under the inspiration of the influential monastery of Lerins. And it was strictly Western in its acceptance; for though a Greek version of it was in existence before the middle of the thirteenth century, it has never received official recognition by the Eastern Church.

A creed, however, the Quicunque certainly is. It consists mainly of two sections. The first is a rather elaborate summary of the developed doctrine of the Trinity. This is followed by an exposition of the doctrine of the Incarnation, which summarizes particularly the church's teaching concerning Jesus Christ as being fully divine and at the same time fully human. "This is the Catholic faith," it concludes, "which except a man believe faithfully, he cannot be saved." The Athanasian Creed was unquestionably drawn up with the Nestorian heresy in view, for its phrasing is such as quite explicitly to refute this heresy. But it is constructive rather than controversial in tone and attitude; and in all likelihood it was designed primarily as a statement of orthodox Christian doctrine for clergy of the Western Church to assimilate and impart in their teaching work.

2. REFORMATION AND POST-REFORMATION DEVELOPMENTS

The Reformation movement of the sixteenth century brought into existence several types of Protestant churches — Lutheran or Evangelical, Calvinist or Reformed, Anglican, Evangelical "left wing" churches represented by the Anabaptists, and Rationalist anti-Trinitarian groups of which the Socinians were the most significant. Each of these churches felt it necessary to issue confessional manifestos expounding its distinctive theological viewpoint. Except for the rationalist groups, all these Protestant churches were in accord with the ancient Christian symbols, especially the Apostles' Creed and the Nicene Creed.

a. *Lutheran Creeds.* Lutheran Confessions were produced during the decade between 1528 and 1537. Of these the most important was the Augsburg Confession, "the most authoritative Lutheran standard." In 1530 the Holy Roman Emperor, Charles V, asked representatives of both Lutheran and Roman

Catholic Churches to present their case at a Diet which he convened at Augsburg, in order "to put an end to discord. . . to make Christian truth stand out and to abolish all that which either party has done or said against the truth" (Paul T. Fuhrmann, *Introduction to the Great Creeds of the Church,* p. 87). The Lutheran statement, called the Augsburg Confession, was prepared by the theologian Melanchthon, with Luther's approval. It consists of two parts. The first twenty-one articles constitute a positive "summary of the doctrines that are preached and taught in our churches." The second part, articles twenty-two through twenty-eight, deals with abuses which had been corrected in Lutheranism, for example, monastic vows, and the denial of the cup to the laity in the sacrament of the Lord's Supper.

Since this Augsburg Confession was intended as a possible basis for reconciliation with Roman Catholicism, some distinctive Protestant principles were not stressed in it. For example, though the Bible alone is appealed to as authoritative, nothing is said of this as an article of faith; the doctrine of *sola Scriptura* is not mentioned. The doctrine of the priesthood of all believers is conspicuous by its absence; and even the problem of indulgences, which had been the immediate occasion of Luther's protest in 1517, receives only passing mention. But the central Lutheran doctrine of justification by grace through faith is clearly expounded, the good works are represented as a consequence, but not a cause, of salvation. And the church is defined as "the assembly of all believers among whom the Gospel is preached in its purity and the sacraments are administered according to the Gospel," – i.e., it is not to be identified with Roman Catholicism. Although this Augsburg Confession was framed in an irenical and ecumenical spirit, the Roman Catholic representatives at the Diet rejected it in a damning confutation, which rendered all reconciliation between Lutheranism and Roman Catholicism impossible.

Differences of doctrinal viewpoint emerged within Lutheranism, principally between Luther himself and Melanchthon, before Luther's death in 1546; and they became still more acute during the following generation. These differences had to do with three main questions. (1) What part does man's will play in his salvation? Luther held that the human will is in bondage through sin, and therefore cannot actively participate, but is passively molded by the divine Spirit. On the other hand, Melanchthon contended that man can and does cooperate, even though the Holy Spirit takes the initiative – a position usually described as synergism. (2) There was a difference of viewpoint with respect to the nature of Christ's presence in the sacrament of the Lord's Supper. All Lutherans agreed that faith alone guarantees the presence of Jesus Christ; but whereas Luther insisted on Christ's bodily presence, Melanchthon believed that his presence is spiritual and not physical – a view resembled that of John Calvin. (3) There was also a sharp difference among Lutherans with respect to the place of good works in the experience of Christian redemption. One group insisted that good works were necessary for salvation; an opposite group contended that good works were not necessary, and even were detrimental – the so-called anti-nomian view. On this question Melanchthon took a mediating position, holding that good works were necessary, but not to salvation.

After a generation of acrimonious controversy the Formula of Concord was drawn up in 1577 to settle the outstanding issues in dispute. This document rejected synergism but appeared to envisage the possibility of man's rejecting God's grace. It denied Melanchthon's view of Christ's presence in the Lord's Supper, insisting that the body and blood of Christ was received "in, with, and under" the elements of bread and wine. But it upheld Melanchthon in insisting on the necessity of good works, not as a cause of salvation, but as its necessary outcome. Though the publication of this Formula of Concord did not end the theological controversies which had divided the Lutherans, along with the Augsburg Confession it became the doctrinal standard for German Lutheranism.

b. *The Thirty-nine Articles of the Church of England.* Roland H. Bainton has said of sixteenth century England that "from this land emanated no distinctive confession and no great work on theology" (*The Reformation of the Sixteenth Century,* p. 184).

Nevertheless, the English sixteenth century Reformers issued several doctrinal statements, beginning with the Ten Articles of 1536. Of these the most important were the Thirty-nine Articles of 1563-71, the official standard of Anglican orthodoxy. These Articles pay due respect to the three ecumenical creeds, Apostles', Nicene, and Athanasian, which according to Article VIII, "ought thoroughly to be received and believed; for they may be proved by most certain words of Holy Scripture." Some of these Anglican Articles are of Lutheran inspiration, for example, Article XI, which asserts that "we are accounted righteous before God only for the merit of our Lord, Jesus Christ, by faith, and not for our own works or deservings"; and this is declared to be "a most wholesome doctrine and very full of comfort." Other Articles are Calvinistic in their viewpoint, for example, Article XVII on predestination, and Article XXVIII which declares that "the body of Christ is given, taken, and eaten in the [Lord's] Supper, only after a heavenly and spiritual manner." The Thirty-nine Articles, however, "form a decisively Protestant interpretation of the Faith" (A. G. Dickens, *The English Reformation*, p. 251). Not only are such specifically Roman Catholic doctrines as transubstantiation, purgatory, and papal supremacy decisively rejected, but such a distinctively Protestant doctrine as the sole sufficiency of Holy Scripture (Article VI) is asserted; and it is decreed that in the Lord's Supper the laity are to receive the cup as well as the bread (Article XXX).

It is doubtless correct to say that the genius of Anglicanism is to be found rather in its Prayer Book and the King James translation of the Bible than in its Thirty-nine Articles. But these Articles prove that the sixteenth century Church of England was by no means indifferent to theological issues; and if they have been variously interpreted in subsequent years, this testifies rather to their comprehensiveness, than to what is sometimes referred to as their "studied ambiguity."

c. *Calvinistic Confessions: The Canons of the Synod of Dort, and the Westminster Confession.* Since Calvinism was theologically minded from its very beginnings in sixteenth century Europe, its churches might have been expected to produce confessional manifestos. This they certainly did. For example, the Reformed Church of France issued its Gallican Confession in 1559, the Church of Scotland its Scots Confession in 1560, and the Reformed Church in the Netherlands its Belgic Confession in 1561. Though these documents differ somewhat in tone and emphasis, they all follow closely the teaching of John Calvin as expounded in his *Institutes of the Christian Religion.*

Other Calvinistic Confessions were issued later, for example, the Second Helvetic Confession in 1566. But probably the most influential of Reformed doctrinal manifestos were the Canons of the Synod of Dort, of 1619, and the Westminister Confession of 1647.

During the early 1600's a violent controversy broke out among Dutch Calvinists over the meaning and implications of the doctrine of predestination. James Arminius (Professor at Leyden, 1603-09) and his like-minded followers did not believe in the Biblical doctrine of election. This Arminian viewpoint was expressed in a Remonstrance issued in 1610, and was replied to in a Counter-Remonstrance the next year. To settle the dispute which thus ensued, the Synod of Dort was convened in 1618. It has been described by Erik Routley as "the most impressive ecumenical gathering in Protestantism before the First Assembly of the World Council of Churches (1948)" (*Creeds and Confessions*, p. 92). The Arminians had sought to make God's election dependent on his foreknowledge of man's decision for, or against, Jesus Christ. But the Synod of Dort rejected this view, declaring that God had elected a certain number of persons to redemption through Jesus Christ and given them the grace of final perseverance, solely because of His good pleasure. The other sinners God has "declared to leave in the common misery in which they have willfully plunged themselves."

After the civil war broke out in England in 1642 between King Charles I and the Long Parliament, the latter body convened an Assembly of Divines to meet in Westminster Abbey in order to give guidance in the task of reforming the Church of England. This Westminster Assembly met 163 times between 1643 and 1648. Out of its deliberations there came, besides such documents as the Shorter Catechism and the Longer Catechism, the Westminster Confession of Faith. This document expresses opposition to Roman Catholicism, for example, it describes the Pope as "that anti-Christ, that man of sin and son of perdition." And it condemns what it calls "the popish sacrifice of the Mass." But its thirty-three chapters are mainly a clear-cut and comprehensive statement of Reformed Church principles, expressing the Calvinistic viewpoint, but influenced also by that Puritan covenant theology which had developed since Calvin's day. The foundation on which it rests is that of Holy Scripture, defined as consisting of the sixty-six canonical books of the Old Testament and the New Testament, whose authority "dependeth not upon the testimony of any man or church, but wholly upon God, the Author thereof." It distinguishes between the invisible church, consisting of "the whole number of the elect," and the visible church, which consists of all "those throughout the world that profess true religion, and of their children." This church, organized in synods and councils, conducts regular worship services, dispenses the two sacraments of baptism and the Lord's supper, and administers discipline among its members. Since God alone is Lord of the conscience, the church enjoys Christian liberty in all spiritual matters, but lives in accord and cooperation with civil magistrates, who are God's appointed servants "for the defense and encouragement of them that are good, and for the punishment of evil doers." Its members are justified, i.e., accounted as righteous, adopted as God's children, and sanctified, through the virtue of Christ's death and resurrection; and they bring forth good works as "fruits and evidences of the true and lively faith." At death the souls of the righteous are received into the highest heaven, and wait for the full redemption of their bodies at the last day. The souls of the wicked, on the other hand, are at death cast into hell, where they remain until the day of final judgment, when they "shall be cast into eternal torments, and punished with everlasting destruction from the presence of the Lord."

This Westminister Confession, which the late Dr. P. Carnegie Simpson characterized as "incomparably the ablest document that ever came from Westminster," was ratified by the General Assembly of the Church of Scotland in 1647; and it has subsequently, with certain modifications, become the subordinate standard of orthodoxy throughout the Presbyterian world.

d. *Anabaptist Confessions.* The Anabaptists were representative of that radical evangelical Protestantism which emerged in the course of the religious revolution in sixteenth century Europe. They did not try to reform and cleanse the already existing church and reinterpret the Catholic tradition. Rather they sought to restore the church to what they considered to be its pristine purity during early centuries before it was established by the Roman imperial government and thereby denatured. Of the confessional statements issued by these groups two stand out as of special significance: the Schleitheim Confession of 1527, and the Dordrecht (Dort) Confession of 1632. The purpose of the former was to emphasize the distinctive tenets of its Anabaptist subscribers, their insistence that the sacrament of baptism should properly be administered, not to uncomprehending infants, but only those who had personally decided to accept Jesus Christ as Saviour and follow him as Lord. These alone also are entitled to participate in the Lord's Supper, from which however they may be debarred, under the so-called "ban," should their conduct not measure up to their profession. This discipline should be applied even to those pastors whom the faithful elect as their ministers in holy things. Such committed Christians should forsake the world, including the state churches of that day, both Roman Catholic and Protestant; and they should refuse to serve as civil magistrates, since such magistracy is of the world, and employs carnal weapons to enforce its decrees.

The Dordrecht (Dort) Confession of 1632 was drawn up by Adrian Cornelis, a bishop of the Mennonite Church. This group was named after Menno Simons (1496-1551), a Dutch Anabaptist whose followers settled into two groups, Frisian and Flemish, after his death. The Dort Confession is a statement of belief on which both groups were able to agree; and it has subsequently enjoyed widespread acceptance among Mennonites, including those in the USA. It differs from the Schleitheim Confession in being not simply a statement of distinctive

Anabaptist tenets, but a comprehensive exposition of Christian truth, and a kind of manual of Mennonite church order.

Basing itself on the Bible, this Dort Confession begins with a statement concerning the Trinity, the Creation, the Person and Work of Jesus Christ, and the offer of salvation to all mankind on condition of repentance and amendment of life. It goes on to affirm the characteristic Anabaptist doctrine of the church as consisting exclusively of committed Christians. This church elects its office bearers – bishops, leaders and ministers, plus deacons and deaconesses, the latter of whom were to consist of "honorable old widows"; and this church so constituted carries out four ordinances (sacraments) i.e., namely Baptism, the Lord's Supper, foot washing, and matrimony. Church members will not take up arms, or swear oaths; but they will pray for civil magistrates, and act as good citizens by paying their taxes and living peaceably. The confession concludes by asserting that at the last judgment all who have died will be raised up, and assigned their eternal destiny. The "good and pious" will reign with Jesus Christ forever, but the wicked and impious will be "cast into outer darkness, yea into eternal hellish torments."

e. *The Racovian Catechism.* Another kind of radical religious movement which emerged in Europe in the course of the sixteenth century was that which is associated with the names of Laelius Socinus (1525-1562), and his nephew, Faustus Socinus (1539-1604). They were Italians who, taking reason as their criterion of judgment, did scheme, as expressed in the Nicene and Athanasian Creeds. Faustus Socinus, after some wanderings, arrived in 1579 in Poland, where he headed up an Anti-Trinitiarian group known as the Minor Church. In 1605 this group issued in Polish, and in 1609 in Latin, its statement of belief, known as the Racovian Catechism, because Racow, from which it was issued, was the church's headquarters. This document was drawn up by Valentine Smalcius and Jerome Moscorovius after the death of Socinus, but its viewpoint is basically his.

According to this catechism, the fundamental Christian doctrine revealed in Scripture is that of the unity of God: "In the one essence of God, there is but one Person." This rules out the doctrine of the Trinity. Jesus Christ was not consubstantial with the Father: his nature was purely human. But he was virgin-born, "lived so holy a life that he approached nearest to God," and after his crucifixion was raised from the dead. The Holy Spirit is not a Person in the Godhead, but a "virtue or energy flowing from God to men and communicated to them, whereby He separates them from others and consecrates them to His service." The death of Jesus was not a propitiation for sin, but rather a revelation of God's nature as love. A Christian is one who seeks to follow Jesus, to be his disciple and imitate his example, and if necessary to submit "even to the most cruel death." The external religious acts or sacred rules – this catechism does not use the word "sacraments" – to be observed by the church are "baptism and the breaking of the sacred bread." Baptism is the right of initiation into church membership, by which converts openly acknowledge Jesus Christ as their master; it should therefore be administered only to committed disciples. The Lord's supper is a purely commemorative rite, recalling Jesus Christ's passion and death; there is no "real presence" of Christ in it. The chief gift which Jesus Christ bestows is that of eternal life, according to John 17:3, by which is meant "not only a life never to terminate, or immortality, but also an existence which is replete with joy and pleasure, and wholly divine, passed in heaven with God and Jesus Christ and the holy angels."

f. *The Roman Catholic Creed of the Council of Trent.* On the confessional level sixteenth century Roman Catholicism responded to the challenge of Protestantism by convening the Council of Trent, which sat, with intervals of intermission, from 1545 to 1563. At this council the Roman Catholic Church clarified its doctrinal position, but not by meeting Protestantism halfway. Rather, it so defined those beliefs which were in dispute as to point up the differences between Protestantism and itself. And in the Creed of the Council of Trent, promulgated by Pope Pius IV in 1564, it summarized those doctrines which the council had defined. This creed is still binding on faithful Roman Catholics. Its subscribers accept "traditions" as well as Scripture as interpreted by the Roman Catholic Church as sources of Christian doctrine. They acknowledge the number of the Christian sacraments as seven; they affirm the doctrine of transubstantiation; they accept the existence of purgatory and the validity of indulgences as proclaimed by the Roman Catholic Church, which is stated to be "the mother and teacher of all churches"; and they swear true obedience to the pope, as vicar of Christ and successor of Peter in the headship of the church.

3. CREEDS AND CONFESSIONS IN THE MODERN CHURCH

The mid-seventeenth century marked the end of the age of great confessions which were produced as a result of the Protestant Reformation. Most such confessions were based on the assumption that the church which produced them would ultimately at least, enjoy a nationwide if not larger religious monopoly. Since this "Age of Reform" – as the period between 1500 and 1650 is coming to be called – the ecclesiastical situation has greatly changed. For one thing, permissive pluralism has come to be the accepted religious pattern in western Europe and North America. Again, Protestantism in general, especially since the eighteenth century, has become less confidently dogmatic than it was in the confession-making era. And virtually all Protestant churches have, particularly in the twentieth century, increasingly come to emphasize God's love rather than his justice, and to lay correspondingly less stress on such a doctrine as predestination. In view of these changes the churches have become less attached to the classical creeds and confessions. Even such ancient symbols as the Apostles' Creed, the Nicene Creed, and the Athanasian Creed, do not enjoy their former authority.

Terms of subscription to some of the Reformation and Post-Reformation confessions have been modified. Thus the Church of Scotland General Assembly, in 1910, authorized its ministers to subscribe to the Westminster Confession in the following terms: "I hereby subscribe to the Confession of Faith, declaring that I accept it as the Confession of this Church, and that I believe the fundamental doctrines of the Christian Faith contained therein." In 1903 the Presbyterian Church in the USA adopted six amendments to the Westminster Confession, including new chapters entitled, "Of the Holy Spirit," and "Of the Love of God and Missions," besides a "Declaratory Statement" which asserted the love of God for all mankind and also the salvation of such as died in infancy. And in 1959 the General Assembly of the United Presbyterian Church in the USA, asserting that "it is the right and duty of a living Church to restate its faith from time to time, so as to display any additional attainments in truth it may have made under the guidance of the Holy Spirit," appointed a Special Committee on a Brief Contemporary Statement of Faith. This committee drew up a document called The Proposed Confession of 1967, consisting of three sections: (1) God's work of reconciliation, (2) The ministry of reconciliation, and (3) The fulfillment of reconciliation. Before these documents can become official, however, they must be adopted by the General Assembly and ratified by the church's presbyteries.

In the course of the present century several new confessional statements have been issued by Christian groups. For example, in 1934 those German churchmen who opposed the attempt of the Nazis to paganize the German Church, issued the Barmen Declaration, in which they vigorously asserted the inalienable sovereignty of God in Jesus Christ as over against all forms of paganism and totalitarianism.

BIBLIOGRAPHY

Briggs, Charles A., *Theological Symbolics.* 1914.

Fuhrman, Paul T., *An Introduction to the Great Creeds of the Church.* 1960.

Gerrish, Brian A., *The Faith of Christendom.* 1963.

Kelly, John N. D., *Early Christian Creeds.* 1950.

————————, *The Athanasian Creed.* 1965.

Leith, John H., *Creeds of the Churches.* 1963.

Routley, Erik, *Creeds and Confessions.* 1962.

Schaff, Philip, *Creeds of Christendom,* 3 vols. 1877.

The Ecumenical Movement

The Ecumenical Movement, may be defined in the words of George H. Tavard, as "that movement of thought and action which is concerned with the reunion of Christians" (*Two Centuries of Ecumenism,* pp. xi-xii).

As such this movement has two main aspects, that of mission and that of reunification. The aspect of mission means that the Christian religion has now been spread, at least in embryo, virtually throughout the entire inhabited globe. This vast movement of Christian expansion has been, in large measure, a recent development. It has taken place mainly during the past two centuries or so. Till the middle of the eighteenth century the Christian faith had established itself permanently, strongly, and securely, only in Europe and the Americas; its hold on Asia, its birthplace, and Africa, where in early centuries it had flourished, was tenuous and slight. But in the eighteenth century the Protestant Christian churches of Europe and North America began a great missionary crusade to preach the gospel to every creature. The usual date given for the opening of this movement is 1792, when at the urging of William Carey, a group of Englishmen formed the Baptist Missionary Society, Carey himself going to India as its first foreign missionary. Within a generation practically all the old line churches, as well as other Christian groups, had committed themselves to the missionary enterprise, and thereupon proceeded to take the Christian gospel throughout practically the whole world. It is mainly because of this great missionary outpouring that Kenneth S. Latourette, the church historian, has called the period between 1815 and 1914 "the great century."

The other, and correlative, aspect of the ecumenical movement, is that which is specifically concerned with reunion among the separated branches of the Christian church now existing in every representative section of the world. This drive towards union is mainly a creation of the twentieth century. Among its causes are the following:

(1) The waste of scarce men of training and experience, and scarce money involved in the overlapping, and reduplication of effort, on the part of many Christian churches.

(2) The realization that the matters on which Protestant Christians are at one, are deeper and more significant than the points on which they differ. Their differences have to do with questions of church worship, organization, administration, and doctrine. But they all agree in their experience and commitment that they are infinitely indebted to Jesus Christ, and have a solemn obligation to serve and obey him as Lord and Master.

(3) Pressure from the foreign mission field has been a highly significant factor in the drive towards Christian unity. In the so-called "Younger Churches" brought into being through the missionary movement, the church differences which developed in the West are less meaningful and tend to hinder the advance of the Christian cause.

(4) A strong factor in this urge towards unity is the increasing realization that unity was desired by Jesus Christ. On the eve of his passion he prayed for his disciples "That they may all be one" (John 17:21). Doubtless this means primarily a unity of spirit and purpose; but it may rightly include unity at every level of action and manifestation, according to the New Testament pattern.

1. FORMS OF UNITY

This drive towards Christian unity has taken several forms. First, there have been organic, incorporating mergers of denominations previously separated. During the present century churches of the same confessional family have reunited; for example, the majority of Scottish Presbyterians in 1929, the Methodists of England in 1932, and the American Methodists in 1939. Impressive as this is, however, Dr. John A. Mackay says that "denominational family relations have still a long way to go before they achieve the oneness that is called for by their common heritage of faith, and by the current needs of the society which they should serve in unison" (*Ecumenics: The Science of the Church Universal*, p. 201). Again, mergers have taken place among denominations of different ecclesiastical parentage and ethos. In Canada in 1925, all the Methodists and Congregationalists, along with over two-thirds of the Presbyterians, joined to form the United Church of Canada. In the U.S.A., in 1957, the Congregational – Christian Churches merged with the Evangelical and Reformed Church to form the United Church of Christ. In India in 1947, the Church of South India was formed, a merger of former Presbyterian, Reformed, and Congregational churches with the Methodists and Anglicans, the latter constituting the most numerous element. The prime significance of this

Indian merger lay in the fact that for the first time churches of the Anglican communion merged with non-Anglican churches on equal terms.

Another expression of the ecumenical movement has been the federations of churches which have been organized in the course of the present century. These federations embrace councils of churches at every level – city, county, state and nation – as exemplified in such bodies as the British Council of Churches formed in 1942, and the National Council of Churches of Christ in America, constituted in 1950 as a merger of previous federative bodies such as the Federal Council of Churches. In such federations, the various cooperating church groups, while retaining their separate identity as churches, pool their resources in order to pursue tasks which they judge can better be done together than separately, such as religious radio programs, and evangelistic missions.

On a larger scale than these church federations within particular nation-states, has been the development of the federation movement at the world level, culminating in the formation of the World Council of Churches in 1948. This movement began with the World Missionary Conference held in 1910 at Edinburgh, Scotland. That Conference of Missionary Societies appointed a Continuation Committee, under the leadership of Dr. John R. Mott, who by 1921 organized the International Missionary Council as an overall international organization seeking to coordinate, supervise, and interpret the worldwide mission of the Christian churches. It consisted predominantly of missionary councils, such as the Foreign Missions Conference of North America, and the National Christian Council of India. This International Missionary Council held significant conferences at Jerusalem (1928), Madras (1938), Whitby, Canada (1947), Willingen (1952), and Accra, Ghana Africa (1957). At Accra it agreed to merge with the World Council of Churches, with which it had been "in association" since that council's formation in 1948. This was effected at New Delhi in 1961, and today the former International Missionary Council is the Division of World Mission and Evangelism of the World Council of Churches.

2. THE FAITH AND ORDER MOVEMENT

The Edinburgh Conference of 1910 had another important consequence in the ecumenical field. It had avoided the discussion of doctrinal issues on which the participating church groups differed. But one of the delegates, Dr. Charles H. Brent, Missionary Bishop of the Philippines of the Protestant Episcopal Church, believed that discussion of such doctrinal differences might well point the way to a larger unity among Christian churchmen. Through his initiative, and that of other Episcopalians, the General Convention of the Protestant Episcopal Church in 1910 passed the following resolution, "That a Joint Commission be appointed to bring about a Conference for the consideration of questions touching Faith and Order, and that all Christian Communions through the word which confess our Lord Jesus Christ as God and Saviour, be asked to unite with us in arranging for and conducting such a Conference."

The outbreak of World War I postponed the holding of such a conference; but in 1927, under Brent's chairmanship, the first Conference on Faith and Order assembled at Lausanne, Switzerland. It initiated discussion of certain disputed questions of church doctrine and practice; and it adopted a statement of the church's message, part of which ran as follows: "The message of the Church to the world is and must always remain the Gospel of Jesus Christ. The Gospel is the joyful message of redemption, both here and hereafter, the gift of God to sinful man in Jesus Christ. . . . Sympathizing with the anguish of our generation, with its longing for intellectual sincerity, social justice, and spiritual inspiration, the Church in the eternal Gospel meets the needs and fulfills the God-given aspirations of the modern world. Consequently, as in the past, so also in the present, the Gospel is the only way to salvation. Thus, through His Church, the loving Christ still says to man, 'Come unto me! . . . He that believeth in me shall not walk in darkness, but shall have the light of life'" (William Adams Brown, *Toward a United Church*, pp. 211-212).

The Lausanne Conference appointed a Continuation Committee of 100 members to convey its reports to their various churches and to take whatever action they might deem appropriate. During the next decade the questions of faith and order which had been opened up at Lausanne continued to be discussed by the Theological Committee; and in 1932 a composite volume on "The Doctrine of Grace" was published as a report of this committee's findings.

In 1937 a second Conference on Faith and Order was held at Edinburgh, Scotland, presided over by Archbishop William Temple of York, who had succeeded to the chairmanship on Bishop Brent's death in 1929. This Edinburgh Conference adopted an Affirmation of Unity which said that "We are one in faith in our Lord Jesus Christ . . . we are one in allegiance to him as Head of the Church, and as King of kings, and Lord of lords. We are one in acknowledging that this allegiance takes precedence to any other allegiance that may make claims upon us.

"This unity does not consist in the agreement of our minds or the consent of our wills. It is found in Jesus Christ himself, who lived, died and rose again to bring us to the Father, and who through the Holy Spirit dwells in His Church. We are one because we are all the objects of the love and grace of God, and called by Him to witness in all the world to His glorious Gospel. . . .

"We desire also to declare to all men everywhere our assurance that Christ is the one hope of unity for the world in face of the distractions and dissensions of this present time. We know that our witness is weakened by our divisions. Yet we are one in Christ, and in the fellowship of His spirit. We pray that everywhere, in a world divided and perplexed, man may turn to Jesus Christ our Lord, Who makes us one in spite of our divisions; that He may bind in one those who by many worldly claims are set at variance, and that the world may at last find peace and unity in Him; to whom be glory forever" (William Adams Brown, *Toward a United Church*, pp. 229-221). This Edinburgh Conference achieved a virtual consensus on the "Grace of the Lord Jesus Christ." Its report stated expressly that "There is in connection with this subject no ground for maintaining division among Churches." But on the crucial questions of the ministry and sacraments no such agreement was reached; as Dr. Norman Goodall says, "This remains the central area of unresolved differences" (*The Ecumenical Movement*, p. 55).

3. THE LIFE AND WORK MOVEMENT

Alongside the Faith and Order Movement there developed a parallel organization known as that of Life and Work. Its chief begetter was the Lutheran, Nathan Söderblom, Archbishop of Upsala and Primate of the Swedish Church; and its basic idea was that Christians might achieve greater unity by working together in social projects of common concern, on the principle that "doctrine divides, but service unites." Söderblom was acutely distressed by the outbreak in 1914 of World War I. Though he was unsuccessful in his appeals for peace while the war lasted, after its conclusion in 1918 he set himself, along with other likeminded Christian leaders as William Temple, and Willoughby (later Lord) Dickinson, of England, to establish an organization on which Christian social concern would find expression on an international scale.

Preparatory meetings were held at Oud Wassenaar, in The Hague in 1919; Geneva, Switzerland in 1920; Peterborough, England in 1921; and Halsingborg, Sweden in 1922; and in 1925 the Universal Christian Conference on Life and Work met in Stockholm, Sweden under Archbishop Söderblom's chairmanship. The declared purpose of this gathering was "to concentrate the mind of Christ as received in the Gospels towards those great social, industrial and international questions which are so acutely urgent in our civilization." More than 600 delegates from thirty-seven countries attended this conference, among them representatives of Eastern Orthodox Christianity led by the patriarchs of Alexandria and Jerusalem. Though this Stockholm conference adopted no official finding it issued an important "Message" to the churches saying in part: "The Conference has deepened and purified our devotion to the Captain of our Salvation. Responding to his call, 'Follow Me,' we have in the presence of the Cross accepted the urgent duty of applying His Gospel in all realms of human life — industrial, social, political and international.

"We have not attempted to offer precise solutions, nor have we confirmed by a vote the results of our friendly discussions. This was due not only to our respect for the convictions of individuals or groups, but still more to the feeling that the mission of the Church is above all to state principles, and to assert the ideal, while leaving to individual consciences and to communities the duty of applying them with charity, wisdom and courage" (William Adams Brown, *Toward a United Church*, pp. 208, 209).

Besides issuing this message the Stockholm conference appointed a Continuation Committee to give continuity to its work; and in 1930 this committee was reconstituted on a permanent basis as the Universal Christian Council for Life and Work. Its declared objective was "to perpetuate and strengthen the fellowship between the churches in the application of Christian ethics to the social problems of modern life" (S. Neill and R. Rouse, *History of the Ecumenical Movement*, p. 553).

In July, 1937 another international conference was convened by the Universal Christian Council. It met at Oxford, England, and took as its general theme, "Church, Community, and State." The 425 members of this conference (of whom 300 were official delegates) represented 120 churches in forty countries. Absent, however, were representatives from the German Evangelical Church, who were refused permission to attend by the Nazi government then in power in Germany. This Oxford conference addressed itself to a whole range of social problems, particularly those posed by the ominous rise of totalitarianism, which by the 1930's was menacing the Christian church and Christian principles over much of the world. The conference in its reports stressed the theme, "Let the Church be the Church"; and it expressed one important way in which this should be implemented by saying that "If the Christian witness is to be borne in social and political life it must be through the action of the multitude of Christian men and women who are actively engaged from day to day in the conduct of administration and industry, and the affairs of the public and common life" (J. H. Oldham, *The Churches Survey Their Task*, p. 44).

4. THE WORLD COUNCIL OF CHURCHES

By 1937 it was becoming clear that the two movements, Faith and Order, and Life and Work, belonged together and should be merged. It was increasingly realized that these two forms of Christian activity were inseparably intertwined, Faith and Order as theological rootage, and Life and Work as practical, ethical fruitage. As early as 1933 some leaders of both movements canvassed the possibility of uniting the two. In line with this, the conferences sponsored by the two movements were both arranged for 1937 in Great Britain, and within a few weeks of each other. Each of these two conferences was asked to vote on a merger of its movement with the other in the World Council of Churches, and both voted affirmatively. A Continuation Committee was appointed, representing both movements, with William Temple, Archbishop of York, as chairman; and in May, 1938 this committee drew up a draft constitution for the projected World Council, and nominated a Provisional Committee to implement the contemplated merger. It had been hoped that the World Council might be formally constituted in 1939, but the outbreak of World War II compelled a postponement. Even during the war, however, the World Council (in process of formation) under the leadership of W. A. Visser t' Hooft, who was later to become its General Secretary, was able to render effective service in such matters as ministering to prisoners of war, and providing money and equipment for impoverished ministers and churches.

The Second World War came to a close in 1945, and in February, 1946 the Provisional Committee met and fixed the date for the First Assembly of the World Council for August-September, 1948, at Amsterdam in the Netherlands. This Amsterdam assembly formally constituted the World Council of Churches, adopting in the main the draft constitution which had been drawn up in Utrecht in 1938. It set up as an organization for the ongoing work of the Council a Presidium of six members, a Central Committee of one hundred meeting annually, and a permanent secretariat. The Amsterdam Assembly also discussed as its basic theme, "Man's Disorder and God's Design" with frankness and penetration; and it issued a message to the churches in which it said that "We bless God our Father, and our Lord Jesus Christ, who gathers together in one the children of God that are scattered abroad. He has brought us here together at Amsterdam. We are one in acknowledging Him as our God and Saviour. We are divided from one another not only in matters of faith, order and tradition, but also by pride of nation, class and race. But Christ has made us His own, and He is not divided. In seeking Him we find one another. Here at Amsterdam we have committed ourselves afresh to Him, and have covenanted with one another in constituting this World Council of Churches. We intend to stay together. We call upon Christian congregations everywhere to endorse and fulfill this covenant in their relations one with another. In thankfulness to God we commit the future to Him" (*The Official Report*, p. 9).

The Assembly is the principal organ of authority of the World Council of Churches, and meets about once every five years. In 1954 it held its second gathering at Evanston, Illinois, with its basic theme, "Jesus Christ the Hope of the World." In 1961 its third meeting was held at New Delhi, India. Here three significant developments took place. The Council restated its doctrinal basis. In place of "The World Council of Churches is a fellowship of Churches which accept our Lord Jesus Christ as God and Saviour," the new basis reads thus: "The World Council of Churches is a fellowship of churches which confess the Lord Jesus Christ as God and Saviour according to the Scriptures and therefore seek to fulfill together their common calling to the glory of one God, Father, Son, and Holy Spirit." Also at New Delhi the International Missionary Council was formally merged with the World Council to become its Division of World Mission and Evangelism. And the Russian Orthodox Church and two Chilean Pentecostal Churches were received into full membership in the World Council.

The World Council is not without its imperfections and limitations. For one thing, it is not as inclusive in its membership as ideally it should be. Two of the largest American Protestant churches, the Southern Baptists and the Missouri Synod Lutherans, do not belong to it. Nor has it captured the imagination and devotion of the rank and file membership of its member churches, having been mainly a matter of high level sponsorship. Nevertheless since the more than 200 churches included in it have a nominal membership of about 300,000,000, or more than a third of the nominal Christians in the world, and since these churches cover a spectrum from Pentecostalism and Quakerism to Eastern Orthodoxy, the Council has become in the words of Dr. John A. Mackay, "The leading contemporary symbol of Christian unity" (*Ecumenics*, p. 209).

5. OTHER ECUMENICAL MOVEMENTS

There are some Protestant Christians and Christian groups which do not participate in this ecumenical movement. Such denominations as the Southern Baptists and Missouri Synod Lutherans have not sought membership in either the National Council of Churches or the World Council of Churches. In addition, some conservative Protestant Christians who were not satisfied with the Federal Council of Churches (which in 1950 merged with other organizations to form the National Council of Churches) organized in 1942 the National Association of Evangelicals. By 1964 this organization claimed a membership of 2,000,000 including thirty-four denominations which, together with individual churches, totaled 28,000 congregations. At the international level, the National Association of Evangelicals participates in a loosely knit consultative body called the World Evangelical Fellowship, which came into being in 1951, with headquarters in London. Another organization, the American Council of Christian Churches was organized in 1941 by the Reverend Carl McIntire, who in 1948 also took the lead in organizing the International Council of Churches.

The Roman Catholic Church is not a member of the World Council of Churches. But relations between Roman Catholicism and other Christian churches have recently become more friendly, especially since the pontificate of Pope John XXIII (1958-1963). Pope John not only received in audience many non-Roman Catholic Christian leaders, but he also accepted the invitation of the World Council to send official observers to its New Delhi Assembly in 1961. He in turn invited Protestants and Eastern Orthodox Christians to send observers to the second Vatican Council which he summoned to meet in 1962. In 1964 the Central Committee of the World Council invited the Roman Catholic Church to appoint delegates "to explore together the possibilities of dialogue and collaboration." Early in 1965 the Roman church responded favorably to this invitation by naming its delegates. Only the future will reveal what will result from this increasing dialogue between Catholicism and Protestantism.

BIBLIOGRAPHY

A. *Official Conference Reports.*

The Stockholm Conference, 1925, edited by G. K. A. Bell, 1926.

Faith and Order: Proceedings of the World Conference at Lausanne, 1927. Edited by H. N. Bate, 1927.

The Churches Survey Their Task: The Report of the Conference at Oxford, 1937. Edited by J. H. Oldham, 1937.

The Second World Conference on Faith and Order, Edinburgh, 1937. Edited by Leonard Hodgson, 1938.

Man's Disorder and God's Design: The Amsterdam Assembly Series, 1948.

The Evanston Report: The Second Assembly of The World Council of Churches, edited by W. A. Visser 't Hooft, 1955.

New Delhi speaks about Witness, Service, and Unity: the Message, Appeal, and Section Reports of the Third Assembly of The World Council of Churches, 1961, edited by W. A Visser 't Hooft, 1962.

B. *History and Interpretation.*

Brown, W. Adams, *Toward a United Church.* 1946.

Duff, Edward, *The Social Thought of the World Council of Churches.* 1956.

Goodall, Norman, *The Ecumenical Movement: What It Is and What It Does.* 1961.

Grant, Frederick C., *Rome and Reunion.* 1965.

Hogg, W. Richey, *Ecumenical Foundations.* 1952.

Mackay, John A., *Ecumenics: The Science of the Church Universal.* 1964.

Rouse, Ruth and Neill, Stephen C., eds., *A History of the Ecumenical Movement 1517-1948.* 1954.

Slosser, Gaius J., *Christian Unity: Its History and Challenge.* 1929.

Tavard, George H., *Two Centuries of Ecumenism: The Search for Unity.* 1960

SECTION 7

PASTORAL

"Should not the shepherds feed the sheep?"
– Ezekiel 34:2

TITLE	AUTHOR
1. The Pastor's Calling	Herschel H. Hobbs
2. The Pastor as Comforter	Wesley W. Nelson
3. The Pastor as Healer	Wayne E. Oates
4. The Pastor as Worshiper	Elvis E. Cochrane
5. The Pastor as Writer	Sherwood E. Wirt
6. The Pastor as Reconciler	James McGraw
7. The Pastor as Administrator	Dick H. Hall, Jr.
8. The Pastor as Overseer	H. Franklin Paschall
9. The Pastor as Teacher	Norris W. Stoa
10. The Pastor as Friend	August W. Hintz

The Pastor's Calling

In Ephesians 4:8-11 Paul adapts Psalm 68:18 to depict the risen Christ's triumphant return to heaven. Through the rejoicing hosts he rides, with conquered death in chains following behind his chariot. In such entries among the ancients, the conquering hero scattered gifts among the celebrating throngs. But Paul says that Christ "gave gifts," not to the heavenly hosts, but to "men" or to those remaining on the earth. And he names these gifts as apostles, prophets evangelists, and pastors and teachers. These were not spiritual gifts bestowed upon various people (I Cor. 12:28), but persons occupying these offices who were to minister to the saints in their growth and service (Eph. 4:12-16). The word "give," *edōke*, implies that Christ had called these persons to serve in these various functions.

To what do they refer? "Apostles" were spiritual pioneers who planted the gospel in new areas. "Prophets" were those with the ability to preach the gospel with unusual power. In modern parlance they might correspond to evangelists. Both apostles and prophets were itinerants with no one established place of service. "Evangelists," perhaps were assigned to given areas, but not to individual churches. They were more like district missionaries working with groups of churches. "Pastors and teachers" refer to one office, and one which was related to one local church. A teacher might not necessarily be a pastor. But all pastors must be "apt to teach" (I Tim. 3:2).

All of these offices were "for the perfecting [mending] of the saints, and for the edifying [building up] of the body of Christ" (Eph. 4:12). Note the progression of thought: full equipment for the saints, that they may render their appointed services, that the body of Christ may be edified. And while each of these "gifts" of Christ had a function in this work, by the nature of its close relation to the local church and offices of pastors and teachers was the most vital in the achieving of this purpose.

1. THE DIVINE CALLING

It has been noted that these persons were *called* to fill specific offices of service. The Christian life itself is the result of one's response to a call from God. He calls men out of darkness into light, out of spiritual death into life (cf. Matt. 11:28-29; John 6:44). The initiative in a saving relation is with God, but the response to the call in the will of man is also involved.

Likewise, God extends a call for service to all Christians. The Great Commission itself was given to others along with "the eleven disciples" (Matt. 28:16-20). It is quite evident that Christians generally understood that they were to be witnesses to the gospel (Acts 6:8ff.; 8:4ff.; 18:26). One of Satan's greatest triumphs over the people of Christ was when he led them to divide themselves into the "clergy" and the "laity." The result was the loss of a sense of responsibility on the part of the latter, as the former was regarded as divinely appointed dispensers of grace. During recent years there has been a wholesome effort to return to the New Testament concept that witnessing is "every Christian's job."

However, in this as in so many other things, one extreme has been replaced by another. Hence, today the attitude is widespread that God calls all Christians on the same basis. This serves to diminish the idea of a divine call being given to certain Christians for specific spiritual services, as over against other honored and useful vocations. For instance, the call of men to be physicians, lawyers, merchants, teachers, farmers, or any other vocation is equated with that of the pastor. Certainly men and women should serve God in whatever may be their vocations. But this is not to say that God, in a special way, does not call certain men to leave the normal pursuits of life to be set apart for some definite place of spiritual leadership.

The word "gave" in Ephesians 4:11 speaks to the contrary. Acts 20:28 clearly indicates that Paul regarded the office of pastor as a definite appointment of the Holy Spirit. In his own case the apostle was quite certain of a divine call in that Christ had placed him in the ministry (I Tim. 1:12). Furthermore, he implied separation from material pursuits for spiritual service as he declared the Biblical principle "even so hath the Lord ordained that they which preach the gospel should live of the gospel" (I Cor. 9:14; cf. Num. 18:8-20; I Cor. 9:1-19). This provision made by the Lord is his recognition that he does call some men in a peculiar way and for a peculiar service.

Biblical history lends abundant support to this truth. In the Old Testament there are the calls of Moses (Exod. 3:10), Samuel (I Sam. 3), Isaiah (6:9), and Jeremiah (1:5). In the New Testament also there is clear evidence of a divine call. Saul of Tarsus received his call shortly after a dramatic conversion experience. Saul became "a chosen vessel unto me, to bear my name before the Gentiles, and kings, and the children of Israel" (Acts 9:15). The apostles were first called into the Christian life (John 1:39-51). At a later time they were called to leave their material pursuits to follow Jesus in a peculiar mission (Matt. 4:18-22; 9:9; Mark 3:13-19). To the eleven Jesus said, "Ye have not chosen me, but I have chosen you and ordained [appointed] you, that ye should go and bring forth fruit" (John 15:16). In John 15:16 and Acts 9:15 the words for "chosen" carry the meaning of a selection from among others, and in this sense from among other Christians.

Therefore, the Scriptures teach the fact of a divine call given by God to specific persons for specific purposes. This does not diminish the sanctity of any vocation dedicated to God's will. But it does enhance the calling of those who are chosen of God for services of a peculiarly spiritual nature.

2. THE PASTORAL OFFICE

The word "pastor" translates the Greek word *poimēn,* which comes from a root word meaning to protect. Basically it means "shepherd." This word is used eighteen times in the New Testament. Eight times it refers to a "shepherd" of sheep (Matt. 9:36; 25:32; Mark 6:34; Luke 2:8, 15, 18, 20; John 10:2). Seven times it is used symbolically of Jesus (Matt. 26:31; Mark 14:27; John 10:11-12, 14, 16). One time it refers to "our Lord Jesus, that great shepherd of the sheep" (Heb. 13:20). Once it speaks of Christ as "the Shepherd and Bishop of your souls" (I Peter 2:25). The only time where *poimēn* is translated "pastor," and the only time that "pastor" appears in the New Testament, is in Ephesians 4:11. Pastor comes from *pastores,* the Latin equivalent of the Greek *poimen.* So the other New Testament uses of this Greek word shed light upon its usage in Ephesians 4:11.

It should be noted, however, that the verb form, *poimainō* is used eleven times in the New Testament. Four times it is rendered "rule" (Luke 2:6; Rev. 2:27; 12:5; 19:15). One time it is translated "feeding cattle" (Luke 17:7), where it might just as well read "feeding sheep" (cf. I Cor. 9:7). In Revelation 7:17 it speaks of the Lamb feeding his sheep. Elsewhere, except Jude 12, it refers to a spiritual shepherd feeding the flock of Christ (John 21:16; Acts 20:28; I Peter 5:2).

One of the most interesting verses dealing with the office of "pastor" or "shepherd" is Acts 20:28. It records an exhortation of Paul to the elders of the Ephesian church (20:17). "Take heed therefore unto yourselves [elders], and to all the flock, over the which the Holy Ghost hath made you overseers (*episkopous,* bishops), to feed [*poimainein,* to feed or tend as a shepherd or pastor] the church of God, which he hath purchased with his own blood" (cf. I Peter 2:25; 5:1-4). In this one verse the ideas of elders, *presbuteros,* bishop or overseer, *episkopos,* and pastor, *poimainein,* are used to refer to one office. While in the course of Christian history these terms have come to be applied to three different offices, it is clear that in the New Testament they were used to refer to three different functions within one office. The plurality of elders in one church is also reflected in Philippians 1:1, where along with "the saints . . . which are at Philippi" Paul also addresses "the bishops and deacons." Here he links the office of bishop with that of deacon, showing that the church in Philippi had more than one of each. Since the letters to the seven churches of Asia Minor (Rev. 2-3) are addressed to "the angel of the church" in each case, (the "angel" was probably the "pastor"), apparently some of the churches had a pastor (elder, bishop) under whom others served in similar but subordinate positions. This was certainly true of Ephesus, Philippi, and Jerusalem (Acts 11:30; 15:4, 22).

The meanings of the terms elder, bishop, and pastor suggest the threefold nature of the office. Elder was originally applied to older men with particular reference to their wisdom. Later it was conferred upon others, but still with the connotation of wisdom. Bishop basically referred to one who was over a group of workmen to direct them in the proper performance of their duties. Pastor was derived from the idea of a shepherd, and carried the thought of the multiple duties of such. Thus the pastor is seen not only in that office but also as a counselor and an administrator. And since the three terms refer to one office, any one of the three may be used as pertaining to the multiple functions as described. It should be noted, however, that, since in Acts 20:28 the verb "to feed" clearly carries the idea of a shepherd, the pastoral idea is the predominant one. The pastoral office is qualified by those of elder and bishop. In other words the duties of counsel and oversight were but functions within the framework of feeding as shepherds.

A study of the pastoral office would be incomplete without a consideration of other terms which are associated with its work: "teacher" and "minister." The former speaks of a function within the office, and the latter connotes more the nature of the discharge of the office.

"Teacher" renders the Greek word *didaskalos.* It is the equivalent of the Hebrew rabbi. This word was used repeatedly in the gospels with reference to Jesus. Of further interest is the fact that one of the most prevalent names for Jesus' followers is the word "disciple," pupil, or learner. The pastor, then, is to be an instructor. The teacher-pupil relationship is one within the larger relationship of shepherd-sheep.

"Minister" in the New Testament translates three different Greek words: *diakonos,* laborer, servant, or deacon; *leitourgos,* public servant or worker; and *hupēretēs,* under-rower or assistant. Each of these expresses a certain nature of the function of the office as minister or pastor.

Diakonos is uncertain as to its derivation. A. T. Robertson sees it as composed of *dia,* through, and *konis,* dust, as one who raises dust in his haste to serve. Thayer rejects this, leaning more to the origin as being from the obsolete *diakō*, allied with *diokō*, suggesting swiftness and diligence in the pursuit of a task or goal. Thus a *diakonos* is one who executes the commands of another, such as one's master. He concludes that it "represents the servant in his activity for the work" (*in loco*). But in the end the final meaning is virtually the same. Jesus used it in the sense of one who serves for the very joy of serving, with no thought as to honor or reward (Matt. 20:26). In the same context he used the verb form *diakoneō* with reference to his own ministry (Matt. 20:28; cf. Rom. 15:8). Paul employed the word *diakonos* to refer to himself and others with reference to their ministry for Christ to men (I Cor. 3:5; II Cor. 3:6; Eph. 3:7; 6:21; Col. 1:7, 23, 25; I Tim. 4:6).

Leitourgos was used of public servants and of religious ministers who presided at the altar. In the New Testament it is used of public officials as God's servants (Rom. 13:6; cf. also *diakonos*, 13:4). It is used also of Christ in his priestly ministry in the heavenly sanctuary (Heb. 8:26; cf. 1:7). Paul used it one time to refer to himself as a "minister of Jesus Christ" (Rom. 15:16). In this sense it carries the dual idea of leading in public worship and of a public proclamation of the gospel.

Hupēretēs basically means an under-rower on a ship. It came to be applied to officers or servants who served under another (cf. Matt. 5:25; 26:58). In the Christian sense Paul used it to refer to himself and Apollos as "ministers [under-rowers] of Christ" (I Cor. 4:1). So the thought in this word is that of subordination. They were "under-rowers" under Christ as the pastor or under-shepherd is under "our Lord Jesus, that great shepherd of the sheep" (Heb. 13:20). Furthermore, Paul allied *hupēretēs* with "stewards," *oikonomous*, or house managers of the mysteries of God. These mysteries were God's secrets pertaining to his kingdom and revealed in his redemptive work through Christ. The minister has the responsibility of teaching these not as a profession but as a stewardship. Note that both *hupēretēs* and *oikonomos* carry the idea of slavery (cf. *doulos*, bond slave, Paul's favorite reference to himself as a servant of Christ, Rom. 1:1).

Therefore, the pastor is not only to be a teacher charged with teaching the mysteries of God. As a minister he is to serve for the joy of serving, with no thought of public honor or reward. These things he is to leave with the Lord (I Cor. 4:2-5). He is to render both private and public service. And in it all he is to remember that he serves not for himself but for Christ.

3. THE PASTORAL MINISTRY

Paul's message to the Ephesian elders is a masterpiece in describing the pastoral ministry (Acts 20:18 ff.). He had spent three years in Ephesus. The itinerant apostle had during that time settled down to the life of a pastor. While he doubtless had directed the spread of the gospel throughout the province of Asia, he had been a shepherd to the flock in Ephesus. In lowliness of mind, many tears, and trials he had given himself fully to this ministry. Both publicly and in house to house ministration (20:19-21) he had served (*douleuōn*, serving as a slave, v. 19) the Lord. He had set an example for these Ephesian elders to follow (20:35). It was in the midst of this message that Paul exhorted them as to their task.

"Take heed therefore unto yourselves, and to all the flock, over the which the Holy Ghost hath made you overseers, to feed [or tend as a shepherd] the church of God, which he hath purchased with his own blood" (20:28). The price which God in Christ had paid for this flock added all the more to the responsibility of the shepherds.

They were to pay careful attention to both themselves and to the flock. This is suggestive of the intimate, personal relationship which must exist between pastor and people. One can hardly understand this unless he recalls the relationship between a shepherd and his sheep. Jesus himself drew upon this fact to relate his own relationship to his sheep. (John 10:3-5). A shepherd gave individual names to his sheep. He did not simply know them collectively but individually. "He calleth his own sheep by name, and leadeth them out" (vs. 3). He might not know by name the sheep of another flock, but he knew his own. Furthermore, his sheep knew his voice, and would not follow another shepherd. At night many flocks shared the same fold.

In the morning a given shepherd would give a certain call. His sheep, recognizing his voice, followed him as he led them forth to water and pasture. Note that he went before them (v. 4). He did not drive them. He led them. And because they knew his voice and he called them by name, they followed him.

What a blessed experience it is when this relationship exists between a pastor and his flock. But it does not happen by accident. It is the result of the pastor living with his sheep, knowing their needs, and sharing their problems. A pastor may preach at his people on Sunday without living with them during the week. But he can preach to them only after he has shared himself with them. To be sure the shepherd must be fed if he is to feed the sheep. He must "study" if he is to cut straight the word of truth (II Tim. 2:15). It is a difficult thing to strike the delicate balance between study time and ministration time. But that balance must be obtained if the shepherd properly is to fulfill his ministry. Many times the sheep do not follow the shepherd in some worthy program because they do not know him. For "a stranger will they not follow, but will flee from him: for they know not the voice of strangers" (John 10:5).

As shepherds the Ephesian elders were to feed or tend the flocks. Either word makes a good translation. Feeding the flock involves the teaching and preaching ministry of the pastor. And tending encompasses a multitude of pastoral duties wherein the pastor identifies himself with the manifold needs of his people. The pastor heart cannot be indifferent to any of these. This emphasizes the importance of the pastor living with his people. He must be among them as one who serves. And no service is so menial but that he should render it with dignity and compassion.

The pastor must rebuke and console. And both must be done with tears. He must "lift up the hands which hang down, and the feeble knees; and make straight [even] paths" for the feet of the flock (Heb. 12: 12-13). He must reclaim the wandering sheep. He must rejoice with those who rejoice, and weep with those who weep. He must become all things to all men as he seeks to lead them to the Saviour, and to enable them to walk in his will and way. Like the great Shepherd of the sheep he should become one with his people, apart from their sins, that under his leadership they all may "come in [into] the unity of the faith, and of the knowledge [full knowledge] of the Son of God, unto a perfect [mature] man, unto the measure of the stature of the fulness of Christ" (Eph. 4:13).

Furthermore, Paul evoked another function of the shepherd, that of protecting the flock. "Grievous wolves" shall enter, not sparing the flock (Acts 20:29). Evidently he had in mind outside worldly forces such as bodily persecution and moral, mental, and spiritual intimidation designed to kill or to scatter the flock. Paul knew only too well the power of the Diana (Artemis) cult and their opposition to the Christian gospel (Acts 19:23 ff.) Revelation 2:1-7 does not mention the Roman persecution connected with emperor worship as falling upon the Ephesian church. But it most likely experienced much opposition from the pagan life of the city itself.

"Also of your own selves shall men arise, speaking perverse [twisted, distorted] things, to draw away disciples after them" (20:30). Heresy from within the church itself would be a major threat. This could refer to the Judaizers and Gnostics. Some see these as the "wolves" of verse 29. It could be either or both. Certainly under the guise of superior Christian knowledge the Gnostics made great inroads in some of the churches of Asia Minor (cf. Col., I John, Rev. 2:12–3:6). In their emphasis upon the separation of the spirit from the flesh, they led many Christians into sinful living. Paul warned Timothy of some in Ephesus who had made shipwreck of their faith (I Tim. 1:20). Revelation 2:2 speaks of false apostles in Ephesus. And John writes of antichrists who went out from Ephesus but who were not truly a part of their fellowship (I John 2:18-19; cf. II John 7).

Against all of these destructive forces the Ephesian elders were to be on the alert (Acts 20:31). Paul had guarded this church for three years. Now it was their responsibility. Apparently they did a good job. For Revelation 2:2-3, 6 speaks of this church's stand in the faith and against the encroachments of evil. They did lose, however, the first love of the glow of their evangelistic zeal, which they were commanded to regain lest they lose their reason for being (2:4-5).

The pastor is to guard his flock. It may be against the blatant forces of evil which openly challenge the church and its ministry. Or it may be against those wolves in sheep's clothing (cf. Matt. 7:15) which attempt to lead the sheep away under the guise of a supposedly more advanced Christian theology. The pastor can contend for the faith without being contentious (Jude 3). He can speak the truth in love, but he must speak the truth as God gives to him to see it (Eph. 4:15). And it is this constant feeding and tending of the flock which will enable it to stand against the contrary winds of doctrine (Eph. 4:14).

Indeed, Jesus said that the test of a good shepherd is the extent to which he will go to protect his flock (John 10:10-15). A "hireling" or a time-server regards the sheep only as a source of selfish gratification or profit. When the wolves approach he looks out for himself, leaving the flock to be ravaged and scattered. But the true shepherd will give his life to protect them. Jesus said, "I am the good [beautiful, in character and service] shepherd: the good shepherd giveth his life for [*huper*, as a substitute for] the sheep" (John 10:11).

If the pastor is to be a true undershepherd he must be willing to do the same. It may mean actual death itself. Or in this day it more likely means that he must lose his life in complete dedication to his calling. This is the point in Paul's word to the Ephesian elders recorded in Acts 20:34. "It is more blessed to give than to receive." This "last beatitude" of Jesus is often quoted in support of the faithful stewardship of one's possessions. The principle certainly applies at that point. But its immediate context relates it to the stewardship of a pastor with regard to his calling.

A study of the pastoral ministry would not be complete without a reference to Psalm 23. "The Lord is my shepherd." David had been a shepherd. He knew the pastoral duties of such. In this psalm he transferred these ministries to the care for him on the part of the Great Shepherd. The pastor will do well, in turn, to parallel his ministry as an undershepherd according to Jehovah's shepherd care for his own. A reading of this beautiful passage in this light will enhance immeasurably the ministerial responsibility of the pastor. When it is interpreted in the light of the life of Jesus — his compassion, love, faithfulness, and sacrifice — it calls for a reconsecration of every pastor to the opportunity which God in Christ has given to him. He is reminded afresh that the Holy Spirit has made him an overseer "to all the flock."

4. THE PASTORAL EXHORTATION

I Peter 5:1-11 is an exhortation by Peter, a fellow-elder, *sumpresbuteros,* to other elders. He claims to be a witness to the sufferings of Christ, and expects to share in the glory of Christ which shall be revealed. And, like Paul, he may expect to share in Christ's glory to the same degree that he has shared in his sufferings (Rom. 8:17).

On this basis Peter exhorts these elders as to their ministry, motive, and method of service. They are to shepherd the flock of God in the full sense of that word, including the overall oversight of it. Their motive in service is not to be out of compulsion but of willingness, not as an hireling who serves for filthy lucre but as a true shepherd out of an eager spirit. The method is not to be one of lording it over their charge as tyrants; they are to serve as examples leading the flock. (But the flock is to be mindful of those who lead them, Heb. 13:7.) Neither are they to court the temporary glory of men. For "when the chief Shepherd shall appear, ye shall receive a crown of glory that fadeth not away" (v. 4).

In the system of multiple elders, the younger are to be subject to the older. Yet there is to be no superior among them. For each is voluntarily to subject himself to the others. They are to be clothed with humility as though each wore the girdle of a slave (cf. John 13:4-17). As such they are not to seek after self-aggrandizement; but are to serve as under the mighty hand of God, knowing that in his own time and way he will exalt them. They are to cast all of their anxiety or worry of life upon God, knowing that "he careth for you" (v. 7).

In the meantime, they are to be self-possessed under all circumstances, and alert, because their "adversary the devil, as a roaring lion, walketh about, seeking whom he may devour" (v. 8). They are stedfastly to stand against him in the faith. At times it may seem to be a lonely vigil. But while they are resisting Satan in their charge, Peter reminds them that others of their brethren are standing with them in the same afflictions. And God himself stands with them all.

Then the fellow-elder pronounces a benediction beyond measure upon every pastor (elder, bishop). "But the God of all grace, who hath called us unto his eternal glory by [in] Christ Jesus, after that ye have suffered a while, make you perfect, stablish, strengthen, settle you. To him be glory and dominion for ever and ever. Amen." (v. 10-11).

BIBLIOGRAPHY

Blackwood, Andrew W., *Pastoral Leadership.* Nashville: Abingdon Press, 1949.

Carver, William Owen, *The Glory of God in the Christian Calling.* Nashville: Broadman Press, 1949.

Garvie, Alfred E., *The Christian Preacher.* New York: Scribner's, 1928.

Lindsay, Thomas M., *The Church and the Ministry in the Early Centuries.* New York: Doran, 1910.

Mullins, Edgar Y., *The Christian Religion in Its Doctrinal Expression.* Nashville: Baptist Sunday School Board, 1917.

Stagg, Frank, *New Testament Theology.* Nashville: Broadman Press, 1962.

Summers, Ray, "Ephesians: Pattern for Christian Living," *The International Standard Bible Encyclopaedia*, Vol. III. James Orr, General Editor. Grand Rapids: Wm. B. Eerdmans, 1949.

The Pastor as Comforter

1. DEFINITION

The Christian ministry of comfort is defined both by Scripture and by human need. The New Testament references to comfort are largely derived from the verb *parakaleo* and its noun form *paraklesis* which, in the context of the general meaning of comfort, are usually translated "comfort," "consolation," or "encouragement." God is a God of comfort (Rom. 15:5; II Cor. 1:3). There is comfort in Christ (Phil. 2:1). The Holy Spirit is called "Comforter" (RSV "Counselor") (John 14:16-17, 26; 15:26; 16:7). Comfort is promised to the believer (Matt. 5:4; II Cor. 1:4; II Thess. 2:16-17). There is comfort in the Scriptures (Rom. 15:4), and in the gift of prophecy (I Cor. 14:3). The apostles engaged in a ministry of comfort (I Cor. 1:4; Eph. 6:22; Col. 2:2; I Thess. 2:11). The apostles were also confident that they themselves would be comforted in this ministry of comforting others (II Cor. 1:7; 7:6-7, 13; I Thess. 3:7-8). Believers are exhorted to engage in the ministry of comforting one another (I Thess. 5:14). Jesus identified himself with the ministry which is described in Isaiah 61:1-2, which was in essence a ministry of comfort (Luke 4:18-19).

The needs of people have constantly required that the pastor give a significant share of his attention to this ministry. Men have always been faced with distress, pain, anxiety, tragedy, violence, and death, and the pastor is able to serve effectively as a shepherd of souls only as he follows the example of his Lord and of the apostles in a ministry of comfort and consolation.

The word *parakaleo* literally means "to call near" or, by implication, "to call to one's side." The implication is that a comforter is one who is called to one's side to serve as advocate, counselor, friend, or in some other like capacity. The word does not always imply the popular concept of comfort. In some contexts it conveys the concept of exhortation and is so translated (Acts 13:15; Rom. 12:8; I Thess. 4:1; II Tim. 4:2; Heb. 12:5). In other contexts it is translated "beseech," "appeal," "urge," or "beg" (Rom. 12:1; I Cor. 4:16; Eph. 4:1; Philem. 9). The Christian ministry of comfort should not be limited to those situations in which the popular idea of comfort is implied. Words of Christian comfort may not necessarily be soothing words. Sometimes they may be exhortations, entreaties or appeals where the basic quality is that of the strength given by a stedfast companion who may be called to one's side who will understand, counsel, and share the need. The basic element of comfort is not so much in the actual form of the words used as in the strength conveyed by the stedfast presence of the comforter. Thus God is an adequate comforter because he remains stedfast and his love never fails (Rom. 8:38-39). There are no possible conditions in which God will fail his people.

2. CONTENT

It is this eternal stedfastness of God which stands behind the gospel, without which it would not be the gospel, which provides the Christian pastor with the content of his message of comfort. God loves us even though we are sinners. He will forgive the greatest of sinners and will not abandon us in the time of moral or spiritual failure. He knows our weaknesses and will continue to accept us apart from our ability to achieve. The promise of eternal life is not limited to a select segment with certain qualifications. Whosoever will may come. The person who has tried and failed, who cannot maintain the standards that are expected of him by his fellowmen, will nevertheless be accepted by God if he will but come. The very reason for despair on the part of one who is unacceptable elsewhere constitutes an invitation to come to God, for God will accept him. Therefore the gospel offers hope which cannot be thwarted by evil, failure, or death. It is this quality of the gospel which makes it a message of unfailing comfort.

The offer of limitless comfort is not inconsistent with God's severity and the fact of God's judgment on sin. An unrepentant and a rebellious attitude is often only a symptom of a deepseated fear of not being accepted. Cynicism and unbelief often result from disillusioning experiences with representatives of the Christian faith who have failed to demonstrate the true nature of God's redemption. It is possible for the Christian religion to become increasingly demanding and legalistic with the result that unbelievers become increasingly cynical. When this happens representatives of Christianity often tend to see the world as becoming more and more confirmed in unbelief and fail to see further possibility of God's continued mercy. Meanwhile unbelievers, seeking for some relief from their distress, often turn to other sources for comfort.

Only when God's mercy is proclaimed without reservation can such attitudes of cynicism and unbelief be dissolved in confidence and faith. The doctrine of God's judgment is not endangered at this point for God's judgment is reserved for the impenitent, not for those who seek his mercy. The pastor has the example of our Lord himself who came not to condemn, but to redeem and who gave himself a ransom for those who did not deserve to be redeemed (John 3:17; Matt. 20:28). Even when the pastor finds it necessary to warn of judgment he does so from an attitude of concern and his warning is intended to comfort by leading to repentance and faith.

In recent times the insights of modern psychotherapy have also served to support the need for the proclamation of the gospel without reservation by revealing how complex are the factors involved in guilt, anxiety, and rejection, and by revealing how difficult it is for men to respond to offers of acceptance which are dependent on their own ability to fulfill certain expectations. There are indications that men cannot become true persons as God intended them to be unless they can enter into a relationship in which they are accepted apart from their own qualifications. It is in the offer of such unqualified acceptance that the gospel is a message of comfort and consolation.

3. THE PERSON OF THE COMFORTER

The nature of the pastor's own personality as comforter is also defined by the implications of the word *parakaleo*. As has already been indicated, it is the unwavering stedfastness of God himself, apart from all worthiness and ability to achieve on the part of man, which makes the gospel a message of true comfort. The pastor is "called near" in order to be a comforter, and the effectiveness of his ministry of comfort will consist most fundamentally in his unfailing stedfastness as Gods representative.

The situation may at times call for a confrontation with unpleasant facts or for exhortation or reproof. The pastor needs adequate training and understanding of human nature so that he will choose his words wisely. Sometimes words have different meanings to troubled persons. Whatever may be said of the words used, however, the comfort still depends on the faithfulness of the comforter who has been "called near" and the confidence of the needy person that the comforter will not desert him no matter what he may do. In his faithfulness the comforter represents God's unfailing stedfastness.

The ministry of comfort requires a high degree of personal integrity on the part of the comforter. He must have sufficient confidence in God and in the gospel so that he can accept himself and be aware of his own weaknesses. He must be particularly aware of mixed motives and of any hidden desires to elicit responses which are satisfying to himself. He must be aware of feelings of insecurity and of any tendency to use the troubled person for his own advantage. His status as God's representative may be both an advantage and a disadvantage. It may be an advantage in that people will look upon him as a man of integrity in whom they may confide with confidence. It may be a disadvantage if it tends to inflate his own ego so that he is tempted to play God by giving answers which are based on solutions the pastor has himself worked out. He must bear in mind that such advice really robs the troubled person of the responsibility of facing his own need and making his own choices.

The pastor may actually find it difficult to listen to the troubled person because his distress seems to be a sign that the pastor has failed to deal with these problems adequately in his ministry. In this case the pastor may be tempted to interrupt the person by telling him that he "should not" or "need not" feel as he does. Such interruptions really constitute a refusal to accept the person as he really is by telling him what he should be. The troubled person needs to know that the pastor regards him enough as a person to hear what he has to say, that he understands him, and that he will not condemn him. His fears and needs are often so involved that he cannot even define them himself until he has begun to share them with the pastor. He will generally be afraid to express his real needs until he has been assured that he will be accepted. If he does not receive this assurance he will withdraw and further communication will be difficult or impossible. He may not know why he cannot continue to communicate with the pastor except that he will be conscious of discomfort or embarrassment when he talks with him.

Acceptance of a person as he is must not be confused with permissiveness or approval of his behavior. The pastor, as God's representative, must, whenever necessary, convey God's disapproval of certain attitudes or behavior. Sometimes he must act with firmness in his dealing with the troubled person. He can do this without rejecting him by continuing to minister faithfully to him and by looking upon him as a candidate for God's grace. Any concept of comfort which yields to attitudes that are contrary to the purposes of God is unfaithful to the gospel and cannot lead to lasting consolation. Even by firmness the pastor represents the stedfastness of God and proves his faithfulness. Often he can do this more effectively by his actions and attitudes than by words. Eventually he will then be able to share the resources of the gospel on deeper and more realistic levels.

The pastor will usually find that the most apparent needs for the ministry of comfort will arise from illness, infirmity, accident, financial distress, and other causes of physical discomfort. In such cases the pastor must be aware of professional, physical, and financial resources available through the church and the community (James 2: 15-16). However, he must bear in mind that most cases of physical suffering also have emotional factors such as fear, anxiety, resentment, cynicism and other problems of the soul. In order to be a true comforter, the pastor must be alert to these factors. He will look upon a person as including body, soul and spirit in a complex relationship and he will seek to minister to him as a whole person. Without seeking to pry but always ready to understand, he will place both the resources of the gospel and of his own person as a Christian minister at the disposal of the person in need of the ministry of comfort.

Increased attention to the complexity of the need for Christian comfort has been a factor in the development of programs of special training in pastoral care in connection with hospitals, seminaries, and other institutions. The pastor who so desires may take advantage of some such program in order to develop valuable professional skills.

4. RELATION TO PSYCHOTHERAPY

Some pastors fear that greater emphasis on psychology will lead to confusion by eliminating theology as the basis for the pastoral ministry. That this may be a danger cannot be denied. There are tendencies to interpret Christian truth more from the perspective of modern psychology than Christian theology. However, the possible misuse of available tools does not justify their rejection. The pastor must always remember that the nature of his work as comforter is defined by the basic concepts of the Christian gospel rather than by modern psychology. Once this matter is settled, he should also recognize that all things are his in Christ (I Cor. 3:21-22), including the insights of psychology.

The pastor needs to understand the difference between psychiatry and the pastoral ministry of Christian comfort, and he must avoid the temptation to try to be an amateur psychiatrist. He should not seek for problems where none exist. He should learn to be alert to any needs which are expressed without delving for additional problems. He should also learn to recognize cases of such seriousness that they should be referred to a professional therapist. Even in cases where referrals are made, however, the pastor must not permit himself to fail to be a stedfast comforter. Where there is mutual respect for the persons and skills involved, a pastor and a psychiatrist can work effectively as a team. The pastor provides the Christian comfort and the psychiatrist provides the needed therapy and neither conflicts with the other.

5. BEREAVEMENT

In the case of bereavement, as in other calls for the ministry of comfort, the content of the gospel and the stedfast presence of the pastor as God's representative are the resources of Christian comfort. The Christian faith does not deny that grief is a legitimate part of Christian experience and believers are not admonished to refrain from grieving (Rom. 9:2; II Cor. 6:9-10; Phil. 2:27; Rev. 21:4). They are, however, given guidance in their grief so that they "may not grieve as those do who have no hope" (I Thess. 4:13). Recent studies confirm the legitimacy of grief. They seem to indicate that grief follows a fairly predictable pattern with various symptoms such as weeping and physical discomfort, fear, loneliness, guilt, and sometimes resentment and hostility. There are, of course, individual differences and no one can predict the precise nature of the symptoms in each case. However, the pastor-comforter will not seek to restrain the bereaved from grieving. Rather he will make available the comfort of the gospel and of his person for the guidance of the bereaved as he passes through the normal process of grief. Any reason for the bereaved to feel that the pastor has put his own comfort and convenience above his concern for the bereaved will constitute a failure to represent the unfailing and steadfast God in the hour of one of life's greatest needs.

Usually many words of comfort will not be needed and much time will not necessarily need to be spent with the bereaved. The many necessary details will usually keep the family of the deceased quite busy. In some cases they will need assistance and in other cases they will prefer to handle these details alone. The pastor should be available for assistance but should not press his services on them.

Expressions of grief are often conditioned by prevailing customs and some Christians mistakenly consider it their duty to suppress their normal grief in order better to witness to their faith. In many such cases the pastor can be of assistance, particularly if he has taken the opportunity in advance to discuss the Christian concept of grief in his preaching or teaching ministry.

Since Christian burial is practiced not only by committed Christians but also quite generally by nominal Christians and even by unbelievers, funeral practices are subject to many influences which are not motivated by Christian concerns. Criticisms have been made from time to time that burial customs have become needlessly commercialized and there has been considerable discussion of the need for a reform of Christian funeral practices. If the pastor feels compelled to engage in such reforms he should first make careful investigation. Some practices which may at first seem superficial have become established over long periods of time because they meet profound needs on the part of the bereaved. This is particularly true of customs which help the bereaved accept the fact of death. It is never justifiable for the pastor to make a charge for the burial of the dead. However, there is considerable difference of opinion concerning the accepting of honorariums which are voluntarily given.

6. THE FUNERAL SERVICE

The funeral service itself will serve at least two purposes. It will be a worship service of the church designed to give glory to God and, as a worship service, it will also be intended to be a service of comfort to the bereaved. The Word of God should be read and other normal elements of worship should be included. The service should be briefer than most worship services. Preaching is always appropriate in evangelical worship, but the funeral sermon should not usually be longer than five or ten minutes.

Eulogies of the dead are generally considered out of order in Christian worship, both because they do not bring glory to God, and because they cannot be honestly given the same emphasis in all cases. This does not mean that no mention may be made of the deceased. Whether a formal obituary be read or informal remarks be made, the statement should be objective, simple, and related to information which is generally known to be true. The gospel of grace should not be refuted by leaving the impression that the basis of Christian hope lies in the qualifications of the deceased.

In planning the content of the service consideration should be given to how the bereaved will interpret each detail. Generally speaking, they will not be able to benefit by exhortation, by discourses which require close attention to logical arguments, or even in some cases to affirmations of hope for the future. A state of grief makes it difficult to concentrate on abstract themes and in a time of sorrow it is difficult to think clearly. Affirmations of the presence of God in the present hour of need will be most effective and such affirmations should be the dominant note of the service. It should be remembered that, particularly in the state of grief, hope and comfort do not result from the ability to reason. The Holy Spirit will comfort in ways beyond human comprehension and if the presence of God is affirmed through proper use of Scripture and on the basis of the gospel, the Spirit will perform his work of comfort.

This emphasis on the affirmation of God's presence in the hour of need is particularly helpful where there are grave questions about the spiritual state of the deceased. The pastor will rightfully question whether he does right in speaking of hope of future blessedness for one who is known to have rejected God's grace to the very moment of death. However, though the situation may be clouded by great uncertainties, God himself will be present to minister to the living through Christ and the gospel. This work of God is beyond understanding and even though the case may seem utterly hopeless, the Holy Spirit may usher the entire congregation into the very presence of the God of grace. The pastor's own confident faithfulness as a servant of God and the content of the gospel he proclaims thus become the resources for comfort.

The pastor should continue to counsel with the bereaved after the funeral. In fact, in the quiet days after others have returned to their own interests there may be greater need for the ministry of comfort than before. Then, if the bereaved are not believers, the pastor may be able to lead them to a knowledge of Christ.

7. CONTEMPORARY NEEDS FOR COMFORT

Secular interests appear to occupy the attention of modern men so that they do not apparently give as much attention to the questions of eternity as they did in the past. However, secularity tends toward an impersonal existence which denies men the comfort of personal relationships. Therefore, the personal presence of the pastor as a stedfast and faithful friend in any time of crisis will always be appreciated. Under these circumstances a greater attention to the ministry of comfort may result in a renewed interest in the gospel with its implications both for time and for eternity. By this means the pastor will often be able to bring men to God through Christ.

The pastor's ministry of comfort is closely related to his pulpit ministry. If in his preaching he is strongly opinionated, coercive and authoritarian, he will not invite the confidence of people in times when they need comfort. However, if he faces the issues and problems of life realistically and sympathetically so that his sermons relate the needs of men to the resources of God; if he is sufficiently confident in the gospel and the forgiveness of God to accept and deal with his own failings so he does not present a superficial image in the pulpit; and if, on the authority of the Word of God, he confidently proclaims the stedfastness of God's grace, his congregation will welcome his ministry as a comforter.

BIBLIOGRAPHY

Blackwood, Andrew W., *The Funeral.* Philadelphia: Westminster Press, 1942.

Bowman, Leroy., *The American Funeral.* Washington: Public Affairs Press, 1959.

Dahlstrom, Earl C., *Helping Human Beings.* Washington: Public Affairs Press, 1964.

Irion, Paul E., *The Funeral and the Mourners.* New York: Abingdon Press, 1954.

Kent, Homer A., Sr. *The Pastor and his Work.* Chicago: Moody Press, 1963.

McNeill, John T., *A History of the Cure of Souls.* New York: Harper and Brothers, 1951.

Oates, Wayne E., *The Christian Pastor.* Philadelphia: Westminster Press, 1951, 1964.

Tournier, Paul., *The Meaning of Persons.* New York: Harper and Brothers, 1957.

The Pastor as Healer

The Lord Jesus Christ gave his disciples "authority over unclean spirits, to cast them out, and to heal every disease and every infirmity" (Matt. 10:1). When he sent the seventy out, he briefed them for their mission by saying, "Whenever you enter a town and they receive you, eat what is set before you; heal the sick in it and say to them, 'The kingdom of God has come upon you' " (Luke 10:8-9). When the seventy returned, they joyfully told him: "Lord, even the demons are subject to us in your name!" (Luke 10: 17). He, in turn, cautioned them as to their motives for rejoicing. They were not to rejoice because they could heal in his name, but because their own names were written in heaven.

Both the command and the caution of Jesus to his followers are inseparable in the work of the pastor as a healer today. We still are commanded to heal the sick. Yet those pastors today who have taken this command seriously today are still in need of caution that their enthusiasm does not make their own ability to heal the center, the "be-all" and "end-all" of the kingdom of God. Consequently pastors today are prone to ignore both the command and the caution of Jesus concerning their work as healers. Some shrink from the whole idea and ignore the command of Jesus. Others "go over board" and make "healing" both the center and circumference of the concern as a Christian. One is irresponsible and the other is idolatrous. A clear path is available between these two pitfalls, however.

1. HEALING AND REDEMPTION

We are redeemed from sin and to life in God when we respond to the act of God in Jesus Christ through faith and renounce all lesser loyalties which would otherwise take first place in our lives. Without this renunciation, we become idolaters of the little "lords" that tyrannize life. The lesser loyalties of life are self-limiting and limit our own capacity to grow into the fullness of the knowledge of God in Jesus Christ. We reach the limits of the growth set for us by the loyalties to family, fortune, passion, and ambition. When growth stops, sickness sets in spiritually. Our idolatry becomes the religious factor in much of our illness. This is not the only factor in illness, for the aging process has limits set to it by God himself. However, these limits are shortened by our wrong centering of life. Many die before their time because of the smallness of that which they worship, the weakness of that to which they give their total allegiance. When we give ourselves to idols, we are possessed by them. Therefore, the pastor as a healer cannot divest himself of his identity as a prophet who challenges the idols to which people give themselves.

One of the contemporary idolatries of American life is the worship of health itself. Preoccupation with obesity, the search for complete relief from all pain, the fear of aging, the use of drugs and especially of alcohol, the expectation of perfection from doctors – these are marketplace topics of conversations. In religion, healing cults abound of both the sophisticated and the unsophisticated varieties. In these cults of healing, health itself is made the "be-all" and "end-all" of life. The pastor as healer must work the works of the Christ who sent him to heal in the midst of Elymas-like magicians who are filled with deceit and villainy, and will not stop making crooked the straight paths of the Lord (Acts 13: 6-10).

In Revelation 22:1ff., the story is told of the river of the water of life. On either side of the river the tree of life grows. The tree of life yields twelve kinds of fruit, one for each month of the year. At no time are the people of God without its fruit. Then the Scripture says that *the leaves* of the tree are for the healing of the nation. Healing is not the fruit. It is the leaves. The leaves contribute to the fruit just as health contributes to the full fruit of the gospel. The fruits of redemption, however, are the end-intention of the gospel, not health itself. Reality requires of us that we look upon health as a temporal good. Healing of every kind is ultimately subject to the power of death. The resurrection itself transcends death but does not remove death from the normal process of earthly life. The pastor, therefore, as a healer does not ask that death be removed from life but that death shall not have the last word about the destiny of man. God's answer in Jesus Christ is that nothing — neither death nor life — can separate us from the love of God in Jesus Christ.

2. HEALING AND PASTORAL RESPONSIBILITY

Pastors have at various times in history interpreted their responsibility for healing in different ways. Present day attitudes toward the pastor's healing responsibility are a mosaic of these different interpretations. Each interpretation has a valid dimension. Each has a marked limitation. The validity and the limitation must be jointly fitted into a larger understanding of the work of the pastor as a healer.

a. *Healing as a Gift of the Holy Spirit.* Charismatic interpretations of healing underscore this responsibility as a gift of the Holy Spirit. I Corinthians 12:8-9 says, "To one is given through the Spirit the utterance of wisdom, and to another the utterance of knowledge according to the same Spirit, to another faith by the same Spirit, to another gifts of healing by the one Spirit." The validity of pastoral healing as a gift of the Spirit is constantly revalidated by the way in which human cleverness and manipulation are likely to turn healing into magic and pastoral care into personal power without the constant leadership of the Holy Spirit. Healing as the gift of the Holy Spirit is validated further by the way in which the most carefully laid plans for healing people through medicine are spontaneously transcended by "a Power not ourselves" that makes for health. Curiously enough, the mystery of health itself is almost axiomatic with those who know most about medicine and their search for the unknown causes of illness and death is more often than not a spiritual quest without the fanfare of a healing service. Similarly, psychiatric criteria for the validity of a religious experience of healing are vividly reminiscent of Old Testament tests of the false prophet and New Testament examples of "trying of the spirits" to see whether they are of God or man.

The limitations of the charismatic healing as a gift of the Holy Spirit are the same today that they were in the New Testament. We are constantly required to test the nature of the spirits that lead us, and not all of them are the Holy Spirit. Also, the activity of the Holy Spirit in the Biblical accounts was not accepted on the word of one man alone, but was validated by the fellowship of believers. Today the so-called charismatic healer often is a "free-lancer" who acknowledges no fellowship of believers and is motivated by the desires for power, publicity, and money. Therefore, the person who relies solely upon the Holy Spirit must take heed to test his leadership of the Holy Spirit by that of others around him who are also in touch with the Holy Spirit. He must constantly re-examine his own temptations to power, exhibitionism, and to a luxury that calls for much money.

b. *Healing as an Expression of a Concerned Community of Trust.* Idolatry is one factor in disease. Isolation is another. Loneliness is the hallmark of all manner of disease. Many diseases "cut off" the patient from "the land of the living." Leprosy was the disease of isolation in the New Testament. Lepers called to Jesus in a loud voice from afar off. Jesus, the Great Physician, never called back in a loud voice. He moved toward them in trust and healing mercy. Tuberculosis was the disease of isolation at the turn of the present century. To a certain extent it still is. Mental illness, both in the times of the Gadarene demoniac and the patient whose family in shame "puts him away" today, is best understood as the withdrawal of a person from community and as the results of the rejection and exploitation of the individual by the community. Of course, there are basic organic causes of mental illness occasioned by the infection, deterioration, and wounding of the central nervous system. But the psychic damage of isolation from the "community of those whose approval one considers most worth while" stands high in the field of causes that underly mental illness. Alcoholism is a combination of direct and side effects of alcohol upon the body and the estrangement of the alcoholic from his family and the "respectable" community at large.

The Scripture at many points describes the fellowship of believers in the church as a "restoring community" of fellow sinners. The vivid expression of this is in Galatians 6:1: "Brethren, if a man is overtaken in any trespass, you who are spiritual should restore him in a spirit of gentleness." This fulfills the law of Christ to bear one another's burdens. This calls for mutual awareness of fault. We are all to look to ourselves lest we too be tempted. The Epistle of James pinpoints the therapeutic power of such a community in these words, ". . . confess your sins to one another . . . that you may be healed" (James 5:16). The maxim of contemporary group psychotherapists is that "By the crowd have they been broken; by the crowd they shall be healed."

The pastor as a teacher is the leader of small groups. The healing ministry of pastors has diminished as we have let our small group ministry go by the board in behalf of large, unrelated crowds of people. The pastor can bring his personal healing ministry to bright leafing of the tree of life by activating small groups of people with common concerns. Families who have retarded children need fellowship with each other. Widows need the support that unadvertized and informal group meetings can afford. Divorcees and the so-called "one-parent" families of the church have hurts that go unmollified with the oil of pastoral concern. Recovered mentally ill persons often relapse into illness from sheer loneliness and lack of fellowship. Alcoholics who are struggling alone to win the battle for sobriety often lose it because of their estrangement. Bereaved people fall into the idolatry of the dead because no instruction and companionship is provided in the spiritual combat with grief.

The Christian pastor in the pastoral epistles is portrayed as one who is "apt to teach" and who communicates "health-giving doctrine." When the pastor activates the power of the intimate and well-defined group on great continuing threats to people's total health as persons, he both teaches and heals. His sermons to great congregations of people become more pertinent to the capacity of each individual in the audience to hear in his own idiom.

c. *Healing as the Implementation of the Unique Role of the Pastor.* The pastor has a place in the life of people, either positively or negatively, which is far more than his own personal individuality or powers to help and hurt people. He wears a mantle of the mercy and judgment of God without the option of putting it on and taking it off at will. He is a man of God, a man of prayer, and a man of care. As such, people come to him seeking help with the painful disturbances of their lives. In this role as a man of God, he cannot "play God" or act as if the wisdom which is his is tantamount to that of God. He has this gift of ministry in earthen vessels in order that the excellency of the power may be of God and not of himself. Nevertheless, the place he has been given by God and by people as well enables him to use the power of that place to heal people's relationships to themselves, to one another, and to God. As such he is a minister of reconciliation. Reconciliation is a kind of healing in its own right.

Soren Kierkegaard said that a man is "disrelated to himself." One of the main tasks of the pastor as a healer is that of healing men and women in their wrong relationships to themselves. These stand as thorns in the flesh of their lives. They may think of themselves as nobodies when God's intention is that they be a person in their own right with integrity and hope. They may think of themselves more highly than they ought to think when God's intention is that they think of themselves soberly according to the measure of faith God has given them. They may think of themselves as something apart from all other men, as unique either in goodness or evil, when God's intention is that they realize the companionship of others both in fault and righteousness.

The pastor, furthermore, is called as a healer of the breaches that separate people from one another. Over half of the personal counseling done by a pastor concerns the conflicts that arise between husband and wife. The inflamed idolatries of money, sex, prestige, and personal vanity rise as high things that exalt themselves against the knowledge of God in the interaction between husband and wife. The fellowship of believers is not without conflict and internecine warfare among its members. The pastor cannot delegate this disorder to the healing hands of others. It is his. He functions as a healer or as a part of the disease. He has no other choice. The community as a whole is beset by conflicts between extremists of every persuasion. The pastor functions not only as a prophet of social justice on major issues of each generation – racial justice, the evils of war and harms of both militarism and pacifism, labor-industry struggles, etc.; the pastor also functions as a healer, a quiet man of reconciliation who represents a totality larger than the passions of contending parties. The pastor who is moved only by passion and not compassion is likely to be misunderstood by those who know only passion, whatever their cause may be. Yet the pastor who moves at his task as healer without empathy for the hurt of his people has yet to learn of the Holy Spirit.

The pastor at heart is a minister of reconciliation between God and man as an undershepherd of Christ. The pastor as a healer of the rift between man and God serves as a minister of introduction of men to God in Jesus Christ. At this point, the work of the pastor as a healer is coterminous with his work as an evangelist. As a healer he brings the good news that God was in Christ reconciling the world to himself.

d. *Healing as the Work of the Church and Its Ministry in Relation to Other Healers.* The pastor as a healer does not work in isolation. Other men of good will, often not even of the fold of Jesus Christ, have assistance to offer in the healing of men and society. Medical doctors lead these men. Social workers, psychologists, public assistance people, nurses, lawyers, and financiers have their disciplines and resources as well. This is a day when the gifts of these equipped and disciplined people are being called upon increasingly by wise and well-trained pastors. Theological schools are equipping pastors through actual clinical training in the care of the sick in the therapeutic teamwork of ministers, doctors, nurses, psychologists, social workers, and others who have been named here. The pastor as a healer today does so in the context of other disciplined persons. The riches of these professions can be used by the pastor in his ministry of healing.

BIBLIOGRAPHY

Doniger, Simon, ed., *Healing: Human and Divine.* New York: Association Press, 1957.

Kemp, Charles, *Physicians of the Soul.* New York: The Macmillan Co., 1947.

Knight, James A., *A Psychiatrist Looks at Religion and Health.* New York: Abingdon Press, 1964.

McCasland, S. Vernon, *By the Finger of God.* New York: The Macmillan Co., 1951.

Oates, Wayne E., "The Findings of the Commission in the Ministry," *Annals of the New York Academy of Sciences,* Vol. 63, Article 3, November 7, 1955, pp. 414-428.

———————, *The Christian Pastor.* Philadelphia: Westminster Press, 1964.

Roberts, David, *Psychotherapy and a Christian View of Man.* New York: Charles Scribner's Sons, 1950.

Scherzer, Carl J. *The Church and Healing.* Philadelphia: Westminster Press, 1950.

Williams, Daniel Day, *The Minister and the Care of Souls.* New York: Harper Brothers 1961.

Young, Richard K, *The Pastor's Hospital Ministry.* Nashville: Broadman Press, 1954.

The Pastor as Worshiper

1. THE LEADER IN WORSHIP

The pastor is a worshiper while at the same time directing the congregation in worship. Leadership is the ability to lead. Christ is the true leader and as the pastor follows him in loyalty and devotion he will in turn be able to lead the people. The true shepherd leads the sheep into green pastures. He does not drive; where he goes there the sheep follow. The pastor must know beforehand exactly the direction he will lead in every worship service. John Calvin said, "The worship of God is the one thing calculated to lift man above the brute creation and to inspire him with hopes of immortality" (Institutes 1.33).

Thus it is that worship serves the purpose of clarifying vision and only as the pastor has a clear vision of God and his Word is he able to open up that vista to his people. Worship is a means by which one may receive a clear knowledge of tomorrow's path. The pastor's task is to act as a guide leading into the right paths. Among other things worship is a confession of spiritual need and this is a joint demand of pastor and people.

It should be a medium for the renewing of exhausted spiritual and moral forces. The pastor needs this reinvigoration even more than others. As he worships with the people they both find a spirit of unity and strength. In no sense must the pastor be apart from or higher than the people.

The parish priest, of authority,
Climbed up in the high church steeple,
To be nearer God, so that he might
Hand His word down to the people.

And in sermon script he daily wrote
What he thought was sent from heaven;
And he dropped it down on the people's heads
Two times one day in seven.

In his age, God said, "Come down and die,"
And he cried out from the steeple,
"Where art Thou, Lord?"; and the Lord replied
"Down here among the people."
(anonymous)

Jesus went away from his disciples and spent hours in prayer preparation before facing the demands of a new day. This the pastor must do daily and not only on Sunday morning. Prayer should become the means by which the mind of Christ is imparted to the leader so that he in turn may be able to interpret the same to his people.

President Woodrow Wilson, who was raised in a Presbyterian manse, said in an address the following pertinent words, "You do not have to *be* anything in particular to be a lawyer. I have been a lawyer and I know. You do not have to *be* anything in particular, except a kind-hearted man, perhaps, to be a physician. You do not have to *be* anything, nor undergo any stirring spiritual change, in order to be a merchant. The only profession which consists in *being* something is the ministry of our Lord and Savior — and it does not consist in anything else" ("The Ministry and the Community").

The great open sesame for the pastor-leader is dependence upon the leadership and direction of Jesus Christ through the Holy Spirit of God. Denis Wortman wrote a poem, "God of the Prophets," from which come these two closing stanzas:

Anoint them priests!
Strong intercessors, Lord!
Anoint them with the Spirit of Thy Son;
Theirs not a jeweled crown, a blood-stained sword;
Theirs by sweet love, for Christ a kingdom won.

Make them apostles!
Heralds of Thy cross,
Forth may they go to tell all realms Thy grace:
Inspired of Thee, may they count all but loss.
And stand at last with joy before Thy face.

These are the leaders in worship! The men who have experienced God, who know God, who worship Him and follow wherever He leads.

As a worshiper the pastor must conduct himself in a dignified manner with propriety, decency, decorum, and in accordance with the rules of ministerial etiquette and ethics. Unseemly joking and a flippant attitude dissipate the spirit of worship and therefore have no place in the pulpit. Unnecessary pacing, jumping about or cavorting over the platform are inexpedient, vulgar, and serve only to induce ridicule. Proper decorum and dignity of speech and action will be more convincing of the truth and more conducive to worship than any amount of dancing and prancing.

2. THE INVOCATION

The invocation at the opening of a worship service is not a formal prayer. Actually it is an act of worship calling upon God for aid, inspiration, and blessing with reference to the immediate service and is to be given in the opening minutes of that service. It may consist of some short but appropriate prayer such as may be found under the heading "Aids to Worship" in the front of "The Hymnbook" of the Presbyterian Church and some others also. Under no circumstances is an invocation to be a lengthy prayer. If a prayer is offered it should never be over two to four short sentences making an appeal to God for the manifestation of his presence or expressing thanks for his presence. The invocation serves the purpose of bringing the minds of those present into the spirit of worship. It is for this reason that no service should begin without asking that God's presence be manifest and that the minds of the congregation be made alive to spiritual truths and put in tune with the Infinite One.

3. THE HYMNS

Singing has always had a large place in Judaistic and Christian worship. The Book of Psalms was the psalter, for use in the religious services of the Hebrew people. They also became the hymns of the Christian church especially during the historical period of the Reformation. Hymns should be and indeed must be, dignified, didactic, and selected to fit the general theme of the hour. The minister should select the hymns to be sung and see that they are in accord with the sermon topic. He must worship in song along with the congregation. If he does not have the gift for singing then he should reverently follow along with the words and make it an act of worship. This is not the time for reviewing announcements to be made, looking up Scripture to be read or casting over his sermon notes. All that should have sufficiently been done well before the service started. Let him worship along with the people and sing in the spirit if unable to do so audibly.

Dean Brown in "The Art of Preaching" wrote in reference to the minister and his attitude during the singing of the hymns in words "Sing yourself! Do it as a means of grace to your own soul! Do it also as a bit of Godly example to your people. The lazy, shiftless minister who announces a hymn and then goes back to his chair and sits down while the people stand up and sing it, as if praising God were no affair of his, ought to be cast out of the synagogue" (p. 207). There is no part of the service which the minister as a leader can afford to neglect or treat lightly. He needs to worship in song as much as does the congregation.

The pastor should also confer with the director of special music in order that the choir numbers and the special soloist may select their numbers to conform to and serve the worship theme.

4. THE SCRIPTURE

Reading from the Scriptures is an act of worship engaged in by congregation and pastor. It should never be done without care, interest, and concern; never merely as a form or routine. The Holy Scripture is God speaking to man and the pastor should read as a prophet, i.e., to bring out the meaning of the passage selected. No Scripture should be read hastily, stumblingly, thoughtlessly, or without clear enunciation. All Scripture should be read with this thought in mind, "God is now speaking, listen to him." In those churches which use a prescribed form or ritual for public worship, the Scripture for the day is printed in the order for the day and thus is apropos for the day but the same rules for reading obtain.

The method, now used by many churches, of having the congregation read a responsive selection from the Old Testament, followed by an appropriate hymn and a selection from the New Testament read by the pastor, helps to build up a worship spirit. This order of reading may be reversed to fit the needs of the occasion.

5. THE PASTORAL PRAYER

The pastoral prayer should precede the sermon. The people expect this and the minister must prepare for it. There can be no true prayer without the leading of the Holy Spirit of God. The man who has learned how to pray by private practice will have no difficulty in approaching God in public.

The pastor must lead the congregation in this approach to God sincerely, humbly, earnestly, and reverently. In the form prayers of a completely liturgical service it is not appropriate to read the prayer in an affected fervor or hollow, pious voice. Those ministers who use this plan must remember that the printed prayers were carefully thought out by someone to fit that day's worship and felt to be the proper approach to God. These are not to be treated lightly, flippantly, or without previous thought. The careless prayer, whether read or spontaneous, induces irreverence and the pastor thus defeats his own purpose.

In prayer the pastor is approaching God in public. He does not speak for himself alone but is standing as a representative of the congregation. Prayers are never to be disguised sermons. When the pastor expresses his own needs, sorrows, aspiration and praise he must express those of his congregation as well. This must be done, therefore, in a generally inclusive way and not in a personal manner. Henry Ward Beecher in the Yale Lectures expressed the oneness of the pastor with his congregation in this way: "Hundreds and hundreds of times as I rose to pray and glanced at the congregation I could not keep back the tears. There came to my mind such a sense of their wants, there were so many hidden sorrows, there were so many weights and burdens, there were so many doubts, there were so many states of weakness, there were so many dangers, so many perils, there were so many histories – not world histories, but eternal-world histories – I had such a sense of compassion for them, my soul so longed for them, that it seemed to me as if I could scarcely open my mouth to speak for them. And when I take my people and carry them before God to plead for them, I never plead for myself as I do for them – I never could" (Vol. II, p. 46). This is an example of the method of a true priestly prayer.

6. THE SERMON

All Protestant services are sermon centered and all parts of the worship program point to that medium of expressing God's truth. To make this meaningful is the responsibility of the preacher which he does not, indeed cannot, share with anyone but God. To take the sacred Word of God and unfold it to a listening audience is a grave responsibility, which cannot be treated lightly. The pulpit is a place dedicated to the dispensing of divine truths. Those truths enter every field which concerns man and his relation to God and his fellow men.

It is doubtful whether the sermon will ever be pushed into a secondary place in Protestant worship, since it is the supreme medium for dispensing Divine truth and edifying the church of Jesus Christ. The sermon must find its source in God's inspired Word, which means that the pastor must become a "man of one Book" thoroughly acquainted with and instructed in the inspired Scripture of both Old and New Testaments. To be effective and productive the sermon must have power, which comes only as the minister is in personal contact with the power of the Holy Spirit. Furthermore, the pastor must by personal experience and contact with his parishioners enter into the problems, sorrows and experiences of life, and he must possess a depth of sincerity with which he speaks his convictions.

The pastor must also be a student for he has to produce at least one sermon every week. In some churches he must produce two sermons each week. In this he is contrasted to the evangelist who moves from place to place, enabling repeatedly to use the same sermons. The pastor has to bring forth that which is new and inspirational and instructive. He is under a solemn obligation to discover, as far as he is able, the mind of the Holy Spirit in selecting his sermon text, topic, and material. Only then can he say "thus saith the Lord," and so be a genuine worshiper himself.

7. THE BENEDICTION

This is to be pronounced by the pastor at the conclusion of the worship service. It is the Lord's parting word of blessing upon the worshipers. Therefore, the spirit of the worship service must be conserved in the benediction, which is a genuine part of worship and not a signal that the service is ended. An extempore benediction made for the moment is usually a farce and serves no purpose. The Scriptural benedictions are those to be used, and may be quoted from memory in a reverent and dignified manner (see e.g., II Cor. 13:14). When spoken reverently and with deep sincerity the benediction will tend to fix the mind of the congregation upon the overall presence of the Holy Trinity, and God's people can leave his house with the assurance of the riches of his grace.

BIBLIOGRAPHY

Beebe, James A., *The Pastoral Office.* Chicago: Methodist Book Concern, 1923.

Blackwood, Andrew W., *Leading in Public Prayer.* Nashville: The Abingdon Press, 1958.

——————, *Pastoral Work.* Philadelphia: The Westminster Press, 1945.

Gunsaulus, Frank W., *The Minister and the Spiritual Life.* Chicago, Ill.: Fleming H. Revell Company, 1911.

Harmon, Nolan B., *Ministerial Ethics and Etiquette.* Nashville: Abingdon-Cokesbury Press, 1928.

Jones, Ilion T., *The Pastor: the Man and His Ministry.* Philadelphia: Westminster Press, 1961.

Kay, J. Alan, *The Nature of Christian Worship.* New York: The Philosophical Library, Inc., 1954.

Macgregor, W. M., *The Making of a Preacher.* Philadelphia: The Westminster Press, 1946.

Palmer, Albert W., *Come Let Us Worship.* New York: The Macmillan Company, 1941.

Plune, Peter H., *Some to Be Pastors.* New York: Abingdon-Cokesbury Press, 1943.

The Pastor as Writer

Most ministers have no idea of the potential of evangelistic literature. The man in the pew normally does not remember nearly all that is said in preaching, but he can take a printed or mimeographed sermon home for further reading or study. This is not to denigrate preaching in any sense. There is nothing on earth to compare with the inspiration of a godly worship service where the Lord Jesus Christ is lifted up, and one's soul is put under the glass, and the hungry sheep are fed. No greater privilege than to preach is given to a man in this life. To witness the Holy Spirit using one's own feeble tongue to bring men and women to a living, personal faith in Jesus Christ brings unspeakable joy to a minister.

Yet with all the glory God gives to the pulpit, the ministry of literature is more far-reaching, more penetrating, and more efficacious. Peter's oratory is known today only because of the faithful reporting of Luke. The echo of the eloquence of Apollos died away in the hills of Asia Minor nineteen centuries ago, but the passion of Paul lives on in the one-fifth of the New Testament which he wrote.

What then shall a pastor put on paper? The obvious material he should consider worthy of publishing are his sermons. There are certain characteristics of a well-written sermon. First, it should have a solid skeleton. It should not only have three or four logical points, but a clear, well-defined, and memorable outline. Secondly, it should have an exciting introduction and conclusion. It is always a thrilling experience to follow a good mind through a perennial human problem to a victorious solution. Sermons are not spy thrillers, but they need to provide a satisfying experience. Thirdly, it should be sprinkled with accurate, contemporary, relevant, and interesting illustrations. Such a sermon should be in print. In print it may literally go around the world and redirect the lives of thousands of people.

There are many outlets open to the minister who is willing to learn how to improve his writing. The church bulletin, the parish newsletter, the local weekly paper, the daily newspaper, the denominational organ, the interdenominational periodicals and even secular magazines are all available. Skill in writing comes from practice. Further, articles may have to be rewritten several times. And the minister-writer would do well to expose his writings to competent constructive criticism.

Many ministers wonder about book-length writing. Every minister should be able to produce at least one good book in a lifetime. The world needs Christian literature. Trained clergy are in a favorable position to produce it.

But a minister should not go about writing a book backwards. He should not crank out their *opus magnificus* and expect the editors to accept and publish anything he has written. Rather, he should first ask an editor or publisher what kind of book is needed. Or if he decides on a topic he could write out a few pages of the opening chapter to suggest how it would read, taking it to a publisher for his appraisal. If he liked the material, the minister would proceed to write the book. If no editor liked it, the book could better remain unwritten, and many hours of futile effort would have been salvaged for productive use.

Neither should a minister drop an unsolicited manuscript of sermons or other ministerial material on the desk of a religion editor. And yet this same editor may be yearning for something spiritually fresh, contemporary, and deep in insight to give to the Christian (and non-Christian) reading world. One goes back again and again to the great classics of our time. Arthur John Cossip preached a message after the sudden death of his wife, calling it, "When Life Tumbles In, What Then?" He had the wisdom to put it on paper. It became a very famous sermon of the twentieth century. Years later he wrote:

> "I know a man who had to pass through an experience even more suddenly devastating than that which befell Ezekiel.

'Son of man, behold I take away the desire of thine eyes with a stroke. So I preached unto the people in the morning. And in the evening my wife died.' A bleak message Yet the prophet was at least granted one full day's warning. But this poor soul had not even a second's. In a twinkling she was gone. And that grim night amid the tumbled ruins of what, ten minutes before, had been a home, he tried to give her, not of compulsion, but as a free gift; and asked that, since he had to bear the pain, he might not miss or lose what it was sent to teach him.

"The years slipped past, and many letters reached him, all of a kind; one from two missionaries in the wilds of Africa. The one had lost her husband, drowned on their honeymoon in the United States, and with that, faith went out, until somebody sent her what that man had written in the dark to study his own soul. And faith revived in her, and she went to the foreign field. The husband of the second, too, was drowned in Africa; and her faith also went to pieces. Until the one, who had been through it all herself, read to the other what had brought her back. And that other, too, came home. And, together, they wrote to the man, whom they will never see, 'You can be absolutely sure that it was not for nothing that your heart was broken. It had to be, in order that two lost souls might be found again.'

"So it was not chance-blown, did not just happen. It had meaning in it: was a plan thought out by God. And the man is content" (*Experience Worketh Hope*, pp. 19. 20).

Literature is the one great untapped resource of the minister in his desire to reach lost men – even in his own congregation – for Jesus Christ.

BIBLIOGRAPHY

Camus, Albert, *The Plague* and *The Fall.*

Dostoyevsky, Fyodor, *Brothers Karamazov.*

Elliot, Betty, *Shadow of the Almighty.*

Evans, Bergen and Cornelia, *A Dictionary of Contemporary American Usage.*

Gosnell, Janice, *Christian Writer's Handbook.*

Koestler, Arthur, *The Yogi and the Commissar.*

Lewis, C. S., *Mere Christianity.*

————————, *That Hideous Strength.*

Paton, Alan, *Cry, the Beloved Country.*

———————, *Too Late the Phalarope.*

Rodale, J. I., *The Synonym Finder.*

Zylstra, Henry, *A Testament of Vision.*

The Pastor as Reconciler

Therefore, if any man be in Christ, he is a new creature: old things are passed away; behold, all things are become new. And all things are of God, who hath reconciled us to himself by Jesus Christ, and hath given to us the ministry of reconciliation; to wit, that God was in Christ reconciling the world unto himself (II Cor. 5:17-19).

The pastor's ministry of reconciliation – what an exciting and yet awesome concept of his calling. In describing this concept of the pastoral ministry Saint Paul uses a word which has its root meaning in the idea of "change," or "exchange." The pastor's ministry of reconciliation is to bring a change in relationships, to bring an exchange of relationships. Those to whom we minister are alienated from God because of sin, and their relationship is therefore wrong. In Christ there is a change from the wrong to the right, and an exchange of unchristian relationships for those which are Christian. Guilt is exchanged for forgiveness, condemnation is exchanged for justification and pardon, and spiritual death miraculously becomes new life in Christ.

The pastor is the "reconciler" in the sense that he is the herald of God bringing the message of redemption to the unreconciled. The pastor sees himself in the pattern of Jesus, whose first public utterance in the house of God was the reading of the word from the prophet Isaiah: "The Spirit of the Lord is upon me, because he hath anointed me to preach the gospel to the poor; he hath sent me to heal the broken hearted, to preach deliverance to the captives, and recovering of sight to the blind, to set at liberty them that are bruised" (Luke 4:18). In the view of Jesus, there is something very much wrong with men. They are poor, they are brokenhearted, they are captive, they are blind and bruised. Something needs changing, and there are some things which must be exchanged.

Hartford's Robert S. Paul sees this as the central and vital factor in the Christian ministry. He writes, "At the heart of this redemptive purpose there is the intention of bringing about reconciliation — a reconciliation that would reach out and embrace man in all of his relationships, to solve the estrangements between brother and brother (Matt. 5:24), between husband and wife (I Cor. 7:11), between nations and races (Eph. 2:13-16), and indeed, between man and the whole cosmic order (Col. 1:20)" (*Ministry*, p. 87). Reconciliation is the fundamental need. Change must take place, and a way found to bring about the needed exchange in relationship. All other human relationships depend upon reconciliation with God.

The pastor who sees his role as the reconciler, then, is more likely to be challenged than frustrated by the demands made upon him by today's parish. In his traditional role as preacher, priest and teacher, he is comfortable and efficient. But in his contemporary role as administrator, organizer, promotion executive and trouble-shooter he must find a way to keep his goals in perspective. He cannot afford the luxury of equating his place in the kingdom in terms of "my teaching, my interests, my theological perspective." This might well lead him into the ecclesiastical trap of expecting people to come to him, adjust to him, adapt themselves to his ideas and his methods; but his ministry of reconciliation rather sends him to the people. He goes where they are, meets them on their ground, and projects himself into their lives and interests. They then hear the word from the Lord, because communication takes place when the chasm of isolation is bridged.

Admittedly, the tension is greatest in that pastor who does not understand why reconciliation is needed even among the baptized. He can very well offer it to the heathen, the pagan, the unbeliever, the non-Christian, but sometimes he is not prepared to offer it also to those in the fellowship of the church who need it. And, it is here he finds it difficult to adjust his thinking and adapt his method. But the need to be reconciled, in its deepest meanings, is not automatically fulfilled once and for all at some point of conversion, nor yet at some time of spiritual victory, or some experience of deep dedication and Spirit-filling. All too typical of religious experience is the description Paul Tournier gives in *Guilt and Grace*: "Our convert . . . is transformed. . . . In the religious community in which he is entering, he finds men who speak with open hearts, even about their own difficulties and their own faults. By hearing these, he dicovers his own, which for so long he had hidden from himself. But little by little, disillusion creeps in. He notices that his spiritual leader is not faultless, that he shows pettiness and moods which are really surprising in such a religious man. And then, in the community there are some rather unpleasant people, who make pretty speeches and a display of virtue, but who lack charity. . . . In the church, they still play the fraternal community game, they still proclaim loudly the mutual charity to which they are seeking to conform; but it is only a façade which hides innumerable repressed judgments. All. . . hold one another as guilty, all are crushed" (p. 101).

The pastor who draws a line delimiting his role to that of bringing reconciliation only to those not yet in the fellowship of the church will find himself hopelessly confused when he sees such deep needs among his church people. He will brood over the discrepancy between the ideal image he has in mind for his sheep, and the real or apparent picture they present as he knows them more intimately.

He will have to spend considerable time helping people find peace with themselves so that they can live in peace with their fellow human beings. This is a vital part in the whole concept of his ministry of reconciliation. It may well be the most vital part, because it is only in the measure that he succeeds here that his parish will be free to release energy and power in the salvation of the lost.

There is a ministry of reconciliation to the needs of families which are threatened with hostilities, misunderstandings, broken lines of communication, and eventual disintegration. These are days of early marriages, easy divorces, social stresses, and family strains. As a testimony to this need, there are 800,000 divorces each year in the United States, and ninety-five percent of these are uncontested. In these divorces, there are approximately 300,000 children involved. R. Lofton Hudson writes concerning this family problem: "These are a very small part of the real story of divorce. The story that matters is one that includes the account of confused children, dirty court proceedings, tears and disappointment, and long years of regrets and loneliness" (*The Religion of a Happy Home,* p. 112). This author should know. He is director of a counseling center which ministers to thousands each year, and according to their records, something like seventy-five per cent of their clients come to them for help because of marriage problems.

What is wrong with the family today? Where have marriages failed? It would be an inadequate oversimplification to answer that the problem is sin. Sin may be the most significant factor in the tragic story of unreconciled husbands and wives, but it is not the only factor. There is such a thing as spiritual need, which the pastor sees as his target. But, there are also such things as physical needs, and also psychological and emotional needs. It is at these points that the pastor is most likely to become confused, for these needs more nearly resemble the spiritual than the physical, and therefore they are often not understood when they are present in the lives of Christians.

Next to his knowledge of God in Christ Jesus, and his thorough understanding of the Scriptures, the pastor needs to know the people to whom he ministers. If he has at least gained a fairly adequate mastery of pastoral psychology, he will be able more intelligently to approach these problems his people are facing. Karen Horney writes of the neurotic person's relationship with other persons — and we have seen that our ministry of reconciliation seeks to change wrong relationships — as reflecting the competitive struggles of our culture. She states in *The Neurotic Personality of Our Time,*

> "The neurotic . . . is driven by a blind, indiscriminate and compulsive urge to disparage others. He may do this even though he realizes that the others would do him no actual harm, or even when their defeat is distinctly counter to his own interests. His feelings may be described as an articulate conviction that 'only one can succeed,' which is only another way of expressing the idea that 'no one but I shall succeed'" (p. 193).

It is somewhat ironical that psychiatry has rediscovered the primary position of love in man's world. The church from its beginning has accepted God's divine love, *agape,* which is self-giving, unmerited, voluntary and boundless; and the church has always claimed to believe it must be given as well as accepted. But, does she need to re-examine her attitude toward those among her fellowship who exhibit neurotic tendencies, lest she sit in judgment upon them rather than offer her healing ministry of reconciliation and love? Certainly not, if intentions and motives are in question; but the failure is not found here. The failure is in communication. The church must overcome the barriers which hinder communication between her pastors and her worshippers; barriers which lead to such neurotic attitudes as Horney describes.

A survey was made recently among ministers from various denominations. These men, about a thousand in number, and from widely different educational backgrounds and theological orientations, pointed to the problem of communication as their primary concern. From their viewpoint, laymen are not opening their lives at any deep level to the meanings of the gospel. Reuel L. Howe discusses this communication barrier, and suggests that the laymen, from their side, see the failure of communication ". . . to lie in the fact that the preacher's sermon, for example, on the free gift of God's love is often heard by them simply as a new and harsher demand to be good. The preaching of 'grace' is heard as a demand of 'law'" (*The Miracle of Dialogue,* p. 20).

It is at the point of communication that the pastor often fails to reconcile those whose problem is identified with psychological weakness rather than spiritual wickedness. It is here that love is more powerful than judgment, for love is creative and judgment is destructive. It is here that a working knowledge of psychology may help him reconcile the disturbed persons whose lives have lost meaning for them, and whose relationships must be changed. And, it is here that the problem emerges as being much larger in scope than the pastor may have realized, as Flanders Dunbar finds ". . . that at least sixty-five percent of patients are suffering from illness syndromes initiated or seriously complicated by psychological problems" (*Psychiatry in the Medical Specialties*, p. v).

Several years ago, David K. Roberts wrote concerning this aspect of pastoral ministry, in which he made an evaluation of pastoral psychotherapy as a means of reconciling those whose problem is emotional rather than spiritual. He stated: "Why does psychotherapy work? The simplest answer is that it provides a situation in which a person can be completely honest with himself and with a fellow human being. Conversely, it provides a situation in which he can discover how much he has deceived himself hitherto; the manner in which his ideal picture of himself . . . has caused him to distort reality" (*Psychotherapy and a Christian View of Sin*, p. 33). Thus, the pastor who seeks to reconcile the "lost" who are right within the doors of his church, must be willing to lay aside the flowing robes of ecclesiastical dogmatism and, in an atmosphere of love and understanding which aids communication, help people to understand themselves and see their needs clearly so that they are able to grow stronger as they exchange their neurotic weaknesses for spiritual power.

This is not to claim that any pastor needs to sacrifice or compromise his convictions concerning right and wrong. It does mean that he can more effectively help people when he is able to accept them as persons; and acceptance is not the same as approval. Acceptance is like *agape*; it means "Neither do I condemn thee; go and sin no more." The question is not really, "What do you think of my behavior?" or, "How do you feel about my weakness?" The question is, "How do you feel about *me*? Will you please try and understand *me*?" Victor Hugo once said that the greatest happiness of life is the conviction that we are loved – loved for ourselves, or rather, loved in spite of ourselves.

A revival of this kind of love is the deep need of our present anxious, hostile, confused and lonely generation. And, it is only to the extent that God-anointed pastors are able to be used of him in bringing their people to reconciliation with Christ that they will become reconciled to themselves, and to one another.

In summary, to be reconciled to God is to be changed from death unto life, but to continue to be reconciled in all of life's relationships means continual growth in grace, and demands the best effort of every Christian and the skillful assistance of the well-trained, dedicated pastor, who knows and loves God, knows and loves the Bible, and knows and loves people. The painful truth is this, that all who need to be reconciled are not outside the church. Some of them come and worship, but they do not feel comfortable about themselves, they do not feel right about other people, and they are not able to meet the demands of life. It is to them that the pastor must "go," not because their souls are more precious than those as yet unbaptized, but because it is in exchanging their hostility, their insecurity, and their immaturity for the substance of sound personal growth in Christian love that the church is going to see more and more of the skeptics, unbelievers, doubters, and sinners brought into reconciliation with Christ. It is then that the "roots" of vital growing faith will have been firmly planted, and it is then that the "fruits" of conversion, new church members, and the coming of Christ's kingdom will be seen in surprising abundance.

BIBLIOGRAPHY

Belgum, David, *Guilt: Where Psychology and Religion Meet.* Englewood Cliffs, N. J.: Prentice-Hall, Inc. 1963.

Dunbar, Flanders, *Psychiatry in the Medical Specialties.* New York: McGraw-Hill Book Company. 1959.

Ferre, Nels F. S., *Making Religion Real.* New York: Harper and Brothers, 1955.

Horney, Karen, *The Neurotic Personality of our Time.* New York: W. W. Norton Company. 1937.

Howe, Reuel L., *The Miracle of Dialogue.* New York: The Seabury Press, 1963.

Hudson, R. Lofton, *The Religion of a Happy Home.* Pittsburg: Pittcraft, Inc., 1965.

Knight, James A., *A Psychiatrist Looks at Religion and Health.* New York: Abingdon Press. 1964.

Roberts, Paul, *Ministry.* Grand Rapids: Wm. B. Eerdmans Publishing Company. 1965.

Roberts, David E., *Psychotherapy and a Christian View of Man.* New York: Charles Scribner's Sons, 1950.

Robinson, Reginald, *Community Resources in Mental Health.* New York: Basic Book, inc., 1960.

Tournier, Paul, *Guilt and Grace.* New York: Harper and Row. 1962.

The Pastor as Administrator

It is impossible to separate the work of ministry from that of administration. Linguistically the two words are cognate and for the Christian pastor they are inseparable. Administration concerns the total care of the church and may be thought of as including "ministry."

There is no typical situation. There are variants in the size of churches, the temperament and training of pastors, the position and disposition of the constituents. Every situation is peculiar. Any situation will present problems. Generally a safe rule in administration would be for the pastor to do as the apostles who asked for the election of men whom they might appoint over the business administration of the church. Then the apostles could give themselves to the more important work of prayer and the ministry of the Word. Thus, more time can be given by the pastor to his spiritual responsibilities. Also, the more people who have responsibility in the work of the church, the more interest will be taken in its general success.

However, the ultimate responsibility for organization, inspiration, supervision, and success must largely be accepted by the pastor. A danger that we face is that we will require that a pastor have thorough theological training without even inquiring as to his preparation for administration. Too often we assume that administration comes naturally. The success of a pastor will largely be measured by his success as an administrator. If the details of administration can be handled in such manner as to become more or less automatic so far as the pastor is concerned, he will then be free for other avenues of ministry. A great many breakdowns among the clergy must be charged to administrative inability, due either to the fact that the calls are too many or the helpers too few.

In moving into a new situation it is not always possible for a pastor to set up the organization which he would like. He must seek to adapt himself to the existing program, and carefully and gradually shift that program to conform more nearly to his ideas. The wise pastor will stay as much in the shadows as possible in making such changes. If he can be adroit enough to plant a seed-thought in the mind of a church leader, then support him when he proposes (probably as original) that idea, the pastor will find much pleasure in seeing interest, initiative and progress increase. In fact, it will often make the difference between success and failure.

Some techniques and procedures may be suggested, which have proved effective in the operation of churches.

1. STAFF AND STAFF RELATIONS

Since churches vary very greatly as to the number and the functions of the staff, it is necessary to give an example of a larger organization with the understanding that variations will be the rule instead of the exception, in which activities will be combined or reassigned as individual cases require.

The problem of choosing associates in a church staff is of paramount importance. The battle may be lost before it is begun, unless the staff is composed of associates of unquestionable character, who have a sense of divine call, who are honest in their stewardship, willing to work, and loyal to the program of the church and to the pastor. This refers particularly to those on the staff who have been ordained. It is desirable also that all secretaries, the custodian, the janitors and maids, be carefully screened as to character, honesty, and dependability. A credit rating should be secured on each person in the employ of the church. And for those who are responsible for the spiritual life of the church, the pastor should be very sure that they practice Christian stewardship and are in harmony with the full beliefs and program of the church. These matters should be settled before employment, if possible, thereby preventing trouble before it begins.

a. *Assistant Pastors.* Very close to the pastor, where this is practical, should be the associate, or assistant pastor, or pastors. Since they labor in the same general field, a very definite understanding should be had as to the type of ministry on which each should major. Most pastorates have numerous shut-ins who require periodic visitation. The ministry to the sick is a constant necessity.

Visiting of prospects and enlistment are vital activities. And where the staff is otherwise limited, and other activities are not provided for, a division of labor in administration of church activities and functions is desirable. For the large church today, a shared ministry is vital.

b. *Ministry of Education.* Where there are ministers, or directors of education, or a minister of education, these persons should be directly responsible to the pastor and should keep him informed concerning all activities. Where it is possible to have a plurality of ministers of education, it is desirable to have one coordinator who will be the director of this division. It should be borne in mind that the primary emphasis here should be on education, with promotion taking a secondary place.

c. *Music Ministry.* Where it is possible to have an employed director of music, this person should be in charge of the music program of the church and, of course, the musicians. The director of music should have a rather free hand in selecting music, but he must also choose that music which complements the theme of the worship services. Many churches now have graded choir systems which include a very large number who receive invaluable training in music and assist tremendously in any worship program. It is not unusual for the number enrolled in the music program to be 10 per cent or more of the total membership.

d. *Business Administrator.* Many churches are finding it necessary to employ someone trained in modern business methods to handle the personnel and the business affairs of the church. This person is in charge of the financial secretary, or secretaries, and other church secretaries except those assigned to the pastor, the associate pastor and the minister of education, and perhaps to the minister of music. He is also in charge of the church hostess and the building superintendent, through whom he supervises the work of the janitors and maids.

Since the pastor must bear final responsibility for the success of each phase of the work of the church, it is necessary that the business administrator be accountable to the pastor and work in close harmony with him at all times. Confusion of the program and misunderstandings can be avoided only in this way.

e. *Job Descriptions.* It is often advisable to have detailed job descriptions for every member of the staff as well as for all employees of the church. In some cases this would be like asking for a job description of a homemaker, but the general outline can at least be made. It will be found to be of great advantage if each member of an organization knows what is required in his position and is held responsible for its fulfillment.

Regular staff meetings, with the administrative personnel, are rather vital in carrying out a church program. These meetings should be held at least weekly at a specified time and with a planned agenda. In the absence of the pastor, the associate, or assistant, pastor would be in charge.

The wise pastor will designate to these, as much as possible of the details of church administration.

2. ORGANIZATION

a. *Governing Body.* Such a body of elders, stewards, deacons, or the like is generally provided for in the basic organization of a church.

b. *Trustees.* In many churches trustees, perhaps three or five, are named as the holders of the title to the property owned by the church. Where the church is a corporation, the chairman of the governing body is normally president of the corporation and its other officers serve as officers of the corporation. The title to the property is then in the name of the corporation.

c. *Finance Committee.* This committee may be a small group, elected from the governing body, either by that body or by the church. This group is charged with the receipt and distribution of all funds in accordance with the adopted budget and the direction of the governing body of the church. Special needs and problems are brought to one of the latter bodies. It is assumed that most churches will have carefully prepared and adopted budgets which anticipate mission responsibilities and local needs.

Some churches have found it very desirable to have a large finance committee which is composed of the governing body of the church plus a like number of men, and perhaps women, of the church. In this way, new members who have outstanding business ability can be enlisted in the work of the church long before they are well-enough known to be elected to office. These added members of the finance committee may be nominated, as is the case in some churches, by a committee composed of the pastor, the chairman, and the vice-chairman of the governing body. With such a large finance committee it may be desirable to have a small executive committee which manages financial matters according to the budget.

In nominating members for the governing board and members of the finance committee (if the larger plan is adopted) the pastor should know something of the financial commitment and the day by day living of any whose names are suggested. There are always some in a church who attend every meeting and show great interest but give little or nothing. If the shepherd of the sheep needs to know about the condition of the sheep, the pastor definitely needs to know the *stewardship temperature* of his members, especially those who are considered for leadership.

3. BYLAWS

a. *Provisions.* For independent churches, carefully prepared bylaws for the governing of the church and the directing of all committees, are necessary. These bylaws should provide for all officers and the method of their election or appointment. The method of calling of the minister, or ministers, of the church and perhaps the number and method of securing a pulpit committee in time of vacancies, should be provided. Terms of office of the governing body should be specified.

Terms of not more than three or four years for service on the governing body of the church have been found desirable. One year should elapse before one is eligible for reelection to the board. Where an unexpired term is being filled, one may be eligible for re-election if not more than two years have been served. In this way more people can be enlisted and any whose service is unsatisfactory can be retired without embarrassment.

The bylaws should specify the time for church conferences, i.e., regular business meetings and the number of members present to constitute a quorum. Provision should be made for special "called meetings" of the church and for regular meetings of the governing board. It is well to designate a set of parliamentary rules to be used (such as Robert's Rules of Order), and to provide for a regular moderator at business meetings.

b. *Committees.*

(1) Exofficio committees. A personnel committee of three, composed of the chairman of the governing board, the chairman of the finance committee (or the executive committee), and the pastor, should be responsible for the employment, dismissal, and supervision of all employees of the church, other than the ministers.

Some churches set up a church foundation to hold and administer, for missions and benevolent purposes, funds or properties received as legacies or built up as endowment. These may be held for general or specific purposes. Half of the trustees of these funds may be elected by the church and half be ex-officio, such as pastor, chairman of the governing body, and chairman of the finance committee.

(2) Standing committees. Either in the bylaws or by resolution, a number of standing committees should be provided for, to be appointed by the chairman of the governing board in collaboration with the pastor. Each committee should have definite responsibility for various parts of the program of the church. A partial alphabetical list of such committees is suggested: Athletics, Audio-Visual Aids, Baptismal, Christian Council (to represent the church in the municipal interchurch organization), Flower, Grounds, Library, Lord's Supper, Missions, Music, New Member Sponsoring, Nursery, Property, Public Address System, Public Relations, Prospective Members, Recreation, Youth Advisory and Ushers. Where there is a Boy Scout troop, such a committee should be set up.

The pastor must be the administrator of all of the work of the church. He is to be designated as an exofficio member of all committees and will find it necessary to keep in contact with their work. The chairman of the governing board should also be an exofficio member of all committees. A well planned budget will include funds, where necessary, for the work of these committees.

4. CABINET

It is desirable to have regular joint meetings of the pastors, the official leaders of the church, and the church staff. This group is called the cabinet, or the pastor's cabinet. These meetings should be held early enough before the monthly meeting of the official governing board to allow time for preparation of their recommendations to that board.

The pastor's cabinet is composed of the employed ministers and directors, the superintendent of the Sunday School, the director of the training organization, the president of the women's missionary organization and the president of the men's brotherhood or other similar groups, together with the chairman of the governing board, the chairman of the finance committee, their vice-chairmen, and the church treasurer and the church clerk. At this cabinet meeting each phase of the church work is reported on and policies and needs are discussed. Here should originate matters to be decided by the governing board or passed on by them to the church. Reports on the various activities of the church are discussed, sent on to the governing board and thence to the regular monthly church business meeting. Each member of the pastor's staff has opportunity to report any need and to make necessary requests to the cabinet. Unusual needs should be discussed by the church staff and agreed upon before the cabinet meeting.

5. SPECIAL RESPONSIBILITIES

a. *Church Budget*. In the preparation of the annual church budget, the pastor must be sure that all necessary items are included. He will be as vitally concerned for the mission side of the budget as for any other. He will be very fortunate if he can develop in his church such a missionary spirit that in setting up the budget the necessary local items are listed and their total would be the amount to be given to missions.

What he has to administer will largely be determined by the pastor's leadership in the subscribing of the budget. If he can report to the cabinet that all staff members have signed cards to tithe into the budget, he can challenge them to join in. Then the governing body should be challenged to tithe; and with such a start, the pastor can urge the whole church to full stewardship. A series of sermons on stewardship at budget time should make it unnecessary to stress the matter of money during the rest of the year.

b. *Building*. When added space is needed, or a new location and building are indicated, it is generally the pastor who must stir up the people and lead them to desire to make the necessary sacrifice to provide the facilities. Here is one of the great tests of pastoral leadership. Not only must he "sell the idea" but he must lead in making plans and in raising funds for the venture. At the same time he must seek out dedicated and able laymen who can and will give wise and aggressive leadership in a building program.

The pastor should insist on employing expert counsel, from his denomination if possible, to help plan for the education plant as well as for the whole building. Normally local architects have not specialized enough in church building not to need outside advice. Too much stress cannot be laid upon the necessity of having adequate plans prepared by specialists in the field. Such a specialist should generally work as consultant with a local architect, especially in the matter of floor plans in order to avoid wasted space and unnecessary ornamentation. Money needlessly spent can better be used for missions and other productive work. Special committees such as plans committee, building committee, finance committee, furnishings committee and the like, should be set up.

The missions program of the church ought not be curtailed, or left static, while a building is erected and paid for. If the mission program of the denomination is caused to suffer, the spiritual welfare of the church, which is as dependent upon missions as the individual is dependent upon stewardship, may be seriously hurt.

6. CONCLUSIONS

As an administrator, the pastor must remember that he is shepherd of the flock and so must be mindful of his spiritual responsibility to those with whom he labors. The attitude of the church staff and their spirit of camaraderie and devotion will have its effect on the whole work of the church. The pastor must be sure of himself and of his long range objectives as well as the immediate operations. He must be firm without being a dictator, positive without being unkind, and cordial without being effusive. His example of unremitting devotion to duty will be the best possible challenge to those with whom he is associated.

The pastor should seek to safeguard the members of the church staff. Unless they have some protection, much of their time will be dissipated by people who are members of the church and feel that they, therefore, have a right to ask special favors of the church staff. Often, they will use up time in visiting which should be given to work. The good administrator will somehow get the idea to the people that the Lord's business is business, and that those who are employed to do certain work should have the privilege of doing that work under one supervisor rather than a multitude of them. Here is a real problem of administration and the pastor must take a firm hand in it.

Administrators should recognize the fact that specialists in various fields covered by the church staff should be more highly skilled in doing their task than the pastor. It will be wise for him to delegate as much responsibility as possible to these associates, and then encourage them in every way. The pastor will not work less, but will accomplish more, if he will see that his associates are assigned the great majority of the details while he seeks to carry out his more exclusive responsibilities to the pulpit and to the people. However, it is impossible for him to escape ultimate responsibility for all the details of the work of the church. As administrator, the pastor must be faithful over many things if he is to be successful in the ultimate goal of giving Christ pre-eminence and of making full proof of his ministry.

BIBLIOGRAPHY

Dobbins, Gaines S., *A Ministering Church.* Nashville, Tennessee: Broadman Press, 1960.

Dolloff, Eugene Dinsmore, *The Efficient Church Officer: His Responsibilities and Problems.* New York: F. H. Revell Co., 1949.

Donaldson, Margaret F., *How to Put Church Members to Work.* F. H. Revell Co., 1963.

Howse, W. L., *The Church Staff and Its Work.* Nashville: Broadman Press, 1959.

Niebuhr, H. Richard, *The Purpose of the Church and Its Ministry.* New York: Harper and Row, 1956.

Powell, Robert R., *Managing Church Business through Group Procedures.* Englewood Cliffs, New Jersey: Prentice-Hall, Inc., 1964.

Robert, General Henry M., *Robert's Rules of Order Revised.* New York: Scott, Foresman and Co., 1951.

Schleh, Edward C., *Executive Management of Personnel.* Englewood Cliffs, New Jersey: Prentice-Hall, Inc., 1958.

St. Clair, Robert James, *Neurotics in the Church.* Westwood, New Jersey: Fleming H. Revell Co., 1963.

Sweet, Herman J., *The Multiple Staff in the Local Church.* Philadelphia: Westminster Press, 1963.

The Pastor as Overseer

1. BIBLICAL TERMS

The word for pastor in the New Testament is *poimēn.* It means a shepherd, one who tends herds or flocks (Eph. 4:11). Pastors guide as well as feed the flock. This ministry of shepherding was committed to the elders who were also overseers (Acts 20:17, 28). Paul says to the elders of the church in Ephesus, "Take heed therefore unto yourselves, and to all the flock, over the which the Holy Spirit hath made you overseers, to feed the church of God, which he hath purchased with his own blood." Peter holds this view, "The elders which are among you I exhort, who am also an elder, and a witness of the sufferings of Christ, and also a partaker of the glory that shall be revealed: Feed the flock of God which is among you, taking the oversight thereof, not by constraint, but willingly; not for filthy lucre, but of a ready mind; Neither as being lords over God's heritage, but being ensamples to the flock" (I Peter 5:1-3). In Acts 20:17, 28 the three terms "elder," "bishop," and "pastor" are brought together. Hence we may conclude that the pastor is an elder or overseer. His work involves tender care and watchful superintendence.

The Greek word for overseer in the New Testament is *episcopos.* It is usually translated bishop. The literal meaning is overseer (*epi,* over, *skopeo,* to look or watch).

The term bishop or overseer indicates the character of the work undertaken. In the New Testament there were to be bishops in every local church (Acts 14:23; 20:17; Phil. 1:1; Titus 1:5; James 5:14). When the singular is used, the passage is describing what a bishop should be (I Tim. 3:2; Titus 1:7). Christ is spoken of as the "bishop of our souls," (I Peter 2:25). The word *episkopē is* rendered "office" in Acts 1:20 (A.V., "bishoprick"); in I Timothy 3:1 "the office of a bishop." It would be better translated "overseership." There is no word for office.

The word *episcopos* in the Septuagint has the generic meaning of "superintendency, oversight, searching" (Num. 4:16; 31:14). The same idea is conveyed in interbiblical literature (I Macc. 1:54; Wisd. 1:6). It is also found in classical Greek. Homer in the *Iliad* applied it to the gods (XXII 255). In Athens the governors of conquered states were called by this name.

In the New Testament it is clear that the appellations bishop, elder, and pastor designate the same office and order of persons (Acts 20:17, 28; Phil. 1:1; I Tim. 3:1, 8; Titus 1:5, 7; I Peter 5:1, 2). Strong quotes Conybeare and Howson, Dexter, and Plumptre in support of this view: "The terms 'bishop' and 'elder' are used in the New Testament as equivalent, – the former denoting (as its meaning of overseer implies) the duties, the latter the rank of the office." It is significant that Jerome held this view. Dexter, in defending Congregationalism, shows that bishop, elder, and pastor are names for the same office: (1) from the significance of the words; (2) from the fact that the same qualifications are demanded from all; (3) from the fact that the same duties are assigned to all; (4) from the fact that the texts held to prove higher rank of the bishop do not support that claim. Plumptre says, "There cannot be a shadow of doubt that the two titles of Bishop and Presbyter were in the Apostolic Age interchangeable." Williston Walker in his *History of the Christian Church* says that this is "the opinion of most modern scholars and seems the probable conclusion." A. H. Newman in his *A Manual of Church History* writes: "The identity of appointed elders and bishops in the Apostolic Age is now commonly admitted by Roman Catholic and Anglican writers and is insisted upon by scholars in general."

The name presbyter or elder, familiar to the Jews, signifies their age and place in the church. The other term bishop or overseer refers to their office. But both evidently have reference to the same person. The office is defined as "ruling" (Rom. 12:8), "overseeing" (Acts 20:17, 28; I Peter 5:2), caring for the flock of God (Acts 20:28). The Greek word *archein,* which means "to rule" in the hierarchical sense, is never used.

Stagg quotes Knox who suggests that the earliest Jewish Christian communities closely followed the Jewish pattern whereby each community was governed by elders (cf. (James 5:14; Rev. 4:4; Acts 20:17). He also intimates that the term *episkopos,* bishop or overseer, was employed sometimes to make intelligible to Gentiles the meaning of *presbuteros,* elder. He says further that elder was a rather inclusive term, used for elders who supervised and elders who served, the seven of Acts 6:3-6 being an enlargement of the body of elders. The elders who presided came to be designated bishops, while the elders who served came to be deacons.

If this be a correct understanding of "elder" as the inclusive term, it would explain why those appointed in the newly formed churches were called "elders" (cf. Acts 14:23); and why in Acts 20:17 those are called elders who actually function as bishops and pastors (Acts 20:28). It would also account for the fact that the varied functions of visiting, praying for and anointing the sick are by James attributed to the elders (James 5:14 f.). In this usage elder described all the functions later attributed to bishops and deacons.

Newman thinks the overseer was chosen from the elders: "It was not uncommon that among the presbyters of a church some one was so eminent for gifts and for elevation of character as to acquire the practical leadership of the body. The permanent chairman of the board of presbyters became the president or bishop of the second century, and his position was analogous to that of a modern congregational pastor."

2. PASTORAL DUTIES

The New Testament presents the pastor, elder, or bishop as a spiritual minister and not as an ecclesiastical dignitary. When referring to the Gentiles' exercising lordship and authority Christ says, "Not so shall it be among you" (Matt. 20:26). He sets the standard for greatness when he says, "the Son of Man came not to be ministered unto, but to minister," and that "whosoever would become great among you shall be your minister [servant]." There is no primacy among the followers of Christ for Jesus Christ himself is the chief corner stone (Eph. 2:20). Peter referred to himself as a fellow elder and not as a monarchical bishop (I Peter 5: 1). The organization and history of the early church establish this view of simplicity. In Acts 1:20, the Revised Version corrects the rendering "bishopric" (given by the King James translators, who were officers of the Anglican Church) to "office," thus relieving the verse of possible ecclesiastical pretensions. The apostles, prophets, evangelists, elders, deacons, pastors and teachers were leaders in the early church, but they exercised their authority in a spiritual, not hierarchical manner.

The pastor of a church is the spiritual leader and minister. His functions are executive and not legislative. Christ is the only lawgiver. In fulfilling this office, the manner and spirit of the pastor's work are of supreme importance. Specifically, the functions of pastors in the New Testament were the administration of discipline, the settlement of disputes among Christians, the conducting of public services, the administration of the ordinances, the supervision of charities, and the general oversight of the church community. Preaching and teaching were also a part of his duties. In modern churches with complex organizational structures and many staff members, it is necessary for the pastor to give general oversight and supervision. A pastor is to be an example to his flock in all things. They are to learn from him in word and deed. Both pastor and people should keep ever before them the major objective of winning men to faith in the Lord Jesus Christ.

3. DEVELOPMENT OF EPISCOPAL IDEA

The episcopal form of church government is the rule of the bishops. Ordination of other church officers can be done only by a bishop who claims descent from apostolic or subapostolic times. This rule is followed in the Orthodox churches in the East, the Roman Catholic Church, and the Anglicans. According to Rome as finally expressed in the Council of Trent, and to the episcopal idea in general, the hierarchical organization, which originated in the third century, existed from the beginning in the New Testament church. But as seen above this position is untenable. The New Testament knows nothing of a centralized authority or a hierarchical organization.

How did the episcopal system come into being? The leadership of the church in the New Testament is based on the gifts of the Spirit. God gave "some apostles; and some, prophets; and some, evangelists; and some, pastors and teachers." The local churches had elders and deacons who supervised and directed the work of the congregation, administered its charity, took care of the sick, and saw to it that services were held regularly. But the early church organization was not centered in office and in law, but in the special gifts of the Spirit. The teaching and preaching, the administration of the ordinances were conducted by the "gifted men" in the congregation. An elder would teach, preach, and administer the ordinances, but he did so primarily because he had the "gift." Teaching, preaching, and administration were not confined legally to any specific office.

At the beginning of the second Christian century, a change took place. A general lack of confidence in the special gifts of the Spirit, a desire for more specific order, and a pressing disregard for proper safeguard against heresy, resulted in a gradual transfer of the preaching, the teaching and the administration of the ordinances from the "gifted men" to the local elders. Perhaps these elders were elected because they possessed some of the special gifts, particularly the gift of teaching. The official functions were now performed by elders only. The ministry of the Word and ordinances became official, which was the beginning of the distinction between "clergy" (chosen ones) and the "laity" (masses).

Important changes occurred in the second and third centuries. The government by a group of elders gave way to a single head, the bishop. The election of the bishop became a legal matter and he alone had the right to preach, teach, and administer the ordinances. It was believed that he was endowed and appointed by God to be the leader of the congregation. The presence of the bishop or his representative was now essential to every valid act of the congregation. In fact, without the bishop there could be no church. In order to be a church, a group of believers must have a bishop and anyone who claimed to be a Christian must be subject to a bishop. The church of the people became the church of the bishops. Outside of this church there was no salvation. Personal communion with God, and the assurance of the presence of Christ could be experienced only by strict adherence to certain outward forms. This momentous departure not only involved a change in the conception of the church and its organization but also a change of faith. To have communion with God one must be in communion with the bishops. The original spiritual priesthood of all believers surrendered to the special priesthood of the clergy.

The Teaching of the Twelve Apostles is a document written to Christians. The date assigned to it ranges from A.D. 80 to 160. It directs: "Appoint for yourselves, therefore, bishops and deacons worthy of the Lord, men who are meek and not lovers of money, and true and approved; for unto you they also perform the service of the prophets and teachers. Therefore despise them not; for they are your honorable men along with the prophets and teachers." Clement of Rome wrote of those in the church at Corinth who had rebelled against their "appointed presbyters." He also spoke of "those who have offered the gifts of the bishop's office" as presbyters.

Ignatius (110-117) has been called the monarchical bishop of Antioch. He exalts in every way the authority of the local monarchical bishop in the churches of Ephesus, Magnesia, Tralles, Philadelphia, and Smyrna. In four of the churches he mentions the bishop by name. Ignatius saw the monarchical bishop as the rallying point of unity and the best opponent of heresy. He makes no appeal to apostolic succession.

By 160, monarchical bishops were well-nigh universal. Cyprian of Carthage (195-258) had a strong formative influence upon the development of church government. A typical high-church man of the epoch, he is said to have done more for the development of hierarchical views than any other man. He said that "The Church is constituted of bishops, and every act of the Church is controlled by these leaders." "Whence thou shouldst know that the bishop is in the Church, and the Church in the bishop, and he who is not with the bishop, is not in the Church." "The bishops are the successors of the apostles, and are chosen by the Lord himself, and are induced into their office as leaders or pastors. The bishop is not only the successor of the historic apostolate, and hence the legitimate teacher of the apostolic tradition, but he is also the inspired prophet, endowed with the 'charismata' or special gifts of the Spirit."

It is admitted by those who espouse the episcopal form of church government that this system is not clearly defined in the New Testament. They say that due allowance is not generally made for the attitude of the apostles and early Christians. It is further stated that the first century Christians were looking for the speedy return of Christ, and consequently did not organize the church in its infancy, as it was afterward found necessary to do. But the fact remains that the episcopal or hierarchical organization is not found in the New Testament.

Nevertheless, the episcopal system developed. What does history say about the wisdom or practical value of it? Throughout Christian history there have been grave abuses of the powers of the episcopal office. At the time of the Reformation, there was a great rebellion against the bishops. They had come to be great, temporal lords immersed in schemes of political and material aggrandizement, and often actually leading their armies in times of war. Many bishops were proud and arrogant, forgetful of their duties to care for the flock with divine patience and infinite love. There is ample evidence in history favoring the New Testament pattern of spiritual democracy in the churches under the headship of Jesus Christ.

BIBLIOGRAPHY

The Ante-Nicene Fathers, Vols. I, V.

Ayer, J. C., Jr., *A Source Book for Ancient Church History.*

The International Standard Bible Encyclopedia, Vol. I.

Newman, A. H., *A Manual of Church History,* Vol. I.

Qualben, Lars P., *A History of the Christian Church.*

Strong, A. H., *Systematic Theology.*

Stagg, Frank, *New Testament Theology.*

Thayer, J. H., *Greek-English Lexicon of the New Testament.*

Vine, W. E., *An Expository Dictionary of New Testament Words.*

Walker, Williston, *A History of the Christian Church.*

The Pastor as Teacher

As we study the New Testament to see what are the sacred duties of the pastor we find that the Lord has indeed called a pastor to an awesome task. The duties are many, the privileges wonderful, the responsibilities staggering. But the opportunities for serving God and helping our fellow men are most remarkable. One of the most exciting, inviting, needed, and appreciated assignments our Lord gave to his pastors is that of teaching. It is enlightening to note how the apostle Paul puts it in Ephesians 4:11. The Lord called "some to be apostles, some prophets, some evangelists, some pastors and teachers." He here refers to various assignments Christ has given in his church. Some are to be prophets, some apostles, some evangelists. But then he puts "pastor" and "teacher" together. This is very revealing. We know that some have been given unusual gifts for the regular class room instruction who are in a special sense "teachers," giving full time to classrooms in schools, colleges, and seminaries. Yet, we note that for the ministry, for the congregations, for the "building up of the body of Christ" the Lord appointed leaders (pastors) who were to be teachers as well as preachers and shepherds of the flock. In other words, teaching was to be a vital part of a pastor's ministry, for there are multitudes who must be "taught" who cannot be reached in classrooms of any school.

This role of teacher as well as preacher and leader is further brought out in II Timothy 1:11 where Paul says, "I was appointed a preacher. . . and teacher." In I Timothy 4:13 and 16 Paul tells young pastor Timothy that his duties include "reading of Scripture, preaching and teaching." In verse 16 he tells this pastor to give special heed to himself and to his teaching. In Titus 2:1 Paul tells pastor Titus that among his main tasks as a pastor, a very important one, is to teach sound doctrine.

The pastor's call gives him much opportunity for proclamation of the Word of God as a prophet and preacher from the pulpit. He is to proclaim and preach the unsearchable riches of God. He is to warn, exhort, and rebuke with authority. These things he ought to do, and not leave the important work of teaching undone. The pastor will find innumerable opportunities to bring God's message to men through sermons on many occasions. But while he is thus busy with sermons and preaching let him fully as much sense his call to rejoice in the privilege of and grasp every opportunity to teach and explain the great doctrines of the faith once delivered to the saints.

The true pastor is in the ministry because he is convinced he was called to it and commissioned by the Lord Jesus. So he earnestly studies the Word of the Lord and then seeks to preach and teach as his Lord teaches in the Word. But he remembers well that Peter says that Christ set us an example that we should follow in his steps. So the pastor studies his Lord's ministry, as well as that of his chief apostle Paul, to see how the Lord and Paul carried out their ministry. He finds that often both Jesus and Paul took their opportunities to stand before large groups and preach sermons. But it is most interesting to see how very often both the Lord and Paul were with small groups where one or more questions were asked. Then in answering these questions a teaching situation at once developed and deep and profound mysteries of the kingdom were explained, or further explained in answer to further questions. This prompts the pastor to look for and use the many similar opportunities that come his way to be a good teacher of the word.

1. THE PASTOR TEACHING HIS TEACHERS

Opportunities for teaching which present themselves to a pastor are many. I serve in the Lutheran Church, which has always stressed the need of a teaching ministry.

Our national boards are regularly arranging for district or area conferences on methods and materials to improve our teaching ministry. Some of this is in the specific area of Sunday School teaching. To such conferences we try to bring with us our Sunday School teachers, and any others who may desire to help us as pastors in the work of teaching both young and old the great truths of God.

Following such area conferences we as pastors meet with our own teaching staff and in turn are "teachers" to our teachers to help them in our total teaching ministry to the congregation. This becomes a challenge as well as a great privilege for the pastor to exercise his call to be a teacher of the Word. Here he must instruct his teachers on the importance of standing on the solid doctrines of the church. He must help his teachers guard against simply an easy pietistic "preaching" of good church morals and following Jesus. His teachers need help to sense their great privilege in helping their pupils learn and hold the outstanding doctrines of the church as re-emphasized so clearly in the Reformation and the earlier great Christian creeds.

2. THE PASTOR'S CATECHETICAL CLASS

To prepare young people for full membership in the church is one of the very specific obligations of the pastor as teacher. In the Lutheran Church this is usually referred to as "The Confirmation Class." The theory back of this teaching is as follows. Our people bring their children to the Lord as infants in the sacrament of baptism, through which we believe the child becomes a member of the body of Christ. The child is then to be nurtured in the Christian faith in its home and in the Sunday School. When this child reaches the eighth grade he enters the pastor's catechism class. The pastor meets for an hour and fifteen minutes to two hours each week with this class. In 1965 the Synodical Board of Education urged pastors to have this catechumen class begin with seventh graders and run for three school years. Then at the end of October, when the child is in the tenth grade, he is welcome to come to the altar with others in his class for the service of "Confirmation." The Confirmation Service is not "graduation," but a service in which each child in turn makes a short confession of his personal faith in Christ. He restates in his own words the declaration of faith in Christ which his parents made for him when he was brought as a child to Christ in baptism. But if the pastor and, or, the the catechumen feels he is not ready at heart to make this confession he is encouraged to pray about it and perhaps continue in the class another year until he is more ready both in mind and in heart to declare this faith in and commit his life to Jesus Christ.

Brief reflection permits one readily to see the great opportunities for the pastor as a teacher in this area with his young people. Here are youth just approaching age sixteen, the year of the highest rate of lasting decisions to follow and serve the Christ. Youth are very impressionable at this age and the young person here has one of the greatest opportunities to learn the "whole counsel of God" and come face to face with the claim of God on his life. In the Lutheran Church, Martin Luther's "Small Catechism" with additional studies or explanation and Scriptural references is used. Thus the youth learn the great doctrines of Christian faith, and memorize and analyze many Bible texts. In this way the pastor can teach his youth and lead them to know the claims of the Christ and consecrate their lives to him.

3. THE MEMBERSHIP CLASS FOR ADULTS

While some churches have been quite hasty about accepting into full membership almost anyone who attends a few Sundays and then applies for membership, the Lutheran churches, as well as many others, ask that all such adults shall first receive instruction in church membership. In this instruction the conscientious pastor will go far beyond a mere cursory explanation of the church and outward show of devotion and loyalty to it. He here has one of the finest opportunities for evangelism and soul winning which come to him.

In such an adult instruction class the pastor will most often not have a very large group, enabling him to give careful attention to helping those of different religious backgrounds. Here he will often have professional people, highly educated people, as well as the more common and less highly trained in the same class. But the pastor need have no difficulty deciding what to teach or how to approach such a class. All people at heart need the same fundamental gospel, that "Christ died for our sins according to the Scriptures" and that "God was in Christ reconciling the world unto himself."

Let the pastor, therefore, seek out people of every background and training around him, invite them to his class, and then sincerely and plainly present the most fundamental doctrines of the Holy Bible and he will often see folks thus "redeemed, restored, forgiven." Let the Pastor not despair if he does not succeed in sweeping in large groups as a result of a short "evangelistic" or "revival" crusade. Some of the most lasting results in evangelism have come through these instruction classes. Let the pastor faithfully teach and explain the "whole counsel of God" to such inquiring adults, for here is a "field white unto harvest." From such classes have come some of the finest Christian workers and leaders in our congregations.

4. BIBLE STUDIES FOR CHURCH AUXILIARIES

Numerous opportunities come to the Pastor to be a teacher for the several women's groups, the men's organizations, young adults, couples clubs, etc., in the congregation. Most of these organizations, especially the women's auxiliaries, have their special programs they wish to carry out, as well as considerable business to transact regarding projects they carry on for church extension and promotion. However, many pastors have found all these groups very willing to have a time for definite teaching of the Scriptures and so they welcome brief Bible studies as a definite part of their programs. Sometimes there may be some willing and able Bible teachers among the membership who can give such Bible studies. But more often it becomes the pastor's responsibility and privilege to be on hand to give these studies. Here he can give consecutive studies in Bible books, or topics of special interest to various groups. The pastor who loves his place as a teacher can find many interesting series of topics as well as chapter by chapter Bible studies for this work. With these groups he would have contact with most of his people and has wonderful opportunities to serve as a teacher of the word.

5. THE PASTOR'S BIBLE CLASS

Martin Luther put the work of preaching the gospel at the top of all vocations, considering it the highest calling to which God will call a mortal. Then he put teaching in second place. It is not strange then that the church not only places great stress on preaching, but also stresses to every pastor that he is to be "apt to teach." Besides openings for teaching as mentioned above the pastor has excellent opportunities for his role as teacher in the Sunday morning pastor's class for adults. A similar pastor's class held some mid-week evening can also be an effective way for the pastor to reach and teach the Word to his people. Usually the pastor has a full hour for each of these classes, hence has ample time to invite questions and discussion. Occasionally certain topics are chosen for study in these classes, such as prayer, the working of the Holy Spirit, personal soul-winning, science and Scripture, and similar topics. However, here are excellent opportunities also to go into Bible Book studies, chapter by chapter to take his people through many of the books of the Bible.

A new method for such study has recently been developed in the Lutheran Church. It is now spreading rapidly among other denominations. It is called the "Bethel Series." The pastor himself first has a very intensive course of study for two weeks. The next October he gathers a small group of his people who are willing to spend several months, once a week, in very intensive Bible study and training. It involves much memory and outlining of Scripture. These people the next fall are the pastor's "Bethel Teachers." Each teacher has a class of fifteen or twenty Bible students from the congregation who also "sign up" to take this intensive course for two years. The pastor continues to supervise the teaching and teaches more in his class who in turn become teachers. This method of study has proven so successful that some congregations which had only thirty-five in the midweek class now have 150 to 300 each week. This has developed great interest in Bible study, and many of these people now crowd the pastor's Bible class on Sunday mornings, eager to go deeper into the Word, to ask more questions, and to share their Christian experiences. Anyone interested in learning more of this method should write to Bethel Lutheran Church, Madison, Wisconsin.

6. SUMMER CONFERENCES AND BIBLE CAMPS

These give many pastors unusually fine opportunities to serve as teachers of the Word to hundreds of youth. Often such camps are also held for family groups, or for adults, and thus again the pastor for a week or two each summer may be their teacher. Such groups going out to some lakeside or mountain camp are usually very eager to study the Scriptures. Here the pastor may have many extra hours of questions and answers in "open forum" sessions.

7. TEACH THE GREAT DOCTRINES OF THE WORD OF GOD

It is the pastor's sacred duty to see to it that his people are taught the great doctrines of the Bible. There is no such thing as "undogmatic Christianity." The Reformation of the sixteenth century brought the pastor his supreme opportunity to teach the Word to a people that now were to have the Word of God in their possession in the language they could read and grasp. Out of this sacred holy book the Reformers brought the great dogmas of the Christian faith. But "When the last great confession of the Reformed Churches was written at Westminister, the feet of those who would bury the heritage of the Reformation were at the door" (*Christianity Today,* Oct. '65).

While the true pastor will teach an evangelical experiential Christianity, he will guard against giving up the great dogmas of the church. Much is heard today that the decisive encounter between God and man takes place no longer in the events of sacred history but in the immediate experience of the soul. To many today what matters is not that Christ was born in Bethlehem (by some considered a legend) but that he is born in me today (of which I am to be sure by trusting in my pious feelings).

While a true pious evangelical Christian experience must be taught, "Christianity is essentially a dogmatic religion, perhaps better, *the* dogmatic religion. None of the great religions of India or of the ancient world has known anything like a dogmatics. Not even the "testimony" of the Mohammedans or the 'Hear, Israel' of Judaism (Deut. 6:4, cf. I Cor. 8:6) is 'dogma' in the sense of the Christian Church" (*Christainity Today,* Oct. '65).

Christian dogma is summarized in the great creeds, which a true teaching pastor will faithfully teach his people, while he is teaching Bible books and the whole counsel of God. The great creeds are the binding doctrinal content of the declaration of faith which Christ required from his disciples when he said; "Whom say ye that I am?" He asked the same from his adversaries, saying, "What do you think of Christ? Whose Son is He?" Amid the confusion of many voices in our day belittling doctrine, the true pastor will faithfully teach the doctrines that have been the common heritage of all Christians.

When the time comes, as it is prophesied, that people will not endure sound teaching, but having itching ears, will turn to teachers to suit their own likings, and will turn away from listening to the truth and wander into myths," then the pastor-teacher is to be especially careful to "preach the word, be urgent in season and out of season, convince, rebuke, and exhort, be unfailing in patience and in teaching" (II Tim. 4:2-4). Let the pastor take encouragement from Paul's word to pastor Titus, "as for you, teach what befits sound doctrine" (2:1). This is the pastor's great work as a teacher under the guidance and inspiration of God's Holy Spirit.

BIBLIOGRAPHY

Bodensieck, J., *The Encyclopedia of The Lutheran Church,* Vol. I. Minneapolis: Augsburg Publishing House, 1965.

Christian Education Monographs, *The Pastor in Sunday School, Leadership,* and *Board of Education.* Glen Ellyn, Ill.: Scripture Press, 1966.

Gerberding, G. H., *The Lutheran Pastor.* Minneapolis: Augsburg Publishing House, 1915.

Kurth, Erwin, *Catechetical Helps.* St. Louis: Concordia Publishing House, 1961.

Storvick, Hortence, *We Learn to Teach.* Minneapolis: Augsburg Publishing House, 1957.

Streng, William D., *The Faith We Teach.* Minneapolis: Augsburg Publishing House, 1962.

The Pastor as Friend

"Let me live in a house by the side of the road and be a friend to man."

(Sam Walter Foss)

A minister of the gospel will be a friend to every man. He serves one who was a friend of all, even publicans and sinners. It is impossible to represent him and not be a friend to man, and the minister who becomes so busy that he has no time to do so loses a vital part of his ministry. Even his sermons, though beautiful, will not be as meaningful.

The minister as friend will love people genuinely. He will love them for their own sake with no ulterior motive. This means taking time to visit with people, and being interested enough to learn about them. The minister as friend will know people, and will call them by name. Jesus spoke of himself as the Good Shepherd: "The sheep hear his voice, and he calls his own sheep by name . . . and the sheep follow him, for they know his voice" (John 10:3, 4). The minister must know peoples' names, their joys and sorrows, their triumphs and defeats. He must always emphasize the needs of others, showing such genuine interest in and concern for their welfare that they will trust him and have confidence in him. He will be concerned about the environment in which people live, and will therefore engage in the struggle to create conditions in which all men can enjoy the abundant life in Jesus Christ.

1. THE MINISTER AS FRIEND OF CHILDREN

Jesus placed great emphasis on children. "Let the children come unto me, and do not hinder them; for to such belongs the kingdom of God" (Luke 18:16). The minister must always be interested in the children around him, knowing them well enough to recognize them and to call them by name. He must be known as a friend of children, not only in his church, but also in his neighborhood. This is a relationship children will remember and cherish as long as they live. It may be a reason they will want to be active in the church in later life.

In the church the minister ought to visit the Sunday School classes where children are studying, spending enough time there to enter into their lesson discussions and explaining the great truths of the church from time to time. He ought also to conduct childrens' training classes in the Christian life, acting as a friend who points the way.

The minister should call in the homes of his people in order to know the environment in which the children are growing, and, thus to understand them and to learn how to be of greatest help to them. When death comes in the home, he needs to help the children understand its Christian meaning. When the child is in trouble, he should extend his help, seeking ways to show him the love of God while not trying to circumvent justice.

2. THE MINISTER AS FRIEND OF TEEN-AGERS

Since Jesus was deeply interested in young people so the minister must also be interested in youth. This is the age when so many are lost to the church. The minister must, therefore, study this age group — listen to their music, hear what they say, read what they read, and study what they write. Without understanding them it is impossible to be their friend. Only as he knows them well will they think of him as one to whom they can turn in their need.

At this age, the young person needs much sympathy and understanding. When young people get into trouble, the minister is needed more than ever. He must stand with the youngster when he stands in the court with a willingness to help redeem the wayward youth, even sometimes accepting the responsibilities of having the boy put on probation to him.

3. THE MINISTER AS FRIEND OF SERVICEMEN

Every church has some of its young people in the armed services, and often there is a group of service personnel in the area where the church is located. As in the case of students, the minister should write these young people away from home, and keep writing regularly even when they do not reply. He must also arrange to visit these young people when they are at home on leave, getting to know them well enough so that they can feel free to talk with him about their personal problems.

The church ought to provide special social

and study opportunities for these young men who may be stationed in the area, arranging for them to be guests in the homes of church members and occasionally in the minister's home. Godless forces are constantly wooing these young people. They need encouragement to maintain the ideals they learned in their home and church.

For the boys who face the draft, the minister as a friend will provide information about branches of the service, and will advise any young men who feel led to declare themselves as conscientious objectors.

4. THE MINISTER AS FRIEND OF YOUNG ADULTS

Throughout our cities there are thousands of employed young people, some married, others unmarried. These young adults face problems others don't face, living as they do in apartments away from home. Supervision is lacking; so without restraints, and because they are making money, they face temptations to "live it up" beyond any other group. Often employed single young adults are lonely, craving companionship and seeking it wherever they can find it. The church must provide it, or they will go where it is available, even that of the wrong kind. The minister must find ways to reach them, though this is not always easy. It may be necessary to arrange for appointments beforehand.

The newly married couples present a different opportunity. They are often so absorbed with each other that they are not interested in getting to know others; yet the minister must find ways to relate to them in order to be available to serve them whenever they need him. Therefore, the minister, or his wife, might teach a young married couples' class, invite them to get together in the manse, and call on them in their own home. They too need the minister as friend.

5. THE MINISTER AS FRIEND OF MARRIED PEOPLE

Because of the many stresses and strains in married life, married people need to know the minister as their friend. If he performs their marriage ceremony, he should spend time with them prior to the ceremony, counseling with them and preparing them for marriage. Then they will know him, and will naturally seek him in time of need. This helps them to understand too that wherever they live, the minister is ready to serve them as a friend who cares.

When marital trouble comes the minister must be available to be a good listener, and then, recognizing his limitations, he must know where to send them for the specialized help they need. Therefore, the minister must know something about the agencies and sources of help available in his community. The minister must always indicate equal interest in each mate, and make himself available to help each one personally. Sometimes he will be the only person who can get the separated couple back together. If the marriage breaks up, the minister must provide understanding for each of the parties, for this is a most difficult time in their lives.

Nothing is more important in ministering as friend to married people than the assurance that they can discuss any problem, even the most intimate, without fear of being betrayed. They must be able to trust the minister to keep personal things confidential.

6. THE MINISTER AS FRIEND OF THE ELDERLY

A large segment of our population consists of elderly persons, and the number is increasing. Old age can be a difficult time in life as the person struggles with loneliness, limited income, and sometimes physical afflictions. Our society is helping to alleviate the suffering of the elderly through the creation of retirement, convalescent, nursing, and rest homes where elderly people can feel accepted and receive the necessary care required at this stage of life.

The minister can show that he is a friend of the elderly by visiting them regularly wherever they are and by arranging for special opportunities of worship and study for them. He must never neglect the shut-ins of the church, but recognize their needs, and seek to help fulfill them. The minister needs to know the source of financial and other kinds of help for the elderly, so that he can advise them wisely in their times of need.

Many churches have clubs for the elderly, meeting once a week or more, often with a variety of programs. Elderly folk do not require a great amount of space, because they prefer table games; so a center can be provided by almost any church. Members of the church ought to be organized to call on the elderly regularly. They also need to be listed for prayer at church services.

With opportunities now available for churches to sponsor retirement homes and to provide other services to the elderly, church leaders need to consider seriously becoming involved in such projects making it possible for old folk to enjoy peace and security in their latter days.

7. THE MINISTER AS FRIEND OF THE HANDICAPPED

Many people in our society are handicapped, physically and/or mentally. These folk need love and encouragement. Life is so difficult for them. Often they feel as if they are alone, that nobody cares. Jesus set the example for the minister in his constant concern for the halt, the blind and the sick.

Some churches provide special services for the handicapped, such as worship in the sign language, social meetings for the handicapped, special transportation to the church for various functions. (Legal protection needs to be provided for people who provide such transportation in case of an accident.) Recovery, Inc., for those who have been in mental institutions is an important group for churches to sponsor.

The minister as friend needs to know what sources are available to help these persons in their need, and must always be able to arrange for specialized help. Then he ought to see those who are handicapped as often as possible. He should work with institutions in his community that seek to serve the handicapped, and will encourage his members to relate to them in order to be used of God in this effective ministry.

8. THE MINISTER AS FRIEND OF THE DISADVANTAGED

There is a great concentration of poor, disadvantaged persons living in our cities. The minister must relate to the poor, for, although they cannot provide financial strength for his church, they need the ministry of the church more than others. They need more than a Thanksgiving basket and a Christmas remembrance. Some churches keep a supply of good used clothing to give to those in need, provide food in case of emergencies, and even some money to be used with discretion in providing relief of various kinds in times of great need.

The minister must always seek to understand the loneliness, the despair, the discouragement and frustations that afflict the poor. Among these is the problem of unemployment. The minister should know where employment centers are located, and relate his people to them. Other disadvantaged people are those imprisoned in city ghettos. These he can help by working for opportunities of equality in terms of employment, education, housing, etc. The minister cannot help engaging in the struggle for social righteousness and justice, even when doing so stirs up opposition, even in his own church.

The minister must also befriend the criminal, the hoodlum, the delinquent, and the ex-convict. He needs to make himself available to minister in jails and prisons, and then to be used of God in helping the convict to be rehabilitated. This will require much patience, faith and love, but as a representative of Jesus Christ, the minister has no choice except to serve such persons.

With the number of alcoholics increasing in our society, the minister must also be involved in dealing with the problem of alcoholism and in ministering to the alcoholic. He must have contact with Alcoholics Anonymous and other organizations that can help the man enslaved by this vicious evil. Some churches have such groups meeting in their building, with the minister available to serve whenever called upon.

The minister must also be a friend of the narcotics addict. Drug addiction is exceedingly hard to break. In some communities there is a fellowship of Addicts Anonymous, similar to Alcoholics Anonymous that can be of help.

The prostitute also needs the friendly help of a minister. He should, therefore, let the people in his neighborhood, including the night people, know that he is available to help, and how he can be reached. It is never enough, however, just to help the victim; the cause must also be dealt with. Hence, the minister must be involved in contending with the overemphasis our society in placing on sex.

Another group of troubled persons who need the minister as friend is the beggar, the "professional bum," who comes to the church door regularly for a hand-out. It is doubtful that the minister's schedule will permit him to spend the time required to minister to these persons, especially when several come to the city church door each day, and it is doubtful that a hand-out helps such persons, especially if it encourages them to continue their way of life, enabling them to go from church to church seeking hand-outs. A clearing house could be set up among churches, with such persons being sent to the center to be "screened" and helped. Often this can be done through the Salvation Army, with each church paying the costs of the help given to each person sent to the center.

9. THE MINISTER AS FRIEND OF THE LONELY, THE SICK, AND THE BEREAVED

The minister must spend time every day with the sick and the lonely of his church, and must always be close to those who face bereavement and must minister to the dying. It means much to the sick for a minister to come with comforting and encouraging words of Scripture and simple, earnest prayer. When one is to undergo major surgery, a visit from the minister the night before surgery is to be performed can be most helpful. Follow-up visits will help the sick to be patient and to have faith and hope.

It is not enough to visit with the bereaved at the time of the bereavement. Visits later are perhaps even more necessary when the full impact of the death of a loved one comes with great force upon the bereaved. When a person is facing death, the minister who helps such a person discover the real meaning of death in Jesus Christ becomes a friend for eternity.

BIBLIOGRAPHY

Barclay, Wm., *Fishers of Men.* Philadelphia: The Westminster Press, 1966.

Green, Michael, *Called to Serve.* Philadelphia: The Westminster Press, 1964.

Hall, Clarence W., *Adventures for God.* New York: Harper and Brothers, 1959.

Howe, Reuel L., *Herein Is Love.* Philadelphia: The Judson Press, 1961.

King, Henry C., *The Laws of Friendship.* New York: The Macmillan Co., 1919.

Marney, Carlyle, *The Suffering Servant.* Nashville: Abingdon Press, 1965.

Price, Eugenia, *The Burden Is Light.* Westwood, N. J.: Fleming H. Revell Co., 1955.

Rutenber, Culbert G., *The Reconciling Gospel.* Valley Forge: Judson Press, 1960.

Stone, John Timothy, *Foot-steps in a Parish.* New York: Chas. Scribner's Sons, 1908.

Thomas, D. Reginald, *Love So Amazing.* Westwood, N. J.: Fleming H. Revell Co., 1951.

Turnbull, Ralph G., *A Minister's Obstacles.* Westwood, N. J.: Fleming H. Revell Co., 1964.

SECTION 8

STEWARDSHIP

"It is required in stewards, that a man be found faithful."
— I Corinthians 4:2

The Minister in Giving and Benevolences

A minister who serves a church in our contemporary society is called to be an exponent and example of Christian stewardship. However effective he may be as a preacher and pastor he will fail to meet the highest challenge of his calling if he does not translate a recognition of God as the Creator and Redeemer of all of life into a sense of holy trust for everything which God gives to men. Stewardship is the end result of a consciousness of the reality of God's creative goodness and of his presence in the world.

Jesus of Nazareth came teaching stewardship. He used the words "steward" and "stewardship" many times in his teachings to emphasize the privilege and responsibility of man in his relationship to God. In his parables he frequently used the idea of a steward as picturing the relationship between the Creator and his creation.

Stewardship has sometimes been a lost word in theological and religious thought. Many ministers have regarded the concept as "old-fashioned." It is well to remember that many of the traditional Christian terms are similarly old-fashioned. The kingdom of God is out of date in a generation when thrones and kingdoms have disappeared before the march of democratic ideas. Yet the word kingdom expresses better than any other the teaching of Jesus concerning the hope that the world may be transformed. The cross is outmoded in a century when men have devised new ways to inflict torture and death upon those whom they regard as enemies. Yet the cross will forever remind humanity of the price which was paid to demonstrate everlastingly the love of God for mankind.

Stewardship is an essential element in the Christian heritage. It was the word which has best pictured the relationship of God to man, and man to his God.

Early in the record of the New Testament

church we find that the word "stewardship" was widely understood and accepted. In First Corinthians Paul wrote: "Let a man so account of us, as of ministers of Christ, and stewards of the mysteries of God. Moreover, it is required in stewards that a man be found faithful" (4:1-2). Later in the same letter he said: "If I do this of mine own will, I have a reward: but if not of mine own will, I have a stewardship intrusted to me" (9:17).

The New Testament sets forth no more challenging picture of the followers of Christ than to refer to those men as stewards who have enrolled under the banner of the Master.

1. THE MEANING OF STEWARDSHIP

Three basic truths are included in the concept of stewardship. *First,* the word implies that someone is the owner. Jesus reminded his followers that God is not only creator and sustainer, but he is the owner of all of life. Centuries earlier the Psalmist had declared: "The earth is the Lord's, and the fullness thereof, the world and they that dwell therein" (Ps. 24:1).

The early apostles stressed the ownership of God. It was said of the early Christians that "not one of them said that aught of the things which he possessed was his own" (Acts 4:32). The whole of life was a gift of God; he was the creator and the giver of all which man possessed. It belonged to him. The early Christians believed this truth, and lived it as well.

In every generation the preached Word has resulted in a similar faith, even in the midst of material success.

Edward H. Faulkner in his "Plowman's Folly" traces the origin of all of life to the soil. He attributes the sources of man's wealth to the soil, the rainfall, and the sun. Man did not create or invent any of these. If all of life — all that we have and are — originated in these three fundamentals, then man should continually give thanks to the creator God. God has given all of life; he is the owner.

In the *second place,* since God is the owner of all things, then man is a trustee of what he is, and has, and can become. Man is a steward. More is involved than the fact that man ought to be a steward. He is a steward by the very nature of the universe of which he is a part.

A new rebirth of a sense of trusteeship is the best hope for a world in which misery, ignorance, poverty and injustice cast their shadows upon humanity. It requires a recognition by professing Christians that life is sacred, and that what we have must be used wisely and well.

Captain Pipon of the British Navy visited Pitcairn Island in the South Pacific in 1813 and later described the people as follows: "Each person considered that whatever he possessed was for the general good." That spirit has prevailed even until now. The people recognize that they have a stewardship. The island upon which they live is a gift of God, their fellow islanders are sharers of that gift. They are faithful in their stewardship. All of society will be transformed if this experience is repeated in every life, every home, and every community. The fact of God's ownership implies that man has a stewardship which begins with the first consciousness of selfhood and never ends while life remains.

The *third principle* involved in stewardship is the necessity that a steward must give an account of the use which he makes of all that is entrusted to him. In Jesus' well-known parable the owner is insistent in his demand: "Give an account of thy stewardship!" Jesus of Nazareth left no doubt that this testing was to be the experience of every man and woman. Somewhere along the road of life — perhaps many times — a voice from the silence speaks with authority and says, "Give an account of thy stewardship!" The voice may be soft and encouraging; it may be harsh with the remembrance of forgotten obligations. But it is insistent, and inevitable.

No minister can adequately present the Christian concept of stewardship without giving emphasis to judgment. However unpleasant the concept may seem to the practicing Christian, it is an essential part of the Biblical and historical understanding of God's relationship to man. The hesitation of the preacher to stress judgment is encouraged by the fact that judgment has usually been associated with guilt and punishment. But the accounting for a Christian steward need not be a feared and awesome day. It can be a day of triumph.

A Christian will welcome an accounting of his stewardship if he has been faithful in the use of his time, his talents, and his means. He will gladly open the records upon which the story of his life is written. He can expect to hear the tribute: "Well done, good and faithful servant" (Matt. 25:23). But if he has been careless and wasteful of his opportunities it is understandable that he may fear the presence of the One who demands an accounting.

2. PHILOSOPHIES WHICH UNDERMINE STEWARDSHIP

The minister who endeavors to lead his people into a deeper awareness of the meaning and obligations of Christian stewardship is immediately confronted by two prevailing personal philosophies which are the antithesis of the Christian point of view.

The first of these is materialism. It is basically the idea that material and physical satisfactions are the final goal and end of life. Materialism is not a problem which is unique in our society. It has been appealing to man in every generation. But the rapid development of man's control over the world of matter has placed a far more abundant store of material goods in the hands of man than was known by any people in the history of civilization.

Stewardship is always an unpleasant burden when the primary interest of man is devoted to the getting and holding of material things. Possessions are not in themselves an evil. Money is not in its nature an enemy of the divine will. God intended money and material things to enrich the lives of his children. If an attitude of stewardship prevails material wealth will be accepted and used with a sense of holy trust. If this outlook on life is neglected then the question of Jesus immediately becomes inevitable, "What is it profited if a man shall gain the whole world, and lose his own soul?" (Matt. 16:26).

The pressure of the material is not always direct. Sometimes the approach is insidious. Often it is expressed in a desire for the ease and luxury which material possessions make possible. In no part of the world is the pressure of the material greater than in the United States. In 1960 the number of manufactured articles in the United States totaled more than 425,000. Compare that figure with those of one hundred years ago when there were only 6,000 articles made and sold in the United States. One hundred years ago the average American had 72 wants and 16 needs; today the average American has 594 wants and 108 articles which he regards as necessities. If the increase in the number of things were a guarantee of greater happiness there might be reason for the Christian minister to accept the principle that material things constitute ultimate values. If the added leisure which has become possible for the average man who benefits from the industrial revolution merely makes him eager for more leisure, or even for a total life of leisure, then something dangerous threatens the society in which the preacher speaks for the eternal.

The minister confronts individuals every day who boast of the comforts of their homes, the speed of their cars, or the amount of money which they have accumulated. The preacher faces an endless battle for the souls of those who are converts to the cult of the material. His strongest ally is a rebirth of stewardship responsibility in those who have declared their allegiance to the God who was revealed in Jesus Christ.

The prophetic message might be more difficult if the average preacher could be convinced that happiness is the end result of the possession of material things. Yet it is evident that those who possess the greater number of luxuries often possess less of the contentment which they hoped to experience. The possessive urge often erodes away their moral and spiritual values. The minister faces a world in which the people he serves are constantly threatened, or are already victimized, by moral and spiritual sickness. He often is driven to a shrill denunciation of material things. He sometimes pleads for "a return to God." Yet the best antidote for the sickness brought about by absorption with physical and material pleasure is a fresh devotion to a life of Christian stewardship – recognizing the source of all of life in the creating power of God, and the need to use his gifts with a sense of holy trust.

The second philosophical concept which claims the devotion of many in our society is humanism. It may be said that humanism is the philosophical result of consuming materialism. It asserts that man will finally overcome the problems of his world by the application of his own intelligence and strength. It holds that faith in God is not necessary in man's battle with the issues which face him. Humanism assumes a confident pose in the power of man to exist and triumph without reference to God. When lust and hatred combine to bring about war he is sometimes disillusioned. Because his faith rests in finite humanity he can only sink into black despair.

Christian stewardship is a practical answer to the blight of humanism. No person who recognizes an obligation to use his gifts wisely and well will remain unaware of God's presence in the world. He will not lose God outside the universe, nor will he glory in the power of man to solve his problems by his own strength. A consciousness of the fact that he has a stewardship will be a daily reminder that man is dependent upon the Creator for the blessings which surround him. He will experience a growing awareness that God is the source of all of life, and he will receive divine power sufficient for each day's need.

3. THE CULTIVATION OF STEWARDSHIP

It is evident that the Protestant ministry has often failed to stress the message of Christian stewardship. The pulpit is persistent in its emphasis upon Christian duty. It is unceasing in its call for the application of the teachings of Jesus to the problems of our society. Its weakness is its failure to indicate the intellectual and spiritual imerative for faithfulness in the awareness of God's creative and sustaining power. A Christian can become as discouraged as any humanist if the urge to virtue is not soundly anchored in an understanding of the providence of God. The idea of stewardship is meaningless unless it begins with a firm faith in the nature of God as the source of all life.

The failure of the church to stress the message of Christian stewardship is reflected in many phases of its activity. It is evident in the increasing percentage of the total population which recognizes no obligation to Christ. While the number of church members has increased, the percentage of the people holding allegiance to Christian principles has decreased. It is seen in the pitifully small portion of the total income of the members of the church which is laid on the altar for Christian causes. It is reflected in the large number of vacancies in positions demanding full-time service for the cause of Christ.

The ministry must bear its share of the responsibility for the failure of the church to be worthy of its stewardship. Often the individual church member has no understanding of the broad and sacred responsibility which is involved in his acceptance of the faith. He often has no conception of the vastness of the trust which was placed upon him when he affirmed his belief in the fatherhood of God.

The widespread neglect of stewardship education and training was revealed in a survey made by the General Board of Lay Activities of the Methodist Church. A questionnaire was sent to a large number of representative pastors in every section of America. One of the questions was worded as follows: "What features of stewardship cultivation have you used that produced definite results?" Most of the answers revealed perplexity as to what was meant by the question. Ninety per cent of those who answered described a stewardship program limited to a concern for budget and finance. The survey made it clear that few pastors make a systematic attempt to interpret Christian obligation in the light of stewardship concepts.

It is probable that a survey of ministers of other religious groups would reveal a similar neglect. Christian stewardship transformed the first century church at a time when there was danger that the early followers of Jesus would be satisfied to await the return of their Lord. A stress upon this essential theme is imperative if the church is to meet the challenge of this changing century.

The witness of numerous individual Christians should be a reminder that an awakened awareness of stewardship obligations holds vast possibilities for the advance of the kingdom. The late Dr. William Mayo, speaking for himself and his brother, said, "The holy money, as we call it, must go into the service of the God whose gifts made it possible, and of the humanity which paid it to us. My brother and I have both put ourselves on salaries. We live within them. The rest belongs to God, and will be used for his service."

No minister of the gospel should hesitate to summon professing Christians to a consecration of their money, their time, and their lives to God. It is an obligation but it involves more than duty. It is the way to victorious living.

4. THE FRUITS OF STEWARDSHIP

Any minister who regularly and systematically trains the members of his church in the obligations of stewardship will be able to measure the results. The fruits of such training can be observed in a new and deeper relationship between a steward and his God, but the results can also be measured in more specific forms. They can be observed in any church and among any group of people.

An acceptance of the stewardship concept will be noticeable in the financial program of the church. No minister can hold before his people the truth that money and possessions are a trust for the strengthening of the individual life and for the extension of the kingdom without something extraordinary happening. The purse is opened because the pocketbook itself is God's.

An emphasis upon stewardship will unlock a reservior of leadership which has never been used for the work of the church. When time and talents are understood to be a loan from God, Christians inevitably ask how best they can utilize their talents and time for the benefit of God's work in the world. In almost every church one can observe a shortage of leadership. People are needed in the church school, in the women's, men's, and youth work. The lack of such leadership can in large measure be satisfied if Christians come to the realization that all of life belongs to God, and that a worthy part of it must be employed in His service.

Furthermore, an emphasis upon stewardship will have an inevitable effect upon the missionary outlook of the church. When God is recognized as the creator of all of life, and the heavenly Father of all the people of the earth, the awakened steward will feel a compelling obligation to share the treasures of faith with those who are less fortunate. The summons to Christian stewardship will never be satisfied until every man and every woman in the world has the opportunity to know and follow Christ.

Finally, the awareness of stewardship obligations is the most effective means to awaken youth to the need to consecrate their lives to full time Christian service – in the ministry, in the mission field, and in other areas of Christian vocation. When young people recognize that all of life belongs to God – that all of life has been loaned by him – it is inevitable that courageous youth in every church will gladly declare: "My life belongs to him: He gave it. I will use it in his service."

The minister has no other key to Christian devotion which can equal the persuasive power of a dedication born out of an awareness of the meaning and acceptance of Christian stewardship.

BIBLIOGRAPHY

Conrad, A., *The Divine Economy*. Grand Rapids: Wm. B. Eerdmans Publishing Co., 1956.

Ely, Virginia, *Stewardship*. New York: Fleming H. Revell, 1962.

Kantonen, Taito, *Theology of Christian Stewardship*. New York: Fleming H. Revell, 1964.

Rolston, Holmes, *Stewardship in the New Testament Church*. Richmond: John Knox Press, 1946.

Thomas, G. Ernest, *To Whom Much Is Given*. New York: Abingdon Press, 1946.

Thompson, T. K., *Stewardship in Contemporary Theology*. New York: Association Press, 1964.

Tithing as an Essential Act of Stewardship

Tithing in its broadest sense means the offering of a proportion, most generally a tenth, of one's material goods to God. Religious practice in every community from ancient times and in every culture has exhibited the custom of offering material possessions in the course of divine worship.

1. TITHING IN THE HISTORY OF THE CHURCH

The history of tithing will be examined and analyzed according to the various motivations, ostensible and real, which have produced both the giving and levying of tithes. Thus people have felt obliged to tithe (1) in order to pay tribute from an inferior to a superior for the support of the priesthood; (2) in order to give thanks for special blessings; (3) in order to care for the poor and needy; and (4) in obedience to a divine economy which will provide for an increase of material blessings from the divine storehouse. In addition we may detect that at times tithes were exacted for the aggrandizement of the fortunes of both clergy and laymen by playing on the credulity of people who were willing to buy their salvation.

The first instance of the tributary tithe is the story of Abram and Melchizedek (Gen. 16:17-20). When Chederlaomer attacked the city of Sodom and took captive Lot, Abram's kinsman, Abram retaliated and routed the aggressors. After the defeat of Chederlaomer Abram met Melchizedek, priest and king of Salem, who brought bread and wine for a sacramental meal in celebration of God Most High to whom thanks was given for delivering Abram's enemies into his hand. Here tribute was acknowledged for the priest of the God who acted in history to favor the triumphant destiny of Abram.

Thanksgiving, not tribute, is the motivation for Jacob in his vow to give a tenth of his goods to the Lord. When he was about to embark upon a precarious journey Jacob made this vow: "If God will be with me, and will keep me in this way that I go, and will give me bread to eat and clothing to wear, so that I come again to my father's house in peace, then the Lord shall be my God, and this stone, which I have set up for a pillar, shall be God's house; and of all that thou givest me I will give the tenth to thee" (Gen. 28:20-22).

This thanksgiving tithe was set down later in the history of Israel as the tithe which was not forced or tributary but a freely willed thank offering. First fruits of flocks and fields were brought to the sanctuary and eaten there as a community festival with families and servants together and the Levitical priests presiding. Every third year the tithe was set aside at home for the benefit of the Levite or stranger who might come to visit, and for the fatherless and the widows. This began a new use of the tithe for charitable purposes, a function which has had tremendous significance in the history of the church until the present day when increasingly government is taking over welfare responsibilities in society.

In addition to the tithe given for the religious festivals in Jerusalem such as Passover, Pentecost and Tabernacles, another tithe was given for the poor, and a third tithe was required for support of the sons of Levi who officiated in the temple at Jerusalem. This is the rabbinical system which is reported in the book of Tobit at a time when the tributary tithe for the priests was collected annually, the festival tithe was due in the first, second and fourth years, and the eleemosynary tithe in the third and sixth years (1:7-8). No tithe was collected in the seventh year since the land lay fallow. Hence although there were three tithes, only two were collected annually.

By the time of Jesus a ridiculous fastidiousness had reduced the practice of tithing to absurdity. The legalism of the Pharisees drew sharp castigation from Jesus for their failure to divide their offering rightly: "But woe to you Pharisees! For you tithe mint and rue and every herb, and neglect justice and the love of God; these you ought to have done without neglecting the others" (Luke 11:42). This critical reference and the fact that tithing is not mentioned anywhere in the epistles of Paul makes it mandatory that we call into question the whole Jewish system of tithing in the light of the gospel. Indeed the early church did not resort to the system of tithes for several centuries even though support of the clergy was recognized from the beginning and alms were given to the poor. The peculiar Christian orientation to the offering is expressed by Irenaeus who described Christians as "those who have received liberty, set aside all their possessions for the Lord's purposes, bestowing joyfully and freely not the less valuable portions of their property" (*Against Heresies* IV, p. xviii).

About the time of Charlemagne, however, the tithe became generally established for the Bishop and clergy, for the poor, and for the support of church property. It was justified by comparing the Christian priests with the Levites even though this lacks exegetical legitimacy inasmuch as priests in the church are presbyters and bishops while the sons of Levi were hieratical. Furthermore enormous practical abuses arose in the late Medieval Period when tithes in some cases became graft money for buying ecclesiastical offices.

The Reformation was largely a repudiation of the scandal of corruption in the high offices of the church. While the evil of simony was routed the church was split asunder and the center of power moved from the church to the state. As the Western world grew more and more secularized the tithe, now collected by the state, was greatly reduced.

Out of this vacuum a new interest in tithing has developed chiefly among laymen who have been inspired by the conviction that God prospers in temporal affairs those who dedicate a definite proportion of their income to his service. They base their belief on Malachi 3:10: "Bring the full tithes into the storehouse, that there may be food in my house; and thereby put me to the test, says the Lord of hosts, if I will not open the windows of heaven for you and pour down for you an overflowing blessing."

2. RIGHT DIVISION OF THE OFFERING

The coming of Jesus has revealed, as in everything else, a new understanding of stewardship. We can see history as the movement of an exciting drama, the climax of which occurs in the third act. It is at this crucial point in the story of salvation that the identity of two characters is disclosed, characters who have been acting in a mysterious way from the beginning but who have been hidden behind strange masks. The Word of God has been speaking and the Spirit of the Lord has been giving life, and because of this dual action and passion of the divine power all creatures have come into being and have moved toward their eternal destiny. But now with the historical incidence of Jesus, Christ and the Holy Spirit become manifest to the elect family of God in a way which radically changes this destiny.

In the first act of the drama of salvation God is found extremely close to the processes of nature. The great pagan religions recognized this with their devotion to fertility and the natural cycle of birth and death. All of life, labor and leisure, found meaning which was expressed through periodic communal festivals of thanksgiving for nature's gifts. Progress and change is abhorrent at this level because there is no thought of an eternal destiny with a real goal in the future. Everything is caught in the cycle of nature which constantly repeats itself. Stewardship becomes a simple matter of dividing a pie. The ethics in such a view rests on the principle of rights in which each man is an island protected by the rule of *suum cuique.* So long as everyone respects what belongs to everybody else justice and peace will be established. And to insure the perpetuation of the system a token offering is brought to the gods with an attitude of appeasement at the least and gratitude at the highest.

This pious awareness of nature's gifts and the need for dividing an offering in recognition of the divine source has sustained men in various civilizations for centuries. High religions and profound philosophies have been built around it from the time of the ancient Indians and Greeks to the present. In modern times some philosophers, like Bergson, Whitehead, and Bernard Meland, have reminded us of the closeness of God to the processes of nature, and in addition they have tried to break out of the static cycle of the ancient immanental view by pointing to a unidirectional process which is proclaimed by the eschatological thrust of the Christian message. For them God is the concrescence of emergent novelty in the creative passage. From this point of view there is no sharp distinction between nature and grace. Indeed grace is conceived as a movement of spirit attending not only the redemptive aspects of humanity, but also with depth and spontaneity grace attends the whole of created realities.

While this philosophy has its appealing depth it still belongs in the first act of the drama. The currently more prestigious philosophy of Paul Tillich even more obviously finds its lines in this act because of his essentially immanental metaphysics. In contrast to the process philosophy of Whitehead, with its place for emergent novelty, however, Tillich holds fast to the more static categories of Plato with his concept of the Ground of Being. As the distinction between the sacred and the secular is wiped out, so the dichotomy between nature and supernature is disallowed. With God as Ground of Being rather than Supreme Being who stands above us, there is an ontological continuity running through all reality. This makes the notion of a divine being coming in the flesh of humanity absurd. The Incarnation, which is the climactic event in the third act of the Christian story, is therefore not appreciated by Tillich, and instead he prefers to look upon Jesus as the example of one who achieved perfect God consciousness. The result of this tradition in theological thinking, all of which is rooted in Schleiermacher, is that a piety of personal stewardship is defined which is limited to grateful response for nature's gifts.

Proof that the story has moved on, however, is demonstrated by a simple observation of the world about us. Man's prowess over nature has changed his life so radically that he no longer sees nature as the giver of his sustenance. Now nature has become only the repository of materials for his artifacts. If he is to be grateful for the real thing in his life, he must be grateful for the intelligence he uses in the manufacture of materials. He lives now, not by the whim of nature for which he formerly shaped his piety as joyful gratitude, but by his inventive genius in manipulating nature. Man limited to a God of natural process or to the Ground of Being is therefore in danger of losing all piety whatever. Being grateful to oneself is scarcely a pattern of piety, especially when this same intelligent self may through fearful miscalculation or defiant greed obliterate all life on this planet.

It is at this point that the revelation of God in the Bible speaks most clearly, calling us out of natural piety into a covenant piety in which our stewardship is directed responsibly to our fellows in the community. Perhaps this is the profound significance of the story of Cain and Abel, in which Cain had to learn the painful lesson that he was his brother's keeper, that right division of his offering included care for others. The stewardship of gratitude for nature's gifts is now replaced by the stewardship of obligation to one's neighbor. Here the second act in the drama of salvation is played with God's covenant with Israel providing the lines of the Torah for the role of stewardship. Now we see God as a person who speaks to his creatures. He is not embedded in the process or being of our reality. He stands over against us in free address. We live by the utterance of his speech and the breath of his Spirit, but since he has made us in his image he never violates our freedom. It is this freedom in which we are addressed as persons which turns simple gratitude into a sense of obligation. When we are obliged to come together, we form communities with law, and as a result history is set on its course.

The ethics of covenant piety rests on the principle of obligation in which all men are brothers in the family which is chosen by God. So long as every member of the family respects his obligation to every other member the family will prosper under the promise of God. "Blessed is the man who walks not in the counsel of the wicked. . . . He is like a tree planted by streams of water, that yields its fruit in its season, and its leaf does not wither. In all that he does, he prospers" (Ps. 1:1, 3). And the offering becomes an obligatory tithe as the legal system becomes more binding. The destiny of the chosen family in history is determined by the faithfulness with which one keeps the covenant. This is no longer a matter of seasonal appeasement or occasional gratitude; this is now ultimate destiny which therefore shapes every moment before God.

But God's revelation does not stop with nature and history. He has come to us in the uniform behavior of the natural process and taught us to be grateful. He has come to us in the unidirectional thrust of history and taught us to be responsible. But he has also come to us in a third act in the unique disclosure of his Son and taught us to be creative as we share his new life in the resurrection community. It is not enough that we recognize our responsible stewardship in the management of the resources God has given us. We must also accept the challenge of the creative development of these resources. We are not only to name and distribute various creatures under our dominion; we are not only to cut up a pie equitably. We must also create and produce new things in a burgeoning economy under the direction of the Spirit.

Man has been trying in his checkered career to tame the wilderness and harness nature. He has been trying to bring order out of the irrational forces of nature and establish a society. Rapidly we are coming to the point where we no longer have nature as our environment, as the thing existing around us which we work. We have instead the society which we have ordered as our immediate environment. Whereas before we had things which could be used for our needs, now we have people who need to be managed. By manipulating people in the organization of our work, we make them things. Instead of loving people and using things, we find ourselves loving things and using people. As St. Thomas Aquinas said, "We use what we should enjoy and we enjoy what we should use and this is the core of sin."

In the resurrection community in which we live in the presence of the risen Christ and by the guidance of the Holy Spirit. This is because we do not live as impersonal parts of a natural process nor as cases in a legalistically constituted community. Our destiny goes beyond nature and history as persons who freely participate in the creative thrust of the Spirit. We live and walk and work by the Spirit and therefore we must strive to find a meaningful place for all persons in this new community.

Rightly dividing the offering cannot mean in the Christian community giving a portion to God and keeping the remainder for oneself. Tithing must now mean dividing the offering variously each moment according as the Spirit directs to satisfy the needs of the moment. While this may appear at first to be ephemeral and antinomian, it will be so only to the legalist who does not recognize either the presence of Christ or the guidance of the Spirit. Every decision to divide the offering will be based upon eschatological awareness that one is not living for the moment but for eternity.

The pressing problem in the modern world is to keep the machine age from dehumanizing and depersonalizing people. It is only the fact of the Spirit working in our midst that guarantees both the freedom to be persons and the reverence of personal concern for everything in the cosmos, great and small. The unique and surprising development in the drama of salvation is the coming of the Spirit. This is what makes us Christians, for it is by the Spirit that we recognize Jesus to be Lord and by the Spirit that we pray to the Father. And it is by the Creator Spirit that we move forward in our destiny transcending ourselves in a creative thrust as participants with God himself as we pass together from glory to glory. "Now the Lord is the Spirit, and where the Spirit of the Lord is, there is freedom. And we all, with unveiled face, beholding the glory of the Lord, are being changed into his likeness from one degree of glory to another; for this comes from the Lord who is the Spirit" (II Cor. 3:17-18).

The work of the Spirit in personal stewardship is to bring men above the natural process and out of the historical community of law into a creative, personal community of resurrection. Here the right division of the offering means that we do not exploit nature and simply give God thanks for it, nor do we organize men only with justice and say we are obliged, but rather we wait upon the Spirit and jump with joy at his spontaneous direction for he will lead us into truth and freedom.

BIBLIOGRAPHY

Cox, Harvey, *The Secular City.* New York: Macmillan, 1965.

Hefner, Philip, ed., *The Scope of Grace.* Philadelphia: Fortress Press, 1964.

Kantonen, T. A., *A Theology for Stewardship.* Philadelphia: Muhlenberg Press, 1956.

Kierkegaard, Soren, *Christian Discourses.* London: Oxford University Press, 1937.

Lansdell, Henry, *The Tithe in Scripture.* London: S.P.C.K. Press, 1908.

Pieper, Josef, *Leisure, the Basis of Culture.* New York: Mentor-Omega, 1964.

Sittler, Joseph, *The Care of the Earth.* Philadelphia: Fortress Press, 1964.

Thompson, T. K., ed., *Stewardship in Contemporary Theology.* New York: Association Press, 1960.

The Church Budget and Stewardship

1. THE EXISTING PROCEDURES

The local church budget is developed and subsequently functions with few fixed guidelines. The basic concepts related to it are very liquid.

Many churches, particularly small ones, do not build a budget. The churches which do build budgets do it in a variety of ways. Far too great a number undertake the task by calling together a very small group — sometimes the group may include only the pastor, the treasurer and one or two others, perhaps the chairman of finance or the financial secretary. Their main source of information is the most recent year's budget. It is a process of looking backward rather than to look up and forward. The only forward look is that which is forced upon them. For instance, if utility rates have gone up, then some increase in the budget must be made. All growth and expansion based on vision and faith are thought of as visionary and therefore out of bounds. This group emerges with pride if they have built "the lowest possible budget."

Then there are churches which build their budgets with a real concern for rendering significant Christian service. Their guiding principle is not how low can we hold the line but how far can we go in doing a great work worthy of the high calling with which they are challenged.

2. A SUGGESTED METHOD

The first step in budget building should be naming of a responsible committee or commission and defining the committee's functions. This committee need not be large but it should be representative of the various program functions in the local church. Budget building should never be left to the control of a small group related primarily to the financial aspects of the church. This is without question the besetting sin of many local churches. Program areas which should be included are education, worship, evangelism, the mission of the church, and social emphases.

The function of the committee in charge of budget building should be clearly defined. The duties include that of initiating the effort, collecting the recommendations, evaluating the suggestions, adjusting requests where advisable and necessary, and constructing a working program. They must also construct a supporting budget which has a chance of being supported by the members of the church. This is far distant from the committee's sitting together for an evening to formulate a budget.

The second step should be to secure all available materials from the denominational agency charged with the responsibility of developing a stewardship and finance program for the local church. Securing these materials does not mean that the local leadership has tied its hands in regard to creativity. This should not be feared and should not deter from getting these materials. There is always plenty of room for originality but the guidance and stimulation coming from those who specialize in this field is almost indispensable. This will help keep churches out of dangerous ruts and help to rescue some from ruts into which they have fallen.

The third step is for the guiding committee to study the material and decide upon the course they are going to follow and it is herewith urged that such course be that of program building as a proper, logical and effective way to proceed.

3. THE PROGRAM IN RELATION TO BUDGET

The fourth step is to build a program. There should be a clear understanding of the term "program" and the term "budget." Budget building is approached through the development of a program for the year ahead. That puts the emphasis on purpose rather than on money. The budget is important but it is determined after the objects of program have been ascertained.

This procedure is that the chief emphasis is to be put on something to be accomplished rather than on an amount of money. People are interested in giving to a cause where they cannot be aroused to give to a "fund" or a "budget" as such. Furthermore, program building puts the emphasis on "kingdom building" rather than "holding the line" or "keeping the wolf from the door." Program building puts the emphasis on people rather than on money. It brings out the spiritual challenge, removing much of the sting of talk about deficits and emergency campaigns. This method assures victory because it puts forth the offensive as a way of getting something done rather than the defensive which frequently means trying to maintain the status quo which is about as unromantic as an appeal can be.

After a local church has decided to take the route of program building, there are some clear procedures which should be followed.

The program committee should meet to do two things, namely, to determine what committees, commissions and organizations should be included in building a program, and then to determine a time and place when the groups can be called together. The program chairman should consult with the leadership of the committees and organizations and gain their consent to cooperate with the plan. And a letter should be sent to all members of the committees announcing the date. It should go out as far in advance as possible and should go over the signature of both the program chairman and respective committee chairmen.

When the time has come for the groups to assemble the first one-third of the evening should be used to explain the meaning of program building to the total group. Those present would then be asked to meet as separate committees, asking such questions as, "What should our committee, our organization, propose to the whole church as a working program for the coming year?" After the suggested program has been decided upon within the various planning groups the estimated cost should be determined. The suggested program and the cost estimates should be given to the general program committee by a designated date.

When the program proposals have been submitted, it becomes the duty of the program committee to evaluate them. Some overlapping will need to be eliminated. Some proposals will be too large and others too small. The costs will have to be totaled and studied. Adjustment must be made where total costs present an unrealistic challenge which the membership could not reasonably be expected to underwrite. On the other hand, some proposals will be too small and an enlarged challenge should be considered by the committee.

When the program committee has decided on the program and proposed costs, the next step will be to submit the report to the proper official body for reaction, adjustment and approval.

4. THE TENTATIVE BUDGET

At this point a serious warning should be raised. The proposals reached through this process up to this time do not result in the budget for the coming year. This is only the tentative budget. The finalized budget which will be the authorized pattern of operation in the area of finance for the following year must come later.

This tentative program and budget constitutes the proposal and challenge to the membership and constituency for purposes of the every member visitation.

5. THE PRE-BUDGET CANVASS

A word should be said here about the so-called pre-budget approach. To put it briefly, the pre-budget concept calls for all the groups working on program building to do their work without stressing costs. If they do estimate costs, nothing is to be presented to the membership to suggest any amount of support which might be needed. The entire drive back of this idea is to go to the people with a far-reaching, perhaps presumptuous proposed program. It would be designed to stimulate the imagination and bring out new and attractive projects which ought to be carried out in and through the church if only the people would catch the vision and become concerned.

The appeal to the membership would be done in small groups, all-church gatherings and in home-to-home visits. When the cause has been presented and discussed the families or individuals should make their commitments for the support of the program for the new year.

This method has been found to be very effective in many churches. However the proposal being made here is a modification of the pre-budget canvass. It is not believed that the pre-budget canvass is a good way to proceed year after year. Instead the compromise position is recommended, namely, that cost estimates be made and presented to the membership but that they should never be described as "the budget." At best they represent the tentative budget. Many feel that it is more intelligible and meaningful if cost estimates accompany the program challenge. This should not present a serious objection if it is made clear that they are tentative, and are subject to the will of the people as they express themselves in the visitation.

6. THE FINALIZED BUDGET

After the canvass or visitation is complete, the group with official responsibility must gather all the facts concerning the results of the visitation, evaluate them, and build the finalized budget. The mistake should not be made whereby the total commitments are made the sole basis for determining the finalized operating budget. In addition to total commitments there are other sources of income to be considered. They are: the loose offerings, the gifts of new members, and the contributions of those who do not make written commitments. The financial secretary should be able to furnish realistic estimates of the probable income from these sources.

Now the operating budget is to be determined. Adjustments are to be made upward and downward. Any drastic changes should be discussed with the chairmen of committees and organization presidents who helped make the proposals. These persons should have an opportunity to express themselves when substantial changes are being made in their proposed program. To be sure, those having official responsibility in the management of the financial affairs must have a high priority in deciding on a budget for actual expenditures but the attitude of domination without a hearing should be outlawed in the church. The challenge of the kingdom should be prior, not the ill-founded notion of any individual.

This matter of kingdom challenge is the heart of the approach being proposed here. The driving appeal should be "How much can we get done this year for Christ and his work," not the idea that to keep all proposals at a minimum is the commendable objective of those in control of finance.

A plea for some element of faith should be injected here. Christ urged, "launch out into the deep" (Luke 5:4). It is not visionary to include some things in a budget for which all support is not easily forthcoming. The church is in Christian work. She should be straining at the yoke to achieve for Christ "while yet it is day." A reasonable challenge containing an element of faith does need to disturb the average church. A conservative deficit at the end of the year can be adjusted without undue difficulty. But in many instances the second mile challenge will have produced new interest and support and perhaps may make it easier to secure the committed portion of the budget.

7. THE STEWARDSHIP OF POSSESSIONS

The Hoosier schoolmaster said, "When you are guessing, guess a plenty." But when people guess at the amount they should give for support of Christian causes they usually do not "guess a plenty." Perhaps the tragedy of the whole matter is that a decision of such prime importance is made a matter of guessing. Nevertheless, take a look at the record of giving in most any church today. There will follow an emphatic impression that there is very little prayerful thought back of the average decision on the question, "How much should I give?" The weekly contribution of many will be comparable to the cost of their daily mid-afternoon refreshments. And the envelope placed on the offering plate on Sunday morning will represent for many a family of substantial means but a fraction of that which they will spend for their Sunday dinner.

It is obvious to every thoughtful person that an answer to this question of giving must be found which is above the level of the casual, careless guess. Effort to find a better answer is not with the motive of getting a few more dollars out of the members of the churches. The motive is distinctly twofold. The one motive is that the spiritual life of the giver may live and grow because "the poorest man in the world is a man with much to live on and little to live for." The other motive is that the cause of God's kingdom may live.

Giving in the church will be more what it ought to be when there is a stewardship of possessions. This includes two things, i.e., tithing and generous giving.

Tithing certainly brings to all Christian people a real challenge. It is embedded in the Scriptures and in theology. There are no grounds except ill-founded legalism, on which to contend that a person is not a Christian nor an acceptable church member if he is not a tither. However, the powerful call directed to Christ's followers to make the coming of his kingdom possible makes the giving of a tenth of net income both reasonable and desirable. Tithing is recommended and every loyal Christian should seriously consider it as a part of his way of life.

While it is a distressing fact that so many have not made a commitment to tithing, it is even more distressing that so many have never given thought to either the matter of tithing or generous giving aside from tithing. The standard for so many has been "What is the lowest amount I can give and still maintain a degree of respect in my church and help get the necessary bills paid to keep the church open?"

To be a generous giver, one must consider that which is spent for non-necessities and luxuries in comparison to that which is given to and through the church. The need of making the program of the church strong in a day when man's highest values are being threatened by a competitive ideology and general moral breakdown calls for generous giving.

8. STEWARDSHIP EDUCATION IN THE CHURCH TODAY

There is a definite increase in a consistent educational program on stewardship in the local church. Churches are voluntarily asking for a stewardship foundation for fund raising rather than an emphasis on methods which might have questionable motivation.

An effective stewardship program for the local church will have two aspects. The one would be the constant year-round emphasis and the other a concentrated period of intensive cultivation. Both are needed and one does not exclude the values to come from the other.

The year-round program should include such features as a section in the church library where stewardship books are assembled to make it easy for interested persons to find them. In this connection, attention should be called to the library of Christian stewardship being developed by the Commission on Stewardship and Benevolence of the National Council of Churches. In this library there are scholarly and very recent works. Every church should have this collection as well as the stewardship material from the denominational headquarters.

Other features of the constant cultivation could be a literature rack stocked with stewardship pamphlets, an annual training course for church school teachers to brief them in stewardship principles and developments.

Most churches are in need of a concentrated period of stewardship education as well as the year-round program. A period should be set aside when a certain phase of stewardship should be studied throughout the church. The subject could be one of the following: stewardship for all of life; tithing; stewardship for children and youth; stewardship of volunteer service.

The month of sustained emphasis should include a series of sermons by the pastor, a reading program for the entire constituency, participation of the organizations of the church. The thinking of the people can be transformed and doors opened for an effective constant emphasis. The spiritual values are high as well as the undergirding of the budget of the church.

BIBLIOGRAPHY

Brattgard, Helge, *God's Stewards.* Minneapolis: Augsburg Publishing House, 1963.

Kantonen, T. A., *Theology for Christian Stewardship.* Philadelphia: Fortress Press, 1956.

Piper, Otto A., *The Christian Meaning of Money.* Englewood Cliffs, N. J.: Prentice-Hall, 1965.

Powell, Luther, *Money and the Church.* New York: Association Press, 1962.

Thomas, Winburn T., *Stewardship in Mission.* Englewood Cliffs, N. J.: Prentice-Hall, 1964.

Thompson, T. K., ed., *Stewardship in Contemporary Theology.* New York: Association Press, 1960.

The Stewardship of Time and Talents

Stewardship means to hold something in trust for some one else. For the Christian it means that all that we possess we hold in trust for God to whom we shall one day have to give an account of our stewardship.

For most people stewardship is related to money or possessions, for it is obvious that we have responsibility not only to God but also to our fellowman for the manner in which we use our money or our possessions. Few would quarrel with the thought that you can judge character by the way people use the things they have, and particularly the manner in which they use money.

But what is money? Surely money is a symbol of something else. After all, a dollar bill is only a small piece of paper. It is what it symbolizes that makes it of value. In commerce and in trade money may be defined as a means of exchange. For the individual money is a necessity if he is to live in our Western society. For money is more than just a means of exchange. It is a symbol of work. In order for most money to be put into circulation some kind of work had to be done.

Such symbols of work are recognized in stores. There they are changed into other symbols of work, perhaps bread. But what is bread? It is a symbol of another man's work, the farmer or the baker. Yet we must go further and ask, What is work? Work takes time. Thus in a certain sense work is time. When we talk of stewardship of money, then, we are really talking of the stewardship of time.

1. THE STEWARDSHIP OF TIME

There are many who feel that since they have little of this world's goods stewardship is no problem for them. They don't have many possessions and the disposal of the little money they have is certainly no difficult problem. It soon goes in the necessities of life, and they have but little for charity or church. Yet this is a shortsighted view. All have a stewardship of time, whether they are poor or rich. God has given us life and life is made up of time. Not only our eight-hour day where we earn money, but time itself is a sacred trust.

Some people think of the stewardship of time in terms of how many hours they spend in church work, how many in social living, and so on. This is important, but the stewardship of time goes deeper. We should note several important things about time if we are to understand our stewardship of it.

First, time is fleeting. God gives us only the present moment. The present quickly becomes the past. There is something relentless, inexorable, and even terrible about the swiftness of time. Life is soon lived and it cannot be lived again. Isaac Watts put it as well as it can be put:

> Time, like an ever-rolling stream,
> Bears all its sons away
> They fly forgotten, as a dream
> Dies at the opening day.

So the stream of life rolls steadily onward and on. We must, if we are to be good stewards, realize for ourselves the tragic transience of life and time. The time we waste we can never recapture. We may be forgiven for wasting our time, but we can never again be given the opportunity to use it.

Yet we live in a society where many people claim to be bored — they don't know what to do with their time, they say, so they "kill time." They seek useless amusement and profitless thrills. They lust, they gamble, they invent all kinds of idle ways of using their time.

This is true not only of individuals, but in national, social and economic life our stewardship of time is often so unworthy of God's gift of life. Perhaps the most far-reaching problem of our age is to find ways in which nations and peoples may properly use time. Consider the time spent in building armaments that might be spent in feeding the world's hungry. Consider the time consumed in much useless advertising that might be used in more productive ways. See how as a society we waste the time of individuals in luxury occupations that contribute neither to depth of living nor to happiness.

Television is one of man's most intricate and startling achievements. We need not go into the statistics of the five or six hours a day the average North American spends in viewing television to indicate how tragically a great invention is used to waste people's time with that which, if not positively dangerous to our society, is, at the least, tawdry and trivial.

The mental drugs in which we thoughtlessly indulge is but one indication of the manner in which we misuse time. Good stewardship here would make all the difference. The trash on our newstands, the vapid and empty melodrama on television, the childish comic books, and the exploitation of the human taste for thrills and adventure exploited by pocket books and all other means of communication alike, need serious consideration by thoughtful Christians. Indeed, it is time the church itself took a good long look at the stewardship of time in terms of our modern culture.

The stewardship of time is to be measured not in length but in depth, not in quantity but in quality. Indeed, it is not how long we live that matters, but what we do with our time on earth. Hours may pass and seem but minutes when listening to great music or reading a worthwhile book. Yet the time we spend reading a detective novel or watching a useless television program may be three hours, but we don't recall a moment of it afterwards. What we put into time is most important. In Hugh Walpole's novel *Fortitude* it is said, "It isn't life that matters but the courage you bring to it." But so often we attribute to time that which ought to belong to our stewardship of it. We say, for instance, that "time heals." But time itself is neutral. Time spent in faith, in hope, in deeds of love may heal life's wounds and soothe life's sorrows. Time spent in brooding over our losses, our bereavements, our suffering, embitters and hurts.

2. THE STEWARDSHIP OF TALENT

There are so many talented people that untalented people easily are discouraged. They are not musical, cannot teach or do public speaking, or lead a church group or even do administrative work. "I have no talents about which I need to exercise stewardship," such people say, or at least think. So often when we think of the stewardship of talents we think of talented people who have unusual gifts of some kind or another. Now, of course, it is good for people with artistic, musical, or leadership gifts to offer them as part of their service to the church. But the real stewardship of talents goes deeper. All people have talents. There are no ordinary people. We need to understand this more than we do when we think of stewardship. Our greatest talent, no matter who we are, is not any particular gift, but our unique and extraordinary life. Our human experience which we can offer to God and our fellow man is our most unusual talent.

Arnold Bennett, seated in a café in Paris, was told he could not possibly write a novel about three faded, unattractive, ordinary-looking, old ladies seated at another table. But he produced an English classic, *The Old Wives' Tale*. For he knew that everyone has a story; all have an experience which is not duplicated by any other living person.

No one ever has the experience of another. The kind of person each one is, his looks, his disposition, and the experiences he has have made him a unique person. Heredity and environment are different for each one of us and therefore make each one of us not ordinary but extraordinary persons. This is our foremost talent. Our joys and our sorrows, our successes and our failures, the heights we have climbed and the depths we have plumbed, make us what we are. Our talent for music, or art, or public speaking is secondary. For there are many artists, musicians, speakers, but only one who will express art or music in our own peculiar way, a way that no other can.

Even our disabilities, our illnesses, the harsh experiences of our life can become a talent that we can offer in service to our fellow man, and therefore to our God. In Thornton Wilder's play, *The Angel That Troubled the Pool*, there is one about to step down into the pool when the waters are troubled and the angel stops him and says, "Without your wound, where would your power be? . . . In love's service only the wounded soldiers can serve." Then another is healed and turns to the one who was refused healing and says, "Come with me to my home. My son is lost in dark thoughts. I, I do not understand him, and only you have ever lifted his mood." Here is a talent made by pain and suffering. We can use our wounds as a talent. Blind people can bring light and life to those who see. The sick people can bring hope to those who are well. The wounded serve best in God's war against sorrow, pain, failure and loss.

All our talents are personal. God uses our good stewardship of them to accomplish his will and purpose on earth. If God wants Stradivarius violins, says George Eliot, then he must have a man called Stradivarius to make them. Or Dorothy Sayers, in her play, *The Zeal of Thine House*, makes William of Sens, the builder of Canterbury Cathedral, say:

"Say God needs a church
As here in Canterbury – and say he calls together
By miracle stone, wood and metal, builds
A church of sorts; MY church He cannot make –
Another but not that. This church is mine
And none but I, not even God, can build it."

The cathedral builder learns later in the play about the danger of inordinate pride, but yet in his human pride he voiced a great truth. God uses our talents to do his work. And the work we do no other can do. The way we sing, or act, or write is our way.

We are then to offer God our inique lives, our personal talents. They cannot be offered by any other person in the world. No one can take our place in the sight of God in this stewardship of our personal talents. This alone we can offer to God, and we do it as we offer it in service to our fellow man. To others also we offer our peculiar talent; it may be of music, or art, or drama, or writing, or even of sewing and baking, of sawing wood or laying bricks. What we offer will be ours. Let what we offer serve God's purpose.

BIBLIOGRAPHY

Berry, William G., *To Be Honest.* Philadelphia: Westminster Press, 1965.

MacMurray, John, *The Structure of Religious Experience.* London: Faber and Faber, 1936.

Teilhard de Chardin, Pierre, *The Future of Man.* London, 1964. (Especially the essays "The Grand Option" and "The End of the Species.")

"Stewardship Explorations" — 1963 Stewardship School Lectures. Toronto: Ryerson Press, 1963. (Especially section IV.)

The Voices of Time, J. T. Fraser, ed. New York: George Braziller, 1966. (Especially essay, "Time in Christian Thought," J. L. Russell.)

New Testament Stewardship

The New Testament, like the Old Testament, is primarily a proclamation of the great acts of God. The New Testament, unlike the Old Testament, finds the culmination of these mighty acts in the life, death and resurrection of his Son, Jesus Christ. In his sermon at Antioch of Pisidia, Paul succinctly presented the central articles of faith in the New Testament credo:

"The God of this people of Israel chose our fathers. When they were still living as aliens in Egypt he made them into a nation and brought them out of that country with arm outstretched. For some forty years he bore with their conduct in the desert. Then in the Canaanite country he overthrew seven nations, whose lands he gave them to be their heritage for some four hundred and fifty years, and afterwards appointed judges for them until the time of the prophet Samuel.

"Then they asked for a king and God gave them Saul the son of Kish, a man of the tribe of Benjamin, who reigned for forty years. Then he removed him and set up David as their king, giving him his approval in these words: 'I have found David son of Jesse to be a man after my own heart, who will carry out all my purposes.' This is the man from whose posterity God, as he promised, has brought Israel a Saviour, Jesus" (Acts 13:16-23, NEB).

The confession declares: (a) God chose our fathers; (b) he made them into a nation; (c) he gave them the land as an inheritance; (d) he raised up David as their king; and (e) he has brought Israel a savior as he promised. This typical Biblical statement of faith follows the form of the oldest and simplest statement in Deuteronomy 26:1-9 which Bernard Anderson calls "the heart of the Pentateuch" and G. Ernest Wright has called the "Hexateuch in miniature."

The synoptic gospels stand in the forefront of the New Testament as histories of the life and death of Jesus Christ, written in the light of his resurrection. The epistles, as G. Ernest Wright has pointed out in *Interpreters Bible,* are an explication of the meaning of the event of Christ in the light of the whole Biblical history of God's work and in the light also of particular situations which the letters were written to confront (*op. cit.,* p. 388). In a word, the New Testament is a statement about God's purpose in sending his Son into the world. In this record there is the affirmation that in a whole series of mighty acts, beginning with the Exodus and continuing through the history of Israel, God has spoken to us in this final age in the Son whom he has made heir to the whole universe (Heb. 1:2, NEB).

In considering the concept of stewardship no attempt should be made to find an adequate definition of stewardship within the pages of the New Testament. The New Testament is not a dictionary where neat little definitions are arranged in alphabetical order. This is not to say that word studies are not useful, but they must be carried out in the context of the whole body of literature which makes up the New Testament.

It may be that one of the reasons why Biblical scholars have given so little attention to the growing body of stewardship literature is that too often such literature has been largely homiletical and moralistic in style and based for the most part upon a proof-text method that is no longer acceptable. It is time that in the consideration of stewardship we move away from the position which uses the Scriptures to support or illuminate a preconceived idea. If we are to make a fresh and new approach to Biblical stewardship, we must allow the Scriptures themselves to shape and determine the content of the term. On the basis of the Biblical material, three considerations begin to emerge in regard to stewardship.

1. The New Testament points pre-eminently to the prior love of God. It celebrates the conviction of the early Christian community that God has acted in history by sending his Son into the world. That act was not in response to nor a reward for good works or good behavior on the part of men. God has freely and graciously acted out of his love for his children. The initiative was clearly his.

In the light of this basic affirmation men are called to accept this gift and to live in its presence. Stewardship thus begins with an act of receiving, of acceptance of a gift that is proffered. God shows forth his love for us in that while we were yet sinners, Christ died for us (Rom. 5:8). The New Testament views stewardly action not as something a person does for God, but as something God does for men. It has been put very succinctly in Ephesians: "We are God's workmanship" (Eph. 2:9). Whatever we are and whatever we are enabled to do, is by the gracious working of God. The transcendent power belongs not to us but to God.

Two key passages set the direction for stewardship. The writer of Ephesians declares, "For it is by grace you are saved, through trusting him; it is not your own doing. It is God's gift, not a reward for work done. There is nothing for anyone to boast of. For we are God's handiwork, created in Christ Jesus to devote ourselves to the good deeds for which God has designed us" (Eph. 2:8-10, NEB). The radical doctrine here is that God has acted prior to and without regard for the good works of men. Indeed good works are actually the evidence of God's working in human life.

The second key passage is in Paul's letter to the Corinthians. "My brothers, think what sort of people you are, whom God has called. Few of you are men of wisdom, by any human standard; few are powerful or highly born. Yet to shame the wise, God has chosen what the world counts folly, and to shame what is strong, God has chosen what the world counts weakness. He has chosen things low and contemptible, mere nothings, to overthrow the existing order. And so there is no place for human pride in the presence of God. You are in Christ Jesus by God's act, for God has made him our wisdom; he is our righteousness; in him we are consecrated and set free" (I Cor. 1:26-30 NEB).

The New Testament carefully avoids pointing to human achievements or accomplishments as a basis for exhorting men to go and do likewise. It constantly plays down the ability and performance of men in order to point to the power and action of God. God is the ultimate source of what believers receive and the gifts come to them freely and graciously. In one of those strange coincidences that appear occasionally in Scriptures, the two verses, I Corinthians 4:7, and II Corinthians 4:7, complement and support each other. "Who makes you, my friend, so important? What do you possess that was not given you? If then you really received it as a gift why take the credit to yourself? (I Cor. 4:7, NEB) And again, "We are no better than pots of earthenware to contain this treasure, and this proves that such transcendent power does not come from us, but is God's alone" (II Cor. 4:7, NEB).

Stewardship then in the New Testament begins not with a definition of man's management of what God has entrusted to him, but with the recognition that God has acted, that the priority belongs to him, that he works through us.

2. The New Testament also points to the new life that is made possible for the believer. It is a life that is set free from bondage. It is a life that is released from obligations. "When anyone is united to Christ he is a new creature: his old life is over; a new life has already begun" (II Cor. 5:7, NEB marginal reading), is the bold assertion of the New Testament.

Stewardship as commonly and widely understood in the contemporary church is a method for getting people to give of their means, their time, and their talents in services and deeds that support and promote the Christian witness in the world. The New Testament, however, sees stewardship as a way of setting people free from a sense of oughtness or obligation. The new creature is set free to use the resources he has – his very life – to enter into joyous, uninhibited fulfillment of life.

The church has been preoccupied for a long time with such questions as: How can we get people to give more? How can we tell the story most effectively so that people will give generously? What must we do in order to enlist the support of people for good and worthy causes? Sometimes the question has been put simply, How can we get people to be better Christians?

The real questions for the church in our time are altogether different. The crucial questions from the perspective of the New Testament are: How can persons be set free from selfishness and greed? How can persons be helped to discover a larger measure of fulness and purpose in life? How can the abilities and resources of persons be released for usefulness and righteousness, for justice and helpfulness?

"The tragedy of life" says Norman Cousins, "is not in the hurt to a man's name or even in the fact of death itself. The tragedy of life is in what dies inside a man while he lives — the death of genuine feelings, the death of inspired purpose, the death of the awareness that makes it possible to feel the pain or the glory of other men in oneself" (*Saturday Review*, Sept. 24, 1965). Stewardship is the key that opens the gate to the glory of life, so that man is set free to use the gift of life itself in such a way that life is renewed and fulfilled.

In addition to the words mentioned earlier from II Corinthians 5:17, two other passages are instructive. In Matthew 23:4, Jesus is reported as saying, "They [the scribes and Pharisees] make up heavy packs and pile them on men's shoulders, but will not raise a finger to lift the load themselves." The persistent practice of church authorities in our day to speak of stewardship as an obligation, as a responsibility, that is often burdensome is readily apparent. But Christian faith is not the imposition of a set of rules or demands upon men; it is an invitation to enter into a life that is set free for lowly service. The greatest person in the Christian order of things is the person who is free to be a servant.

The second passage is John 10:10 (NEB). "I have come that men may have life, and may have it in all its fullness." The great tragedy in the life of the rich young ruler was not that he was rich, but that his riches had restricted him and had become a burden to him. Jesus meant to set him free so that his life really might be full. He went away sorrowful not because he had great possessions, but because his possessions had taken such a hold on him. Stewardship in the New Tetament sense moves in the direction of setting men free so that they might experience life in all its fullness and richness.

3. It is only after the New Testament points to the prior love of God and the new life made possible in Jesus Christ, that it speaks of a calling or a vocation. "But you are a chosen race, a royal priesthood, a dedicated nation, and a people claimed by God for his own, to proclaim the triumph of him who has called you out of darkness into his marvellous light" (I Peter 2:9 NEB). It is through this people who are literally God's possession that he fulfills his purpose and performs his will in the world. The church, the community of living disciples, becomes the instrument through which God works.

Many a modern interpretation of stewardship has been plagued by the idea of proportionate giving as if the Christian were called to give a portion of his income such as a tithe, or a portion of his time — so many hours a week to worship and Christian service — or a portion of his energy and abilities. But this leads to spiritual schizophrenia. Where sophisticated Christians delude themselves by thinking that they can set aside a part of themselves and their resources as sacred and are thereby given license to use the balance in any fashion whatsoever, a tension is set up that can lead to serious difficulties. The New Testament knows of no such splitting of life. Someone has said, "It doesn't take much of a man to be a Christian, but it takes all there is of him."

Stewardship in its broadest sense is the offering up of a whole life to God — a life wholly integrated with and totally committed to God's will. The appeal of the New Testament is "to offer your very selves to him: a living sacrifice, dedicated and fit for his acceptance, the worship offered by mind and heart" (Rom. 12:1, NEB). A man's whole nature is called for and not some single section that is regarded as holy or sacred.

The New Testament points beyond itself in such a way as to guide the church in this present age. This is at once the reason for and the excitement about New Testament studies in the church. They instruct, yet from them also new light is constantly breaking forth.

It is becoming increasingly clear that stewardship is not confined to the church, nor directed toward the support of churchly programs and activities solely. Stewardship in its broadest sense is directed toward the world.

In a brilliant passage that sets stewardship in the context of the growing secularization of our society, Harvey Cox writes:

> "The coming of the secular city is a historical process which removes adolescent illusions. Freed from these fantasies man is expected to assume the status of sonship, maturity, and responsible stewardship. His response to the call must include a willingness to participate in the constant improvisation of social and cultural arrangements which will be changed again and again in the future. The acceptance of provisionality is part of maturity. So is the need to exert one's own originality. No one supplies the steward with a handbook in which to look up procedures by which to cope with every problem in the garden. He must be original" (*The Secular City*, p. 121).

Joseph Fletcher in an unpublished address, "Stewardship, the Christian Vocation in an Opulent Era," lists such things as urban renewal, rapid transportation in metropolitan areas, aid of education, anti-poverty programs, massive public works and research and development projects such as dams, reservoirs, water and air pollution services, etc., and he concludes: "This is where stewardship counts in the modern world, and it is only petty and picayune apart from it. It is a big world we live in."

It is entirely in keeping with the spirit of the New Testament to see stewardship stretching and extending the church's concern until it takes in the whole world.

The ministry of the modern Christian, if it is to bear the marks of authenticity, must be a ministry similar in purpose to Christ's. His ministry was marked by his readiness to be used of God. Just as Mary sang in the *Magnificat*, "Behold the hand maiden of the Lord. Be it to me according to thy word," so Jesus opened his life fully to the will and purpose of God. Traditionally Jesus is depicted as yielding himself to God's will in the agonizing and painful experience of the Garden of Gethsemane. But could it be possible that the agony and pain was associated with the very human struggle to impose his will on God? If so, the prayer of "Not my will, but thine be done," must have been the cry of victory and not a lament of surrender. In any event, the New Testament affirms that Jesus was the instrument, the "effective agent" through whom God was accomplishing his purpose to reclaim and reshape human life.

Jesus was not put to death because he went about doing good, or because he taught men to love one another, or because he was a worker of miracles. He was destroyed because the claim was made that God was working through him. Such a claim was blasphemy to the "defenders of the faith." If Jesus could be the agent, the instrument of God's love and will then it would be possible for every man to be such an agent and that is a claim that threatens the very order of human existence. But it is just the claim which the church makes when it calls all men to a life of stewardship.

The passages that are traditionally associated with stewardship in the New Testament have not been dealt with. Stewardship can be rightly understood only in terms of the central content of the New Testament, and not in terms of separate parables, sayings of Jesus, word studies or selected texts. Stewardship according to the New Testament is not the product of a determined, stoical, grim effort to serve God. It is, rather, a free, happy, life-fulfilling experience open to all who become the agents of God's purpose and will.

BIBLIOGRAPHY

Brattgard, Helge, *God's Stewards*.

Rolston, Holmes, *Stewardship in the New Testament Church*.

Money and Missions

Money and missions have been bound together from the very beginning of the Christian movement. As Jesus carried out his earthly ministry, he and his disciples used money to satisfy their basic needs. John explains the absence of the disciples while Jesus talked with the Samaritan woman beside the well by saying, "His disciples had gone away into the city to buy food" (4:8). John also points out twice in 12:6 and 13:

28, "Judas had the money bag," indicating he acted as treasurer for the group.

The apostle Paul needed money to finance his missionary journeys. Rather than be indebted to others, however, he supported himself by his own labors (Acts 20:33-34), accepting only occasional personal gifts which came as spontaneous expressions of love from some of the churches.

But Paul did not hesitate to challenge Christians to give money when there was a great need to be met. Some of the most profound New Testament teaching on the subject of stewardship is found in Paul's letters to the Corinthians. He urges them to share generously in the offering for the Jerusalem church whose people were in dire need, challenges them by reporting the generous response of others, and points out to them that "giving proves the reality of your faith."

Paul's point of view on the missionary supporting himself was shared by William Carey, British Baptist and father of the modern missionary movement. He and his associates at Serampore, near Calcutta, William Ward and Joshua Marshman, knew that money was needed to carry out their mission, but they were committed to the idea that every missionary should, as soon as possible, support himself by finding employment in the country to which he went. The original buildings at Serampore, erected by the pooled earnings of the missionaries and still in use, are silent testimonies to the success and complete dedication of these men.

The fact that Paul and others managed to support themselves during their missionary labors does not negate the statement that money and missions have been bound together from the earliest days of the Christian movement. It merely shows there is more than one way to support the mission of the church. In the mid-twentieth century, in a money economy, the need for financial support for missions is clearly evident. There is no go-into-all-the-world mission without people who go and people who give. God still calls for full-time professional missionary life and full-time financial commitment.

1. DEFINITIONS

At this point some definitions are in order. The terms "mission" and "missions" are frequently used interchangeably. While they are definitely related, there is an important distinction between them. The mission of the church is the proclamation of the gospel on all frontiers of unbelief. Missions are those organized activities by which the church fulfills its mission.

Most Protestant church members have a rather narrow concept of missions. They think in terms of overseas or so-called "foreign missions." As a consequence, two views have developed which have resulted in curtailing the funds available for the total mission of the church. On the one hand, there are the foreign missions enthusiasts who are disturbed when they find that a major portion of the dollar they give through denominational channels is used for forms of mission other than overseas work. On the other hand, there are those who believe either that the church has no right to carry Christianity to nations which have their own religion and culture, or that with the spread of Communism in so much of the non-Christian world it is foolish to give money for overseas work since it will probably all be lost to us.

2. A BROAD CONCEPT OF MISSIONS

There is need for broadening the concept of missions. Missions have been defined as those organized activities by which the church fulfills its mission in the world. If this definition is valid, then it becomes clear that overseas missions, while highly significant and important, are not the only forms of mission.

Some frontiers of unbelief, against which the church must move, are to be found in every community. Therefore, if the local church is effectively confronting unbelief in its own community, it is engaged in missionary activity, and money contributed and spent in its community is money for missions.

At the same time, no local church can fulfill its calling by carrying out a purely local mission. It must share in a wider mission. There are frontiers of unbelief and need throughout America that are too great for any one church to confront alone. Vast social concerns, such as juvenile delinquency, civil rights, alcoholism, international affairs, work among migrants, care for the aging and the handicapped, come within the scope of the mission of the church. Wise strategy calls for a council of churches in the area or for the denominational board of home missions to become involved. Money contributed and spent through these channels and used for these ministries is also money for missions.

Moreover, there are frontiers of unbelief that must be confronted by the gospel in the inner city and in rural areas, among Indian Americans, and on college campuses. One of the greatest mission fields in the world today is the college and university campus in America. Anyone working with college or university students and faculty is a missionary. Money given and spent for work in these areas is also money for missions.

In addition to all these areas of work, every denomination renders a wide variety of services to its local congregations as a part of equiping them for mission. Training young men and women for the ministry and related church vocations, publishing books and teaching materials, providing tools and helps in the work of evangelism and stewardship, counseling in the field of church extension and church buildings, are only a few of the many services provided. These, too, are a part of the mission, and money is needed to make possible this kind of missionary activity.

Thus it becomes abundantly clear that a broader concept of missions is needed, one that embraces the wide spectrum of all forms of mission, if the task of the church is to be properly understood in the space age. Because of the complexity of modern life and because of the immensity of the problems that confront the church, there is need for increased financial support if the church is to fulfill its mission.

3. MISSIONS AS MOTIVATION FOR GIVING

"Stewardship and mission are inseparable," says Dr. John Thompson Peters, former stewardship executive in the United Presbyterian Church in the U.S.A. He goes on to say, "Stewardship without mission is hopeless. Mission without stewardship is helpless."

Throughout the history of Christianity the challenge to support missions has been a major factor in motivation for giving. As a general rule, individuals and churches that have responded generously to this call to support the wider mission of the church have also given generously to support the churches in their local mission. In churches operating on a dual budget, where members make separate pledges to local expenses and to missions, it is usually the members who pledge to missions who are most likely to be regular and generous in their giving for the church's local program. Each generous act makes the next more likely and easier, for generosity begets generosity.

Annually the Commission on Stewardship and Benevolence of the National Council of the Churches of Christ in the U.S.A. publishes *Statistics of Church Finances*, summarizing the financial reports of nearly fifty major Protestant bodies in the United States and Canada. Contributions totaling $2,986, 493,255 were reported by 47 communions in 1963, for example. Of this amount $558,666, 682 is reported under benevolence, including homes and overseas missions, education and publications, relief work abroad, etc.

These figures represent only the contributions channeled through the churches. The American Association of Fund-Raising Counsel estimated the total philanthropic giving for religious, educational, hospital, health, welfare, recreation, character-building and cultural programs reached the level of $10.6 billion in 1964. Of this amount 49 per cent, or approximately $5.2 billion, was for religious purposes.

All these figures when taken by themselves look impressive. Against the background of national personal income, however, they are not very imposing. Total philanthropic giving represents only 2.1 per cent of the nations personal income, while contributions for religious purposes equal a mere one per cent.

Close analysis of *Statistics of Church Finances* reveals a greater cause for concern when one looks at the per member giving record. The average Protestant gives just $70.00 per year to his church. This amounts to $1.34 a week or 19¢ a day. Even more shocking is the discovery that out of every dollar that comes into the treasury of the average Protestant church, 81.5¢ is used locally and only 18.5¢ is allocated for the mission of the church beyond its own community. The budget of the average church reveals a self-centeredness that indicates either a lack of understanding of the total mission of the church or else a complete lack of concern for it.

Here and there congregations are beginning to catch a vision of their full responsibility. They are saying, "We ought to be as concerned for the wider mission of the church as we are for our local work." They have expressed this concern realistically by setting a goal of what is called "fifty-fifty" or "dollar-for-dollar" giving – i.e., a dollar for the wider mission of the church for every dollar spent on the local program. Such a goal is not impossible. Some churches have already reached it. A few have even gone beyond it. Most congregations can achieve this level if they desire to do so. What is required is a sincere application of proven methods of challenging individual Christians to a deeper commitment in their stewardship of money, coupled with a church policy of increasing the benevolence share of the total budget by two or three per cent each year. This kind of commitment would make possible significant advances in the total mission of the church.

4. RESPONSIBILITY FOR SECURING

Since money and missions are bound together and since more money is needed for missions, someone must be responsible for raising the money. It is really a shared responsibility – shared by the denomination, the minister, and the lay leaders of the congregation.

In recent years the number of denominational stewardship departments has increased significantly. Many of these departments now have a staff of experienced field workers, available to assist congregations in developing a sound stewardship program. In the Commission on Stewardship and Benevolence of the National Council of Churches stewardship executives from many communions share plans, programs and materials in the areas of stewardship and benevolence promotion. A conscious effort is made to maintain a balance between proven methods and techniques of fund-raising and a solid Biblical and theological content.

As a result of these developments, no church needs to continue to use antiquated and ineffective methods in the field of stewardship. A growing body of resource material – books, manuals, pamphlets and audio-visuals – is available. Training programs for ministers and laymen are conducted by all major denominations. As the level of stewardship understanding and commitment is raised, more money becomes available for the church's mission locally and around the world.

Within the local congregation the responsibility for securing the money for missions is shared by the minister and the lay leaders. But the minister must take the lead, for he is the chief steward. He has had the advantage of more specialized training. His attendance at conferences, his study and reading, all make it possible for him to gain a wider knowledge and a better understanding of missions than his laymen. In his pulpit ministry, in his personal contacts and in his work with committees he will demonstrate a vital concern for the wider mission of the church and will challenge his people to give generously for its support. Therefore, the minister becomes the eyes of his congregation, the horizon lifter.

Many ministers fail to understand this responsibility, or else they shy away from it, believing they should not become involved in money raising. They have a mistaken notion that money matters are not spiritual. This attitude is supported by the trustees who say to the minister, "You take care of the spiritual matters and we will take care of the finances."

What is needed here is a re-examination of our basic assumptions. Jesus had more to say about how men get and use their material possessions than he had to say about prayer or forgiveness or eternal life. He must have considered it a spiritual concern to have given so much attention to it. If he were conducting his public ministry in today's world with its money economy, he would undoubtedly place even greater stress on this subject, for our excessive preoccupation with money and material things is sapping our spiritual strength. After Paul concludes his marvelous exposition of the resurrection in I Corinthians 15 his very next word in 16:1 (NEB) is, "And now about the collection in aid of God's people" – a missionary offering. Apparently Paul felt it belonged on a high spiritual level. Money matters are spiritual matters, and the minister cannot afford to ignore them.

But the minister cannot carry the full responsibility for securing the money for missions. He needs the support and active participation of lay leaders. Each congregation needs a responsible board of missions which will work with the minister in this area of church life and program. Members of this board will seek to become well-informed and will, in turn, educate the entire congregation. They will be responsible for building the church's benevolence budget, for seeing that the proper balance is maintained between local expenses and missions, and for working toward the goal of dollar-for-dollar giving. With the proper sharing of responsibility between the denominational stewardship office, the minister, and a responsible board, money so desperately needed for missions will be made available.

The question is often raised as to the relative merits of a unified or consolidated budget compared with a dual budget in the matter of securing money for missions. Under the unified budget method, members make a single pledge in support of the church program and a per cent of the total is allocated for missions. With a dual budget, members make separate pledges for local expenses and for missions, and the missions pledges determine the amount of the missions budget. Many churches have recently moved toward the unified budget because it simplifies the bookkeeping and the work of the treasurer. There is no conclusive evidence that one method is superior to the other in terms of the money given to missions. Either system will produce money for missions provided the minister and church leaders are convinced of the importance of the wider mission of the church. Neither system will work effectively if this concern is lacking. There is some evidence, however, that in a succession of years of economic reversal for a church, there is a stronger temptation to cut back on mission support in churches operating on a unified budget than in those whose individual members determine the amount they wish to give for missions.

5. RESPONSIBLE USE OF MONEY

One further aspect of the subject of money and missions deserves attention. It is the responsible use of the money that is given. There is a basic stewardship of the gospel in which every Christian has a part, but there is a special stewardship incumbent upon all who administer mission programs or funds. It is not alone a matter of spending funds carefully and wisely. Good stewardship of the gospel requires a constant evaluation of all mission work with a view to terminating that which is outdated and ineffective and moving out into new forms of mission.

There is no question but that mistakes have been made in the past, some with the very best of intentions. Relationships between the so-called sending and receiving churches are of great importance. They are also very sensitive. It is always difficult to have funds, as mission board's do, to administer them in a work for and with an underprivileged or underdeveloped group, and at the same time maintain a spirit of understanding and mutual respect. Financial assistance dispensed in a paternalistic manner creates serious problems and often does more harm than good.

Bishop V. S. Azariah, the first Indian bishop of the Anglican Church, in his book *Christian Giving,* traces the picture of this kind of relationship, pointing out the lasting harm done thereby to some of the younger churches. He goes on to tell of several church bodies that have made remarkable progress and that are live and vital. A study was made of a number of churches to find out how far the duty of Christian giving was understood by Christians and how far the churches were able to maintain their work without help from the West. "It was found," writes Bishop Azariah, "that there were very great differences between the churches. . . . It was not always the richest churches which had made the greatest progress; much more seemed to depend on the kind of teaching that had been given to the Christians from the beginning, and on the extent to which they had been led to see Christian giving as part of their duty toward God." He follows this with a description of several churches in which specially good progress toward self-support had been made. In every case clear teaching had been given from the start on the duty of Christian giving. It was Bishop Azariah's conviction that even those in abject poverty need to give something. "Sacrificial giving," he writes, "is one of the essential elements in promoting true spiritual growth."

6. CONCLUSION

We return to our starting point and state once more that money and missions have been bound together from the very beginning of the Christian movement. There seems little likelihood that this situation will lessen. In fact, there is every likelihood that the need for funds to support missions will increase.

The Apostle Paul puts the matter very directly when, after declaring that "every one who calls upon the name of the Lord will be saved," he raises a series of pointed questions: "But how are men to call upon him in whom they have not believed? And how are they to believe in him of whom they have never heard? And how are they to hear without a preacher? And how can men preach unless they are sent?" (Rom. 10:13-15 RSV).

Paul's word indicates that in the final analysis there are only two groups of Christians. There is that relatively small group who carry the message of the gospel to to those who need to hear it, wherever they may be, and there is that large group of those who make it possible for the first group to go. Both groups are important to the life and vigor of the church. God still calls for full-time professional missionary life and full-time financial commitment. Money and missions are bound together inseparably.

BIBLIOGRAPH Y

Brattgard, H., *God's Stewards.* Minneapolis: Augsburg Publishing House, 1963.

Kantonen, T. A., *A Theology for Christian Stewardship.* Philadelphia: Muhlenberg Press, 1956.

Keech, W. J., *The Life I Owe.* Valley Forge, Pa.: Judson Press, 1963.

Powell, L. P., *Money and the Church.* New York: Association Press, 1962.

Rolston, H., *Stewardship in the New Testament Church.* Richmond: John Knox Press, 1959.

Stewart, J. S., *Thine Is the Kingdom.* New York: Charles Scribner's Sons, 1956.

Thomas, W. T., *Stewardship in Mission.* Englewood Cliffs, N. J.: Prentice-Hall, 1964.

Thompson, T. K., *Stewardship in Contemporary Theology.* New York: Association Press, 1960.

The Old Testament and the Tithe

1. STEWARDSHIP IN THE NEW AND OLD TESTAMENTS

It has been stated that the Old Testament contains more stewardship teaching than the New and that, for the steward, the Old is a more articulate handbook. It is difficult to make such an assessment, particularly in view of the parables, the proportion of Jesus' teaching devoted to the use of resources, and the Pauline appeals.

Nevertheless, when it comes to tithing, the most clear rooting and understanding is precisely in the Old Testament. The Gospels refer to the tithe only three times. One of these references (Luke 18:12) is contained in a parable which compares unfavorably a Pharisee with a tax collector. Those to whom Jesus told the story are described as trusting in themselves "that they were righteous and despised others." The Pharisee, justifying himself in private prayer before God, offered as evidence of his goodness, "I give tithes of all that I get." Indeed, he was not merely fulfilling the law; he was going beyond in tithing all his income, while the Deuteronomic requirement (Deut. 14:22-23) was for the products of agriculture only.

While tithing is related to the negative side of the contrast, it would be unwarranted to assume from that fact a distaste by Jesus for the tithe itself. And certainly we can find here no clear affirmation of the tithe.

The tithe is in the Gospels at two other points, parallel passages in Matthew 23:23 and Luke 11:42. Again the Pharisees are involved: "Woe to you, scribes and Pharisees, hypocrites! for you tithe mint and dill and cummin, and have neglected the weightier matters of the law, justice and mercy and faith; these you ought to have done, without neglecting the others." Here is a clear endorsement. While there is a placing in perspective of "weightier matters of the law," there is also with relation to the tithes, *these you ought to have done.* Only three times the Master employed that strong term, ought, once on the giving of tithes. Still, there are critical textual problems with the phrase "these you ought to have done, without neglecting the others," and it would be a mistake to try to understand fully the mind of Christ on the tithe from so scant a fragment.

No mention of the tithe is made by Paul. This is a curious and puzzling omission by a man for whom the law became a major issue to be plumbed in its relation to the gospel.

Hebrews 7:1-10 contains the only New

Testament treatment of tithing outside the Gospels. Here, the passage deals with Abraham's giving a tithe to Melchizedek, and how the latter was thereby honored. The focus is not on tithing, but on the priesthood, with some parallels drawn between Melchizedek and Christ our High Priest.

It is apparent that the pages of the New Testament do not present anything like a comprehensive treatment of tithing. Despite this, we can still say that tithing is integral to the New Testament. The relative silence may be understood from the tithe being assumed by Jesus, by Paul, and the other writers. The life and faith of the people to whom they were speaking included tithing. It was a regular practice, not needing to be established. It was to take them beyond this basic kind of commitment that Jesus talked of the "weightier matters of the law."

And in our exploration of the tithe in the Old Testament, the understandings and the implications we draw for ourselves will certainly be influenced by what we know of stewardship in the New Testament.

2. MEANING OF THE TITHE

The word tithe means simply the tenth part. As it is used in Scripture, it is always related to belief in God and the setting aside of a tenth of certain possessions for special use as commanded by God.

The Biblical references to tithing or the giving of the tenth are all included in the following passages: Genesis 14:17-24; 28:20-22; Leviticus 27:30-33; Numbers 18:21-32; Deuteronomy 12:5-14, 17-19; 14:22-29; 26:12-14; II Chronicles 31:2-12; Nehemiah 10:35-39; 12:44-47; 13:4-12; Amos 4:4; Malachi 3:8-12.

One must see the faith context for the tithe to understand its role in Hebrew life. The Old Testament begins with the creation story. Its central truth is that God is Creator. And when Abraham gives a tenth to Melchizedek the priest (Gen. 14:17-24) both men speak of "God Most High, maker of heaven and earth."

God has not only created, he has maintained ownership. "The earth is the Lord's and the fulness thereof, the world and those who dwell therein" (Ps. 24:1). Though man is to have dominion (Gen. 1:26) over the earth, he is not an absolute owner. He is always responsible to God for whatever he has. To remind man of this responsibility, God established certain laws relating: (1) to life itself – the giving of the first born (Exod. 22:29); (2) to property (c.f. Amos, Lev. 25:25-28); (3) to time – the day, "the seventh day is a sabbath to the Lord your God" (Exod. 20:10); even the year, "A jubilee shall that fiftieth year be to you" (Lev. 25:11).

Man is subject to God as his creature, and must ultimately answer to God for all he possesses. Even when David brought an offering in the presence of the assembly, he prayed, "But who am I, and what is my people, that we should be able thus to offer willingly? For all things come from thee, and of thine own have we given thee" (I Chron. 29:14).

T. A. Kantonen in *A Theology for Christian Stewardship* in a rather negative appraisal of the tithe, feels that there is a peril of implication that having given God his 10 per cent, one has discharged his stewardship and may do as he pleases with the remaining 90 per cent (p. 20-26). If such peril exists, it is radically foreign to the Old Testament, for the tithe symbolized the whole. Says T. M. Taylor, "Among the ancient Hebrews . . . the corn and oil offerings, the first fruit cereal offerings, the wine libations, the first-born lamb were all interpreted as symbolic of the belief that the entire crop, the whole grain harvest, the annual yield of olive oil and wine, and all one's flocks and herds were God's gift to man. . . . Each of these offerings of portions of man's substance amounted to a recognition that man owed all he had to the God who had given him of his bounty" (*Stewardship in Contemporary Life*, p. 86).

Even the calling, the election of the Hebrew people, was symbolic that all men belong to God. They were not set apart for their own privilege, but to be "a light to the nations."

Thus, for a covenant people, the tithe must be seen as a link between God the Creator and the elements of his creation, between a system of belief and a means of expression, and between God Most High and "a wandering Aramean." (Deut. 26:5).

3. DEVELOPMENT OF TITHING AMONG THE HEBREWS

The giving of the tenth extends backward

into the far reaches of antiquity. Gifts were in the form of produce or the spoils of war; they were occasional and they were regular. In some instances, it was a tribute to the gods of the people; at other times, it was more like a tax which supported the king or the priests. The amount was not always the same. Egyptians, for example, were required to give a fifth of the harvest to Pharaoh (Gen. 47:23-26).

For the Hebrews, the tithe was introduced by Abraham. Returning from victory over the confederate kings, Abram presents a tenth of his spoils to Melchizedek, king and priest of Salem (Gen. 14:17-24).

Jacob sought to negotiate with God (Gen. 28:20-22). If God would give him food, drink, clothing and safety, of all that was given, Jacob would return a tenth. "Bargaining with God" may offend the sensitivities of the modern Christian, but for a covenant people, accustomed to reaching agreements with God, the vow by Jacob posed no such problem.

In Deuteronomy the people are admonished to "Take heed that you do not offer your burnt offerings at every place that you see; but at the place which the Lord will choose" (Deut. 12:13-14). This is the call for a central sanctuary. Once the tithes were brought to the central place, they were to be consumed with rejoicing before the Lord. The tithe was to include all the yield each year. If the distance to the central sanctuary was too great to transport the tithe offerings, provision was made for selling the tithe, going with the money to the sanctuary, and then buying whatever gifts might be desired — oxen, sheep, wine or "whatever your appetite craves." The Levites (tribe of priests charged with caring for the sanctuary, teaching and expounding the faith) were to be remembered, for they inherited no property of their own.

At the end of every third year the tithe was to be stored in the villages rather than taken to the central sanctuary. This tithe was for the Levites and the needy — the fatherless, the widow, the sojourner. A special confession was to be used in the sanctuary that year (Deut. 6:13).

A Leviticus passage (27:30-33) adds to the harvest offerings described in Deuteronomy, a tithe of the herds and flocks. Such a tithe was to be selected mechanically, "every tenth animal of all that pass under the herdsman's staff." The fruit of the land or the trees could be redeemed by adding a fifth to it; the animal tithe could not be redeemed — that is, it could not be used for human purposes. Some scholars have advanced the idea that the animal tithe was added to the land harvest because the latter failed to provide adequate financial support for the work of the priests.

In Numbers 18:21-32, the Levites are given instructions on the tithe. They are also to present a tithe of the tithe they received from the people of Israel. Here the selection of the tenth is not mechanical, it is "from all the best of them." The principle of giving the best is crucial, and Eli's household is judged harshly for honoring his sons above God "by fattening yourselves upon the choicest parts of every offering of my people Israel" (I Sam. 2:29).

The faith of Israel was not just a moral code; worship, including the giving of offerings was integral to the laws governing the affairs of men. Indeed, ethical behavior grew from their obeisance to God. This relationship between faith and works is at best in tenuous balance, and just as the problem occupied Paul and James in the New Testament, Amos is concerned when cultic acts become ends in themselves. Harsh words he has for the rich "cows of Bashan." They oppress the poor, and crush the needy, but continue religious acts, including sacrifices and the giving of tithes. No amount of tithing can atone for failure in the weightier matters of the law, "justice and mercy and faith." In his warnings, Amos is representative of the prophetic attitude toward the priestly system of Israel.

We may be tempted to think that all Hebrews willingly and gladly gave their tenth. That is error. The tithes were not automatic. Hezekiah found it necessary to command the giving of tithes and offerings (II Chron. 31:2-12). And Malachi cried with outrage, "Will a man rob God? Yet you are robbing me. But you say, 'How are we robbing thee?' In your tithes and offerings . . . Bring the full tithes into the storehouse" (Mal. 3:8-10).

There are apparent differences in the regulations on tithing between Deuteronomy and Leviticus. Deuteronomy prescribes a feast in a central sanctuary with the tithe, except for the third year. Leviticus requires all the tithes to be given to the Levites. Robert Paul Roth in *Stewardship in Contemporary Theology* comments as follows: "With this background the rabbinical system established three tithes. The book of Tobit shows that it was expected of a good man to give an annual tenth to the sons of Levi who officiated in the temple at Jerusalem, another tenth for the religious festivals each year in Jerusalem, and a third tenth for the poor (Tobit 1:7-8). It is generally believed that in the rabbinic system the first tithe was collected annually, the second was due in the first, second, fourth, and fifth years, and the third in the third and sixth years. Hence there were two tithes annually except the seventh year in which the land lay fallow" (p. 135).

Later rabbinic tradition on the tithe became quite elaborate and intricate. The absurdity and foolishness of the regulations found disapproval in Jesus, and is fair warning to any modern who would try, legalistically, to define all situations in calculating the tithe.

4. PURPOSE OF THE TITHE

In the Old Testament, offerings were placed on the altar and burned. There was no utilitarian function to be served. Part of the tithes were eaten in a feast of rejoicing. These gifts met only the need of the giver to present a part of themselves unto God. They are gifts similar to that presented by the woman who spilled the precious ointment on the feet of Jesus. To the disciples, it was a waste. To Jesus it was a beautiful act. And to the woman, who asked nothing in return, it was adoration in spontaneous expression.

The motives for tithing in the Jacob passage (Gen. 28:20-22) are more complex. Surely, it was promised as a measure of gratitude. This is a high motive, though not without its problems. Suppose God provided no bread, no clothing, no safety. What becomes of gratitude? It would be incorrect to assume from Jacob that the Hebrews were grateful only when prosperous. Job, his flesh nearly destroyed, continued to affirm the righteousness of God.

Unmistakably, there is a thread of belief that the faithful tither, (the faithful in any faith relationship) will be rewarded. Malachi is the most explicit: "Bring the full tithes into the storehouse, that there may be food in my house; and thereby put me to the test, says the Lord of hosts, if I will not open the windows of heaven for you and pour down for you an overflowing blessing." We have seen much abuse of the idea of reward — so much that we have taken it out of our teaching. We do well to remember that Paul has a parallel passage saying that liberality in giving brings an increase in resources: "He who supplies seed to the sower and bread for food will supply and multiply your resources and increase the harvest of your righteousness. You will be enriched in every way for great generosity, which through us will produce thanksgiving to God; for the rendering of this service not only supplies the wants of the saints but also overflows in many thanksgivings to God" (II Cor. 9: 10-12).

Further, the noted Quaker, Henry Cadbury, in the Shaffer Lectures for 1946, calls our attention to the absence in the teaching of Jesus of an altruistic motive. "The Gospels," he says, "so far as they represent Jesus as appealing to motive at all, are, to our way of thinking, exceedingly utilitarian in their sanctions" (*Jesus: What Manner of Man*, p. 104).

The giving of the tithe was also that the giver might learn to fear God. Deuteronomy 14:23 specifies the offerings that are to be made at the sanctuary. The practice is "that you may learn to fear the Lord your God always."

For the people of Israel, the tithe was a means to support the Levites and the priestly system. In many ways, it was akin to what we know as taxes, though one must recognize the close identity between "church and state" in the Old Testament. When resources are needed, attention is called to the tithe — this is apparently in the background of Malachi's statement. Later, Christians drew a parallel between the tithe for the support of Levites and that for the ministry of the church. Thus, tithing was for the benefit of the person, for Israel as they were served by the priests, and for all men, as the Hebrews became a "light to the nations."

5. THE TITHE FOR TODAY

With the publishing in 1963 of *God's Stewards* by Helge Brattgard, there has developed a new theological interest and understanding of the tithe within the framework of the meaning of the law and the gospel. Brattgard brought a corrective to stewardship thought, saying that it could not be based upon gospel alone – it must also be related to law. "It is not right to ask whether the steward idea should be based on the Law *or* the Gospel. It must rather be based on the dialectic between the two. But in this tension between Law and Gospel, the Law is constantly being overcome by the Gospel" (p. 167).

The Christian is enjoined to tithe not simply because it was an Old Testament law. The 10 per cent is not fixed for the follower of Christ just because Abraham gave Melchizedek this proportion. The practice of Christian tithing grows out of the Hebrew tradition and it is there that we discover its rich meanings. Tithing is found within the total context of Jewish law, a law which Jesus came not to destroy but to fulfill, and a law which Paul called sacred in its ability to convict us of sin, to prepare us for that which is to come, and to provide standards even in the presence of freedom. Thus, tithing has its roots in Hebrew faith, but is also watered and nurtured in the Word of the New Testament.

Tithing is related to the "ought" in faith, to obedience, to discipline. While there is no absolute proportion in Christian giving, Paul counsels that we ought not do less than the Jewish law requires. Even apart from the Jewish law, there remains the matter of establishing standards, and the Christian would do well to at least begin where he has Biblical precedent.

BIBLIOGRAPHY

Brattgard, Helge, *God's Stewards*. Minneapolis: Augsburg Publishing House, 1963.

Cadbury, Henry J., *Jesus: What Manner of Man*. New York: The Macmillan Company, 1947.

Kantonen, T. A., *A Theology for Christian Stewardship*. Philadelphia: Muhlenberg Press, 1956.

Roth, Robert Paul, *Stewardship in Contemporary Theology*, T. K. Thompson, ed. New York: Association Press, 1960.

Taylor, Theophilus M., *Stewardship in Contemporary Life*, T. K. Thompson, ed. New York: Association Press, 1965.

Laymen as Good Stewards

While Jesus was on earth carrying out his ministry, he at the same time trained men to continue the work of the Kingdom after his ascension into heaven. But Jesus did not stop with the twelve. "The Lord appointed seventy others, and sent them ahead of him, two by two, into every town and place where he himself was about to come" (Luke 10:1). "The seventy returned with joy, saying, "Lord, even the demons are subject to us in your name" (Luke 10:17). When the brethren gathered in the upper room, following the Ascension, there were about one hundred and twenty. It is very clear from the Gospels that Jesus used men to advance his cause. Yet the fact is He did not ask all he called to "leave their nets." "Jesus did not call all his adherents to follow Him. He selected a small group to be eye-witnesses in order to become fundamental witnesses to the world" (Berkhof and Potter, *Key Words of the Gospel*).

He called laymen to follow him before they fully knew who he really was. Months of close fellowship passed before anyone of them could say, "Thou art the Christ, the Son of the living God." Sometimes they were woefully dense. They all stumbled and fell. Peter denied knowing him. They all fled on the night of his betrayal. Yet he never gave up on them. He never deserted them. He loved them all. It was his desire that each one called would prove to be a good steward.

Today's church should be producing good stewards. This is one thing Christ meant when he said, "Follow me and I will make you." Yet it can be said without fear of contradiction that lay people are "God's frozen people." According to Hendrik Kraemer, "In all our criticism and sometimes near despair of the institutional Church, it should never be forgotten that many powers and possibilities really exist in it, but often in captivity; exist as frozen credits and dead capital" (*A Theology of the Laity*, p. 176). There are many reasons why this tragic condition exists. Not the least is the fear in the minister himself. He feels threatened by boisterous and quick acting laymen. But sometimes ministers are guilty of jealousy and are envious.

One of the greatest stumbling blocks to good stewardship is the misunderstanding which exists between the roles of the clergy and laity. The clergy are considered professionals and the laity amateurs. This invites the amateur to leave the field to the professional. But there is only one ministry and one mission as there is only one Lord. The clergy and the laity are actually engaged in the same task. They are co-laborers. Together they are responsible to God for the health and well being of the church and fellowship. They are both needed to help win all the areas of the world for God, the Father. All too often the laity feel that if they pay the bills, they need do no more. Good stewards will gladly pay the bills, but they will also become part of the Christian team doing the Master's work. All too often the clergy have thought of themselves as a group apart, who feel that they alone should do the work. The time has come to let everyone know that no steward or minister can do it alone. We must pay and pray and work together.

Some laymen have been misled into thinking that the Lord's work is easy. But if we are to develop good stewards, ministers must share the truth about their own trials and tribulations, and failures. Leslie Weatherhead told his British brothers that such confession would do much to strengthen and encourage laymen in their struggles. Sometimes clergymen set the ideal so high laymen get discouraged. Whether we deliberately do so or not, we encourage them to draw the false conclusion that we are attaining ourselves, that we hit the mark every time, that we are constantly inspired and because of our prayer life know exactly what to do in every situation and are never in doubt nor ever discouraged. This is a false image of the minister, but many lay people have been encouraged to have it. Yet it sets a great gulf between minister and layman and makes team work almost impossible unless the gulf is bridged. If the laity are to be effective, they must be taught that the work is not easy. It will call for the best from minister and laymen alike.

To be good stewards, laymen need to know and understand what the church is. Many churches are proud of themselves just as they are and thus have "sacralized themselves." Where such ideas prevail, ministers grow weary trying to get their best lay people to come in and help. J. H. Oldham reminds us that this is the very thing many of the ablest people will not do. These lay people are determined that the church must be willing to change if their abilities are to be used.

There are many lay people who hold false ideas about the nature of the church. They think the determining factor should be their own pleasure. So they shop around for a church like they do for a car. But Elton Trueblood is right when he points out that a church is not something to which you go as it is something that you are in. He says, "We can go to a railroad station or to a motion picture theatre or to a ball game; but a church is something which demands a wholly different human relationship — the relationship of belonging. If a man is really in — really belongs to a church, he is just as much a member of it when he sits at his desk in his business house as when he sits in a pew at his meetinghouse. The point is that the relationship, if real, is continuous, regardless of time and place and performance" (*The Company of the Committed,* p. 19).

The great revolution which is taking place in religion is having its effect upon the idea of a good steward. There was a time when a tither was considered a good steward. If anyone did anything beyond what the ordinary church member did, which was little if anything, he was thought to be a good steward. But today there is a more adequate understanding of who a good steward really is. He is one whose whole life is committed to following Christ in all areas of his daily activity.

One activity which still takes a large part of a steward's time is his vocation. Though the work week is getting shorter and leisure time is lengthening, the bulk of his time is still related to his work. Every steward should be encouraged to make a good witness for Christ, to be a good neighbor, to be considerate and helpful to those who work with him. He should be encouraged to turn out a good product, to cooperate with the boss, and to be a good representative of the concern for which he works. If he is an employer, he must be encouraged to pay an honest wage and look out for the well-being of those entrusted to him. Christian stewards should be encouraged to do the best they can in the situations in which they find themselves. There is no doubt that this is difficult in a technological society in which Christian principles are not the guiding motive. It is not a simple matter either for a Christian steward to quit one job and find another more in keeping with Christian ideals. It might just be that he is the very man to help make the place where he is working more Christian. But all stewards should strive to be good stewards of Christ at their work whether they be clergy or laity.

All stewards can witness in their homes. "Where two or three are gathered together in my name, there am I in the midst of them" (Matt. 18:20). Usually we limit this great truth to a small prayer group meeting where only a few are present. Certainly the early Christians thought of it in relationship to their homes. Could not the "two" be a husband and wife, or the "three" father, mother and child? At a time when there are many cracks in the foundation of the home, the Christian witness is urgently needed there. The home is basic to society. The home is where the life of love should be tested and shared and revealed. Children should learn through their homes that their father and mother are Christians. They should see them at prayer and hear them read the Word of God. The home should support and strengthen the church in every possible way. Children should be brought up to understand that a Christian is one who actively works in the church and supports its worldwide program. There is no better place than the Christian home to tackle the problem of human diversity. Today many homes are built in the suburbs to escape the big city with its many problems and to avoid peoples of various cultures and races. The best place to try for racial and cultural understanding is in a Christian home. A mature Christian home should not be a constant refuge from the world but a home through which the world passes and is exposed to love. If Christian people would invite peoples of other cultures and races into their homes, this would add greatly to understanding and increase good will among men. The Christian home must so witness that Schaller's prediction will not come true. In *Planning for Protestantism in Urban America* he says, "Tomorrow may find the Protestant churches the last segregated institutions in many communities. For many persons it will continue to be the one place left to which they may go with confidence that Negroes will not come in and sit down beside them."

The child should learn in the Christian home that life is a gift from God and is sacred. Parents should teach their children that talents are given to be used and shared. If Christian parents would help their children to think beyond the getting of money to a life of unselfish service, we would not have the human shortages that we do. In every area of life where people work with people, we are understaffed. We do not have enough stewards with a service motive.

Nels Ferre reminds us that the "very nature of the body of Christ, the true Church, is to be a community of continual concern for the world" (*God's New Age*, p. 50). Since this is true, a good steward must be helped to see clearly the problems of the world. There has been one indictment against Christians and the church which should not be. "The trouble with the Church is that it is blind. It closes its eyes to the troubles of the world. The people of the Church refuse to face the facts of life — of prejudice — of poverty — of brutal power." Unfortunately, this indictment is all too true. Hendrik Kraemer reminds us that when the church becomes serious about its missionary and ministerial calling for the world, two difficult roads in particular have to be trodden. One of them is "the road towards overcoming the scantiness of its knowledge of the world of today, and its ignoring of what really goes on in the world under the surface" (*op cit.*, p. 177).

There is little point in urging stewards to go forth and witness unless they know the true nature of the world they are going forth to win, and the specific nature of the problems they are called upon to face and solve. This calls for seminars, discussions and dialogues. Books concerning the world situation need to be made available to all stewards. There are many Christian scholars and teachers, as well as politicians, labor leaders, and industrialists who can be called upon to help in this vital area.

But Christianity is more than a way of knowing about the problems of the world. It is even more than a way of thinking. It is basically a way of living. For all stewards the Christian way of living is love. The good steward will not only be encouraged to tell what Christ has done for him, but he will try also to live the life of love. This will demand experimentation, discovering new techniques, seeking new ways to express self-giving and outflowing love.

We need to experiment to find new jobs for good stewards. Far too many say that all the jobs are already taken. But the pastor can share with these stewards the names of persons and families who do not know Christ. He can encourage stewards to prepare themselves adequately for this demanding task by instructing and visiting with them; and by discussing the problems which arise out of visiting the unchurched. The pastor can encourage stewards to visit those members who have "grown cold." It is shocking how many there are who are in this category. This is one of the hardest tasks in the whole Christian fellowship. It calls for unlimited patience as well as a willingness to allow those who are visited to unburden themselves.

A steward should stay alive all his life. Many who retire from their employment retire from the church. But they must be helped to see that no one can. Each person has to account for his own discipleship, and the retirement years might easily be the freest and the most creative for good stewardship.

New jobs must also be found that love finally flows into every area of life. J. B. Phillips reminds us that "to Christ the most serious sin was not the misdirection of the love-energy, which might be due to ignorance or mere carelessness, but the deliberate refusal to allow it to flow out either to God or to other people." Experimentation is absolutely necessary if love is to flow out. People must be helped to give themselves. The old idea of stewardship was too restrictive. No one has all the techniques. No one has all the answers. Stewards must be encouraged to do what Jesus called the first disciples to do – to launch out into the deep. Now it must be the deep of the world – the skyscrapers and alleys in our cities; the suburbs and slums in our towns. Good stewards will seek to demonstrate their love for God and their neighbor in as many ways as possible. This does not mean to ignore the old idea. The choir loft should still be filled. There should be enough ushers every Sunday. Church school classes must be fully staffed. Financial support must be given for local and world missions; help must be given to the poor, the unfortunate and the aged. Hospitals and colleges must still be assisted. But this is only the beginning of stewardship.

The church is the people of God who are trying to live the life of Christ. Good stewards will attempt to live the life of Christ in every area of life. No one knows all the areas, but stewards, clergy and laity alike must encourage each other to venture forth in love. If the world is to be won for God, the Christian fellowship must be as serious about research and experimentation for Christ as big business ever thought of being. If stewards launch out the Holy Spirit will give guidance. This is what a group of stewards found out recently when they began the "Meals on Wheels" program. A small group of concerned stewards knew there were sick and needy people in their community who could not prepare their own meals. What could they do about it? They talked with the doctors, the hospital administrators, and the Red Cross. The doctors said they would supply the names. The Red Cross said they would investigate to see each case was valid. The hospital agreed to prepare the meals according to dietetic specifications. The stewards agreed, at their own expense in time and gasoline, to distribute the meals five times a week. They have been doing so now for more than two years, regardless of the weather. Those who started this service of compassion say they were led by the Holy Spirit. If stewards will be obedient to the call of Christ and follow in love the direction of the Holy Spirit, no one can tell how far love will lead them nor yet how high love will lift the world.

Every steward knows that sometime there will be an accounting. Christ made it quite clear that every steward would have to give an account of his own stewardship. May it finally be that all who face him, clergy and laity alike, will give such an honest and creative account of flowing love that each one will hear from the Master's own lips, "Well done, good and faithful steward, enter thou into the joy of thy Lord."

BIBLIOGRAPHY

Cox, Harvey, *The Secular City*. New York: Macmillan.

Davies, J. G., *Worship and Mission*. London: S.C.M. Press.

DeWolf, L. Harold, *A Hard Rain and a Cross*. New York: Abingdon Press.

Jones, Tracey K., Jr., *Our Mission Today.* New York: World Outlook Press.

Kilbourn, William, *The Restless Church.* New York: Lippincott.

Rose, Stephen C., ed., "Who's Killing the Church?" *Renewal Magazine.*

Stewardship in a World of Abundance

Christians need to be honest with God. Each and everyone of us is on trial. The churches, and especially ministers, have for too long been too defensive about asking for money for God's work. I believe the church should lay it upon the hearts of men and women that they have a responsibility to God and that they should give of their money in an open, direct, and honest manner. The attitude that a minister should be interested solely in the spiritual aspects of the church and not the material side of life is pure folly. Our spiritual life is simply the way in which we order our material lives.

Our Lord talked freely about possessions and money. He knew that money and possessions represent our effort, energy, time, and talents. When we are selfish with our possessions we are withholding ourselves. Since money represents power and prestige and security, our attitude toward money can become a spiritual disease.

The Psalmist said, "The earth is the Lord's and the fullness thereof, the world and those who dwell therein" (24:1). The idea that you can separate the spiritual from the secular did not originate with God. The spiritual and the material are inseparable; each area affects the other. Jesus Christ is Lord of all of life, including our money and our possessions. Our Lord is interested in how we make our money and how we spend it, both as individuals and as a church.

The idea that a church needs hard-headed business men and bankers to run the financial side of the church and spiritually-minded men to look after visitation and the so-called spiritual aspects of the church is erroneous. We need our most dedicated and spiritual leaders giving oversight to the financial matters of the church.

Many a church can trace its decline and fall to the minister who timidly heeded the advice of a self-appointed oracle who said, "Never speak of money from the pulpit." The people who object to a minister speaking about Christian stewardship are not the generous givers; they are those who have a guilty conscience. They are the people who say behind the minister's back, "I wish the minister would preach the gospel." The preaching of stewardship is a very important phase of the gospel. We need to look at this emphasis of the gospel honestly and prayerfully.

There are three attitudes that we may have toward our money and our possessions in this world of abundance.

1. WE CAN SQUANDER IT – LIKE THE PRODIGAL

We may play the prodigal with our money and possessions by throwing them away. The prodigal son, in the parable that Jesus told, took his inheritance, which he begged from his father, and went into a far country. He wanted to be happy. He wanted to get away from the restraining influence of his father and live his life the way he wanted to live it. The number of men and women and young people who waste their money in a vain attempt to be happy would fill the largest city in the world. Such people learn too late that the amount of our money and possessions does not determine our happiness. Happiness is not dependent upon one's possessions. One's joy in living does not increase in proportion to his increasing income or possessions. Often the very opposite is true.

2. WE CAN HOARD IT – LIKE THE RICH FOOL

In the parable of the rich fool Jesus said, "A man's life does not consist in the abundance of his possessions" (Luke 12:15). Jesus said this rich man wanted to accumulate all his money for himself rather than to use a portion on others. Because of his attitude Jesus called him a fool. So is everyone else who centers his life on himself and his possessions to the exclusion of being rich toward God.

The rich man was a fool because he thought he was responsible for the increase of his possessions. Ultimately it was God who had furnished the farmer with his crops. This farmer made a great mistake when he decided that his abundant crop should be hoarded. Laying up treasures for self is the opposite of being rich toward God.

The rich man was also a fool because he thought he could live only in the material realm. True life has no connection with wealth, for often wealth chokes the very channels through which life would flow. Happiness can be had without wealth, but it is impossible to be happy without faith in God.

The rich man was a fool because he gave no thought to eternity. This farmer forgot that there is a God who rules both time and eternity. He was making material preparations for many years, but he made no preparation for eternity. It is wise for us to give thought to our financial security for future years, but it is also an evidence of prudence when a person gives time, effort, and energy in spiritual preparation for both this life and the life to come.

God holds us responsible for the use of our money. The Bible teaches that no believer has a right to enjoy this world's goods while his brother is in need. The apostle Paul made this point very clear to the Corinthians when he urged upon them to help those less fortunate. Paul said, "I do not mean that others should be eased and you burdened, but that as a matter of equality your abundance at the present time should supply their want, so that their abundance may supply your want, that there may be equality" (II. Cor. 8:13-14). In times of prosperity we should help those who are in need.

3. WE CAN USE IT FOR GOD – LIKE THE GOOD STEWARD

The good steward in Jesus' parable (Luke 12:42-46) acted during his master's absence exactly as he would have acted if the master had been present. Contrary wise, the evil steward used his position to serve his own selfish interest. He took advantage of his master's absence. Jesus points out that the good steward will be advanced and be given greater responsibility while the poor steward will be punished and will lose his position.

A good steward is a person who faithfully manages the affairs and assets of his Lord and Master. God has entrusted the world and all it contains to us. We are responsible for the way in which we use our stewardship that God has placed in our hands. A steward works with what is not his own, however, for he must give an accounting of that for which he is responsible.

The spending of our money tells how important God is to us. We learn what Americans believe, not by what the historians may say, but what the cash register shows. The way we spend our money is one of the most accurate ways of reflecting our sense of values. We in America are a most favored people. The words abundance and luxury are written everywhere across America. While we account for 7 per cent of the world's population, we own nearly 50 per cent of its wealth. American Protestant groups contribute approximately three billion dollars a year to our God, yet we spend on ourselves, according to the U. S. Department of Commerce: eight billion dollars for tobacco; eleven billion dollars for intoxicants; twenty-two billion dollars for recreation; and thirty-seven billion dollars for clothing and accessories.

When Paul wrote his second letter to the Corinthians he chided them for their poor stewardship. He challenged them by holding up the splendid example of the Christians in Macedonia who gave with sacrificial abandon. Paul gave the secret of their generous stewardship when he said of the Macedonian Christians that "They first gave themselves to the Lord" (II Cor. 8:5).

Merely to tithe our income and feel we have done our duty to God is too easy and cheap. God is interested, not just in our tenth, but in how we spend the other nine also. The cross is the symbol of Christianity. We should nail our selfish egos to the cross and let Christ rule our lives and manage our time, talents, and treasure.

There is a joy and deep satisfaction in sacrificing for one's children. There is also a satisfaction that many receive in sacrificing for their nation, whether they are in uniform or just paying taxes. Someone has figured out that the typical American citizen works two and a half hours a day to pay his taxes to the government. As we think about the hundred and fifty minutes of every working day that we give to support our nation, we must consider how many minutes a day we give to the Lord in prayer, family worship, serving those in need, and witnessing to our friends and loved ones; how many minutes a day do we work for God.

BIBLIOGRAPHY

Keech, William J., *The Life I Owe.* Philadelphia: The Judson Press, 1963.

McMullen, John S., Stewardship Unlimited. Richmond: John Knox Press, 1961.

McRae, Glenn, *Teaching Christian Stewardship.* St. Louis: The Bethany Press, 1954.

Rolston, Holmes, *Stewardship in the New Testament Church.* Richmond: John Knox Press, 1946.

Shedd, Charlie W., *How to Develop a Tithing Church.* New York: Abingdon Press, 1961.

Thomas, G. Ernest, *Spiritual Life through Tithing.* Nashville: Tidings Press, 1953.

SECTION 9

WORSHIP

"O Come, let us worship and bow down;
Let us kneel before the Lord our maker."
– Psalm 95:6

The New Testament Basis

Worship may be briefly described as an adoring mental attitude toward God and an outward expression in corporate speech and act. It recognizes God's holiness, goodness and love and reverently tells God so. Apart from the fact that worship is divinely commanded ("Thou shalt worship the Lord thy God," Matt. 4:10) it has an inherent reasonableness. If God is utter perfection, then he ought to be praised.

From time to time we shall be using the words "liturgy" and "ritual." It should be clearly understood that in so using them we are not necessarily thinking of written prayer books and forms of divine service which must not be changed. Liturgy means "what is said in public worship," whether it comes out of a prayer book or spontaneously from the heart of the officiating minister or the congregation. Similarly we are taking the word ritual to mean "what is done in public worship," whether it is always done at a particular stage in the service in accordance with a rubric or written directions in a prayer book (e.g. "then shall the minister turn to the Lord's Table") or quite freely by the minister or congregation. In this sense some ritual is inevitable. Does the congregation stand for the hymn? Does it kneel for the prayer? Does the minister walk to the lectern to read the Word of God or to the pulpit to proclaim it? Are bread and wine taken to communicants? All this is an elementary form of ritual and we mean here no more and no less than this. It is convenient to have at our disposal single words which sum up the worshippers' words and deeds. We are not implying that a prayer book must be used nor are we advocating ritualism.

In Christian worship it would seem desirable to avoid the extravagant and the extreme on the one hand and the barren and colorless on the other. Are we to bring in theology? Or, remembering that most worshippers have had little if any training in theology, are we deliberately to exclude it? These and similar questions make us look for guidance. Is there any norm or standard by which we may test our existing worship or plan our future services? There is such a standard and it is found in the New Testament.

In recent years New Testament scholars have turned their attention to the liturgical interests and purposes of the writers of the Gospels. Philip Carrington has seen Mark's Gospel as a series of Scripture lessons tied in with the Christian Year (*Primitive Christian Calendar*). Aileen Guilding has related John's Gospel to the ancient Jewish lectionary system (*The Fourth Gospel and Jewish Worship*). Again, some have sought to disentangle the various early Christian hymns which may be embedded in the text of the New Testament. Joachim Jeremias calls the Prologue to John's Gospel (1:1-18) a Logos-hymn (*The Central Message of the New Testament*), and Ralph P. Martin has found other hymns (*Worship in the Early Church*). All such investigations have their value and place, for they go to show that the New Testament arose in the context of a joyful, worshipping church. It was not coldly written by a committee and kept in the church safe for security.

But all these are ultimately questions of "introduction." Without discountenancing or ignoring the work of such scholars we hope rather to concentrate on the text itself in our search for the New Testament norm. Those who read Greek are referred to the lexicons, concordances and commentaries. It is sufficient to mention the cultic words *latreuō*, *latreia*, and *proskuneō* with its picture of prostration or homage, and *leitourgia*. It may be helpful for the purposes of illustration to recall that at Athens *leitourgia* meant public service by a private citizen at his own expense. An example today would be an ambassador whose expenses abroad were far in excess of his official salary and were made up out of his own pocket.

In worship there are two parties involved, God and the worshiper(s). This is the simple implication of our original definition, though it ought to be remembered that worship will not be understood by those who do not know it as an experience from the inside. The mere observer can see only so much. The nonbeliever can see a man on his knees and he may know that it is called prayer or worship, but he cannot really see or know a Christian engaged in worship. The natural man receiveth not the things of the Spirit of God. From various parts of the New Testament we are able to piece together the evidence which will give us a composite concept of the object of Christians' worship.

1. THE GOD WHO IS WORSHIPED

a. *He Is the Living God.* This is brought out clearly in a context of worship. ". . . how much more will the blood of Christ, who through the eternal Spirit offered himself [as an offering] without blemish to God, cleanse your conscience from dead works to worship [*latreuein*] the living God" (Heb. 9:14). The same thought is present in Hebrews 11:6, "he who approaches (cf. Heb. 7:25) God must believe that he exists." Existence here must mean living because the text goes on to speak of his action: he proves to be a rewarder of those who seek him.

At Lystra sacrifice (another word for worship) was about to be offered to Paul and Barnabas. They swiftly intervened with a loud protest and the gospel command to "turn from these vain things to the living God" (Acts 14:13ff). Heathen worship was about to begin but the apostles called for conversion to the true God, the first step in Christian worship. Note the contrast between the vanities and the living God. An idol is nothing (I Cor. 8:4), but "it is a frightening experience to fall into the hands of a living God" (Heb. 10:31). In similar fashion the Thessalonians "turned to God from idols to serve the living and true God" (I Thess. 1:9).

b. *He Is the Lord.* This term points to "the personal, legitimate, comprehensive sovereignty of God" (Werner Foerster). The object of worship does not react to men's worship like a thing (e.g., a tape-recorder or a computer); we are concerned with a "He" and not with an "It." He has authority, not despotic power immorally gained and arbitrarily exercised; his authority is grounded in his own being and nature. He is ruler over the worshipers and over the whole of nature and the affairs of men, and his control is absolute. Human freedom itself is in his hands.

Evidence for this is found in Acts 4:24ff. It is not necessary for our present purpose to go into any difference between *despotēs* and *kurios*, both of which are used in the passage under review. The "despot" is addressed in verse 24 and is quoted (Ps. 2:1f.); and God uses the word *Kurios*, Lord, of himself. Here we see men engaged in worship. True, it is not a regular Sunday morning service with its usual "form," and it may not be the whole church gathered together. But it is still worship: it is a spontaneous and unanimous crying out to God as a result of bad news. He can help for he is the Lord. Herod and Pontius Pilate were gathered together . . . "to do what Thy hand and counsel predestined to take place." The "counsel" means the divine will; the "hand" means the divine power; and responsible and therefore lawless (2:23) men were plastic in the divine hand. Personal sovereignty could hardly be expressed more strongly. It is superior to human threats (4:29) and hostility (vss. 26f.).

In Matthew 4:10 and Luke 4:8 the verbs for "worship" are used. "Thou shalt worship the Lord thy God and him only shalt thou [religiously] serve." In the battle and victory of the temptation our Lord showed that the object of worship is the Lord, and his teaching is reflected in the church-at-worship in the episode in the Acts. It will continue so forever. "And the throne of God and of the Lamb will be in it, and his servants will worship him [*latreuō*] . . . because the Lord God will shine upon them" (Rev. 22:3 ff.). Similarly in Hebrews 8 there is the association of "throne" with the language of worship, and the thrice repeated "saith the Lord," and "the Lord" in verse 2. In Philippians 2:9-11 the exalted Christ is given the name which is above every name, the name of Lord. "Lord" calls for kneeling and confession — worship.

c. *He Is the Creator.* Israel, it has been said, knew God as Lord before she knew him as Creator. But the nation did come to know him as Creator and this knowledge was taken over by the church. In the significant passage already discussed we find lordship and creation closely linked in worship: "Lord, thou who didst make the heaven and the earth" (Acts 4:24). This is virtually a quotation from Exodus 20:11 LXX and Nehemiah 9:6 (II Esdras 19:6 LXX); and from Psalm 146:6 (Ps. 145:6 LXX). The atmosphere of worship is unmistakable.

When Paul was before the Council of the Areopagus he began his address with a reference to Athenian worship. They were piously but ignorantly worshiping *sebasmata*, in this case images. He proclaimed "the God who made the world and everything in it," who needs nothing and gives everything to all (Acts 17:22 ff.). The implication is that men should worship him and should begin in repentance (vss. 30 f.).

The same apostle maintained the link between worship and the Creator when writing of unrighteous men who suppress the truth. From the creation onwards they have known that God is God ("his eternal power and deity"), but in spite of such knowledge they did not glorify him as God or give thanks to him. On the contrary they became idolators and "reverenced and worshipped the creation [what had been created] to the neglect of the creator." Moved with devout feeling Paul cannot refrain at this point from a burst of praise: "who is blessed for ever; amen." The "amen" crowns both the thought of worship and the worship itself (Rom. 1:18 ff.).

The Revelation, which describes heavenly worship in language drawn from the earthly scene, reflects the thought of Paul. "Worthy art Thou, our Lord and God, to receive the glory . . . because thou didst create the universe" (Rev. 4:9). Creation is due to God's will. The Creator is also the Sustainer, as Paul showed at Athens and the Revelation maintains in the use of the word "Almighty," or "Controller of All" (*pantkokratōr*).

If the Jewish people have rejected their undoubted Messiah (Acts 13:4; Rom. 9-11), it would seem that their worship is an anachronism, being based on the Old Testament alone. Christians have not discarded the Old Testament, for it is fulfilled and included in the New. Its place in Christian worship must therefore be observed.

d. *He Is the God of the Old Testament.* Paul worshiped in the synagogue (Acts 13:14 f.), and in his address there said that "the God of this people Israel" (vs. 17) "brought unto Israel a Saviour, Jesus" (vs.

23). "The God . . . of our Lord Jesus Christ" (Eph. 1:3) is the God of the Old Testament, finally revealed. The Christian apostle, Paul, said, "In accordance with the way which they call a sect I worship (*latreuō*) the God of my forefathers" (Acts 24:14). Here is the ancestral God, worshiped (because known) in a new way. The standard was set in the new movement, the "Way." The same God is worshiped but in Christ (Acts 24:22, 24). The speech of Stephen is relevant here (Acts 7).

What was Paul's practice is given a theological foundation in the Epistle to the Hebrews, particularly in chapters 8-10. The God who gave the old covenant is the God who inaugurated the new, and in his exposition the author draws freely from the levitical cult, using ritual terms in profusion. In particular he has in mind the Day of Atonement (Lev. 16). Christ our high priest is a minister (*leitourgos*) of the sanctuary in heaven (8:2). There was in existence a priesthood for the repeated offering of gifts and sacrifices, a priesthood which religiously serves (*latreuousin*) the copy and shadow of the heavenly (8:3 ff.). He has offered (*prospherein*) himself (9:14), and has obtained a more excellent ministry (*leitourgia*) as the mediator of a better covenant (8:6). The new covenant was promised by God (Jer. 31:31 ff. is fully quoted).

e. *He Is Present in the Worship.* Paul pictures a meeting of the whole church with the prophetic gift exercised by all. If an unbeliever comes in, he will be convinced by all, examined by all, the secrets of his heart will become manifest, and he will fall upon his face and worship God, frankly saying that "in reality God is among you" (I Cor. 14:25; cf. Isa. 45:14; Dan. 2:47; Zech. 8:23). "In reality" is no trick of the imagination or no wild assumption; God is really present when Christians worship. He dwells in his temple, the believing church, and moves among them and welcomes them (II Cor. 6:16 ff.; Lev. 26:12; Ezek. 20:34 LXX).

God's presence is seen in the song of Moses and the song of the Lamb in a context of worship. "All the Gentiles will come and will worship before Thee" (Rev. 15:4). "Before" (*enopion*) means "in the presence of," as we see from Luke 13:26.

All this should prevent us from holding the arid view that worship is no more than "going through the motions." God is present.

f. *He Has an Attitude to the Worship.* "Let us worship God acceptably," says the writer to the Hebrews (Heb. 12:28). The meaning is that we please him if we receive the unshakable kingdom with thankfulness and if our consequent worship combines reverence and awe. (Not "fear" in the usual sense; we are to approach God with "boldness" [Heb. 4:16].) If we do not receive the kingdom or if we lack gratitude, reverence or awe, then to that extent we fail to please him. He is present and he notices our worship.

In accordance with his understanding of Christianity as a life of worship, the writer to the Hebrews can think of the doing of good as a sacrifice which is well-pleasing to God (Heb. 13:16). Christians must not forget to do good; and when they have done it, God does not forget it (Heb. 6:10). Paul mentions this same line of approach. The Philippian gift was "an odour of a sweet smell, an acceptable sacrifice, well-pleasing to God" (Phil. 4:18). God notices and appraises. He has an attitude. And his attitude is not directed to the external aspect only.

g. *He Is the Knower of Hearts.* When Peter and the brethren were seeking a twelfth apostle to take the place of Judas, they prayed: "Thou, Lord, the Heart-knower of all men" (Acts 1:24). Peter used this word later at the Council of Jerusalem. God the Heart-knower had testified to the Gentiles by giving them the Holy Spirit. He had cleansed their hearts by faith (Acts 15:8). This refers to the inner life rather than to the outer actions like kneeling. The One who knows men's hearts can penetrate beyond the outer expression, sincere or insincere, and can recognize the presence of faith. He is Almighty God, unto whom all hearts be open, all desires known, and from whom no secrets are hid. It ought to be observed that this involves the knowledge of the deepest thoughts and feelings of the individual. The Lord, who knew men in his dealings with them, knows them at their worship (Cf. John 2:24 f.; 6:70).

God is described as "the one who searches the hearts" (Rom. 8:27). Gerhard Delling speaks of his "probing insight" (Cf. I Cor.

4:5; Rev. 2:23; Heb. 4:12 f.). If he knows us so well, can we be sure of a welcome when we approach him? Is he "glad to see us" or does he merely tolerate us or even wish to reject us?

h. *He Is the One who Invites and Responds.* "Draw near to God," says James, "and he will draw near to you" (4:8). It seems at first as if the initiative is with men. But God has already come near in Christ and there is a standing invitation to draw near offered both to the world and to the church. The evangelistic invitation says "Come unto me . . ." and the ecclesiastical invitation says that "there remains a rest for the people of God. . . . Let us be eager to enter in" (Heb. 4:9ff.). The initiative is not with men. God has drawn near to men in Christ, soteriologically; men respond by drawing near to God in worship; then God responds by drawing near to worshipers, experientially.

"To draw near" is an Old Testament term for the sacrificial ministry of priests (Exod. 19:22; Ezek. 44:13), which has been transferred to all spiritual worship (Heb. 4:16; 7:19; 10:19 ff.). When men thus draw near to God in Christ, he "receives them into his society" (Rom. 14:1-3; 15:7; cf. Acts 28:2; Philemon 17).

i. *He Is "for us."* It is not an undue strain on exegesis to apply Romans 8:31-39 to worship in particular. The intensity of the "for us" can be measured only by the cross. In worship it means that he listens to us. Worshipers in both Old and New Testaments are called "those who invoke, call upon (the Name of) the Lord" (see Acts 2:21; 7:59; 9:14, 21; 26:16; Rom. 10:12 ff.; I Cor. 1:2). Calling upon God is the expression of faith (Rom. 10:14), and in I Peter 1:17 refers to Christian worship, perhaps especially to "Father" in the Lord's Prayer. God is not deaf, inattentive, or unwilling. For he is the Receiver of requests (Acts 4:29 ff.). In a sense he is the one who surprises (Acts 13: 2 f.). He has called us into his surprising light (I Peter 2:9), and in worship the Word, read or preached, brings home anew to us his wondrous excellencies. He is rich and generous towards all who call upon him (Rom. 10:12), and in a niggardly world Christian worshipers rejoice to discover time and time again the purpose of the incarnation surprisingly fulfilled (II Cor. 8:9). It is a gift of God which cannot be bought (Acts 8:20). Worshipers need never be disappointed.

j. *He Is Ever Constant.* "I am the Lord; I change not," so wrote the prophet Malachi (3:6). Its thought is reflected in Psalm 102:27, "Thou art the same" (cf. Heb. 1:12), and its New Testament counterpart is seen in Hebrews 13:8, "Jesus Christ the same yesterday and today and for ever." The moods of nature change; the face of the sky is smiling or angry; colors vary with the seasons; the decay of autumn is an annual pointing to the final dissolution of all things; but God in Christ changes not. God's revelation in his Son does not need correction or supplementary addition. He abides faithful. In worship therefore our welcome is certain.

k. *He Is to Be Praised and Glorified.* The opening words of the *Te Deum Laudamus* mean strictly "We praise Thee *as God*." This is the ultimate aim of all life and all worship. We see the church doing it in Acts 2:46 f., and we are exhorted to do it in Romans 15:6.

2. THE CHRISTIANS WHO WORSHIP

The apostle Paul determined to know nothing but Jesus Christ and him crucified (I Cor. 2:2). By this he meant a leaven, or a flavor, which was to be dominant in all theological thought and in all activity. This has a special application in worship.

a. *They Are Men of Faith.* "Without faith it is impossible to please God; for he who draws near to God must have the faith that he exists and proves to be the rewarder of those who seek him" (Heb. 11:6). It was by faith that Abel offered a fuller sacrifice (vs. 4). Abel was not a Christian but he is an example to Christians. It is similar with the two patriarchs. Abraham offered Isaac by faith (11:17). Moses celebrated the Passover by faith (11:28). "Let us approach God in the full assurance of faith" (Heb. 10:22), without doubt or hesitation. The ground of such faith is the sacrifice of Christ. The eagerness with which it is exercised is due to a further reason.

b. *They Are "for God."* In a passage already noticed (Acts 4:24 ff.) the worshipers see the arrogant and vain conspiracy of the heathen: kings standing at the ready and rulers gathering together "against the Lord and against his Christ." This is exemplified in the crucifixion of Jesus – "against thy holy servant Jesus." But they are overruled by the divine will and power. The worshipers call on the Lord to aid them "to go on speaking thy Word with all boldness." They obviously do not stand with the opposition but with the Lord. That they should be "for God" exclusively is suggested by II Corinthians 6:16 ff. with its teaching on "separation." "What agreement has the temple of God with idols?"

c. *They Are Men of Intellect.* By this we do not mean that they are solely scholars. The sacrifice of praise is the fruit of lips confessing to his Name (Heb. 13:15). That is to say, they say something. There is an intellectual content in worship. Paul will pray "with the understanding" (I Cor. 14:15), in full possession of his mental faculties. The new covenant of Jeremiah 31 is concerned with the understanding (*dianoia*) and the heart (*kardia*), the center of the inner, mental life. The Word (*logos*) or message of the cross has to be preached in rational words, though it is not "rationalist" (Heb. 8:10; 10:16). The early hymn in I Timothy 3:16 is virtually a sung creed; only a mind can understand it.

d. *They Are Spiritually Minded.* As God is Spirit, they worship him in spirit and truth (John 4:23f.). They worship him with their bodies when they kneel or sing, but it is possible for this to be a mere external act (see Matt. 15:7 ff.; Mark 7:6 f.). True worship is from the heart, consciously done "to the Lord" (Col. 3:23). God, as Spirit, is not limited by space and time. He may be found in Christ, everywhere and always. We have our sacred places like church buildings, and our sacred seasons for our discipline like Sunday worship. But God does not dwell in buildings which he never leaves (Acts 7:48); nor is he to be found only at stated times. Regularly "going to church" is for the good of our souls, but if we say that we cannot worship except in a building and at fixed hours, we have become unspiritual. This is not an argument for the abandonment of our church services. It tells us rather that the God whom we meet in the regular public worship may still be the object of our prayer and praise in the intervals between the services.

The New Testament recognizes the place of the externals in worship, but when these become an end in themselves something else has taken the place of the living God. This is idolatry. Though the scene is a Christian church building, it is still idolatry. An idol is a nonentity and is at the same time a spiritual danger (I Cor. 8:4; 10:19 f.). Idolatry may invite divine chastisement (I Cor. 10:5-11; 11:30). The worship of Christians must be spiritual.

e. *They Are Men of Experience.* They are not strangers to the Lord but have tasted and seen that the Lord is gracious. It was in an atmosphere of worship (Col. 1:9 – praying; 1:12 – giving thanks) that Paul led up to the apparent quotation of "an already existing hymn" (Ralph P. Martin) in Colossians 1:15-20. Christians, as "rescued," are in the light and in the kingdom; they have redemption, the forgiveness of sins. In another figure it is as "cleansed" men that Christians worship (Heb. 9:14; 10:22). Again, they have been reconciled to God. "We" were reconciled (Rom. 5:10 f.; II Cor. 5:18). They are children of God and have the Spirit of adoption to prove it. They cry "Abba, Father," because the witnessing Spirit in their hearts likewise cries "Abba, Father" (Rom. 8:14 ff.; Gal. 4:6).

In all these varied categories one fact stands out. The men described know the meaning of "experiential" religion. They have crossed the line from unbelief to faith and they know it.

f. *They Actually Draw Near to God.* It may be doubted if this can be explained further to a non-Christian, any more than the color green can be "explained" to a man blind from birth. The Christian who has already done it will know what is meant by drawing near. What we do when consciously and deliberately we begin to say our prayers, that we do when we begin to worship. This is a privilege of believers, because God is unapproachable (I Tim. 6:16), except in Christ (Heb. 4:16; 10:22; James 4:8).

g. *They Are Not Boastful but Bold.* The Pharisee is the classic example of the boastful man. He thanked "God" for his accomplishments, but prayed to himself, contrasting himself with other men. The publican humbly confessed, repented and asked for forgiveness. The authentic Christian, even when he comes in a renewed repentance to God, is sure of the answer to his prayer. "There is no condemnation to those who are in Christ Jesus" (Rom. 8:1); "we have an Advocate" (I John 2:1). Christian worshipers as such do not boast in their own achievements (I Cor. 1:29), though they do in Christ (Phil. 3:3). They do not approach God in levity but with reverence and awe (Heb. 12:28). They have a high priest who as a result of his victorious battles with temptation is able to sympathize with them in their weakness. He knows the strenuous spiritual efforts required to overcome. He understands; therefore let us draw near with boldness (Heb. 4:15 f.). The word does not mean effrontery, but rather confidence. It is the opposite of hesitation. It takes God at his word. It is not self-reliant but is "in Christ" (Eph. 3:12).

It may be that there are hesitant Christians, doubtful not of God's rich mercy but somehow doubtful of its application to them. Such bounty seems almost beyond their reach. Or they have not been adequately instructed in the doctrine and experience of Christian assurance. But there can be no question of the ideal set before us. Boldness is part of the pattern of worship which should be manifest everywhere.

h. *They Exhibit Unanimity in Worship.* "With one accord, with one mind [*homothumadon*], they raised their voice [not 'voices'] to God" (Acts 4:24). No doubt there were "all sorts and conditions of men" present, but they were united in one specific impulse and purpose: prayer for the divine assistance in continuing to speak the Word.

Here we see unanimity exhibited as a fact in worship. It is also inculcated as an ideal. In Romans 15:5 Paul expresses the wish that God may give his readers a unanimity to match the mind of Christ, "in order that with one accord [*homothumadon*] you may with one mouth glorify the God and Father of our Lord Jesus Christ." Such agreement in worship is fostered by ethical agreement (see Rom. 12:16; Phil. 2:2; 4:2; Acts 4:32).

The ideal of unanimity is strikingly illustrated and taught in Matthew 5:23f. If there is a "disagreement" the offering of a gift on the altar must be postponed until reconciliation has been effected. Unreconciled men should not worship together.

i. *They Have a Spirit of Expectancy.* Paul visualized an occasion when an unbeliever attended a meeting of the gathered church in which the Spirit of prophecy was moving strongly (I Cor. 14:23ff.). Convicted by the prophetic Word, he would sink down in worship because "God is in reality among you." There are no doubt Christians who "come to church" ill-prepared and thoughtless; but they ought to come expecting the presence of God.

Paul visualized the situation and expected the Spirit's working. In Acts 13:2 there is an actual instance of the Holy Spirit's call when men were at worship. Men who meet with him in worship regularly go to the service expecting a blessing, whether it is encouragement for their spiritual pilgrimage or a challenge and call to future service. And as they have already received his boundless mercy they know that their recognition and praise of it is but the beginning of an endless story.

j. *They Know Their Own Inadequacy as Worshipers.* Worship has a content. The worshiper "tells" God with gratitude who he is and what he has done. "O Lord, open thou my lips; and my mouth shall tell the story in thy praise" (Ps. 51:15). But with the deepest sense of indebtedness and the warmest joy in God's grace in Christ, our knowledge is incomplete and our language inadequate. Christ's riches are unsearchable (Eph. 3:8). Like territory awaiting exploration there are vast areas which have not been "surveyed." Even with tongues loosened by the Spirit we cannot tell the full praise of God. God's gift is indescribable (II Cor. 9:15).

3. THE BACKGROUND AND HORIZON OF WORSHIP

a. *Background.* After a fearful list of sinners who will not inherit the kingdom of God Paul exclaims: "And such were some of you" (I Cor. 6:11). But now they are in the kingdom — justified. The background of worship is the former sin and unbelief, now put away, forgiven and forgotten. For others the background is one of privilege. "We," says Paul, "Jews by nature and not sinners of the Gentiles . . . even we set our faith in Christ Jesus" (Gal. 2:15 f.).

These factors of the background, sin and unbelief, and privilege, may be regarded as past.

But there is another factor, which is in the present. The secret of public worship is private devotion. Paul was not a preacher in public and a practical atheist in private. He had an intense life of prayer. He prays, gives thanks, makes request (Rom. 1:8-10; I Cor. 1:4; Eph. 1:16; 3:14). The Christ who speaks in him (II Cor. 13:3) lives in him (Gal. 2:20). Corporate worship is fresh and living when it comes from men who worship in private (Matt. 6:6).

b. *Horizons.* Public worship also has its wide horizons. There is first the vision of the unseen. Our eyes are not on the temporary "things seen" but on the eternal "things not seen," and we yearn to put on the heavenly habit(ation) (II Cor. 4:18; 5:2, 7). We advance in our moral and spiritual journey by means of faith, not sight; for faith can see the invisible (Heb. 11:27). This is illustrated in William Cowper's hymn:

> Jesus, where'er Thy people meet,
> There they behold Thy mercy-seat:
> Where'er they seek Thee, Thou art found,
> And every place is hallowed ground.
>
> Here may we prove the power of prayer,
> To strengthen faith and banish care;
> To teach our faint desires to rise,
> *And bring all heaven before our eyes.*

There is also the wider horizon of missionary endeavor and danger. Paul's ministry receives aid in prayer: many will pray for his deliverance from danger and many will give thanks for the gracious answer (II Cor. 1:11). This implies an outlook far beyond the limitations of the walls of a building or the local interests of a local church.

In addition even in worship a "political" awareness is joined to an ecclesiastical and evangelistic outreach. Prayers of all kinds, petitions, intercessions, thanksgivings, are to be offered for all men, for kings and all in prominent positions, with a view to social tranquillity and religious piety and seriousness (I Tim. 2:1ff.).

4. CHARACTERIZATION AND BEHAVIOR

Christian worship is not a rarity. It must not be compared, for example, with a man's attendance at church for his own wedding. It has a continuity and persistence, and involves effort. It requires alertness and wakefulness (Eph. 6:18; Col. 4:2 f.). Regularity is to be observed: weekly (Acts 20:7; I Cor. 16:2; Rev. 1:10) or even daily (Acts 2:46). A place of meeting is obviously necessary. Early worship is seen in the temple (Acts 2:46; 3:1; 5:12), and in various private homes (Acts 5:42; 20:8; Rom. 16:5; I Cor. 16:19; Col. 4:15; Philemon 2). But no "special" place is essential for spiritual worship. If a house were too small to accommodate the whole church it is possible that different sections met in different houses. Paul and Silas worshiped in prison (Acts 16:25), and at Tyre all the disciples with wives and children seem to have knelt and prayed on the shore (Acts 21:5 f.).

Worship is addressed to God; but in a secondary sense mutually in the congregation: "speaking to one another with psalms and hymns . . . singing . . . to the Lord" (Eph. 5:19). Worship is for the Lord alone; stimulus is for one another. Worship thus has value and is not to be neglected (Heb. 10:25); and the church is not to be despised (I Cor. 11:22).

Worship must be reverent. It must also exhibit decorum. Paul reveals this in his discussion of "hats in church" (I Cor. 11:4 ff.). Paul's sensitiveness to public decorum is also apparent in his horror at an unbeliever's opinion that the whole church is out of its mind (I Cor. 14:23). Again, it is not fitting that some subjects should even be mentioned in public (Eph. 5:3). Behavior counts (I Tim. 3:15). The principle of Titus 2:10 may be extended: the doctrine is to be adorned in all things.

The principle in James 2:1ff. is "no respect of persons." The wealthy are not to be treated specially to the neglect of the shabby and poor. James is opposed to false distinctions. To all we should exercise the brotherly courtesy of the faith. "Thou shalt love thy neighbor" (James 2:8).

While thinking of behavior we might well give some attention to the reaction of the congregation to long sermons. At Troas at the breaking of bread Paul "kept on" until midnight; and after the episode of Eutychus he went on until dawn (Acts 20:7-11). It is a salutary reminder to churches today. "A Christianity of short sermons is a Christianity of short fibre" (P. T. Forsyth).

5. THE PATTERN OF WORSHIP

We have seen that in the New Testament Christians were to be found in the temple and in the synagogue. The time came when they were not welcome in the synagogues (Acts 13:46, 50 f.; 14:21 ff.). But they took something of the synagogue with them. It can hardly be questioned that "the earliest Christian meetings and meetingplaces were modelled on the pattern of the synagogues" (Paul P. Levertoff). The services here were simple rather than ornate (Luke 4:15-21; Acts 13:14 f.), and the church followed them.

A simple "order of service" has been detected by some scholars, notably Ralph P. Martin, in I Thessalonians 5:16 ff. Here we see prayer and thanksgiving; an association of the Spirit with prophecy, which probably implies *preaching*; receptive listening, but not gullibility; and the whole rounded off with a *blessing* (vs. 23). Some may feel that this is an austere diet of worship, while others will see in it a flexible order which can be modified according to need and circumstance.

Finally, there are two standards by which worship may be judged. First, it must glorify God. Secondly, it must "build" the worshipers (I Cor. 10:23; 14:3f., 12, 17, 26). The activity of building is secondary, not primary; but this, too, is for the glory of God (I Cor. 10:31).

BIBLIOGRAPHY

Abba, R., *Principles of Christian Worship,* 1957.

Bartlet, J. Vernon, *Encyclopedia of Religion and Ethics.*

Clarke, W. K. L., ed., *Liturgy and Worship.* London, 1932, 1947.

Cranfield, C. E. B., "Divine and Human Action: The Biblical Concept of Worship," *Interpretation,* XXII, 1958, pp. 387-398.

Cullmann, Oscar, *Early Christian Worship.* London, 1953.

————————,*Baptism in the New Testament.* London, 1950.

Delling, G., *Worship in the New Testament.* London, 1962.

Dix, G., *The Shape of the Liturgy.* London, 1945.

Dugmore, C. W., *The Influence of the Synagogue upon the Divine Office.* Oxford, 1944.

Flemington, W. F., *The New Testament Doctrine of Baptism.* London, 1957.

Herbert, A. S., *Worship in Ancient Israel* (Ecumenical Studies in Worship). London, 1959.

Higgins, A. J. B., *The Lord's Supper in the New Testament.* London, 1952.

Hopwood, P. G. S., *The Religious Experience of the Primitive Church.* New York, 1937.

Jeremias, J., *The Eucharistic Words of Jesus.* Oxford, 1955.

————————, *The Central Message of the New Testament.* London, 1965.

Kay, J. A., *The Nature of Christian Worship.* London, 1953.

Macdonald, A. B., *Christian Worship in the Primitive Church.* Edinburgh, 1934.

Martin, R. P., *An Early Christian Confession: Phil. 2:5-11.* Tyndale Press.

————————, *Worship in the Early Church.* London, 1964.

————————, "An Early Christian Hymn: Col. 1:15-20," *The Evangelical Quarterly* XXXVI, 4, 1964.

————————, "Aspects of Worship in the New Testament Church," *Vox Evangelica,* II. London, 1963.

Maxwell, W. D., *An Outline of Christian Worship.* Oxford 1945.

Michell, G. A., *Eucharistic Consecration in the Primitive Church.* London, 1948.

Micklem, N., ed., *Christian Worship: Studies in Its History and Meaning.* Oxford, 1936.

Moule, C. F. D., *Worship in the New Testament.*

Nielen, J. M., *The Earliest Christian Liturgy.* London, 1941.

Otto, R., *The Idea of the Holy.* Penguin Books, 1960.

Schnackenburg, R., *Baptism in the Thought of Saint Paul.* Oxford, 1964.

Smith, W. S., *Musical Aspects of the New Testament.* Amsterdam, 1962.

White, R. E. O., *The Biblical Doctrine of Initiation.* Grand Rapids, 1960.

The Old Testament Background

For a full study of the detailed requirements of Old Testament worship, reference must be made to Bible dictionaries and such other works as de Vaux, *Ancient Israel: Its*

Life and Institutions, Pt. IV (Eng. trans., London and New York, 1961) and A. S. Herbert, *Worship in Ancient Israel* (London, 1959). The scope of this essay is to notice the features of Hebrew worship which have a particular bearing on the worship of the Christian church — for the temple, the synagogue and the Old Testament Scriptures were highly influential in the life of the early Christian worshiping community.

It is a tantalizing feature of the Old Testament that, even though it shows clearly the centrality of the worship of Jahweh, the God of Israel, in the national life, it never provides us with any full description of one such act of worship, whether an isolated sacrifice or a major festival in Jerusalem. Some special orders of service are described, e.g., Solomon's dedication of the temple (II Chron. 5-7), and certain stipulations about the way in which sacrifices should be offered are given (Lev. 6-7), but we do not see the whole picture, with spoken liturgy, ceremonial action, and detailed rubrics all included. Some conjecture is therefore called for, and it has been applied with some degree of success to the study of the Psalms.

1. LITURGY OF WORD: THE PSALMS

Since Gunkel's commentary was published in 1926, the Psalms have been viewed no longer as isolated compositions from different periods of Israelite history but as ritual forms which owe their continued existence, if not their original composition, to the use that was made of them in the regular life of the Jerusalem temple. Read thus, at least some of them can be recognized as liturgical compositions for festival occasions or for particular religious moments in the life of the individual worshiper.

It is often possible to identify differing voices in the wording of psalms as, for instance, in Psalm 24, which describes a procession of worshipers approaching the temple on Mount Zion. As they draw near they cry out:

> Who shall ascend the hill of Jahweh?
> Who shall stand in his holy place?

Another character, a priest or the gatekeeper of the temple, replies in the words of the entry formula (cf. Ps. 15):

> He who has clean hands and a pure heart,
> Who does not lift up his soul to what is false,
> And does not swear deceitfully.
> He will receive blessing from Jahweh,
> And vindication from the God of his salvation.

One of the leaders of the procession then vouches for the sincerity of his company with the words:

> Such is the generation of those who seek him,
> Who seek the face of the God of Jacob.

The next section of the psalm may be a later part of the festival liturgy or, more likely, it indicates that these words were being spoken by the main festival procession as it approached the temple carrying with it the ark of the covenant as the symbol of Jahweh's presence. They therefore demand admittance for the ark:

> Lift up your heads, O gates,
> And be lifted up, O ancient doors!
> That the King of glory may come in.

From behind the doors comes the demand for the password:

> Who is the King of glory?

The implication is that these doors will only be opened to the true God who belongs there. There is some suspense as the first reply, "*The Lord,* strong and mighty, the Lord mighty in battle" is not apparently accepted, and the question is repeated. This time the special cultic name of the God of Israel is used: "*Jahweh of Hosts,* He is the King of glory," and the procession is welcomed in through the open doors.

This kind of search for liturgical situations reflected in the Psalms has enabled students of the Psalter to identify the following categories of psalm: ark liturgies e.g., Ps. 24, 68, 132), songs of Zion (Ps. 46, 48, 76, 87), songs of pilgrimage (Ps. 84, 122), royal psalms in which the king features prominently (Ps. 2, 20, 21, 101, 110, 132), thanksgivings to be used either privately when a vow-sacrifice was offered or corporately by the whole nation after some great act of deliverance (Ps. 30, 67, 116, 124), and laments or penitential psalms which again could be for either individual or corporate use (Ps. 51, 70, 80).

One of the burning issues of more recent years has been the extent to which the Psalms reflect the existence of an annual

(New Year?) festival in which Jahweh's enthronement as King of the universe was celebrated. According to Mowinckel's reconstruction (*The Psalms in Israel's Worship*, 2 vols, Eng. trans., Oxford, 1962), year by year Jahweh's triumph over the primeval powers of chaos and their allies, the kings of the earth, was ritually re-enacted, the ark as the symbol of Jahweh's presence was carried in procession to the temple, and Jahweh was proclaimed king with the cry "*Jahweh* mālakh" (The Lord has become king, cf. Ps. 93:1; 97:1; 99:1). Jahweh's covenant with his people through the Davidic king was then renewed for another year, and the congregation of Israel faced the future with fresh confidence.

Variations of this theory have been many, but for us the common denominator of them all is that they recognize a similar liturgical pattern in a number of psalms with the following recurrent themes:

a. A recitation of Jahweh's marvelous acts. These consist not only of his great acts in creation but also of his deliverance through the exodus from Egypt and the settlement in the promised land, a redemption which the Israelites never tired of retelling.

b. The conflict between Jahweh (or the spokesman of the psalm) and his enemies, variously described as the powers of evil, the kings of the earth or the waters of the deep. Thus subsequent generations who used the psalms were never allowed to forget the reality and power of evil, spiritual as well as physical, with which the true followers of Jahweh were constantly engaged in battle.

c. The eventual triumph of faith after near defeat. Invariably Jahweh gave victory, which in Hebrew is synonymous with salvation. However downtrodden the little kingdom of Judah might be, the hope of eventual triumph was thus kept alive through the cult.

d. The renewal of Jahweh's covenant with his people in righteousness. Acts of worship were designed to end up with a restored relationship with God so that, like the publican in the parable, the worshiper left the temple "justified."

e. The part played by the Davidic king who is called Jahweh's son, his beloved, and his anointed (messiah). It follows from this that all such psalms have a legitimate right to be understood messianically even by the most cautious exegete.

All these aspects of the liturgy of the Psalter have considerable bearing on the worship of the Christian church in every generation. How many Christian liturgies bring home to their users so effectively these great Biblical truths of God's redemption, the conflict with evil, the promise of victory, and the justification of the believer?

2. LITURGY OF ACT

a. *Festival*

The Jewish year was broken up by three major festivals with long histories behind them — Passover, Pentecost and Tabernacles. These all had agricultural origins and at some stage in their development they became associated with God's redemption of Israel.

Passover, or the Feast of Unleavened Bread, was celebrated from 14 to 21 Nisan, the first spring month of the year: agriculturally it represented the time of offering the firstfruits of the barley harvest (Lev. 23:10 f.), but its theological connection was with the Exodus from Egypt (Exod. 12:17). Leviticus 23:6 suggests that the first day only was the Passover commemoration. Pentecost came seven weeks later (Lev. 23:15) at the completion of the barley and wheat harvests, and was originally called the Feast of Weeks. In post-Biblical Judaism it was historicized as a memorial of the covenant of Sinai, but there is no indication of this tradition in Scripture.

The Feast of Tabernacles, or Ingathering, was a seven-day festival in the seventh month (Tishri 15-21), almost exactly balancing Passover in the calendar. It came at the time of grape and olive harvests for which temporary dwellings were erected in the fields. It combined all the joyfulness of a great harvest thanksgiving with a commemoration of the wilderness wanderings in the peninsula of Sinai (Lev. 23:42 f.). It is characteristic of Hebrew religion that the great agricultural festivals of the year were used as theological commemorations, in much the same way as the Christian church has taken over pre-Christian festival periods and associated them with the major events of Christ's life.

Other great days of the Jewish year were the Day of Atonement (Tishri 10; see Lev. 23:26-31), and the Day of Acclamation (Tishri 1: see Num. 29:1-6), which could have been a New Year Festival at a time when the calendar year began in the autumn. Apart from these and the later festivals of Purim (Esther 9) and the Dedication (I Macc. 4:52; John 10:22), there was, of course, the regular routine of new moons, sabbaths, and the daily offerings each of which had its own ritual of sacrifice described in detail in Numbers 28-29.

b. *Sacrifice*

The different kinds of sacrifice required represent differing aspects of the Israelite's relationship to his God. The burnt offering (*eōlāh*) was essentially an act of giving, as the whole animal was consumed with fire to be "a pleasing odour to the Lord," and so it represented the homage of the offerer. The cereal offering (*minchāh*) was not an animal sacrifice, though it usually accompanied one, but an offering of flour, baked cakes or raw grain (Lev. 2:1-16). After a token portion had been burnt the remainder went to the priests. It thus served as a contribution towards the maintenance of the ministry. The peace offerings (*shelāmīm*) were sacrifices of communion; they incorporated both the ideas of gift and fellowship-meal. Their aim was to maintain friendship with God and it is easy to see why the vow, the thank offering and the freewill offering (Lev. 7:12, 16) were regarded as subdivisions of the peace offering, for they were all expressions of good relations with the deity.

The thought of atonement was never completely absent from any of these forms of sacrifice, but the guilt and sin offering (*āshām, chaṭṭā'th*) were intended more specifically for the atonement of sins, both moral and ceremonial, whether committed consciously or unwittingly. There does not however appear to have been any sacrificial atonement for sins "with a high hand," i.e., deliberate violations of God's law like murder and adultery.

Apart from the sin offerings, sacrifices were mainly joyful occasions and were accompanied by singing and dancing, music and trumpet blowing, the waving of branches and shouts of jubilation. The Psalms are particularly rich in words expressing various degrees of exultation. This fact illustrates a significant feature of Old Testament worship, namely, that it was essentially a happy procedure, and thankfulness for past mercies was never far from the minds of the worshipers. The prayers of David (I Chron. 29:10 ff.) and Solomon (II Chron. 6:4 ff.) concentrate characteristically on objective worship and thanksgiving rather than on lengthy petition.

The chief cause for gratitude was ever the great act of redemption from Egypt, the prototype of which every subsequent act, like the return from exile, was but a reflection. Hebrew religion always looked back into the past ("Remember that you were a servant in the land of Egypt") and it expressed itself, appropriately, in the tangible form of the sacrificial system. For sacrifice involved giving to God and to his service through the priesthood, and giving *irrevocably*: the fire on the altar saw to that. So the gift was an act of self-deprivation, for it consisted of meat and produce, the necessities of life as far as the giver was concerned. Nor was any member of the community exempt from this obligation. Graded offerings were allowed for those who were poorer, but no one except the unholy and those who opted out willfully were excluded from offering what they could. Furthermore, the ritual made it clear that only the best was good enough for God ("a male without blemish"), and Malachi spoke strongly against those who thought anything would do (1:6-14).

By offering his gift, however, the Israelite did not lose the gift. He gained God's favor; not as it were by a bribe, but in accepting his sacrifice, God bound himself in some way to the giver. Hence the frequency and popularity of the communal meal, or peace offering.

Alongside all this and deeply underlying it was the offerer's sense of unworthiness before a holy God and his continual need for cleansing through the efficacy of the sin offerings. This sense of sin was not always felt, however, and when it was lacking the whole system could easily degenerate into the debauch that non-Israelite festivals frequently were. That is why the prophets attacked the sacrifices, denying that God wanted it at all if sincerity and obedience to his laws were missing (Amos 5:25; Jer. 7:

22; Hos. 6:6; cf. 1 Sam. 15:22 f.). The act must be subordinate to the motive.

3. WORSHIP IN THE SYNAGOGUE

There was much more to Old Testament religion than what went on in the temple or at earlier cult centers. One of the more enduring results of the exile was the development in Judaism of the nonritual element which grew into the later synagogue movement. The origins of this may be traced to Ezekiel's Babylonian ministry (14:1) or to Ezra's practice of reading and interpreting the Law to the people, but the Old Testament contains no positive reference to synagogue worship and we have to go to post-Biblical sources for our knowledge of it.

Jewish piety in the closing centuries before Christ was centered in the Torah. From its study there arose the personal devotion of prayer, fasting and acts of righteousness, three aspects of religion on which our Lord had cause to comment in the Sermon on the Mount (Matt. 6). C. W. Dugmore (*The Influence of the Synagogue upon the Divine Office*, London, 1964) shows that "the first followers of Jesus continued to join in the worship of the synagogue and to keep *Tōrāh*. They formed, as it were, a new sect or party . . . within Judaism, differing from their orthodox Jewish friends only in their acceptance of Jesus as Messiah." As the rift between Jew and Christian increased, churches became more and more independent but they still were little more than Christian synagogues (see James Parkes, *The Conflict of the Church and the Synagogue*, London, 1934). The extent to which early Christian liturgy borrowed from synagogal forms is debatable, but it seems likely that both in its pattern of ministry and in its forms of worship the church looked back mainly to the synagogue and only minimally to the temple.

The daily synagogue service in the first century A.D. probably began with the invocation "Bless ye the Lord who is to be blessed." Then followed the two main elements, common to both morning and evening services, of the *Shema'* and the *Tephillah*. Basically the *Shema'* was a recitation of the Jewish creed, consisting altogether of Deuteronomy 6:4-9; 11:13-21 and Numbers 15:37-41, though the first sentence was the most important and probably the original part. This was accompanied by four blessings, two before it and two after it, the earliest of which was the *Yōtzēr*:

> Blessed art Thou, O Lord our God, King of the world,
> Former of light and Creator of darkness,
> Maker of peace and Creator of all things;
> Who gives light in mercy to the earth and to those who live thereon,
> And in His goodness renews every day, continually, the work of creation.
> Let a new light shine over Zion and Thy Messiah's light over us.

The other part of the service, the *Tephillah*, was mainly prayer expressed in the form of benedictions. The present Eighteen Benedictions contain a few which are later than the first century A.D., the most famous of which is the twelfth which in its older form prayed that Christians and heretics would "perish as in a moment." These benedictions covered a variety of themes, praise, prayer for spiritual and material blessings, and supplication for those in need. The Maccabean fourteenth benediction is not untypical:

> Have pity, O Lord our God, on Israel Thy people,
> On Jerusalem Thy city, and on Zion the dwelling-place of Thy glory,
> and on Thine altar, and on Thy palace,
> and on the kingdom of the house of David, the Messiah Thy righteousness.
> Blessed art Thou, O Lord, the Builder of Jerusalem.

In addition to creed and prayers, the Scriptures were read on Sabbaths and holy days, each day having two lections, from the Pentateuch and from the Prophets. This was frequently followed by exposition of the passage by a suitably qualified member of the synagogue or a distinguished visitor (cf. Luke 4:20 ff.; Acts 13:15 ff.). The psalms, especially the Hallel psalms (113-118), were in regular use in the temple and on certain festival occasions, but their use early spread further afield and at a very early date they were an established part of the daily synagogue services.

BIBLIOGRAPHY

Kidner, F. D., *Sacrifice in the Old Testament*, 1952.

Hooke, S. H., ed., *Myth, Ritual and Kingship*, 1958.

Lamb, J. A., *The Psalms in Christian Worship,* 1962.
Leslie, E. A., *The Psalms,* 1949.
Micklem, N., ed., *Christian Worship,* 1936.
Ringgren, H., *The Faith of the Psalmists,* 1963.
Rowley, H. H., *Ritual and the Hebrew Prophets.*
Welch, A. C., *The Psalter in Life, Worship and History,* 1926.

Medieval Worship

The most important single source of information about medieval worship is the various service books in use both in the East and in the West. They were compiled for different purposes and they have come to us from different periods. If a reader at mass had to read a passage from the Old Testament, or from the Acts, the Epistles or the Apocalypse, he resorted to the *Epistolarium*; if another had to read the lesson from the Gospels, the *Evangelarium* was at hand, or perhaps the *Liber Comitis* was available for both of them. The priest used his *Sacramentarium,* though it still contained forms for rites which had become reserved in the course of time to the bishop, as well as forms used by the priest at baptism, marriage, the visitation of the sick, the burial of the dead, forms which were later gathered into a separate book known as the *Manuale,* the *Rituale,* or the *Sacramentale* The *Kalendarium* indicated the approach of festivals, and the *Martyrologium* of days sacred to the memory of saints and martyrs. The *Ordinale* guided the clergy in the conduct of worship, while the *Compotus* helped them to calculate the date of Easter. In more frequent use were the *Psalterium* for reciting the daily office, and the *Sermologus* and the *Homilarium,* aids for the preacher in preparing his weekly sermon for the instruction of the faithful.

The service book in the earlier years of the period indicated the mode of worship peculiar to a district. Variations were frequent and no one uniform rite was followed throughout large geographical areas. Gradually, however, local forms tended to give way to more widely accepted uses, and uniformity increased.

Under Charlemagne, the church of Gaul adopted the Roman liturgy, but incorporated in it elements peculiar to Gallic liturgies, and later this Gallic and Roman amalgam displaced the liturgy used in Rome itself. Of this combination, the *Gelasian Sacramentary* is the best known representative. It belongs to the seventh century. The *Antiphonary of Bangor* in Ireland (A.D. 680-691) preserves the choir office of the Celtic church. In England the *Use of Sarum* (Salisbury) became important. The Roman rite followed in the cathedral was modified during the Middle Ages and by 1457 nearly the whole country had adopted the order of service in use at Salisbury. In 1549 the Reformers largely adopted it for the *First Book of Common Prayer* of Edward VI, in the preface of which it is described as a "local" form which the new book was designed to replace.

In the East, the *Euchologion* was used; it contained the text of the three eucharistic rites of St. Chrysostom, St. Basil, and the Liturgy of the Presanctified, with the invariable parts of the Office and the prayers used in the celebration of the sacraments. The earliest manuscript of it, the *Codex Barberinus,* probably originated in the eighth century. Rites in the East quickly became uniform and service books homogeneous.

The center of worship was the Eucharist and here also the general tendency was towards uniformity. The Eastern tradition, fixed in essentials before the close of the fourth century, was based on the rite of the church of Jerusalem with some modifications introduced from Byzantium, the Byzantine rite which Constantinople attempted to force upon all churches subject to the imperial edict. The considerable changes which were characteristic of the East before the seventh century ceased by the ninth, when the eastern liturgy became stereotyped.

The western rite of the Eucharist consisted of Roman and Gallic elements; the eastern rite was the Byzantine liturgy. Some of the differences between the two are notable. The service in the East began with the *Prothesis,* namely, the preparatory devotions and vesting of the ministers, the washing of hands, the preparation of the oblations, that is especially, the cutting of the bread, the censing of the church, and the blessing pronounced by the priest standing before the table. The preparations were followed by litanies, antiphons, and prayers, together known as the *Enarxis*. At this point the *Liturgy of the Catechumens* began with the procession to the table with the Gospel-book and with the singing of hymns concluding with the *Trisagion*. In the West, however, the service began with the *Mass of the Catechumens* which until the sixteenth century included the recital before the altar of Psalm 43, mutual confession, and prayers. Subsequently in the West, these were not accounted part of the mass which properly began with the *Kyrie*, an eastern litany which survived in its three responses *Kyrie Eleison*, and with the *Gloria*, an eastern private psalm in use from the fourth century. The two liturgies coincide in the Epistle, the Alleluia, and the Gospel, which in the West was followed by the *Nicene Creed* inserted here before the eleventh century, except in Rome, and in the East by the Litany, the Prayer of Supplication, and the Dismissal of the Catechumens. At this point in both East and West, the mass, or Liturgy of the Faithful, began with the Offertory, followed in the East by the Nicene Creed. The second part of the Canon in both East and West was similar up to the Benedictus. In the West at this point certain prayers followed for the church, and then the *Prayers of Oblation and Consecration*. Afterwards in East and West came the narrative of the Institution and the *Anamnesis*, the memorial of the Passion, Death, Resurrection and Ascension, followed in the East by the *Great Intercession*, and in the West by the *Consignation*, the signing with one species over the other, and the *Elevation*. In both rites at this point the *Fraction* and *Commixture* were the prelude to the *Communion*. Prayers, Thanksgiving, and the Dismissal concluded the service. From the seventh century in the West a simplified form, *Low Mass* came into use, in which there was no singing and the priest officiated with only a server, and a century later, the canon was recited inaudibly. At about the same time unleavened bread was used, and it was placed in the communicant's mouth instead of in his hands. The reserved elements were kept in a *Pyx* shut up in a sanctuary cupboard, the *Aumbry*, or in a receptable hanging over the altar. They were used for the communion of the sick but they were not associated with any special devotions. In the East the bread which had been blessed but not consecrated was distributed to people who had not communicated; the remnants of the consecrated bread were eaten by the children.

In the East, the African custom of taking home consecrated bread (Tertullian, Cyprian) for private communion, endured until the eighth century. The dipping of the bread in the consecrated wine was widely practiced and although forbidden by the Third Council of Braga (A.D. 675), it was popular again by the eleventh century, and forbidden again by the Council of Westminster (A.D. 1175). In the West the laity had ceased to drink the cup by the thirteenth century when the Synod of Lambeth (A.D. 1281) restricted it to the celebrant. During the Middle Ages the laity was present at mass but rarely took communion. The service was largely the concern of the celebrant alone; the congregation took the opportunity of saying their private prayers during the course of the mass. With the development of vernacular languages in the West, Latin became a learned language known only to priests who were often themselves not very familiar with it, and increasingly the mass became a priestly ritual rather than the common worship of the people of God.

In the fifth century mass was sometimes said in private houses, and masses of a semi-private character in chapels annexed to large churches. According to the Gelasian sacramentary, masses were said for travelers, rain, good weather, cattle, children, the sick, and there were several masses for the dead. Throughout the Middle Ages *Votive Masses* were said, and chantries were built where the chantry priest could say or sing mass for the repose of the soul of a founder, his relatives, and his friends.

The theology of the mass was increasingly elaborated and ultimately received its precise and authoritative formulation at the Lateran Council in 1215 when the *Doctrine of Transubstantiation* was defined as the belief that at the words of institution the whole substance of the bread and the wine is converted into the whole substance of the body and blood of Christ, only the accidents or appearances remaining. Later in the century, St. Thomas Aquinas developed this doctrine in Aristotelian terms of substance and attribute. The doctrine thus defined in the High Middle Ages had its roots in what was already the remote past. Some patristic writers tended to minimize the genuine reality of the bread and wine after consecration, and in 831 Paschasius Radbertus was teaching a form of transubstantiation. The natural substance was annihilated after consecration and only the appearances remained. Berengar of Tours criticized crudely materialistic accounts, and in the pope's presence was forced to admit that after consecration the true body and blood of our Lord Jesus Christ are sensibly, not only in the sacrament but in truth, touched and broken by the hands of the priests, and bruised by the teeth of the faithful. They were indeed physically eaten with the mouth. The doctrine of transubstantiation, designed to correct grossly materialistic accounts of the sacrament, is one of the chief distinctions of medieval theology. Whether it succeeded in correcting popular error is doubtful. Perhaps it is worth noting that what is characteristic of it is the assertion that Christ is present in the elements because after consecration they undergo a specific change. The "how" of the change, that is the conversion of the substance, is chiefly important. It was the metaphysical account of the change which the Twenty-Eighth Article of the Church of England repudiates: "Transubstantiation (or the change of the substance of the Bread and Wine) in the Supper of the Lord cannot be proved by Holy Writ; but is repugnant to the plain words of Scripture, overthroweth the nature of a Sacrament, and hath given occasion to many superstitions." Berengar and Wycliffe had argued long before that accidents could not exist without the substance in which they inhered.

The doctrine of transubstantiation encouraged belief in the virtue of the eucharistic sacrifice. In it, according to popular opinion, if not according to theologians, the church had power to present the material body and blood as a repetition of the sacrifice of the cross whose effect was unlimited for whatever purpose the church applied it. Consequently the number of masses greatly increased, and they were applied to the living and to the dead. Every priest was expected to say mass daily and daily to communicate. The religious, monks, nuns, and friars frequently communicated, the laity rarely, however often they might be present. Mass was heard on Sundays and on holy days in church, or, among the aristocracy, in private chapels, but the congregation was present to witness a divine drama really and not only symbolically enacted before them, rather than to participate in a common act of worship which in fellowship with the Redeemer they offered to God. They witnessed a miracle rather than participated in God's gracious and redemptive act. In the thirteenth century the priest began to raise the bread above his head and to ring the sanctuary bell before and after consecration, in order to display to the congregation the host which called for their adoration. To adore precipitately was idolatry, to refuse was sacrilege. Subsequently the Reserved Sacrament was also adored.

Daily worship was offered in the churches as early as the fourth century, and it was ordered, regularized, and perpetuated by the coming of monasticism. In the eighth century St. Benedict arranged for his monks to sing eight offices during each day and night – Vespers at sunset, Compline at bedtime, Nocturns and Lauds at 2 a.m. or at dawn, Prime on rising for the day, Terce at 9 a.m., Sext at noon, and None at 3 p.m. The Psalter, recited weekly in its entirety, was the basis of worship, with passages of Scripture, prayers, and such hymns as the *Gloria in Excelsis* and the *Te Deum*. Litanies (Greek: supplication) were used in Antioch towards the end of the fourth century. In the eighth century the Office of the Saints was introduced into the Daily Office, and a century later, Charlemagne introduced a liturgical innovation by uniting the Gallican and the Roman uses. Later the Daily Office was modified to include the Office of the Blessed Virgin and the Office of the Dead.

The Daily Office was revised in the twelfth century, and abbreviated, chiefly by using shorter passages from Scripture. The number of festivals to be observed was increased and the Office of the Blessed Virgin was introduced. The Franciscans extended this revision in 1241 by shortening still more the Scripture passages and by introducing legendary material to be used on saints' days, whose number was increased. The *Ave Maria* was sung before and after each Office of the Blessed Virgin. The friars popularized this Daily Office which became the basis of diocesan uses such as that of Sarum. Secular priests said Matins and Lauds overnight, Prime, Terce, Sext, and None, in the morning, Vespers and Compline in the afternoon. In the Anglican Book of Common Prayer the Order for Morning Prayer, often popularly known as Matins, is based on the medieval Matins, supplemented from Prime; Evening Prayer, or Evensong, is based on a conflation of Vespers and Compline in the Sarum use. The medieval layman did not concern himself with the Daily Offices except to some extent on Sundays, though the bell from the neighboring monastery reminded him that the monks were hallowing time by the *Opus Dei,* and that punctuality was important in the ordering of his secular affairs.

Processions were characteristic of medieval worship. There were processions in church before mass on Sundays and on some holy days; on Wednesdays and Fridays in Lent, on Palm Sunday, Ascension Day, and Corpus Christi, the procession made its way through the churchyard, and on Rogation Days and on St. Mark's Day through the streets and the countryside. From about the tenth century at Rogationtide, a procession went round the parish boundaries to beat them and the boys of the parish with willow rods. The Major Rogation on April 25th was imitated from the pagan Robigalia when a procession went through the cornfields to pray for the defense of the crop from mildew.

The parish priest delivered a sermon at mass on Sundays and on holy days, with the help of a Homilarium, if he were sufficiently wealthy or conscientious. In the fifth century St. Augustine used to preach on the lesson appointed for the day, and his sermons were normally expositions of Scripture which were continued in the services for two or three days. The Middle Ages produced no preachers of the excellence of Augustine or Chrysostom, but they nevertheless produced many great preachers, and preaching played a considerable part in the worship, the education, and the public life of the time. Pope Urban II, Peter the Hermit, and St. Bernard of Clairvaux by their preaching aroused their contemporaries to rescue the Holy Places from the infidel Moslems, and the Crusades were the result. The preaching of the Dominicans with their careful intellectual training was directed to the suppression of heresy, especially that of the Albigenses; the Franciscans with their imagination, simple style, and evangelical fervor, appealed to great numbers of ordinary folk and in Berthold of Regensburg produced a widely popular evangelist. Theologians of the highest eminence such as Albertus Magnus, Thomas Aquinas, and Bonaventura, were also great preachers, and perhaps rather more surprisingly, so were the mystics, Eckhart, Henry Suso, and John Tauler. Preaching was based on Scripture interpreted according to the canons received from the early church, and diligently studied and expounded in the monasteries. In many churches preaching was poor and the preacher well-nigh illiterate, who had no readier access to the Bible than his parishioners, and as little trained in the understanding of it. Oft-told legends of the saints, moral tales, illustrations drawn from local events and from gossip about them, often made up for what the preacher lacked in knowledge of the Bible and the creeds about which he was chiefly concerned to instruct his hearers.

In the thirteenth and fourteenth centuries, three new festivals were appointed. Pope Urban IV instituted the Feast of Corpus Christi (1264) in honor of the sacrament of the Altar. By the following century it was universally observed in the West; the services were arranged by St. Thomas Aquinas who composed for them the hymns *Lauda Sion* and *Pange Lingua.* Pope John XXII instituted the general observance of Trinity Sunday in 1334, though it had been locally observed ever since the tenth century. It was especially popular in England, perhaps because it was associated with Thomas à Becket who in 1162 was consecrated bishop on that day. From this Sunday Carmelites, Dominicans, and the Sarum Missal, reckoned the Sundays before Advent; in the Roman rite they are counted from Pentecost. In 1389 Pope Urban VI instituted the Feast of the Visitation, but it had been observed by the Franciscans on the prompting of St. Bonaventure since the General Chapter of 1263. The Feast of the Annunciation had already been observed for nearly six hundred years. The Trullan Synod had ordained that it should be kept as a feast even though it fell in Lent. To avoid this unseasonable collocation the church in Spain had for long kept the Feast on December 18th, but by the eighth century it was universally celebrated on March 25th. The Book of Common Prayer in the Alternative Calendar (1928) describes it as the Annunciation of Our Lady, the only place in the book where this term is applied to the Blessed Virgin.

The Cult of Mary had been important in the East after the Council of Ephesus and probably before; in the West its theological basis was strengthened in the Middle Ages by Anselm (c. 1036-1086) who taught that Mary must possess all the privileges of a creature in keeping with her status as the Mother of God, and by Duns Scotus (c. 1264-1308) who formulated the Doctrine of the Immaculate Conception which was ultimately defined in 1854. Devotion to Mary considerably increased during this period. The Little Office of Our Lady is first known in the tenth century and was adopted by the Camaldulensians, by the Cistercians, and later, by the secular clergy. Popular piety expressed itself in the Devotion of the Rosary, said to have been founded by St. Dominic (1170-1221) though, in fact, it developed under Cistercian and Dominican influence, and in the *Angelus,* which as a morning devotion first appears in the fourteenth century, and as a midday devotion, a century later. May was regàrded as the month of Mary. Pilgrimages of all kinds played an important, not to say a spectacular, part in popular religion, and the shrine of Our Lady of Walsingham attracted pilgrims from many parts of England and from abroad.

The rites of baptism, marriage, and burial underwent little change during the Middle Ages. In the Orthodox and other eastern churches, the mode of baptism was submersion, and in the West this was also the mode of the Ambrosian rite. It seems to have been used fairly widely throughout the Middle Ages. From the eighth century onwards, immersion was practiced, that is, the candidate stood in the water which was also poured on his head. When infants were baptized they were usually dipped in the font. Affusion, that is the pouring of water over the candidate's head, was not generally practiced until the close of the Middle Ages.

In the East, confirmation immediately followed baptism, even the baptism of infants, the priest using oil which had previously been consecrated by the bishop. In the West the bishop administered the rite as originally he administered baptism. Since the bishop could not be present at every baptism, confirmation became separated from it and was not regularly administered. In the later Middle Ages it was conferred as soon as convenient after the seventh birthday. The bishop anointed the candidate's head with oil, tapped him on the cheek in token of the spiritual warfare in which he would be engaged, and laid his hands on his head in blessing. The doctrine of confirmation was discussed with special reference to its institution. St. Thomas Aquinas believed that it was instituted by Christ, St. Bonaventura that it was instituted by the Holy Spirit through the successors of the apostles, and Alexander of Hales, that it was instituted by the Council of Meaux in 845.

Marriage banns were read on three separate Sundays or on holy days, the church following Roman law regarding the basis of marriage as consent. An impediment to marriage was constituted by affinity which was decided according to complicated rules which also applied to spiritual affinity between godparents and the baptized. The first part of the wedding service took place at the entrance to the church. The priest put the questions and the couple made their vows in English. Gold, silver, and the ring were put on the priest's book. The ring was blessed, sprinkled with holy water, and placed on the first finger of the bride's right hand in the name of the Father, on the second in the name of the Son, on the third in the name of the Holy Ghost, and on the fourth finger, where it remained, at the Amen. The bridal party went with the priest to the altar while he recited Psalm 128; he said prayers at the altar step and when the couple had made their way to the south side of the presbytery, he began Nuptial Mass. A blessing on the marriage was pronounced immediately before the communion. It was held that the bride and the bridegroom were the ministers of this sacrament, the priest being present only as a witness.

The Churching of Women followed childbirth. Psalms 121 and 128, the *Kyrie,* the *Paternoster,* versicles, and prayers were said at the church door, the mother was sprinkled with holy water and then admitted to church with the words, "Enter into the temple of

God that thou mayest have eternal life and live for ever."

On his way to the Visitation of the Sick the priest recited the seven Penitential Psalms, and when he arrived at the house, invoked the blessing of peace. In the presence of the sick he said the *Kyrie,* the *Paternoster,* versicles, and prayers. He examined him in the creed, exhorted him to patience, faith, hope, and charity, heard his confession, and said prayers.

Unction was originally an anointing for the healing of the sick and this usage was not wholly forgotten, though the rite was generally reserved for the mortally ill and was held to convey the remission of sins. Peter Lombard (c. 1100-1160) is the first known writer to use the term Extreme Unction and in the Middle Ages it was given a place among the seven sacraments. The *Viaticum* – provision for the journey – was the Holy Communion given to the sick at the point of death.

While the body was being prepared for removal to church, psalms and prayers were said followed by Vespers, Compline, and the Vigils of the Dead. The priest said Requiem Mass and the Burial Service was held. In the fourth century it was an occasion of rejoicing and mourners wore white; by the eighth century, however, black was worn and prayers were offered for purification and for deliverance from hell. At the burial, antiphons, kyries, and prayers were said in church. The priest censed the body and sprinkled it with holy water. On the way to the grave, psalms were sung; the grave was censed and blessed. When the body had been laid in it with committal prayers, earth was sprinkled on it in the form of a cross. After more prayers and psalms, the procession returned to church singing a penitential psalm. Requiem Masses were said for the dead on the third, ninth, thirtieth, and three hundred and sixty-sixth day after death; black vestments were worn in a setting provided by pictures in stained glass and on church walls of the pains of hell and purgatory and of the joys of heaven.

In the Middle Ages, Christian worship was already very ancient. Its roots ran down into the Old and New Testaments; it inherited and preserved a rich legacy from the early church. Its main outlines, its "shape," had been fixed centuries before, and there were no revolutionary changes either in doctrine or in ceremonial, though there was considerable adaptation to Christian needs within the limits laid down by the living tradition of the church. Its great strength was its firm basis in Christian theology; in worship doctrine came alive, and whatever may be thought of some of the contents of that doctrine, the advantage of having it daily portrayed in action, speech, music, painting, and architecture, can scarcely be denied. Medieval worship was centered on God; it would have been impossible without a belief in the God of which the doctrines of the Holy Trinity and the Incarnation speak. No matter how unskilled in theology a worshiper might be, he could scarcely take part in the worship of the church from his early years without being confronted and claimed by the universal faith. Moreover, he became aware that the faith claimed the whole of his life. From his earliest hours to his last some Christian rite or ceremony, some form of worship, threatened his sins, confirmed his good resolutions, hallowed his joys, and reminded him of God's claims upon him. Religious devotion and human weakness turned into shot silk the material of medieval life. Even when the Middle Ages were passing away and the old order was falling into decay, merchants still headed the pages of ledgers, recording sometimes dubious profits, "In the Name of God." And when the medieval worshiper committed sin, he did not regard it as "bad form or psychological" but as sin against God's holiness who had appointed, largely in the Middle Ages, an elaborate penitential system for his restoration.

The kind of worship men offer to God ultimately depends on their conception of his nature, so that if they change the way in which they think of him and of his relation to mankind, they will also change their worship. This is the explanation of the far reaching changes which took place at the close of the Middle Ages. Medieval Christians had thought that God in his holiness communicated grace to men through the divinely appointed channels of the church and its sacraments. Worship involved participation in the sacramental life of the church which hallowed and sanctified the life of men and made them Christians. The Reformers thought of grace as the outgoing of the active and redemptive love of God to the sinner which elicited his penitent response. Everything depended upon a man's personal response to the love of God. Grace was communicated not so much through the institutionalized church as through God's immediate confrontation with the sinner, and his response in faith conceived not so much as knowledge of the contents of revelation as in committal to him who revealed himself in Christ. Evangelical and Reformed worship expressed this confrontation with God revealed in his Word.

BIBLIOGRAPHY

Dix, G., *The Shape of the Liturgy.* London: Dacre Press, 1945.

Hardman, O., *A History of Christian Worship.* London: University of London Press, 1937.

Jungmann, J., *The Early Liturgy.* London: Darton Press, 1958.

Maxwell, W. D., *An Outline of Christian Worship.* Oxford: Oxford University Press, 1939.

Micklem, N., *Christian Worship.* Oxford: Oxford University Press, 1936.

Norman, J., *Handbook to the Christian Liturgy.* London: S.P.C.K., 1944.

Reformed Worship

The Protestant Reformation of the sixteenth century had as its objective the reforming of the church which had become decadent theologically, morally and spiritually. To accomplish this, Martin Luther, the Wittenberg professor, sought to remove from the church whatever came into conflict with Biblical teaching. The church must once again become "a pilgrim church," oppressed, humiliated but at the same time bearing its testimony to the gospel. This understanding of the church often resulted in his retaining ceremonies and symbolism which he felt were useful although they had no Scriptural warrant. To John Calvin, on the other hand, the only means of reform was the reestablishment, as far as possible, of the early church on strictly Biblical principles. When this had been accomplished, the church could then go forth conquering and to conquer under its king, the risen victorious Christ.

The Reformed churches, which look back to Calvin as their originator, have spread over the whole world from the Genevan starting point. With them they have carried Calvin's views on doctrine, discipline, and worship so that they have tended to establish a general pattern of worship which, while it may differ from church to church and from country to country, yet has a basic structure that makes it possible for anyone of Reformed background to understand. At the same time, one must also recognize that nearly all churches which call themselves Reformed have not always manifested an unswerving loyalty to the principles of Calvin. They have experienced theological declines coupled with the rise of rationalism, sacramentalism, or pietism. Consequently one can notice in the history of these churches that at times strenuous efforts have been made to change the forms of worship. Usually those who sought such changes endeavored to find support for their ideas in the teaching of Calvin, even if they had to twist his views to fit their purposes. Yet in spite of all such efforts, Reformed forms of worship have generally remained fundamentally the same.

1. THE ESSENCE OF REFORMED WORSHIP

In truly Reformed thinking the worship of God is essentially spiritual. This means that it does not consist in outward actions, but comes from the very core of man's being, his heart. All men have a need for such worship, since that basically is what differentiates them from animals (Calvin, *Institutes,* 1:3:3). True worship must also be "in the Spirit" of God, for men cannot worship in a true spiritual manner unless God's Spirit enables them to do so. And for the Christian all such worship must involve his faith in Christ as his Savior and Lord, for only by such faith will his worship be acceptable in the sight of God, since Christ is the only mediator between God and man. Such worship alone is true worship, which man expresses in praise, prayer, and in listening to what God has to say to him.

Yet the Christian because of the earthbound character of his existence and because of the deep sinful corruption of his heart cannot attain to true spiritual worship without the assistance of external aids. For this reason God gave to Israel the ceremonial law that it might be a schoolmaster to bring them to Christ in true faith and worship (Calvin, *op. cit.*, 2:7:1). In the present age, although Christ has come and the church has received the gift of the Holy Spirit in his fullness, man still needs aids in his worship albeit of a different type from those given to Israel. By such aids and assistance the believer is enabled the more easily to lift up his heart in true worship, and to have communion with God whereby he grows in grace and in the likeness of Jesus Christ.

In Reformed thinking, God alone can determine the character of these external aids to worship, for he it is who is the object of worship. Just as in Old Testament times God set forth the ceremonial law, so in the present age he indicates how men should approach him in worship and fellowship (Calvin, *op. cit.*, 2:7:16). The first table of the Ten Commandments set forth the basic principles for divine worship, and these man must obey at all times. The New Testament applies these commandments in general to the church as it has existed since Christ's Ascension. Therefore, the final authority for all the principles of the worship of God lies in the Scriptures of the New Testament.

The Scriptures, however, provide for this age no detailed description of the external forms of divine worship. They lay down only the basic rules. For common order, however, that there may be no confusion and everything may be conducted with decorum and decency, some form of application of the rules is necessary. Consequently, the church always needs to devise some ceremonies and liturgical procedures in accordance with basic Biblical requirements. While the Christian may accept such acts as necessary for proper order, he must not feel that they are necessary for his salvation, nor is he out of misguided zeal to seek to devise various ceremonies merely for their esthetic or emotional effect. All things must be done for the edification of the church, which means growth in the knowledge and understanding of the Triune God according to the Scriptures (Calvin, *op. cit.*, 4:10:27ff.; Westminster Assembly of Divines: *Directory for the Public Worship of God*, p. 137).

Because of this, Calvin and his followers during the four following centuries, have held strongly to the view that there is nothing sacrosanct about a service book. Calvin believed that a particular form of service which might be quite suitable for one era or one country might prove completely unsuitable for another. Furthermore, prayers of one kind and in one language might be completely unsuitable to other situations and races. Even the matter of kneeling in prayer depended largely upon circumstances. Consequently, Reformed churches have generally refused to have a fixed liturgy which congregations must follow at all times. The Church of England's *Book of Common Prayer* because of its compulsory character therefore, helped to cause the division between the Puritan dissenters and the established church (Westminster *Directory*, p. 135). As Calvin put it: "It is of little importance what days and hours are appointed, what is the form of the places, what psalms are sung on the respective days" (*Op. cit.*, 4:10:31). No service book was ever regarded as possessing divine authority.

2. THE ELEMENTS OF REFORMED WORSHIP

Divine authority alone applied to the elements that all public worship should contain. First came prayers which Calvin held could be either spoken or sung. Then in response to these God spoke to the worshipers through the reading of the Scriptures and their exposition in the sermon. Finally, the Word received physical embodiment in the sacraments of baptism and the Lord's supper, whereby the believers received the divine blessing (Calvin, *Forme des Prieres, Opera Selecta*, P. Barth, D. Scheuner, eds., 1952, II, 13f.). In Calvin's mind all worship must gather around these three specific focal points.

Calvin set forth his views on church worship first in Strasburg where he adapted some earlier service books to his own use. In Geneva later he worked out fully his concept of the liturgy of the service in his *La Forme des Prieres*. John Knox, when he came to Geneva at the head of the group of English refugees who had left Frankfurt because they would not use the *Book of Common Prayer*, prepared a somewhat modified version of Calvin's work, and that in turn became the service book of the Scottish reformers. Other Reformed churches such as those in France, Holland or Germany, either adopted or adapted Calvin's liturgical plan. Probably one of the best examples of adaptation is the Westminster Assembly's *Directory for Public Worship* which became the norm for English speaking Reformed churches down to the present century. But no one has followed Calvin slavishly, for with Calvin they have felt that adaptation lay within their powers. Only in recent years have some made attempts to bring about radical changes, and then always in the name of Calvin. In most cases even the most thoroughgoing innovators have usually claimed that they only sought to restore the proper balance between the three elements of public worship. One must, therefore, examine carefully the nature of these elements in order to understand their mutual relationships.

a. *Music.* One important innovation of the Protestant reformers in public worship consisted in the reintroduction of music as a part of the congregation's participation. During the Middle Ages either the choir had done all the singing or there had been no music at all. Luther, in the early days of the reform movement, taught his congregation to sing not only psalms but also hymns sometimes set to popular tunes. This custom soon spread, and, although Calvin stressed the use of psalms only, singing became an important part of the service. In his *La Forme des Prieres,* he devotes considerable space to explaining the importance of singing. He employed the French poet Clement Marot and the musician Louis Bourgeois to prepare a psalm book. His example was followed wherever his influence made itself felt, so that the psalter came to form the very basis of Calvinistic or Reformed public worship.

Although Calvin had not specifically rejected the use of non-Scriptural hymns, he undoubtedly felt that the inspired psalms provided the best means of praising God. The Reformed churches usually held this position for the next two centuries, most of them being even more insistent on the exclusive use of the psalms than Calvin. However, in the various evangelical revivals which took place during the latter part of the seventeenth and during the eighteenth centuries paraphrases and hymns came into more common use with the result that by the middle of the nineteenth century a good many Reformed churches had adopted them for public worship. Some, however, have refused to accept this innovation down to the present, insisting that the psalms alone are suitable for the church to sing.

Another point of difference between Reformed churches has been the propriety of employing a musical instrument to lead the singing. During the Middle Ages organs did not always occupy their present positions of honor in the churches and in the services. With the coming of the Reformation, the Calvinistic tendency was to sing without instrumental accompaniment, in imitation of the synagogue services upon which the Reformed cult was partially patterned. However, in the eighteenth and nineteenth centuries organs were gradually introduced into Reformed churches, often causing serious divisions. Some churches, particularly those in the highlands of Scotland and their offshoots, still do not employ organs, believing that God can be worshiped properly only by the human voice.

b. *Prayer.* While the "singings" of the Reformed churches are usually held to be one form of prayers, spoken prayers also occupy an important place in the service. The minister "leads in prayer." He does not pray to himself nor for himself alone. His responsibility is to lead the congregation in their prayers. For this reason he prays in a manner commensurate with the congregational devotions. Moreover, all those in attendance should take part by listening intently to the prayers of the minister so that at the close they may truly say "amen." The congregation thus prays with the minister in their own hearts, although they do not necessarily speak any words, except perhaps in the recitation of the Lord's Prayer. For this reason the prayers in the service have often received the name of "Common Prayers."

In none of the Reformed service books does one find any attempt to employ required forms of prayer. Calvin in his liturgy tended to summarize and suggest prayers, rather than compose them for verbatim repetition. In the Westminster *Directory* the same point of view rules in opposition to the Anglican practice as set forth in the *Book of Common Prayer.* The Westminster divines felt that the required use of set prayers tended to encourage laziness on the part of ministers and also hindered them in the exercise of gifts which God had bestowed upon them. While they believed that all public and common prayers should deal with certain matters, they also held very strongly to the view that how the prayers should be offered depended upon the one who led the service, that he might speak spontaneously to God.

What were the topics for prayer? Calvin and those who followed in his footsteps believed that every service should commence with a prayer of adoration and praise which also included petitions that the Holy Spirit would come upon the worshiping congregation in order to enable them to worship "in spirit and in truth." Prayers following these should present the worshipers' confession of sins and thanksgiving both for divine grace and pardon, and also for all God's other benefits to his people. Finally would come intercession for others, not only for the church, but for all classes and conditions of men including the civil rulers. At the close of the service prayers of thanksgiving for God's blessing in the service were also offered. Various orders and sequences for these prayers in relation to singing and the hearing of the Word appear in different service books, for no one insisted that there existed any divinely required pattern. The sequence of prayers outlined above provided a logical order, but the way it fitted into the structure of the service depended largely on those in charge.

Calvin had favored the use of both the Lord's Prayer and the recitation of the Apostles' Creed. For various reasons some of those who came after him felt that the use of the Lord's Prayer fostered the following of set forms, while the constant recital of the Apostles' Creed tended also to formalism. For these and other reasons some of the Reformed churches, particularly those in the Scottish tradition, have often tended to neglect both these elements in the service of public worship.

c. *The Word.* Central to the service was the Word of God, the Scriptures of the Old and New Testament. This the Reformed churches symbolized in the buildings that they erected after the Reformation by placing the pulpit in the center of the front of the church. Even many pre-1800 Anglican churches had this form. Although the Christians' prayers and praise held important places in the service, much more important was the fact that God spoke to them from his Word. He spoke to them, showing them how he desired to be worshiped, and also revealed to them his words of judgment and grace.

For this reason the reading of the Scriptures in the congregational service occupied one of the central places. This was particularly true in the early days when a good many of the worshipers could not read for themselves. Calvin and those who came after him usually followed the practice of reading consecutively through both the Old and New Testaments at each service. Such a practice meant that even though one might not be able to read at home, at least one did hear the Scriptures read continuously on each Lord's Day. Furthermore, the custom of reading the psalms and of singing metrical versions of them very frequently gave further instruction to the uneducated. Later Reformed churches have tended to neglect this practice of consecutive readings, nor does it seem of such great importance in a day when most possess their own Bibles and can read them privately. The important thing in all of this, however, was the belief that God through the Scriptures addressed his people.

d. *The Sermon.* Mere reading, on the other hand, did not provide all that was necessary, for most could not perhaps understand what the Word of God had to say or how they should apply it to their own lives. The Christian needed assistance by way of explanation and practical application for everyday life. To this end a good many of the early Reformed preachers would preach on one of the passages read in the service, giving a running commentary on a section of the chapter. This came to be known as the homily. Later, however, more artistically formed sermons with a central theme based upon a single verse or part of a verse became common.

Whatever form the sermon took it has always remained central to the Reformed service, for it is the Word of God to man in his existential situation. Those of the Reformed tradition have always recognized its position of importance, and have stressed its necessity as the core of the service. By its very nature it formed the element in the service which specifically and clearly called men to decision in answer to God's Word. Repentance, faith, and praise all should result from the proclamation of the Word, for the minister holds the position of a herald of God. In a sense the sermon by its interpretation, application, and exhortation brings the service to a climax in which man within his own heart answers to the call of the Most High God.

e. *The Sacraments.* Coupled with the sermon in the thinking of Calvin and later Reformed leaders went the sacraments of baptism and the Lord's supper, for the sacraments are in Augustine's words "the visible words of God." They make clear in a physical and symbolical sense the gracious work of God in Christ Jesus. As Calvin repeatedly pointed out, God had given them to men because of their finitude and their corruption that he might constantly remind them through the physical elements of what he had done for them. Yet the sacraments themselves possess no power or efficacy, but only as Christians receive them in faith. For this reason the sacraments always remain subordinate to the Word which determines not only their form but also their meaning.

Another characteristic of the sacraments in Reformed thinking is that they are congregational rites. Such things as private communions or private baptisms had no place in early Reformed churches. Both sacraments provided physical representations of the blessings of the covenant relationship, which meant not merely the believer's relationship to God, but also his relationship to all other believers. Both baptism and the Lord's supper indicated the believers' unity with each other in Christ as well as with Christ. With this in mind they insisted that the sacraments could be administered only in the public worship of the church. The sacraments should form an integral part of such worship.

Baptism was usually administered on some specific Lord's Day set aside for that purpose, although the time largely depended upon the decision of the congregational authorities. The celebration of the Lord's supper by its very nature held a somewhat different position. All recognized the importance of having it frequently, but usually left the matter of how frequently to the local church. Calvin at first advocated that the communion should be celebrated once a week, but when the Genevan authorities objected to this practice he agreed that it should be dispensed once a month in rotation in each of the four churches of the city. In other countries practice has varied widely since a good many have feared that too frequent celebration might lead congregations to ignore its significance. In the highlands of Scotland one communion a year became the custom, with the whole of the week preceding devoted to special services of preparation. Most common, however, is the practice of a "quarterly communion."

Whenever the sacraments were celebrated great stress was laid upon the fact that they possessed no magical or mechanical character. Nor did they consist merely in symbolic acts which constituted memorials of long past events. Rather those who received them must do so in faith, trusting in Christ as their Savior and looking unto him to make the sacraments effective in their hearts and lives. When so received the Holy Spirit working within the believers' hearts enabled them more fully to appropriate Christ as their Savior and Lord. Because of this insistence upon faith on the part of the recipients of the sacraments, Reformed churches have always tended to "fence" the sacraments lest known unbelievers should receive them and thus make a mockery of them.

f. *The Benediction.* Every service closes with God's benediction given by the minister to the congregation. Worshipers have had fellowship with God, offering unto him their praise and prayers, listening to his Word and perhaps receiving the sacrament as a support to his Word. God then sends them away with his blessing and the promise of his peace as they go out into the world to serve him in everyday life.

In describing Reformed worship, an attempt has been made to set forth the basic principles laid down by Calvin and elaborated later by those who agreed with his views. In recent years, however, partially as a result of the Oxford Movement in the Church of England and partially because of the rise of rationalistic views within the Reformed churches themselves, one finds that ritualism and sacerdotalism have tended to revive. Increasingly have Reformed churches in new services books stressed ritual and symbolism as "acts of worship" and necessary aids to true communion with God. Simultaneously a tendency to go back to the authority of the early church rather than to the Scriptures only has manifested itself. The outcome of this trend is that not only have non-Biblical practices become part of Reformed worship services, but the structure and focus of the services have tended to change, with the sermon receiving less attention and the sacramental aspect more.

True Reformed worship, in spite of this, remains basically the same. It emphasizes the fact that all worship of God must be spiritual, to which external circumstances and acts merely give aid and assistance. Because of this spiritual character of such worship the church remains free to deal with the details of the service, but always under the rule of Christ in the Scriptures of the Old and New Testaments. When his Lordship is acknowledged and his rule obeyed, man can truly glorify and enjoy God, which is the chief end of his existence.

BIBLIOGRAPHY

Barth, P., and Scheuner, D., eds., *Opera Selecta,* 1952.

Calvin, John, *Institutes of the Christian Religion.*

MacLeod, Donald, *Presbyterian Worship.* Richmond, Va., 1965.

Martin, Ch., *Les Protestants Anglais refugiés à Genève au temps de Calvin.* Genève, 1915.

McMillan, Wm., *The Worship of the Scottish Reformed Church.* London, 1931.

Westminster Assembly of Divines, *Directory for the Public Worship of God.* Edinburgh, 1957.

The Sacraments or Ordinances

The life of a Christian congregation and its worship lie in the closest possible relationship, for worship, in which the Word of God is proclaimed and the sacraments administered, is the life-giving center of the congregation. In worship the congregation meets with God, and through the vehicle of Word and sacrament receives his life and power. In this sense it can be said that the congregation lives by its worship of God. But Christianity has too frequently been regarded as solely a system of belief or else as a way of holiness for the individual, and in this way, the formal liturgy of the church has been disparaged as an external act, unimportant, or less spiritual than the private prayer in which the individual soul holds communion with God. Such views display not only an inadequate approach to Christian worship, but also seriously misrepresent New Testament Christianity. Where instruction is seen as the only essential, Christianity can easily degenerate into an arid intellectualism; where personal devotion receives undue emphasis, the priority given in the New Testament to the church is ignored. But Christianity as a religion appeals to the whole man, and not merely to the mind; it is a religion of the community, not merely for the individual, and in both respects it is the sacramental nature of Christian worship which is the safeguard against deviation. The sacraments, employing material objects with particular, declared significance, appeal not only to the mind, but to every aspect of the personality; though individually received, the sacraments are essentially corporate acts. It always denotes a deviation when objection is taken to the fact that the sacraments are material signs and an attempt is made to spiritualize or intellectualize them. It also denotes a deviation when the individualistic aspects of the sacraments are stressed at the expense of their corporate nature.

In full New Testament Christianity, the two sacraments maintain a vital position. Not only are they of divine command, but they give objective form to divine truth. From this standpoint the patterns of sacramental worship assume a real importance, for what is done is not of our own choosing, but of God's volition.

1. PREACHING AND THE SACRAMENTS

The New Testament sets sacramental worship in the context of the preaching of the Word. The two go together; they form one whole, each part dependent upon the other, and this fact has been insufficiently recognized.

It has been customary, in histories of the early church and of liturgy, to distinguish sharply between gatherings for the proclamation of the Word and gatherings for the performance of the sacramental acts. In this way, two essentially different forms of gathering for worship are postulated, the one corresponding to the Jewish synagogue service, which was exclusively a ministry of the Word (including readings from Scripture, preaching, prayer, blessing, and perhaps the singing of psalms), the other being a gathering, in the normal life of a congregation, for the Lord's supper, though at certain times a gathering for the admission of new converts in baptism. It is affirmed that by the time of Justin Martyr (c. A.D. 150) the two gatherings had become united, and the evidence for this is Justin's description of a Sunday gathering of Christians, which includes a ministry of the Word followed by the breaking of bread (Apology I: 67). This view, however, ignores much of the evidence of the New Testament. It is obvious that baptism depends upon the preaching of the gospel. Though the act of baptism may not always be in the context of preaching, the sacrament is a meaningless symbol without the prior preaching of the gospel (Acts 2:37-41; 8:12, 30-39; 10:44-48). The same is true in the case of the Lord's supper, which in New Testament times was a full meal, and not the ritual meal it had become by Justin's period. In this rite, however, it is not the missionary preaching which is the setting for the sacrament, but that expounding of Scripture necessary to edify the congregation. Admittedly, there are texts which speak of teaching only (Acts 5:42), and others which speak of breaking bread only (Acts 2:46), but that does not necessitate a distinction between two forms of gathering, particularly when the rest of the evidence points to one gathering. Acts 2:42, describing the worship activity of the Jerusalem church, may indicate a community gathering for instruction and fellowship in the context of a meal with its attendant prayers; from Acts 20:7-12 we learn that Paul preached a sermon on the Lord's day at the gathering for the breaking of bread; the implication of I Corinthians 11:17-20 is that the Corinthians assembled as a church in order to eat the Lord's Supper, and it was most probably at this assembly that the "edifying" practices mentioned in I Corinthians 14 were expected to take place (I Cor. 14:26).

We are in a position then to see that Justin's pattern of a ministry of the Word to edify, followed by the breaking of bread, was no innovation, but a continuance of New Testament practice. If there is an innovation it is in the reduction of the common meal to one of a ritual nature, but this can be traced to Paul's teaching in I Corinthians 11:20-22.

From this basic position of the liturgical unity of Word and sacrament, we can begin to examine the necessary features and patterns of the sacramental services.

2. THE BAPTISM RITE

From apostolic times, to be a Christian has never been a matter of inward conviction only, nor yet of mere enrolment; the two are necessary. There must be a real response of faith to the gospel message; there must also be the reception of the sign of the divine covenant in the sacrament of baptism, which has consisted invariably of the use of water, accompanied at an early date, though perhaps not invariably, by the laying on of hands.

The New Testament gives no detailed description of a baptismal liturgy. In fact, it is not even explicit as to the mode of application of the water, nor as to the wording of the formula used when the water is applied to the candidate, a point which deserves special attention. Acts 2:38; 8:16; 10:48; 19:5; Romans 6:3; and Galatians 3:27 speak either of Baptism "into the name of the Lord Jesus," or, of baptism "into Christ," while Matthew 28:19 gives a Trinitarian formula, though whether this verse is theological rather than liturgical (i.e., has reference to the Trinitarian character of the sacrament rather than to liturgical forms) is debatable. A variety of practice, in this respect, seems to have characterized the post-New Testament church. The Didache, composed in Syria probably in the early part of the second century, mentions a use of the Matthean formula, but the Acts of Paul and Thecla, written in the mid-second century, depict Thecla as baptizing herself "in the name of Jesus Christ." In the Western church, an expanded form of the Trinitarian formula was common until the fifth/sixth century, as witnessed by Tertullian, Hippolytus, Ambrose, and many others. The candidate received a triple baptism corresponding to the mention of each person of the Trinity, who was confessed by the candidate prior to each application of the water. The advantage of this mode of baptism lies in the way the sign of the divine covenant is intimately combined with the candidate's confession of faith. We can only speculate as to why the simple Matthean formula displaced this longer Western form, though a reason may be advanced in the unsuitability of the creedal interrogation so closely linked with this form, in an age when infant baptism was becoming the norm (see E. C. Whitaker, "The History of the Baptismal Formula," *Journal of Ecclesiastical History*, Vol. XVI No. I, April, 1965).

An integral part of baptism in the New Testament is the candidate's act of faith. This is necessary not because an assurance of the candidate's conversion is required, but because it belongs to the permanent character of the Christian that he is a person who believes certain things. Hence, in this baptismal covenant between God and man, the divine side is represented by the baptismal washing, and the human side by the candidate's confession of faith, a form first fully expressed in the Biblical account of the baptism of the Ethiopian eunuch at the hands of Philip (Acts 8:36-38 Western Text). On the basis of this text, the core of the confession is belief in Jesus Christ as the Son of God. If, then, the baptismal rite is to contain these two vital elements — washing with water and a confession of faith — it is essential to relate the pouring of the water to the making of the act of faith, and this would apply even in the case of infant baptism, where the candidate is represented by sponsors. It is important to emphasize that this practice of infant baptism, where it is followed, should adhere to the same pattern of adult baptism. The household baptisms of the New Testament probably find a reflection in the Apostolic tradition of Hippolytus (c. A.D. 215), according to which the children precede their parents into the baptismal water.

The position in the initiatory rite of the laying on of hands with prayer for the Holy Spirit (Acts 8:15-17) is controversial. The importance attached to this act will vary according to the degree in which the Holy Spirit is associated with the act of baptism. The New Testament, however, gives two accounts of this rite following upon baptism (Acts 8:14-17; 19:1-7), but whether this practice was universal cannot be definitely established, though the custom of the early church in viewing baptism, anointing with oil, and the laying on of hands as together comprising initiation into the fullness of the Christian life, is evidence of the widespread practice of this rite.

On the basis of these remarks, what should be the structure of a Scriptural and evangelical baptismal rite? The sacramental action should be set within the context of a declaration of the gospel, with particular mention of man's sin, and God's provision of salvation through Jesus Christ. This may be done by readings from Scripture and a sermon. From this foundation the baptism can proceed, the pouring of the water being obviously related to the candidate's confession of faith in Jesus Christ. Immediately following the baptism there might be laying on of hands with prayer for the Holy Spirit. The service could end fittingly with a declaration of the benefits received in baptism, and of the responsibilities assumed by the candidate. It goes without saying that the setting of this initiatory rite is one of prayer. The sacrament is administered in the sight of God and is an appeal in faith to him.

3. THE RITE OF THE LORD'S SUPPER

If the New Testament gives few specific details regarding the composition of a baptismal rite, this is far from the case with regard to the Lord's supper, which from the earliest days of the Christian church appears to have consisted of instruction followed by the breaking of bread. Without denying the essential unity, it will be convenient to treat these two parts of the Eucharist separately, and where possible attempt a reconstruction.

In essentials the instructional part of the Eucharist consisted of readings from the Scriptures and exposition — features well-known to the first Christians from their synagogue background. At Nazareth, Jesus Christ read and preached from the prophetic lesson in Isaiah (Luke 4:16-30); at Pisidian Antioch, "after the reading of the law and the prophets" Paul expounded their meaning in a sermon (Acts 13:15-41); in Justin's account of Christian worship, he records: "On the day called Sunday an assembly in one place is held of all who dwell in cities and in the country; and the memoirs of the Apostles or the writings of the Prophets are read for as long as time allows. Then, when the reader has ended, the president makes a discourse admonishing and exhorting [his hearers] to imitate these good things."

(Apology I:67).

Following upon Paul's directions to the churches to read his letters at their gathering (Col. 4:16; I Thess. 5:27), it becomes obvious how the New Testament writings took their place alongside those of the Old Testament, until finally they displaced the latter in most eucharistic liturgies by the beginning of the Dark Ages – a lamentable fact which needs rectifying in an evangelical Eucharist.

With the Scripture readings goes closely the exposition or sermon. The mere reading of Scripture is not a full ministry of the Word. To achieve this there must be, under the guidance of the Holy Spirit, an opening of the meaning of the Word and its application to the current situation of the congregation. Churches which omit a sermon in the eucharistic context are neither ministering the Word nor placing the sacrament in its Scriptural setting.

The question now arises, should this first section of the Eucharist contain other elements of worship – collects, creed, intercession, penitence – as is customary in many existing liturgies? We search in vain for these additional features in any Biblical account of the Eucharist, but their non-inclusion in the Bible is no reason for paring the ministry of the Word to its bare essentials. Many of the additions of subsequent centuries are perfectly consistent with Biblical patterns and principles, and we can benefit from these enrichments. Some form of prayer, perhaps of the collect form, would be a natural introduction to the readings; a creedal declaration, though a late liturgical innovation (*c.* 500 in the Eastern Church, not until 1014 at Rome), is an appropiate form of affirmation in the Scriptural faith following on the ministry of the Word; intercession may also naturally arise from the sermon, and the precedent for its inclusion at this point goes back to Justin's Apology. But at whatever point the intercession is included, it is vital (and this applies also to the Thanksgiving prayer later in the service) that the prayer is that of the whole congregation. The congregation is the priesthood of believers and prayer is their duty, not just that of their leaders. For this reason, a litany form of prayer is best, since the congregation actively participates.

Problems of a theological character attach to a penitential section. The qualification for participation in eucharistic worship is faith in Jesus Christ, but if participants approach as the redeemed, what emphasis should be placed on penitence? Some form of confession is clearly desirable and necessary, but is an absolution essential? Is not the receiving of the sacrament itself "for the remission of sins"? Where should a confession occur? The Didache places it in close relation to the meal itself, but an equally suitable place might be before the instruction as a preparation for the whole worship-action. Questions such as these affect the psychology as well as the theology of eucharistic worship.

The ministry of the Word has often (particularly in the churches of the Reformation) been used as a separate act of worship, but for completion it needs the sacramental meal, for which Scripture provides definite form.

The pattern of the Eucharist proper is governed by what Jesus Christ did at the Last Supper. That evening he took bread, thanked (or blessed) God, broke, and gave the bread to his followers. At a later point in the meal, He took a cup of wine, thanked (or blessed) God, and gave it to His followers to drink (I Cor. 11:23-25). These seven actions were later reduced to four, an understandable process once these significant actions were removed from the context of a full meal, and a process, the progress of which may be reflected in Mark 14:22-24 and Matthew 26:26-28 – two passages which make no mention of a gap between the taking of the bread and the taking of the wine. The four actions which remain are: the taking of the bread and wine; the thanksgiving, or blessing, over the bread and wine; the breaking of the bread; and the distribution of the bread and wine. Whatever else may be added to the sacramental meal, these four features are essential and must not be obscured.

The first action of taking the bread and wine is simply that of preparing the meal. Before the Last Supper, Peter and John were sent ahead to make the necessary arrangements (Luke 22:8), and it would appear that at Corinth the participants brought with them their own provision for the common meal (I Cor. 11:21-22). It was their conduct at the meal, and not this practice of bringing the necessary food, which Paul condemned. On these grounds it would seem right to give some definite part to the congregation at the taking of the elements. However, to convert this action into an offering to God either of the first-fruits of creation, which was the custom of the early church, or of tokens of the life and labors of mankind, which is a characteristic view of the modern liturgical movement, is to go beyond the warrant of Scripture. From this standpoint, though it is traditional, a collection and presentation of alms, at this stage in the service, is capable of gross misinterpretation. It should be reserved until the end (cf. Justin *op. cit.*).

The taking of the bread and wine is followed by the thanksgiving. In essence this is the grace before the meal, and a number of passages in the Gospels show it to have been our Lord's habitual custom to offer such prayer (Mark 6:41; Matt. 15:36; Luke 24:30), though his exact words are never recorded. In the case of the Last Supper the words "This is my body . . . This is my blood" are not the thanksgiving, but are connected with the distribution of the food. The actual offering of thanks most probably followed Jewish precedent – that over the bread being a recognition of God as universal King and provider of food; that over the cup (particularly if this meal was a Passover meal, and the cup, the "cup of blessing") a prayer containing three strands: a thanksgiving for the vine, and for all God's providence over his creatures, a thanksgiving for the covenant he made for the redemption of his chosen people, and a prayer for the reuniting of all his faithful people in his everlasting kingdom. If this was indeed the case at the Last Supper, then we are justified in constructing a eucharistic prayer on this basic pattern, and including with it the account of our Lord's actions and words in the upper room as the warrant of what the people of God do at the sacrament. In constructing such a prayer, it must not be forgotten that we perform the sacramental action "in remembrance" of Jesus Christ (I Cor. 11:24-25). There must be adequate mention of the salient features of the Christ-event (incarnation, passion, resurrection, ascension and second coming) to make this obvious, and the wording must be such as to make it clear that the remembrance is with a view to man's appropriating of Christ by faith, and not for the recalling of Christ's sacrifice before the Father – a theory based on an interpretation of the word *ava vnaisd.*

In all the accounts of the Last Supper special mention is made of the Lord "breaking" the bread. To "break bread" in New Testament usage need mean no more than sharing a meal, but the careful mention of this action would seem to give it a special significance and this is underlined by the teaching of I Corinthians 10:15-17, in the light of which the breaking of the bread can be seen as the sharing of the one bread among the many in the one body. This action then has great point in visibly demonstrating the unity fellowship aspect of the sacrament, a feature difficult to convey in other ways.

The fourth action in the sequence is of course the meal itself. Whether or not there is need for words of administration is debatable, but, having already used Christ's own words of distribution in the recital of the institution narrative, partaking in silence would seem the best procedure.

If the act of partaking the bread and wine is the climax of the whole service, is there need for anything to follow this? The early tradition in both East and West was a brief post-communion prayer of thanksgiving and then dismissal, but to this various elements were added in the course of time. The note of thanksgiving is appropriate, but this is the point at which mission can also be emphasized. The meeting of believers with the Lord is not a private function for a pious few; the sacrament has a purpose for the church. In the sacrament the incorporation of the church in Christ the Sent One is revitalized so that the church may be effective in the world to extend his kingdom. Hence the need to re-echo, at the close of the Eucharist, the command of the ascending Christ: "Go into all the world and preach the gospel." In this, the sacrament achieves its purpose; the church renewed in Christ, that her mission be renewed in the world.

BIBLIOGRAPHY

Cullmann, Oscar, *Early Christian Worship.*

Dix, G., *The Shape of the Liturgy.*

Hahn, W., *Worship and Congregation.*

Jones, I. T., *An Historical Approach to Evangelical Worship.*

Martin, R. P., *Worship in the Early Church.*

Stibbs, A. M., *Sacrament, Sacrifice and Eucharist.*

Particular or Special Services

One *Oxford Dictionary* definition of worship is: "Honour with religious rites." On special occasions the religious rite or service is often just a prelude or an appendage to the occasion. Honouring with religious rites – but who is honoured? Since God "looketh on the heart" (I Sam. 16:7), the special service must be designed to bring people into the presence of God with true heart worship. Such services are also an opportunity for the presentation of the gospel, the divine plan of salvation from sin and death.

1. WEDDINGS

A marriage can be a threefold or a twofold contract: legal, physical and religious, or merely legal and physical. For many the religious ceremony is shallow formality. Some couples are married by a civic judge or registrar of marriages; others prefer the veneer of religion, a church service. Since marriage is an illustration of Christ's love for his Church, persons wanting a church service should be carefully counseled by the minister. Marriage according to God's Word must be explained fully, with emphasis upon the significance and solemnity of the vows to be taken. The claims of Christ and the way of salvation must also be presented, with prayerful hope that they will receive Christ as Savior and so begin their married life together as Christians.

Legal requirements will have to be explained and these can be obtained from denominational handbooks or from the appropriate civil authorities. Certain words are required by law to be said during the service; without them the ceremony will be null and void.

A Christian couple will have hymns that they would like included in the service, ones with special significance for them. Nonbelieving couples will need guidance in this. Likewise some soloists have strange ideas about the suitability of solo pieces. The pastor should oversee such selections for suitability and guidance should be given regarding dress, deportment, etc. Nothing must detract from the bridal party and congregation entering into the spirit of worship for the glory of God. For the sake of non-Christian relatives the solo should be a testimony and a witness on the part of the couple who have requested it.

With respect to the choir and organist the minister must also make this part of the service subservient to his theme. A preliminary discussion will take place with organist and choir master. Organists must be warned about ornate embellishments, or about continuing their voluntaries, wedding marches, etc, too long after the bridal procession is in position, to the nervous embarrassment of all.

The spirit of praise should predominate – prayers, hymns, organ music, choir pieces and solos all contributing to this spirit. Joy, however, must not overshadow the solemnity of the actual "wedding." It is helpful to have the congregation sit for part of the service, standing for the pronouncement that the two persons are now "man and wife."

In the address the purpose of God-ordained marriage must be explained, with warnings against the prevalent views of easy divorce. Finally the gospel should be clearly presented. If the bride and groom are Christians then they must be reminded of the importance of the family altar, of Christian hospitality in their new home, and of Christian service within the fellowship of the church.

2. FUNERALS

A funeral is "a burial of the dead with observances" (*Oxford Dictionary*). These observances, usually religious in nature in nominally Christian countries, are generally according to denominational tradition. Common to all evangelical churches, however, are certain principles. Legal formalities must be observed although most of them can safely be left in the hands of the mortician. Usually the only legal requirement for the minister is the signing of the Register of Burials or Cremations.

At the service in church or at the graveside there should predominate the notes of thanksgiving, comfort, intercession, and the evangel.

The minister will generally lead the coffin and mourners in procession. Often Scripture sentences are read aloud as this is done, usually a blending of words of comfort and expressions of hope and victory over death.

Hymns will usually be the choice of near relatives who remember the favorites of the deceased or those which had some spiritual influence. If left to the minister he can choose suitable hymns of thanksgiving and triumph as well as ones of heavenly hope and comfort.

Thanksgiving will be of two kinds, general and particular. General thanksgiving includes gratitude to God for his creation, preservation and provision; for being the fountain of all life; for being unchangeable in a world of change and decay; and for the comfort and strength he alone can give in the dark hour of bereavement. This thanksgiving centers round the fact of Calvary and the resurrection of Christ from the dead.

Particular thanksgiving is for the life and works of the deceased. If the person being buried has been a practicing Christian, serving Christ through the local church, this will present no problem. Great care is necessary, however, when making reference to unbelievers who have died. It is so easy to give a false hope to sorrowing relatives. In the same way caution must be exercised in giving comfort. What comfort can be given to non-Christian relatives of a non-Christian deceased person? The Scriptures are clear — the death of an unbeliever is but the first step into a lost eternity.

General thanksgiving will, in the main, be incorporated in public prayer. Particular thanksgiving, and the comfort, will probably form part of the address. In that address will be the worship of witness or the proclaiming of the evangel. At no other time are people's hearts so open and receptive to the gospel as at bereavement. The issues of life and death, time and eternity, sin and salvation, must be placed before them.

Intercession must conclude the service. The minister must intercede with God on behalf of the mourners. Somehow they have to carry on life as usual with an empty place in the home and family circle. Widows and widowers, orphans — these need the prayers of intercession that they may know divine care and consolation such as the world cannot give.

At the committal the above principles of worship need to be applied in miniature. There will be no address but in Scripture reading and in prayers the notes of thanksgiving, comfort, and intercession must again predominate.

Formality must be eschewed. It is so easy to go through a form of service as printed in some denominational handbook, impersonally, without feeling.

3. CIVIC AND NATIONAL OCCASIONS

"In a Christian community, worship comes first absolutely and all the time, for it is the expression of our love of God and our loyalty to the risen Lord" (C. Cleal, *Adventures in Christian Obedience*). But worship must be related to the needs of the community in which the Christian lives. The apostles commended respect for authority, civic and national, within the sphere of Christian worship. Those in high position of rule or government are to be prayed for, and this the minister will do in his Sunday services and at his mid-week prayer meetings. Besides that the church will seek to infiltrate pagan society through the individual witness of its members. Where committed Christians hold civic or national appointments, or are engaged in public service and local government, they will have opportunities for evangelistic witness.

The civic and national powers-that-be sometimes come to the church, or are invited, for special services of a social, national, or international nature. Denominational handbooks and other aids usually only suggest suitable Scripture readings, and the hymn books have but a small section entitled *Our Country and Our Citizenship* or *National and International.* Thus a civic service is often little different from an ordinary worship service, except for these special hymns, prayers, readings and the attendance of some local dignitaries.

It is these latter that pose a problem for the evangelical pastor. If they are not Christians, then how can they worship as well as watch others worship? Ought they to take part in the service (e g., a Bible reading) as so many expect to do? Some are unfamiliar with the Scriptures, others are uneducated, and so the Word of God is read in an almost unintelligible way. Protocol also has to be observed. The dignitary must sit in such-and-such a seat. He must not be preceded by this or that one. Usually such persons come in uniform or civic insignia, and the regular worshiper finds he is looking at man instead of worshiping God. These difficulties will be dealt with as we study sample occasions:

a. *National Day of Prayer.* Usually this is asked for by the reigning Monarch or President, and occurs during a major war. During World War I it was a day of "prayer and fasting"; in the midst of World War II the people of Britain were called to a day of "prayer." We no longer link prayer with fasting, and we do not seem prepared to humiliate ourselves before God.

Humiliation must be the first note in any such special service. Wars are the result of human sin and sin must be confessed and repented of before we can expect God to act on our behalf.

Prayers should be offered for one's own country, one's allies, and for the enemy. Rather than praying for victory, prayer should be made that the cause of righteousness and justice may prevail. The days have surely gone when clergymen blessed guns, bombs, and other instruments of destruction in the Name of God. Our main concern is for righteousness and peace to prevail, and that during the remainder of the conflict the people will be strengthened and comforted in whatever disasters and privations may come their way.

The great opportunity for the preacher is in the sermon. Many people will be attending by "royal command." The gospel must be preached in all simplicity, with directness and challenge. Only as the human heart is changed by the miracle of the new birth will men and women be able to live together peaceably, having found "peace through the blood of the cross."

For such a national occasion it is best if the minister (perhaps assisted by chaplains of the armed forces) conducts the service himself. There would be so many representatives of civic and national bodies that it would be too difficult to single out a few to take part. The National Anthem also presents a difficulty. If played first then it displaces God to whom worship should be first addressed. If placed last it again prevents the last note of the service being distinctly Christian and spiritual. The best place is just before the benediction.

The above principles also apply to such national occasions as victory celebrations, or the signing of an armistice or treaty.

b. *The Death of a King, Queen, or President.* "The king is dead; long live the king!" This age-old cry reminds us of the continuity and succession of authority and government. It does not imply that the person and reign are soon to be forgotten. Gratitude must be given for the past; respect must be paid to the dead; hopes and prayers and loyalty for the future must find expression in Christian worship.

The coronation of a Monarch or the installation of a President will be a national religious ceremony in a Christian country. But local churches will also wish to share in the mourning and the thanksgiving. The minister who has the task of arranging such a service for his own locality would do well not to try to copy in miniature the national ceremony. That will have been heard on radio and watched on television. He must arrange a suitable service of personal dedication in which there will be audible and silent vows of loyalty, promises of prayer support for the health and strength of the one in high office, and that he or she will give a religious lead to the country, observing God's Word, his Day, and his house of prayer, for "righteousness exalteth a nation; but sin is a reproach to any people" (Prov. 14:34).

For the sake of the non-churchgoer the sermon must be evangelistic in content. Having stressed that the powers that be are "ordained of God" (Rom. 13:1), the congregation must be made aware of the fact that God is sovereign (I Chron. 29:12), that his Son will one day "reign from sea to sea and shore to shore." Since he will return only for his own, allegiance must be given him now by receiving him as Savior and Lord.

Here is a fine opportunity for the Ten Commandments (with the addition of selected New Testament commands) to be read or repeated by the congregation.

c. *Local Celebrations.* Individual Christians are not *of* the world, although *in* it. The church is a community within a community, and when the neighborhood to which the church is committed to serve celebrates some special event, the church is often asked to take part.

It may be a sorrowful occasion such as a local disaster: flood, or famine, an accident on land, below ground, in the air or on the sea, etc. It could be the installation of a Mayor, or the visit of royalty or nobility to the town. A famous school or university might be celebrating its opening, extension, or observance of many years of educational influence.

The same principles that applied to weddings, funerals, civic and national occasions apply here. The various aspects of evangelical worship must be included, evangelical preaching taking precedence over all else. The minister is not merely gracing the occasion; he is there as the Lord's ambassador to present his message with dignity, urgency, and authority. It is important to "speak to the occasion." Without preaching a "social gospel" the gospel must be preached in its social setting. C. H. Spurgeon's *Sermons for Special Occasions* (Kelvedon Edition, Volume I, 1958) is invaluable. Here are evangelical sermons for Memorial Day, Mothers' Day, Labor Day, Thanksgiving Day, etc.

4. DEDICATION OF A CHURCH BUILDING

"The Most High dwelleth not in temples made with hands" (Acts 7:48), and the phrase "the house of God" (I Tim. 3:15) really means God's household or family, the "living stones" (I Peter 2:5) of the church. On the other hand as Christianity outgrew the house meetings of the New Testament period special buildings had to be erected to accommodate the congregations and to act as a center for evangelistic and educational (in the sense of the church's Bible teaching ministry) activities.

Such a building should have a special service dedicating it to the worship of God and the work of the gospel. In such a service there will be thanksgiving first of all, that God implanted the thought of a house of prayer in the mind of a group of believers. Then will follow thanks for the provision of the site, the required money, and the erection of the building without harm or loss of life to the workmen. All this may well be done in the open air, before the building is formally opened. This is an excellent witness to non-Christian bystanders, reminding them of the purposes of the church.

Thanksgiving will be followed by dedication, the giving over to God for his use the actual building with all its effects, that it might become a house of prayer, a center of evangelism, a source of comfort, a place for the celebration of the ordinances or sacraments, the preaching of the Word, etc. A carefully worded statement is best here, read aloud with the people standing, followed by the singing of the *Te Deum*, a psalm, or a suitable hymn. Denominational handbooks will give guidance as to the best form of wording. Then follows the prayer of dedication.

The evangel comes next. This is the first time the gospel will be proclaimed within the new building. Much prayer in preparation and during delivery will be required of all members. If the Holy Spirit blesses this initial preaching of the Word it will be a divine seal upon the occasion. It is a mistake to have too many taking part at this service of dedication (representatives of other denominations can speak at a subsequent meeting). The opening service is one of thanksgiving, dedication and proclamation. Within the proclamation of the gospel will come teaching regarding the nature of the church, its function, etc.

When the sermon is over the final note must be one of rededication on the part of the membership. The gospel that has just been preached must go on being preached by the lives and lips of every church member.

5. CHURCH FURNISHINGS AND MEMORIALS

When a new church has been opened there is usually a great deal of furnishings and fittings to be dedicated. They may have been the individual gifts of generous donors (or of a group or society within the church membership) and mention of them will be made at the opening ceremony. Later an official dedication of stained glass windows, lecterns, communion table, organ, piano, memorial tablets, pulpit, etc. has to be made. The dedication of these gifts must bring glory to God and not to the donor. Due thanks must be given to the donor, but all glory must be given to the God in whose service these gifts will be used. From a practical point of view, the minister should advise donors to have any inscription plaques fixed in some unobtrusive place on the gift. Often they are given too prominent a place and man rather than God is honored. For the same reason it is inadvisable for the minister to walk to the article for the act of dedication. It may be in a somewhat inaccessible place; acoustics may not be as good as from the usual place of speaking; and the congregation will be straining themselves to see what is going on. It is best if the gift is mentioned and described from the pulpit and the dedication taken from there.

Thanksgiving, intercession, and witness will predominate: thanksgiving for the Holy Spirit having prompted generosity in the heart of the donor; intercession for the spiritual use of the gift in the service of God and the gospel (beautifying the house of prayer, drawing mind and heart and spirit towards God in meditation and contemplation, inspiring Christian service and devotion, helping believers to make melody with heart and voice); and finally witness to the saving grace of God in Christ, that is, that the dedicated gift may be used for the saving of souls and the extension of Christ's kingdom.

BIBLIOGRAPHY

Abba, R., *Principles of Christian Worship.*

Cleal, C., *Adventures in Christian Obedience.*

Lloyd-Jones, D. M., *The Presentation of the Gospel.*

Martin, R. P., *Worship in the Early Church.*

General or Regular Services

The spirit of worship is always more important than its form or order. Provided the spirit is right, irregularities or even omissions may be readily excused. The publican in our Lord's parable confined himself exclusively to supplication and confession, in that order, and in the eyes of many his worship would come under criticism as being both defective and disordered. In fact, he was commended in comparison with the Pharisee, and not only so, but it is implied that he had offered to God something acceptable, and therefore of genuine worth.

In the ecstasy of the immediate post-Pentecostal era, with its intense awareness of the presence of Christ, and the power of the Spirit, order could be a matter of indifference, and there is a sense in which to a fully enlightened congregation today the same might still be true. However the more deliberate the effort of those who formulate the liturgy, and the less enlightened the minds of those who follow it, the more important it becomes that the order should be correct, reflecting not whim or fancy, but deep theological and Biblical conviction. It is not merely a matter of doing things tidily. The form is there to instruct and to guide.

In asserting that worship is not necessarily invalidated by the lack of a liturgy, we in no way deny the desirability nor indeed the inevitability of liturgy if worship is to be more than a rare and isolated approach to God.

It is interesting to reflect that of all the prophets Jeremiah came nearest to saying that the externals of religion are of no account, and in the New Testament Paul boasts that his own ecstatic spiritual experiences outshine any to which his contemporaries can point. In spite of this Jeremiah envisages ultimately a return to Jerusalem, and an implied return to temple worship, while it is Paul who calls for things to be done decently and in order.

In fact the alternatives do not lie between liturgy and no liturgy, but rather between a liturgy produced haphazardly and stereotyped mainly through unconscious habit, or one which is the result of careful thought and deliberate expression. It is conceivable that the man who proudly claims emancipation from liturgical forms may be more rigid in his worship than the man who, consciously devoted to liturgical principles, yet feels himself free to vary the liturgy not haphazardly, but of set purpose, as occasion may suggest or demand.

The greatest danger is to dogmatize. Of course there are important constituents whose habitual absence will impoverish worship. Of course there is a logical sequence to which attention should be given. If all members of a worshiping community were uniform in their Christian standing and experience, this norm could be uniformly applied. But congregations are made up of individuals, and individuals are at varying stages of development. The average congregation is as much a figment of the imagination as the average man. The point is worthy of some elaboration.

Were it the case that all Christians came to worship with a due sense of the majesty of God, tempered by a consciousness of their own creatureliness and sin, and joined with the realization of God's grace and mercy to all men, the logical sequence of adoration, confession, the New Testament Word, and intercession would be the sensible and necessary order of liturgy. But few will in fact come in such a well-balanced state. One will be dominated by the sense of his guilt and folly evidenced by the sin into which he has fallen. He cannot begin to worship God until he has confessed and been forgiven, and become reconciled to God. Another will be overwhelmed by the sorrow of his experience, quite unable to contemplate the majesty of God until first there has been ministered to him the comfort and consolation of the gospel. A third will be torn by the spirit of anxiety for some loved one in desperate need, and irregular as it may seem to some, he can do no other than anticipate the intercessory prayer, and plead the cause of his friend before the throne of grace.

To say that all of these should have prepared themselves before coming is to envisage an ideal, but to be woefully ignorant of the reality. The minister who deliberately deviates from the norm, out of compassion to his flock, must not be summarily condemned as ignorant or careless. Those who seek logical perfection in worship are entitled to do so. They are not entitled to sneer at the supposed imperfections of those who think and feel differently.

However, the same examples which make a case for flexibility of order, emphasize the value of a comprehensive and orderly liturgy. For one thing it ensures fulness. To fashion the service on the basis of a dominating theme may indeed drive home some particular truth to those who need to heed it, but there will be those who go away unhelped unless the other aspects of Christian worship have also found a place within the service, and have not been neglected in the eagerness of emphasizing a part. In short it may be said that the service is not to be determined by personal taste or preference, nor even by some particular purpose which may relate to a section of the congregation. The liturgy is to be as comprehensive and catholic as the gospel itself.

1. THE CALL TO WORSHIP

The opening words of the liturgy which at first may merely have served the purpose of indicating that the service was about to begin, or which took the form of a greeting exchanged between the officiating minister and those who had assembled, has now rightly become a call to worship couched in the words of the Scripture to encourage those who seek to approach to God. The fact that the words are those of God, and not of men, emphasizes the initiative of God in man's salvation, and expresses an order which is true at every other point of the liturgy also. Fitting as it may be that some word of aspiration and approach might be included, indicating the summoning of the whole man, to seek after and worship God, yet it remains true that no such approach could ever have been contemplated, far less sustained, apart from the gracious words of encouragement so freely distributed throughout the Scripture, which provide ample justification for a joyful and thankful coming into the presence of God. This truth the liturgy must express, and thus the scene is set for the congregation to bring its adoration which should ideally be thoroughly objective at least in its first expression. God as the Eternal Creator, Sustainer, and Redeemer will be its theme, but inasmuch as the Eternal has manifested himself in time, there seems no good reason that thanksgiving for the mercies of God in personal experience should not immediately follow. An existential element in such worship is by no means out of place, and if God is experientially known in his encounter with men, there must inevitably be the recognition on the part of the worshiper of the "I" as well as the "Thou."

2. CONFESSION

There is much to be said for introducing as a rule, a prayer of confession early in the liturgy. Scripture bears out the fact that a sense of sin is often awakened when the holiness of God is contemplated, and as soon as the congregation is ready there should be opportunity of confession followed by the assurance of forgiveness. There are heights of exultation and joy in worship which can only be realized within the freedom which comes to those whose sins are forgiven. On the other hand it must not be forgotten that there are other ways by which the conviction of sin comes about. The setting forth of God's requirement laid down in the law may accomplish it. Even a realization of the kindness of God may be salutary in its effect. As the apostle puts it, the goodness of God is seeking to lead us to repentance. In view of this the confession of sin should not be limited to one single point in the liturgy, as if it could be accomplished once and for all. Men, even good and godly men, need to be called to repentance again and again. To say that the conviction and confession, and forgiveness of sin may well come again later in the service is not to hold back the course of Christian experience which the liturgy traces, for a sense of sin is by no means incompatible with the most developed sainthood. We must not then be surprised or alarmed if certain elements of the liturgy which logically can be differentiated and put in order are in fact gathered up in one supreme moment of blessed intercourse with God through Christ.

3. HYMNS AND THEIR PSYCHOLOGY

That the service should be interspersed with hymns is justified both on the grounds of principle and expediency. If each hymn corresponds in theme to the particular part of the service into which it is injected, it will not only prolong and thus emphasize the theme, but inasmuch as the congregation will participate, there will be a tendency more and more for the spirit which the officiating minister seeks to exemplify to be reproduced within the worshiping community. Such forms are a part of true worship, and the fact that at the same time they minister to human frailty by gaining and holding the attention does not therefore mean that they must be regarded as unworthy devices alien to the spiritual character of the exercise.

A fuller word may perhaps be spoken at this point about the psychological aspects of liturgical form and order. No one doubts the necessity of objectivity in worship, so that every part is of the nature of dialogue, God speaking to man, and man speaking to God. No one would wish to fall into the attitude of the brother who in commending a prayer declared it to be the finest he had ever heard "offered to a congregation." On the other hand it must not be forgotten that there are certain forms which encourage a response as well as express a response, and this aspect is not to be neglected. Perhaps it is a mistake to distinguish too sharply between a service of worship, and an evangelistic service. The primary function of the liturgy is worship, but there is no reason why in the process it should not instruct, or even evangelize. The church can bring no better offering to Christ than a liturgy which in its offering gathers to itself an increasing company of participants.

4. THE CREED

What are we to say concerning a creed, and if we admit it, at what point should it come? The original purpose of a creed was no doubt to safeguard the purity of the church, especially at a time when there was coming into it a host of people with heathen background. The simplest confession of faith which might well have sufficed needed to be elaborated, lest the simpler form understood in some heathen fashion should prove inadequate. Again, because of error which arose within the church, the creed served also to ensure the purity of the church and its orthodoxy. If such tests are to be applied today, they belong to a different setting from that of the liturgy. Nevertheless the form to which they have given rise may well be incorporated into the worship of the church. For the creed is the exultant cry of the church which delights to fill out the content of its worship by introducing a brief succinct summary of that great wealth of truth which forms the background of all our thinking, but which if it were included in anything other than summary form would prove to extend the liturgy beyond its reasonable bounds. If the creed is set to music, that is all the better, for it is always fitting that beauty and truth should go hand in hand.

5. THE SERMON

The Word of God will have been heard and recognized in the call to worship and in the great creedal statements, which are based upon the Scriptures, and which summarize them. Now there comes the particular application of some portion of the Word. If the reading of Scripture immediately precedes the sermon, it will declare the indissolubility of the two. If they are separated for the sake of convenience, then there is all the more reason why their relationship should be borne constantly in mind. It is when the Word of

God is read before the people systematically, and thus in all its varied aspects, and when the preaching follows faithfully the Word which alone can be its inspiration that the congregation is delivered from the whims and fancies, the idiosyncrasies, and the narrow confines of interest which are liable to characterize the clergy. Many of the topical utterances which pass as sermons would never have been born if the pure marriage of the Scripture and sermon had not become adulterated.

6. PRAYERS

The position of the prayers will be seriously influenced by considerations as to the nature of prayer, and as to those who may legitimately and effectively offer it. The early practice of dismissing all but the faithful at the conclusion of the sermon before the church turned to prayer was justified on the grounds that prayer is offered in the name of Christ, and only those who are truly in him may share in this part of the liturgy. Thus enquirers of all kinds, some of slight attachment, and even catechumens who had accepted the faith but had not yet been admitted to the church through the sacraments, might legitimately hear the Word of God and its exposition, but when the church turned to prayer there was no place for them within the assembly. This arrangement involved no difficulties when the different categories were clearly delineated and recognized, but in the atmosphere of an age when the committed are often less decisively marked out, and the uncommitted less aware of their limitations, its administration involves problems of tact and discernment hitherto unknown. We may very well question whether the presence of the uncommitted is a serious disadvantage providing they bring to the situation a spirit of reverence. If as is frequently the case in the Lord's Supper, some are permitted to be present and to "observe" without participating, then how much more may they be present when the prayers of the church ascend to God. Their dismissal is no more necessary than that a father at family prayers after the reading of the Word should dismiss those of tender years and immature experience before the household and its interests are committed to God in prayer. All present will share in the posture of prayer, and follow its form. Whether or not they participate in a true and valid sense becomes an academic question, not affecting the form or administration of the liturgy. We may safely rest in the assurance that "The Lord knows those that are his." Once we have taken up this position the point at which the prayers enter into the liturgy becomes unimportant. Indeed there is no reason why they should not be varied or broken up as occasion may suggest.

There should not be too sharp a distinction between prayers of a general or particular character. Otherwise there will be a tendency to feel that the latter would best be omitted from the liturgy altogether, and be offered in private. To do this would deprive the private prayers of the inspiration and guidance which come from participating in true devout corporate prayer. Obviously no officiating minister is fully aware of the personal interests and concerns of each individual member of his congregation. Far less is he capable of framing a prayer that will adequately express those needs. He must confine himself at this point to the task of leading and directing the prayers, the substance of which will be provided by the members of the congregation individually. Thus there will be achieved the unity of prayers which are specific, and yet at the same time corporate; personal, and yet offered within the fellowship of the church. Necessity will dictate what is in any case desirable, namely, that the participation of the congregation should by no means be confined to the uttering of the "Amen," but should be constant throughout.

The question whether the Lord's Prayer was first intended to be a pattern for prayer or a summary of all prayer matters little. It lends itself to liturgical use whether or not this was originally in mind. Long usage, and relative familiarity among the people even in these days, assures it of its place, traditionally at the close of the intercessions, though not necessarily so.

7. THE OFFERING

It is important that the spirit of worship should not be dispelled by the collection which is the prelude to the gifts being offered to God. For this reason the mechanics of the operation should be orderly and swift without being hurried. It should be late enough in the service to enable the gifts to be made within the setting of the declaration of God's kindness and mercy towards men, and the receiving of forgiveness, for "to whom little is forgiven, the same loveth little." At the same time, coming after, and not before forgiveness will guard against any idea of merit, for it is astonishing how even in Protestant circles the very basis of forgiveness can be misconceived. Contrary to the dogmatic assertion of some, it should not be so late in the service as to form its culmination. For true as it is that the preaching of the Word is to draw forth a response of which the offering might well be the token, it nevertheless is fitting and true to Protestant theological emphasis that the final thought within the liturgy should be one of God and of his grace. To this the benediction rather than the offering will contribute.

For the sake of convenience we have divided the liturgy into its component parts, and discussed their arrangement. But essentially it is a whole. Just as any celebration of Good Friday anticipates the joy of Easter morn, and just as the rejoicing of Easter Sunday is tempered by the remembrance of the cross, so in the liturgy we contemplate the fulness of God's relationship with men. The more familiar we are with the liturgy in its totality the more we shall appreciate it as rehearsing the boundless and eternal mercies of God.

BIBLIOGRAPHY

Benoit, J. D., *Liturgical Renewal.* London: S.C.M. Press.

Davies, Horton, *Worship and Theology in England 1690-1850.* Oxford University Press.

Dix, Dom Gregory, *The Shape of the Liturgy.* London: Dacre Press.

Jungmann, Josef A., *The Early Liturgy.* Darton, Longman & Todd.

Micklem, Nathaniel, *Christian Worship.* Oxford: Clarendon Press.

Underhill, Evelyn, *Worship.* Nisbet.

Aids to Worship

The purpose of worship is expressed in the succinct words of the Psalmist: "Give unto the Lord the glory due unto his name; worship the Lord in the beauty of holiness" (29:2; cf. 96:9). Thus the primary purpose of worship is not moral uplift nor ecstatic feeling nor aesthetic pleasure; on the contrary, worship means giving to God that of which he is worthy (the root word means "worth-ship"), that which is his due.

This provides us with a criterion by which to judge the propriety of traditional and accepted aids to worship. The question which we must ask is this: Do they give glory to God? Do they enable us to worship the Lord in the beauty of holiness?

1. MUSIC

The Bible bears clear witness to the fact that music, both choral and instrumental, has its appropriate place in the activity of public worship. We are, the Psalmist says, to praise God in his sanctuary, employing, in the service of praise, trumpet and harp, stringed instruments and high sounding cymbals (150:3-5). We are, the Apostle Paul says, to use psalms and hymns and spiritual songs when singing and making melody in our hearts to the Lord (Eph. 5:19).

Every true revival has been accompanied by the experience of joy spontaneously expressing itself in music and in song. Thus the Methodist Revival, for example, was associated with a wealth of music for the people. Nothing but the best is good enough in worship. This means that our offering of music and of song must be the best that we can make it. We do not, Augustine points out, honor God by willfully disregarding the laws of symmetry and soundness. Calvin insists on two guiding axioms: music is for the people, so it must be simple; music is for God, so it must be modest. We need to regulate music, he insists, "so that it is useful and not pernicious."

We need to bear in mind that true worship is only possible through genuine participation on the part of the congregation. Luther taught his people to sing by composing chorales, and Calvin, in like manner, put the psalms to simple tunes. Solos and anthems are not necessarily excluded, provided they do not derogate from the congregational nature of the service. They must be fully integrated into the general structure of the service, not be intrusive. The service of public worship is neither the time nor the place for virtuoso exhibitions by either organist or choir, lest we neglect the glory of God for the praise of men. The congregation must not be reduced to the role of passive spectators at a performance. The problem becomes acute in relation to cathedral services where ornate settings and special chants are traditionally employed. The problem, though difficult, is not insoluble. The function of the choir is to lead the praises of the people, to help, and not to hinder, the activity of worship. What applies to organs applies to all other instruments of music.

We must show a proper concern with what is sung. We are to sing, the Apostle insists, not only with the spirit but with the understanding also (I Cor. 14:16). What matters, Jesus says, is worship in spirit and in truth (John 4:24). We must take heed to the doctrine (I Tim. 4:16). We must not contradict the truth which we believe by the unthinking repetition of words which are theologically suspect. There must be a proper marriage between sound and sense, between music and words. Thus, if music is to aid the service of worship it must be modest, not flamboyant; it must be genuinely congregational, and serve the cause of truth and edification.

2. ARCHITECTURE

"A church that is interested in proclaiming the gospel," it has been said, "must also be interested in architecture, for year after year the architecture of the church proclaims a message that either augments the preached Word or conflicts with it. . . . If the gospel of Christ is worthy of accurate verbal proclamation week by week, it is also worthy of faithful architectural proclamation, where its message speaks year after year."

When God gave the children of Israel the tabernacle he provided detailed instructions concerning its form and arrangements. Church architecture is not a matter of indifference; it is a matter of the utmost theological importance.

For the medieval church the mass was the focal point of worship, and Gothic churches were designed for this purpose. What we believe about the gospel will determine the design of the sanctuary. That is why the Reformers rightly replaced the altar with the Lord's table. An altar implies both a sacrifice and a priest, but the New Testament recognizes no sacrifice other than that sacrifice which was offered by our Lord Jesus Christ, once for all, and no priesthood other than the unchangeable priesthood of Christ in heaven. At the Lord's table we are not concerned with "repeating" the sacrifice of Calvary; on the contrary, our concern is "remembering" it. We do not offer Christ afresh as a sacrifice for sins; on the contrary, we offer the sacrifice of praise and thanksgiving for an accomplished victory and a finished work.

Those who number themselves among the heirs of the Reformation recognize the centrality and abiding authority of the Word of God. Not only must the Bible be prominently displayed; the architectural design must make possible its proclamation. In the medieval church it was sufficient for the mass to be offered; evangelicals insist that the sacrament is meaningless without the interpretative word of the gospel. "Faith cometh by hearing and hearing by the word of God" (Rom. 10:17). Is the church designed, architecturally and acoustically, to make possible the preaching of the Word? This is the determinative consideration. Is the pulpit unobstructed? Is the church functional? Is it designed to serve the needs of a worshiping community?

New churches should not slavishly reflect the styles and fashions of a bygone age. The church needs to proclaim, by its outward design, that it belongs to the present. The gospel is a message for the here and now. Gothic architecture was a breathtaking achievement in the thirteenth century but is an anachronism in the twentieth. What is required is not a faked and fictitious imitation of the past but an authentic and honest expression of the faith in the materials and forms of today. We then indicate the timeless relevance of the gospel for all men, at all times, in all places.

On the mission field we ought not to suggest that the church is a foreign importation and simply another facet of western civilization. We ought to adopt a form of architecture which is truly indigenous. We ought to baptize into Christ, as far as this is possible, local art and native music. What needs to be avoided is the contamination of the faith by associations which are pagan. Watchfulness is, of course, required. Nevertheless, the Biblical principle is clear: to bring all things into captivity to the obedience of Christ (II Cor. 10:5).

3. SYMBOLISM

When a man shakes hands it is a symbol of friendship; when a man salutes his nation's flag it is a symbol of patriotic pride; when a man gives a girl a ring, it is a symbol of the eternity of his love. Symbols are a non-verbal mode of communication, expressing thoughts too deep for words. Symbols belong to the pattern of our common life. They also belong to the life of religion. That is why our Lord Jesus Christ provided tangible symbols as instrumental means of grace. He took the common things of life – water and bread and wine – and, by the interpretative word, made them effective signs and sure witnesses of his love and grace.

The baptismal font or the baptistry, within the body of the church, speaks of Christ's baptism of death (Luke 12:50) and of our identification with him in death and resurrection. Likewise the sacrament of the Lord's table speaks to us of the body of Christ broken upon the cross and of the blood shed for our redemption, and of the communion which we now have with God through him. It also reminds us of his future coming again. Thus, through the water of baptism and the broken bread and the outpoured wine the gospel is dramatically proclaimed.

The question is to what extent it is permissible to use additional symbolism to proclaim the gospel. The early Christians adorned their catacombs with a wealth of symbols portraying the reality of their new found faith. Jonah was a sign of Christ's resurrection. The fish (as well as being a mnemonic for "Jesus Christ, Son of God, Saviour") was a reminder that Jesus fed the multitude with loaves and fishes, and commanded his disciples to be fishers of men. The first and last letters of the Greek alphabet, the alpha and the omega, spoke of Jesus, the first and the last. The ark spoke of the church. The heavenly creatures in Ezekiel's vision spoke of the four gospels. Of all symbols the cross was the most precious.

The English Reformers believed that in their day the cross had become an occasion of idolatry. They therefore ordered the removal of all crosses from the furniture of the church, finding Biblical justification in the action of Hezekiah, who destroyed "the brazen serpent that Moses had made: for . . . the children of Israel did burn incense to it" (II Kings 18:4). Nevertheless, significantly enough, the English Reformers retained the sign of the cross in baptism.

There have been, down the ages, two schools of thought: those for whom symbols are a snare and a hindrance to faith, and those for whom symbols are a stimulus to worship and an aid to faith. The Cistercians aspired to "follow, naked, the naked Christ," and believed "that nothing savouring of pride or superfluity should be left in God's house." Antonio, a Dominican, wrote: "The reprobate Cain is the first of whom we read that he built a city and therefore houses. . . . spacious palaces and excessive buildings beyond what is convenient are not pleasing to God; the patriarchs lived in tents." By contrast, Gregory the Great commended the use of paintings in churches. They enabled the illiterate, he explained, to read upon the walls what they could not read in books. Centuries before, Quintilian remarked that pictures are the books of those who cannot read.

Luther, in contrast to the iconoclastic practices of some of his followers, recognized the positive value of art. "I do not hold that the Gospel should destroy all the arts," he said, "as certain superstitious folks believe. On the contrary, I would see all arts, and especially that of music, serving Him that hath created them and given them to us." Calvin saw the danger of idolatry: "Seeing that the art of painting and carving images cometh from God, I require that the practice of art should be kept pure and lawful." He made one important proviso: "We think it unlawful to make any visible representation of God, because he hath himself forbidden it, and it cannot be done without detracting, in some measure, from his glory."

It is in the light of these principles that Christians will decide whether it is legitimate to embellish and adorn churches with appropriate Christian symbols and works of art. One critic justly observes: "If they are allowed to become ends-in-themselves, and so to dominate the proceedings that attention is drawn from the table to the wall, then, the better they are as works of art, the worse they are as liturgical adjuncts." The guiding principles are that the subject matter be appropriate and the artistic execution honest. It is a commentary on the situation which exists today that a stained glass window in Coventry Cathedral interweaves Biblical symbols with the psychological insights of Freud and Jung.

Christians believe that "every good gift and every perfect gift is from above" (James 1:17), and that each gift of God is to be "received with thanksgiving" (I Tim. 4:3). Art is a gift of God; there are those, therefore, who argue that works of art ought to be received and not rejected, provided they serve the cause of reverence and truth.

BIBLIOGRAPHY

Bevan, Edwyn, *Symbolism and Belief*. Collins: The Fontana Library, 1962.

Bruggink, Donald J. and Droppers, Carl H., *Christ and Architecture*. Grand Rapids: Eerdmans, 1965.

Ferguson, George, *Signs and Symbols in Christian Art*. Oxford University Press, 1954.

Routley, Erik, *The Church and Music*. London: Gerald Duckworty, 1950.

——————, *Church Music and Theology*. London: S.C.M. Press, 1959.

Stafford, T. A., *Christian Symbolism in the Evangelical Churches*. New York: Abingdon, 1942.

Constituents of Liturgy

In the examination of the distinctive parts involved in a worship service it is important to keep constantly in mind the following salient points.

(a) The necessity of maintaining an overall unity. Each phase must have a relation of harmony with the others and with the particular theme or doctrine which is being emphasized. Avoid fragmentation.

(b) The value of the development of a sense of catholicity in worship. We are not isolated congregations approaching God, each on its own, but we are integral parts of the whole fellowship of Christian believers, the body of Christ, extending through space and time.

(c) The need to consider growth and nurture in an ongoing program of worship, in building the Christian character and moving forward in Christian living and experience. In a sense one might say that each occasion of divine worship is part of a serial — to be continued.

(d) The importance of being willing to share what we are and have with one another. We come to God's house not only to receive but also to give. There should be an attitude of sympathy towards any who join with us, especially those burdened in soul, mind or body. We worship that we may witness.

(e) In each opportunity of worship there should be a note of expectancy, an air of excitement as we come anew into this great and wonderful experience of the presence of God.

(f) Thorough and careful preparation of each detail in the liturgical program is of prime importance. The very best of which we are capable is the least we can offer. The awareness of the presence of the living Christ in the midst of his worshiping community will challenge us to strive for meaning, dignity and depth in our preparation as well as in performance.

(g) Do what you are supposed to be doing. When you are supposed to be praying, PRAY. When you are supposed to be praising, PRAISE. When you are supposed to be listening, LISTEN. Where this axiom is applied, worship will be dynamic, transforming, enriching.

1. MUSIC

a. *Hymns*. The hymns for each service should be of the particular season, doctrine, or theme of the day. Each hymn in the service should be relevant to that particular part of the service in which it occurs. The following is a fairly generally observed pattern.

(1) The opening or processional hymn. This sounds the call to worship and sets the tone for the entire service. Here we lift up our hearts and raise our voices in praise to God who is the object of our worship. This is a hymn of praise, a *Gloria Tibi*. This hymn should be strong, joyful, triumphant, and have dignity. The tune should be one which is stirring and bold. All of this would still apply in those churches where the practice is for the choir to enter quietly, or where there is no choir, and the hymn would be sung a little later in the service.

(2) The second hymn usually comes adjacent to either the prayers or a lesson.

This hymn should be of a more devotional nature, more quiet and restrained, in keeping with the spirit or mood the worshipers have attained.

(3) The next hymn will probably be just before the sermon. It should be a hymn which contains a message in preparation for the preaching of the Word of God. The type of sermon will indicate the nature of both words and music in the hymn chosen. An evangelistic sermon will require a hymn with the ring of the gospel. A sermon with a doctrinal emphasis calls for a hymn which relates to the particular teaching.

(4) There is usually a hymn following the sermon. This is in a sense an Amen. Here the congregation gives assent to the spoken word and makes an act of dedication to God, a pledge to fulfil his purpose and obey his will. This hymn will be of a more personal kind. It, too, should be related directly to the theme presented.

(5) The closing hymn is the grand climax. This (both words and music) is what the people carry away with them from the service. The more impressive the hymn, the more lasting its effect. It should be a hymn that is strong, stirring, convincing, and convicting. Its echoes will ring beyond the church into the home. It can gather together all that has happened in the service and be the link between the sacred and the secular.

(6) There are variations from the above. Notably, the children's hymn. Children are an invaluable part of the Christian family and their presence should be encouraged and recognized by having some part of the service that is theirs. A children's hymn sung in the midst of the service will help them to feel that they really belong. It will also remind the older members of their responsibilities towards the young.

(7) Some general practical considerations. The hymn is pre-eminently the congregational part of the musical service. To ensure their own interests the congregation should have found the "place," stand when the choir stands and begin to sing with them. The pitch should be within the range of the majority so that for the average person the singing may come easily and without strain. Each congregation will tend to develop its own tempo. Most congregational singing is too slow. There should be good movement avoiding the temptation to drag. Careful study should be given to the treatment of each type of hymn. This, of course, requires strong leadership, but it will make singing much more exciting and interesting and avoid monotony. For example, a Bach chorale calls for a treatment of stately dignity, while an evangelistic hymn will move with more vigor and liveliness. Congregations should be encouraged to broaden their repertoire. Most hymnals have many good hymns and tunes which lie neglected. Each minister should develop a definite method of introducing new hymns. The choir and children can learn them readily and usually with enthusiasm. A sympathetic gradual introduction of the "new" will enrich the congregation's hymnal vocabulary and excite the taste for more. The old favorites should be retained because of their rich associations but sung with less frequency.

For the worship of God the church should strive for the best in words and music. Beauty, truth and holiness should be obvious tests of the best in church music. It should speak to the praise and glory of God; it should reflect man's aspirations for the highest; it should be clothed in language that is marked by clarity and conviction. Obscurity and tawdriness should be avoided. The tunes should be carefully selected so that they fit the words and enhance them

b. *The Choir.* The function of the choir is to lead the worship of the congregation in both the said and sung parts of the service. A church service is not the setting for a concert or recital. The use of anthems or solos requires careful consideration and cooperation. They have their place as men and women with God-given talents dedicate their gifts to God in the exercise of those talents. Yet all musical offerings should be considered in the light of their relation to the whole service. They should make a real contribution, rather than tend to disrupt or disturb the general pattern of worship. The members of the choir should continually strive to increase their effectiveness and widen their repertoire. It is wise that they recognize their limitations; struggling beyond their powers can often be disastrous.

c. *The Organ.* The instrumental music forms a background for the whole service as well as providing constant leadership. Here again, the standard of only the best for God should prevail. Prelude, postlude and incidental music should be carefully planned to be in harmony with the main theme of the day. The organist can be most effective in inculcating the spirit of reverence and devoutness among all in attendance.

d. *The Psalter.* The Psalter has been called the Hymn Book of the Old Testament. The congregation has the right to an active participation in psalms and canticles whether sung, chanted, or recited. There are various methods that can be used in the reading of the Psalms. There is the pattern of alternate verses between minister and congregation, alternate half verses, the division between choir and congregation, the recital of the entire Psalm in unison. Each congregation will develop the formula which proves of most value and meaning to it.

2. THE PRAYERS

a. *The Individual in the Congregation Setting.* Devotional preparation before a service is essential for the worship to have real meaning. This is expected of the minister but applies with equal force to the members of the choir and to the congregation. Before each service there is the need of a time of quiet during which each seeks to become aware of the presence of Christ, to examine his inner self and to await with expectancy what God will bring in the way of new truth, stronger faith, clearer understanding. In the time of quiet devotion we prepare to offer to God renewed dedication and faithfulness. Periods of silence before, after, and even during a service enable the individual to realize that not only is he trying to reach for God but that God is reaching towards him. Few people are able to capitalize on the golden opportunities afforded by silence.

b. *The Liturgical or Set Prayers.* When the minister says, "Let us Pray," it means just that. It does not mean, "Listen while I pray." Together, we come to the throne of grace. When a Prayer Book is used the people can follow along with the minister, word for word. This should be done with no hurry or rush. Due time should be allowed for each person to find the right page. In the liturgical prayers we share in the heritage of devotion which has come to us from the ages. We use language which has stood the test of time, which has been a source of inspiration to people of many traditions within the Christian family. Words become ours which have been used to express with beauty and depth the needs and longings of men. There is, of course, the danger of familiarity bringing, not necessarily contempt, but at least lack of reality and concern, lack of a sense of real involvement, especially if the rendition is inadequate.

A valuable and proven form of the liturgical prayer is contained in the litany. This form, with its short petitions and brief answers does serve to involve people in greater participation and attention.

c. *The Prepared Invocation or Intercessions.* Some ministers find that this type of prayer requires as much preparation as a sermon. In his study the minister considers the needs and aspirations, the hopes and temptations, the joys and the sorrows of his people. He gathers all together and brings it in their name before God. It is an act of intercession which the people can easily follow especially if there is sufficient paragraphing of petitions. It also can have the advantage of speaking most directly and intimately to their condition There is danger if it becomes too ornate and flowery. Also it can become just another sermon either preaching to the people in another guise or preaching to God, telling him what the preacher thinks he ought to know and do.

d. *Extempore Prayer.* The expression means not only "on the spur of the moment" but also "in relation to the times." This is prayer uttered in response to strong feelings and urgent needs of the moment. Where there is a spirit of real devotion it can mean that the Holy Spirit of God breaks through and takes over control in leading the worship of God's people. The most effective of these prayers are direct and to the point. There is certain psychological value when the leader feels the people are right with him before God. There is danger in the temptation to wander and be overly long. This will distract the people. When their concentration is gone it is time to stop. Brief, simple, direct utterances have usually the most meaning and value.

e. *Prayers in Unison.* Traditionally this has been practiced in the saying of the Lord's Prayer, versicles and responses, general thanksgivings and confession. It is of great significance when people unite in common utterances expressing humility or gratitude, common needs or devotion. There is real value when that which is common to all can be said in common. Here the sense of participation and involvement can come alive.

f. *The Amen.* This is a most significant act on the part of the congregation in response to prayers uttered on their behalf. It is at once an expression of aspiration and of acceptance. Therein is intended their earnest desire that God's will may be done and that they themselves may become involved in the fulfillment of God's will. When the Amen comes from the heart there is no need to speak of volume.

g. *The Content of the Prayers.*

(1) Adoration. "Lo, God is here, Let us adore." Here there is the humble recognition of the sovereignty of God. We bow in reverence before him who is the Almighty, Father, Savior and Lord.

(2) Humility. This is expressed in acts of confession and contrition. Here is a humble recognition of ourselves as unworthy, as suppliants asking God for forgiveness, for cleansing, for grace.

(3) Thanksgiving. Here we show gratitude to God for all that in his mercy he has done and is doing for and through us. Herein is a recognition of God as the only source of grace, power, love and redemption.

(4) Petition. Here we bring before God the needs of his children, recognizing that in him alone there is full understanding and compassion, wisdom and mercy. We acknowledge his love and power and our need and duty to cooperate with him in the fulfillment of his divine will. Petition necessarily involves dedication.

h. *The Voice.* The prayers should be spoken in a natural voice stressing clarity of enunciation. Sloppiness, carelessness, mannerisms and idiosyncrasies are unworthy and distress a devout congregation. Sincerity of heart, concentration of mind, singleness of purpose are naturally revealed in oral expression. This will bring a similar response of attitude from the people. To mean what you say and say what you mean is most productive and will overcome many handicaps.

3. THE LESSON

a. *Introduction.* For many people, the portions of Scripture read in the church services constitute their only exposure to the written Word of God. God is speaking to his people through the pages of Holy Writ. The teachings of the Christian church are founded upon the whole Bible. It is important, therefore, that readings should come from both the Old and New Testaments in each service. When planning a season's program, the Law and the Prophets, the Gospels and the Epistles should all be included in any well balanced scheme of presentation. A certain discrimination needs to be exercised. Some passages are definitely obscure and seemingly unedifying, impractical for public use; at the same time many sections full of rich nourishment are never tasted.

b. *Patterns of Selection.*

(1) The Lectionary. The original reasons for setting up a Table of Lessons were: To set the highest possible standard of choice; to establish uniformity in the whole church; to ensure the most adequate readings for specific occasions which stressed the major Christian doctrines; to promote a growth and progression through the Church Year; and to read as much as possible of the Bible in the course of each year. In some churches adherence to the schedule is mandatory. Others permit occasional variants. There is strength in unity. There is at the same time a freshness in wise variation.

(2) The Principle of Free Selection. Each minister who follows this pattern would be well advised to adopt or prepare a Table of Lessons as a basic guide for the year's operations. This will serve at least as a reminder of the necessity of adequate Scriptural foundation for the teachings of the major seasons in the Christian calendar. The principle of progressive growth and development in the Christian life should be observed. The lessons should relate directly to the theme of the sermon on each occasion.

c. *Preparation.* Each lesson should be studied in depth well in advance. If the minister employs Readers, these need plenty of advance notice for preparation. It is wise to read the lessons in several versions, carefully considering words to be stressed; thoughts, ideas, images to be emphasized; where to pause; the correct pronunciation of difficult words and unusual names. Inadequate preparation can ruin the reading of a lesson. Avoid being too casual in the handling and treatment of the Holy Bible. Preparation should be begun, continued and ended in prayer, seeking God's guidance for illumination, understanding and ability of expression. As we make ready to read God's Word to God's people we need to pray that God's message may come through and that God's will may be done and his holy name honored through the service of his ministers.

d. *The Delivery.* Congregations which are accustomed to the style of language of a certain version may be disturbed or even resent the introduction of more modern translations. When this is done the people should be told why. An occasional variation in the text used will bring a freshness of vision and insight. The church members should be encouraged to follow the reading of the lessons with their own copies of the Bible. When this practice is followed it is helpful to introduce the lesson in a way which will facilitate the finding of the passage.

The reader should always be vividly aware of the process involved during the reading. The message comes from the printed page, through the eye of the reader, to his mind and understanding. Then through his speech to the ear of the listener, thence to his understanding. The reader should feel the message in his very soul. Where there is action or imagery he needs to visualize what is taking place as if he were there himself. When this happens the whole scene, picture, idea or teaching will come alive in the heart and mind of the listener. It is more likely then to result in acceptance and action. The reader should be alert to the need of continual speech training to improve performance and eliminate unreality and defects.

4. THE SERMON

While this area of worship is given fuller treatment elsewhere, it is important to insert at least a note here to stress the place of the sermon in the context of liturgical detail. The sermon is an essential part of the worship program. It is not more important nor is it of less importance than the other constituent parts. The areas of praise, prayers and lessons should harmonize with and prepare for the sermon. The preaching of the Word should complement and endorse all that has gone before. In some churches the sermon is all-important. This tends to the aggrandizement of the preacher. In other churches the sermon is considered an insignificant detail. This can result in an overbalance of the ceremonial. The minister should strive for a happy medium contributing all to the glory of God.

5. THE ANNOUNCEMENTS OR NOTICES

There are two schools of thought concerning this matter. The first is that giving of notices disrupts the smooth rhythm of the worship sequence, introducing a discordant note. They are regarded as being irrelevant and out of place, causing an irreverent break in the mood of worship which is difficult and at times impossible to recapture. Where this view prevails announcements during the service are eliminated and all information necessary to be conveyed is contained in a leaflet or bulletin. Congregations soon become accustomed to such procedure. The posting of notices on a bulletin board is usually of little or no value as very few can see it at a time; too many notices add to confusion; and it is difficult to keep the board up to date. Where the rule is "no announcements," an occasional departure from the practice can have a startling effect, especially if the notice is of paramount importance.

Another attitude is that what goes on in the name of the church is something which concerns the whole congregational family. As fellow members of this Christian community adults should know what the children are doing. The activities of the young people need the support and interest of all. In the fellowship the activities and concerns of one group are the concerns of all. What happens in the life and work of organizations is really an extension of the activities of Sunday worship. The reading of announcements as a means of conveying information is regarded as part and parcel of the spiritual life of the congregation. To be effective, notices should be short and to the point. There is always the danger that this period will become the occasion of another sermon thus weakening the impact of the sermon proper when it comes.

Whatever method of communication is used, the important thing is to relate the activities of the Christian family in areas of service, fellowship or witness to the fellowship in worship. The people have a right to know what their fellow members are doing. If properly organized and presented the giving of notices can be a worshipful experience and will draw the family more closely together.

6. THE OFFERING OR COLLECTION

The word collection suggests passing the hat and receiving a token gift from unconcerned donors. The word offering suggests a sacrifice, costing the donor something to give. It is symbolic of the offering of ourselves to God. It is a recognition within the area of worship of stewardship; a reminder that all we are and have belong to God. We present our offering as a recognition of this and as an expression of our gratitude to God for his many mercies. The offering is received by the minister and dedicated to the service and glory of God. Thus both giving and receiving are in themselves an act of worship and form a natural constituent in the liturgy. Where this is more fully realized there is liable to be shown a greater response in generosity.

7. THE BENEDICTION

This is the grand Amen of the service. It is more than a mere dismissal of the congregation. It involves commitment and assurance: a committing of ourselves, our worship, our life into the care and keeping of God. It is an expression of assurance of God's good will towards us as we move from the place of worship. The blessing is usually couched in the Trinitarian formula. Here we are made aware that as we leave God's house his presence goes with us. We depart confident that God the Father, our maker and preserver; God the Son, our Savior and Lord; God the Holy Spirit, our sanctifier will be our God as we go to face again the challenge of daily living.

BIBLIOGRAPHY

Brenner, S. F., *The Way of Worship.* New York: Macmillan Co., 1944.

Delling, D. G., *Worship in the New Testament.* London: Darton, Longman and Todd, 1962.

Forder, C. R., *The Parish Priest at Work.* London: S.P.C.K., 1959.

Horton, D., *The Meaning of Worship,* New York: Harper & Brothers, 1959.

Reed, L. D., *Worship, A Study of Corporate Devotion.* Philadelphia, 1959.

Roach, C. C., *For All Sorts and Conditions.* Greenwich, Conn.: Seabury Press, 1955.

Shepherd, M. H., *The Worship of the Church.* Greenwich, Conn.: Seabury Press, 1959.

Spence, H., *Praises with Understanding.* London: Royal School of Church Music, 1960.

The Christian Year

In the history of worship there are two fairly distinct traditions. On the one hand, there are those brought up in a tradition of worship according to a fairly rigid pattern, based on a prescribed prayer book with a number of set prayers and a fixed choice of Scripture lessons. Many evangelical Christians would avow that such an aid to worship as the Book of Common Prayer is a divine gift to the church through the ministry of spiritually minded men, and they find a sense of enrichment in worship as they are thus linked with many Christians in a common order of service. On the other hand, there are those who find something almost repellent about the very word liturgy with its suggestion of written, set forms of worship which may deprive the leader of worship of the opportunity of following the immediate guidance of the Spirit as he seeks to meet the specific needs of the individual congregation.

It is not the purpose of this article to discriminate between these two traditions and to defend the one which the author finds most congenial; one must not fall into the contemporary ecumenical fallacy of assuming that Christian unity depends upon everybody doing the same things in the same way. What is necessary is to point out that both traditions may fail to offer real worship to God through the development of staleness and monotony. Within the so-called liturgical tradition the leader of worship has the resources of devotional aids which have been prepared by men who may well be more capable than he himself is, and at the same time the use of a written form does enable the congregation to play a full part in the service and actively demonstrate the doctrine of the priesthood of all believers instead of sitting passively in their pews. But it cannot be denied that such worship may easily become monotonous and dead — monotonous because there is a real danger of vain repetition in the regular use of the same form of words, and dead because the form of service used may fail to express the needs and aspirations of the worshipers both by its use of archaic words and phrases and by its failure to arise from the immediate situation of the church. Within the so-called free tradition the leader of worship has a rich opportunity of becoming the sympathetic guide and spokesman of the congregation as they enter the presence of God. He can adapt his conduct of the service to their particular needs in a way that no prayer book can ever do. But it is sadly true that it is equally easy for free worship to become monotonous and dead through the continued repetition of stereotyped phrases and thoughts as they regularly emerge from the subconscious mind of the leader. Moreover, it may well be that Thomas Cranmer was much more free from personal idiosyncrasies than many leaders of free worship who are unconsciously blind to their own limitations and peculiarities.

The great task of all leaders of worship is, therefore, to aim for a form of worship which will be vitally related to the needs of the congregation and bring them into living contact with their God. A popular maxim assures us that "variety is the spice of life," but there is plainly no place in worship for variety merely for the sake of variety. Variety in itself is no guarantee of vitality; what matters is the factor which controls and finds expression in the variety. In any attempt to bring life into worship the way ahead must be by a recollection of the main principles which govern the pattern of worship. In the opinion of the present writer these are two. In the first place, the basic pattern of worship is that of proclamation and response — proclamation of the Word of God and the opportunity of human response to that Word. And in this pattern the cardinal factor is the proclamation of God's Word through the reading of Scripture and the exposition of the Word. We are tempted by the use of the word service as a name for a diet of worship to assume that the all-important thing is the service that we do to God by our prayer and praise, but it needs to be emphasized that the supreme thing which happens in worship is that God graciously serves us. The pattern of worship is one of devine prevenient grace arousing the response of human faith. Hence the central fact in worship is the proclamation of the Word of God, and it may well be that the general pattern of our worship ought to be drastically altered so that the preaching of the Word is neither the climax of the service to which everything else is merely a preliminary nor an addendum to the service after the Order of Morning or Evening Prayer has finished, but rather the center of the service and the foundation of our response to God in prayer, praise and offering.

The second basic principle of worship, which follows immediately from the first one, is that the Word of God which alone can stir up the worshipers to true worship must be proclaimed in all its fulness; the whole counsel of God must be declared to the congregation so that they may make their response to the totality of divine revelation and offer to him a worship which is as rich and variegated as his own revelation to them in the Scriptures. This principle gives us our clue for gaining a living variety in worship. Life and variety will not be human works offered to God. They will be the human response to a proclamation of a living and rich Word to men by God himself. Variety in worship will spring out of the plenitude of the divine encounter with men in the Word.

According to this understanding of the situation, the task of seeking life and vitality in worship is in effect the task of presenting the Word of God to the congregation in a living and full manner. One manner in which this may be achieved is by observance of the Christian year, which indeed is already built into the structure of most prayer books and is followed with varying degrees of faithfulness by the advocates of free worship. There are two great advantages in following this system. First, the basic pattern of the Christian year is Christocentric and lays the main emphasis upon the supreme revelation of God to men in Jesus Christ, the living Word. The leader of worship who follows the Christian year finds himself making an annual journey through the life of Jesus from its foreshadowings in the Old Testament through the incarnation and epiphany to the climax in the passion and Easter and then to the outcome of that life in the birth of the church at Pentecost. The second advantage of following this course is that it compels the leader of worship to remember certain Biblical themes which he might otherwise overlook, whether unconsciously or deliberately. It is salutary, for example, to be reminded of the Second Advent during the season of Advent and thus avoid the temptation to look back to Bethlehem without at the same time looking forward to the consummation of the Kingdom of God; and many of us might fail to preach about the Trinity if it were not for the occurrence of Trinity Sunday.

On the other hand, observance of the Christian year also has its defects. The structure which has been handed down to us by tradition is by no means completely satisfactory. After Trinity Sunday the inspiration of the compilers evidently dried up and we are treated to a long series of "Sundays after Trinity." Some items (such as the Annuciation and various saints' days) appear to be placed quite arbitrarily and upset the even tenor of the main theme, while Rogation Sunday has long since lost its original significance for most of us. Most important of all, many aspects of divine revelation are passed by with no mention. There is also the danger that one may follow the pattern too pedantically and mechanically, always taking the appointed theme for the day and never mentioning any topic out of season.

These points are clearly not arguments against the use of the Christian year, but rather indicate the need for individual discretion and liberty in the use of it; the Christian year was made for man, not man for the Christian year. More important is the question whether other possible methods of worship may help to overcome its defects.

The observance of the Christian year is often coupled with the use of a lectionary, i.e., a planned course of Bible reading. Such a course need not be tied to the Christian year, and equally the Christian year need not demand a lectionary as an indispensable adjunct. Its use is open to the same objection as has already appeared within these pages with regard to following a fixed liturgical form. A lectionary may become a chain instead of a guide, and the leader of worship may fall into the temptation of following it slavishly (and lazily) instead of asking what new Word God may have to utter to his congregation. It is probably also true that a lectionary may confine itself to a limited number of selected passages from the Bible, and fail to cover the whole content of the Biblical revelation. Nevertheless, the basic principle is a sound one. In general the leader of worship should plan his reading of the Scriptures so that the whole counsel of God is declared to the congregation in the course of time.

Many leaders of worship, especially in the "free" tradition, find that they achieve a combination of comprehensiveness and continuity in their reading from Scripture by working systematically through various books (or extended portions), expounding them from the pulpit, and generally constructing their services around them. In this way, the content of Scripture is systematically and comprehensively brought before the congregation, and over the years the various parts of Scripture will be covered in worship without that repetition of well-known passages and limitation of treatment which is the inherent danger in traditional lectionaries. There is very much to be said in favor of this type of treatment. Certainly it is true that the most effective contemporary evangelical ministries are based on this principle. The method of treatment need not, of course, always be that of following through a particular portion of Scripture, but some of the great themes of the Bible may be followed through from time to time. And it goes without saying that the preacher will not feel himself compelled to follow any rigid pattern but will at all times seek the guidance of the Spirit as he prepares for worship.

Conduct of worship according to the Christian year and conduct according to a Scriptural scheme do not represent two opposing principles, but rather two methods of securing a living variety in worship which may very fruitfully be used in conjunction with each other. Within the pattern of the Christian year there is great scope for the systematic presentation of the Word of God in the Scriptures, and by the use of the Scriptures in this comprehensive fashion the defects of the traditional Christian year may be adequately overcome. There is much to be said, for example, for letting the Christian year begin in September or October (at the end of the holiday season) and devoting the autumn to a consideration of God's Word to Israel in preparation for the coming of Jesus; a scheme of worship may be built around an Old Testament book or a general survey of the great acts of divine redemption in Israel. The second major part of the Christian year runs from Christmas to Ascension Day, and the obvious choice of theme for this period will be one of the Gospels. It is worth remembering that, despite their basic similarities, our four Gospels each present a highly individual portrait of Jesus, and the preacher who exerts himself to bring out the distinctiveness of the Gospel portraits will preserve himself and his congregation from a monotonous and drab presentation of the life and ministry of Jesus. Finally, in the third part of the Christian year, from Pentecost to the end of the summer, the appropriate theme will obviously be the life of the Christian and the church from the Acts and Epistles.

This general pattern is capable of endless variation. In particular there must be some measure of variety between morning and evening services of worship. The author assumes that there will be two services of worship Sunday by Sunday. Whatever be the age of this tradition and however limited its geographical extent, he is firmly persuaded that in some shape or form the church must carry on two services week by week, one addressed to the unconverted and of a basically evangelistic character, and the other addressed to the converted and of a basically edificatory character. Local circumstances may determine the form of this pattern in detail, but that the pattern must contain these two elements is a matter of basic principle. The existence of these two needs within the congregation will call for two different types of treatment. For there is no virtue whatever in having two Sunday services which slavishly follow each other. One of the author's principal complaints against the Book of Common Prayer is that Morning and Evening Prayer are so alike to each other. With regard to the general theme of the services, the Christian year may furnish the basic structure for either evangelism or edification, but the need for carrying on two diets of worship week by week will force the leader to seek out different approaches within the same basic Scriptural framework.

It is not the purpose here to discuss in any detail the general conduct of worship. Our concern is with the basic principles which must determine the attainment of vitality from week to week. Inevitably for one who belongs to the Reformed tradition these basic principles have been concerned with the presentation of the Word of God which is the very center of the Christian service and to which our worship must be a response. Liturgy thus arises out of the Word and the preaching of the Word, and it would appear to be doctrinally false for the order to be reversed. Yet it would be wrong to assume that the approach adopted here makes preaching all-important and ignores the other elements in the service. What is being suggested is that the whole of a service of worship should be vitally related to the proclaimed Word of God. Naturally this does not mean that, for example, when the appointed Scripture theme is Ephesians 6: 10 ff., all the hymns sung should come from the "Temptation and Conflict" and "Militant and Triumphant" areas of the hymn book. Rather, the service as a whole should form a unity in which the various elements of praise, confession, response and petition are not arranged and expressed haphazardly but are integrated into an organic whole. The point is that when some such attempt as this is made the leader of worship will find himself freed from the monotony in prayer which so often deadens worship and forced to express himself (and the congregation) in prayers which will partake of something of the richness of divine revelation.

A further point which needs some emphasis is that adoption of this general principle for the structure of services of worship will help to free us from the strange assumption that services ought to follow the same general pattern from week to week. This is simply not so. There is no one perfect pattern for the church service, and different aspects of the gospel require different treatment. The Word of God will not always be proclaimed in the same manner; it may not even require always to be expounded in a sermon, but may come home to the hearts of the people simply through the Scripture reading or through the words of a hymn or through its visible presentation in the sacrament. Again, as was indicated earlier, an evangelistic service may require a completely different treatment from one meant primarily for those already within the Christian family. In this connection, it may be worth remembering that there is perhaps a danger in trying to dictate too rigidly what ought to be the response of each individual member of the congregation to the gospel, and that one must beware of attempting to force every individual present to express his response in the same fashion.

This point leads to some consideration of the place of the congregation in worship. Since we have emphasized that the primary element in the service is the proclamation of the Word of God, it follows that the basic direction of the service must be in the care of the minister who seeks to discover the Word from God for each particular occasion of worship and who seeks to hide himself so that Christ alone may be seen and glorified. It may therefore seem to be unjustified to follow the principle of holding a meeting of a "worship committee" to discover what popular taste wishes to be included in the service. But the doctrine of the priesthood of all believers should find expression in a greater element of participation by the congregation in the conduct of worship. Thus the church's intercession ought to be guided by the informed sympathy of the members as a body and not merely by what a minister may think ought to be the subject of their prayers. Moreover, when a congregation is able to take part in the worship other than simply by joining in the singing of hymns, there is much more scope for variety in the form of service, a variety which will serve to remind them that response to God is indeed a common act of the congregation.

If the principles advanced in this article are sound, there is no excuse for dulness or deadness in our worship. Where these occur, it is because our apprehension of the Word of God is itself shoddy and lifeless. The way to living worship will always be by a fresh knowledge of the living Word rather than by attempts to copy other people's ways of worship or to indulge in sheer novelty. Undoubtedly the leader of free worship will greatly benefit from a study of the church's rich tradition of worship, just as the leader of liturgical worship will gain richly by practicing the spontaneity and freshness of freedom, but in the end the chief route to living worship is by a renewed encounter with God in the Scriptures and by a renewed asking of the question, "Lord, what wilt Thou have me to do?"

BIBLIOGRAPHY

Coffin, H. S., *The Public Worship of God.* Philadelphia: Westminster Press, 1946.

Dearmer, P., *The Parson's Handbook.* London: Oxford University Press, 1924.

Kay, J. A., *The Nature of Christian Worship.* London: Epworth Press, 1953.

Scott, A. B., *Preaching Week by Week.* New York: Richard R. Smith, 1929.

SECTION 10

EDUCATION

"These things command and teach."
– I Timothy 4:11

	Title	Author
1.	The Ministry – a Teaching Ministry	Kendig Brubaker Cully
2.	The Exposition of Scripture – a Teaching Ministry	J. Edward Hakes
3.	The Work of the Bible Class and Sunday School – Teacher of a Class	Martha M. Leypoldt
4.	Using the Weekday for Religious Education	Charles Tyrrell
5.	Church Organizations for Teaching	Robert K. Bower
6.	Preparing the Laity to Teach	John Mostert
7.	The Christian School	John F. Blanchard, Jr.

The Ministry — a Teaching Ministry

kerygma — didache

In recent years New Testament scholars have used the terms *kerygma* and *didache* very frequently. It is important for purposes of understanding the implications of these terms for pastoral theology and religious education to have some clear understanding as to what they denote.

The Greek word *kerygma* refers to the setting forth of the basic gospel of Jesus Christ – God's redemptive action in and through his mighty acts performed in and by Jesus of Nazareth, the Christ. The word is derived from *keryssein,* "to preach," and the resultant noun refers to that which is preached, the proclamation itself.

The *kerygma* refers to the presentation of the message of Jesus Christ by heralds, who were sent forth ("apostles"), commissioned to declare to an unbelieving world those saving acts by which God through Christ had brought salvation to mankind. It has often been pointed out by modern scholars that this proclamation underlies every writing in the New Testament. It becomes explicit at many points, but even where it is only implicit, it is the ground-message on which all else is founded.

"For the word of the cross is folly to those who are perishing, but to us who are being saved it is the power of God," Paul writes to the Corinthians. "For since, in the wisdom of God, the world did not know God through wisdom, it pleased God through the folly of what we preach to save those who believe. For Jews demand signs and Greeks seek wisdom, but we preach Christ crucified, a stumbling-block to Jews and folly to Gentiles, but to those who are called, both Jews and Greeks, Christ the power of God and the wisdom of God. For the foolishness of God is wiser than men, and the weakness of God is stronger than men" (I Cor. 1:18-25).

It was this commission and zeal to preach the gospel that found expression in the New Testament books. The basic *kerygma* can be seen in one of its earliest strands in Chapter 2 of the Acts of the Apostles.

C. H. Dodd, to whom the scholarly world is indebted for his careful delineation of the *kerygma,* has outlined the sequence of the kerygmatic utterances in the primitive Christian preaching: the age of fulfillment now at hand, the fact that this fulfillment has taken place through the ministry, death, and resurrection of Jesus Christ, God's exalting Jesus as messianic head of the new Israel, the Holy Spirit's continuing Christ's power and glory in the church, and the consummation of the messianic age in the return of Christ. The proclamation always ends "with an appeal for repentance, the offer of forgiveness and of the Holy Spirit, and the promise of 'salvation,' that is, of 'the life of the age to come,' to those who enter the elect community." As it is expressed in the words of Peter, "Repent, and be baptized every one of you in the name of Jesus Christ for the forgiveness of your sins; and you shall receive the gift of the Holy Spirit. For the promise is to you and to your children and to all that are far off, every one whom the Lord our God calls to him" (Acts 2:38 f.). (See C. H. Dodd, *The Apostolic Preaching and Its Developments,* Harper & Brothers, 1936, pp. 24-29.)

Jules Laurence Moreau has pointed out that the word *kerygma* implies "three factors in the preaching: announcement of sin and judgment (man's situation before God); proclamation of God's saving act in Christ; and the appeal to accept God's saving act of forgiveness and to live as becomes those who have been forgiven of all sin by God who alone has been wronged and who alone can forgive." (See "Kerygma" in Kendig Brubaker Cully, ed., *The Westminster Dictionary of Christian Education,* The Westminster Press, 1963, pp. 364 f.).

It was out of this basic *kerygma* that the apostles and their successors went forth into the ancient world to proclaim the gospel and to win converts to the growing church.

Closely related to *kerygma* is the word *didache.* C. H. Dodd, again, performed a notable service in detecting these two basic strands and pointing out their relationship. The *didache* is that part of the gospel which refers to the teaching based on the proclamation: ethical and moral exhortation, the ways in which Christians who have responded to God's saving act in Jesus Christ will now live in the world. It would be wrong to separate the *didache* from the *kerygma,* as perhaps Dodd tended too sharply to do, since the two are intertwined always in Paul's writings, for example. But it is certainly true that many sections of the epistles are largely didactic in tone, suggesting a kind of prebaptismal catechesis. Examples of writings in the New Testament that are essentially didactic are I and II Timothy and Titus. In the Gospel according to Matthew we see the arrangement of materials with a teaching motivation apparently in mind. It has been suggested by some scholars that the format of the gospels was in part dictated by catechetical necessities or purposes. It is evident that Jesus himself taught as well as preached, heralding the kingdom of God, but also instructing the disciples, as in the teaching material of the Sermon on the Mount.

In Paul's writing we see the close correlation between *kerygma* and *didache* in a passage such as Galatians 5, in which Paul follows his discussion of the freedom of the Christian with exhortation of a moral nature such as "stand fast, therefore, and do not submit again to a yoke of slavery." Those who are in Jesus Christ are called upon to live differently toward one another than they would have done under the old system of law. Freedom is not to be used "as an opportunity for the flesh," rather, "through love be servants of one another." He sets forth in very explicit terms "the works of the flesh" as opposed to the "fruit of the Spirit," which will be exemplified in "love, joy, peace, patience, kindness, goodness, faithfulness, gentleness, self-control." "Let us have no self-conceit, no provoking of one another, no envy of one another."

It should be noted that no "general law" of moral behavior is enunciated in the New Testament writings. Always the *didache* rests upon and is derived from the *kerygma.* Thus we should not expect to look into the New Testament to find universal laws of moral behavior, for example. These are the ethical-moral modes of behavior for those who are called into the kingdom, who have given assent to the redemptive action of God through Christ, who are now impelled and enabled to live in the world as his followers and as integrally a part of his body, the church.

The implications of the relation of *kerygma* and *didache* for Christian education have been increasingly studied in recent years. Among the first serious Protestant studies of this type was Iris V. Cully's *The Dynamics of Christian Education* (The Westminster Press, 1958). She pointed out that the very proclamation of the good news is teaching," not in the sense of imparting information, but "the dynamic word through which a redemptive experience is mediated. The way in which it is proclaimed as well as the fact of its proclamation gives a ground for interpreting the experience. When the words are appropriated by the person and he is turned around – accepting the forgiveness of God, finding new life in Jesus Christ – then he has the ground for interpreting the experience" (p. 48). The *kerygma* at many levels yields teaching as the church seeks to understand the moral implications of the gospel, as it interprets the redemptive events in the life of the Christian community through fellowship, and as it faces the apologetic task – interpreting its life to the world.

Roman Catholic writers also have been engaged in a search for the meaning of a kerygmatic catechetics. This is evidenced in a work like *Modern Catechetics*, edited by Gerard S. Sloyan (The Macmillan Company, 1963).

The implications of the *kerygma-didache* relationship for pastoral theology and preaching have not yet been fully explored, but there is evidence that this dialectic is entering increasingly into the actual execution of pastoral counseling and preaching. The tendency for preachers in the earlier part of the twentieth century to preach didactically, on one hand, emphasizing socio-ethical behavior oftentimes unrelated to the basic proclamatory task, has come in for thoroughgoing evaluation in recent decades; likewise, evangelistic preaching which aimed at perpetual reconversions without the provision of nurturing *didache* for those who already had committed themselves to Christ, has been reexamined. The basic postulate of the most influential pastoral counseling theories of the present is that solving another's problems for him without helping him face the ambiguities of life in terms of personal decision cannot stand up under the most penetrating understandings of the human situation, let alone the basic relationship to God, who calls to repentance but simultaneously provides the means for forgiveness and hope through faithful living.

BIBLIOGRAPHY

Cully, Iris V., *The Dynamics of Christian Education*. The Westminster Press, 1958.

————————, *Imparting the Word: The Bible in Christian Education*. The Westminster Press, 1962.

Cully, Kendig Brubaker, ed., *The Westminster Dictionary of Christian Education*. The Westminster Press, 1963. Articles: *Didache* by Robert M. Grant; *Kerygma* by Jules Laurence Moreau.

Dodd, C.H., *The Apostolic Preaching and Its Developments*. Harper & Brothers, 1936.

Sloyan, Gerard S., ed., *Modern Catechetics*. The Macmillan Company, 1963.

Wright, G. Ernest and Fuller, Reginald H., *The Book of the Acts of God*. Doubleday & Company, 1957.

The Exposition of Scripture — a Teaching Ministry

Ministers who take seriously the Scriptural injunction to "preach the word" (II Tim. 4:2) and who recognize that there is an obligation concerning *didache* for all who, in their pulpit activities, would be faithful to the *kerygma* (cf. N. J. D. White's treatment of II Timothy 4:2 in *The Expositor's Greek Testament*), will find that expository preaching is by far the most appropriate method of sermonizing. In fact it could be said that it is the only kind of pulpit discourse which can truly be called preaching.

Traditionally, expository preaching has been thought of as one of the three ways to sermonize, to be distinguished from the topical and the textual approaches. Thus it has been conceived of almost exclusively in terms of homiletical structure. Whereas the preacher's choice and the textual sermon deals with a single statement of the Scriptures, the expository sermon "comes mainly," according to Blackwood in his *Expository Preaching for Today*, "from a Bible passage longer than two or three consecutive verses." Blackwood's definition is typical of those given by Broadus, Meyer, and other great expositors and authorities on homiletics of past generations.

Contemporary definitions of expository preaching, however, tend to be expressed in terms of sermon content. Miller, for example, in *The Way to Biblical Preaching*, insists that "truly biblical exposition is limited only by the broad principle that the substance of one's preaching should be drawn from the Bible." He defines expository preaching as "an act wherein the living truth of some portion of Holy Scripture, understood in the light of solid exegetical and historical study and made a living reality to the preacher by the Holy Spirit, comes alive to the hearer as he is confronted by God in Christ through the Holy Spirit in judgment and redemption." On this premise he maintains that "all true preaching is expository preaching, and that preaching which is not expository is not preaching."

It is impossible to argue successfully against Miller's ideas at this point if one agrees with Ramm, in his *Protestant Biblical Interpretation*, that "the preacher is a minister of the Word of God. He is not a person who has a full and free right of sermonizing before a group of people. If he is a true minister of God, he is bound to the ministry of the Word of God." Thus, by whatever procedures he may prepare and deliver his sermon, the truly Biblical preacher will be restricted to the expounding (i.e., the explanation and/or interpretation) of God's truth as inscripturated in some passage of the Bible. If he fails to be an expositor of God's Word, he simply is not preaching. As Ramm reminds us, the preacher's "fundamental task is not to be clever or sermonic or profound, but to minister the truth of God." This requires that *all* sermons be expository, in the true sense of the term. Littorin sums it up well in his *How to Preach the Word with Variety* when he says that "only in exposition, well prepared and presented, can one sound the very voice of God in the ears and hearts of the people before him."

Historically, expository preaching has its roots deeply embedded in the Judao-Christian tradition. As Glen points out in the 1959 Smyth Lectures which have been published as *The Recovery of the Teaching Ministry*, "the pulpit tradition inherited from the Protestant Reformation, and indirectly from the Jewish synagogue, demands that the pulpit assume a major responsibility for teaching." The custom among the post-exilic Jews is described by Sherrill in *The Rise of Christian Education*: "As Hebrew became an unfamiliar language except to scholars, it was necessary to translate. One verse from the Torah, or as many as three verses from the prophets, would be read. Then the translator would render it, giving it to the people in their own tongue. He was not permitted to read his translation, but must give the sense in a free interpretation. It is easy to see how naturally this free translation with explanation would pass into the homily which is a more formal discourse based on portions of Scripture. It is not certain when this became a part of the service, but it was familiar in the time of Jesus. The detailed expounding of Scripture might last until late afternoon." Thus the expository sermon, at least in embryonic form, was a familiar phenomenon among the people of God by the time the New Testament age began.

Our Lord is called by F. B. Meyer, in his *Expository Preaching*, "the Prince of Expositors." Of him Luke says that "beginning at Moses and all the prophets, he expounded (*diermeneuen* – explained) unto them all the scriptures the things concerning himself" (Luke 24:27). Although Luke is no more explicit than this, this brief comment does indicate Christ's expository treatment of the Old Testament.

Luke describes the Apostle Paul's ministry in similar language. When, during his first imprisonment in Rome, the leaders of the Jewish community visited him, to them "he expounded (*ektitheto* – unloosed or explained) and testified the kingdom of God, persuading them concerning Jesus, both out of the law of Moses, and out of the prophets" (Acts 28:23). He too preached expositorily. And this appears to be characteristic of the New Testament throughout. "It is instructive," says Meyer, "how much of the New Testament is expository of the Old."

This apostolic practice of expounding the Scriptures continued during the early centuries of the church's history. But, when the Scriptures were supplanted by religious ceremony and the clergy became priests rather than preachers of God's Word, a long hiatus developed in the history of expository preaching. This was not broken until the eruption of the Protestant Reformation and the rediscovery of the principle of *sola Scriptura*. An important consequence of this was the replacement of the mass by the preaching of the Word of God. Caemmerer reminds us that both of the great Reformers "Martin Luther and John Calvin presented expositions of the entire Bible." The reappearance of expository preaching and the success of the Reformation are far from being merely coincidental.

In the English speaking world the expository sermon is for the most part a heritage from the Scottish Presbyterians and the English Free Churchmen (cf. F. R. Webber's *History of Preaching in Britain and America*, Parts One, Two, and Three). Out of this tradition came such pulpit luminaries as Lawson, Brown, Eadie, Maclaren, and G. Campbell Morgan – expositors all. Archibald Alexander, Princeton Seminary's first professor, was from a Scottish background and both by his teaching and example introduced expository preaching to the United States in the first part of the nineteenth century. G. Campbell Morgan, on his frequent visits to America, was perhaps the most potent single influence in demonstrating the advantages of the exposition of the Scriptures to congregations in this country.

The construction of an expository sermon depends on these three essential steps: the selection of the Scriptural passage to be expounded, the exegesis of the text, and the application of the truth derived therefrom to the contemporary situation. The homiletical structure is comparatively irrelevant, as long as it is in accord with sound communication theory.

The choosing of the particular Biblical excerpt to be expounded is crucial. The wisest choice results from a knowledge of the will of God and an understanding of the needs of one's congregation. Prayerful waiting upon the Spirit for guidance and an intelligent insight into the needs of the audience combine to lead the preacher to the phrase, verse, paragraph, chapter, or book from which, in a single sermon or in a protracted series, he will confront his hearers with the living Word of God. Apart from these, the minister may bring the wrong message in that it will be inappropriate to the particular situation faced at the existential moment of his preaching the sermon.

Second, and equally important, is the exegesis of the text. Littorin is right when he insists that "exegesis is always, without variation, the parent of exposition." The only legitimate handling of the Scriptures is to lead out (literal meaning of "to exegete") that, and only that, which God has written in.

At all costs eisegesis, rightly called by Cleland in his *Preaching to be Understood* a "homiletical sin," is to be avoided. By means of this "leading into" the passage ideas not present, the text, to use Cleland's figure, "becomes a magician's hat. The sermonic rabbit which the preacher pulls from the hat was not originally in the hat. He found the rabbit in the hat because he put it there." Congregations may be amused by the thaumaturgic appearances of these sermonic rabbits, but such homiletical legerdemain is a fraud, unworthy of the prophet who must, if he is to be faithful to his God-given assignment, preface his message with the "Thus saith the Lord." Exegesis is the only honest way to deal with the Scriptures. No one is exempt from its demands. Every preacher must ask the same question which John Brown, a pulpit craftsman of the last century, asked himself when an idea occurred to him as he examined his text: "This is true and it is important, but is it the truth taught in this text?" If it is not in the text, it cannot be in a sermon which professes to be an exposition of the text.

For an explication of the hermeneutical rules of *grammatico-historical* exegesis, the reader is referred to such sources as Ramm's *Protestant Biblical Interpretation* and Mickelsen's *Interpreting the Bible*. Ramm's work also includes a four-page list of books which he considers a "minimum bibliography for exegetical work." To ascertain what the writer of a Biblical statement was saying to his contemporaries and to state those same ideas in today's idiom involve the exegete in hard work. This is why preachers have studies in their home or at their churches. Nothing less than the sound, honest exegetical treatment of the passage will suffice.

Yet, an expository sermon cannot be a mere recital of the findings of study. It is more than a commentary; it is a sermon. Ramm correctly says that one of the dangers of exegesis is that "it is likely to stop with exegesis and not press on to the feeding ministry of the Word of God. It should result in a truly Biblical teaching and preaching ministry in which relevant application is made to listeners." The truth of God in the passage being expounded must be made contemporary in the fullest sense. It must be made relevant to the particular congregation to which it is delivered at the particular moment in which it is being heard. Members of the audience, after having listened to an expository sermon, must be able to answer not only the question, "What does God say in this text?" but "What does God say *to me* in this text?"

Thus a sermon appropriate for yesterday may not be germane today. The same sermon cannot be preached in the chapel services of both a college and a penitentiary. The sermon delivered to an adult congregation will differ greatly from the message given at a junior church service. To be sure, the truth of God is forever settled in the heavens. But its application must of necessity differ from audience to audience.

The advantages of expository preaching are numerous. Some of these accrue to the benefit of the preacher himself. As Broadus, in his monumental *Treatise on the Preparation and Delivery of Sermons* says, "It is one of the benefits of expository preaching that it compels the preacher to study." It demands on the preacher's part a rigorous exploration of the Scriptures in depth. Thus he becomes increasingly better acquainted with the truth of God. The exegesis which exposition requires is an excellent discipline by which he becomes ever more knowledgeable in the area of his distinguishing specialty – i.e., God's special revelation of Christ in the written Word.

Along the same line, expository preaching spares the preacher from yielding to the besetting ministerial sin of "riding hobbies" in the pulpit. As F. B. Meyer has said, "No other style of preaching can so completely guarantee immunity from an indulgence in special crochets and fads." It is normal for each pastor to have his own personal preferences for certain sermonic themes. His natural inclinations, however, will often lead him to an overemphasis of his favorite subjects. The best safeguard against falling prey to his proclivity is systematic exposition. In this way a preacher is more apt to communicate the whole council of God.

The principal gain, however, will be realized by the congregation. "Expository preaching," as Littorin says, "is the door to an educated constituency." Members of churches where the exposition of the Scriptures is the regular practice will be adequately grounded in that which is Christianity rightly so called. They will learn, intellectually and experientially, true Christian doctrine.

Teaching is the only effective antidote to ignorance. And that an alarming illiteracy of distinctive Christian belief exists in the typical Protestant church can be well documented. Mullen, in his *Renewal of the Ministry*, claims that "Never before in our church history have so many enrolled church members known so little about the Bible." Evangelicals must especially beware of the temptation to exempt their own constituencies from this diagnosis of doctrinal illiteracy, particularly if the basis for doing so is the ability of their church members to recite Bible verses or to repeat cliches which have an orthodox sound. If the church's aim for the occupant of the pew is an intelligent understanding of the faith and a demonstration in life of Biblical principles, it must be conceded that ignorance abounds even in the most orthodox churches.

Miller correctly attributes this ignorance to a departure in the American pulpit from the centrality of Biblical preaching. "A famine is abroad," he laments, " 'not a famine of bread, not a thirst for water, but of hearing the words of the Lord' (Amos 8:11)." The absence of truly expository preaching is a major contributing cause of the prevailing Biblical deficiency among lay people which threatens the health of the church.

In the interest of providing spiritual nurture for God's growing children, the diet must be enriched. Church members must be fed both the "milk" and the "meat" of revealed truth. Blackwood suggests that too often "we underestimate the capacity of God's people to digest sermonic food." The minimum weekly requirements of all Christians for spiritual nutriment call for regular expository preaching.

There are also certain pitfalls which must be avoided by the expositor. One of the most dangerous of these is a lack of unity and progress in the exposition of the message. Blackwood reminds us that "Critics of preaching say that the average expository sermon has neither beginning, middle, nor end. Like a ball of twine, it simply unwinds." This criticism usually applies to so-called expository sermons which are in reality verse-by-verse running commentaries. It is the lazy man's caricature of exposition.

The remedy for this is twofold. First, a goal for the sermon must be made explicit in the thinking of the sermon builder. No man ever reached his destination without knowing what it was. Before constructing the message the preacher must know what he wants to accomplish. Second, a well-organized outline must be prepared. At times the outline may appear in the very structure of the passage. More frequently, however, it will be the responsibility of the preacher to organize the divinely revealed truths in a logical and orderly arrangement. Either way, an outline is essential for unity and progression.

Another snare to be avoided by the minister who would preach expositorily – and by all preachers who would teach through their sermons – is the assumption that people learn merely by hearing the truth articulated. Many specialists in learning theory have concluded that the lecture method is one of the poorest techniques for teaching. Yet practically all preaching is lecturing. How many preachers, nevertheless, ignoring the basic principles of learning process, persist in soliloquizing in the pulpit before a passive audience. It should be no surprise that so little of what is said is really learned.

Every preacher who would teach through sermons must understand how people learn. It cannot be said that one has taught unless someone has learned. And God has so constructed men, and hereditary and environmental factors have so influenced the organism that he has designed, that human beings tend to learn in certain ways which the educational psychologists, by God's common grace, have discovered. These must be utilized, if a congregation is to learn from the preacher.

One such principle which cannot be overlooked is that of dialog between teacher and learner. In other words, there must be interchange between pulpit and pew. Passivity in the congregation inhibits real learning. Yet how can there be dialog between a preacher who speaks uninterruptedly for a half-hour and his listeners who sit in reverential silence before him? The answer is that each member of the congregation must be provoked to *think*. His mind must be active, even though his body is inactive. There can be dialog between pulpit and pew, even though the responses from the congregation are not expressed audibly. Indeed, there must be such dialog for learning to take place.

It is impossible here to present an adequate treatment of the important aspects of learning theory. The reader is referred to the bibliography in the author's *Introduction to Evangelical Christian Education*. Let every pulpit-teacher familiarize himself with the psychology of learning.

Sermons with cognitive content, as contrasted to messages which can only excite the emotions or entertain an audience, are essential to the maintenance of the faith as well as to the building of the church. There can be no better content in sermons than the Word of God. Expository preaching is the means by which that Word is taught from the pulpit. Consequently, as Mickelsen says, "The crucial question to ask oneself at the close of every sermon is: did the word (the proclaimed truth of God) become alive to me and to my hearers?" The preacher who can answer this question in the affirmative has really preached.

BIBLIOGRAPHY

Arndt, William F. and Gingrich, F. Wilbur, *A Greek-English Lexicon of the New Testament*. Chicago: University of Chicago Press, 1957.

Blackwood, Andrew W., *Expository Preaching for Today*. New York: Abingdon-Cokesbury, 1953.

Broadus, John A., *A Treatise on the Preparation and Delivery of Sermons*. New York: Hodder and Stoughton, 1898.

Caemmerer, Richard R., *Preaching for the Church*. St. Louis: Concordia, 1959.

Cleland, James T., *Preaching to Be Understood*. New York: Abingdon, 1965.

Glen, J. Stanley, *The Recovery of the Teaching Ministry*. Philadelphia: Westminster Press, 1960.

Littorin, Frank J., *How to Preach the Word with Variety*. Grand Rapids: Baker Book House, 1953.

Meyer, Frederick B., *Expository Preaching*. Grand Rapids: Zondervan, 1954.

Mickelsen, A. Berkeley, *Interpreting the Bible*. Grand Rapids: Eerdmans, 1963.

Miller, Donald G., *The Way to Biblical Preaching*. New York: Abingdon, 1957.

Moulton, James H. and Milligan, George, *The Vocabulary of the Greek Testament*. Grand Rapids: Eerdmans, 1963.

Mullen, Thomas J., *The Renewal of the Ministry*. New York: Abingdon, 1963.

Ramm, Bernard, *Protestant Biblical Interpretation*. Boston: Wilde, 1956.

Sherrill, Lewis J., *The Rise of Christian Education*. New York: Macmillan, 1944.

Webber, F. R., *A History of Preaching in Britain and America*. Parts One, Two and Three. Milwaukee, Wisconsin: Northwestern Publishing House, 1952.

The Work of the Bible Class and Sunday School — Teacher of a Class

The Sunday School is an influential instrument for the teaching ministry of the church. The Bible is the basic book used in the teaching program which is designed for children, youth, and adults. The message of the Bible must be presented in such a way that lives are changed through human instrumentality and the working of the Holy Spirit.

1. THE TEACHING–LEARNING PROCESS

Learning involves change. The teacher is responsible to assist in bringing about changes within the lives of the students in his care as both the teacher and the pupil are sensitive to the work of the Holy Spirit in their lives.

Effective learning involves three aspects: cognitive, affective, and motoric conduct. The cognitive aspect of learning involves a body of knowledge that is to be known or understood. The affective aspect of learning involves changes in feelings, attitudes, and appreciations. The motoric aspect involves the doing of Christian acts. The culmination of learning results when the motoric aspect is evidenced. Knowing with the mind and feeling with the emotions should result in action. The Holy Spirit works through the Word of God and the intellect and emotions of individuals so that visible evidence of learning is seen in the lives of people. Effective teachers, therefore, will not only stress the cognitive aspect of learning but will also give adequate attention to the affective and motoric conduct of their pupils.

Effective learning results when both the teacher and the learner are active participants in the teaching-learning process. Ralph Tyler has stated that it is not so much what the teacher does but what happens to the students that is important (*Basic Principles of Curriculum and Instruction*. Chicago: University of Chicago, 1956, p. 41).

The functions of the teacher are to guide, probe, give direction, provide resources, and stimulate thinking, feeling, and action in his students. The learners actively participate through the following experiences: listening, discussion, writing, asking questions, reading, participating in role playing and drama, participating in projects, etc.

2. APPROACHES TO THE USE OF THE BIBLE

Ralph D. Heim suggests that there are two approaches to teaching the Bible: the factual and the functional approach ("The Use of the Bible in Religious Education," in *Religious Education*. Marvin J. Taylor, ed. New York: Abingdon Press, 1960, p. 55). The factual approach stresses the mastery of Biblical content. The functional approach uses the Bible primarily as a resource to effect changes in living as related to specific situations. Jesus' teaching ministry exemplifies the use of Scripture to deal with specific situations. Paul's epistles taught spiritual truths as a result of certain problems which the early churches faced.

The factual approach involves only the cognitive aspect of learning while the functional approach gives attention to all three aspects: cognitive, affective, and motoric conduct. Both the factual and functional approaches use the Bible and each approach has its place. The use of merely one of the approaches, however, will result in ineffective Christian teaching.

3. RESOURCES AVAILABLE TO THE TEACHER

A Sunday School teacher should have many resources at his disposal. These will be considered in two categories: resource materials and resource persons.

a. *Resource Materials*

Resource materials include a variety of printed matter and audio-visual materials. The Sunday School teacher who desires to be effective needs the following resource materials for his use.

(1) *Teacher's book*. The teacher's book usually provides the basic resource for the Sunday School teacher. This lesson material, provided by the Sunday School, is a part of a pattern of an overall teaching program of the school. The teacher usually uses this

basic resource as his starting point for his teaching program.

(2) *Pupil's book.* When a pupil's study book is provided, the teacher must be acquainted with its contents.

(3) *The Holy Bible.* The teacher's books are based upon Biblical teachings. The teacher should always refer to any Biblical passages that are listed in the teacher's books. The Biblical passages should be read within the context of the passage in which it is found. It should also be considered in the light of the entire gospel and message of the Bible. The teacher must be dedicated to an enlightened interpretation of Scripture, being careful not to take one verse or a part of a verse of Scripture and use it carelessly.

The numerous translations and paraphrases of the Bible can be very helpful to the Sunday School teacher. The message of the Bible put in language that is understandable to its readers and that takes into account the current use of words can make the Biblical message more meaningful. The Sunday School teacher is advantaged to have at least four or five translations at his disposal.

(4) *Bible concordance.* A complete Bible concordance provides a teacher with a record of the use of every word in the Bible. The words, listed alphabetically, are followed by a record of every Biblical passage where this word is found. The teacher who uses this resource may find additional Bible verses than those listed in his lesson book that will assist him in his study of the topic which he is to teach. An abridged Bible concordance also serves a useful purpose but needs a little more skill and time in its use.

(5) *Topical concordance.* The topical cordance provides a series of Biblical passages listed under numerous topics and subtopics.

(6) *Bible dictionary.* This resource provides information about people, events, places, and words used in the Bible. A concise description is given under each listing and the dictionary also provides Biblical references on specific topics.

(7) *Bible commentary.* Some publishers have printed a commentary on the Bible in one volume. Since each verse or series of verses of Scripture is commented upon, one can see that only very general statements can be made. The teacher who has at his disposal one or two complete sets of Bible commentaries is fortunate. Much insight can be gained into Bible doctrine and theological interpretations given by scholars in their fields.

(8) *Bible atlas.* Information about the geography of Biblical lands and specific places gives the Sunday School teacher background material to assist him in understanding the settings where Biblical events took place.

(9) *Books on specific subjects.* A good church library or public library will provide books written on specific subjects that will be a good supplement to the information in the teacher's book.

(10) *Audiovisual materials.* Films, filmstrips, records, maps, flannelgraph, flat pictures, objects, and other audiovisual materials can be of great assistance to the teacher. Much learning takes place through the eye gate. The more senses which are used simultaneously by the learner the more possibility that sustained learning will result. For example, the visual sense supported by the auditory sense renders more effective learning than the auditory sense alone. Care needs to be taken by the teacher to use audiovisual materials to assist in achieving specific goals rather than to fill in time.

(11) *Magazine articles.* The teacher needs to read current periodicals to keep up with current thinking in religious and secular fields. Many magazines have a yearly index which make particular topics of concern readily accessible.

(12) *Books on understanding the various age levels.* Only when the teacher has an understanding of the individuals whom he is teaching will he be able to be an effective teacher. Although each person is an individual unlike any other person, God has designed a physiological and psychological pattern of growth that is gradual and progressive in the life of an individual. This pattern of growth follows certain developmental stages that are common to people at definite periods of life. The teacher should therefore be acquainted with the particular age group he is teaching.

(13) *Books on teaching techniques.* There are many ways by which the teacher can involve the student in the teaching-learning

process. The teacher needs to have in his possession a book on techniques for the particular age group which he is teaching. Some books combine the developmental tasks of the age group as well as the techniques of teaching in one volume. These would be appropriate for the teacher with a limited amount of time at his disposal.

b. *Resource Persons*

(1) *The Holy Spirit.* The Holy Spirit is the teacher's Teacher. Dependence upon him as one's guide is needed in order to be led aright in the selection of materials and activities that will assist the pupils in deeper insights into the meaning of God's Word for their lives.

(2) *Experts.* When a particular topic is studied, the teacher may know a person in the community who is competent in the area of concern. A personal conversation may assist the teacher in securing sufficient information to use during the class session. The resource person may refer the teacher to specific resource materials for him to do some more research on the topic. Sometimes the teacher may request the expert to come to the class to be a resource person to answer questions that the students may have on the subject.

4. HOW TO USE THE RESOURCE MATERIALS

a. *Select the Kinds of Resources that Are Needed.* The resources that the teacher will use at any one time or in preparation for any one session will depend upon the topic which he is studying and also the age group which he is teaching.

b. *Read Widely.* A teacher should always be sufficiently knowledgeable about a subject that he is to teach so that he will have command of the teaching-learning situation. This will mean that a teacher will have to read widely on the subject under consideration. He will need to know more than what he will be able to present during the class session. The additional store of knowledge that the teacher has will enrich his own life. When discussion is used during a class session, the teacher will have a reserve of information that will be helpful to him in answering some of the questions that the students will ask. Additional background material may also be supplied when appropriate.

c. *Select What Material Is Appropriate for the Class in the Time Available.* With the broad knowledge of the teacher, he will need to select those materials that will be understandable to the students that he teaches and that will meet their needs. The teacher will need to determine the amount of material and the kinds of activities that will be appropriate in the limited time available to him.

d. *Provide Resource Materials during the Class Session.* Knowing where information is available is important for a teacher. He will not have complete information about a subject but should know the sources that are available to find answers to questions that are raised. Having some of the resource books, such as a concordance, commentaries, translations, and/or Bible dictionaries in the class will be helpful at times to look up answers immediately when they are asked. This has two values. One is that the immediacy of the situation makes learning more possible and meaningful. If a question cannot be answered immediately, a student may not be sufficiently motivated to seek for the answer at a later time. The second reason is that students will become acquainted with the resource materials and learn how to use them.

5. THE TEACHING UNIT

A teaching unit includes the study of a topic or participation in a project that extends over a period of time, usually several weeks. The study includes a unifying goal with specific goals for each session that assist in achieving the overall, unifying goal towards which all content and activities are directed and planned.

a. *Reasons for Developing a Teaching Unit*

Whichever format a teacher's book follows it is important for a teacher to plan for an entire unit of study rather than study one lesson at a time. The reasons for this procedure are listed below.

(1) *Unit planning provides for continuity in the study plan.* Provisions can be made to carry the theme in a progressive arrangement of content and materials for study and action. The weekly periods of study can be linked

with each other so that each session follows the preceding session in logical order.

(2) *Unit planning provides an opportunity to use variety in teaching procedures.* Knowing that a routine procedure tends to disinterest on the part of students, a teacher should plan to incorporate various techniques of teaching during the unit of study. Variety can be used in the order of the techniques presented as well as in the kinds of techniques used. Care should be taken to involve the students as much as possible in the teaching-learning process.

(3) *Unit planning provides for an opportunity to order teaching resources or invite resource persons in advance.* When audio-visual materials are to be used, adequate time is needed to order such materials so they will be available on the appropriate day. Audio-visual equipment also needs to be reserved in advance. Any other resource materials may need to be purchased or reserved for ready use. When resource persons could assist the teacher in a specialized area of study, contacts can be made in advance for this person to participate at the appropriate time.

(4) *Unit planning provides for an opportunity to give assignments to students.* When a teacher plans in advance he knows what materials will be covered in the succeeding studies. He will, therefore, know what kinds of participation and study will be needed on the part of individuals or the entire group.

(5) *Unit planning allows for flexibility in the study program.* When a teacher plans for a series of class sessions he can arrange for the emphases in the unit of study that are most needed and pertinent for the students whom he is assisting to learn. A certain emphasis may need to be studied by the group for a period of several weeks and some less important emphasis may need to be eliminated.

(6) *Unit planning provides for an opportunity to meet the needs of individuals in the class.* In preparing the lessons, individual students should be kept in mind.

(7) *Unit planning can provide for pupil-teacher planning.* In the initial preparation of the unit, cooperative planning can be done between teacher and pupil. A selective group of pupils or the entire class may be given opportunity to react to materials that are relevant to them and suggest activities and projects that will encourage meaningful learning.

b. *Planning the Teaching Unit*

A teacher should prepare to teach a unit of study by using the following sequential pattern:

(1) *Pray for God's guidance.*

(2) *Read the entire unit of study* from the teacher's book from the beginning to the end. Read it carefully to see the overall purpose and impact of the study.

(3) *Read relevant materials* in the appropriate resources and *contact resource persons* when necessary.

(4) *Consider the pupils in the class.* The good teacher knows his pupils and their needs. Mental, physical, psychological, social, and spiritual needs all require attention.

(5) *Determine the overall objective of the study unit.* The teacher should write this in his own words. Many curricular materials list unit objectives but the teacher should always evaluate this objective in the light of his own pupils and adjust the aim to provide for meaningful learning experiences.

(6) *Determine the length of time the study will cover.* This is necessary in order to prepare the learning experiences that will be possible within this length of time.

(7) *Make a chart of the teaching unit.* Draw vertical lines between which to place appropriate headings: objective, Scripture, learning experiences, techniques, and resources. Draw horizontal lines to fit the number of lessons in the unit of study.

(8) *List the objectives for each session in the unit.* Care should be taken to see that the objective for each session follows a logical pattern and also assists in achieving the overall objective of the unit.

(9) *Select the content to be covered.* The content will include the verses of Scripture to be studied and other related materials. The curricular materials may provide too much material for the teacher or the suggestions may be irrelevant to the class' needs. At this point the teacher must be very selective, both in relation to the amount of

material that can be adequately covered and also in relation to the needs of the class.

(10) *Select the kinds of learning experiences that will be provided for the students to achieve the objectives.* It is important for the teacher to realize that it is what happens to the students that is important. The more that they are involved in the teaching-learning experience the more learning will take place. Learning experiences in which the students may participate may include the following: listening, reading, research, participating in projects, memorizing, visiting appropriate people and places, participating in role playing or drama, discussing problems that need solutions, writing answers to questions, etc.

(11) *Select the techniques of teaching to be used.* The techniques should all be designed to achieve the objectives set forth. James Berkeley suggests that every teacher should include in each class session the following four fundamental arts: telling, asking, showing, and providing work. He suggests that these methods should be used in various ways and in different combinations, giving variety and meaning to the class sessions (*You Can Teach.* Valley Forge: Judson Press, 1957, pp. 34-46).

(12) *Determine the kinds of resources needed.* Resources may include materials, such as newsprint, drawing paper, pencils, audio-visuals, or resource persons. Provide for securing these resources in adequate time for their use on the appropriate date.

(13) *Prepare each Sunday's lesson in detail.* Organize the learning experiences, content, and techniques of teaching for each lesson in such a manner that the content of the lesson will follow a logical and sequential pattern. Determine how the lesson will be introduced, developed, and concluded. Prepare each lesson in detail after the previous lesson is completed so adjustments can be made and the needs of the students determined at the particular stage of the sequential learning experience.

(14) *Provide for evaluation during and at the end of the teaching unit.* Involve the students as much as possible in the evaluation procedures.

6. PLANNING A CLASS SESSION

A class session is a period of time when a group of persons meet together for the purpose of learning about the Bible and its meaning. The length of the class session usually varies from thirty minutes to an hour in duration for adult, youth, and some classes for children. Where an expanded session is held for children, the duration of time usually extends to a two hour period of study, worship, and meaningful activity appropriate to the age level. The longer period is needed when students are actively involved in the teaching-learning experience.

In order for the teacher to design an adequate learning experience for each class session, certain definite steps are necessary. These follow a sequential pattern that constitutes a lesson plan. The teacher needs to use the following outline of procedure:

a. *The Objective.* The class session is devoted to achieving a specific purpose toward which all experiences are planned.

b. *The Introduction.* In preparing for the class session, the teacher asks himself the question, "How will I best introduce the subject or activity in such a way that I can motivate the students to learn?"

c. *The Development.* The teacher asks himself the question, "What kinds of learning experiences can I provide for the students that will assist in achieving the goal? What is the best order of these experiences so that maximum learning will take place?"

d. *The Conclusion.* The teacher asks himself the question, "How can I conclude the session so that all the learning focuses on the achievement of the goal? How can I plan for these experiences to be evidenced in the lives of the students?"

BIBLIOGRAPHY

Adkins, George, H., *Tools for Teachers.* St. Louis, Missouri: Bethany Press, 1962.

Caldwell, Irene S., *Teaching That Makes a Difference.* Anderson, Indiana: The Warner Press, 1956.

Edge, Findley, B., *Helping the Teacher.* Nashville: Broadman Press, 1959.

Leavitt, Guy P., *Teach with Success.* Cincinnati, Ohio: The Standard Publishing Foundation, 1956.

LeBar, Lois E., *Education That Is Christian.*

Westwood, New Jersey: Fleming H. Revell Co., 1958.

Lederach, Paul M., *Learning to Teach.* Scottdale, Pa.: Herald Press and Newton, Kan.: Faith and Life Press, 1964.

Little, Sara, *Learning Together in the Christian Fellowship.* Richmond, Virginia: John Knox Press, 1956.

Soderholm, Marjorie E., *Understanding the Pupil*: Part I – The Pre-School Child; Part II – The Primary and Junior Child; Part III – The Adolescent. Grand Rapids: Baker Book House, 1962.

Swain, Dorothy G., *Teach Me to Teach.* Valley Forge: Judson Press, 1964.

Zuch, Roy B., *The Holy Spirit in Your Teaching.* Wheaton, Illinois: Scripture Press Publications, Inc., 1963.

Using the Weekday for Religious Education

The church has an educational responsibility. That it should teach on Sunday is a settled question, but what its weekday teaching task should be has not been finally answered. The problem is complicated because it depends upon political as well as practical considerations. When the American church was displaced as the educational agent by a state supported school system in the nineteenth century, two general patterns emerged: the Roman Catholic Church elected to develop the parochial school while the Protestant churches settled for the Sunday school. In neither case did the answer prove to be adequate and the search for a viable solution continued.

While the Sunday school remained central in the church's program, experiments were tried in weekday religious education. These may be considered under the headings, the use of free time and the use of public school time for religious instruction.

1. FREE TIME CHURCH EDUCATION

In rural America the church had Sunday, but the increasing complexity of the emerging urban society broke down the simple formula of six days for work and one day for worship and rest. The church, like the world, had to adjust to a new time schedule. It was evident that the educative process required the weekday as well as Sunday.

a. *Vacation Church School.* At the turn of the century the religious education movement in America began to expand into the weekday as the summer vacation church school and the weekday church school.

Like the Sunday school of Robert Raikes, the vacation church school gained prominence first in the cities where it served the underprivileged children. Thus, while there are records of vacation church schools in Boston, Massachusetts (1866), Montreal, Canada (1877), and Hopedale, Illinois (1894), the movement is traced to the school of the Epiphany Baptist Church in New York City that alerted a city missionary to its feasibility. Robert G. Boville, having already observed the school in Montreal, was inspired by the Epiphany venture to begin similar programs in blighted areas of New York City in 1901. In 1905 he became the leader of the new enterprise at the invitation of the Federation of Churches of New York City. The program passed through several stages, becoming a concern of the International Council of Religious Education in 1923, and an integral part of the organization in 1927. To implement the program, curricula were prepared by denominational publishing houses and the Interdenominational Committee on Cooperative Publication of Vacation and Weekday Church School Curriculum. The interdenominational materials covered six areas of interest, one for each year of a six-year cycle.

A number of forms have marked the development of the vacation church school venture. While local churches may conduct their own schools, rural communities and city areas where like-minded churches cluster have established cooperative programs which pool personnel, resources, and space to improve the educative process. A common plan has been to set a period of ten days with a two and one-half hour school day while another plan has telescoped the same hours into one week by planning a five-hour day. In a few situations one day per week sessions are held throughout the summer whereas in crowded areas of the cities full day sessions may extend for eight to twelve weeks. Some churches have scheduled the school for evening hours and have used them for family education. Two theories have been held concerning the recruitment of leadership. One is that teachers who serve in the Sunday church school are in a position to follow through because they have established rapport with the pupils of their age group and have a comprehensive view of subject matter and teaching goals. On the other hand it is contended that volunteer teachers with limited time and other commitments should be excused for summer teaching and that the best interests of the program are served when a separate staff is assigned to the vacation school.

The organization of the vacation school has also been marked by various plans. In churches where it has been regarded as an integral part of the whole enterprise, the program has been administered by the committee charged with the total educational responsibility. The budget has been comparable to that spent for an equal number of hours in the Sunday school. The curriculum has been selected to serve the unique need of this phase of the year's purpose. Teachers who know both the characteristics of the age group to which they have been assigned and the subject matter of the curriculum have been assigned and the subject matter of the curriculum have been recruited. Resource leaders have been called into service to augment teaching in special areas of interest and need.

The vacation church school has been established as an important part of the educational program but now new problems confront the movement. In a day of intense competition for the time of the child, the church could lose its option unless it takes a defiant stand against organizations which would erode its effectiveness. Given such a positive stance, it may establish a program of excellence which is worthy of respect by the church and the community.

b. *Summer Camps and Conferences.* Perhaps no enterprise of the church has changed so radically in purpose and procedure as the program which is now known as camps and conferences. As an organized activity, it can be traced back to the religious camp meeting which served both as a revival effort and a recreational outlet for those whose lives were drab and routine. A radical change was inaugurated at the Methodist camp meeting held at Chautauqua, New York, in August 1873 when the "Chautauqua Sunday School Assembly" was instituted. Under the leadership of Bishop John H. Vincent and Lewis Miller the effort to provide normal training for Sunday school teachers was given a dramatic lift. By the close of the nineteenth century two trends became evident. One was the movement to convert camp meeting grounds into summer conference sites and the other was the development of camps for boys and girls. In 1880 George W. Hinkley established a camp for his parish in Rhode Island. About 1887 the Y.M.C.A. took over a camp that had been developed for boys by Sumner F. Dudley. The first church camp to be organized on a permanent basis was established at Lake Geneva, Wisconsin, in 1914.

Before proceeding with the development of this phase of church life, it will be necessary to differentiate between the terms camp and conference. In an article "Camps and Conferences" Maurice D. Bone writes: "Defined simply as an experience of living in the out-of-doors in the Christian community, the camp tends to emphasize the living together, while the conference tends to emphasize study. The camp makes greater use of the situation in which the camp is located, involving boys and girls, families, and adult programs in exploration, trips, discoveries, camp fires; while the conference tends to concentrate on classes, study, the use of visual aids, and the relationship of its experience to the local church, with an exphases on leadership training in many areas" (*Religious Education, a Comprehensive Survey,* p. 215).

The church summer camp and conference program has been developed according to age groups. At each level there are characteristics germane to the interests and needs of those who are served.

Camping for juniors has taken two forms: the first is the day camp. Boys and girls sleep and take breakfast and the evening meal at home. During the day, from about 9:30 to 3:30, they are at a camp, park, or farm for their program. The design emphasizes the living situation rather than formal instruction. The second form is the resident camp. Since 1950 there has been a swing away from what was originally the junior edition of the youth summer conference to an emphasis upon outdoor living. Experience has indicated that small groups should live together in relation to other small groups where the campers have freedom and responsibility. The total camping group in any one area is limited to sixty campers and leaders.

Church camping for junior highs started about 1925. At first there were camps for boys and others for girls but it was not long before major denominations began to experiment with co-educational camping. In the beginning sites for the program were state parks or similar facilities but now much of the camping is done at church camps which are designed for junior high outdoor living. The pattern is basically the same as that described at the junior level.

Senior high camps and conferences. Where the program has taken the form of a conference the stress is upon formal learning based upon a central theme. Experimental projects have been introduced so that senior highs learn by doing. Having started as a conference, the senior high venture now options camping. Those who participate engage in work camps, visit mission stations, and take pack or canoe trips. Through these activities the welfare of the individual becomes important, especially as he relates to others in small groups which engage in a variety of experiences. It is regarded as essential that both the camp and conference experience be tied to the program of the local church by insisting that the group from each church shall be accompanied by an advisor from that church, and by integrating Sunday school and fellowship materials into the resources for camps and conferences.

Family camping has emerged in recent years. Whether the sponsor is an area organization or a local church, the program highlights family living. The family hikes, fishes, explores, and sometimes cooks together. The leadership comes family style with the leaders living with their own families.

The concensus is that camps and conferences will expand and continue to serve a unique purpose in the church.

c. *Free Time Weekday Church Education.* Except for the vacation church school and the weekday religious education movement which uses public school time for instruction, there has not been a concerted effort to use the weekday for church education. To be sure, free time during the week has been used for club work and limited weekday sessions but no clear and distinct pattern has emerged. Now there are pressures which may alert the churches to their opportunity. The new stresses on excellence in education and on learning how to learn have pointed up the weakness of one hour Sunday school sessions. The spiraling cost of plant construction has reinforced the need for a staggered use of church educational facilities. In some communities the weekend has become travel time so regular church school experiences are being planned for week days. Travel distance to the church has encouraged the clustering of activities.

The pattern which is now taking shape is cued to the junior high-adult span. Consider a youth program which is planned for a single block of time during the week. Beginning with free activity, a schedule of three hours provides time for work groups, individual study, interacting small groups, assembly, and time for a meal together.

The future use of free time for education in the church may depend on two factors: a rediscovery of the importance of education by the church and a convincing demonstration of the value of church education to its constituency.

2. CHURCH AND STATE EDUCATION

Both the church and the state recognize that through education they are responsible for the conservation of moral and spiritual values. The church will affirm, and many within public education will confirm, that a complete education should include religious instruction. For the church this means that all children have the right to education in religion as one phase of the total learning experience. But in a nation committed to separation of church and state, where state supported education is central, how can adequate religious instruction be assured?

The state requires that a child shall be educated but the parent may decide, within limits, what that education shall be and who is to provide it. So long as parents were willing to accept either the state or the church to perform the educational task there was no conflict but when it seemed that both agencies were needed to make their unique contributions to the education of the child a question of the division of time arose. This situation has produced one of the major problems of the twentieth century.

a. *Weekday Religious Education.* One

answer to the relation of church and state in education has been weekday religious education. E. L. Shaver defines a weekday church school as "a school set up by the churches singly or in cooperation, in which the attending pupils are excused from their usual public school program, at the written request of parents, to go to a church or other building to receive religious education" (*Remember the Weekday to Teach Religion Thereon*). A later definition is much more explicit: "The purpose of weekday religious education is to help children and youth to interpret public school education in the light of the on-going revelation of God within human experience and in his son, Jesus Christ" (*Weekday Religious Education Guidebook*).

Historically, weekday religious education can be traced back to the first decade of this century. At the Interfaith Conference, meeting in New York City in 1905, a Lutheran minister, George U. Wenner, proposed Weekday Religious Instruction. The recommendation was addressed to both schools and churches and called upon public school authorities to give one half day per week for this purpose. At the first meeting of the Federal Council of Churches of Christ in America in 1908, action was taken on this issue. In 1911 the General Council of the Evangelical Lutheran Church moved to secure the cooperation of other Protestant churches in promoting weekday instruction in religion. At the second meeting of the Council in 1912 a report by George U. Wenner reinforced the resolution adopted in 1908.

While resolutions were being debated and approved by denominational and interdenominational bodies, cities and states were experimenting with the plan. What may have been the first effort to relate religious instruction to a state supported school was the North Dakota plan initiated in 1911. By this plan high school credit was given for Bible study. To facilitate the project, the faculty of the University of North Dakota worked with the North Dakota State Board of Education to prepare a syllabus upon the assumption that one-half unit of credit would be given for Bible study. In Colorado and certain other states comparable plans were tried but by 1924 the International Council of Religious Education concluded that the plan was not as successful as they had anticipated because the emphasis was upon Bible study and not religious instruction and the idea of credit became too important. However, the program which set the pattern for secondary schools was established by the Mormons in Salt Lake City in 1912 when they established a church supported school in a church owned building where courses in religion were offered during the school day for credit to students enrolled in the public high school. Programs of religious education at the secondary school level, often with provisions for credit toward graduation, are in operation in a number of cities. However, the program at the elementary level has been more widely accepted. Credit for the initial effort is given to Superintendent William Wirt of the Gary Public School System. While the venture began in 1913, it was 1914 when some five denominations established schools in their churches. In 1917 the plan was revised and by 1923 there were 4000 pupils enrolled.

Since the program of weekday religious education involves an arrangement with the public schools, it is obvious that church-state relations would be called into question. A number of cases were brought before lower courts but an early state court decision and two United States Supreme Court decisions should be cited. In 1926 the president of the American Free Thinkers Society brought suit in New York against the program on the grounds that it violated the principle of separation of church and state. The court upheld the validity of the weekday church school program in White Plains, New York and subsequently the state legislature amended the school code to excuse pupils for religious observances and instruction. In 1945, Mrs. Vashti McCollum, in the Champaign case, brought suit against the program in that city. When it reached the United States Supreme Court, the plea of Mrs. McCollum was upheld on the grounds that public school buildings were used and this constituted a violation of the First Amendment. Since the Court did not ban all released time programs, schools continued pending later decisions. In 1952 the United States Supreme Court ruled against the suit brought by Tessim Zorach and Esta Gluck. It upheld the New York law and permitted schools which did not use public school buildings and did not depend on the aid of the public school system.

Based on United States Supreme Court decisions, the legality of weekday religious education is assumed so long as these conditions are met: (1) public school buildings are not used; (2) administrative help of public schools is not used to enroll pupils; (3) parents consent to the release of their children for religious instruction.

There are two general plans for weekday religious education. One is "dismissed" time. By mutual agreement between the public school and the church, the public school is closed at a scheduled time each week and the children are free to enroll in courses in religion or engage in other activities. The arrangement more frequently used is "released" time. During a period, or periods, mutually agreed upon by school and church authorities, pupils are released from the public school at the request of the parents to go to a church school for religious instruction. Usually a staggered schedule is adopted so that the grades are released to meet at different hours throughout the week. This plan is necessary where professional teachers are employed to do the instructing.

A variety of curricula are in use throughout the country. Some have been developed by city or state councils of churches to meet local needs. Certain denominations have produced materials which are broadly conceived to meet the needs of interdenominational schools. However, since weekday religious education is usually a community venture it is assumed that there should be a curriculum which is published cooperatively for Protestant schools. Therefore, the Cooperative Series is produced by the Interdenominational Committee on Cooperative Publication of Vacation and Weekday Church School Curriculum.

Since classes in religion must meet off public school property, various arrangements have been made for space for the program. Where schools are located in proximity to the churches, the facilities of the religious institutions are used. In some communities pupils are taken by buses to the churches. Cities like Fort Wayne, Indiana and Dubuque, Iowa use trailer classrooms. Some cities with programs at the secondary level have erected buildings near the high school to provide facilities for religious classes.

There is not an established practice for the recruitment of teachers. Some communities use volunteer instructors but the most successful programs have been staffed by paid teachers. Conversely, when schools have been closed the cause has often been due to poor teaching and lack of church support.

The financial responsibility for the weekday religious education operation resides in the churches, the cost of the total program being allocated proportionately to the participating churches. The budget must be large enough to cover rent and utilities, text and reference materials, audio-visual tools, and salaries, if teachers are paid.

b. *Shared Time.* Shared time, otherwise entitled dual school enrollment, has emerged as a viable option in the debate over the preferable time for religious instruction. This education concept has been defined as "the division of time of school children between public schools and church schools: certain subjects would be taught in the public schools to all children; other subjects – specifically those of religious content – would be taught to all or part of the same children in church schools of the parent's choice" (Harry L. Stearns, *Christianity and Crisis,* Sept. 18, 1961, p. 154).

In the writing of Erwin L. Shaver this concept was advanced as early as 1956 as "the complementary school plan." He referred to "the growing practice in many communities throughout America of having children, whose primary enrollment is in a parochial school, take some of their courses in the public school, even to the extent in one reported instance of a 'fifty-fifty' program" (*The Weekday Church School,* pp. 146-147). This option was one among several advanced by writers of this period. Others were (1) the extension of the parochial system as a valid Protestant expression of its educational purpose; (2) the development of a "common core" of religious belief to be taught in the public schools; (3) the objective teaching of religious facts as part of the total body of truth to which pupils should be exposed.

While the subject was a matter of academic discussion, the theory had been applied in practice. Limited use of dual school facilities can be traced back to 1913 when the Pittsburgh, Pennsylvania public schools provided a shared time course in the practical arts. The Hartford, Connecticut public schools had such an arrangement for pupils of parochial schools as early as about 1930.

What brought the shared time option to public notice was the mid-twentieth century debate on the question of federal aid to education. The law was written so as to prohibit the use of tax funds to aid or support private or church schools. Yet the question remained concerning the large segment of the citizenry who for conscience sake supported their parochial schools while they carried their share of the financial burden for public education. At this moment the shared time plan is being promoted as the most feasible option.

The primary consideration of the merits of the plan is not that of financial adjustment but whether it will provide for the full education of children which includes religion. But our pluralistic society places restrictions upon freedom to teach when it limits what can be taught in the area of religion. Shared time presents one way by which the parents can assume their primary responsibility to determine the nature of their child's instruction and to employ both the church and the state as their agents in providing a full education.

It is clear that those churches with well-established parochial school systems are in the best position to take advantage of the new program. Parochial schools discontinue the teaching of subjects which have only peripheral religious meanings and dismiss their pupils to the state supported schools for such instruction while retaining their perogative to teach religion and those other subjects which can only be taught properly within a religious context. Such an arrangement relieves the pressure on classroom space, teaching personnel, and facilities.

Whether the plan would provide benefits for those churches which do not have a parochial school system is now only a hypothetical question. The verdict belongs to time where it will be decided by the resolve of such churches to finance a program, educate teachers, provide space, and consolidate resources for the common good.

Properly conceived, it could provide for an integration of subject matter which is not now possible. It is suggested by some, for instance, that children could receive instruction in the public schools in such subjects as literature and history. Parallel teaching could be done in the church schools with the latter giving the distinctive focus which is enhanced by the religious perspective. When doctrine is taught it could be made relevant by reference to and illustrations from public school experience.

The shared time plan presents problems. It does force a compromise in the philosophy of education of churches with parochial school systems. They regard education as an integrated whole. The Catholic Church, writes O'Neil C. D'Amour, "sees religious truth as permeating the entire curriculum. It feels that there can be no true understanding of science, mathematics, social studies, or even of oneself without an understanding of God and religion" (*Religious Education*, Jan-Feb., 1962, p. 30).

On the other side, questions are raised about the concessions to be made by the public schools which could undermine the integrity of the system. The components of subject matter in the public school represent a framework of wholeness according to the philosophy of the system. If parts of the curriculum are assigned to other agencies would the public school become an educational cafeteria instead of an integral system? The plan might foster confusion rather than clarity. In each school points of view would be expressed which were not congenial to instructors in the opposite institution. These differences of opinion would be modified and reinterpreted. At an advanced level such differences are the life-blood of education but for children they can be detrimental.

School administrators are also concerned about practical matters. How will the school day, the school week, and the school year be divided? Essentially, through the addition of religion courses the content of the total subject matter will be increased with added pressure to extend the length of the school day and the school year. Will the school plant need to be expanded, especially in those areas where construction and equipment are most expensive as in shop, laboratory, and physical education? What new formulas need to be devised to record credits and ascertain the requirements for graduation?

A thorough survey of the use of the weekday for religious education would include nursery and kindergarten schools, the new emphasis upon adult education, a realistic look at the responsibilities of the Christian home, leisure time activities, and the expanding needs for leadership education. A program worthy of the purpose of the church could take on tremendous proportions. Such an enterprise would require a wholehearted commitment to Christian education, supported by dedicated leaders and an adequate budget. It would likewise demand a rethinking of values and time schedules on the part of those who teach and those who learn. Planning for such a program would require a new assessment of community resources, the unique contributions of key agencies, and a reappraisal of state-church relations. Yet it would be in accord with the commission of the Great Teacher: "Go therefore and make disciples of all nations, baptizing them in the name of the Father and of the Son and of the Holy Spirit, teaching them to observe all that I have commanded you; and lo, I am with you always, to the close of the age" (Matt. 28:20, RSV).

BIBLIOGRAPHY

Bennett, John C., *Christians and the State.* Scribners, 1958.

Blanshard, Paul, *Religion and the Schools: The Great Controversy.* Beacon, 1963.

Bower, W. C., Hayward, P. R., *Protestantism Faces Its Educational Task Together.* Nelson, 1949.

Cope, Henry Frederick, *The Week-Day Church-School.* Doran, 1921.

deBlois, Austen K., Gorham, Donald R., *Christian Religious Education: Principles and Practice.* Revell, 1939.

Dierenfield, Richard B., *Religion in American Public Schools.* Public Affairs Press, 1962.

Lotz, Philip Henry, *Current Week-Day Religious Education.* Abingdon. 1925.

———————, ed., *Orientation in Christian Education.* Abingdon-Cokesbury, 1956.

McKibben, Frank M., ed., *Report and Interpretation of the First National Conference on Weekday Religious Education,* Division of Christian Education, National Council of the Churches of Christ in the U.S.A., 1956.

Price, J. M., Chapman, James H., Carpenter, L., Yarborough, W. Forbes, *A Survey of Religious Education,* 1959.

Shaver, Erwin L., *The Weekday Church School.* Pilgrim, 1956.

Taylor, Marvin J., ed., *Religious Education: A Comprehensive Survey.* Abingdon, 1960.

Vieth, Paul H., ed., *The Church and Christian Education.* Bethany, 1947.

Magazines

Cope Henry F., "The Church and the Public Schools in Religious Education," *Religious Education* 10:566-74, 1915.

The Gary Plan, *Religious Education,* 9:392-93, 1914; 10:42-45, 1915; 10:259-64; 1915; 10: 559-65, 1915; 11:221-26, 1916; 11:226-30, 1916; 11:345-49, 1916.

International Journal of Religious Education, March 1956, May 1958, April 1960, June 1960.

Mutch, William James, "The Madison Religious Day School," *Religious Education,* 9:386-89. 1914.

The New York Plan, *Religious Education,* 10:46-49, 1915; 10:559-65, 1915.

The North Dakota Plan, *Religious Education,* 8: 225-31, 1913; 10:264-68, 1915; 11:20-27, 1916.

Wilson, H. B., "High-School Credits for Bible Study in Kansas," *Religious Education,* 10:574-78, 1915.

Church Organization for Teaching

The scope of Christian education has been described as ranging from the teaching dimension of the preaching function to the structuring of the educational environment. Of course, almost every activity has some educational value. Present day practice, however, would tend to include the following educational agencies under the aegis of Christian education: (a) board of Christian education, (b) Sunday church school, (c) Sunday evening fellowships (including youth groups), (d) Boys' groups, such as the Boy Scouts, Boys' Brigade, YMCA programs for boys directed by church personnel in church facilities, (e) Girls' groups, such as the Girl Scouts, Pioneer Girls, Campfire Girls, and groups sponsored and directed by the Women's Missionary Societies within the churches, (f) leadership training programs, (g) family life education, (h) vacation church school (daily vacation Bible school), (i) camps and conferences, (j) weekday church school (k) junior church, and (l) full-time Christian day schools.

Several of the above agencies will be described here. Many of the others will be described elsewhere in this volume under their own or related headings.

1. BOARD OF CHRISTIAN EDUCATION

The board of Christian education (or committee on Christian education) is the official church body charged with the direction and administration of the educational program of the church. Its main function is to set policy in respect to personnel, curriculum, and physical facilities. The membership usually consists of those elected by the congregation to the board, or of duly appointed persons representing the various educational groups within the church. It is customary for the pastor and the minister or director of Christian education to hold ex officio membership on this as well as on other boards and committees. In order to operate efficiently, a chairman should preside at the meetings and carry out whatever functions are delegated to him. The continuity of the program is provided for in most churches through the election of board members on a three year basis, with one-third of the membership retiring each year.

Ideally, a board is a policy making body which does not concern itself with working out the details of a program. It may do limited long range planning, approve the curriculum to be employed, approve teachers, workers, and others who are to serve in the program, and make arrangements for the evaluation of the effectiveness of teaching and of the adequacy of the facilities. In practice, however, it is only boards in the larger churches which can limit themselves to broad policy-making activities and delegate all remaining functions of a specific nature to others. Smaller churches usually expect board members not only to set policies but to implement them to a greater or lesser degree, depending upon the availability of volunteer or paid personnel.

The board is expected to maintain and improve the program through the use of such processes as (1) planning, both long range and short range, (2) organizing, so that line and staff relationships are clear, (3) delegating, a process which must be followed as a church increases in size, (4) staffiing, i.e., the enlistment, training, and recruitment of educational personnel, (5) coordinating, which is a process of arranging activities so that there is a minimum of conflict and a unified effort in moving toward the objectives established for the program by the church and board, (6) controlling, which includes receiving reports, allocating the budget according to a plan, checking on the progress of plans, and evaluation of the educational program.

In regard to the Sunday church school, the board will be expected to make policy decisions about such matters as whether certain classes should be coeducational or not, what the ideal class size is for each age level, to what extent teachers may depart, if at all, from the prescribed curriculum, how the available classroom space is to be assigned, and to what extent teachers will be permitted to purchase and be reimbursed for teaching aids. The appointment or dismissal of permanent teachers, also, will be a board responsibility.

Policies of importance with reference to the youth fellowship groups include the appointment of youth counselors or sponsors, rules of behavior at social events sponsored by the groups, the usage of church property, methods for resolving conflicts between church activities and those desired by the young people, special benevolent or missionary projects, and the honoraria to be given invited program guests (speakers, musicians, and others).

Church sponsored camp and conference programs is another area for which the Christian education board is responsible. When children and youth are transferred over to the church's care for either a short or long period of time, there are problems of transportation, insurance, adequate adult supervision, provisions for first aid and medical care if needed, etc. Neglect of any of these items could involve the church in some form of legal action, particularly in the case of minors.

The vacation church school (or daily vacation Bible school) is still another educational function over which the board has supervision. A satisfactory curriculum must be selected and approved. If the school is to be conducted in cooperation with other churches, the board's sanction is necessary. Perhaps the primary concern of the board in this area is that of appointing a director for the school and making periodic checks with him in respect to implementation of the steps leading to the opening of the school.

The recruitment, enlistment, training, and retention of teachers and leaders for the Christian education program is probably the most difficult task of the board. The board, however, along with the cooperation of the pastor can create a climate within the church for facilitating this work. With a regularly scheduled, annual program of leadership training which receives pastoral support, teachers, helpers, and leaders of every kind are far more easily persuaded to accept positions in the church. Methods frequently employed for training potential leaders are: (1) the church's own annual or semiannual leadership program, emphasizing Bible, church history, administration, and teaching methodology, (2) annual orientation and planning retreats for church boards and officials, (3) laboratory or demonstration schools where teachers may observe master teachers in action, (4) community or city-wide leadership training schools which often draw their faculty from theological institutions, (5) church library materials, (6) occasional substitute teaching, (7) observing other educational programs, (8) church manuals and handbooks which provide information on how to draw up a lesson, how to use audio-visual aids, how to conduct a discussion, etc.

Churches with large memberships may decide to form committees to serve under the board of Christian education. If so, then one member of the board is appointed chairman of a committee and is made responsible for a single educational area. He then recruits from one to three non-board members to help him with his committee work. Although the listing of areas differs from one church to another, the following is an example of the types of committees commonly used: Sunday church school, youth fellowship, boys' groups, girls' groups, leadership training, family life, camps and conferences, vacation church school, missionary, library, and weekday church school (released time).

The coordination of the educational program, involving a number of groups as it does, requires that the board utilize as many techniques and methods of communication as possible. Organizational charts, administrative handbooks, master calendars, church bulletins, ex officio memberships for the ministerial staff, periodic reports, and regular monthly meetings all contribute to the creation of a unified, well-integrated program when these are guided by well-formulated policies laid down by the board.

2. SUNDAY CHURCH SCHOOL

Perhaps the most influential organization designed for instructional purposes in the church is the Sunday church school. Beginning in England as a lay movement in the eighteenth century, it soon spread to the United States and added to its total enrolment year by year until it reached a point oftentimes equivalent to fifty per cent or more of the total church membership within Protestantism.

The desire of Robert Raikes, the founder of the modern Sunday school movement, to educate needy children was joined by increased knowledge of teaching methods for children to form a wholly new organization within the church. Johann Amos Comenius (b. 1592), a bishop of the Moravian church, and Johann Heinrich Pestalozzi (b. 1746), a Swiss educational pioneer, developed a methodology which stressed: (1) the understanding of study material instead of rote memorization, (2) using materials suited to the abilities of the child at each age level rather than highly abstract adult materials and experiences for all ages, and (3) learning by observation and activity rather than by the acquisition of precepts alone.

Through the contributions of Raikes, Comenius, Pestalozzi and others, the Sunday church school began to develop a form of its own which was distinguished from the common worship service through its grading both of materials and of its members. It was not, however, until the beginning of the twentieth century that churches began to grade materials and pupil personnel on a wide scale. Pastors and lay leaders began to realize the importance of grading the curriculum of the church so that the concept of grading today extends as far as the establishment of junior churches for children through junior age or the inclusion of a brief children's sermon in the regular worship services.

In the vast majority of Sunday schools, volunteer workers function as superintendents, department heads, teachers, secretaries, pianists, and librarians. If there are any paid educational personnel, they are part of the permanent church staff and serve as ministers or directors of Christian education, or, in some cases, as associate ministers with responsibilities in the Christian education field.

The organization of the Sunday school is usually by divisions in the smaller churches, consisting of the children, youth, and adult groups. In moderately large churches, the organization may take the form of departments: Nursery (up through age 3), Beginners and Kindergarten (through ages 4 and 5), Primary (ages 6-8 or grades 1-3), Junior (ages 9-11 or grades 4-6), Junior High (ages 12-14 or grades 7-9), Senior High (ages 15-18 or grades 10-12), College age, and Adult. For exceptionally large churches, grading may be done by individual age or grade levels insofar as there are sufficient students to form a class. Otherwise, combinations of the above patterns are used depending upon the circumstances.

The curriculum of the Sunday school may be one of three types: (1) group or cycle graded, covering a two or three year period and used by smaller churches with sufficient students in a department but not in a grade to make up a class, (2) closely graded, providing a different lesson for each age or grade, and (3) uniform series, employing a single topic for all age levels so that children, youth, and adults within a particular family will be encouraged to prepare the Sunday school lesson together at home. There are both denominational and interdenominational (or nondenominational) materials available, some of which claim varying unique characteristics, ranging from a heavy emphasis upon the use of the Scriptures to the incorporation of newer educational techniques or greater application of the Scriptures to present day social and personal problems.

With the increasing trend toward two Sunday morning worship services, churches are putting their educational facilities into greater use by conducting the Sunday school in two sections, usually running simultaneously with the services (9:30 a.m. and 11:00 a.m. are the generally accepted hours). For all practical purposes, this results in a duplication of the classes in the children's division, keeping young people's groups together (for morale purposes) so they meet at only one hour, and maintaining the adult classes as units but assigning them to one of the two periods. A few churches have worship services at 8:30 a.m. and 11:00 a.m. with Sunday school at 9:30 a.m., but the problem of recruiting sufficient staff for all three periods has been a difficult one to date.

3. YOUTH FELLOWSHIPS

The Sunday evening youth fellowships which are to be found in most Protestant churches had their primary origin in the Christian Endeavor Society — a movement which began in the latter half of the nineteenth century. Its purpose was to provide opportunity for both Christian service and fellowship for young people as well as to foster the development of good citizenship. Many churches, interested in developing denominational loyalty, eventually constructed their own programs and renamed their Sunday evening youth groups as "fellowships." The general objectives, however, of the original group were retained and eventually expanded to include five areas: faith, witness, world outreach, citizenship, and fellowship.

The program topics of youth fellowships ordinarily reflect the five area objectives so that in any one quarter, experiences will be chosen which focus on all of the objectives to a greater or lesser degree, depending upon the needs of the participants. Programing often takes the form of dividing an entire youth group into committees representing each area and making the committees responsible for the conduct of the youth meeting. The committee on faith might be responsible for the program on the first Sunday of each month, the committee on witness for the program on the second Sunday, the committee on world outreach for the program on the third Sunday, etc. Variations of this arrangement have been successfully tried (for instance, a whole month of programs might be given over to the subject of witnessing). Along with the group-sponsored programs, there are often outside speakers invited in, Christian motion pictures or filmstrips used, debates, symposiums, missionary presentations, reports, and other features employed.

Because young people discourage easily and are inexperienced, it is advisable to obtain mature adults to guide the young people in their planning and presentations. Psychologically, it is best for young people to experience success most of the time if they are to be sufficiently motivated to continue their interest in the group and support it loyally month after month. In addition to the adults who guide the program on Sunday evenings, it is a practice in some churches to recruit three or four additional couples for each youth group and ask them to serve as "social sponsors," taking turns functioning as chaperones and as adults responsible for the group at their social events.

Fellowship groups have, in the main, consisted of Junior High, Senior High, and College age young people. However, since many churches with evening services are desirous of providing educational opportunities for the entire family, groups are now being established at the adult and children's levels which run concurrently with the youth fellowship programs. Most fellowship groups are scheduled for the period prior to the Sunday evening service, or, if the church does not conduct an evening service, then the fellowship groups may meet during that time period.

There is little doubt but that in our highly impersonal society with its high population turnover and with its lack of concern for the spiritual and emotional needs of people, the fellowship groups in the churches have an unparalleled opportunity to provide an evangelistic emphasis and a much needed environment of closeness, acceptance, and belonging which is so desperately sought after by man in his loneliness today.

4. VACATION CHURCH SCHOOL

An early twentieth century development, the vacation church school (also termed the daily vacation Bible school) is an effort to inculcate during the summer vacation period additional knowledge of the Scriptures and the principles of Christian conduct. Special curricula are designed by denominational and interdenominational publishing houses focused primarily on the children's division, but may include those of junior high school age. If youth and adult classes are included in the school, as they are in some areas of the United States, the materials used with these age levels are largely of the leadership training type (courses in Bible, church history, teaching methodology, church doctrine, etc.) or they may stress family life information with emphasis on child, adolescent, or adult psychology.

The usual time period for vacation church schools is in the two to four weeks immediately following the closing of public school while the children are still accustomed to an educational routine. Occasionally, these schools are scheduled for a two week period in the latter part of August when the students are "played out" and appear to be interested in a change in their daily program. The hours of the day devoted to this work are in the morning, running in most cases from nine to twelve. However, if the church desires to include young people and adults in the program, then all classes are scheduled in the evenings so that the entire family attends the school. This is particularly useful in churches equipped with air conditioning or situated in areas where the summer evenings are cool.

Since it is customary for families to plan their summer vacations several months in advance, the person charged with directing the school frequently begins to recruit department superintendents and to select the course of study six to eight months prior to the school's opening. Most of the teachers and helpers are asked to commit themselves to the program at least three months before the school begins, and preferably four to six months before if it is scheduled for the month of August.

For churches with limited memberships, interchurch schools may be arranged and the necessary instructional and administrative leadership drawn from the cooperating churches. Whether the school is sponsored by one or several churches, an assessment of the program should be made at the end so that subsequent schools will incorporate the findings in their plans and thereby provide for continuous improvement. The areas to be evaluated will generally include those of worship, instruction, fellowship, handicrafts, and recreation. If a special program is planned for the closing day, this, too, should be included in the evaluation in order to determine its effectiveness.

5. CAMPS AND CONFERENCES

Camps and conferences are not traditionally considered to be instructional groups. They, nevertheless, provide an environment within which remarkable behavioral changes often take place. Insights are acquired regarding one's personality characteristics, opportunities are made available for developing skills in creating friendships and in cooperating with others, decisions which influence the entire course of an individual's life are frequently made, knowledge of the Scriptures is broadened and deepened, and a greater love for God and those within the redemptive community often results.

The type of instruction is more of an informal nature, but, example, accompanied by genuine personal concern, may teach young people and adults more about the love of God and the practical application of Christian principles than would several years of lessons or lectures. The need for this kind of learning experience is perhaps greater today than in the past. Due to the social factors of population explosion, geographical mobility, automation, and the general impersonal attitude pervading society, small group experiences with a high degree of personal closeness such as are found in camping are crucial for communicating the message that there are persons who care about the individual.

Long range planning should characterize this program as well as other programs in Christian education. Thus, a camping or conference plan should begin to take definite form a year in advance. This implies the necessity of decision making at an early date regarding camp site, financing, major speakers, and the director. By the sixth month, the additional matters of programing, the enlistment of counselors and food arrangements should be very close to settled.

Counselors should be given orientation training prior to the camp opening. This may involve the use of lectures and discussion, the examination of charts and handbooks, and other devices such as maps, motion pictures, filmstrips, role-playing, and a panel discussion by officers or former officers of previous camps.

Three very common types of camps are: (1)resident, (2) family, and (3) day. In the case of the resident camp, there are permanent structures providing sleeping and eating accommodations, hot and cold running water, a chapel, and recreational facilities. Usually, these are attended by children and youth. Family camps involve both adults and their children, having as their major purpose the strengthening of family relationships through the use of lectures by special speakers, discussions, planned activities for the entire family, question and answer sessions for parents and young people, and general living-together experiences in a Christian atmosphere. Day camps are one week or more in length, are designed for children, and involve transporting them to a camp site within easy traveling distance where they spend the day hiking, eating, playing games, listening to Bible stories, and studying nature. They are usually gone for a period of approximately six hours (e.g., 9 a.m. to 3 p.m.) and return to their homes for the balance of the day and night.

The present trend in camping philosophy is to avoid splitting the activities into (a) religious and (b) secular. Christian living is a *total* process and since camping is not only to be like life but *is* life, all activities are permeated with Christian beliefs and values thereby providing a unified experience in living without any artificial dichotomy characterizing the programs.

BIBLIOGRAPHY

Bower, Robert K., *Administering Christian Education.*

Cully, Kendig Brubaker, ed., *Westminster Dictionary of Christian Education.*

Hakes, J. Edward, ed., *Introduction to Evangelical Christian Education.*

Leach, William H., *Handbook of Church Management.*

Lotz, Philip H., ed., *Orientation in Religious Education.*

Taylor, Marvin J., ed., *Religious Education.*

Preparing the Laity to Teach

1. PRINCIPLES

a. *Biblical Antecedents and Philosophy*

It has become axiomatic among evangelical Protestants that the educational task of the church cannot be accomplished by the clergy alone. There must be the dedicated, intelligent service of the laity.

This concept of lay involvement in the teaching ministry of the church stems from the character of New Testament Christianity, both the example and teachings of Christ, and the essential character of the Christian life. Our Lord during his earthly ministry gathered about himself a group of followers, then taught and trained them so that they might in turn reach and teach mankind. The doctrine of the universal priesthood of all believers (I Peter 2:9) gives rise to the preparation of the laity for teaching as well as other kinds of lay ministries. In Ephesians 4:11-12, it is stated that God gave us pastors and teachers to prepare the saints for the work of serving (*diakonias*), and the history of the early church evidenced extensive lay participation in Christian service.

The concept that the whole church is to be involved in the work of Christ is of vital significance. Evangelical Christianity and the work of the church can be sustained only if consecrated laymen volunteer for the task of teaching and seek to prepare themselves for the responsibility involved in this task. The church must rely on the voluntary leadership of laymen for the main segment of its educational program. Professionally trained leaders, as ministers and directors of Christian Education, give inspiration, supervision, and coordination, but laymen carry the main burden of the task.

b. *Historical Development*

The assuming of responsibility in the preparation of the laity for teaching has increased markedly during the past century. This has come as a concomitant outgrowth of expanded interest in the broad area of religious education and the Sunday School movement. In the 1880's the American Sunday School Union promoted leadership education by providing teacher helps based upon the educational concepts of that day. In its *American Sunday School*, a magazine for Sunday School teachers, it purposed "to place within the reach of every Sunday School teacher the improvements in this system and information on subjects which may render their labors easy and efficient."

Sunday School conventions were initiated in 1832 with the first National Sunday School Convention. During ensuing years many suggestions and propositions were put forth for the preparation of Sunday School teachers – such as the institution of normal colleges, courses for Sunday School teachers, and voluntary community organizations to instruct Sunday School teachers. During the middle of the century classes for the training of teachers were established in various parts of the country, the first of these being organized in 1857 by John H. Vincent, a pastor in Joliet, Illinois. He led in the formation of what was known as the Sunday School Institute for the Northwest, under the Cook County Sunday School Association. In 1867 he organized a "normal college" for Sunday School teachers, with courses in Bible and Bible-teaching methods. The American Sunday School Union appointed Henry Clay Trumbull in 1871 as a specialist in training laymen to teach in the Sunday School. Then in 1874 the Chautauqua Sunday School Assembly was begun by Dr. Vincent, this constituting a summer institute program for the training of Sunday School teachers. This teacher training concept spread to many local communities. Regular courses of study were provided and diplomas awarded. The development of standard forms of teacher training lessons also took place during this period.

Just prior to and following the turn of the century, many local church groups became interested in the training of Sunday School teachers. Concise teacher training manuals (by Hurlbut, Oliver, etc.) were used and occasioned interest even among those who did not aspire to teach.

The International Sunday School Association formally recognized the teacher training movement in 1896. In 1903 it appointed a Committee on Education, and in 1904 a Teacher Training Section. In 1910 the Sunday School Council of Evangelical Denominations was established and in 1922 it merged with the International Sunday School Association to form the International Sunday School Council of Religious Education. The name of this organization was later abbreviated to International Council of Religious Education. In this organization both lay and professional concerns were combined. The World Sunday School Association was formed in 1907, its name being changed to the World Council of Christian Education and Sunday School Association in 1947.

Graded lessons, introduced in 1909, laid stress upon specialization in the training of teachers. During this period denominational efforts toward the training of teachers also increased tremendously. To illustrate, the Southern Baptist Convention had done very little in this area before 1900. But at this time the slogan "A certificate for every teacher" incited many to prepare for teaching. Since that time the Southern Baptist Convention has greatly expanded its efforts with the publication of textbooks and manuals. A vast host of laymen have been reached through this program over the years.

Evangelical leaders organized in 1930 as the International Institute Council of Christian Education. Since other kinds of schools became interested in the teacher training concerns of the Council, it was renamed the Evangelical Teacher Training Association in 1931.

Present provisions for the preparation of lay teachers are both numerous and varied in character. The program conducted by the National Sunday School Association and by its affiliate state and regional associations has done much to stimulate interest in leadership education. Many Protestant denominations sustain active programs through their boards of Christian education and their publishing houses. There are also independent religious publishing houses that are making extensive contribution to this field (e.g., Scripture Press, Gospel Light, David C. Cook, and Moody Press). Of vital significance is the contribution being made by Christian colleges – both general and specialized. In many such institutions the Christian education programs are especially designed to prepare for lay participation in the teaching ministry of the local church.

c. *Content and Method*

As is true in the area of general education, there is some difference of opinion as to what ought to be stressed in programs to prepare the laity to teach – whether it be the content of teaching or the method of teaching. First efforts were focused more on content than techniques. Teaching in the early American Sunday School followed the catechetical plan of teaching by means of questions and answers. This was followed by stress on memorization of portions from the Bible, catechism, and hymns. As demonstrated in the Uniform Limited Lessons System, the next development was the selection of various passages of Scripture for Sunday School lessons, accompanied by teachers' helps. The *Standard Course* and the *Advanced Course*, developed in 1910 by the International Association emphasized mostly content – the Bible, but included some material on method. Then in 1926 the International Council of Religious Education modified the *Advanced Course* to the *Standard Leadership Course* which is still used today. This marked a shift in emphasis from content to method, assuming that individuals taking the course possess sufficient Bible knowledge.

It should be noted that a number of organizations have sought to achieve balance between content and technique in their leadership training programs. This has been true, for example, among the Southern Baptists and other denominational groups. It is also true of the program of the Evangelical Teacher Training Association, with its *Preliminary Training Course* and its more extensive *Standard Training Course.* Both courses train lay teachers in both Bible content and teaching methods. An *Advanced Certificate Course* has been added since this association was first established. The *Preliminary Course* is designed for church and community leadership classes; the *Advanced Course* for groups having more highly developed teacher training programs; and the *Standard Training Course* for active member schools – seminaries, liberal arts colleges, and Bible colleges. All these courses are more or less evenly divided between Biblical studies and teaching techniques.

2. PROGRAMS

a. *Programs in Institution of Higher Education*

There are now hundreds of colleges and seminaries that include courses in Christian education in their curricula. While some schools have only a few introductory or general courses in this field, many provide undergraduate majors or minors. As evidenced by the program of the American Association of Schools of Religious Education and the broadening concerns of the American Association of Theological Schools, theological seminaries and graduate schools of theology are showing increased interest in this field. Christian education courses offered in graduate schools of theology are naturally oriented to professional Christian education ministries or are designed for providing assistance to the prospective pastor in the Christian education program of the local church. This is also true to some degree in the undergraduate schools which have complete departments of Christian education and provide majors in this field.

It should be stated, however, that the many Christian education programs offered in Christian colleges make a greater contribution to preparation for lay teaching than to the training of professional directors of Christian education. A few liberal arts colleges require that all students take at least a general course in Christian education. A yet greater concern that students receive instruction in Christian education is evident in the more specialized Christian colleges which emphasize Biblical and church vocational education. These schools are variously known as Bible colleges, Bible institutes, or Bible schools (some cannot be distinguished in name from the Christian liberal arts colleges). The majority of these schools have among their stated objectives preparation for lay ministries and require that all students take courses in Christian education. In a recent survey conducted by the Accrediting Association of Bible Colleges it was found that Christian education departments not only prepare professional workers in the field of Christian education and supplement the training of pastors, missionaries, and ministers of music, but practically all students become involved in the educational program of the church after they leave college. The Bible college movement must therefore be regarded as a vital force in preparing the laity for teaching. The survey disclosed that at least 80 per cent of the 25,000 students enrolled in Bible colleges are taking one or more courses in the field of Christian education. No other class of schools is preparing so many.

Certain Lutheran and Reformed groups conduct Bible institute programs devoted to preparation for lay ministries – especially that of teaching. The Board for Parish Education of the Lutheran Church – Missouri Synod – in its publication, *Leadership Education Through Bible Institutes,* stresses the importance of lay training for leadership education. The several inter-synodical Lutheran Bible institutes now train many lay workers each year. Other major denominations such as the Southern Baptist and the American Baptist maintain specialized schools which have training for lay teaching among their major objectives.

b. *Adult Education*

Another development in recent years is the provision of adult education courses in various colleges – courses that purpose to assist in preparing for lay teaching. These are mostly evening schools or classes conducted by Bible colleges located in urban areas. One institution, for example, has an evening school enrollment of nearly 1,000 students, and the majority of these are taking courses in order to become better teachers in their local churches.

A significant type of program conducted by a number of Christian colleges for the training of the laity in both Bible content and Christian education methods is the correspondence school. Professionally accredited specialized colleges report nearly 30,000 students enrolled in such courses. There are furthermore a number of Christian colleges that provide summer school programs especially structured for the purpose of preparing the laity to teach.

c. *Other Organized Programs*

In addition to the organized institutional efforts being made to train the laity for teaching, there are a variety of programs being conducted on national, state, community, and local church levels. Among evangelical groups the National Sunday School Association has done a great deal to stimulate adult education programs through national conventions, workshops, and seminars. This is an interdenominational organization organized to promote Sunday School work. It was developed out of a concern of evangelical leaders for the general health of the Sunday School movement in America. The vitalization of the Sunday School has been one of its major objectives. In accomplishing this purpose it has developed new uniform lesson outlines, extensively promoted Sunday School conventions – both national and regional, conducted research programs, and issued many publications to promote the evangelical Sunday School and to help teachers in their work. Over fifty regional Sunday School associations are now affiliated with NSSA. The estimated circulation of its Sunday School lessons is now over three million and some seventy denominations are included in the Association's constituency. It operates from a new office building located in Wheaton, Illinois.

Present denominational efforts for the training of lay teachers are exemplified in the Christian education program of the Lutheran Church – Missouri Synod. One of the chief aims of this Association of Lutheran Churches is the promotion of Sunday School work. As revealed in its early constitution, one of its majors aims has been to train teachers. Consequently all synodical officers provide leadership in this area. Its General School Board established in 1914 and its General Sunday School Board established in 1920 were merged into a Board of Christian Education in 1932. The Board of Parish Education was formed in 1944. To it is assigned the area of adult education and the promotion of Lutheran secondary schools. Leadership training activities include the recruitment and training of teachers, publication of textbooks and curriculum guides, publication of lesson material and manuals for teachers, development of Sunday School associations, conventions and workshops, and adult education in Biblical studies. A vigorous program of lay leadership training in as many as ninety evening Bible institutes is being conducted by the Synod.

One of the oldest and most extensive Christian education programs for the training of the laity is that of the Southern Baptist Convention. From its beginnings, Christian education has been one of the chief concerns of this Convention. The present Sunday School Board which promotes Sunday School work as well as the Training Union was established in 1891. This Training Union now has a total membership of nearly 2,400,000.

The American Baptist Convention has also stressed Christian education in the local church. Its Board of Education and Publications publishes Christian education materials. The Judson Graded Curriculum serves many of the ABC churches. The Convention also sponsors conventions and workshops on the national, regional, and local levels. For example, over 200 conferences attended by more than 30,000 persons are conducted at its Green Lake laboratory school each summer.

Another illustration of denominational effort is that of the General Assembly of the Presbyterian Church, which elects a Board of ministers, laymen and women to promote Christian education concerns. A new curriculum "Faith and Life" was offered by the Board in 1964.

Confronted with opportunities in the important task of educating the laity for teaching, numerous publishing firms are going well beyond the role of publishing literature to the conducting of research programs in adult leadership education, holding seminars for pastors and lay leaders, and carrying on leadership training courses in affiliation with educational institutions. Scripture Press, for example, has initiated a program of "leadership training institutes." Instructors in Christian Education and in Biblical Studies are engaged to conduct six Tuesday evening classes. Sponsorship of such leadership training institutes has been extended to other parts of the United States and is proving highly successful.

d. *Leadership Training Curricula*

The curriculum of the *Standard Leadership Course* of the International Sunday School Association consisted of ten units of Child Study, Pedagogy, Old Testament Teaching Values, New Testament Teaching Values, Message and Program, and Teaching Work of Church, along with thirty units each of Departmental Work, and electives. Only slight modifications have been made since this program was conceived. Observable in this curriculum is the stress on the process rather than the content of teaching.

The *Preliminary Course* of the ETTA is evenly divided between the study of the Scriptures and Christian education method courses. Its *Advanced Certificate Course* adds twenty-four units of Biblical Doctrine and twelve units each of Bible Introduction, Evangelism, Vacation Bible School, and Missions. Textbooks are provided for each course. *The ETTA Standard Training Course,* offered in member schools and leading to the Teacher's Diploma calls for a minimum of twenty-four semester hours, ten semester hours in Biblical Studies and fourteen semester hours in Christian Education.

Typical Christian education courses either required of or recommended for students enrolled in Christian colleges are: The Educational Work of the Church (Introduction to Christian Education), Principles and Methods of Teaching, and Christian Education of Children or Christian Education of Youth. These three subjects normally total nine semester hours. In addition to these, a broad variety of as many as forty Christian Education subjects are being offered to serve the needs of both professional Christian Education directors and lay teachers. These include such courses as Educational Psychology, Curriculum, Philosophy of Christian Education, Visual Aids, Storytelling, and Practice Teaching.

e. *Motivation*

The concept of motivating the pupil to learn is frequently stressed. Of genuine significance also is the need of inviting the laity to become involved in the teaching ministry of the church. Relevant questions are: What subjective factors in the life of a Christian layman incite him to become thus involved? What part does the pastor and the Christian education director play in this process? How may such motivation be sustained?

It goes without saying that most factors which normally motivate an individual to train for a vocation or profession are not apropos here. Participation in the teaching ministry of the church is of a voluntary character and rewards are regarded from a spiritual rather than material perspective. What then are some of the basic factors which provide motivation?

(1) There must first of all exist *an intelligent understanding of the Scriptures and a vital experience of saving faith in Christ.* In this framework of spiritual life and discernment it becomes a matter of supernatural rather than natural motivation. With the living Christ in the heart and life, and, concomitantly with the indwelling Holy Spirit working within, it is appropriate to expect that there exist the inner motivation to incite the individual to engage in the work of Christ.

(2) Flowing from the spiritual life is a natural *concern for the spiritual need of others.* Apart from such concern and need, the church's teaching function becomes meaningless. Rationale for the implementation of the church's purpose to teach lies in the spiritual needs of its constituents, and it is for the individual Christian to recognize such need and seek ways of meeting it.

(3) There must also be in the heart of the Christian layman *a conviction concerning the essentiality of the church's educative responsibility toward its people.* Christ's command to his disciples, "to teach," must penetrate the will and incite the individual believer to appropriate action.

(4) The foregoing factors lead to a *desire toward self-improvement.* How can I develop my ability as a teacher? What should I teach? How should I teach? — These become relevant questions and in turn, lead the Christian layman to investigate and take advantage of opportunities for training.

(5) Externally it is the *pastor's role* to provide necessary means of spiritual growth. It is also his duty to remind the Christian layman of his responsibilities, then to help him find ways to prepare to meet them. With regard to the latter, the development of a strong program of training the laity for teaching, whether locally or through assistance of an outside agency, ought to constitute a vital challenge and a significant aspect of his labors. Under his guidance the Christian education director (in churches engaging such) plays an active role in making provision for the preparation of the laity. Securing appropriate instructional materials, conducting local teacher training classes, stimulating participation in denominational, regional, and national adult leadership programs — these are some of the efforts that may well come within the scope of his interest. Any such efforts, whether carried on by the pastor, the Christian education director or other church leaders, are of importance in sustaining an effective program of preparing the laity to teach.

BIBLIOGRAPHY

Cully, Kendig B., *The Westminister Dictionary of Christian Education.* Philadelphia: The Westminster Press, 1963.

Eavey, C. B., *History of Christian Education.* Chicago: Moody Press, 1964.

Gable, Lee J., *Encyclopedia for Church Group Leaders.* New York: Association Press, 1959.

Gaebelein, Frank E., *Christian Education in a Democracy.* New York: Oxford University Press, 1951.

Gwynn, Price H., *Leadership Education in the Local Church.* Philadelphia: The Westminster Press, 1952.

Hakes, J. Edward, *An Introduction to Evangelical Christian Education.* Chicago: Moody Press, 1964.

Person, Peter P., *The Minister in Christian Education.* Grand Rapids, Michigan: Baker Book House, 1960.

Taylor, Marvin J., *Religious Education.* New York, Abingdon Press, 1960.

Vieth, Paul H., *The Church School.* Philadelphia: Christian Education Press, 1957.

Witmer, S. A., *Education with Dimension.* New York: Channel Press, 1962.

Witmer, S. A., *Report: Preparing Bible College Students for Ministries in Christian Education.* Wheaton, Illinois: Accrediting Association of Bible Colleges, 1962.

The Christian School

The increasing secularism of American society is becoming distressingly evident in our classrooms. This has naturally resulted in a secularizing of the thinking of the children of the church.

Alarmed by this, a significant number of churches have re-examined their responsibility to their school children. It is evident that the Biblical principles for the education of children and young people can only be fully applied in a Christian School. Therefore, many churches have established Christian day schools as an integral part of their total church program.

The value of this dimension in the local church program is increasingly evident. Families are drawn to the total program church. Children are rooted and grounded in the Lord Jesus Christ and his Word. Young hearts are prepared to respond to the challenge of complete dedication of life, talents, and resources to the cause of Christ.

Expensive facilities are used six days a week instead of one. By careful planning both the Sunday and weekday programs are more adequately housed and equipped.

When properly planned, executed, and followed-up the church sponsored Christian day school can effectively serve also as a missionary agency for community outreach. Families can be claimed for Christ when the Christian school opens the door and all the agencies of the church combine for maximum spiritual impact.

1. THE SCRIPTURAL BASIS FOR THE CHRISTIAN SCHOOL

The threefold imperative of the Great Commission, Evangelize, Enlist, and Educate, concludes by commanding the activity which is the special responsibility of the Christian school – "teaching them to observe *all things* whatsoever I have commanded you."

The ministry of the Christian school must begin with the saving gospel of our Lord Jesus Christ but it dare not stop there. Christian leaders and parents see with increasing clarity that the "whatsoever" of I Corinthians 10:31 includes the study of history, science, psychology, literature – the whole curriculum. This is to be done "to the glory of God." Only the Christian school can educate in the manner that God commands.

This command is specifically applied to Christian parents (and thus to the church) when the Holy Spirit said through Paul, "And, ye fathers, provoke not your children . . . but nurture them in the chastening and admonition of the Lord" (Eph. 6:4). This New Testament phrasing is a simple summation of Old Testament teaching to the people of God: "And thou shalt teach . . . thy children [diligently]" (Deut. 6:7), and "Train up a child" (Prov. 22:6).

This is the responsibility of Christian parents, especially in the midst of a secular society that is delegating direction and control of education to the state. Christian parents must be aware of the increasing spiritual sterility of state controlled education. As God leads they must assert their divinely assigned responsibility and through the fellowship of believers – the church – move to educate their children as he commands.

Only the Christian school strives to "bring *every thought* into captivity to the obedience of Christ"; so that "in *all things* he might have the pre-eminence." When Christian children from Christian homes are thus educated in Christian schools the cause of Christ will be strengthened by a growing host of young men and women ready to hazard their lives in the service of God and the proclamation of the gospel.

2. CHARACTERISTICS OF EDUCATION THAT IS CHRISTIAN

What one believes concerning the origin of the universe, the purpose of history, and the nature of man determines the fundamental impact of education. It was with this in mind that Prof. Norman Harper said, "It may be possible to separate church and state, but it is impossible to separate education and faith."

The Christian school is not unique in its educational equipment or in the shape of the desks that it uses. The Christian school is unique in the way it shapes the minds of its students. The molding of minds and the developing of Christian thought patterns is the result of several characteristics that are unique to the Christian school.

(These are the convictions of all Christians. We are presenting them with their special implications for education.)

a. *The Bible Is a Unique and Special Revelation of God to Man.* Its information and principles are to guide and control as men seek deeper understandings of the universe and their fellows who inhabit it. Its instruction most effectively and realistically prepares us for the here and now while the faith it inspires prepares us for the hereafter. The Bible is not worshiped in the Christian school, nor is its impact restricted to the chapel or Bible study period. Rather, its vital principles and supernatural faith infuse all school centered activities with a divine dimension.

b. *God Is.* Only the Christian school proclaims the reality of the supernatural. Only the Christian school proclaims the characteristics of a supernatural God as he is revealed in the Bible. The church cannot proclaim to its young people an infinite God who is concerned for all of life and learning, and then shut him off in an isolation booth for six days a week.

As we proclaim the primacy of spiritual values, we must acknowledge the primacy of spiritual forces and the supremacy of spiritual power. Only the Christian school teaches in this framework. At the same time we must teach the reality of Satan and sin. Our children will not be prepared for spiritual warfare unless the leader of the enemy is known and his forces are identified.

c. *God Is Relevant.* There are many who recognize "The Great Designer," "The Uncaused Cause," or "The All-Pervading Spirit of the Infinite Universe." These acknowledge a god and then set him outside our universe. Only the Christian school teaches that God is relevant. He is relevant to the forces of science, to the unfolding of history, and to the complexities of man. He is personally relevant in the power of prayer, in the provision of guidance, and for perseverance in service. In many special ways the Christian school looks beyond the simple moralities of shallow faith and shows its students the deep dimensions of God's relevance to our time. At the same time the Christian school teaches its students to sort out the fundamental problems of their own lives and to see the relevance of God's provision to their own need.

Permit us to interrupt the flow of this presentation for a moment. Some will say, "What does this have to do with elementary school children? or even young people in high school? These are concepts to be studied in college or seminary." Philosophy is not taught, it is caught. The Christian school communicates a world-view long before its students can say, "*Weltanschaung*." By re-enforcing what is communicated in the Christian home and church the Christian school is helping to establish the foundation that the Holy Spirit will use to keep young lives in the center of God's will.

d. *Man Is a Spiritual Being.* Every Christian recognizes this truth, but few appreciate the impact of education that ignores or denies it. We stand aghast at the mounting reports of "man's inhumanity to man" and fail to recognize that a key reason for men acting like animals is that all through their schooling they have been taught that they *are* animals. God created man a spiritual being. Man was given dominion over the animals because he is of a different order of creation. Schools that ignore or deny this cannot possibly educate the whole man properly. Only the Christian school with its recognition of the spiritual nature of man and his responsibility to God is preparing its students for effective living and Christian commitment. The materialism of our age will be most successfully countered by proclaiming and presenting the spiritual values of the Christian faith. We will not strengthen the Christian cause by being merely anti-materialistic. (Our young people will be drawn to explore for themselves the evils we so loudly deplore.)

The Christian school presents spiritual values and truths as more enduring than time or substance. A young life that is saturated with these principles cannot easily turn to merely material pursuits.

e. *Truth Is Absolute.* The tragic futility of non-directive rebellion against the conformities of relativism is increasingly evident A man needs a rock on which to anchor his lever as he endeavors to move the world (or any small part of it). The Christian school plants in the lives of its young students the words of our Lord as he said, "Heaven and earth shall pass away but my word shall not pass away." God has revealed that which is eternally good, true, and beautiful. The Christian school communicates these concepts and strengthens young lives on firm foundations with well-defined guide lines as they move with steadfast purpose toward eternally important goals. This instruction concerning the nature of truth helps to deliver the Christian student from the bondage of a majority vote or common practice. Truth is not determined in this fashion. His march, whether with majority or minority, will be paced to a different drum beat.

f. *Education Alone Is Not Enough.* It has been widely held since at least Aristotle that if men *knew* the good they would *do* it. Hence the mounting emphasis on education. The search for knowledge and the efforts to educate more children more effectively is based on the faith that man is inherently good. This faith permeates the curriculum and administration of American education. The Christian school builds on the revelation that "all have sinned and come short of the glory of God." It teaches that even as we master the skills necessary to maintain dominion over all the rest of creation, man himself must acknowledge the sovereignty of God. "There is none other name under heaven given among men whereby we must be saved." We must teach our children that the greatest tragedy is to "gain the whole world and lose our [eternal] soul."

The subtle impact of education that speaks of "the spark of the divine" in every man, but ignores the demands of divine sovereignty will have tragic effects. It will empty our churches and end in death and destruction as political and social institutions reveal the tyranny of conformity that finite fallibility demands.

It is commitment to Christ that leads to the more abundant life. It is his Word that sets men free. Only the Christian school gives its pupils the privilege of relating all of this learning to these fundamental facts of eternal truth.

The practical impact of this conviction gives an evangelistic thrust to all education that is truly Christian. The eternal value of the soul must be set above the academic values of the intellect. Education that fails to establish this hierarchy is not Christian, nor is it truly education in its deepest dimension. It should be pointed out in this connection that since the Christian school gives proper priority to spiritual values, it *must* demonstrate competence in its academic activities. There are various avenues of child and youth evangelism in which the church may legitimately engage that do not have academic implications. When we choose to operate a Christian school, it must be thoroughly Christian and academically competent.

3. THE OUTREACH AND OBJECTIONS OF THE CHRISTIAN SCHOOL

There are various working definitions of "What is a Christian school?" In significant measure the outreach of a school will be determined by the local answer to this question. The objectives of the Christian school will apply to all, differing only in emphasis and manner of attack.

Some suggest that a school is Christian when the administration and a majority of the faculty are Christians. Apart from the problems of satisfactorily defining "Christian" in this situation, enough has already been presented to indicate the inadequacy of this definition.

Many citizens of the United States have felt that the united practice of certain "Christian" exercises constituted a school as Christian. Thus there was a great outcry about "paganizing" our schools when Supreme Court decisions outlawed compulsory prayer and Bible reading. When, three and one-half years later, the court refused to review a ban on voluntary prayer, it became crystal clear that our public schools were no longer an adjunct of the church.

This confirmed the analysis of certain discerning observers who had been questioning the value of prayer to the Creator before studying evolution or the logical consistency of reading the Christmas promise of "peace on earth" through the ministry and work of Christ and then presenting the United Nations as the only hope for world peace.

There is wide agreement that administration, faculty, curriculum and religious exercises must all be Christian to have a Christian school. There are many who suggest that these are the essential element, and, having these, to throw open their doors to any family whose children meet the academic and behavior standards of the school.

a. *Outreach.* The Christian school that operates with this missionary motive uppermost faces special problems as it deals with parents who do not understand the fundamental characteristics of education that is Christian. They frequently use evangelistic efforts to bring their children to a personal faith in Jesus Christ. It naturally follows that children from unchurched homes cannot be taught or disciplined on the basis of their personal responsibility to God. Their standards of conversation, conduct, diligence, and recreation are often so diverse from the Christian culture of the sponsors and Christian parents of the community that valuable pupils and support are forfeited.

It must always be remembered that no Christian school needs to lower its spiritual, academic, or behavior standards in the hope of increased gifts or enrollments. A clear statement of standards and a prayerful maintaining of them will be honored by the Lord.

The sponsors of a Christian school with a missionary outreach must always be careful to maintain control of the governing elements in the school organization. The board, the administration, and offices of the parent organization must be unitedly and firmly committed to the Christian convictions and their application that brought the school into existence.

In this setting there must be a special awareness of the Christian school responsibility to the unchurched families of the school. God has made some special promises to families and everything possible must be done to transform the family of children who come from homes where Christ is not honored.

Another view of the Christian school vigorously insists that Christian pupils are essential. The Christian school exists to serve Christian homes. Since the schooling of children is now carried forward by persons professionally prepared for that service, and since Christian parents are responsible to God for the education of their children; it is essential that Christian children be instructed in a thoroughly Christian fashion. These Christians are not unaware of our responsibility to win the children for Christ. They identify the Sunday School and related activities as the evangelistic outreach for the children of the community.

This Christian school exists to provide instruction and environment that reinforces the teaching of the Christian home and church. The united impact of these three key forces in the life of a child produces committed, well-qualified soldiers for the cause of Christ.

The sponsors of a Christian school that exists primarily to serve the children of Christian homes must continually impress its students with their responsibility to communicate the gospel of grace to an unbelieving world. We dare not draw aside from the world in Pharisiac isolation. Rather, we are to nurture and admonish our children so that as mature adult Christians they can serve God and their fellow men with understandings developed from earliest childhood.

Let no one suppose, however, that because a school exists to serve Christian families there is no need for an evangelistic alertness. God's Word makes it clear that we become members of the family of God through personal faith in Jesus Christ. Children from Christian families need to be led to a personal faith if they are to possess a dynamic Christianity. (If the term "church-related" is substituted for "Christian" the above statement becomes an imperative directive.)

Another word should be added for the instruction of those who regard the Christian school as a means of grace. It operates in obedience to at least three great truths of Scripture: (1) fathers bring up your children in the nurture and admonition of the Lord; (2) Suffer the little children to come unto me; and, (3) bring every thought into captivity to the obedience of Christ. Not one of these, nor all of them makes or keeps a child a Christian.

Christian schools are operated in obedience to God's commands, but no Christian school makes or preserves Christians. That is God's business. Christian adults, parents and church leaders, provide instruction, nurture, admonition, even discipline as God directs, but it is his Holy Spirit that works in the heart of each child. When God does not permit the Christian school to see the harvest for which it labors, it must continue to cultivate and irrigate in the assurance that God will give the increase.

b. *Objectives*. While the outreach of Christian schools will differ as local conditions and divine direction differs, there is remarkable agreement concerning the objectives of the Christian school. Specific statements of objectives will contain from six to sixteen statements, and emphasis will vary from school to school. All Christian schools seek to accomplish the following objectives:

(1) Personal salvation and spiritual commitment.

(2) Personal maturity and growth.

(3) Academic competence above average.

(4) Social usefulness to God and country.

In the Christian school a profession of faith is the first of the spiritual objectives. From this beginning should come the commitment of life, ability and material possessions that will strengthen the body of Christ in both pulpit and pew. This vision is nurtured during these formative school days.

Since effectiveness in life rests ultimately upon personal characteristics, the Christian school seeks to develop responsibilty, dependability, respect for authority, cooperation and related attitudes. As Christian convictions make their impact upon the students of the Christian school they come to maturity with a perspective that cannot be imparted in any other educational institution.

Academic competence is the responsibility of the Christian school. Because of its Christian commitment, it must honor the Lord with a mastery of intellectual tools above the average. It evaluates curricular fads and frills as well as pedagogical innovations, and "holds fast to that which is good."

Because "no man lives to himself" the Christian school strives to implant an understanding of the divine concern for society generally and the fellowship of believers particularly.

4. THE CURRICULUM OF THE CHRISTIAN SCHOOL

Externally the curriculum of the Christian school will not usually differ significantly from that of other schools. The chief and expected difference is the presence of Bible study and Christian religious exercises. In some states the law imposes a basic curriculum on all schools, public and private.

Internally the Christian school curriculum will be permeated with a different philosophy as the characteristics of education that is Christian manifest themselves in every course. Thus Christian children are given the academic competence that the world requires and they are led to see the divine and eternal dimensions to all that God has done.

Some specific observations:

Bible: Mastery of content. Great themes of instruction. Practical applications of the principles it establishes.

Language Arts: Competence in expressing and comprehending thought. Value of the written word and the spoken word.

Fine Arts, including literature: Art to the glory of God, not "art for art's sake." Christian discrimination in subjects under consideration and presentation. Role in opening doors for a Christian testimony.

History: Communicate the historicity of the Christian faith. Restore the sense of our Judeo-Christian heritage to balance the Greeco-Roman influence. A Christian philosophy of history and time. Proclaim the sovereignty of God in the events of history. Study how men's actions (history) reflect his nature (revelation).

Science and Mathematics: Study of the divine order and attributes as unfolded in the material universe. Creation. Limitations and competence of science.

Practical Arts, including Physical Education and Business: Avenues for the service of God.

5. THE STUDENTS IN A CHRISTIAN SCHOOL

The students attending a school at a given time are there because of their interest and the admission and retention policies of the school. Comprehensive policy and procedure statements can be secured. These general questions touch upon most of the critical areas.

"Do you limit your enrollment to Christian students?" No, this is impossible. Some applicants have never been given the opportunity to make a profession of faith, others who claim to be Christians do not understand the full dimension of the term, while some, in the upper grades can give satisfactory answers despite the fact that they have never entered into the new life. The key spiritual characteristic to investigate is the applicants attitude toward authority. A reference from a former teacher wherever possible will give the most reliable report. The Scriptures describe Satan as "the lawless one" and children to whom this term applies will damage the Christian school. It is well to remember that the school will be dealing with the child. Children are the ones being admitted, not parents. It is harder to get valid information about children, but the effort will be well rewarded.

"What are the academic qualifications for admission to a Christian school?" Unless the school has special provision for special instruction we suggest that no candidate with a report card average below C, or, an achievement battery average more than one-half year behind the grade in which applicant is enrolled; or, an I.Q. below 90 be admitted. Some will point out that not all Christian children will meet these standards. Is a policy that excludes some children worthy of the cause of Christ? It is not, but until his church is providing the financing of an educational program that meets the academic needs of all children we must use available resources to carry on the best program possible. Certain limitations must therefore be established. On the basis of national averages the suggested qualifications open the Christian school door to more than 85 per cent of the total school population. Achievement test scores are becoming increasingly important for admission decisions. A few schools are operating summer programs to bring applicants up to standard in reading and arithmetic especially.

"Does the Christian school accept problem children?" Not unless it is specially dedicated to that ministry or does not want to expand its ministry beyond the dedicated group of original patrons. Behavior problems in children are the result of some spiritual deficiency before application is made to the Christian school. Unless there is evidence of a specific spiritual decision in the life of the individual or family that changes the other factors, the Christian school cannot expect significant changes in problem children.

"Can the physically handicapped child benefit from the Christian school?" If the handicap does not hinder the learning process the Christian school can be a real benefit. Here the handicapped child can learn to make his contribution to the normal world. At the same time he serves as inspiration for kindness and consideration that will enrich the lives of his fellow students.

6. THE TEACHER IN THE CHRISTIAN SCHOOL

The special mission of the Christian school demands teachers who are not only in doctrinal agreement with the sponsoring Christians but also demonstrate a vital and attractive growth in the Christian life. Of equal importance is a comprehension of the implications of a Christian philosophy of education throughout the total curriculum.

The Christian school teacher must be professional in training and outlook. Although teaching certification does not automatically result in this it does assure that certain professional courses have been taken. Christians who are called to teach are not faithful to their calling without preparation for it.

One who enters the role of "teacher" must realize that from that moment his life is not his own. In appearance, language, interests, attitudes, diligence, and many additional attributes the teacher exerts a tremendous influence, sometimes surpassing even the parental example. A teacher may meet the measure of all these standards and be as ineffective as "sounding brass or a tinkling cymbal." The concern (or "love") that is most effective in the classroom is aptly described by St. Paul when he says, "The servant of the Lord must not strive but be gentle unto all men, apt to teach, patient, in meekness instructing those that oppose themselves."

7. THE ORGANIZATION OF A CHRISTIAN SCHOOL IN THE LOCAL CHURCH

While the pastor has a key role in any church-related Christian school, his first concern must be the development of lay leaders who will bear the operating and professional burdens of the school. By instructing the congregation concerning the place of the school in the total program of the church, by encouraging those who have a vision for the Christian school, and by facilitating the organizational relationships, the pastor will make his best contribution.

Every church-related school should have a school board whose sole responsibility is the operation of the day school. This board must have some member(s) who also serve on the governing bodies of the church to facilitate maximum two-way involvement. All members of the school board should be members of the sponsoring church. (This requirement need not be a condition for membership on board committees.)

The school board shall determine the distribution of the operating responsibilities. It is most important that responsibility for the daily operating of the school be assigned to one full-time employee. This may be a teaching principal but he must be at the school during school hours. (Since whole books have been written about Christian School Board responsibilities we will simply list them in our bibliography.)

When a church is planning new construction for both day school and Sunday use, much can be done to make efficient provision for both if the school board is involved in the design of the facilities. Day school use of almost all the church facilities and equipment can multiply and deepen the impact of the related expenditures for the cause of Christ.

Christian schools are also operating under parent-controlled or independent self-perpetuating board organization. If the local interest and situation indicates that one of these approaches would best serve the cause of Christ, information can be secured.

8. THE ROLE OF THE CHRISTIAN SCHOOL IN AMERICAN SOCIETY

The Bible proclaims that "righteousness exalteth a nation," and through the centuries the Christian ethic has made its social impact through the service and leadership of individuals committed to that principle. The social importance of the Christian school is its education of multiplying thousands of children with an understanding of their responsibility to God, their fellow man, and themselves. However, there is mounting evidence that American society is rejecting the righteousness that is from above and is endeavoring to achieve greatness through governmental rather than divine morality. At some point we must say to our society "We ought to obey God rather than man."

The Christian school will increasingly serve the Christian minority in American society. It will help to maintain the Christian testimony by communicating a knowledge of the Bible and its implications in all of life. I will challenge all who come within its influence to personal faith in Jesus Christ and to a dedication of mind and strength to the service of eternal truth and true freedom.

The Christian school will be increasingly important to the preservation and strength of the Christian church as long as freedom continues in American education.

BIBLIOGRAPHY

Byrne, H. W., *A Christian Approach to Education.* Grand Rapids: Zondervan, 1961.

Clark, Gordon H., *Christian Philosophy of Education.* Grand Rapids: Wm. B. Eerdmans, 1946.

Fakkema, Mark, *Christian Philosophy and Its Educational Implications.* Chicago: Christian Schools Service, Inc.

Fuller, Edmund, ed., *The Christian Idea of Education.* New Haven: Yale University Press, 1957.

Gaebelein, Frank E., *The Pattern of God's Truth.* New York: Oxford University Press, 1954.

———, *Christian Education in a Democracy.* New York: Oxford University Press, 1951.

Jaarsma, Cornelius R., *Fundamentals in Christian Education.* Grand Rapids: Wm. B. Eerdmans, 1953.

———, *Human Development.* Grand Rapids: Wm. B. Eerdmans, 1961.

Lowie, Roy, *Christian School Administration* Wheaton, Ill: National Association of Christian Schools, 1966.

Lunsford, C. Roman, *The Church-Related School.* Sepulveda, Calif: Los Angeles Baptist School Society.

Rushdoony, Rousas J., *Intellectual Schizophrenia.* Philadelphia: Presbyterian and Reformed Publishing Co., 1961.

Vimont, William H., *Pupil Selection for Christian Classrooms.* Indianapolis, Ind: 8810 Pendleton Pike, Lot 303.

SOURCES OF INFORMATION ON CHURCH-RELATED SCHOOLS

General Council of the Assemblies of God. Mr. Hardy W. Steinberg, Department of Education, 1445 Boonville Ave., Springfield, Mo. 65802.

Los Angeles Baptist City Mission Society. Department of Baptist Day Schools, Rev. C.

Rowan Lunsford, Executive Secretary, 9825 Woodley Ave., Sepulveda, Calif.

Southern Baptist Convention. Education Commission, Mr. Rabun L. Brantley, Executive Secretary, 460 James Robertson Parkway, Nashville 3, Tenn.

National Fellowship of Brethren Schools. Rev. C. R. Taber, Executive Secretary, 909 S. Buffalo St., Warsaw, Indiana.

Protestant Episcopal Church. Rev. Clarence W. Brickman, Executive Secretary, Unit of Parish & Preparatory Schools, 815 Second Ave., New York, N.Y. 10017.

Religious Society of Friends. Miss Harriet L. Hoyle, Secretary, Committee on Education, 1515 Cherry St., Philadelphia, Pa. 19102.

The Lutheran Church – Missouri Synod. Dr. Wm. A. Kramer, Secretary of Schools, 3558 South Jefferson Avenue, St. Louis, Missouri 63118.

Wisconsin Evangelical Lutheran Synod. Mr. Emil Trettin, Executive Secretary, 3512 W. North Ave., Milwaukee, Wisconsin 53208.

The American Lutheran Church. Dr. C. Richard Evenson, Board of Parish Education, 422 S. Fifth St., Minneapolis, Minn. 55415.

Evangelical Lutheran Synod (Norwegian). Prof. Sigurd K. Lee, Bethany Lutheran College, Mankato, Minn.

Synod of Evangelical Lutheran Churches (Slovak), Rev. John Kovac, President, 4126 Blow St., St. Louis, Mo.

Church of the Lutheran Confession, Rev. Paul Nolting, Secretary, 710 S. Grove, Sleepy Eye, Minn. 56085.

Mennonite Christian Day Schools. Mr. Ellrose D. Zook, Editor, Mennonite Yearbook, 610 Walnut Ave., Scottdale, Pa.

National Association of Christian Schools. Rev. John F. Blanchard, Jr., Executive Director, Box 28, Wheaton, Ill. 60187.

National Union of Christian Schools. Mr. John A. Vander Ark, Educational Director, 865 – 28th St., S. E., Grand Rapids, Mich. 49508.

Index of Subjects

Index of Persons